A CURIOUS MAN

A CURIOUS MAN

THE STRANGE & BRILLIANT LIFE OF ROBERT 'BELIEVE IT OR NOT' RIPLEY

NEAL THOMPSON

rh
BOOKS

Published by Random House Books 2013

2 4 6 8 10 9 7 5 3 1

Copyright © Neal Thompson 2013

Neal Thompson has asserted his right under the Copyright, Designs
and Patents Act, 1988, to be identified as the author of this work

Ripley's, Believe It or Not!, and Ripley's Believe It or Not! are registered
trademarks of Ripley Entertainment Inc.

All interior photographs © Ripley Entertainment Inc.

First published in the United States in 2013 by Crown Archetype, an imprint of
the Crown Publishing Group, a division of Random House, Inc., New York

First published in Great Britain in 2013 by Random House Books

Random House, 20 Vauxhall Bridge Road,
London SW1V 2SA

www.randomhouse.co.uk

Addresses for companies within The Random House Group Limited can
be found at: www.randomhouse.co.uk/offices.htm

The Random House Group Limited Reg. No. 954009

A CIP catalogue record for this book
is available from the British Library

ISBN 9781847947208

The Random House Group Limited supports the Forest Stewardship Council®
(FSC®), the leading international forest-certification organisation. Our books
carrying the FSC label are printed on FSC®-certified paper. FSC is the only
forest-certification scheme supported by the leading environmental organisations,
including Greenpeace. Our paper procurement policy can be found at:
www.randomhouse.co.uk/environment

Printed and bound by CPI Group (UK) Ltd, Croydon, CR0 4YY

For Mary, always

For Sean and Leo

Ripley's Rambles

ADEN
Afghanistan
Ajmer-Merwara* ALASKA Albania ALGERIA
Andorra ANTIGUA Arabia ARGENTINA
Armenia AUSTRALIA Austria AZERBAIJAN
Azores BAHAMAS Bahawalpur* BALI
Baluchistan BARBADOS Baroda* BASQUE
Bechuanaland BELGIUM Bengal* BERMUDA
Bihar & Orissa* BOLIVIA Bombay Presidency* BOSNIA
Brazil BRITISH GUIANA* British Honduras* BULGARIA
Burma Canada CAPE ZONE Cape Colony* CELEBES*
Central Provinces (Africa)* CEYLON Channel Islands
CHILE China COLOMBIA Corsica COSTA RICA Croatia
CUBA Curaçao CYRENAICA* Czechoslovakia*
DALMATIA Danzig* DELHI Denmark DJEBEL DRUZE*
Djerba DOMINICAN REPUBLIC Dutch East Indies*
EAST PRUSSIA* Ecuador EGYPT El Salvador ENGLAND
Er Rif* ESTONIA Finland FIJI ISLANDS Formosa* FRANCE
French Guiana FRONTIER PROVINCES (IRAQ)
Garden of Eden* GEORGIA Germany GIBRALTAR
Greece GUADELOUPE Guatemala HAITI Hawaiian
Islands HERZEGOVINA Holland HONDURAS Hong
Kong HUNGARY Iceland ININI TERRITORY* Iraq
IRISH FREE STATE* Isle of Man ITALY Jamaica
JAPAN Java JEHOL* Johore KARELIA*
Kashmir-Jammu* KENYA COLONY* Khairpur* KOREA

* No longer exists or has been renamed

Kurdistan KWANTUNG* Lapland LATVIA Lebanon
LIECHTENSTEIN Lithuania LLÍVIA Luxembourg MACAO
Madeira MADOERA Madras MALLORCA Malta
MANCHUKUO* Martinique MEXICO Mombasa
MONACO Montenegro MOROCCO Mozambique
NATAL* Newfoundland NEW ZEALAND Nicaragua
NORTH CAUCASUS Northern Ireland NORTHERN
RHODESIA* Norway ORANGE FREE STATE* Orkney
Islands PALESTINE Panama PAPUA*
Paraguay PERSIA* Peru PHILIPPINE ISLANDS*
Poland PORTUGAL Puerto Rico PUNJAB Quelimane
RAJPUTANA Rhodes SAAR Sahara (French)*
ST. CROIX St. Lucia ST. PIERRE-MIQUELON St. Thomas
Samoa SAN BLAS San Marino SARDINIA Sark
SCOTLAND Serbia SHETLAND ISLANDS Siam* SICILY
Sinai SINDH Southern Rhodesia* SOVIET RUSSIA* Spain
STRAITS SETTLEMENTS* Sudan SUMATRA Suriname
SWAZILAND Sweden SWITZERLAND Syria
TONGA ISLANDS Tanganyika* TANGIER Tchad*
TRANSJORDAN* Transvaal* TRINIDAD
Tripolitania* TUNISIA Turkey UGANDA
Ukraine UNITED PROVINCES United States
URUGUAY Vatican City State
VENEZUELA Virgin Islands
WALES Württemberg* YUCATÁN
Yugoslavia* ZANZIBAR Zara

**PASSPORT
OFFICE**

An Enhanced Way to Experience this Book!

Unlock exclusive content, such as video, image slideshows, and more, using Ripley's Believe or Not! app.

The app features oddSCAN™ image recognition technology to detect and unlock hidden content.

STEP 1 - Get the app to Use oddSCAN™

Ripley's Believe It or Not! app is available FREE for Apple and Android devices.

Scan the QR codes to the right to find the app for your device, and download it right away.

STEP 2 - Download the Ripley Bio Bundle

All the exclusive content associated with this book is available as a free in-app download accessed within the oddSCAN™ section of the app.

STEP 3 - Find the oddSCAN™ logos

Look inside the book, in the middle photo section, for the oddSCAN™ logos located at the bottom of the page.

Use your smart device and frame the whole page.

POINT. SCAN. UNLOCK.

It's that simple!

Bucktoothed LeRoy Ripley, age eight. "Everyone at school picked on him because he was so different," a classmate would later say. "Not one of the guys," said another.

Though he'd later claim to have sold his first drawing at age fourteen, Ripley was actually eighteen when this cartoon was published in *LIFE* magazine, in June of 1908. He was paid $8, which inspired him to pursue cartooning.

At far right with the *San Francisco Chronicle* art staff, 1912. After moving to San Francisco in 1909, Ripley was fired from his first newspaper job, at the *San Francisco Bulletin*—"My work was poor," he admitted—but was quickly hired at the *Chronicle*.

oddSCAN ▶ SCAN THIS PAGE TO UNLOCK EXCLUSIVE CONTENT

The freakish breaks all rules; it seems beyond belief because it fails to make any sense; it upsets comforting notions. The freakish is the ultimate avant-garde, a finger in the eye of the buttoned-up bourgeois vision of ordered life, like a tattoo parlor in the midst of a holistic spa.

—"O, Believers, Prepare to Be Amazed!"
Edward Rothstein, *New York Times*

Our daily life is so cut and dried that we get relief from fairy tales. Except Ripley's fairy tales are true, and this excites people. They like to learn that nature makes exceptions. These are fairy tales for grown-ups.

—Norbert Pearlroth

In the middle of the Syrian Desert, halfway between Damascus and Baghdad, the half-breed vehicle with twelve sand-surfing balloon tires came to a stop at an indistinct pile of rocks bordered by a scrawny stand of palm trees. It was time for lunch.

Passengers stepped off the car-bus into the brutal heat, including two Americans, one of them more portly and distinctly American than the other.

Robert L. Ripley was dressed in his preferred global traveler's outfit—black-and-white wing tips, knee-high socks, white shorts, and a short-sleeved shirt. Atop his head sat a wide-brimmed pith helmet. As the tour bus staff handed out bagged sandwiches, Ripley withdrew his own lunch: a thermos of scotch and soda. He turned and offered a swig to his traveling partner, an earnest young Mormon from Utah named Joe Simpson, who worked for Ripley's boss.

Newspaperman William Randolph Hearst had hired Ripley in 1929, paying him more than $100,000 a year and making Ripley one of the best-paid journalists in all of newspapers. Simpson's job was to protect and serve the famed and famously erratic cartoonist, a role that veered from traveling secretary

to photographer to drinking partner. That night, Ripley's caravan stopped at the sprawling fortress compound called Rutbah
Wells, whose gates lifted as a small crowd gathered to greet the
new arrivals. Ripley emerged from his vehicle to hear the dis-
tinct drawl of his friend, Will Rogers: "Hi, Bob. Where d'you
think you're goin'?"

Rogers was headed the opposite way, toward Damascus,
while Ripley was trying to add two new countries to his list,
Iraq and Persia, part of his relentless search for material for his
increasingly popular cartoon and its lucrative offshoots: books,
films, radio shows and, currently on display at the Chicago
World's Fair, a kooky museum and performance hall called the
Odditorium.

After a three-hour stopover at the bustling Rutbah encampment, Ripley said good-bye to Rogers and reboarded his bus,
which drove on through the sweltering night. At dawn, 250
miles later, Ripley spotted the sun-sparkled minarets of Baghdad's mosques.

✳ ✳ ✳

RIPLEY HAD BEEN TRAVELING the world ever since moving to New York as a skittish rookie newspaper cartoonist in
1912. In recent years, thanks to his six-figure salary from Hearst
and even more income from other ventures, he'd ramped up
his travels, accumulating more than 130,000 miles in the past
two years alone—more than half the distance to the moon—
ranging from South America to North Africa, Fiji to Singapore,
Indian holy cities to war-wracked China. His current journey
had routed him through Naples, Alexandria, Tel Aviv, Jerusalem, Haifa, and then Damascus. His real goal was the Garden of
Eden, in Iraq, then on to Persia and, finally, forbidden *Russia*.

At the Tigris Palace Hotel in Baghdad, Ripley washed away

two days of Syrian Desert dust and walked among the ancient city's coffeehouses, jotting his first impressions of Iraq in a journal: "never see women. men everywhere, talking and drinking–smoking . . . they talk constantly . . . they are talking about nothing at all."

Ripley had been warned that Iraqis didn't always appreciate the arrival of "unbelievers" in their towns, that visitors were sometimes injured for failing to respect local customs and protocols. Despite such warnings, Ripley and Simpson pointed their cameras at everything, which usually drew curious and sometimes angry crowds, especially in poor and remote villages. At a school in Najaf, where cross-legged men studied the Koran, a group of locals surrounded them, gesturing urgently at Simpson's camera and shouting at Ripley, who later called them "a strange mixture of humanity, paralytic, half-blind, dirty, ragged, and altogether unfriendly."

In the city of Ur, he and Simpson found a secret canteen that sold cold beer and, despite a sign warning NO DRINKING ON THE PREMISES, tossed back twenty-one bottles between them, then fell asleep on an overnight train ride to Basra, where they finally reached the purported site of the Garden of Eden. An unfaithful husband and Prohibition violator, Ripley was both familiar with and fascinated by sin, which he once called "the curse of the human race—although it is very popular."

He was disappointed not to find an intact version of the biblical garden where man's first sin allegedly occurred. "NO APPLES. NO FIG LEAVES," he complained. Instead of the Tree of Knowledge of Good and Evil, from which Eve had plucked the forbidden fruit, Ripley found only a dead stump.

Still, before getting back on the road, he was sufficiently inspired to strip naked and have Simpson take pictures of him posing, Adam-esque, behind a palm tree.

3

Back in Baghdad, Ripley drank German beers at a café near Maude Bridge, then dressed in the white robe and *keffiyeh* head-dress he'd purchased, to the amusement of a nearby crowd. An overnight train ride delivered him to Persia, his 153rd country, where he drank beer for breakfast and began mapping a route home.

* * *

DURING THE DEPRESSION, as Americans in a pre-television era sought affordable means of escape and entertainment, Ripley the traveling cartoonist provided both.

A connoisseur of mosts and bests, of fastest and farthest, of the weirdest and freakiest that the world could offer, his cartoons and essays appeared in hundreds of newspapers around the globe, in dozens of languages, and were read by many millions. His life's mission was to prove to readers that veracity and reality were elusive—King George I of England never spoke English; Aesop did not write Aesop's Fables; Buffalo Bill never once shot a buffalo; Lindbergh wasn't the first man to fly the Atlantic—and that sometimes you can't recognize truth until someone shines a light.

"I think mine is the only business in which the customer is never right," Ripley once said. "Being called untruthful is, to me, a compliment. And as long as I continue to receive the lion's share of this odd form of flattery, I don't worry about a wolf being at my door."

Fans yearned to see their own strange accomplishments, their disfigurements, and their curious misfortunes reimagined inside a *Believe It or Not* rectangle. But Ripley, never content to rely on volunteers, roamed constantly, always searching for strange facts and exotic faces for his cartoons. He met beggars and bedouins, headhunters and heads of state, royal highnesses and holy men, most of these forays funded by Hearst, whose publicists dubbed Ripley the Modern Marco Polo.

An insecure and effete kid named LeRoy, with terrible buckteeth and no shoes, Ripley had grown into an athletic and self-assured young man who always seemed to have luck and an influential patron in his corner. Once he stumbled onto his Believe It or Not concept (on the verge of age thirty), he was smart enough to parlay it into more than a newspaper cartoon, transforming and expanding himself from artist to radio and film star, to museum curator, to unlikely playboy-millionaire.

His goofy everyman perception of the world, his limited education and simplistic worldview, his naiveté . . . turns out, it all meshed with that of his core readership.

The shy, awkward misfit-loner had become champion of the freakishness of others. By celebrating weirdness, he made it mainstream, becoming one of the most widely read and influential syndicated cartoonists of his day—and among the best-traveled men in history.

More than entertainment, his global dispatches gave readers hope.

＊　＊　＊

DURING THE SEVENTEEN-HOUR DRIVE from the Iraq border to Tehran, Ripley was stopped nearly every hour by police. He complained bitterly about the "deadly barrenness and dryness" of the police-controlled country.

Ripley had hoped to escape Tehran by plane and fly into the Soviet Republic of Georgia, anxious to slip into the USSR and finally witness the collectivist, communist regime that Stalin had recently formed. Unable to secure a flight, he and Simpson decided to drive to the Persian-Soviet border, where they would walk across into Azerbaijan and then drive to Georgia—an ambitious and potentially hazardous route that would require passage through the snow-packed Caucasus Mountains.

When Ripley and Simpson finally reached the Aras River Bridge, across which lay Soviet territory, they waited two hours for the Persian border patrol to arrive and awaken their sleeping chief. Sullen officials took their time searching each piece of Ripley's luggage, which had multiplied to more than a dozen pieces in recent weeks with a surging accumulation of trinkets, carvings, and artwork.

When the guards finished with each bag, they'd carry it to the middle of the bridge and drop it in a growing heap. Ripley and Simpson were finally allowed to cross to the middle of the bridge, where they were ordered to "Halt!" Persian soldiers told them to wait while they finished their tea.

Across the bridge, young and twitchy Soviet soldiers stared coldly, aiming their bayonets as if primed for attack. Already Ripley had been at the border for more than four hours, the longest crossing in his two decades of travel. The sky grew dark as he and Simpson, hungry and cold, tired and angry, stood beside their rumpled pile of bags, hour after hour, in no-man's-land. Just thirty yards away sat their unreachable transportation: a donkey-pulled wooden carriage and its bored-looking driver.

Meanwhile, editors back in New York waited for their well-paid, peripatetic cartoonist to *please* send another batch of popular and profitable *Believe It or Not*s.

Isaac Davis Ripley, whose son would one day explore all corners of the earth, fled his dead-end Appalachian home at age fourteen and headed west. He didn't get far before the Ohio River blocked his path. Unable to pay for a ferry crossing, Isaac swam solo across the turbulent river, eventually making his way to Northern California, seeking gold but instead finding work as a carpenter and cabinetmaker. By 1889, having settled in Santa Rosa, he fell in love with a woman fourteen years younger.

Lillie Belle Yocka's family made their own risky journey toward dreams of a sunnier California life. The Yocka clan left Westport Landing (later called Kansas City) in the late 1860s, joining a straggly crowd along the Santa Fe Trail. During the westward journey, Lillie Belle was born in the back of a covered wagon, and she spent her childhood in a Northern California encampment on the banks of the Russian River.

On October 3, 1889, Lillie Belle—twenty-one and pregnant—married thirty-five-year-old Isaac Ripley, their union earning a brief mention in the *Sonoma Democrat*. Isaac built a cottage on a postage-stamp lot on Glenn Street, with intricate wood trim that looked like icicles.

A son arrived five months later, although the exact year and date of birth would remain a lingering mystery. Possibly to prevent profilers from revealing his mother's premarital pregnancy, LeRoy Robert Ripley would never admit to being born on February 22, 1890; on passport applications and other documents he'd declare 1891, 1892, 1893, or 1894 as his birth year. He'd also later claim to have been born on Christmas Day or Christmas Eve.

Isaac and Lillie named him LeRoy but usually called him Roy. Only later in life would he adopt his middle name. A daughter, Ethel, arrived three years later and the family moved into a two-story bungalow Isaac built on Orchard Street, in a quiet grid of streets, home to saloon keepers and dentists, milliners and hops brokers.

✳ ✳ ✳

LEROY WAS LEAN and slight, socially timid but full of energy. He had a ball-shaped head and high forehead, a tousled mop of hair above comically jutted-out ears, a freckled and often-dirty face. His most notable feature was an unfortunate set of protruding and misaligned front teeth, a crooked jumble that practically tumbled from his mouth. When he smiled, it looked like he was wearing novelty teeth. He usually kept his mouth closed, lips stretched to hide his dental deformity.

He suffered from a debilitating shyness, caused largely by his disfigured smile, and by a stutter that filled his speech with *uhs, ums,* and frozen words. Ripley carried himself in ways meant to shield his smile and stutter from others: hunched inward, chin tucked down, shoulders drawn forward, a protective stance. He seemed fragile, almost effeminate, and years later would admit to feeling embarrassed about his "backwardness."

Though thin, he grew to be fast and fit. A tireless neighborhood explorer, he ventured into the orchards north of town and probed south into the beckoning city. Mostly, he preferred to be alone. Barefoot, wearing carpenter's overalls or knickerbocker pants and a ragged straw hat, the curious, dreamy boy roved and reconnoitered, collecting bottle caps, cigar bands, and the baseball cards that came inside cigarette packs. He amassed a set of nails bent in the shape of each letter of the alphabet, keeping them in a cigar box under his bed.

At the one-room Lewis School, he was forced to wear shoes. He owned a single beat-up pair and would stuff newspaper into the holes and gloss them over with shoe polish. Once, he actually made a pair of shoes from folded-up newspapers, tied together with string and caked black with polish. "He wasn't fooling anyone," said one classmate. When his clothes began to fray and tear, his mother crafted new outfits by recycling old dresses and leftovers from her laundry jobs. In his flower-print pants and shirts, LeRoy was cruelly mocked. *Hey kid, why are you wearing a dress?*

At lunchtime, while the other boys chased girls around the water pump and outhouse, Ripley sat beneath a tree, drawing pictures or reading books about pirates or explorers. In class, students were required to stand and recite poems or essays, but Ripley's stutter made this an excruciating nightmare. Hunched over at his desk, he constantly scribbled and sketched in his notebooks. One teacher would smack him upside the head whenever she caught him copying scenes out of his history book instead of paying attention to the lessons.

"Everyone at school picked on him because he was so different," a classmate would later say. "Not one of the guys," said another.

After a bad day at school he'd escape to the attic of his house to draw or carve letters into the roof beams. Other early artistic inclinations included defacing his bedroom wall and chewing on pencils.

✳ ✳ ✳

THOUGH IT WOULD become an epicurean mecca, the land of Ripley's youth—known by the Pomo and Miwok Indians as *Sonoma,* or Valley of the Moon—was more Wild West than wine country. A few years past its cowboy-and-Indian days, Santa Rosa and nearby Sonoma and Napa could be dangerous and deadly. When Ripley was a toddler, the *Sonoma Democrat* reported in breathless detail how Indians had looted a winery, adding: "The red-skins have been on a wild debauch."

Also full of debauch were the newspapers. LeRoy learned to read in a lively two-paper town whose editors practiced what would soon be called yellow journalism. The *Democrat* and its rival, the *Santa Rosa Republican,* cackled with stories of murderous deeds and accidental deaths, divorces, suicides, and all variety of lunacy, a daily "news of the weird." People plunged off railroad trestles, lost limbs beneath train wheels, became mangled by farm machines. They shot each other over card games, stole horses, robbed banks. The *Democrat* was especially poetic in its depictions of death, offering vivid descriptions of "putrescent" bodies "lying in pools of blood."

Santa Rosa's children were kept close to home and warned to stay away from the streets of downtown, especially Chinatown and its alleged opium dens. With his parents working—Dad as a carpenter, Mom taking in laundry and sewing jobs—Ripley had the freedom to ramble. A shoeless ragamuffin, he scampered through streets and alleys, avoiding the train and trolley traffic but irresistibly lured to Chinatown, where he'd peek into the laundries, restaurants, and shops. The proprietors, all men, puffed on long bamboo pipes and beckoned the curious kid, offering peculiar treats like lychee nuts.

Ripley found Santa Rosa's small Chinese community exotic and bizarre. He was awed by the strange clothes, the spicy food smells, and the hand-lettered signs whose symbols looked like hieroglyphs. On the few occasions his parents took him to San Francisco, the highlight was always a brief glimpse of shambling Chinatown.

By 1900, Santa Rosa was home to six thousand farmers, timbermen, miners, vintners, and railroad workers—a vibrant downtown of dusty roads clotted by horse-drawn carts, bicycles, and livestock. The region had attracted a variegated mix of romantic eccentrics, including Thomas Lake Harris, charismatic leader of an alternative-lifestyle "Brotherhood of the New Life" commune, who extolled the virtues of wine, tobacco, and sexuality. As one Sonoma County historian put it, Santa Rosa and its environs was a land of "explorers, rancheros, vintners, artists, writers, athletes, movers & shakers & dreamers."

Among the dreamers was famed horticulturalist Luther Burbank, who created hundreds of fruit, flower, and vegetable varieties at his agricultural laboratory—a thornless cactus, a white blackberry, a "New Seedling Cherry," the result of grafting two hundred cherry varieties onto one tree. Burbank considered California an unconquered land, a new world where a man who avoided alcohol and tobacco "has ten thousand chances of success."

ℰ BELIEVE IT! ℑ

Burbank's prized creation, the perky perennial he named the Shasta Daisy, took seventeen years of trial and error.

✳   ✳   ✳

THE SANTA ROSA of his childhood taught Ripley many things, not least of which was to appreciate off-kilter hobbyists, obsessives, and fanatics, the kind who would years later become targets of his own journalistic curiosity. Ripley's hometown confirmed that you could be both odd and fascinating, obsessive and successful.

Even Ripley's mother's church had an appealingly curious backstory. In 1873, congregants of the First Baptist Church, having outgrown their place of worship, felled a 275-foot redwood; sawed and sliced it into studs, beams, and planks; hauled it to town; and assembled a new church from the single tree. Isaac Ripley had been among the builders of the structure that earned headlines as "The Church Built of One Tree."

Evidence that a town of death and debauchery could also be a place of magic and wonder was found on the city's stages, too. The Athenaeum Theatre hosted a unique medley of entertainment, from Shakespeare to vaudeville to minstrel shows. Newspaper ads hawked the "world's greatest cornetist" and the "world's most marvelous dancer." The nearby Novelty Theatre hosted lowlier acts: a midget show, a bone-playing musician, a boxing kangaroo.

Santa Rosa was also a regular stop on the circus circuit, visited by Tom Thumb's "Smallest Human Beings in the World" and Buffalo Bill's "Wild West Show." The Ringling Brothers Circus visited annually, and when Barnum & Bailey's "Greatest Show on Earth" arrived in town, the *Democrat* described its "troupe of wonderful midgets [and] a giant who stands nearly eight feet tall—All these curious people . . . living wonders."

For a kid who was mocked and teased for his funny looks and shabby clothes, his balky speech and his pathological dread of girls, Santa Rosa proved to be an ideal hometown, a place where the unusual was acceptable, where a person could be a bit peculiar and still succeed.

"Anybody who is born in Santa Rosa must turn out to be either an artist or a poet, for the spirit of the hills gets into your blood out there," Ripley would say years later, calling his home "the quaintest little town in the United States."

* * *

BY THE FALL OF 1904, when he entered Santa Rosa High, Ripley had grown taller and stronger, filling out his scrawny frame and showing signs of athletic prowess. In the spring of his freshman year he joined the baseball team, though he remained an awkward, eye-averting doodler. "No one thought he would amount to much of anything," said a classmate.

In the presence of female classmates, he showed a laughable insecurity. Teachers recalled seeing him run when girls came near and classmates would later remember him as "not much of a ladies' man." His one true female friend, who had roamed with him through downtown and among Chinatown's alleys, was Nell "Nellie Bell" Griffith. By high school, Nell had grown into a dark-haired beauty, a poet and basketball standout. Though she'd tell classmates that she and LeRoy were just "very close friends," Ripley clearly thought it was more than that.

Nell never seemed bothered by Ripley's gawky looks. She knew he was "awkward," but also funny, smart, and artistic. Nell's parents owned an orchard, where she and Ripley often played among the rows of trees. Ripley once upset a bees' nest and ran away screaming—a scene that he captured in a pencil drawing, which he presented to Nell.

In class, Ripley began letting classmates lean over his shoulder to watch him draw amusing caricatures of peers and teachers. Among his popular sketches were those of the balding, bespectacled history teacher, Charles T. Conger, despised by students and teachers alike, whom Ripley posed in what he called "some of his favorite attitudes": sitting at his desk with arms spread wide; sitting on a stool pointing a long ruler at the blackboard. Conger didn't appreciate the likenesses, but others did, and classmates' reactions to his drawings marked the first time Ripley stood out for reasons other than his crooked teeth and stammer.

Notebooks, textbooks, sheets of scrap paper—no empty space was safe from Ripley's eager pencil. His happiest, purest school moments were with a pencil in his right hand, a clean white space before him. His family couldn't afford art supplies, so he hoarded butcher paper and used a cutting board as an easel. Though he never took drawing lessons, he practiced relentlessly, sitting in front of a mirror to study his own lips, eyes, and facial muscles, then drawing his own expressions on crumpled scraps of butcher paper, smiling, scowling, frowning.

He once splurged on a five-cent postcard featuring a painting called *The Wedding Feast,* and practiced copying the scene, over and over. He would follow his sister and mother around, sketching them as they cleaned dishes, washed clothes, or hung laundry, pleading with Ethel or Lillie Belle to sit or stand still for just a few minutes. "Pose for me just a little while, will you?" he'd ask, and they usually gave in.

As he prepared to enter his second year of high school, in mid-1905, Ripley seemed to be settling into a comfortable routine. He'd started making a few friends, and had begun making a less-than-negative impression on classmates. The bucktoothed young misfit was beginning to feel *normal.*

That's when everything changed.

* * *

ISAAC RIPLEY WAS A GLUM, gruff, and serious man, judging by the scant few surviving photographs: the corners of his mustachioed mouth were pulled low and his deep, dark eyes were typically pinched into a scowl. He must have seemed especially forlorn that Friday night in September of 1905.

Ripley's grandmother, who had recently moved to Santa Rosa, had died of a lung hemorrhage that summer, and Isaac was still mourning his mother's death. After dinner on the night of September 15, he felt a crushing pain in his chest. Lillie Belle summoned the local physician, Dr. Jesse, who gave Isaac some medicine to ease his discomfort. A few hours later, just before midnight, Isaac was beset by another attack. Within thirty minutes he was dead, his wife and children by his side.

Ten days shy of his fifty-first birthday, Isaac was buried at the Odd Fellows Cemetery, just blocks from his home. A choral quartet sang as Isaac's brethren from the carpenters' union and the Woodmen of the World lowered his casket into the ground. LeRoy and sister, Ethel, stood beside their mother, who held in her arms the newest family member, sixteen-month-old Douglas.

Alone with three children, Lillie had no apparent skills with which to find a decent job. She began renting out a room to tenants, baking bread, continuing to take on needlework and the laundry of others while looking for a nursing job. Somehow, she was determined to keep her fragile household intact.

Short, tough, and attractive, she had always been the dominant parent, quick-witted and sharp-tongued. With a pouty mouth, dark skin and eyes, narrow waist, and shapely hips, even Ripley's classmates thought his mother was "quite attractive." Though he'd later speak adoringly of Lillie, Ripley "never spoke much about his father," according to one longtime friend. "And the impression is left, somehow, that he did not think too much of him."

Ripley tried to continue in the pose of a typical high school kid, joining the yearbook and school newsletter staffs in his sophomore year. His first credited drawings were published in *The Porcupine* just weeks after his father's death, including a caricature of the football team's fullback. His mother thought little of her son's drawings, though. Without a family breadwinner, she needed her son to find a job. He reluctantly started delivering newspapers before school but quickly decided that early-morning newspaper delivery wasn't for him, and by early 1906 he had quit.

Leaving his newspaper job kept Ripley safely in bed the morning of April 18, 1906, the deadly and historic day that he'd rarely talk about as an adult.

In downtown Santa Rosa, the Fourth Street trolley was preparing for its morning runs and Chinatown's laundrymen began washing the day's clothes. On that otherwise normal morning, paperboys were among the few people outside before dawn, loading up copies of the *Press Democrat* to hurl onto steps and stoops. Among the headline-wielding delivery boys were Charles Shepard and brothers George and Willie Bluth. They would be the first to die.

As the deadliest earthquake in US history began to inflict its devastating wrath, sixteen-year-old ex-paperboy LeRoy Ripley was asleep at his Orchard Street home.

Just past five a.m., miles to the west and deep beneath the Pacific, slabs of earth began to wrench and buck, sending shivers along the San Andreas Fault, the recently discovered jagged crack in the planet. Estimated between 7.9 and 8.3 on the Richter scale, the quake ripped up and down America's western shoreline, heaving earthen grumbles that began rocking Northern California and sending quivers as far north as Oregon and as far south as Los Angeles.

The timbers of the Ripley house twisted and bowed, and the cottage that Isaac had built seemed about to implode into splinters. Pictures popped off walls, beds and furniture danced, dishes fell and shattered. Ripley and his family sprinted out the front door, across the small front yard and onto the dirt-paved street, which undulated as if liquefied. No place felt safe.

Santa Rosans were used to occasional seismic episodes; Ripley had experienced dozens and older residents had survived hundreds. But this felt different. Houses jumped, swayed, and moaned. During an excruciating sixty seconds of tremors, Ripley's town was torn apart. Local plant king Luther Burbank would later describe how everything moved in all directions at once, the "violent vertical and horizontal vibrations . . . a twisting back and forth . . . all this tipping from side to side."

Trees jumped like pogo sticks, streets rose and fell like ocean swells. Seemingly indestructible brick-and-mortar buildings imploded. The courthouse, the Athenaeum, department stores, and banks wiggled and fell, crushing or trapping occupants. One witness later described scenes of sheer chaos: "With fires advancing unchecked, people were crawling out through the rubbish, bleeding and half-dressed, covered from head to foot with lime and sickening dust."

Downed electrical wires crackled and sparked, a broken gas line caught fire, and eight people died when Haven Hardware exploded. A blaze at Rochdale's grocery store swept through downtown, killing Eli Loeb, whose wife's legs had to be amputated to save her from the fire. One man found himself trapped beneath a large timber and with flames prowling nearer begged someone to shoot him, but no one could get close.

Flames raged unchecked all morning. The Occidental, Saint Rose, and Grand hotels all "fell as if constructed of playing cards, and in the heaps were buried the hundreds of lodgers," the *San Francisco Bulletin* would report the next day.

The *Press Democrat* would describe its own losses. During the first rumblings, employees had rushed from the building. A press operator named W. S. Lindley was last to reach the exit, and as he got to the door the outer wall collapsed, falling away from him and onto three paperboys and Lindley's fellow pressman, Milo Fish, who left behind a wife and six children. A fourth paperboy burned to death.

As the terrible day came to a solemn close, Santa Rosans could see a deep glow to the south. They weren't the only ones to experience death and destruction.

✳ ✳ ✳

DAYS AFTER THE FIRES had been doused, Ripley visited San Francisco by train to see the destruction for himself, climbing atop Nob Hill to look out at a heartbreaking panorama that he'd one day describe as "a mass of smoking ruins as far as the eye could see."

While it would historically be known as the Great San Francisco Earthquake, Santa Rosa sustained proportionally more damage than any other city and, with at least a hundred dead, a higher per-capita death toll. The headline in a joint earthquake edition of San Francisco's newspapers declared, SANTA ROSA IS A TOTAL WRECK.

↩ BELIEVE IT! ↪

Millions of gallons of wine, stored in casks in warehouses, ruptured and spilled, turning Santa Rosa's streets into red rivers of wine, whose bouquet attracted the discerning noses of farm animals. Residents soon found drunken pigs and dogs staggering in the streets.

When the smoke cleared, the heart of Santa Rosa was revealed to have been churned into absolute carnage. The dome above the stately courthouse, as one writer put it, had "collapsed like a fallen wedding cake." City Hall was gone. The hotels, the beloved theaters, and even Chinatown, all gone. The children of Santa Rosa would weep to learn that even Reed's candy store was now ash and rubble.

It was suddenly a busy time for carpenters, and Santa Rosa could have used the skills of a man like Isaac Ripley, who had been dead now for half a year.

The earthquake would remain a dark scar on Ripley's childhood—second in a double dose of tragedy. In less than a year, his otherwise comfortable life had been unmade by the dual cataclysms of his father's death and the quake, the defining events of his youth. With streets still littered with debris, schools reopened within a month. But the earthquake ignited in Ripley a far-fetched goal: to leave his busted-up hometown, just as Isaac had done.

At Santa Rosa High, he got help toward that goal from an unlikely patron.

* * *

FRANCES LOUISE "FANNY" O'MEARA, daughter of a feisty Oregon newspaperman, started teaching English in the late 1880s and would dedicate her entire life to Santa Rosa High. "Beloved" is how most graduates would describe her, as well as "tenacious" and "strict." Said one: "She saturated us with poetry and filled every day with such lively imagination." Ripley adored O'Meara, often addressing her as "Mother."

Six months after the earthquake, in the fall of Ripley's junior year, O'Meara assigned an essay about John Greenleaf Whittier's poem "Snowbound." Ripley hated writing compositions and, especially, reading them aloud. O'Meara would cringe at Ripley's stuttering attempts to recite for his classmates. Knowing that he liked to draw—the evidence was all over his notebooks—she decided to allow him to turn in his assignment in the form of a drawing.

The next day, Ripley handed in a sketch entitled "The Coming of the Snowstorm Told." In black-and-white, it conveyed the mood of Whittier's whiteout: *No cloud above, no earth below / a universe of sky and snow!* The next day, Ripley arrived early to class and handed O'Meara another drawing, a living-room scene drawn in pencil of Whittier's snowbound family.

The drawing had "so much feeling" that O'Meara declared it "a masterpiece" and posted it prominently at the front of the classroom. O'Meara realized she could spare Ripley the mortifying experience of reciting his essays aloud. "You like to draw," she told him. "Now, when I assign a paper to the class, if you would rather draw a picture, I'll take the picture as a paper."

Ripley would turn in dozens of drawings, from Shakespearean scenes to Longfellow's village smithy. O'Meara considered Ripley's art more than just boyish efforts at avoiding essays. He took each assignment seriously, researching the historical details. She'd hang them above the blackboard to use as teaching aids and kept them stacked and numbered in a closet. (The drawings would be lost in a 1921 fire that leveled the school.)

* * *

MEANWHILE, Ripley had begun spending more and more time on the baseball diamond, having discovered an agile, loose-limbed adaptability that earned him time at left field, second base, and even the pitcher's mound. "He was one of the best ballplayers we ever had," said a classmate.

Ripley started playing for local semi-professional "bush league" teams, and let himself dream of one day playing for his favorite team, the New York Giants. But Lillie Belle told her son he was too smart to waste time on art and baseball and encouraged him to choose a trade to pursue after high school—if not sooner. "Get a *real* job," she'd say. He earned some money drawing posters and advertisements for one ball team while working various odd jobs—loading fruit and vegetable wagons, painting neighbors' porches, doing yard work. Some weeks he took home as much as $15.

By his senior year, he'd found part-time work polishing headstones at Fisher & Kinslow Marble Works, which had crafted the tombstone atop his father's grave. Old man Fisher, a jolly man in a solemn profession, even let Ripley create a couple of tombstone designs. But Ripley soon quit, rejecting tombstones as "too gloomy." His mother suggested he consider the ministry while warning that if he insisted on becoming an athlete or an artist he faced the "thoroughly enjoyable prospect of slowly expiring at an early age of starvation."

Ripley tried convincing his mother there was money to be made in the popular new phenomenon called *comics*. The success of *Hogan's Alley*, introduced in Joseph Pulitzer's *New York World* in 1895 and featuring a bucktoothed, barefoot immigrant known as the Yellow Kid, had ignited a fierce competition for dominance in the new world of the funnies. Comics had since become newspaper staples, luring a new generation of boys toward the newspaper business.

Santa Rosa's papers weren't yet carrying regular comic strips; the *Press Democrat* lost its cartoonist years earlier. But down in San Francisco, the *Bulletin, Chronicle, Call,* and *Examiner* all employed staff artists and illustrators, some earning $1,000 a year or more—*drawing pictures for a living.*

With that kind of money in comics, Ripley decided to give it a shot. In late 1907 he mailed a one-panel cartoon to *LIFE* magazine in New York. The sketch showed a pretty woman standing beside a wooden washtub, steam curling up from the water as she wrings clothes through hand-cranked twin rollers. She wears a thin hint of a contented smile, her hair drawn back in a tight bun, sleeves rolled up, her dress draped to her ankles.

Playing with homonyms—*belle/bell, wringing/ringing*—his caption read: "The Village Bell Was Slowly Ringing." In the bottom right corner he signed "Ripley '07."

* * *

WHILE WAITING for *LIFE*'s reply, Ripley continued drawing cartoons for the school newsletter, *The Porcupine*, where he had been named "staff artist." In early 1908, he began working on drawings for his commencement program. Graduation was now less than six months away.

As high school drew to a close, Ripley posed with the rest of the yearbook staff wearing a new suit and tie his mother had saved for. In this and other photos, it was apparent that Ripley had matured into an oddly striking specimen. With his stuck-out teeth and jutting ears, his long nose and greased-back hair, he had a vaguely Dracula-like appearance. Instead of grotesque, though, he now looked almost menacing. Other high school photos show him with expressions that look variously as if he's about to snicker, or has a barely contained secret, or is crazy or scared—as though he *knows* something about you.

Such facial expressions were often the result of attempting to hide his buckteeth behind constantly pulled-shut lips. But a mouth like Ripley's simply refused to be hidden. When he laughed or smiled, spoke or ate, teeth spilled out, especially when he stuttered. Letters *b*, *f*, and *p* were particular nuisances, and Ripley frequently wrestled with the choices facing some-one who couldn't afford expensive dentistry. He could avoid the world, crawl into a hole, become a monk or a hermit. Or he could create a defiant "I am who I am" persona. Buoyed by the confidence gained from his artwork and athleticism, he chose the latter.

It showed in his emerging style of dress and his dimpled and unabashedly toothy smiles in certain photos. No longer a barefoot street rat in overalls, he often wore a white shirt and thin black tie with his new graduation suit. Later, as his income allowed, he would complement the suit with bow ties, hats, and nice shoes—efforts to distract people's attention, to stand out and be noticed for something other than his catastrophe of teeth.

One person had seen this self-assured side of Ripley all along. After their childhood days of romping around Santa Rosa, Nell Griffith had watched the real LeRoy Ripley slowly emerge through high school. For his part, Ripley considered Nell his best friend. But in the love letters he'd begun writing he made it clear he was now ready for more.

* * *

SANTA ROSA HIGH'S CLASS of 1908 commencement was held on a warm June night, an overflow crowd spilling out of the auditorium as graduates received their diplomas. It was, as the newspaper put it, "a happy event in the lives of their fathers and mothers," who clutched copies of the commencement program, its cover featuring a boy in cap and gown, diploma in his hand, drawn and signed "By LeRoy Ripley."

Ripley, however, was not among the twenty-eight graduates that night. Despite Miss O'Meara's best efforts to help him after his father's death, he had left school that spring. The story he'd tell years later was that it was time to find a job and help his family. One problem with that story is the lack of evidence of gainful employment. Instead, there's much evidence of baseball playing, with Ripley's name appearing regularly on the local sports pages through 1908.

Rumors tittered among classmates. *Did he get kicked out? Did he just get bored with it all?* Among the nastier rumors was that Ripley was so poor his mother had turned to prostitution. He'd been a mysterious presence in their school. Other kids liked him fine, they just didn't understand him. Maybe they'd never been able to get past the discomfort of seeing those terrible teeth up close. Maybe they judged him, unable to dispel memories of the stammering elementary school misfit. Or maybe Ripley was the one who pulled back, not letting others get close.

"He was modest and shy, but he couldn't be pushed around," one classmate said.

The timid boy had grown into a young man who was far bolder, smarter, and more ambitious than he let on. Not wanting to be viewed as "a goofy kid from a farm town," as he once put it, he'd already decided to leave the farm town behind. However, even the nearest city seemed beyond his reach.

"San Francisco was where I wanted to go," he confessed many years later. "It wasn't fifty miles away, but it could have been Peking for all the hope I had for ever living there."

Yet, when he received good news from New York, those fifty miles suddenly seemed like less.

LIFE's editors decided to publish Ripley's "Village Bell" cartoon, which ran in the June 18 issue of the magazine—five days after his classmates graduated without him. The poised and pretty "Bell," a dead ringer for Ripley's mother, appeared in the lower-left corner of page three. A letter soon arrived from New York containing his $8 payment. Amazed that his hobby was worth $8 per drawing, he realized that cartooning might indeed be his way out.

That summer, Ripley earned the attentions of a patron who would help him leave Santa Rosa, introducing him to the newsman's life, a life beyond all dreams.

"A high and narrow string bean of a boy" was Carol Read Ennis's first impression of LeRoy Ripley. An attractive freelance writer, she visited Santa Rosa in the summer of 1908 to profile Luther Burbank for the *San Francisco Call*. While renting a room at the Ripley home, Ennis often saw her landlady's son curled beneath a tree, scribbling in beat-up sketch pads when he was supposed to be weeding the garden.

But she felt the bucktoothed high-school dropout had "a

terrific dynamo of unharnessed energy" and decided to make him her pet project. Just as O'Meara had perceived something special in Ripley, Carol Ennis saw a talent where others saw a fantasist, promise where others saw indolence.

"Do you know anything about politics, Roy?" Ennis asked him.

"Not a thing," he admitted, confessing that what he really cared about was baseball.

Ennis suggested he work up a series of cartoon panels about the upcoming presidential race. Ripley drew a few political and sports sketches, which Ennis took to San Francisco and began peddling to friends and colleagues.

By fall, Ripley's portfolio had reached the desk of Fremont Older, the man who had turned the moribund *San Francisco Bulletin* into one of the largest papers west of Chicago. Older handed Ripley's drawings over to his brother-in-law, Hiland L. "Hy" Baggerly, the paper's sports editor, and in February of 1909 Ripley received a letter. "Just came back in time to receive your cartoons, which are very good," Baggerly wrote. "They are so good I have decided to give you a trial, providing we can agree upon a salary." Baggerly offered $8 a week and the promise of a $2 raise "if you make good."

"I think you have a great future," said the editor who helped launch the careers of such pioneering cartoonists as Rube Goldberg and Thomas "Tad" Dorgan.

Though he'd later claim to have started his newspaper career at age sixteen, Ripley was about to turn nineteen. Lacking a diploma or any prospects, he willingly hung up his baseball mitt and wrote to tell Baggerly he was "tickled." He would save Baggerly's letter the rest of his days, and Ennis would remain a lifelong friend.

The *Press Democrat* soon published a brief item, headlined

ROY RIPLEY IS A STAFF ARTIST NOW. He would never live in Santa Rosa again.

* * *

WHEN SANTA ROSANS visited San Francisco, though traveling fifty miles south, they called it "going up to the city." When Ripley went up to the city in 1909, he wore his best clothes—his graduation suit, a huge bow tie, a straw hat perched high atop his head—but still felt like "a gawky youth . . . a wistful rube."

After a Northwest Pacific train ride to Sausalito, he took the ferry past Alcatraz and across the bay to the Embarcadero. From there, walking up Market Street, he stopped at the Block Mercantile Co., a curio shop filled with antique weapons, stuffed mermaids, Asian tools, and a life-size, eerily realistic wooden statue of a Japanese man, which Ripley coveted. Atop Nob Hill, where he had stood dumbstruck three years earlier watching the ruined city smolder, he looked out from the steps of the elegant Fairmont Hotel onto a resurrected San Francisco.

Since the earthquake and fire, the resilient city by the bay had surged ahead, a new stone-and-brick metropolis replacing the wooden city that had burned to cinders. Even Chinatown had rebuilt, with an effort toward pagoda roofs, paper lanterns, and Oriental architecture, looking more exotic and colorful than before.

Ripley loved what he saw, even though the only affordable lodging he could find was *beneath* the city, in a one-room basement apartment on McAllister. The $5 weekly rent would leave just a few dollars a week for food and other basics. He adapted quickly, learning to hop on and off cable cars, wandering through Chinatown, just as he had in Santa Rosa. Though he considered city life to be "thrilling and daring," his lone fear was losing Nell. She'd worried the big city would change him, but Ripley assured her by letter that he'd only change for the better.

When he arrived at the three-year-old Bulletin Building off Market Street and reached the top-floor art room, Ripley was told his job was simple: a cartoon a day, if not more. His first professional cartoon ran on his birthday, February 22, 1909: a bucktoothed baseball fan's head emerges from a flower-shaped baseball. The caption: "A Spring Blossom." The signature: "Rip '09." During his first weeks, he worked tirelessly, producing more than three dozen full-size cartoons and scores of smaller illustrations.

He even wrote his first article—"By Rip," said the byline— about a fighter who had caused a stir in New York by breathing pure oxygen between rounds. In sticking to familiar territory, he mostly focused on baseball. When the minor-league San Francisco Seals prevailed in a twenty-four-inning battle against the Oakland Oaks, Ripley sketched Father Time writing in his "Baseball History" book, "This is the greatest yet."

Six months into his new job, however, his lack of training as either journalist or artist began to show. His drawings still resembled his high school newsletter work and Ripley worried that his limited knowledge of sports "made the job doubly difficult." He hadn't even found his signature yet, still experimenting with "Rip," "Ripley," occasionally "R" or "R2." Coworkers tried to encourage him, but Ripley could tell that his boss, Baggerly, might be having second thoughts.

* * *

AS A CHILD, Ripley's exposure to art had been limited to the illustrations in his adventure and history books. He received little encouragement at home or at school, and would later say that his youthful art training consisted of teething on a pencil as an infant, drawing on his bedroom walls, and scrawling on his schoolbooks. "Who did I study under?" he'd say when asked who taught him to draw. "I studied under the stars in Santa Rosa."

In San Francisco, Ripley was suddenly working along-side—or in the shadow of—cartoonists who were taking the concept of illustrated newspaper entertainment to new levels. At the time, sports photography was still an imperfect format, with photos playing a secondary (and blurry) role to cartoons. Sports cartoonists gave readers a visual summary of last night's game or a preview of tomorrow's. Relying heavily on caricature, they also gave intimate portrayals of the personalities of sport.

Cartoons had migrated to all sections of the newspaper, and a golden era for cartooning was under way. In fact, Rip-ley arrived in San Francisco shortly after the nation's first daily "comic strip" had appeared in print. While working in the *San Francisco Chronicle*'s sports department, Bud Fisher drew a tall, chinless, mustachioed gambler called Mr. A. Mutt. A year later he paired Mutt with a short, bald guy named Jeff. Though it wasn't yet called *Mutt and Jeff,* the cartoon was hugely popular and Fisher was soon earning an unheard-of $45 a week at William Randolph Hearst's *San Francisco Examiner.*

Two of Ripley's predecessors had been lured to New York by larger salaries and readerships. Thomas Aloysius Dorgan, known as "Tad," had started at the *Bulletin* at age fourteen, only a year after losing three fingers on his right hand in a freak accident. He now worked for Hearst's *Evening Journal* in New York. Tad's successor at the *Bulletin*, Rube Goldberg, had also moved to New York, where he earned $50 a week drawing his popular *Foolish Questions* cartoon. (Example: A father asks his pipe-smoking son, "Son, are you smoking that pipe again?" The son's reply, "No, Dad, this is a portable kitchenette and I'm frying smelt for dinner.")

✌ BELIEVE IT! ✧

Through the early 1900s Tad coined dozens of American slang terms, including "for crying out loud," the "cat's meow," the "cat's pajamas," "hard-boiled," "drugstore cowboy," "Yes, we have no bananas," "twenty-three, Skidoo," and "as busy as a one-armed paperhanger."

San Francisco had become an important training ground for anyone hoping to actually make a *living* drawing pictures for newspapers. Goldberg later said San Francisco was where he honed his craft, borrowing ideas from others and learning to trust his personality. "Personality is all-important in any creative art," said the man who would later create *Mike and Ike* and *Boob McNutt*. "If you have personality, it will show in your drawing."

Ripley worked among other pioneering cartoonists at the *Bulletin*—Herb Roth, Hype Igoe, and Paul Terry, soon to be household names. Like many cartoonists, Ripley borrowed heavily from techniques that had evolved over the previous decade. Characters "spoke" in overhead balloons; exclamation points meant surprise; question marks meant confusion. Puffs of dust behind someone's feet meant motion, buzzing z's meant sleep. Such pioneering devices had become universal by 1909. Still, there was plenty of room for innovation, yet Ripley struggled to find his own ideas and to trust his own sheepish personality.

His recently honed self-confidence now weakened, Ripley was learning that a talented artist wasn't automatically a talented cartoonist.

Many of his early efforts suffered from clutter and cliché, a hodgepodge of recycled techniques. His drawings were top-notch and his talent shined bright when he sketched realistic portraits of sports stars, especially facial close-ups. But his cartoony cartoons just weren't that funny, distinguished, or sophisticated. Ripley struggled with a nagging feeling that he didn't quite belong. "It was a hard grind," he'd later confess.

His boss seemed to agree. Four months after hiring him, he changed his mind.

* * *

RIPLEY WASN'T ANGRY about getting fired in June of 1909. Like Miss O'Meara and Carol Ennis, Hy Baggerly had taken a chance on him, and Ripley would remain "everlastingly in debt." He would similarly dote on O'Meara and Ennis, one day lavishing them with gifts, flowers, and limousine rides, signing letters "ever devotedly." Still, losing his job confirmed the feeling that had gnawed at Ripley during his early months in San Francisco, that he was still just an "uncultured" boob.

"My fellow workers felt sorry for me . . . and did everything possible to help me along," he'd later say. "But my work was poor. I was too young."

Maybe his mother had been right—with no art training, he had been unequipped for an artistic career and should have kept working with tombstones. He remained a fatherless kid from the country, thrown into the sophisticated big city whose societal rules he'd yet to master.

"I'm as yet a stranger in a strange world," he wrote to Nell. "And such a strange world, too!"

He had hoped to convince Nell to join him in San Francisco, suggesting by letter that they could be together "forever." Now he was jobless.

After his firing, he wandered the narrow, spice-scented streets and alleys of Chinatown, where he could mingle unselfconsciously, slurping cheap noodles and listening to shopkeepers tell stories of the old country in chopped-up English while puffing on their bamboo pipes. Just as Santa Rosa's small Chinatown had been an enticement, he was fascinated by the exotic people in their long gowns, the shops and aromas of the nation's liveliest Chinatown. At a time of loneliness and near poverty, having lost his first real job, with a $5 weekly rent to cover and a widowed mother counting on his contributions, he found the Chinese to be kind and generous, a "truly civilized people."

"When I was hungry, they fed me," he'd say years later when asked about the origins of his love of all things Oriental.

He would soon meet men who had actually visited the places he learned about in Chinatown—Peking and Nanking, Shanghai and Canton—further stoking a passion for Asia that would slowly grow into an obsession. But before he could even dream of visiting China, he needed a job.

He had made it to San Francisco, but it might as well be Peking without an income.

Three years after the earthquake, San Francisco had rebounded beautifully, as had its journalism—the *Call, News, Post, Chronicle, Examiner,* and *Bulletin* all thriving in modern new buildings. The city that launched the careers of Mark Twain (the *Call*) and Sinclair Lewis (the *Bulletin*) continued to bolster its reputation as a lively literary town whose competitive cluster of publications vied for the attentions of more than half a million readers.

Determined to remain a San Francisco newsman and not skulk back to Santa Rosa, Ripley gathered a portfolio of drawings and one foggy June morning slipped through the front doors of the *Chronicle,* whose post-quake headquarters was just a block up Market Street from the *Bulletin.* His timing was just right. The *Chronicle*'s sports cartoonist, Harry Hershfield, had injured his eye and was unable to keep up with his assignments. When Ripley arrived—admittedly scared and "mute as a dumbwaiter"—Hershfield suggested, *Let this young fellow do it.*

"The boy is good," Hershfield told sports editor Harry B. Smith, after looking at Ripley's work. "Give him a chance."

Smith offered Ripley a trial run at $10 a week, two dollars

more than he'd been making at the *Bulletin*. Barely two weeks after his final cartoon had run in the *Bulletin*, his work was suddenly appearing in the pages of his former competitor, sometimes on the front page.

This time, Ripley wasn't taking any chances. Immediately after starting at the *Chronicle*, he signed up for his first-ever art classes.

Five mornings a week he studied in a downtown classroom, learning about the proper size of an ear, proper head-to-body proportions (an eight-to-one ratio), and the best materials (Gillott's pens and Bristol or Ross board). After class, he'd report to the *Chronicle*'s art room and toil "like a madman," drawing hundreds of cartoons and seeking advice from anyone willing to critique him. Most nights, he stayed until ten—long after the others had left. He ate cheap Chinatown meals, collapsed in his basement apartment, and was back at art school by eight thirty a.m.

Within a few months, Ripley felt he had finally become "a passable artist."

* * *

RIPLEY HAD LEARNED a valuable lesson about his new profession: fear and uncertainty were the side effects of being paid to do what he loved. "An artist is a natural coward," he'd tell an interviewer years later. "He's always afraid of losing his job."

That fear inspired him to draw constantly, obsessively: editorial-page cartoons, slice-of-life scenes, political rallies, car shows, dog shows. He caricatured theater stars and businessmen, no topic too insignificant that it couldn't be rendered by his pen. For a short article about a drunk cat that jumped to its death, he offered *two* sketches. (Said the cat, midair: "Farewell cruel woild.") He sketched actors, comedians, acrobats, magicians, and once, a man who could "walk" up and down stairs on his head.

"The Chronicle is an excellent place to work," he wrote to Nell Griffith late that summer of 1909. "And everything is most agreeable."

Editors loved his enthusiastic productivity and rewarded him with steady raises that would lift his weekly salary to $20. He had been sending money home to his family but now decided he was making enough to invite his mother and brother to join him in the big city. When his sixteen-year-old sister, Ethel, got married and left home, Lillie and Doug moved into the small McAllister Street apartment. Ripley reported to Nell that Santa Rosa now "seems well rid of the Ripleys."

By letter, he repeatedly urged Nell to visit too. "I tell you it is hell to live so apart!" he wrote.

In the fall of 1909, Nell finally gave in. She stayed at his apartment for two days and toured the city with Ripley, his mother, and his brother. Before heading back to Santa Rosa, she gave him a sultry picture of herself. Ripley soon wrote to tell her the photo had become "a stimulant to my imagination of you."

In increasingly romantic letters, calling her "honey girl" and "dearest friend in the world," he practically begged her to move to San Francisco. "I don't know of anything more pleasing or beautiful than that friendship in which each one trusts the other, and where frankness is enjoyed by both!" Ripley wrote. "I hope ours is, or will be of that kind. Do you?"

But Nell soon began backing away, telling him they lived too far apart. Then, when Ripley visited Santa Rosa that Christmas, Nell broke his heart. She didn't envision a future as Mrs. LeRoy Ripley, she said. In fact, she'd begun dating another ex-classmate, a handsome Santa Rosa High football star.

Ripley kept writing letters—"I want to see you!"—but in time he reluctantly accepted that he might become nothing more than a warm memory of Nell's youth, "something to look back upon, maybe to think about sometimes," he told her.

In one of his final letters to Nell, he somewhat pathetically told her that he hoped his own life mate would appear "in the misty distance of the future," and that she and Nell might become friends. But so far, "that girlie of the future is not in sight yet," he wrote. "If she was, I would be too busy to look."

Fortunately, after the breakup, Ripley found himself distracted by the assignment of a lifetime.

* * *

AFTER LESS THAN A YEAR at the *Chronicle*, Ripley was picked as lead cartoonist to cover the upcoming fight between retired champion Jim Jeffries and Jack Johnson, the first black heavyweight champ. Under pressure from sportswriters and cartoonists, including Ripley, Jeffries had agreed to emerge from retirement. Scheduled for July 4, 1910, the highly anticipated and racially charged battle—"The Great White Hope" versus "The Big Black Menace"—had grown into one of the biggest sporting events in US history. A few *Chronicle* old-timers grumbled about the new kid getting such a plum assignment, but sports editor Harry B. Smith insisted the job was Ripley's.

He spent a few weeks at Jeffries's training camp north of Santa Cruz, drawing daily cartoons of the aging boxer's workouts. At night, Ripley and the other journalists would gather for drinks on the hotel's front porch or around a campfire. A newsman's uniform at the time was typically a slouchy gray suit, wrinkled white shirt, dark tie, and fedora. Ripley stood out in his straw hat and knickers, sitting awkwardly among rumpled older men. He kept his head down and legs tucked beneath him in the humble, protective pose he often struck in the face of intimidation or embarrassment.

Photos of Ripley at Jeffries's camp show a clean-shaven man-boy among mustachioed men, a timid child who'd been allowed to stay up late with the grown-ups.

Yet, when the old-timers got him talking, they found Ripley to be an oddly funny fellow, and a bit of a perky smart aleck. They particularly liked one of Ripley's cartoons that showed a huddle of sportswriters rolling dice outside Jeffries's gym. ("Seven! Come eleven!")

He'd been assigned plenty of sports events during his first year as a cartoonist, and had used those opportunities to study the habits and language of more experienced artists and writers. Having lost his father at such a young age, Ripley looked to other men for lessons on how to be manly. He was savvy enough to know that the upcoming fight loomed larger than any event he'd covered. If he played it right, it could be a turning point in his journalistic apprenticeship.

⁕ ⁕ ⁕

THREE WEEKS BEFORE the big day, the fight was moved from San Francisco to Reno, Nevada. Writers, celebrities, and fans stormed the lawless desert city, conquering its saloons and gambling houses. Ripley considered Reno "a riot—a seething cauldron of the sporting clan."

He was soon mingling with the biggest names in newspapers. At dinner one night, he met two of his *Bulletin* predecessors, Rube Goldberg and Tad Dorgan. Also sitting at the table was the famous and famously troubled *Call of the Wild* author, Jack London, who had been hired as part of the *Chronicle*'s "fight team"—making Ripley, for the moment, colleagues with America's most famous writer.

Full-page *Chronicle* ads touting its "corps of experts" showed a pubescent-looking LeRoy Ripley, who would be stationed ringside with London. When London learned that Ripley was from Santa Rosa, just a few miles from his estate at Glen Ellen, he offered to take a look at Ripley's drawings, which had taken on a grittier, moodier quality during the weeks leading up to the fight. Despite the many racist depictions of Johnson—big lips and an apelike head—Ripley had drawn one serious portrait, a near-perfect likeness titled "The Dusky Champion—And His Golden Smile." London was impressed by Ripley's work and encouraged him to keep at it.

Ripley became so "overawed" by his encounters with London and others that he almost missed the fight, nearly sick with nervous indigestion. On fight day, more than 16,000 spectators gathered to watch "The Battle of the Century," scheduled for *forty-five* rounds. Sitting a few feet from center ring in the journalists' section with London, Ripley watched as Johnson slowly ripped Jeffries apart.

In Ripley's post-fight cartoon, Jeffries is depicted lying on his side as a wide-eyed crowd looks on.

"When the old champion went down and out," reads the caption, "there was not one cheer for the victor!"

* * *

THE FIGHT HAD been an exhilarating chance for Ripley to meet the top men in his field, including journalist and author Peter B. Kyne, a California newsman turned novelist who advised Ripley to take his talents to a bigger stage. "If I was a kid your age, you know what I'd do?" Kyne said. "I'd go to New York."

Others, including London, also suggested that Ripley leave San Francisco behind. Noted *New York World* columnist Ned

Brown even offered a letter of introduction if Ripley made it to Manhattan. "You should be in New York with Tad and Goldberg," said Brown.

By the time he'd returned to San Francisco, Ripley was fixated on the idea, even though New York was "a long way off—almost out of the question." Plus, with his mother and brother now living with him, and the whole family dependent upon his income, Lillie would never comprehend his need to ditch a steady job for the hope of a better life nearly three thousand miles away. Yet, from Reno onward, he dreamed about nothing else.

The theme of Ripley's tenure in Nevada could be distilled into two words: *go east*. Meeting London, a model of masculinity to Ripley's generation, had a particularly lasting effect. In fact, London's success story—a poor California kid who succeeded in his art form and became an adventurer-traveler and a wealthy but sad-drunk celebrity—would echo throughout Ripley's life.

He told Nell Griffith by mail that while he was still "getting along swimmingly" at the *Chronicle*, "I hope to be in New York in a while—and from there to Europe!"

✳ ✳ ✳

IT HAD BEEN nice to come home to McAllister Street each night and serve as a father figure to brother Doug, who never knew his dad. For Ripley, his own father figures had become newsmen like London and Kyne, whose influence far outweighed Ripley's mother's view of a sensible future. Ripley *loved* the work of a sports cartoonist, loved being around elite athletes and cheering/jeering crowds and important journalists, especially people who might help advance his career.

The encouragement from men he'd met in Reno and the maturing of his cartoons emboldened Ripley to finally take a chance and ask for a raise. Ripley walked into the office of the *Chronicle*'s bulldog managing editor, John Young, and asked for another $2.50 per week.

"Who are you?" Young demanded of the cartoonist whose name appeared daily in the man's paper. "And in which department do you work?"

Ripley later heard that Young often played dumb when he suspected someone was looking for money. The editor told him he'd "look into the matter," but each time Ripley renewed his request, he got the same *Who are you?* brush-off.

Finally, he boldly told Young one day that if he didn't start getting $25 a week, he would quit.

"Very well, Mr. Ripley," Young said. "We're a happy family here, and we don't want any dissatisfied employees on this newspaper. You are free to leave immediately."

Realizing too late that he'd accidentally quit, Ripley did what he often did to clear his head.

He walked through Chinatown.

* * *

UNABLE TO FACE his mother with the bad news, and barely able to breathe, he wandered for hours and finally stopped at the San Francisco Press Club, where he planned to throw back his last drinks as a member and then resign. Fortunately, just hours after losing his job, Ripley found Peter Kyne at the bar.

"I'm in a fine fix," he told Kyne. "I've been fired from two papers here in two years. I'm a failure even before I start."

Kyne told Ripley the same thing he'd told him in Reno.

"Take a chance, kid. Go to New York," he said. "You'll never get anywhere unless you start somewhere."

Kyne also told Ripley not to panic about his sudden lack of employment. "We'll try to get you something," he said.

Something appeared quickly in the form of an aging actor, singer, and self-proclaimed womanizing brawler looking for someone to illustrate his autobiography.

As a child, Joe Taylor had crisscrossed America with a minstrel show, then ventured in his teens to Hawaii. In his twenties, he joined a troupe touring Shanghai, Hong Kong, and Singapore, surviving knife-slashing pirates and killer typhoons. In China he witnessed twelve prisoners beheaded by a sword-wielding executioner.

Ripley was enthralled by Taylor's tales, such as getting a shave in Manila from a barber using a butcher's cleaver. Ripley chose that particular scene as one of twenty-five he illustrated for Taylor's memoir. The result of the unlikely collaboration between eighty-three-year-old Taylor and young Ripley was a 250-page book, *Joe Taylor: Barnstormer.* Taylor gave Ripley a much-needed dose of cash—$100—and a book credit: "Illustrated by Ripley."

"Accidents have always been a boon to me," Ripley would later say, counting Taylor's memoir among the turning points of his charmed post-quake career.

Equally important, Taylor had stoked Ripley's curiosity about the great wide world beyond California, especially the Orient.

✳ ✳ ✳

ALTHOUGH SAN FRANCISCO was just a three-year stint, a way station between Santa Rosa and his soon-to-be-real home of New York, Ripley's time in the reborn city had been transformative, a period he would come to view as more educational than any college.

As Ripley grew from tentative teen into cocksure young adult, San Francisco had exposed him to the competitive world of newspaper cartooning and the riskier world of *possibility*. He met men who had traveled the globe, hedonists and self-indulgers who had tasted the fruits and women of exotic lands, men who wrote books and drank whiskey, smoked opium, got divorced and made lots of money, men who knew how to live large.

Though Ripley would become one of the great global travelers of his day, he had thus far never ventured beyond Northern California, except for the head-spinning visit to the Babylonian streets of Reno. He considered San Francisco "my hometown" and referred to himself as "a westerner at heart."

Setting course for New York, then—with little money, no confirmed job, lugging just a portfolio of drawings and the names of a few contacts—was not only Ripley's first gutsy adventure, but would forever loom as the boldest. He was twenty-one.

He said good-bye to his family, boarded an eastbound train, then dozed in his wooden seat as one American panorama linked with another: San Francisco to Sacramento, Ogden to Cheyenne, Kansas City to St. Louis, Louisville to Nashville to Cincinnati, where he felt snowflakes touch his face for the first time.

During the dirty two-week crossing he imagined himself enacting a modern version of his parents' cross-country journey, but in reverse. Eating from butcher carts and warming himself near the coal stove, he rolled farther north and east toward an uncertain future.

After safely making his way across the country, Ripley got off the train lugging a battered trunk containing all of his possessions: some clothes, an extra suit, his baseball glove, and a flat-pack portfolio of drawings. Tucked deep in his pants pocket was $15, the last of his cash.

One look around told him that he was *not* in New York. He had accidentally disembarked one stop too soon, in New Jersey. It was cold, it was nighttime, and he had no idea how to cross the Hudson River. Swimming as his father had during his cross-country journey was no option—Ripley couldn't swim. Looking confused and lost, he caught the attention of a man who offered to guide Ripley into Manhattan via the newly opened train tunnel that ran beneath the Hudson.

"You're a real westerner, and I like your style," the man said.

Emerging from the subterranean tube onto the streets of midtown Manhattan, Ripley gawked at the skyscraper forest and the humming, starlit city. Ripley's new buddy helped him find a cheap, closet-sized hotel room to stash his trunk, and at dinner introduced him to two friends. One claimed to be an insurance man, the other a judge. Ripley thought the judge's gnarled, cauliflower ear looked suspiciously like the ear of a boxer.

When the insurance man pulled out a pair of dice and suggested they shoot a friendly game, it finally dawned on Ripley that the yokel was being scammed. He explained that he couldn't play—"All my m-money is in ch-checks," he stammered—but offered to meet them again at nine o'clock the next morning. He excused himself and scurried back to his hotel, where he propped a chair against the door and hardly slept. At seven a.m., he arose and checked out—a precarious entry to a new life.

⁂ * ✳

WITH INCOMING SHIPLOADS of immigrants and a rising literacy rate, New York journalism was thriving, sustained by dozens of news publications. Atop the heap loomed Joseph Pulitzer's *New York World*, an innovative and cartoon-friendly newspaper that was the first stop in Ripley's job search. At the domed Pulitzer building—among the tallest of New York's sky pokers—he sought out Ned Brown, who in Reno had offered to help him find a job.

ᴄ BELIEVE IT! ᕲ

In 1895, the World *launched the seminal* Hogan's Alley *cartoon, whose barefooted star character in an oversized yellow shirt earned him the nickname "The Yellow Kid." In his* New York Journal, *William Randolph Hearst created his own yellow-kid cartoon, a blatant knockoff that stoked the feud between him and Pulitzer. Their subsequent attempts to outsensationalize each other in print birthed the term "yellow journalism."*

But the *World* had been in turmoil since Pulitzer's death a few months earlier, and wasn't hiring. For days, Ripley visited other

45

newspapers, struggling with his portfolio on slushy, snow-slick sidewalks but unwilling to trust himself to the decade-old subways. Feeling as low as he could remember, he began wondering if he'd made a mistake. It didn't help that he had no overcoat.

Ripley finally asked a street-corner newsboy for directions to the *Globe and Commercial Advertiser*, and was soon lost in the street maze of Greenwich Village, yet another complication in his already sloppy introduction to the streets of New York.

One of the city's oldest papers, founded in 1797 by Alexander Hamilton and first edited by Noah Webster (of dictionary renown), the *Globe and Commercial Advertiser* had sunk into relative obscurity, a quaint, thin rag sometimes called "the old-time *Globe*." Editor Henry J. Wright and his staff were struggling to change that perception, in part with eye-grabbing cartoons meant to offer the immigrant and working class a more exciting alternative to the dull-gray text that remained the dominant style of the city's papers.

When Ripley arrived at the *Globe*'s front door, daily circulation had been hovering for years around 100,000; the *World* reached six times as many readers. But *Globe* readership was growing fast, thanks largely to the front-page political cartoons of its popular and populist new artist, J. N. "Ding" Darling.

Ripley was eventually led to the office of sports editor Walter St. Denis, a short-tempered Canadian who had been seeking a new style for his sports pages. St. Denis left Ripley waiting for more than an hour, but when Ripley finally got the chance to spread out his drawings, St. Denis liked what he saw, the mix of art and humanity. He called in Ding Darling for a second opinion.

Darling's initial opinion was that the lean, anxious, and disheveled young Ripley was dressed more for gardening than a job interview. Ripley wore a thick woolen army shirt and, due to the snow, had rolled up his trouser legs, exposing scuffed and worn-out shoes. Darling felt sorry for Ripley but was impressed by his cartoons and smitten by his innocence and eagerness.

"The boy's got something," Darling finally told St. Denis. "Hire him for six months, and if he doesn't make good, I'll be responsible for his salary."

* * *

RIPLEY STARTED AT THE *GLOBE*, in the chilly first days of 1912, at $25 a week. He found a small room in a boarding-house on West Sixtieth Street, a short walk to Central Park. Though *Globe* headquarters was at Globe Square in Greenwich Village, Ripley's office would be in lower Manhattan atop the new Singer Building, built by the sewing-machine company in 1908 and briefly reigning as the world's tallest building.

In addition to Ding Darling (who would later win two Pulit-zer prizes), Ripley's new colleagues were an elite clan. The paper had recently hired such recognizable artists as H. T. Webster and H. A. MacGill, and would soon hire Carl "Bunny" Schultze, each of whom developed America's earliest serialized daily comic strips. As in San Francisco, Ripley's coworkers would be some of the most innovative artists in the business. The timing of his assimilation into this rare gathering couldn't have been better.

The *Globe* had recently partnered with Associated Newspa-pers, a newly formed syndicate (housed in the Singer Building) that distributed stories and cartoons to dozens of midsize papers. Syndication had proved to be a boon to newspapers and their car-toonists. Bigger papers got extra mileage from their cartoons by selling them to smaller papers, which in turn published cartoons that their staffs couldn't otherwise produce. The upside for car-toonists was having their work exposed to a nationwide audience, and some of them were becoming the country's first media celebrities. For Ripley, this meant his cartoons would be distributed nationally by Associated Newspapers and seen by hundreds of thousands of newspaper readers across the United States.

So when Ripley's name first appeared in the *Globe*'s pages—atop a cartoon about the boxer Abe Attell, on January 18, 1912—in a nicely poetic twist, it also appeared three thousand miles away, in the *San Francisco Bulletin*.

* * *

THE *GLOBE* BILLED ITSELF as "New York's Oldest Newspaper" but had lately begun acting like a scrappy upstart. Its editors had been hiring new talent and investing in new printing presses. It sold for a penny and most days devoted two full pages to sports. Ripley quickly became a steady presence on those pages, his cartoons appearing at least every other day, sometimes daily, always in the top center, swallowing the top fourth or more of the sports pages.

In addition to drawing, Ripley began writing in earnest. He launched a series of illustrated stories about Olympic athletes headed to Sweden that summer. In a series called Hardest Battles of Ring Stars as Told by Them to Ripley, he interviewed boxers about their most grueling fights. He created a recurring cartoon character, Demon Dug, named for his brother but clearly based on his younger self. A mop-topped, dirty-faced, mischievous kid in knickers, Dug couldn't stay away from the baseball diamond, lost his schoolbooks, played hooky, broke windows, and got dragged home by the ear by his mother.

As a writer, Ripley developed an ease with the tough-guy language of the pugilist, describing one boxer as "a cold-blooded proposition [who] fought cruelly and unceasingly." He also showed signs of wit. After winning a fight, one hard-drinking fighter was "in the best of spirits (and the best of spirits were in him)." It was no small achievement for an unproven newsman to hold his own among the *Globe*'s sports scribes, who ranked among New York's best.

BELIEVE IT!

One of Ripley's colleagues, Mark Roth, was sometimes credited with coining a new name for the New York Highlanders baseball team—the Yankees.

Globe veterans were impressed by Ripley's prolific output, even if they found him quiet and a little odd. Sportswriter Sid Mercer considered him "a plain lad" and columnist Herb Corey called him the "trembling artist." But Ripley attracted a loyal patron in Associated Newspapers' founder, George Matthew Adams, a minister's son from Michigan who felt Ripley was "un-spoiled . . . a modest chap."

Baseball continued to dominate his cartoons, his arrival in New York coinciding with the start of the preseason. His apartment was close to the Ninth Avenue El, which delivered him to the northern tip of Manhattan, home to the Polo Grounds and the New York Giants, whose pugnacious fireplug of a manager, John McGraw, was now part of Ripley's sports beat. Instead of just drawing cartoons and portraits of McGraw, though, what Ripley really wanted was to play for him.

* * *

AN ENDURING HIGHLIGHT of Ripley's pre-celebrity legacy was that after his modest success in California's bush leagues he came within striking distance of a professional baseball career.

Ripley would perpetually claim that after arriving in New York he immediately went chasing that *other* life dream.

The story goes like this: In February of 1912, Ripley joined the Giants for a train ride to Marlin, Texas, to cover spring training workouts for the *Globe*. When coaches learned Ripley had played semi-pro ball, they invited him to work out with the team. One coach thought Ripley showed "considerable promise and ability," and McGraw allegedly told Ripley that with a few years in the minors he might become a big-league prospect. During a scrimmage, Ripley was called in to pitch, and in one reporter's retelling McGraw called Ripley "the best curve-ball pitcher I've seen in a long, long time."

The story continues: Ripley reared into his windup, whipped his arm forward, and felt a sharp snap. His arm had broken in a ninety-degree fracture, a jagged edge of bone actually poking through the skin. In less gruesome versions, his arm "shattered," though sometimes it was just a broken finger. Later reports would claim that Ripley signed a minor-league contract with the Giants, *then* broke his arm. Yet, while there is an impressive picture of Ripley wearing a Giants uniform and swinging a bat, his name doesn't appear in any Giants statistics or record books, or in any news stories about spring training from 1912 to 1914. The writer Damon Runyon saw Ripley at the Giants' training camp in Texas one year and remembered him more as a poker player than a pitcher.

Ripley loved the story of his flirtation with pro ball—as would future PR men, honing the Ripley legend—even if they all overreached in the retelling. Regardless of the true version, the results were the same. Ripley viewed the injury as "a godsend" and "a great thing" because it forced him to choose between competing career paths. "It ruined me as a baseball player," he'd say. "And it made me a cartoonist."

∗ ∗ ∗

SOMETIME DURING HIS first year at the *Globe*, Ripley's editors decided it was time for their young artist—who had continued to sign his cartoons "Rip" or "Ripley"—to have a real first name. "We can't have a 'LeRoy' in the sporting department," Walter St. Denis said.

"LeRoy" apparently wasn't masculine enough for a sports cartoonist/reporter, so Ripley willingly adopted his middle name, Robert. He became Bob or Rip to his new East Coast friends, still Roy to his mother and siblings, who must have been shocked to receive a letter containing the first "By Robert Ripley" clipping. He'd soon reclaim LeRoy for his middle initial, becoming Robert L. Ripley.

Soon after adopting his new name, Ripley was given an unexpectedly plum assignment, which the *Globe* announced in January of 1913 in a large headline across the top of the sports page: RIPLEY IS OFF FOR EUROPE TODAY. Beneath that appeared a six-column Ripley self-portrait, with slightly underexaggerated buckteeth, wearing a plaid cap and striding across the ocean, a pencil in one hand and sketch pad in the other. In a balloon, Ripley asks Europe, "Well, whatcha got?"

At the time, overseas travel was rare, expensive, and risky. Crossing the Atlantic was an astonishing perk for a rookie staffer and an inexperienced traveler. It was also a reflection of the editors' trust in Ripley's ability to turn his overseas travels into a series of entertaining stories and cartoons. Ripley was thrilled, and hoped his first taste of the world beyond America's shores would not only provide material for a unique new style of cartoon but also guide him toward his eventual big idea.

Instead of traveling directly to Europe, Ripley first sailed through the Mediterranean and visited Egypt. In Giza, he toured the ancient pyramids and in a nearby sandlot noticed a group of men in long gowns playing something like baseball. Using a skinny bat, they had modified the game: eight men per team; eight outs per inning; one strike and you're out. But they played as aggressively as any bush leaguer and were especially vocal in taunting opponents and umpires. Ripley pulled out his sketch pad and started working on a cartoon of Egyptian ball-players wearing "headache towels," as he called their turbans.

As he continued on to Europe, he kept his reporter's eye narrowly focused on sports. Either by habit or under editors' orders, he seemed unwilling to expand his curiosity and test his pen on non-sports topics, unsure of his footing outside the familiar comforts of an arena or stadium.

In Rome he visited the Coliseum, the alleged birthplace of professional boxing, where sixty thousand spectators once watched enslaved fighters pound each other with studded leather gloves called cesti. In Germany, he witnessed a bizarre sword-fighting contest called Mensur, in which duelers swiped at each other's faces. The goal wasn't so much to *win* as to suffer an opponent's blade without flinching. The inevitable scars were borne with pride, scabbed badges of honor. After witnessing a duel, Ripley watched in awe as a doctor stitched the loser's face together without eliciting a wince from the patient.

In France he attended an oddly collegial boxing match at the Cirque de Paris. With plush seats and carpeting, it seemed more opera than prizefight. Only once did he venture outside the pre-planned itinerary, putting his provincialism on full, unapologetic display. In Paris, he went looking for the boxer Georges Carpentier, whom he hoped to interview. "I wanta see Carpentier!" he told his taxi driver, certain that his request was delivered in "perfectly good English." When the confused taxi driver responded in rapid-fire French, Ripley grew flustered and then angry. He began repeating his instructions, but louder. *"CAR-pen-TEER!"* he finally shouted.

Eager to get back to English-speaking New York, he became emotional on the ship's deck as he spotted the faint outline of the Statue of Liberty, the gargoyled spires and peaks of Manhattan. When the ship docked at Hoboken, New Jersey, Ripley suddenly realized he had no money left. He offered to help another passenger with his luggage so he could earn a dollar for the ferry ride to New York.

* * *

THE *GLOBE* ANNOUNCED his return with another six-column cartoon of a caricatured Ripley hugging New York City and kissing the new Woolworth Building. Stacked behind him on the ship's deck was a pile of "sketches." Though the *Globe* offered no explanation for the bold overseas stint, a balloon quote above the cartooned *Globe* building suggested that his editors might have been eager to have their productive new artist back.

"Hey," it read. "Come on, get busy."

Ripley wasted no time, launching a months-long series of stories and cartoons that introduced readers to his take on Europe, and to his clever and curious mind.

His first cartoon was accompanied by a story about the Egyptians he'd watched playing the game they called *leep el tabe*. "What a spectacle it was—a baseball game at the base of the pyramids!" He called the Coliseum "the Madison Square Garden of the Roman days" and the Cirque de Paris "the Madison Square Garden of Paris." He described the pretty female ushers at the Parisian boxing match and the "terrible open gashes and streaming blood" of the Mensur fighters.

His style was casual, colloquial, even a bit irreverent. He admitted to drinking beer in Germany and relied heavily on slangy contractions—*y'know, dontcha, y'see.* He sang the praises of Parisian women but revealed an uneasy distrust of most foreigners and their strange ways. He was the perfect yokel American, never mentioning that King George of Greece had been assassinated during his time abroad.

It amounted to a remarkable series of global dispatches from a mere sports cartoonist, and an entertaining diversion for *Globe* readers. New York's sportswriters and illustrators typically covered baseball, boxing, and horse racing, with lesser sports relegated to an occasional inch of type at the bottom of the page. To read about Egyptian baseball and German Mensur was, in the view of many readers, fascinating.

In his first year and a half at the *Globe*, Ripley had developed a reputation as a cutting-edge journalist and a darn good read. He settled into a steady grind, scurrying across New York to cover games, scouring the city by foot and train, day and night, cranking out cartoons by the score. He averaged two dozen cartoons and/or columns a month through late 1913, expanding his scope to cover billiards, auto racing, horse racing, polo, tennis, and golf.

His work contributed to the *Globe*'s upticking circulation, now above 130,000. Associated Newspapers acknowledged his contributions by offering a two-year contract and bumping his salary to $60 a week.

* * *

IN EARLY 1914, Santa Rosa's *Press Democrat* published a story about the success of its homegrown dropout of an artist. His syndicated cartoons were being published in thirty papers and the *Press Democrat* boasted that Ripley, a proud "product of Santa Rosa," had become wildly popular back east. Later that year, just before the holidays, Ripley managed to return home for the first time in nearly three years. He hopscotched by train across to San Francisco, where he visited friends and former coworkers, including E. T. "Scoop" Gleeson, a sportswriter he'd first worked with at the *Bulletin*.

ᘓ BELIEVE IT! ᘔ

Gleeson is credited with coining the term "jazz." At the San Francisco Seals' spring training camp in 1913, players called the bubbly spring water "jazz water." When a few Seals began playing ragtime-style music with some local musicians, Gleeson said the tunes had "pep" and "jazz."

Gleeson decided to interview his former colleague and write a story about Ripley's blossoming career. Beneath the headline RIPLEY RETURNS TO SCENES OF HIS EARLY TRIUMPH, Gleeson's story described how his formerly shy friend had matured since leaving San Francisco, how Ripley "dresses quietly but with good taste . . . and converses with all the freedom of a campaign manager."

When Lillie Belle read the story, she felt proud of her son's surprising success. She'd managed to witness the planting of the seeds, the gestation of his career. But she would not enjoy her son's achievement for long, or see his burgeoning fame. In mid-1915, Ripley received word that his mother had become gravely ill, suffering from sudden heart failure. He immediately sent a telegraph.

Dear Mom, Hope you are recovered, Mom. I want you to be well and jolly when I come home. When you are unhappy then I am unhappy. So be of good heart, Mom, is the earnest wish of your loving son, Roy.

Ripley boarded the first westbound train. During a stopover in Chicago he received a Western Union wire from his sister. "All thought Mamma would die during the night," she wrote. "Heart stronger today." Two days later, in Colorado . . . "Another bad night," Ethel wired. A similar message reached Ripley in Nevada, and he wired back, urging his sister to "Do all possible" and telling Ethel he was on the "fastest train," due to arrive in Santa Rosa before noon the next day, a Monday.

A trackside shed fire near Truckee, California, delayed Ripley's train just before dawn on Monday. When he reached Sacramento, just hours from home, he learned he was too late. Lillie Belle had died during the night. Just forty-six, she was buried beside Isaac at Odd Fellows Cemetery. The *Press Democrat* praised her as "a well-known resident" with a "wide circle of friends." The paper also noted that, due to his train's delay, "the cartoonist who has made such a success of his profession" had been unable to say good-bye.

* * *

RIPLEY HAD PREVIOUSLY PROMISED his mother that he would always look after Ethel and Doug. Now he faced a difficult decision. Should he bring eleven-year-old Doug back to New York? Or stay in California and go back to the *Bulletin* or *Chronicle*? Either way, could he become a substitute *dad*?

As a boy, Ripley had always been on the outside, different from the other kids, unhandsome and goofy, picked on and mocked, a fatherless stutterer, a high school dropout. Even now, he often considered himself an overgrown adolescent and "just a boy," and if he returned to Santa Rosa he'd bear a new label: *orphan*. Yet, having traveled to Egypt and Europe, having crisscrossed America and made New York City his playground, he knew he had finally outgrown the awkward, solitary kid he'd been in Santa Rosa. Just as his pioneering parents and grand-parents had ventured into unknown lands in their day, he too had become a pioneer of a sort.

His upbringing had somehow instilled in him a desire to travel and explore. He had outgrown his childhood shyness and timid-ity to become the type of person who could appreciate a baseball game beneath the Egyptian pyramids. But as Doug's caretaker, further long-distance travels would be harder to come by.

So, despite the promise to his mother, he made his decision. Uncertain days loomed ahead, with the crescendo of artillery across the Atlantic. New York was no place for Doug. Rather than uproot him, he decided it'd be best for Doug to stay in California. Ethel and her husband, Fred Davis, now lived in Sacramento, where Fred made furniture and Ethel worked as a nurse. But living with his big sister was apparently not an op-tion for Doug—the two were not close. Family friends offered to let Doug live with them in Santa Rosa, and Ripley agreed to send money until Doug was old enough to come to New York.

Ripley then endured a contemplative train ride east, a somber commute between the two influential cities of his young-adult life. Though it had once loomed as an unthinkable destination, he now considered San Francisco just "a horse town" and would not return to Santa Rosa for fifteen years. Back in Manhattan, he plunged even deeper into the social and sporting circles of the city that was now his true home.

CHAPTER

6

Gaining confidence as a cartoonist and a New Yorker, Ripley began to dress the part. In a mid-teens photograph, he poses hands on hips beside a stone wall in Central Park, wearing a checked suit whose long-tailed coat is cinched at the breast by a single button. Narrow, cuffed pants terminate a few inches shy of the ankle, accentuating shiny two-tone shoes. His hair is shaved to a stubble on the sides, long and slicked back on top. He looks pleased with himself, smiling his deformed smile.

Though his misaligned and protruding teeth can't be ignored, in most photographs from this period Ripley looks somewhat stylish and almost handsome. In a city and a profession full of extroverts, the nerdy introvert was finding a middle place where he could fit in.

During his first years in New York, he'd stuck cautiously with San Francisco connections, socializing with former *Bulletin* and *Chronicle* colleagues Paul Terry and Herb Roth (who was now cartooning for the *New York World*). Through 1916, Ripley extended his range and befriended other ambitious young transplants, including a pretty young art school grad, Vyvyan Donner. She and Ripley would attend Sunday-night dinners at the Greenwich Village apartment of Helena Smith-Dayton, an ex-reporter turned artist and filmmaker. One magazine called Smith-Dayton's weekly dinners "a Washington Square institution at which the notables from all the professions gather." Donner would later recall the cocktails, dancing, and laughter of those "wonderful gatherings at Helena's."

Other nights found him playing pool at Jack Doyle's Billiards Academy in Times Square or sitting ringside with Tad Dorgan or Damon Runyon at Madison Square Garden, the world's largest indoor sports arena, which had become like Ripley's second office. Around this time (and most likely at a barroom), Ripley met the man who would become his closest male companion, a short, balding, crag-faced cartoonist who was as odd-looking as him but funny as hell—a real life Jeff to Ripley's Mutt.

✶　✳　✺

AS A SPORTS CARTOONIST in Philadelphia and Washington, DC, Arthur "Bugs" Baer had drawn insects with baseball bodies, calling his ball-shaped creatures "bugs" and earning himself a nickname. Now writing a humor column at the *New York World*, Baer was developing a reputation as a master of one-liners, having coined the quip "What this country needs is a good five-cent cigar." (Comedian Milton Berle would later confess to mimicking Baer's style.)

ℰ BELIEVE IT! ℱ

Baer would bestow upon George Herman "Babe" Ruth
the nickname "Sultan of Swat."

This cigar-smoking, whiskey-drinking storyteller was the perfect sidekick for someone as shy and self-conscious as Ripley. A natural showman and entertaining social butterfly, Baer knew the best nightclubs and parties. He schooled Ripley in the subtleties of celebrity and the fine art of self-promotion. Soon after the two became friends, Baer and Ripley approached Jack Curley, the pudgy promoter who had helped broker the 1910 Johnson-Jeffries fight in Reno, with an idea.

Born and raised in San Francisco, Curley had run away from home to work as a reporter at the *Chronicle*—it was becoming a theme of Ripley's life, these links back to San Francisco. Curley was fired for fabricating stories and eventually took up sports promotion, which led to his role brokering the Reno fight. Ripley had gotten to know Curley fairly well since Reno and occasionally caricatured the tubby man in the *Globe*'s sports pages.

A likable yet shady character, Curley had recently turned to professional wrestling. The working class and the upper class alike thought it was a hoot to watch costumed men named "Americus" and "The Terrible Turk" scrum with each other. Ripley acknowledged in print that they might be "cheap press agent stunts," but he felt Curley had revived "a grand old game" and considered the Masked Marvel "one of the best wrestlers in the United States." Well-dressed and polite, Curley would claim with a straight face, "I have never promoted a wrestling match that was not absolutely honest."

The idea Ripley and Baer brought to the savvy promoter was a wrestling match in which the two minor celebrity cartoonists faced each other at the Lexington Opera House, as a warm-up act before the main event. Like George Plimpton would years later, they wanted to perform as athletes instead of journalists for a change, participants instead of spectators. They'd take home $150 apiece and Curley could pocket the rest.

Ripley and Baer decided they'd give the crowd a good show, then Ripley would flip Baer onto the mat for the win. But after ten minutes of insults and trash talk to amuse the crowd, Baer decided he didn't want to be the loser, and instead of taking the fall he threw Ripley hard on his back. Ripley squirmed free, but minutes later Baer—only 148 pounds, but squat and athletic—had Ripley on his back again, and kept him there.

When Ripley later tried to collect his $150 cut, Curley told him he'd given the full $300 to Baer. Curley similarly told Baer that he'd given the money to Ripley, and the two amateur wrestlers seethed for months before realizing Curley had scammed them both.

The stunt earned some publicity in a few papers, easing Ripley's disappointment over the lost paycheck. Fortunately, losing $150 would hardly break him. His salary had soared in the past four years to nearly $100 a week.

* * *

RIPLEY COULD FINALLY AFFORD to dress well and eat well—no more cheap Chinatown meals—but he remained thrifty. After paying $35 a month for his first apartment, he moved into a brownstone on Fiftieth Street with Paul Terry, his former *San Francisco Bulletin* colleague. They split the $40 rent and slept on cots in the small bedroom. Some weeks, the roommates hardly saw each other. Terry had recently left newspapers altogether, convinced that the future of cartoons was on the big screen. He had begun producing animated films and would soon form his own production company, Paul Terry Productions.

BELIEVE IT!

Terry would eventually produce more than 1,300
"Terry-Toons" cartoons, including Mighty Mouse *and*
Heckle and Jeckle.

Many of Ripley's peers were venturing into the uncharted waters of film, and all across New York innovative cartoonists were expanding their craft. Yet, while animated cartoons were making progress, they were still experimental. The public received the bulk of its information and entertainment from newspapers, and newsprint remained the primary medium of the cartoonist. In fact, due to a steep rise in literacy, circulation was flourishing, and some cartoonists were becoming fabulously wealthy. Bud Fisher was earning $78,000 a year from his syndicated *Mutt and Jeff* cartoons, and boys across the country were enrolling in mail-order art classes, hoping to become the next Tad Dorgan or Rube Goldberg, each making six-figure salaries.

ᶜ BELIEVE IT! ᵔ

In the late teens, an obsessive childhood doodler named Walt Disney began attending art classes, fascinated by newspaper cartoonists and "hoping that some day I, too, would be on the staff of a big newspaper." Rejected by the Kansas City Star *and other papers, he turned to animation.*

Ripley studied the work of artists who were pushing the boundaries of illustrated entertainment, particularly Tad, who was both artistic and prolific. "He had no restrictions or limitations," Ripley would later say. Still, Ripley worried that he spent too much time mimicking his heroes.

The mid-1910s were filled with rags-to-riches stories of cartoonists who toiled through multiple experiments before latching on to a clever concept that separated them from the pack.

Inside the black-and-white cardboard covers of schoolboy notebooks, Ripley collected articles about peculiar athletic feats and peculiar people. On slow news days, he'd flip through the notebooks and cobble together sketches about such achievements. One cartoon, entitled *The Iron Man,* featured men who walked or ran long distances, like John Ennis, who crossed America on foot in eighty days. Another, called *Some Famous Kicks,* profiled the longest field goal and the most kicks in a row. In *Some Jumps* he featured extreme skiing and ice-skating leaps, and in *Some Baseball Records* he offered hard-to-believe swings of the bat. Turning to football, *Gridiron Oddities* included a 105-yard touchdown by a player who hid the ball under his jersey and a game in which Harvard beat Exeter, 158–0.

Ripley's knack for locating and depicting odd facts proved especially useful during the winter lull, a dry period for athletes and the men employed to draw them. On one of those slow days in December 1916, the enterprising cartoonist skimmed through his scrapbook, pulled together a few notable feats of athletic endurance, and drew a sketch for each. One man had stayed under water for six minutes, another skipped rope 11,810 times, while another ran 623 miles in 142 hours, and two men once boxed to a draw after seven and a half hours. He called this cartoon *UNUSUAL RECORDS*—a harbinger of his eventual "big idea."

Other slack days, he'd whip up another sketch of Demon Dug, who ached all winter for baseball season. *Globe* readers would see Dug in bed, sulking: "No Baseball, an' no football, a-a-aw! Woe is me—I'm a woe!" Dug and his ragamuffin friends reflected Ripley's admiration for the outcast and the underdog. The cartoons featuring endurance and achievement, meanwhile, showed Ripley's appreciation for winners, people who were the best at something.

Readers seemed to appreciate the mix, especially this emerging focus on the off-the-wall accomplishments by those striving to be fastest, longest, farthest, and best. Said the *Globe* in a promotional ad: "If you really appreciate art and literature combined, you can't afford to miss Ripley."

He was onto something, but his progress—and the good-time New York parties—were soon interrupted by war.

*　*　*

WHEN THE FIGHTING in Europe first began, Ripley joked in print about America's apathy, possibly conveying his own. One cartoon showed a man at a ball game holding a newspaper covered with headlines about war. "War?" says the sports fan. "Who cares?" But as the United States committed itself to battle in the spring of 1917, World War I became the dominant theme of Ripley's cartoons, especially after he was exempted from military service.

The recently passed Selective Service Act required Ripley to fill out a draft registration card, on which he listed his age as twenty-five (he was really twenty-seven) and his occupation as "artist, writer, cartoonist." Asked whether he had any family members dependent on him for support, Ripley wrote that he was responsible for "two dependents," including a "brother under 12." (Doug was still living with family friends in Santa Rosa, and Ripley had continued to send money.) Ripley's request for an exemption was granted that summer of 1917, and his status as Doug's financial caregiver kept him stateside during the final sixteen months of the brutal conflict.

Though he never discussed his apparent willingness to avoid military service, it seems Ripley preferred being a fan rather than a participant. Intrigued by the idea of battle but not inclined to fight, he seemed content to cheer from the sidelines.

He tried to play his own wartime role, profiling athletes

at the Annapolis and West Point military academies. He visited military training bases, spent time aboard the USS *Texas*, promoted Liberty Loans and Red Cross donations. He turned sketches of sports contests into battlefield skirmishes, aerial dogfights, torpedo launches, and hand-to-hand combat. Team managers became "generals," players "soldiers." He even got Demon Dug and friends into the act, playing "war" instead of baseball or getting chased by a truant officer in a sketch titled "The Retreat of the Allies."

His patriotism was unabashed, as he doggedly portrayed American athletes as *the best*: "Englishmen are boxers; Americans are fighters." When a US athlete/soldier died, he gave them a sober sendoff. The death of a Yale track star resulted in a dramatic half-page sketch of Johnny Overton running on the track and, beneath that, being killed midstride on the battlefield. The title: "Johnny Overton's Greatest Race."

In Ripley's reverent view, which he repeated over and over, American soldiers were the best "in the world" because many of them were *athletes*. He frequently depicted Uncle Sam as a muscle-bound ballplayer or boxer. "Remember," he wrote at the time, "WAR is merely athletics." American ballplayers "make excellent grenade tossers," he said, while the throwing ability of the Germans was "on par with our schoolgirls."

Some of Ripley's wartime sketches were used as recruitment posters, as was James Montgomery Flagg's drawing of a finger-pointing Uncle Sam—"I Want You for U.S. Army"—which was reprinted millions of times during the war. Such posters were part of a massive domestic propaganda campaign run by the Committee on Public Information, which promoted patriotic newsreels, photos, and magazine and newspaper articles. The committee's Bureau of Cartoons supplied the nation's top cartoonists with suggestions and news tips via the weekly *Bulletin for Cartoonists*. George Creel, head of the Committee on Public Information, viewed the work of Ripley and other cartoonists as a "constructive force for shaping public opinion and winning the war."

His patriotic, pro-athlete cartoons earned approving letters to the editor. In response to one of Ripley's athlete/soldier profiles, a reader named Frank Seng wrote, "That kind of cartoon does more to mobilize the sentiments and feelings of the people than any number of stories. It gives us a victorious attitude, which is essential."

On November II, 1918, Armistice Day arrived, and with it peace. Though he had avoided serving overseas, Ripley had loved the wartime assignments, traveling to Army bases and Navy ships, mingling with interesting new people and playing his part. World War I had stoked Ripley's competitive spirit (*war is athletics*) and presented a challenging artistic diversion. But in late 1918 he went back to being just a sports cartoonist. Compared to the real war, baseball and boxing seemed a tad boring.

* * *

WORLD WAR I had transformed the pages of American newspapers into daily adventure stories. Afterward, readers' hunger for drama and intrigue in their daily paper lingered. Readers also now wanted to know more about the world, particularly the strange-sounding places they'd heard about—obscure lands such as Luxembourg and Romania, the exotic corners of Europe, the Balkans, and the Ottoman Empire.

At the same time, soldiers returned home with a taste for the adrenaline and dangers they'd been exposed to in war. In pursuit of such thrills, some began attempting risky feats—scaling the world's peaks, flying airplanes long distances—striving to accomplish something bold, to be first, fastest, or best.

All of which provided Ripley with cartoon fodder. The aftermath of war would slowly alter the trajectory of his cartooning, and his life.

Before the war, he had experimented with various serials that celebrated impressive sports feats and the overlooked Everyman. Wartime took him in a different direction, allowing him to give readers dramatic life-and-death scenarios. Those cartoons felt more *thoughtful* than anything else he'd done. "The ability to think is perhaps a greater asset to the cartoonist than the ability to draw," he'd one day write, in a manuscript he titled *How to Draw*.

After the war, Ripley resumed his search for a niche cartoon that combined all of his skills and interests. The "unusual records" concept had been headed in the right direction, except that it focused almost exclusively on sports. What he really wanted was to indulge his desire to learn about the wonders of the world, to share that curiosity with readers, and to find a consistent and unique artistic style that would "please the great majority."

World War 1 had allowed him to abandon typical "cartoon" drawings and create newspaper *art*. In his *How to Draw* book (which was never published), Ripley revealed how much thought he gave during his early New York apprenticeship to the craft of pen-and-ink cartooning, to the importance of facial features and muscle and bone structure. Ripley also felt an obligation to get the details of his drawings just right. During the war, he made sure he put foreign soldiers in their correct uniforms, to avoid complaints from readers miffed by imperfections. If he couldn't conjure the details from memory, he'd call down to the *Globe*'s "morgue," the library where old articles and photos were stored. He relied heavily on those photos for accuracy, calling the morgue "an invaluable aid."

He also continued assembling his own morgue, pasting more clipped-out newspaper articles and magazine photos into his scrapbooks. During and after the war, these clippings began veering away from sports, becoming more reflective of the postwar fascination with dangerous places and extreme activities. He truly believed that this hodgepodge of quirky scraps might someday "prove of the utmost assistance." In other words: You never know when scraps will make a meal.

✻ ✳ ✾

IN MOST VERSIONS of Ripley's breakthrough moment, the original *Believe It or Not* cartoon (which wouldn't adopt its exclamation point with any consistency until the 1930s) came about on a sluggish winter afternoon in late December 1918. With the war ended, football season over, and baseball season a few months away, Ripley allegedly found himself at a loss for a cartoon topic.

"I was bereft of ideas," he would later claim.

So he dug into his rainy-day notebook collection, sifting through clippings of ambitious athletic endeavors. He chose nine such feats and drew a miniature cartoon for each. Ripley would later claim that "Believe It or Not" was the original title idea. Other times he'd concede that his first idea for a title—"Champs and Chumps"—was not good enough and he offered editors "Believe It or Not" as an alternative title.

Years later, looking back on that day, he said he wasn't entirely sure whether his choice of those four words was "sudden inspiration" or "unconscious accident."

Either way, Ripley was not thrilled with the result and he

left the office that night "very disgusted." He considered the cartoon a throwaway and "a stinker." (In other retellings, he'd claim he was in a hurry to get out the door—he and Bugs Baer had a double date.)

Ripley's editor, Walter St. Denis, had different recollections, later insisting that not only were "believe it or not" *his* words, but the cartoon had been his idea in the first place, that *he* had thrown a stack of clips about odd sports feats onto Ripley's desk and instructed him to come up with a catchy compilation.

Neither recollection was quite right. The original "Believe It or Not" cartoon appeared in the December 19 *Globe,* and it was unequivocally titled "Champs and Chumps." It wasn't an entirely new concept, since it resembled the "unusual records" compilations Ripley had been experimenting with in recent years. Still, something about the layout, the choice of oddball feats, and the appreciative tone Ripley used in describing them seemed quirky and fresh.

Among the nine champs and chumps were J. Darby of England, who jumped backward twelve feet, eleven inches; M. Pauliquen of Paris, who stayed underwater for six and a half minutes; and an unnamed "chap" who walked backward across America. Three of the odd feats involved variations on the hundred-yard dash: one man ran it backward in fourteen seconds; another hopped it in eleven seconds; two men finished in eleven seconds in a three-legged race.

Regardless of who originated the idea, St. Denis agreed with Ripley that it wasn't one of his better cartoons, calling it "just guys who did some screwy athletic stunts." When a few readers wrote in to praise the cartoon, however, St. Denis told Ripley to keep collecting ideas and produce another champ-chump compilation once he had enough material.

According to subsequent legend, another "Believe It or Not"

appeared a week later, followed by another, and soon it was appearing twice a week, then a daily feature—*and the rest was history* . . .

In truth, Ripley's screwy-stunt cartoons were hardly an overnight success, and there was no sudden change in his fame, income, or prospects. He was still a sports cartoonist, covering fights, ball games, and dog shows. In fact, the second "Believe It or Not" cartoon—the first with that exact title—wouldn't appear for another ten months, in October of 1919. A third "Believe It or Not" wouldn't appear until 1920, and only sporadically after that.

Ripley had found his niche, he just didn't know it yet, and wouldn't fully realize what he had stumbled across for at least two more years. Until then, he would continue to view cartooning as a hard grind. "There is no shortcut to success in the field of cartooning," he wrote in his unpublished book. "It is only by hard work and constant practice that [the cartoonist] can hope to prepare himself to conquer the difficulties that will constantly besiege his path."

Indeed, such difficulties were coming, not least of which was an ill-advised marriage to a beautiful teenaged dancer.

Orphaned by parents who died young—Isaac at fifty, Lillie at forty-six—Ripley, nearing thirty, thought constantly of his health.

As a child he used to read *Physical Culture* magazine, published by eccentric fitness guru Bernarr Macfadden, a flamboyant bodybuilder, nutritionist, and health advocate who could tear a deck of cards in half. Though some doctors branded Macfadden a fake and a kook, he railed against "pill-pushers" and processed foods, inspiring millions of acolytes with claims that exercise, fasting, and a heavy intake of milk could help a man live to 150.

BELIEVE IT!
*Macfadden died at age eighty-seven after refusing treatment
for a urinary tract infection.*

Ripley considered himself "an ardent follower of the great health-preacher." Into his late twenties, he remained obsessed with "firm hard flesh, supple muscles, the alertness of health," as he once put it.

It wasn't mere vanity. A late bloomer, Ripley had begun dating. To make himself attractive to women, he had his work cut out for himself. There wasn't much he could do about his fanged teeth or jug ears, so he exploited what he had—dressing colorfully and maintaining a muscular physique.

Having spent the bulk of his adulthood among the nation's finest athletes, he had learned to emulate their workouts. After taking up boxing in San Francisco, he began sparring at the New York Athletic Club, occasionally entering the ring with his heroes, including Jack Dempsey and Georges Carpentier, both club regulars. He also visited the New Jersey health farm and gymnasium created by his boxer friend Freddie Welsh, another Bernarr Macfadden apostle.

ℰ BELIEVE IT! ℈

One of Welsh's camp visitors was F. Scott Fitzgerald, and some historians believe Freddie Welsh (real name Frederick Thomas) was the model for Jay Gatsby (real name James Gatz). One clue is that a woman named Myrtle Wilson had been injured in a car accident with Welsh. In The Great Gatsby, *Myrtle Wilson is struck by Daisy Buchanan, driving Gatsby's car.*

Ripley also took up tennis and golf, partly because they relaxed him but also, judging by photographs, because they allowed him to wear knee pants, argyle socks, and wool caps. He wasn't much for running—"Laborious exercise, to my mind, is harmful," he once said—but he loved a good long walk. He'd often forgo buses and taxis and walk from event to event, at times covering five miles on foot.

Ripley found that when he wasn't exercising or walking, he became tense and grumpy. This renewed vigor for physical fitness led him to take his New York Athletic Club membership to a new level by joining the subset of members, the so-called confirmed bachelors, who actually lived there.

Known mostly by its acronym, the NYAC had been founded in 1868 by a group trying to promote amateur "manly sports" in America. Thirty years later it moved into a spectacular new headquarters on Central Park South. With a marble swimming pool, billiards and card rooms, a dark wood-paneled dining hall, full gymnasium, and handball courts on the roof, it was the ultimate boys' club.

Some of the world's top athletes called the NYAC home, including Olympic medalists whose success in the 1908 and 1912 Games contributed to its prestige. By the time Ripley moved in, around 1919, membership had reached an all-time high of roughly five thousand. George M. Cohan was a member and had introduced his World War I tune "Over There" at the NYAC; Teddy Roosevelt, who died earlier in 1919, had been an honorary member.

Ripley wasn't interested in the NYAC's more popular sports—trap shooting, swimming, water polo. Instead, he joined a small group known as the Killers' Club, devotees of handball, the sport that would captivate him to the point of obsession. He didn't have many hobbies, but when he found one he loved, he immersed himself.

☀ ☀ ☀

IN CHOOSING THE NYAC as his new residence, Ripley joined nearly two hundred others who lived at the main headquarters. Ripley's room, number 59, was more like a large closet than an apartment. The low-ceilinged studio barely contained his bed and drawing table. He showered in a communal bathroom. But it cost just a dollar a day, as did dinner. Plus, he spent very little time in his room. After a day at the *Globe*, he'd pull on his sweatshirt and shorts, lace up his high-top sneakers, then head to the handball courts.

"It is the most natural thing in the world to slap a ball with the hand," he once said of his new favorite sport. "It quickens the eye. It refreshes the nervous system, it gives the body an electric vitality and resilience." The modern game was said to have originated in English prisons of the Middle Ages—inmates bounced balls against cell walls. In New York the sport took root on street corners, Irish immigrant kids hitting balls against tenement walls. As handball's popularity grew, NYAC members converted their roof into courts and shoveled off winter's snow to play year-round.

Ripley's first and most frequent opponent was his pal Bugs Baer, a competitive and testy foe who flung his pudgy little body heedlessly about the court, as if rubberized. Sometimes the two teamed up for doubles matches, winning so often they began entering citywide tournaments.

Over the next few years Ripley would play in dozens of tournaments, including the annual national championship tournament, traveling regularly to Milwaukee, Chicago, Detroit, and Cleveland. One newspaper would later refer to him as "one of the leading handball players of the country."

Ripley viewed handball as the perfect all-around athletic endeavor: "It polishes down my raw nerves after I've been working overtime." He would encourage anyone who'd listen to play handball "when you're emotionally wrought up . . . You simply cannot play this game hard and think of your troubles at the same time."

✳ ✳ ✳

THE NYAC and its handball courts offered Ripley an invigorating male culture, a place where his buckteeth and stutter mattered less than his competitiveness and physical performance. Being an athlete made him feel special, just as being a talented high school artist had helped him feel less of a misfit.

In the same way that his loud clothes sought to draw attention away from his face and teeth, Ripley's athleticism offset his odd looks and mannerisms. Sportsmen were *supposed* to be eccentric, he'd learned after years of covering athletes. In fact, for a man who still felt like the only bumpkin in New York, the NYAC was a perfect home. Because, for all his insecurities, Ripley loved to be around people and *hated* to be alone. At the bustling club, with its meat-and-potatoes restaurant, its amply stocked bar ringed by a brass foot rail, its parties and sporting events, he had access to a built-in network of friends.

Ripley also learned, thanks to Bugs Baer, that being an athlete earned other privileges—mainly women. Baer had recently moved to the gossip-savvy *New York American*. William Randolph Hearst hired him after reading Baer's description of Yankees baseball player Frank Stephen "Ping" Bodie (whom Ripley had known in California's bush leagues) and Bodie's failed attempt to steal second base. "His head was full of larceny," Baer wrote. "But his feet were too honest."

With a hefty new salary from Hearst, and a growing reputation as a hard-drinking night owl who could crack wise on cue, Baer introduced Ripley to a repertoire of lively nightspots: Perry's Gluepot, the Times Gate, and Churchill's. They'd gorge on lobster at Rector's or head up to Columbus Circle to eat wild game at Tom Healy's Golden Glades Cafe, where ice-skaters performed on an indoor rink. Or they'd visit the stage doors of Broadway's theaters, waiting for actresses and dancers to emerge and invite them out for drinks. At times, his and Baer's saucy exploits were recounted in the gossip pages.

A favorite haunt was Jack Doyle's Billiard Academy, a renowned newspaper hangout. Doyle once hosted a pool tournament for journalism's elite, and Ripley beat one famous newsman or cartoonist after another to become co-champion.

Ripley found himself caught up in a giddy postwar euphoria, embracing a heady new lifestyle rich with athletic and social pursuits and hobnobbing with celebrities. He started taking dancing lessons. His taste in clothes grew incrementally flashier—three-piece suits with knicker-length pants, bow ties, two-tone shoes and spats. He sometimes wielded a walking stick. Baer liked to tell his friend that he looked like "a paint factory that got hit by lightning."

The idea was to prove that the bumpkin could fit in, that the big city wasn't too big for Roy Ripley. He had money in his pocket too, thanks to his cheap new living quarters and some cash earned from drawing illustrations for another book, a retired Army colonel's memoir, to be published later in 1919.

With his bachelor's lifestyle revolving around clubs, cafés, and bars, it was a great disappointment when America launched its nationwide experiment in abstinence. Ripley called the Eighteenth Amendment, which would prohibit alcohol consumption starting in 1920, a "foolish law."

Possibly inspired by the looming threat of limited access to legal drink, Ripley decided in the spring of 1919 to treat himself to a journey. On his passport application he wrote that he was traveling to Havana for "health and recreation." It would be his first departure from American soil since his 1913 travels to Egypt and Europe.

*　*　*

NOT LONG AFTER his return from Cuba, Ripley stunned Baer and other friends with the news that he was engaged to be married.

Ripley had previously expressed pride in his bachelorhood and, typical of the boys' club attitudes of the day, an immature understanding of the fairer sex. Maybe it was inevitable that amid so much testosterone Ripley would develop caveman-like views toward women. He swapped dirty jokes in the NYAC's locker room and at the Friars Club bar. In print, he would acknowledge a passion for the company of a shapely woman and a well-made cocktail. Yet, for someone who was mostly raised by his mother and who remained close to his sister, he revealed an astonishing lack of savvy about women.

In general, he felt women required too much time and effort—"Time to woo 'em, win 'em, and time to keep 'em," he'd grouse—and that women had become "spoiled with the gallantries of the ages." After losing his first love, Nell Griffith, he often professed doubts that he'd ever find the right woman. In more petulant moments, he'd disparage Manhattan's female office workers as "the most tragic sight in our cities."

Terrified of finding himself in a "matrimonial wreck," he had seemed happy to pursue the single life. Then again, his petite bride-to-be was no office girl.

✳ ✳ ✳

SOME NEWSPAPER ACCOUNTS said Beatrice Roberts was born in Manhattan to a well-heeled Jewish family. Other accounts said she was a Texas-bred Italian from the cowboy flatlands outside Waco. In truth, she came from a blue-blood Boston family with lineage to the *Mayflower*. Born in Medford, Massachusetts, one of six kids, she had been a teen beauty queen before moving to New York, harboring dreams of a dancer's life.

Her first New York jobs were modeling. Curvy and dark-eyed, with pouty, twin-peaked lips, her face appeared on billboards and in magazines. Beatrice danced on Broadway and in shows directed by Ned Wayburn, a *Ziegfeld Follies* choreographer. She played piano and sang, but her most bankable talents were her high-kicking legs and a pretty face, talents recognized by a man who knew how to nurture young girls' dreams.

Florenz Ziegfeld had created his *Follies* in 1907 and launched many careers over the next quarter century, including W. C. Fields, the actress-singer Fanny Brice, and the singing Cherokee-American Will Rogers. Future Hollywood stars such as Lillian Gish and Bette Davis got their start as Follies Girls. The *Ziegfeld Follies* combined music, comedy, and dance, shot through with innuendo and sex appeal. One Ziegfeld biographer called the 1919 *Follies*, featuring a nude Lady Godiva character atop a horse, "a union of lovely music and lovely girlflesh."

Many *Follies* dancers found their way to an audition with Mr. Ziegfeld at age thirteen or fourteen, and were onstage soon after. Marrying one of Ziegfeld's teens was considered a badge of honor, as impressive as landing a young starlet would be years later. (Bugs Baer would marry a Follies Girl too.) Beatrice briefly danced alongside a Follies Girl named Marion Davies, soon to become William Randolph Hearst's infamously public mistress.

Ripley's first date with Beatrice had been the night he drew his "Champs and Chumps" cartoon in late 1918. She would have been a week past her eighteenth birthday at the time; Ripley was a decade older. They may have been introduced by Bugs Baer, who'd started performing comedy routines in vaudeville shows and would invite Ripley to parties with dancers and singers. Or maybe one of Ripley's NYAC pals—Ziegfeld comedian W. C. Fields or *Follies* composer Robert Baral—introduced them. One writer described her as "a prominent figure in the Ziegfeld Follies on account of her statuesque beauty."

Despite his affinity for the single life, Ripley was moved by her beauty. In a pattern that would later repeat itself regularly, Ripley fell in love quickly, poetically, and passionately. She called him Roy, he called her Bea. They played tennis, walked through Central Park, went to dinners and Broadway shows. In the summer of 1919, he posed for a portrait—his hair slicked back, wearing a bow tie and a suit—and gave her a framed copy: "To Beatrice, With Affection, Roy." She responded with a photograph of herself, posed in mid-pirouette: "To Roy—My Boy."

They married on October 23, 1919, in Newark, New Jersey, then honeymooned in Atlantic City, strolling along the boardwalk and posing for touristy photos. Ripley wore his NYAC handball uniform to the beach—a tank top and tight shorts that revealed his muscular limbs—while Beatrice wore a black bathing suit and a polka-dot sun hat. In photographs, Ripley seems truly happy. Possibly, after so many years of insecurity about his strange looks, he was elated to have landed a *model* and a *dancer.*

Back in New York, however, they both began to wonder if they'd been hasty.

* * *

MAYBE HE'D HAD an inkling from the start, for when Ripley told friends about the end of his bachelorhood, he seemed uncomfortable with the news, and not particularly enthused. "We're married," he'd say, with no further explanation.

One sign of ambivalence was his unwillingness to give up his room at the NYAC. He told Beatrice he wasn't ready to cohabit, that he would be traveling too much and didn't want to commit to a house or apartment just yet. The newlyweds spent nights in midtown hotels—a suite at the Tavern Inn on West Forty-eighth Street or at the spectacular Hotel Marie Antoinette on Broadway. Though Beatrice didn't mind the nice hotels, she must have wondered what she'd gotten herself into.

Prior to wedlock, Ripley had dated other young women, and Beatrice apparently didn't trust her new husband to entirely give up his old lifestyle. It didn't help that Ripley, in addition to spending nights alone at the NYAC, would disappear for days at a time—on assignments or touring with boxer pals—while Beatrice remained in Manhattan. She phoned him constantly, suspicious that Ripley might be seeing other women, but he always insisted he was being faithful.

Still, the whole arrangement felt too bizarre for Beatrice, who had expected a more conventional union. She wanted to be doted on, and her husband's failure to meet her marital expectations triggered loud arguments on the nights they actually shared a room. She would accuse him of drinking too much or flirting with waitresses, and he'd argue that she had too much time on her hands and too vivid an imagination.

"There should be a law to compel suspended animation among wives during the afternoons," he once said. "A wife can get into more trouble to present her hardworking spouse on his return at night than a chorus of Pandoras."

In more introspective moments, Ripley would admit that for a devoted bachelor with limited knowledge of the female mind, an attempt at domestic stability was probably a bad idea. While he truly cared for Beatrice, he had gotten used to living simply and somewhat rootlessly. His NYAC apartment was more a locker room than a home, a sloppy place to change clothes or sleep before getting back to the clubs, the baseball stadiums, the handball courts. Regardless of whom was to blame, the marriage was on the rocks and coming apart fast. Ripley was relieved, then, when the *Globe* decided in mid-1920 to send him on the road.

* * *

THE FIRST CARTOON to actually carry the *Believe It or Not* title had appeared on October 16, 1919, a week before Ripley and Beatrice wed and ten months after the initial "Champs and Chumps" cartoon. After settling into his uneasy union with Beatrice, Ripley's interest in the year-old feature seemed suddenly rejuvenated.

Each of the *Believe It or Not* cartoons he produced in the first half of 1920 featured a medley of odd athletic feats—a wrestler who tested his neck strength by hanging himself (he survived); a pool shark who sank 23,000 balls; a Babe Ruth home run that flew 600 feet. Ripley also weaved random sketches that skewed from modern sports: Alexander the Great's courier, who ran 150 miles in a day, or Olympic hero Melancomas, who stood with arms outstretched for two days.

In response to this new energy, Ripley's editors decided to send him to cover the 1920 Olympic Games in Antwerp, Belgium, which would be one of the crowning journalistic achievements of his early career, placing him in the front row for another important moment in sports history, just like the Jeffries-Johnson fight. For Ripley, the Olympics also offered a much-needed escape from his marital woes and his disgruntled wife. But it wasn't the cushiest assignment.

In late July, he sailed to Europe with the US teams, including three dozen NYAC members. Athletes and newsmen complained about the bad food on the USS *Princess Matoika*, the cramped sleeping quarters, and the lack of training facilities. Ripley sketched athletes on the *Matoika*'s deck praying for land and complaining that the ship was just "a cattle boat." In Antwerp, events were scattered miles apart and frequent rains turned running tracks into muddy ruts. Water for swimming events was dank, dirty, and frigid. Ripley found Belgians to be rude, overweight, and uninterested in the Games.

⌇ BELIEVE IT! ⌇

Hawaiian swimmer Duke Kahanamoku (controversial, due to his darkish skin) won two of the forty-one gold medals taken by the United States: more than twice as many as the next most successful team, Sweden.

But the Games gave Ripley the chance to veer further from covering traditional sports and to stoke his curiosity about the history and oddities of sport. One dispatch described the origins of the marathon, the fabled run by a foot soldier from the Battle of Marathon to the city of Athens. After delivering his message, "Rejoice, we conquer!" the runner collapsed and died. In September, after a month away, Ripley sailed home on the SS *Imperator*. His spoiling marriage awaited.

＊　＊　＊

RIPLEY AND BEATRICE passed their first wedding anniversary in the fall of 1920. Though they'd lived apart for most of that year, they were still husband and wife and they tried occasionally to reconcile, usually with terrible results. They once got into a marathon shouting match at the Hotel Marie Antoinette. Another night, beckoned by an anonymous caller, Beatrice found her husband dancing with another woman at a Broadway café. When she confronted him, he dragged her to the street and put her in a cab.

Over the next year, Ripley further distanced himself from his young bride, traveling to handball tournaments with Bugs Baer, his partner in sport and in drink. It's possible that the onset of Prohibition had contributed to Ripley's refusal to give up his NYAC apartment and settle down with Beatrice. He referred to his kind as "the great criminal element," so it helped to have a bed at the NYAC, just a few blocks north of the notorious stretch of speakeasies along Fifty-second Street, known to house more illegal pubs than anywhere in the city, where secret chutes were built into the walls to dump liquor during a bust.

Through 1921, Ripley began cranking out a steadier stream of *Believe It or Not* cartoons, averaging roughly two a month. Though they still largely contained sports feats, he'd begun featuring more non-sports vignettes, such as the man who ate sixty eggs a day for a week and a man named Martin Laurello who had a "revolving head." He scavenged gossip rags and stuffed his notebooks full of news clippings about hard-to-believe facts and feats, the stranger the better.

As his marriage dissolved and his personal life got messier, his cartoons seemed to grow incrementally weirder. He'd slip in a sketch of a man who never shaved, a man who ate glass and nails, a man who crossed the English Channel on a mattress, a man who stood on one leg for twelve hours, and a 147-year-old man who could lift two hundred pounds. He also presented to readers a billiards player with no hands who sank 799 straight balls, and another who sank 46 straight with his nose.

Signs of Ripley's marital strife sometimes slipped into print. In a mid-1921 essay titled "The Female of the Species," he derided America's female athletes as inferior to their European counterparts. "What is the matter with the American girl?" he asked in print, stating that European women excelled in "stage, opera, science, and letters . . . [and] how about beauty?" He felt American women suffered from "strained nerves" and too many soda-fountain lunches. In an unpublished article advocating physical fitness for women, he fretted that every beautiful woman inevitably "begins to fade."

> After that she begins her desperate fight with cosmetics to save the remnants of her girlishness; she develops a warped "office-girl" figure, spongy muscles, listless eyes . . . Then there's nothing left except bitter, lonely spinsterhood.

Despite Ripley's outbreaks of chauvinism, and his fights with and absences from Beatrice, she still loved him. She gave him a sultry photograph of herself that summer of 1921, signed "Your lover girl." But against so much competition—from nightclubs to baseball games, boxing matches to handball courts—she eventually realized there was nothing to salvage. In December of 1921 she filed papers requesting a formal separation, charging her husband with "cruel treatment," "excessive indulgence in intoxicants," and a "fondness for other young women." A judge granted the separation and awarded Beatrice a monthly alimony of $125, plus $750 in legal fees. Her attorney told the press he'd "made several appeals to Mr. Ripley to do the right thing by his wife," but Ripley's failure to do so had forced Beatrice to bring her complaints to the judge.

Ripley declined to publicly defend himself, allowing the accusations of womanizing, alcoholism, and physical abuse to stand.

Finally, the marriage went down in flames one night after

Beatrice followed him to the Great Northern Hotel and up to Room 304.

He and another woman had shared a quiet dinner and a few drinks, then returned to his room for a nightcap. One thing led to another. Clothes were removed.

The romantic mood was suddenly interrupted by urgent knocking at the door, and then shouting, then *pounding*. Somehow his spouse had found him. Ripley emerged, flustered and wearing only a bathrobe, to find Beatrice accompanied by two other men (an elevator operator and a shoe salesman, he'd later learn—in court). He tried to block them from seeing his companion, but Beatrice could tell the other woman was "scantily attired."

When the shouting died down, Beatrice announced that she was finally, completely through with him. She'd let a judge decide the details.

CHAPTER

8

Exactly one year after his noisy split from Beatrice, Ripley landed the assignment and the adventure of a lifetime.

"All my life I have waited for this day—the day when dreams come true," Ripley told readers in his first dispatch from afield, on December 1, 1922. "To go 'round the world is a youthful dream. Now is the time, before it is too late . . . from the New York Athletic Club and back. Impossible to go further than that."

A decade after escaping San Francisco and landing a fruitful partnership with the *Globe*, Ripley ceased to be a mere sports cartoonist as he embarked on a journey that would change everything. Over the next four months, he would travel by train, steamship, army transport, rickshaw, sedan chair, elephant, horse, camel, and on foot. The journey would test his skills as an aspiring adventurer and offer readers a rare firsthand look into the non-Western world. It would provide rich new material for subsequent *Believe It or Not* cartoons, leading Ripley in a new artistic direction—more worldly, more weird.

The unexpected around-the-world expedition would also

introduce him to the country whose people and culture would transfix him for the rest of his life.

✳ ✳ ✳

TRANSGLOBAL TRAVEL REMAINED a rarity among the masses, such journeys typically undertaken only by the military, merchants, or true explorers. In recent years, attempts at luxury cruise travel had ended badly: the *Titanic* in 1912; the *Lusitania* in 1915.

❧ BELIEVE IT! ☙

Among the Titanic *victims were NYAC members whose bodies were identified by the leather key tabs imprinted with their membership numbers.*

The RMS *Laconia*, owned by pioneering British steamship operator Cunard, had been launched in late 1921 to replace the original *Laconia* (sunk off the Irish coast in 1917 by German U-boat torpedoes). The luxury ocean liner now sought the ambitious distinction of becoming the first passenger ship to circle the earth. Having his name on the passenger list made Ripley feel like some modern-day Magellan or Marco Polo, and Ripley proudly called the *Laconia* "my houseboat around the world."

Unlike previous assignments, confined by stadium walls and sports teams' schedules, the itinerary would be mostly in Ripley's hands. Instead of writing about others, as he had during World War I and at the Olympics, Ripley would be his own leading man. He was expected to file a dispatch every day or so, accompanied by a sketch or two, for the next four months. But where he went, whom he met, and the stories he told . . . that would all be largely up to him.

The *Globe* offered "Ripley's Ramble 'Round the World" series to dozens of newspapers who subscribed to the Associated Newspapers syndicate. The inaugural dispatch was accompanied by a logo of a caricatured Ripley in full stride, wearing a jaunty cap, bow tie, and knickers, a huge sketch pad under one arm, and wielding a pen like a sword in the other hand.

Ripley first boarded a Lake Shore Limited train bound for Chicago, then west on to Las Vegas, Los Angeles, and San Francisco, where he'd meet the *Laconia.* As the lights of New York faded, and the train window framed only darkness, Ripley lay back on the shelf-bed of his sleeper car, suddenly wondering if he was ready to leave his comfortably urban and urbane lifestyle behind. Now entirely on his own, away from friends and mentors, responsible for describing the world to millions of readers, he felt scared—a "fear that creeps toward your throat," he'd later call it—as he watched his hometown recede from view.

* * *

THE TRANSCONTINENTAL RAIL journey was his first return to California since his mother's death seven years earlier.

His solemnity fizzled upon reaching Los Angeles, where he toured Hollywood studios, watched Charlie Chaplin act in a few scenes, and joined up with three traveling companions who would make cameo appearances throughout the Ramble: Jack Davidson, an actor who had appeared in fifty films (including *The Winning of Beatrice* and *The Wild Girl*); May Allison, Davidson's costar in *The Winning of Beatrice*, also the star of nearly fifty films; and Allison's new husband, Robert Ellis, a prolific actor, screenwriter, and director, whose most recent film was *A Divorce of Convenience*. Ripley's otherwise extensive journal keeping offered no commentary on the eerie similarity between his Hollywood friends' films and his own life—*Beatrice, wild girl, divorce . . .*

The foursome traveled to San Francisco and Ripley played tour guide, showing his companions a few favorite haunts—the Barbary Coast, the Cliff House, Mission Delores, and the Hotel Fairmont, where he'd witnessed the smoldering city days after the earthquake—as well as his humble old basement apartment. He introduced them to Coffee Dan's, an underground speakeasy accessed through a hidden wall leading to a playground slide that deposited guests onto the barroom floor. Inside, they ordered "ham and eggs"—code for liquor. Ripley told Jack Davidson the place had the spirit of San Francisco "before the fire."

The ship left San Francisco the next morning, steaming through the burly shoulders surrounding Golden Gate Bay. Slightly hungover, Ripley grew woozy and melancholy watching San Francisco shrink in his wake. He had eagerly left for the East Coast a decade earlier, but still felt pangs of homesickness for Northern California.

"Once again I leave home," he wrote in an essay, revealing to *Globe* readers that his Ramble might become more than a mere travelogue.

Why any one place should forever hold enchantment for the reason you are born there is a mystery. But like cats and birds we are pussy-footed and pigeon-toed and our footsteps lead toward home. . . . The Eskimo longs for his northern bleakness and his ice hut, the cowboy dreams of the wide open towns and prairies of the west, the old salt is looking out to sea . . . and down in the hold of many ships are dead Chinamen's bones going home to China.

In his sketch of the *Laconia* disappearing over the horizon, smoke from the stack spelled "Goodbye."

* * *

DURING HIS FIRST DAYS aboard the *Laconia*, Ripley met the other pioneering travelers who would visit remote parts of the world while also sipping martinis in the ship's saloons, perfectly legal since the *Laconia* sailed under the British flag. Among the passengers were ten honeymooning couples, five ministers, thirty widows, twelve millionaires, and, as Ripley told readers, "one of the best known prohibition enforcement officers New York ever had."

Ripley was soon taunting his Prohibition-restricted readers: "You folks at home have doubtless forgotten the saloon," he said. "Let me tell you . . ." The ship's most popular bar, unobtrusively called A Aft, was filled with "American law-breakers." A beer cost fifteen cents, a whiskey twenty cents, and a bottle of champagne $6. A sign on the wall gave helpful advice to wine buyers: WILL PASSENGERS KINDLY GIVE THEIR ORDERS FOR WINES IN ADVANCE, SO THAT THEY MAY INSURE THEM BEING SERVED AT THE PROPER TEMPERATURE.

Two weeks after leaving New York, Ripley spotted the shimmering Hawaiian archipelago. Onshore at Hilo, he was surrounded by slender, dark-skinned native girls who welcomed Ripley with effusive alohas and piled garlands around his neck. He was instantly smitten, calling the Big Island "an emerald jewel set in the sea."

Though the Prohibition officer searched passengers disembarking at Hilo, to prevent anyone from bringing alcohol ashore, Ripley had developed a knack for sniffing out liquor wherever he went. He and his friends found a local resident who offered some Hawaiian moonshine, *okolehao*, distilled from pineapple and the root of the Ti plant. Ripley bragged in print about the smile that *okolehao* put on his face. Paraphrasing Shakespeare and the Bible, he wrote: "Oh Mule! Where is thy sting?"

At the Moana Hotel on Waikiki Beach in Honolulu, Ripley reunited with Duke Kahanamoku, a local swimming and surfing legend whom he had met at the 1920 Antwerp Olympics. Kahanamoku introduced Ripley to "surf riding," which Ripley attempted to describe to readers: "These bronze-skinned natives paddle on a board . . . to a distance upward of a mile, where they catch a likable wave and then mount to their feet and stand upright."

Ripley tried surf-riding in an outrigger canoe and later enjoyed a tribal hula dance at midnight. He considered the Hawaiian Islands "a land of romance and happiness," although he worried that the Hawaiian race—"the most lovable and hospitable race on earth"—was being eradicated by disease and the influence of Japan, China, and America. He thought Honolulu was too full of US soldiers and sailors to be a novelty. Then again, he felt comforted by the strong military presence. "And that means that the outpost—the frontier, if you will, of America—is safe from foreign aggression," he wrote, nineteen years to the day before the Pearl Harbor attacks.

Reluctantly, he left Hawaii, worried that he'd never experience "such genuine, whole-hearted hospitality again." Then again, having earned a blistering red sunburn, he looked forward to the cold, legal beer aboard the ship.

* * *

FOUR DAYS LATER, after roiling through a twelve-hour storm, Ripley spent a sullen Christmas at sea, thinking of Christmases gone by. His morose holiday worsened as the ship struck the edge of a violent typhoon, and Ripley hunkered in the A Aft saloon beside a snarling man from New Jersey named Sam. Ripley's drinking partner complained miserably about the weather, regretting his decision to spend a month at sea just to see "a lotta Chinks."

When the *Laconia* finally passed through the howling winds of the typhoon, the clouds broke and Ripley was able to leave the bar, walk onto the deck, and witness a spectacularly setting sun. It looked like a giant blood-red orange melting behind Japan's white-tipped Mount Fuji, the perfect welcome to Asia.

A month after leaving New York, Ripley began to find his travel-writer voice in Japan. Instead of focusing on Prohibition and saloons, he started to weave history lessons with cultural analyses, travelogue and random cogitations, weird facts and personal opinion, the type of wide-ranging commentary that would decades later be called *blogging*. He sometimes exposed his biases, sharing hints of racism and stereotyping that had previously made cringe-inducing appearances in his cartoons.

"The Japs and the Jews are the only civilized peoples with a fundamental religion of their own," he wrote in a dispatch on Shintoism. He called the Japanese religion a "strange faith," but was impressed that it preached "love of nature, patriotism, love of family, and filial reverence." He was equally impressed by the Japanese emphasis on ceremony, though he found it frustrating that it took so long to get a cup of tea. He toured temples and shrines, Tokyo's red-light district ("bizarre and brilliant"), and spent New Year's Eve amid the "kaleidoscopic throng" of the Ginza ("the busiest, noisiest, unhandsomest, and most flamboyant of all streets").

He found Japan to be "a hive of industry" where "everybody seems to be pushing or pulling something." As with his remarks about America's military presence in Hawaii, he presciently assessed Japan's military affairs, troubled by the ubiquity of naval vessels and the rampant construction of "massive and murderous" battleships.

Despite his passionate curiosity about the world, Ripley could be a lazy traveler, and sometimes a boor. Just as he seemed to relish opportunities to divulge his chauvinism (and possible alcoholism) in print, he rarely hesitated to put his provincialism on full display. He considered it too much work to learn even a few phrases of his host country's language, unabashedly speaking English at all times. As he'd done in Europe years earlier, when someone didn't understand him, he spoke *louder*.

"Rickshaw man!" he yelled at a driver in Kobe. "Do you speak English?"

"Darn near," the man replied.

In one dispatch he described the Japanese language as so complicated "the Japs can't learn it themselves." It was sometimes hard to tell whether his oafishness was tongue-in-cheek, but he insisted that he could travel anywhere speaking English alone: "Simply speak up and let the other fellow do the worrying."

He was equally unflinching with readers when he confessed, after reboarding the *Laconia* for the next leg of the journey, that he was surprised that he liked Japan so much. "I never thought I would, being born and raised in California and holding the western idea of the Jap," he said.

Folks back in New York must have gagged at a few comments from their otherwise civilized and sophisticated friend, remarks that would proliferate as the trip wore on. Ripley seemed to be trying out different traveler personas, waffling somewhere between small-town yokel and streetwise foreign correspondent.

* * *

AFTER A BRIEF STOP in Manchuria, the ship reached the ancient Chinese city of Tsingtao, and Ripley's first thought upon landing in the country he'd long dreamed of was that "human life is the cheapest thing in Asia." China was both beautiful and horrible, he quickly learned, an uneasy dichotomy that he'd confront in many future travels. He first witnessed the horrible. Along the wharves, he and the other tourists were beset by the local poor—clots of alms-seekers tugging at his sleeves and cuffs.

"I wonder what China is going to look like if this collection of deformities, rags, and leprosy is a sample," he wondered aloud.

After Tsingtao came Shanghai, which astonished him as "one of the most interesting and cosmopolitan places in the world." He and his actor friends dined on bird's nest soup and shark's fin. While touring the old city by rickshaw, he was again swarmed by beggars as he rolled through foul-smelling alleys "thronged with a noisy mass of humanity, the existence of such that I never would have believed." He saw crawling lepers with twisted limbs and at one point was chased down a cobbled alley by a man dragging another man strapped to a board, his hands and feet eaten away by leprosy.

"It is not pleasant to be chased by a thing like that," Ripley reported, heedless of his insensitivity. "Surely there is no lower form of life to be found than in this decayed old poverty-stricken spot."

Still, even in his disgust Ripley found his curiosity aroused by China and its people. Unlike his fellow first-class passengers, who shopped for trinkets and postcards, he frequently ventured off the itinerary in search of a more authentic experience, discovering in himself an unexpected facility with improvised exploration. In Hong Kong, he left the others for an impulse drive around Repulse Bay. On Formosa, he insisted on making a side train trip to see the headhunters he'd read about, though he was disappointed to find the men corralled behind barbed wire, looking "more like lounge lizards than blood-thirsty cannibals . . . I could lick them all myself."

At Formosa, the *Laconia* had anchored offshore and passengers were delivered from the pier to the ship by small shuttle boats. When a sudden storm kicked up, a dozen tourists were thrown overboard from the shuttle and had to be rescued by a Japanese warship. Laughing at their cuts and bruises, Ripley considered the rescue a thrilling highlight. Anytime the trip became ridiculous or dangerous, Ripley grew giddier, as if it were all a game.

In fact, he seemed surprisingly fearless at times, less afraid of gun-toting soldiers than alms-seeking beggars. When he learned about military skirmishes in Canton (as Guangzhou was then called), he asked the US consul for permission to visit. His request was denied, so he and Bob Ellis negotiated with local military leaders for passage on a midnight transport boat out of Hong Kong. Like a Boy Scout on his first campout, Ripley gushed with excitement: "They say it is very dangerous and we are strongly advised not to go," he said. "But I have always wanted to be a war correspondent like Herb Corey."

Squeezing through flotillas of houseboats, Ripley's boat arrived in Canton at dawn. He and Ellis then walked nervously among the soldiers of Sun Yat-Sen's revolutionary army, part of the Kuomintang, which battled Chinese warlords and regional armies in an effort to unite the fractured Chinese Republic. The soldiers must have been surprised and/or amused to see Ripley in town, wearing a herringbone suit, knicker pants, a bow tie, and boyish cap, his sketch pad always in hand. Among the uniformed soldiers and poorly clothed locals, he stood out like a clown at a funeral.

One soldier finally snatched Ripley's sketch pad and accused him of being a spy. "I no like strange soldiers," the man yelled before Ripley's guide came to the rescue. He and Ellis then climbed into sedan chairs, each borne on the shoulders of three men who plunged into the labyrinthine streets of the ancient city, into the "evil-looking alleys" and the "mystic, foul-smelling center" of what Ripley breathlessly discovered to be the *real* China.

After spending the night at the deserted Victoria Hotel, he and Ellis returned to Hong Kong the next day, and Ripley felt that in Canton he had experienced a more genuine taste of China than he would in a year in Hong Kong or Shanghai. Those cities, he scoffed, had been built mainly by Europeans.

As the *Laconia* steamed toward its next stop, Ripley was sorry to leave China, which had repulsed, appalled, and dazzled him. He worried that it would now be impossible for anyplace else to top "the vast, old decaying land of the Celestial."

*　＊　＊*

COASTING INTO MANILA, he thought about Magellan entering the same port four hundred years earlier. The bay, crammed with warships flapping with American flags, made Ripley swell with patriotism and pride. "Our Uncle Sam has done well with his most pretentious colonization effort," he wrote.

Halfway around the world at this point, he had come to fancy himself a far more adventurous traveler than his high-class compatriots, whom he mocked for their petty complaints about heat and food. He scorned those wearing Gallagher and Sheans—"the concrete helmet which distinguishes all tourists of tropical climes."

ℰ BELIEVE IT! ℈

*Ed Gallagher and Al Shean were a popular vaudeville act,
earning $1,500 a week at the 1922 Ziegfeld Follies.
(Shean was uncle of the Marx Brothers; Gallagher married a
Follies Girl.) In their most famous skit, Gallagher parodied an
American tourist, wearing a white suit and
pith helmet.*

"Why a human being will wear such a human lid passeth all understanding," claimed Ripley, who would one day adopt the exact same traveling costume.

Again, he seemed embarrassed by the timidity of the parochial American traveler, even as he was clearly afflicted by the same backwater lack of international sophistication. One moment he could be the keen and curious observer, the next he'd be the insensitive doofus. He had been tickled by the "pidgin English" many Chinese used to converse with tourists, but also found Chinese merchants too shrewd and aggressive—"a Jap or a Jew hasn't a chance with him," he wrote.

And yet, emboldened by his adventures in China, he was now eager to leave the Philippines and reach India. Along the way he visited Java, Singapore, and Rangoon, but India beckoned loudly. "Can India offer more wonders than Japan or China, especially China?" he wrote one night in his journal. "It seems impossible . . ."

In the meantime, he was finding his rhythm as a correspondent—and having a blast. In playful dispatches home he teased his audience, a mischievous tool he'd wield in future cartoons. After visiting a beer garden in Java he declared, "I went to bed and slept with a Dutch wife." The next day he explained that a Dutch wife was an oblong pillow, and that the previous night was "not as romantic as it sounds." He kept razzing those suffering under Prohibition with stories of exotic drinks and taverns. When it got cold, he told readers, he "drank gin to keep warm." When it was hot, he drank beer. He discovered "Chota Peg" (whiskey and soda), and raved about noontime Gin Slings at John Little's Department Store in Singapore, the recipe for which he shared with readers: "Let me whisper . . ."

Upon reaching India, however, his tone shifted, from playful to shocked and somber, and Ripley's question about whether anything could top China was quickly, horrifically answered.

⁎　⁎　⁎

THROUGHOUT THE RAMBLE, he frequently declared, aloud and in print, often with unambiguous authority, that something he had witnessed was the best or worst or most or least *in the world,* which would become his pet three-word tic. Repulse Bay was "the most beautiful in the world"; the Javanese were "the cleanest people in the world"; Singapore "the most cosmopolitan city in the world"; the Hooghli River in India "the most dangerous in the world." Buddhists were "the happiest people on earth"; and a Chinaman was the "most virtuous and most honest man in the world," but also "the dirtiest."

He was blatant about these statements, and seemed to care little about redundancy or contradiction (or insult). If he felt it at the time, that was truth enough. But in the city of Benares— "the most remarkable in the world"—he discovered a place in no need of hyperbole.

"I have traveled 20,000 miles and have seen no place which so baffles description as this," he reported. "Here in India cows are sacred, little girls are married at the age of three, the dead are fed to vultures, holy men sleep on beds of nails, and a man may marry as many wives as he wants. What a motley mixture of mystery!"

India introduced Ripley to the devout Hindu ascetics and beggars known as fakirs. (He sometimes called them fanatics or "wretches.") These men performed inhumane, self-flagellating acts to prove their sanctity. One man had been sitting on a bed of nails for twelve years, while others kept their arms aloft all day—Ripley called them "up-arm men." Some never clipped their cuticles ("nail men") and others hung upside down from limbs like monkeys ("tree men").

The holy city of Benares seemed to be an epicenter for the extremes of Hindu spirituality, home to what Ripley called "the weirdest collection of humanity on the face of the earth—demented, delusioned, diseased, and devout." One of the few white faces, he roamed streets clotted with goats and sacred cows, gawking at the blood and bones scattered about, at the "insane worshippers" and wild-eyed beggars. Walking along the banks of the Ganges River, he watched in amazed horror as a woman, with no sign of emotion, set afire the body of her recently dead husband, using a long pole to make the fire burn faster as vultures circled overhead.

"Not a pleasant site [*sic*]," he wrote that night by kerosene lamp, concluding: "You are never so dead as when you die in India."

Similar "burning ghat" ceremonies were held all along the riverbanks, and Ripley returned three days in a row to witness numerous cremations. Meanwhile, orthodox Hindus bathed in—and drank—the same murky water in which human ashes were being scattered, in which dead bodies floated, and into which sewage seeped. Ripley worried whether leprosy was contagious, but seemed unable to turn away from the corpses and deformed beggars. In home-movie footage Ripley gapes as a man pierces his own tongue with a bicycle spoke; he gives coins to a gnarled beggar who walks on all fours; he walks among the half-clothed poor, skittish but agog.

"Nowhere on earth can you see such a weird cross-cut of human life," Ripley wrote. "All this pagan panorama."

In contrast to the horrible, Ripley also witnessed the sensational. At the Taj Mahal ("the most beautiful building in the world"), he was relieved to enjoy such dazzle after the squalor of Benares. In Jaipur ("a kaleidoscope"), he watched a rainbow-like wedding procession led by an elephant carrying the bridegroom through the streets. But death was never far away. The wedding party marched past a man carrying his dead son wrapped in thin red gauze.

"Funerals and weddings are continually passing each other," he wrote back to America. "Such is life."

India fascinated, revolted, beguiled, and *moved* him. His hotels were wretched, his mattresses festered with bedbugs. Still, he disparaged those who "travel for the sole purpose of mailing picture postcards back to envious home folks," and he continued to explore outside the safe bubble of the tour company's itinerary.

In Delhi, he and Jack Davidson bribed their way into the sacred Jama Masjid mosque during midday prayer. When they were spotted, furious elders dragged them out a side gate as worshippers shouted and jeered. In Calcutta, wanting to visit the famous Black Hole dungeon, he hailed a cab and yelled, "Black hole!" The driver nodded enthusiastically, and after an hour of meandering they stopped beside a miserable riverside structure. The driver pointed and said, "Black hole!" Ripley walked through a door and was hit by the sight and smell of partially cremated bodies. The driver had delivered him to a burning ghat, where Ripley watched a young boy attempting to burn his father's corpse. He left wondering if the boy's meager supply of wood would get the job done.

Back aboard the *Laconia*, Ripley confessed to readers the origins of his now-sated curiosity about India. He had once dated "a little blond sweetheart named Jean" who had lived in India and had given him a book of Kipling's poetry, in which she'd underlined her favorite verses. Among them:

> **If you've 'eard the East a-callin', why you won't 'eed**
> **nothin' else.**
> **No! you won't 'eed nothin' else, but them spicy garlic**
> **smells,**
> **an' the sunshine an' the palm-trees, an' the tinkly**
> **temple-bells.**

Ripley would pen eight dispatches from Benares alone, and a total of 26—out of roughly 120 total—from India, "that enchanting land of squalor and splendor." As the *Laconia* cruised west, he summed it all up: "A strange country is India. . . . It is a common thing to die here."

✳ ✳ ✳

AS HE HEADED toward the Middle East, his thoughts turned to God. Though his mother had been Christian and Ripley believed in a Christian version of God, he was hardly devout and sometimes admitted to having mixed feelings about Christianity. But in recent weeks he had been exposed to Shintoism, Buddhism, Hinduism, and witnessed the extreme and painful lengths to which people go to prove their devotion. So now, sailing toward Egypt, he found himself pondering the mysteries of Islam.

"For the life of me I cannot make up my mind whether the

vaunted power of the prophet is a myth or not," he admitted to readers. At the same time, he couldn't deny the anxiety that most Westerners felt for "the fanatical Muslim," with his robes, his daily prayers, his fierce piety. "Always it seems the European statesmen have lived in dread of the power of Islam," he wrote—once again, with eerie premonition. "The fear of Jehad has been upon the Christian world for ages."

At such moments, Ripley displayed a surprisingly well-calibrated cultural tuning fork. Ever the self-absorbed American, dark-skinned non-Westerners confused and unsettled him, eliciting insensitive commentary (similar to his chauvinistic remarks about women). Then again, he was capable of astute and prophetic observations—on Japan's aggressive military buildup and the threat of the "fanatical Muslim." Even so, he seemed at the same time able to find compassion and respect for the Other.

Ripley admired the restraint of Muslims, as well as Buddhists and Hindus. He reluctantly envied their ability to shun liquor and felt something close to shame that "the only people in the world who drink are Christians." He realized that, except for fellow passengers, he hadn't seen anyone drunk since Coffee Dan's in San Francisco.

In Jerusalem, however, he became downright enraptured at being at "the center of the world . . . my Holy City!" At St. John's Hotel, near the Church of the Holy Sepulchre, he couldn't believe he was near the spot where Christ died, the tomb where Jesus was briefly buried, the pathways "trodden by His feet." But he was also keenly aware of the ancient city's sizzling religious tensions. Rioting between Arabs and Jews had gone underreported in the American press, he realized. He learned that Palestinian Arabs were intent on preventing Zionists from controlling the Middle East, which he found not surprising since 90 percent of Palestine was Arab.

Still, he remained wary and distrustful of Islam, comparing the Mohammedan (as many Westerners then called Muslims) to the "Ku Klux Klan" for their head-to-toe white robes. Ultimately, he hoped that the potential dangers of Muslim fanaticism and threats of jihad were empty, that "the rising tide of his faith is only a ripple."

Again, the two sides of Ripley the traveler were on display—the ethnocentric American buffoon, and the curious anthropologist. He appreciated the "otherness" of the world but didn't necessarily want to get too close or, God forbid, shake its hand—an attitude that would change in time.

One thing he did admire about Islam was a man's ability to marry numerous women and to divorce them simply by repeating "Thou art divorced" three times.

He called their method of divorce "a great idea!"

* * *

CROSSING THE MEDITERRANEAN toward Europe, Ripley suddenly longed for home, his enthusiasm sapped. A Monaco casino looked beautiful on the outside, but inside was foul, smelly, and filled with American gamblers. In southern France, he thought Nice was "nice" and Marseilles was "quaint."

Though he'd sent eight dispatches from Benares, he would send just eight from Paris and Rome combined. The European stopover that intrigued him the most was Pompeii's ruins: "the deadest town I was ever in—and I am not excluding Philadelphia."

In Paris, he watched the funeral procession of actress Sarah Bernhardt and spent a day with Georges Carpentier, the boxer. He played tennis with Molla Mallory, one of the world's top-ranked female players, who had lost in the finals at Wimbledon six months earlier. When Mallory beat him 6–0, 6–0, Ripley blamed the previous night's drinking and smoking. "I didn't come over to play tennis, anyway," he griped.

One day he introduced himself to a stunning Peruvian woman named Carmela and they walked the gaslit streets and shared what he'd later coyly describe as "some wonderful moments." Ripley promised to visit her in Lima. "I'm a man of my word," he told Carmela, calling her "my little dark-eyed señorita."

Yet, after China and India, Europe seemed like an indulgence. Even while standing before Rodin's hunched-over *The Thinker,* he wondered aloud: "If he is thinking of man, he cannot think very much." Before sailing home, Ripley grew philosophical about his global odyssey, and shared some of his thoughts with readers: "Paris is all things to all people. You can find good and bad and indifferent here just the same as you can in Santa Rosa, California—my home town."

Ripley eagerly boarded the massive RMS *Aquitania,* bound for New York, then slipped into a glum reverie as the journey of a lifetime drew to an end. During the five-day westward crossing, completing his circle around the globe, he had plenty of time to look back on the strangest months of his life.

In his cabin one night, Ripley began cataloguing the world's cities of wonder. Benares ranked first, he decided, followed by Canton ("a vast rabbit warren of slant-eyed humanity"), then Jerusalem, Rome, Cairo, and Paris. Seventh on his top-seven list was New York, whose buildings were soon twiddling on the horizon.

"There is no city like Benares," he wrote in his Ramble's final dispatch. "But there is no place like home. . . . Columbus was right. The world is round."

Gliding into New York harbor at dusk, he felt exhausted and dejected, thinking back on Cairo ("a plundered land")

and Monaco ("Man is a gambling animal!"). He found himself wondering how so many could be starving in India and China—"Oriental millions wallowing in filth, ignorance and starvation"—while America was so full-fed. But he admitted that, whatever miseries he had witnessed, and whatever "waves of pessimism" he felt, he wasn't ready to reform the world.

"I can't reform myself!"

In his journal, which he did not share with readers, he wrote: "Why should the spirit of mortal be proud—ideals and actualities are far apart."

CHAPTER 9

Encircling the earth had rewired Ripley. The poverty and hunger he'd witnessed *haunted* him.

"If this world suffers from anything more than another it is malnutrition—malnutrition of brain and belly," he wrote in one of many stories that continued to appear for months after his Ramble. "What the world needs most is one God and one square meal!"

Certain sights and smells would linger forever, from the Chinese man with deformed hands like lobster claws to the smoke rising off burning corpses beside the Ganges to the man with two faces and one eye: "the most horrible living thing I have ever seen." It was now unavoidable that this uneasy fascination with the "demented, delusioned, diseased, and devout" of the world would alter the tone of his cartoon.

He had already come to realize that sports feats alone couldn't sustain his *Believe It or Not* series. After his Ramble, he grew even less interested in the strange things people did in the name of sport, and more fascinated by the inexplicable things people did for their gods. His cartoons began featuring oddities of a more freakish nature: the "Hanging Hindu," whom Ripley had seen dangling from a tree, a hook dug into his back; the "Hindu Sky-Facer," whom Ripley had watched stare directly at the sun with milky and withered eyes; the "Ever-Standing Man," who had been on his feet for twenty years, balanced on a crude wooden rack.

Gruesome became a new staple of Ripley's *Believe It or Not*. Friends and colleagues thought he seemed refreshed by his big adventure, liberated to finally be able to indulge his long-gestating desire to draw and write about something other than sports. From admirers who appreciated the eccentric new tenor of his work, requests trickled in . . . *Would Mr. Ripley speak to our organization? Write a story for our magazine? Donate a drawing to our charitable group? Cash to our orphans' home?*

Back at the *Globe,* he started hunting for a translator to help him mine even more believe-it-or-nots from the stacks of foreign books and magazines he'd collected from around the world. But just as he was getting back to work, he found his career jeopardized by a new employer, ominously known as "The Grocer."

⚹ ⁎ ✳

FRANK A. MUNSEY owned three New York papers: the *Sun,* the *Evening Telegram,* and the *Herald.* In mid-1923, for $2 million, he added Ripley's *Globe* to his collection, boosting his overall circulation and putting him in league with William Randolph Hearst as one of the city's top newspapermen.

As a pioneer of inexpensive printing on untrimmed pulp paper, Munsey had helped create dime novels and "pulp" magazines in the early 1900s. Unlike Hearst, who spent money freely and recklessly to perfect his papers and expand his empire, Munsey was a penny-pinching horse trader with a reputation for selling, merging, or dismantling his possessions, earning such nicknames as "The Great Consolidator" and, because he also owned grocery stores, "The Grocer."

Since 1891, Munsey had purchased sixteen papers, sold six, consolidated or closed seven, and by 1923 owned just the three. As Munsey's biographer put it, he was like an engineer monomaniacally focused on building a huge dam, but indifferent to the homesteads that would be flooded—"No man in the newspaper field was more hated than Munsey."

As a cartoonist, Ripley had good reason to fear Munsey's purchase of the *Globe*. Back in 1920, when Munsey bought the revered *New York Herald*, he instructed the art director to fire cartoonist J. Norman Lynd, adding, "He'll know what it's for." It turned out that four years earlier, Lynd had drawn a caricature of Munsey as a gravedigger, knee-deep in a *Daily News* grave, the headstones of other dead newspapers behind him. Munsey never forgot a slight. A week after buying the *Herald* he shut it down, merging it with the *Sun* and putting hundreds out of work. On the *Herald*'s last night, employees met in the newsroom for drinks and toasts as a bugler played "Taps." One competitor said Munsey had "the talent of a meat-packer, the morals of a money changer, and the manner of an undertaker."

For Ripley, the *Globe*'s new ownership and uncertain future spoiled an otherwise happy return from abroad. Despite the success of his Ramble and the steady popularity of his cartoons, Ripley's future was suddenly as uncertain as it had been in a decade.

At such a tenuous time, it didn't help to get bad publicity.

* * *

RIPLEY'S GROWING RENOWN among New York journalists meant his personal life was subject to scrutiny. And the failing marriage of a world-traveling cartoonist and a high-kicking Follies Girl gave society writers a sordid story line. Ripley's as-yet-unresolved split with Beatrice became fair game for the *Globe*'s gossip-hungry competitors, the type of story that up-and-coming columnist Walter Winchell liked to call "hot news." Various headlines began to appear through mid-1923:

FORMER 'FOLLIES' GIRL IN COURT AGAIN
EX–STAGE BEAUTY SUES CARTOONIST
CARTOONIST'S WIFE SUES FOR DIVORCE

Such stories were usually accompanied by photographs of Beatrice in a long gown, draped in furs, wearing a fashionable hat, and looking entirely pissed-off.

In her latest complaint, Beatrice wanted a judge to make their two-year-old separation permanent. She wanted a divorce. When her lawyer tipped off the press, writers responded with lurid stories about the couple's troubles, citing "new evidence" submitted by her lawyer, including a detailed account of the night in late 1922 when Beatrice found Ripley and his "scantily attired" friend at the Great Northern Hotel.

When the New York Supreme Court agreed to hear the case, Beatrice, now living on Madison Avenue, appeared at the hearing in "a costly fur-trimmed, hand-embroidered gown," as one columnist described it. The newspapers called Ripley her "stalwart, handsome husband." But the judge had harsher words, claiming that Ripley's poor husbanding skills and extramarital affairs were sufficient evidence to grant Beatrice the divorce.

Ripley's refusal to publicly deny Beatrice's accusations left an impression of guilt. At times, all he would say was that marriage had been a "rough voyage." Other times, he'd pretend the marriage never happened at all. In rare introspective moments, he would acknowledge that he was simply "too temperamental" to be a good husband. Losing his father at age fifteen had denied him a grown-up's perspective on love and marriage. And after leaving Santa Rosa, he had mostly lived and worked among newsmen and athletes who harbored manly views on women and wedlock.

His own chauvinistic views inevitably continued to appear in print. Women "are fast causing modern man to degenerate into a mechanical toy for their sole amusement," he declared in one article. Elsewhere he wrote: "The husband of today is little more than a slave with the divine gift of writing checks." America would be happier, he believed, "if husbands did not quarrel with their wives. And men were masters in their own houses."

✳ ✳ ✳

RIPLEY HAD BEEN THRIFTY in his New York lifestyle, living for a dozen years in modest quarters and owning few possessions. Though his *Globe* salary had quadrupled to $100 a week, his savings began dwindling after the divorce.

In addition to $200 monthly payouts to Beatrice, plus legal fees, he had continued sending money to California. His brother, Doug, after living for years with his surrogate Santa Rosa family, had moved in with his older sister Ethel and her husband in Sacramento. Doug was a difficult young man, disinterested in school or work, and he'd sometimes disappear into the woods for days at a time. He declined his older brother's invitation to come live with him in New York, and Ripley felt bad that he couldn't do more for his family.

In a letter sent after the divorce became final, he complained to Ethel about the heavy price of his failed marriage. "I received my divorce on Friday 13—not so unlucky after all," he wrote. "It cost me a great deal more money than I had and leaves me in debt up to my neck. But I think the relief from worry will permit me to earn a little more." He promised to send Ethel more money "as soon as I get some—I am going to work hard."

He signed the letter "Lovingly, Roy," and then added, in reference to both his Ramble and his recent woes: "The world is round, but a little bumpy."

Unfortunately, Frank Munsey soon made good on his reputation as a newspaper killer.

* * *

IN ANNOUNCING HIS PLANS to merge the *Globe* with the *New York Sun*, to create a "bigger and better newspaper," Munsey insisted he was doing New Yorkers a favor by pruning the "oversupply of evening newspapers." Munsey was unsentimental about such consolidations, claiming "there is no greater menace to society than newspapers that are struggling to keep alive."

Ripley's last cartoon appeared on May 31, 1923. Three days later, the *Globe* published its final issue, ending its reign as the nation's oldest paper. Among the five hundred employees to lose their jobs were "good men and women, for the *Globe*'s staff had been notable," wrote George Britt in a 1935 biography of Munsey.

Ripley landed on his feet, finding a spot at the *Evening Telegram*, which Munsey had purchased in 1920. But he felt unsettled by the recent tumult. He'd recently enjoyed the peak experience of his life on the Ramble, then became roiled in a painfully public divorce. That was followed by the premature end to his entrenched position at the *Globe* and a forced separation from longtime editors and colleagues. All of it threatened his shaky finances and his ability to support Doug.

So when he started at the *Evening Telegram,* he decided he needed a little help. At first, all he really wanted was someone to help him decipher the foreign-language publications he'd gathered during his Ramble, someone who could help breathe new life into *Believe It or Not.*

What he found was more than a mere translator. He found a business partner and ally, a man who similarly appreciated the eccentricities of the world.

* * *

NORBERT PEARLROTH WAS BORN in Tarnow, in the ancient Austrian section of Galicia. He was tall, handsome, and always the smartest in his class, possessing a near photographic memory of anything he read. In his youth, Pearlroth had devoured books of all types, and found at an early age that other languages came easily.

Before the war, he had attended the university in Krakow, where he breezed through his studies with plenty of time to earn extra money doing homework for classmates. One day he saw a newspaper ad for a series of encyclopedias printed in German called the *Library of Entertainment and Knowledge* and decided to buy it with his homework earnings. World War I upended his plans to become a lawyer, as Tarnow remained a dangerous battlefront throughout the war. (It became part of southern Poland after World War I.) So Pearlroth fled to America and by 1923 was married, living in the Bronx, and commuting into Manhattan to work at a bank.

Through a mutual friend, Pearlroth learned that a newspaper cartoonist was seeking a linguist and translator. Pearlroth was fluent in Italian, French, Russian, Polish, Yiddish, Hebrew, and more. He sometimes studied three languages at a time, and could quickly figure out the basics of any language.

"Tell me something odd," Ripley said to Pearlroth when the two first met, sometime in late 1923. Ripley had gotten into the habit of asking new acquaintances, *What's the strangest thing you know?* He'd figured: you never knew who might have a bizarro story that could be worked into a *Believe It or Not* cartoon. In recent years, his schoolboy notebooks had grown fatter with handwritten ideas added among the clipped-out articles, partly the result of asking questions of strangers.

Pearlroth served up a factoid that day about a California church built from the wood of a single redwood tree. At first, Ripley seemed confused. *Is this guy making fun of me?* Pearlroth later said he had no idea the First Baptist Church of Santa Rosa—the so-called Church Built of One Tree—was Ripley's parents' house of worship. When Pearlroth explained that he'd learned of the church from his *Library of Entertainment and Knowledge* encyclopedias, Ripley grew excited.

"*I'm* from Santa Rosa," he declared. "And I *know* that church."

On the spot, Ripley offered Pearlroth a part-time job. "I'll only need you for an hour a week," he said, suggesting payment of $25 a week.

To Pearlroth, the deal sounded too good to be true. Twenty-five bucks an *hour?* But working for Robert LeRoy Ripley, Pearlroth soon learned, would be more than an hour-a-week commitment.

Ripley must have known that he'd found a unique and potentially valuable assistant. The two men were kindred spirits in some ways, opposites in others. Ripley was the shy kid who'd found success based on his alleged knowledge of the world. Pearlroth was the handsome supergenius who'd found comfort in a private, solitary pursuit of scholarship. Ripley was athletic and social, a drinker and womanizer. Pearlroth was bookish, a faithful husband, and a devout Jew. Both shared a passion for oddball scraps of information, and Pearlroth was attracted to Ripley's enthusiastic, if naïve, quest for the mysterious arcana of humanity.

"Our daily life is so cut and dried that we get relief from fairy tales," Pearlroth said years later, in a rare interview about what drew him to Ripley in 1923. "Except his fairy tales are *true*, and this excites people. They like to learn that nature makes exceptions. These are fairy tales for grown-ups."

In time, Pearlroth would quit his bank job and commit himself to the most eager and enigmatic boss he could have imagined. Pearlroth would soon be exploiting, on a daily basis, his beloved *Library of Entertainment and Knowledge* collection, from which he would learn that birds had no sense of taste or smell, that a Brazilian butterfly had the fragrance and color of chocolate, that the dental nerve of an elephant weighed twelve pounds. Armed with such off-kilter curiosities, Pearlroth would help Ripley take *Believe It or Not* to unexpected new heights, and a rare and symbiotic relationship would bloom.

But not without some setbacks.

* * *

THOUGH RIPLEY HAD BEEN WELCOMED at the *Evening Telegram* in mid-1923, he soon became a twice-burned victim of Frank "The Grocer" Munsey's obsession with consolidation. Munsey merged the *Evening Telegram* with the *Evening Mail*, which he purchased in early 1924. Again, scores of employees lost their jobs.

Ripley was replaced by a sports cartoonist named Ed Hughes, whose sketches and columns seemed near replicas of his own, including assorted *Believe It or Not*–style bests and mosts in sporting achievements. Even Hughes's signature looked like Ripley's.

Ripley wasn't quite jobless, since Associated Newspapers agreed to keep him on its art staff. Still, for the first time he would not be affiliated with a local newspaper. Instead, his cartoons would be produced solely—and infrequently—by Associated Newspapers, appearing nationally, but *not* in New York.

Until now, he had worried little about imitators or competitors. But without a home at the *Globe*, his *Believe It or Not* concept began losing momentum, allowing Hughes and others to offer similar hard-to-believe-themed cartoons. *Believe It or Not* slowed to a trickle through 1924, the start of an awkward new career phase. During this period of semi-employment, weeks could go by with Ripley not being in print at all. He tried to stay busy writing and drawing on a freelance basis for magazines, including the NYAC's in-house newsletter. He pitched a book about his Ramble around the world, but couldn't find a publisher. Putting his love of handball into print, he authored *Spalding's Official Handball Guide*, which was published in late 1923. A year later he edited and illustrated *The Everlast Boxing Record*, a book of essays by well-known sportswriters.

Ripley sent copies of the handball and boxing books to his brother, but in an exchange of letters with his sister he learned that Ethel was struggling to help Doug finish high school. "Keep him at it and he will thank you some day," he wrote. He and Ethel then agreed by mail that, due to his financial woes and her troubles with Doug, they should sell the family house on Orchard Street. Ripley told his sister the house "seems to be a source of trouble and expense."

* * *

BY LATE 1924, Ripley was looking back gloomily on two volatile years. The end of his marriage, Doug's truancy, and the sale of the Santa Rosa house had all combined with the lingering effects of the death of the *Globe* and his premature departure from the *Telegram*. Signs of melancholy crept into his work. When an earthquake leveled parts of Japan—including places he had visited—Ripley drew a stunning visual commentary, an illustration of a Japanese man lying amid the ruins as an angel hovers above. "Tokio and Yokohama will rise again," Ripley wrote in the caption. "San Francisco rose again—greater than ever . . . spirit never dies!" In that year's Christmas cartoon, he sketched two raggedy orphans huddled beside a woodstove, from which hang two socks. The caption: "Empty Stocking."

Later he would use words like "indolent," "disillusioned," and "easily annoyed" to describe the simmering depression that vexed him through the mid-1920s. He felt his characteristic optimism replaced by despondency. He had worked hard during more than ten years in New York and had proven himself to be more than just a sports cartoonist. He was an athlete, an author, a lecturer, a world traveler, and, as he liked to consider himself, a circumnavigator. He had even been invited to join the prestigious Circumnavigators Club, whose membership included arctic explorers Richard Byrd and Robert Peary.

But now he was divorced and an orphan, an underemployed cartoonist and not really a New York newsman. Though he'd found an able assistant in Pearlroth, he felt unmoored and alone. He'd lost his wife and, in the bloodbath of Frank Munsey layoffs, had lost his editor and mentor, Walter St. Denis.

In the past, others had come to Ripley's rescue at crucial moments, patrons who helped him survive school (Miss O'Meara), escape Santa Rosa (Carol Ennis), and reach New York (Peter Kyne). Now, facing the most difficult period of his adult life, it was up to him to find a reserve of resilience and mettle for a comeback, to regroup and then regain his edge as America's purveyor of oddities. A firm believer in the restorative effects of a road trip, he began planning another big adventure.

* * *

A YEAR EARLIER, not long after his divorce was finalized, one of Ripley's few *Evening Telegram* cartoons had featured his brother/alter-ego, Demon Dug, hiding behind a tree, spying on a girl who is walking arm in arm with another boy. The cartoon was titled "A Bachelor's Decree."

From his hiding spot behind the tree, Dug mutters, "I'm off wimmen for LIFE!"

That's how Ripley initially felt after his divorce. In an interview with the "We Women" columnist Betty Brainerd, Ripley was asked why such a successful artist wasn't yet married. At first, he told Brainerd that he simply didn't have the time. Then he warmed to the topic and let loose a tirade on the virtues of bachelorhood: "I tremble when I look about at the matrimonial wrecks around me. Divorces grow more common every day and domestic squabbles fill the dockets of the courts and the pages of the newspapers. Ninety percent of the troubles that afflict us are due directly or indirectly to men and women fighting with each other."

Ripley had declared, to friends and in print, that he "never had a voyage as rough as that one on the sea of matrimony." But there was something unresolved about his drawn-out split from Beatrice, some emptiness that handball and boxing couldn't fulfill.

If he couldn't find what he needed in New York, he decided it was probably time once again to search abroad for what was lacking. His global Ramble had changed him. And when the world got bumpy and life became a torment, he now knew, the surest cure was to skedaddle.

Then again, with Prohibition soon to celebrate its fifth birthday, maybe all he really needed was a stiff drink in a less puritanical land.

CHAPTER

10

In the Peruvian town of Juliaca, twelve thousand feet above the Pacific, Ripley trudged through the rain toward his hotel, across a small plaza and past huddled groups of Peruvians who seemed "as joyless and sullen as this bleak and bare highland."

It had been a long day's train ride, followed by a soggy walk through town, and he was soaked and shivering. At the hotel, he asked the proprietor to start a fire so he could dry off. The proprietor refused: "No fire in Juliaca."

Stunned, Ripley asked how he was supposed to get warm.

"Go to bed," said the proprietor.

Ripley stormed off into the cold, rainy night, muttering that he was "not going to bed at seven o'clock in the afternoon if I can help it." Finding no bars or anything of interest except a windmill, he walked back to the hotel and went to bed in his dank, windowless room.

The next morning, after a chilly, sleepless night, Ripley walked back to the town plaza and stopped in front of the windmill. He started counting the windmill's revolutions, hopping from one foot to the other to stay warm, wondering why he'd again decided to roam so far from the comforts of home.

As if on cue, a stranger tapped him on the shoulder. His name was Miller. He was English, now living in Juliaca. Curious to see another Westerner in town, Miller invited Ripley to dinner that night, along with his wife and an American couple, also named Miller. "We're the only white people in this place," Miller said.

At dinner with the four Millers, Ripley huddled beside the kitchen stove, warming himself while describing to his hosts his latest adventure—a lengthy tour through South America. He described his sail through the Panama Canal and his recent visit to the corpse of Saint Rose, in Lima, casually mentioning that his California hometown was named for Saint Rose. The wife of the American Mr. Miller then jumped up, realizing the cartoonist was the former "LeRoy" Ripley.

"That's my home! I went to Santa Rosa High," she practically shouted. "I *remember* you. You used to play on the baseball team!"

And suddenly Ripley was reminded why he traveled. Because even in a place like Juliaca—"the most dreary, dismal spot on Earth"—life could surprise him.

Ripley laughed and reminisced with his new friends, joking that it really is "a small world after all."

* * *

HE HAD LEFT NEW YORK in late January of 1925 aboard the SS *Santa Luisa*, a remodeled World War I transport ship. Associated Newspapers announced Ripley's *Ramble 'Round South America* in a series of promotional ads, promising readers they'd "learn things about South America that are not found in books."

Though Ripley was toting stacks of research material supplied by Pearlroth—about Peruvian guano production, Chilean gauchos, Uruguayan silver mining, and the life of conquistador Francisco Pizarro—what readers would mostly learn about was Ripley's pursuit of women and wine.

Ripley made it clear from the start that he'd be taking this Ramble less seriously than his previous journey to Asia. He began this trip, thanks to a farewell party with friends, nursing a throbbing hangover. While passing through the Panama Canal, the ship stopped in Cristobal, a city straddling Prohibition-restricted American territory and unrestricted Panama. Ripley's first great South American discovery, therefore, was how quickly waiters at the Washington Hotel could scamper into Panamanian territory and return with cold champagne.

Freed from Prohibition's shackles, Ripley drank like an acquitted convict. One night he met Panama's president, Rodolfo Chiari, who spoke enthusiastically to Ripley in Spanish, while Ripley slurred right back—in English. Life aboard ship began too early for Ripley's tastes, a dilemma he solved by staying up all night. In Lima, he was invited to dinner with city officials, but his dress clothes had been sent ahead to the next city, and Ripley arrived in less-than-formal attire. In his eagerness to loosen up, he ignored the local custom of offering a toast before each sip of wine and began to drink at will. Every time he lifted his glass, the others scrambled to do the same. Sheepish and exhausted, woozy from a lack of sleep and too much wine, he topped off the night with an embarrassing bloody nose.

Such episodes did little to prompt an attempt at sobriety. During a stopover in Pisco, he walked off the ship, down the pier, and straight to the Gran Hotel in search of Pisco Punch, a cocktail made of the Peruvian-Chilean liquor *pisco*, which he'd first tasted in San Francisco. His drinking partner, an Italian count, called it *"agua ardiente"* (fire water) and Ripley called it "kerosene," then announced, "We're both correct!"

"Give me the tropics!" he crowed in print. "They suit my indolent nature well." At one point Ripley seemed to realize how his dispatches might be perceived by readers, and he soon admitted he had been on a quest. He never mentioned Beatrice or the recent divorce but made it clear he'd been looking for love.

* * *

BEFORE LEAVING NEW YORK, Ripley had sent a telegram to Carmela, the "dark-eyed señorita from Lima" he'd met in Paris. He had promised to visit her, never imagining he would ever reach Peru. Then came his divorce and an unexpected assignment to South America. He wired Carmela and apologized for the two-year lag, but reminded her that he was "a man of my word," and said he desperately hoped she'd be happy to see him.

Carmela never responded, but from the moment he left New York he had been praying she would be waiting at the pier. When he disembarked in Lima, Ripley anxiously scanned the crowds but never found Carmela's lovely face. He soon learned that his señorita was a *señora*, married with two children.

Unabashedly, Ripley confessed all this to his readers. "A woe is me," he wrote, sounding like a moody schoolboy with hurt feelings—like Demon Dug. "I am indeed a woe; I never did have any luck."

After the failed reunion, Ripley was determined to find another dark-eyed señorita. Like a romantic adolescent, he was back on the prowl.

In the southern Peruvian city of Arequipa, beneath the smoky pinnacle of the volcano El Misti, he stayed at a well-known boardinghouse run by Ana Bates, a salty-tongued woman who called everyone "Sonny Boy" and whom guests called Tia. The Quinta Bates boardinghouse was a favorite destination of movie stars, writers, and royalty. Clark Gable loved to visit and drink Pisco Sours; Noël Coward came for a two-day visit that turned into a month.

There, Ripley met Bates's stunning niece, Consuelo, which in Spanish means "consolation." At eighteen, she was half his age, shy and beautiful, and "chic and charming," Ripley wrote in his journal. "When she speaks Spanish it is like a rippling brook, and her English is sweet melody."

One night, he and Consuelo ascended to the roof garden and looked out at the moonlit El Misti. Ripley told Consuelo the volcano reminded him of Mount Fuji in Japan, and when she asked which was more beautiful, he confessed that he preferred Fuji.

"I could never lie to you," he told her. "And I am a pretty good liar, too, by the way."

Ripley later described the scene atop Misti in a dispatch home, telling readers things he should have told Consuelo: "She is modest and unspoiled and when she talks with you, tingling half-moons of guilt creep up your spine, although you have done nothing wrong; and you feel ashamed of the life you are leading, although it is nobody's business but your own."

Readers might have found it strange and even a bit creepy to read such confessional revelations from a newsman, but he seemed unable to hide his desperate and almost juvenile romantic pursuits—early signs of an earnestness, an unfiltered honesty, and naiveté that would endear him to readers.

* * *

ACROSS LAKE TITICACA and into Bolivia, he found that a bruised heart could be healed by a stunning landscape and a fiery cocktail. When he first spotted the city of La Paz, tucked into a chasm between towering mountains, he was dumbstruck. It looked exactly like someone had flung the city of Reno into the

Grand Canyon and he declared the high-altitude city of clouds to be "the most startling sight I have ever seen!"

Inspired by La Paz, and shamed by his recent sullenness, Ripley did what he often did when he felt aflutter. He drank. As he had on his first Ramble, Ripley spilled much ink on the topic of drink, openly declaring himself a Prohibition violator by complaining that the Inca corn liquor *chicha* tasted "almost as bad as the stuff we get in New York." He described how the Incas attached bouquets of flowers to poles outside their saloons: "Beautiful, isn't it? Flowers instead of padlocks!" When he met drinking partners, he amiably introduced them to readers, who thus became acquainted with an Irishman named Heavy and a Scotsman named Ferguson, whom Ripley dubbed one of his three favorite Scots, along with Haig & Haig (a brand of scotch).

While descending from the jagged Bolivian highlands to the Pacific coast, a fourteen-thousand-foot drop in half a day, he visited a tribe that once decapitated enemies, skinned their heads, and shrank them to the size of a baseball—his first exposure to the shrunken heads that would become a *Believe It or Not* emblem. (He bought one for $100.)

Pearlroth had provided history books for Ripley to mine, but Ripley only dug into this cache when there wasn't a woman or a drinking partner worth mentioning. His favorite book was William H. Prescott's *Conquest of Peru*, which chronicled Spanish conquistador Francisco Pizarro's plunder of the Inca Empire. "I am traveling the same road Pizarro trod!" he boasted to readers. "How I admire that villainous old fellow."

For days, he remained fixated on Pizarro. Passing through once-great cities such as Cuzco, he was horrified to witness how completely the Spanish conqueror and his men had trashed Inca culture. Ripley felt Pizarro's greed for gold and his treatment of the Incas were black spots on "the darkest page in all Spanish history."

ᘓ BELIEVE IT! ᘒ

In Cuzco, Pizarro had imprisoned Inca emperor Atahualpa
for refusing to cede control of Peru. Pizarro offered to spare the
emperor's life if he filled a room with gold, silver, and jewels.
Atahualpa complied. But instead of freeing the emperor,
Pizarro had Atahualpa executed.

In between drinking bouts, he occasionally found his poetic travel-writer voice, vividly describing "Indians with burden-bent backs trudging silently and stolidly" and "little fields where grim-faced Indians are plowing the unwilling land with bent sticks." One day he could be lyrical—"bright ponchos gleamed through the twilight of the nave and a faint chant came from the cloister"—and the next philosophical: "The vanity of man grows weak before the majesty of the mountains."

But on this trip, with or without Pearlroth's well-intended research materials, Ripley was at his most entertaining as the goofball American traveler. While traversing the Andes toward Buenos Aires, his train stopped for the night and passengers swarmed the town's few hotels. Ripley had been drinking with a German named Hans, who spoke fluent Spanish and offered to get them each a room. Hans secured two rooms but then bumped into a fellow German and gave away Ripley's key.

When Ripley learned Hans had double-crossed him, he begged the hotel clerk for a room, but there were none. The clerk offered Ripley a bunk in a room with three Chilean men. Afraid to be alone with three dark-skinned strangers, Ripley sat in the lobby, writing in his journal by kerosene lamp, wishing he'd stayed in Santiago, where he'd briefly met a woman whose smile had warmed his "soft and vagrant heart," as he put it in his journal. When his roommates were asleep, he crept into the room, slept a few hours in his clothes, then left the "evil-looking hombres" before dawn.

* * *

BY NOW, Ripley had grown keenly aware of the typical American's unworldliness and national arrogance. He knew South Americans laughed at the ignorance of their northern neighbors. "We are too prone to think of South America as one country when as a matter of fact it is made up of a dozen different countries," he added, proving his point.

In Buenos Aires, he continued to play the bumbling gringo. Among stylish men and women in Parisian-influenced clothes, Ripley stood in the hundred-degree heat of a midday plaza wearing the cream-colored linen suit he'd bought in India. With his sweat-darkened armpits and his sunburned and peeling skin, he was not a pretty sight. He wondered why people seemed to be staring at him until he realized he was the only man wearing a light-colored (and sweat-stained) suit.

Ripley was hardly a typical yokel, even if it was becoming his shtick. He continued to boast that learning other languages was "more a pleasure than necessity" and that his California dialect had served him well. And while he enjoyed meeting new people from other lands, all conversations had to be conducted in English.

* * *

SIX WEEKS into his Ramble he had explored more of South America than an average American might see in a lifetime. After journeying by rail into the Andes and across the continent's belly, Ripley finally felt a weight lifting, relieved to be far from "the static and cross-word puzzles and the rest of the wrangling world," as he put it.

Still, on this particular trip, with the shadow of divorce still looming, what he yearned for more than natives and their culture was the company of a stiff drink and/or a fiery young woman. In Buenos Aires, he managed to coax an attractive Australian named Whupsie Strelitz to spend an afternoon with him. She agreed to meet the next morning in her hotel lobby, and Ripley arrived to find Whupsie's stern-looking mother standing beside her, wanting to know their destination.

"To the cemetery!" he told Whupsie's mother. For their date, Ripley took Whupsie to the "City of the Dead," as La Recoleta Cemetery was known. They strolled among the graves of Argentine presidents, poets, scientists, and soldiers.

Two days later, Ripley met Maggie, a New Yorker who had been living in Buenos Aires. Maggie agreed to spend a day with Ripley and they walked along the Rio Tigre, then drank champagne at the High Life café with another couple. But when Ripley invited Maggie to dinner, she said no, claiming she didn't want to send the wrong message to the locals that she was "a bad woman."

"You must remember that Buenos Aires is not the Bronx," she said.

The next morning he waved good-bye to Maggie, who grew smaller and smaller on the pier as Ripley sailed to Uruguay and then up the coast to Brazil. At sea, he reflected on his eight weeks on the southern continent, and somewhat morosely summarized his limited success with women, a failure he blamed partly on the women. The movies and musicals back in New

York had led him to expect streets filled with dancing Latinas wrapped in shawls, roses clenched in their teeth.

"I am beginning to believe that the famous Spanish señoritas are a myth," he said.

Playing the lovestruck Yankee was part of the woe-is-me persona he'd begun honing in print. And he reluctantly one day acknowledged to readers that maybe Latina women simply weren't interested in *him*. At the thought of it, Ripley spent a melancholy and reflective few days sailing toward Brazil.

The reason Ripley so desperately sought female companionship was that he hated being alone. And he wasn't much for drinking alone, either. His first stop in Rio was a beachside bar, where he met an American journalist, Dick Hyman, and happily agreed to let Hyman interview him for the *Brazilian American Weekly*. While watching a rainbow of locals stroll past. Ripley joked that the biracial couples "would make a Southern gentleman forget himself."

The following day, Ripley again sought out Dick Hyman (soon to become a business partner and a lifelong companion), who found Ripley to be nothing like the man he expected. Ripley was appealingly shy, thought Hyman, a man primarily interested in his work—and women. At dinner that night, Ripley couldn't take his eyes off Hyman's girlfriend, Helena, whom he described without chagrin as "beautiful, with black eyes and snowy teeth, a true Brazilian."

In a sign of Ripley's still-strong readership back home, Hyman's father read Ripley's "Ramble" in his local paper, the *Kansas City Star*. Ripley had incorrectly described Helena as Hyman's fiancée, and Hyman's father sent an urgent telegram begging his son to reconsider.

Helena thought Ripley was adorable, and even coaxed him into trying a few words of Portuguese.

"Luco! Luco!" she said.

Ripley agreed that he was a bit crazy, until Helena explained that *luco* meant "good," or at least that's what it sounded like to Ripley.

* * *

ABOARD THE USMS *American Legion* for the two-week journey home, Ripley rejoined his Scottish friend Ferguson. He was happy to be at sea, sleeping late, roaming the decks, warming himself at night with cocktails. He considered a good ship on smooth seas to be "a floating paradise to lazy people."

During those last days, Ripley seemed to realize how often he had written about two particular topics. In the last of his South American dispatches he wrote:

> I have talked so much about South American drinks and women that I guess you think I am too fond of both . . . I admit that they have had their moments; and you must admit that they are interesting subjects. Or would you have rather heard about the "business opportunities of the Southland" or the "cattle-raising statistics for the fiscal year"?

He may not have found love, but Ripley returned to New York with a rekindled love of travel and a broader perception of the world. The seventy-two-day trip had cost $750—ten bucks a day. Ripley considered it a pittance, and felt that Americans were too stingy when it came to spending on travel.

"Traveling is easy. Traveling is cheap," he wrote. "People should travel more, but they put it off. Don't wait until you are too old . . . Travel will often show you the faults of our own country, but it will make you love it all the more!"

As he neared home, Ripley thought about what awaited him in New York. He didn't own a house or a car. His bank account was under assault by payments to Beatrice, his brother, and his sister. His personal possessions at the NYAC could fit in a steamer trunk. Yet, by traveling so far and wide, he hoped he was gaining something more valuable than material wealth. What he lacked in physical or monetary possessions was offset by what he called "a broader and more tolerant nature."

* * *

BACK IN NEW YORK, however, Ripley didn't always display tolerance.

South American women had large behinds and too many babies, he wrote, and their husbands—"little fellows" who talked too much but spoke no English—beat them weekly to keep them happy. The men were "dirty and coarse" and "sheiks of shirk!" They rarely smiled, he said, because theirs was "a short life and a weary one."

He meant for such comments to be taken lightly, but it was hard to disguise the sense that the continent had let him down. Having seen women torch their husbands' corpses and religious men hanging from trees, it now took a lot to wow Ripley. In the twelve years since his first overseas trip, he had explored more than two dozen countries, and in China and India had dug deep, taken risks, mixed with locals, and explored their politics and history, their gods and idols, their freaks and fanatics.

In South America, though, instead of aggressively pursuing temples and holy men and cannibals as he had in Asia, Ripley had mostly sought out the company of North Americans or other Westerners. Women and wine had been the journey's theme. South America, it turned out, simply wasn't peculiar enough for Ripley.

The only bit of history that invigorated him was the story of Pizarro, whose mummified body he'd visited in Lima and whose route of plunder he'd followed across the continent. "What a man he must have been!" Ripley wrote. "He destroyed a civilization of a continent and the nation of the Incas; and now he serves as a peep-show." But Ripley showed little empathy for the conquered, describing Peru's natives as having "strong backs and weak minds."

Some letter writers complained of Ripley's crass characterizations of Latin Americans, while others defended his casual style of foreign reportage, blaming the critics for having a "woeful lack of sense of humor." Some said they couldn't *wait* to visit the places Ripley so vividly rendered with his pen. "I have read few things that have given me more pleasure," said a writer named Charles Noonan. "Rip has revealed South America to us so alluringly that we all wish we could go there."

Just as Marco Polo's fantastic tales of Asia had incited awe and disbelief, Ripley's far-fetched travelogues and bold-ink cartoons, plus his likably odd personality, gave newspaper readers a new way of looking at the world. He was becoming a voice for the people, bringing the world's weirdness to their doorsteps each morning.

At the time, anti-immigrant forces were trying to shut America's doors to outsiders, a movement bolstered by a recent ban on Japanese immigration and by newly elected president Calvin Coolidge's declaration that "America must be kept American." Amid such nationalistic fervor, Ripley attempted to dispel misperceptions and suspicions about the strangers beyond America's borders. With radio still in its infancy, most people learned of other cultures from books or newspapers. Ripley's conversational reports from far-off lands differed greatly from the textbooks and tabloids. Reading about shrunken heads, señoritas, and strange drinking partners was like sitting barside with an avuncular tippler who slurs, "Let me tell you about the time . . ."

He was hardly a Marco Polo, and neither could he put himself in company with *real* adventurers like polar voyager Roald Amundsen or travel lecturer Burton Holmes. Ripley freely admitted that he liked nice hotel rooms and good bars, that he was terrified of speed and heights. He considered himself an explorer of a particular sort, but far more intrepid than a mere tourist, whom he held in contempt. "Most people I meet should not be allowed by law to travel," he once said. "They see as much in a subway."

While he dressed increasingly like the typical tourist—the Gallagher and Sheans pith helmet he once disparaged, plus khaki shorts, knee socks, and two-toned shoes, were becoming his trademark traveling outfit—Ripley's off-the-beaten-path approach to foreign travel carried its own brand of risk. He wasn't looking for new routes to the North Pole but for dark shadows, hidden deformities, and secret rites. He didn't necessarily seek physical adventure (preferring to keep his hands and shoes clean), but he did confront the people and their cultures. A self-taught ethnographer and anthropologist, what he sought most was *information*. He asked countries to show him their warts and sores, their maimed and poor, their crazy old uncles, their torture chambers, and their dead.

"The more I see of the world the more I like it," he had summed up in his final South American dispatch.

It's a pretty good little old place after all, and I have little time for the gloomers who are eternally shrieking that this old mud ball is rolling to the bow wows. I am satisfied to take my chances with this one, thank you, and not worry about the next . . .

You must carry along with you a lively imagination and plenty of romance in your soul. Some of the most wonderful things in the world will seem dull and drab unless you view them in the proper light.

CHAPTER 11

Frank "The Grocer" Munsey died from a ruptured appendix at his New York City home in late 1925. He was a lonely old man with few friends, no heirs, and a legacy as a newspaper killer. Said Baltimore's curmudgeon columnist H. L. Mencken: "I am glad Munsey is dead and I hope he is in hell!"

By selling, folding, and merging his newspapers he had personally put thousands out of work. Of the sixteen newspapers he'd bought over the course of twenty-five years, he died owning just two, the *Telegram* and the *Sun*. Neither would survive, sealing his legacy.

⌘ BELIEVE IT! ⌘

Munsey's estimated net worth was $40 million, most of which he left to the Metropolitan Museum of Art.

Munsey had been more than a little responsible for the two recent years Ripley spent in newspaper limbo. Walter Winchell would later describe in his column how Ripley, after the *Globe* shut down, had "faded from the Metropolitan scene," unable to find a job because an "army of imitators underbid him . . . pirating his style so well that editors hired them and told Rip he was too expensive."

But Ripley never slowed down or gave up. In fact, after his South American Ramble he dove back into an exhausting schedule of boxing matches, illegal cocktails with Bugs Baer at secret Midtown speakeasies, and daily games of rigorous handball. His NYAC room was often splashed with evidence of the bachelor's lifestyle: empty bottles, butt-filled ashtrays, scattered newspapers, art supplies, and sweat-stained workout clothes.

One benefit of his part-time employment was being able to spend more time on the NYAC's handball courts. A loud and aggressively competitive player, lunging for every shot, Ripley was soon back in peak physical shape, slapping the pink Spalding No. 101 handball better than ever.

Alone or with a partner, he traveled regularly to tournaments in the Midwest through 1925. In Chicago, he defeated the Chicago Athletic Club's best player, Avery Brundage, who had been a world champ. At the National Championships in Cleveland, Ripley lost to top-ranked Maynard Laswell, who went on to win the tournament. At the annual NYAC championship, he reached the finals and found himself facing Jim Kelly, an Irishman and former world champion, considered one of the best to play the game. Kelly had won his first world title in 1909 and in recent years had mentored Ripley, who in his handball book called Kelly "a master of the game."

Before a stunned and drunken crowd, Ripley upset the master to become the 1925 NYAC singles handball champ.

While he would continue to play in local and national tournaments over the next few years, Ripley's handball playing would begin tapering off in 1926, squeezed aside by the sudden demands of an unexpected job change. His period of limbo was about to end.

✳ ✳ ✳

IN JUNE OF 1926, Ripley traveled to England to cover the prestigious horse race known as the Derby, as well as the Wimbledon tennis tournament and the British Open golf tournament. On that trip, Ripley decided to attempt a stunt: to wirelessly send his Derby cartoon from London to New York.

When jockey Joe Childs whipped the stallion Coronach to victory, Ripley quickly sketched the horse crossing the finish line. Then he rushed to the Ambassador Hotel, where his sketch paper was wrapped around a cylinder and, using radio facsimile technology—similar to the fax machines of the future—was transmitted line by line across radio waves to the United States. The cartoon was then delivered by airplane to newspapers across the country.

It was touted as the first transatlantic cartoon transmission, and in a few years the same technology would be used to transmit newspaper photographs by telephone. The feat caught the attention of editors at the creaky old *New York Evening Post*, who felt they could use a promising brand like *Believe It or Not* and its innovative creator.

Alexander Hamilton had founded the *Evening Post* in 1801 (four years after he'd launched the *Globe*). A century later, it was being run by Henry Villard and his son, Oswald, who had helped found the National Association for the Advancement of Colored People (NAACP) and the American Civil Liberties Union (ACLU). When pro-German accusations against Oswald Villard during World War I crippled circulation, he sold the *Post*, which suffered through several halfhearted ownerships.

The *Post* was briefly owned by a group of New York business leaders that included Franklin Delano Roosevelt. But the paper hemorrhaged money and circulation until Cyrus Curtis came to the rescue in 1924. Curtis published a handful of magazines, most profitably the *Ladies' Home Journal* and the *Saturday Evening Post,* two of the largest circulating publications in the world. With wealth rivaling J. P. Morgan's and Henry Ford's, Curtis had no problem meeting Ripley's salary request of $200 a week.

ℰ BELIEVE IT! ℰ

When income taxes were first made public in 1925,
Curtis reported earning $5 million, putting him fifteenth
on the list of America's wealthiest men, one slot ahead
of J. P. Morgan. In terms of relative wealth,
he remains one of the richest men in
world history.

The *Post* introduced Ripley on August 16, 1926: "Believe It or Not, Ripley's returned!" Days later, a subscriber named M. E. Farrington wrote, "I have been an admirer of Mr. Ripley for many years and have often wondered which of the New York newspapers would again treat the public to his fine work."

He'd be making ten times what he'd first earned at the *Globe* in 1912, but in terms of circulation Ripley was moving backward. The *Evening Post*'s readership was a measly 33,000— one of the lowest in the city, and laughable in comparison to the top-ranked *Daily News,* with 633,000 readers.

At the *Evening Post,* Ripley would still be affiliated with Associated Newspapers, which meant his syndicated readership would continue to extend far beyond New York City. He would be starting over with new editors and coworkers—the third job shift in three years—but he was relieved to be anchored to a

New York paper, even if the *Post*'s gray and serious pages desperately needed the levity Ripley was hired to bring.

Ripley introduced himself to readers with a short, enthusiastic article, promising that his *Believe It or Not* cartoons "are all true."

"I have traveled the world over searching for strange and unbelievable things," he wrote in his *Post* debut.

> I have seen white negroes, purple white men, and I know a man who was hanged but still lives . . . Believe me when I tell you about the man who died of old age before he was six years old; the river in Africa that runs backwards; oysters that grow on trees; flowers that eat mice; fish that walk and snakes that fly.

Ripley's perseverance during his time in Munsey-inflicted purgatory had finally paid off, as had hiring Norbert Pearlroth, who stuck by Ripley through the recent ups and downs. Ripley now decided to make a salesman's pitch to his new readership, a new guarantee: "If by chance any reader should doubt any of the facts depicted in my cartoons, I will be glad to explain and prove the truth of them if he will write me." Slowly, he was learning to be a showman.

✳ ✳ ✳

WITH HIS NEW SALARY, Ripley could afford to rent more of Pearlroth's brain. In the three years since they'd met, Ripley had discovered that Pearlroth was far more useful than a mere translator. An autodidact and a "walking encyclopedia," as he'd later be described, Pearlroth seemed to possess a bottomless supply of curious and interesting facts, memorized from the books he read constantly. Ripley phoned Pearlroth daily at the bank where he still worked, hungry for more material.

Soon, with Pearlroth's help, Ripley was introducing readers to such characters as James Thompson of New Mexico, who crossed America by wheelchair; Mary Rosa, a Nantucket toddler who found her mother's ring on the beach twenty-one years after it had been lost; two Russian brothers who slapped each other's faces for thirty-six hours; and Haru Onuki, a Japanese prima donna he'd met (and begun dating), who required a full day to prepare her hair, which then stayed in place for a month.

With America growing more urban and urbane, newspaper readers had developed Jazz Age tastes in new forms of journalism, and publishers were tripping over themselves to accommodate. Cartoons, photographs, and color printing were more popular than ever, as were sexy, gossipy stories. Leading the way (up or down was a matter of debate) were the half-sized papers called tabloids. *The Daily News*, created in 1919 as the nation's first true tabloid, was followed in 1924 by the *Evening Graphic*, founded by Bernarr Macfadden, the fabulously wealthy health guru whose magazines Ripley had read as a boy and whose athletic lifestyle he'd emulated.

Macfadden's credo—"sex on every front page, big gobs of it"—had prompted Hearst in 1924 to enter the tabloid game by creating the *New York Daily Mirror*, which Hearst described as "90 percent entertainment, 10 percent information."

Critics likened tabloids to addictive drugs, fretting that they'd precipitate the demise of American culture. They quickly became the highest-circulation publications in New York, boosted by their pictures and the everyman reportage of gossip writers like Walter Winchell, the *Graphic*'s Broadway columnist. As Winchell's biographer later put it, readers had grown tired of dreary stories about "mice in China" and would rather read of celebrity indiscretions and peccadilloes.

Ripley wanted to give readers *all* if it—the mice in China, the pictures, the gossip and innuendo, the slang and the sex, the information and the entertainment. Ripley the salesman was finally ready to invest the bulk of his artistic talent, his peculiar personality, and his relentless energy solely in *Believe It or Not*.

He was finally ready for his high-wire act.

* * *

ON MAY 20, 1927, Charles Lindbergh departed from muddy Roosevelt Field on Long Island and aimed his fuel-stuffed *Spirit of St. Louis* eastward. Thirty-three treacherous hours later, the lanky aviator touched down at an airfield outside Paris and was swarmed by 150,000 spectators cheering his non-stop flight across the Atlantic. Only two dozen years past the Wright brothers' first flight, he had achieved the unachievable, the unbelievable—crossing an ocean in a day and a half, flying more than three thousand miles, alone through the night, through storms and without sleep. It was the most daring and astounding achievement of its day.

The feat captivated the world and made Lindbergh an instant international hero. He began touring the world in a relentless series of appearances and lectures.

Months later, Pearlroth was at the New York Public Library, conducting research for Ripley, when he picked up a British newspaper someone had left on a table. It carried a story about one of Lindbergh's speeches, in Liverpool, where he explained that a number of other aviators had previously flown across the Atlantic, though none had flown solo. Pearlroth felt "electrified" to discover how many others had crossed the Atlantic before

Lindbergh. He dug up more details and consulted with Ripley, who crafted a risky *Believe It or Not* shocker.

Ripley's sketch showed Lindbergh's *Spirit of St. Louis* flying through dark clouds, beneath which read this heretical caption: "Lindbergh Was the 67th Man to Make a Non-Stop Flight over the Atlantic Ocean!" The cartoon appeared on February 14, 1928, just one day after Lindbergh was feared to have been lost at sea during a flight from Cuba to St. Louis. Ripley's cartoon declared that not only was the famed aviator *not* the first to successfully cross the Atlantic, he wasn't even in the top *fifty*.

It sounded absurd, even anti-American, as some angrily claimed. It was as if someone recklessly asserted that George Washington wasn't the first president, that New Jersey wasn't really a state, that Pluto wasn't a planet. The reaction startled even Ripley, who was assailed by telegrams, phone calls, and many thousands of letters—some containing unprintable language. Three days after his Lindbergh cartoon, during a lecture to the Corps of Cadets at West Point, Ripley defended his statement, explaining how two English aviators, John Alcock and A. Whitton Brown, had flown nonstop from Newfoundland to Ireland in 1919, and that two dirigibles later made transatlantic crossings, carrying thirty-one and thirty-three men, respectively. By omitting the word "solo" from his statement, Ripley was able to justify ranking Lindbergh as sixty-seventh.

"His almost incredible statements are very often challenged by skeptical readers," reported West Point's newspaper. "And his remarks sometimes need a substantial argument to verify their truth."

A few weeks later Ripley spoke at a society luncheon in New York, where he introduced himself as the man who had been called a liar "more often than any other living person."

Seemingly overnight, Ripley found himself entering a new career phase, the moment when "unbelievable" and "liar" converged.

Instead of acting defensively, Ripley immediately struck the pose of the noble truth-teller who considered it high praise to be called a fibber. Being accused of lying by so many people, Ripley realized, was the best publicity he could have hoped for. If someone tagged him as a fabulist, he'd say, "I do not mind it a bit . . . I feel flattered!" He was becoming the embodiment of what H. L. Mencken once said about liars: "The men that American people admire most extravagantly are the most daring liars; the men they detest the most violently are those who try to tell them the truth."

* * *

EVER SINCE CHILDHOOD, Ripley had displayed what an early profile writer called a "bottomless, off-kilter curiosity." Nothing was safe from the musings of a man whose mind was "uncluttered by culture," as one colleague put it: *Everything was new to him."*

Indeed, inspiration could come from anywhere. One night a friend's casual use of "hi-ho" as a form of address got stuck in Ripley's brain and became spiced with remnants of his Chinese dinner, inspiring a vivid dream about the Chinese men he'd once seen carrying bundles and marching along the Bund singing, "Hi! Ho!" He awoke at dawn and sketched his dream. Days later, on April 5, 1928, the *Evening Post* published a cartoon entitled "The Marching Chinese," featuring seemingly endless rows of Chinese men. The caption declared that if all the Chinese people in the world were to march four abreast past a given point, "they would **never** finish passing though they marched forever and ever!"

Befuddled readers had to wait a week for Ripley's explanation. Based on the estimated Chinese population (600 million) and the estimated birth rate (10 percent), he calculated that each new generation of Chinese marchers would replace the previous one, which meant the Chinese could "march on and on, forever."

The Marching Chinese was a bigger hit than Lindbergh, and would remain one of Ripley's personal favorites.

With Pearlroth now in on the scheme, Ripley created more cartoons that seemed intentionally designed to earn skeptical if not outright angry letters. Napoleon crossed the Red Sea—on *dry land.* Buffalo Bill never shot a buffalo in his life. (He shot bison.) US naval hero John Paul Jones was not an American citizen, did not command a fleet of American ships, and his name wasn't Jones. Ripley even found a way to state that "George Washington was not the first president of the United States." The subsequent explanation was that John Hanson, when he signed the Articles of Confederation, was briefly "president of the United States in Congress assembled."

Ripley encouraged Pearlroth to help him find such startling statements, to engage and enrage readers. In short, Ripley loved to be called a liar because of the mischievous joy he took in proving his shockers true. One admiring writer said Ripley was "always waiting, with his authority in his hand, like a club."

By mid-1928, *Believe It or Not* was syndicated in a hundred papers in North America, and Associated Newspapers claimed that Ripley had ten million loyal readers. Other papers in the Associated Newspapers family began claiming Ripley as their own, crowing in print that he "worked" for them, with ads appearing in the *Kansas City Star, Chicago Daily News, Pittsburgh*

Chronicle-Telegraph, and even Ripley's former hometown paper, the *Santa Rosa Press Democrat.*

An editor at Louisville's *Courier-Journal* called Ripley "more than a sports cartoonist . . . He is a student, an artist and a popular psychologist."

* * *

WITH THIS NOTORIETY came speaking invitations, and Ripley discovered that a cupful of liquor could tame the stage fright that had dogged him since childhood. So when the Nomad Lecture Bureau asked him to talk on stage about his travels and draw a few sketches, Ripley agreed to take his *Believe It or Not* stories on the road.

He gave dozens of lectures—to schools and art clubs, to the Brooklyn Rotary Club, at the annual convention of the Kelvinator Corporation, and once sailed for a month aboard a Canadian cruise ship to perform as part of the nightly "Programme of Entertainment." At some lectures he was billed as the "World's Biggest Liar," and Ripley kept stoking the theme. In a speech to a group of athletes, he joked, "It makes no difference what I say, you won't believe me anyway." At most of his lectures, he was asked the same question: *Where do you find the things you draw about?* Speaking to the Advertising Club of New York, he explained that he got some ideas from readers, some from encyclopedias, and some, like the "Marching Chinese," in his dreams. Instead of thanking Pearlroth as a collaborator, Ripley claimed full credit, telling audiences that he found his material "here and there, day and night; through observation, conversation, and edification. I am constantly searching . . . Everywhere, all the time."

By mid-1928 he was receiving at least a hundred letters a day, many purporting to have found an error in Ripley's work, others gushing with praise. One *Evening Post* reader wrote, "My favorite article in your paper is 'Believe It or Not' by Ripley." A competing newspaper even praised Ripley's sports sketches as "better than photographs, because his pictures show the real action and the spirit of the contestants."

After just two years at the *Post*, he was becoming something of a celebrity. The *Post* hired an extra person just to read Ripley's mail, and offered to hire Pearlroth full-time. Thanks in large part to Ripley's sudden infamy, the *Post*'s circulation more than doubled between 1926 and 1928.

*　*　*

THE SCHOOLBOY NOTEBOOKS Ripley had started compiling years earlier were initially filled with clipped-out articles and handwritten notes about sports, with a particular preference for *endurance* and *going the distance:* the hundred-hour dance marathon, the seventy-four-day swim marathon, the man who ran two and a half miles every hour of every day for forty days, or the men (they were almost always men) who biked or walked or rode motorcycles from New York to Los Angeles.

After his Asian and South American travels, the notebooks became cluttered with freakier foreign entries—shocking or nauseating tidbits like the West African tribe that played rugby using a human skull instead of a ball. More recent notebook entries had grown playful and diverse, with fun facts and puzzles and unsolved mysteries, which Ripley called "queeriosities"— there is no lead in a lead pencil (it's graphite); a cuttlefish is not a fish (it's an octopus); it takes two years to make a billiard ball.

Armed with these notebooks, and fueled by Pearlroth's findings, Ripley continued to expand beyond sports and to explore the pull of his eccentric inquisitiveness.

He had always had an affinity for underdogs and outcasts,

since he often felt like one himself. Now he could more fully indulge his fascination with the characters that P. T. Barnum and his progeny had been exploiting for decades on the carny circuit. For the first time, Ripley gave sideshow freaks a place in the daily newspaper, introducing readers to a widening cast of oddballs: sword swallowers, people who ate glass, a man who nailed his tongue to a piece of wood, another who lifted weights with a hook sunk through his tongue, a woman missing the lower half of her body. Other notables included the one-armed paperhanger, the man who hypnotized fish, and the man burned by an electrical wire whose brain was permanently exposed. He sketched men with horns, a child cyclops, an armless golfer, a fork-tongued woman. There were fish that climbed trees, wingless birds, four-legged chickens, peg-legged cows.

He also loved quirks of language, word puzzles, and palindromes. What was the longest curse word? *Forty letters.* How many four-letter words are there for God? *Thirty-seven.* Though he never finished high school, he had developed his own unique mathematical skills. One cartoon, featuring a man with a knife in his chest, said that if three witnesses to a midnight murder told two people, who told two more people, and so on, "everyone on earth would know about it by morning."

Everything had a *Believe It or Not* to offer—science, religion, literature. A coin the size of a nickel made of star matter would weigh 200 pounds; a bundle of spiderwebs no larger than a pea, if untangled and straightened out, would reach 350 miles; a ship weighs less sailing east than sailing west. And the shortest letter ever mailed? That would be Victor Hugo's one-character missive to his publishers, inquiring about his *Les Misérables* manuscript. The letter: ? And the reply: !

Clearly, Ripley was no longer a sports cartoonist. A decade

past that December day when he'd stumbled into his first "Champs and Chumps" cartoon (and twenty years after his first cartoon in *LIFE*), *Believe It or Not* had become not only a regular feature in US newspapers, but a catchphrase that was seeping into the nation's consciousness.

The *Believe It or Not* concept was like some gold mine he'd been sitting atop, unsure of how to mine it or how deep to dig.

* * *

THE 1920s were evolving into a decade of the possible. New technologies—radio, moving pictures, vacuum cleaners, electric razors—had reached mainstream status. Recently unveiled mass-produced products were flying off shelves and influencing the nation's brand-conscious allegiances: Wonder Bread, Eskimo Pies, Kleenex, Wheaties, Butterfinger candy bars, and Chanel No. 5 perfume. Ripley's brand was that of a liar who always told the truth.

He now regularly provoked readers, *I dare you to prove me wrong.* That was his trademark. His cartoon now carried a new tagline: "Full proof and details on request." And the *Evening Post* helped market their "falsely accused liar" with advertisements promising, "Ripley Will Prove It" and "He Will Send You Proof."

In reality, he couldn't always prove it. In striving for a folksy style, he sometimes erred, and there were frequent efforts to trip him up. A man who signed his letter R. Van Winkle griped that in an effort to be "independent and funny" Ripley sometimes distorted history. The writer asked, "What is the use of writing nonsense instead of facts?" When one cartoon described how a Frenchman poured thirteen pints of wine into a vase and quaffed it in one breath, *Time* magazine consulted two doctors who declared it "impossible." Ripley was able to refer *Time* to the French history book in which Pearlroth had found the story.

Ripley tried to deliver it all with a wink, and most readers accepted the hint of charlatanism, knowing that some of Ripley's statements couldn't possibly be proven or disproven, that it was all for fun. Yet, while he loved being called a liar, he hated to be wrong, knowing it would damage the cartoon if he developed a reputation for sloppy reportage. More than ever, he needed Pearlroth to prove him right.

Pearlroth had by now quit his bank job to work full-time on Ripley's staff, which had grown to include a secretary and two assistants who handled Ripley's mail and checked facts. Pearlroth's official title was "linguist," his facility for multiple languages allowing Ripley to accurately publish oddities from places he didn't actually visit. As a stickler for accuracy, Pearlroth helped Ripley provoke with confidence, to push *Believe It or Not* to the brink of falsehood without tumbling over.

"When I first started to draw these cartoons, I wasn't so careful about details," Ripley admitted in a late-1920s interview. "But now I want things to be right. If a costume is to be of a certain period, I make it of that period. People write to me from Singapore, from Calcutta, from all over the world about my cartoons, and it gives me great satisfaction when they tell me, 'I've been there' or 'I've seen that fellow and your cartoon was right.'"

But for Ripley to remain the fact-wielding authority, he couldn't admit that his secret helper was a brainy ex-banker from Brooklyn.

They may have been partners, but they lived in very different worlds.

* * *

ONE OF RIPLEY'S favorite haunts was the 300 Club on West Fifty-fourth Street, the speakeasy run by Mary Louise "Texas" Guinan, an actress and chorus girl who had divorced her cartoonist husband and found her calling as a saloon keeper. With scantily clad dancers and free-flowing alcohol, Guinan's place became a favorite of such celebrities as Al Jolson, George Gershwin, Irving Berlin, and Walter Winchell, and Guinan's greeting to patrons—"Hello, suckers"—would enter the lexicon.

❧ BELIEVE IT! ❧

The most infamous of New York's Prohibition-era gin joints, Guinan's 300 Club netted $700,000 in 1926 alone. Each time she was arrested, Guinan swore she never sold an alcoholic drink in her life—patrons brought their own, she'd claim. And the dancers? The club was so small they had to dance in patrons' laps.

Other nights Ripley attended rowdy parties at Rube Goldberg's apartment with Bugs Baer and Damon Runyon, sharing cocktails with the Marx Brothers, George Gershwin, and Fanny Brice. One night, the petite shimmy-and-shake Ziegfeld star Anne Pennington performed a raucous dance on the hardwood floors while Harry Houdini swallowed sewing needles and pulled them out of his throat, all threaded on a string.

Pearlroth, meanwhile, didn't seem to mind toiling in the shadows, happy to be quietly contributing to Ripley's "fairy tales for grown-ups."

Early each morning Pearlroth rode the subway into Manhattan. Most days he'd go straight to the New York Public Library's main branch on Fifth Avenue, and he'd be one of the first to ascend the front steps between the twin lion statues. He'd grab a card catalogue tray, sift through it and select ten or more books, then find a spot in the cavernous third-floor reading room. He always turned off the reading lamps, preferring the natural light beneath the towering carved-wood ceiling.

Skipping lunch, he'd wander about, scanning shelves, collecting more books, scribbling notes until his eyesight grew blurry. He learned to make Photostat copies, so that Ripley had pictures to copy for his sketches. Librarians came to know Pearlroth by name and would often have to ask him to leave at closing time. He'd arrive home well past dinner, and rarely saw his wife and children during the week.

Though the hours he devoted to his employer caused friction within his family, Pearlroth felt he had found, somewhat remarkably, the dream job. Research and information had long been his hobby, but now he got paid to spend time among dusty history and reference books. What Pearlroth sought day in and day out were facts and truths that made his heart race, evidence that life wasn't "boringly uniform," that there were "glorious exceptions"—the Moroccan emperor who fathered 888 children; the Hindu who married his daughter to a tree; the Slovak who ate 150 hard-boiled eggs for dinner; the two German railroad workers who drank 352 glasses of beer in seventeen hours. "Curiosity is a fundamental human trait," Pearlroth would gush.

Even if they aren't aware of it, people hunger for the "astonishing but true." Pearlroth was proud to be contributing to cartoons that "satisfied a human urge to flee from the daily grind into the realm of the incredible."

By now, Ripley had also learned that what readers loved more than the elite celebrity athletes he'd spent his career featuring were pictures and stories of underdogs and misfits. They wanted the grotesques, the geeks, the goofballs—they wanted less *champ*, more *chump*. For someone who often felt like the ultimate "goofy" outsider, he had at long last begun featuring the imperfect people and performers who were a reflection of the less-than-perfect LeRoy Ripley.

As something of a misfit himself—obsessive, eccentric, monomaniacal—Norbert Pearlroth also left his mark on *Believe It or Not*, but it was Ripley's show, and always would be. Pearlroth's complicated and semivisible role, established from the start, would be that of Ripley's behind-the-bushes voice of authority—his Cyrano.

As he helped Ripley stoke and feed his newly invigorated cartoon, Pearlroth offered to expand his job duties and help prepare travel itineraries for his boss, knowing that Ripley considered travel "an unfailing source of oddities." In fact, Pearlroth seemed to want Ripley to more regularly flee his daily grind, but, for the benefit of the cartoon, in a way that involved more precision, preparation, and purpose. "You can't just take off for a country and ask the natives where their curiosities are," he once told Ripley. "You have to come primed, you have to already know about them."

So when Pearlroth learned that Ripley would soon travel to Amsterdam for the 1928 Olympic Games, he suggested a side trip—*to Hell.*

* * *

INSTEAD OF SAILING directly to Europe, Ripley first visited Iceland and then Scandinavia. In Norway, in the coastal city of Trondheim, he bought a train ticket for the town that was on Pearlroth's itinerary. Ripley's visit to the small village of Hell would ever after loom among his proudest little side trips. Though hardly an adventure, it was a perfect reflection of his offbeat explorer's sensibilities and his appreciation for tongue-in-cheek travel. He loved describing his "descent into Hell."

There wasn't much to see. Just a train station and a few vine-covered cottages. Ripley had befriended a woman (either on the train or on the ship from Greenland) and she snapped photos of him standing beneath the HELL sign, looking dapper in a three-piece wool suit and tie, a wool cap tilted just so.

Ripley wrote an article and drew a cartoon depicting himself and his lady friend having a cocktail—*"Skaal!"*—beside the train station. (Ripley would later tell a colleague that he'd spent the night with his new friend—a one-night tryst in Hell. Another new discovery: for some hard-to-believe reason, women *liked* him!)

The subsequent headlines in US papers would read: RIPLEY GOES TO HELL.

"It has frequently been suggested that I come here," Ripley wrote. "Hell is delightful! . . . Hell is restful, quiet and pleasant . . . Dante must be mistaken."

In a nod to the letter writers who were always asking for proof and information, he explained that Hell meant "gentle slope" in Norwegian.

"Go to Hell!" Ripley advised his readers. "I mean it."

The *Evening Post* admen had a field day. Not only had he visited fifty-three countries, Ripley had been to Hell and back.

M. Lincoln "Max" Schuster was a savvy editor and marketer, with a nose for the public's tastes. With his equally acute partner, Richard L. "Dick" Simon, he'd published the first-ever book of crossword puzzles in 1924, inspired by Simon's aunt, a fanatic crossworder who wanted more than her newspaper's one-a-day puzzle.

❧ BELIEVE IT! ❧

Joseph Pulitzer's pioneering World *introduced the first crossword puzzle on December 21, 1913—a diamond-shaped puzzle created by an English journalist, who called it a "word-cross." Later renamed "crossword puzzle," it become a regular* World *feature, and other newspapers quickly copied the idea.*

With only a shared secretary between them, Simon & Schuster published *The Cross-Word Puzzle Book*, which came with a cute little pencil attached. It was an instant bestseller and within a year the duo published three more crossword-puzzle books, selling more than a million. After a few flops (including a failed Joseph Pulitzer biography), they signed popular gossip writer Walter Winchell to a book deal, and by 1928 Simon & Schuster had established itself as a serious publishing house.

Now Max Schuster wanted Ripley to put a collection of *Believe It or Not* cartoons and essays between hardcovers. Schuster had been wooing Ripley since his 1926 start at the *Evening Post*. He often wrote with praise or suggestions, sometimes promising to dig up curiosa for Ripley if he'd only stop by Schuster's office.

"Renewed congratulations on the way your work grips the popular imagination," Schuster wrote in late 1927. "I never miss an issue."

Schuster knew it might be tricky to sell Ripley in book form. "The big problem now will be to consider Ripley as a writer as well as an artist," he said in one of his letters, while insisting that a *Believe It or Not* collection could be a hit.

For many months, Ripley demurred, claiming that he was just a newspaperman, "just a two-cent man," not an author.

In time, Ripley realized that, with Pearlroth often providing more than he could use, a book might be the perfect place for his backlog of material. So, to Schuster's great relief, he finally signed a two-page contract.

In the book's introductory chapter, Ripley wrote that his humble sports-cartooning career now relied solely on the idea that "truth is stranger than fiction." He thanked a few of the groupies he'd attracted, folks who mailed in *Believe It or Not* suggestions, but he failed to mention Norbert Pearlroth. In fact, throughout Ripley's entire career it seems as if he never once credited Pearlroth in print, having decided that he would be the solo explorer, Pearlroth the invisible staffer geek.

Ripley submitted the final pages to Schuster in late 1928, including a quote from Thomas Moore at the end of his introductory chapter:

This world is all a fleeting show,
For man's illusion given.

* * *

RIPLEY'S 188-PAGE BOOK went on sale in January of 1929, for $2.50. The response was immediate, widespread, and uniformly laudatory.

Reviewers of all journalistic tiers declared it an instant classic and crowned Ripley "the Marco Polo of our time." The *Akron Beacon Journal* called it "an odyssey of oddities," and the *Sioux City Journal* declared it perfect "for anyone who likes the queer and the unusual."

Compared to Ripley's "repertory of freaks," said one writer, carnival barker P. T. Barnum looked like a schoolboy stamp collector. According to *Vanity Fair*, Ripley had resuscitated "the dying art of dinner conversation." The most glowing review came from William Bolitho, writing in Pulitzer's *World:*

> Such books are rare. It pricks the sluggish mind and coaxes the doubtful one to a true realization that the world, and life, is miraculous and interesting. Read Ripley and see with what wild eccentricity, what infinite good spirits, what fantastic jokes the world is administered. This is a pamphlet for truth, for the incontrovertible truth that life is miraculous, breathless and good to live.

Bolitho compared Ripley to such iconic explorers as Marco Polo, Sir John Mandeville, or Herodotus, calling him "the equal of them all."

"He is not merely retailing empty wonders to make yokels gape. His research is for the very highest type of curiosity, the unbelievably true," Bolitho continued, predicting a long shelf life: "It will drift about the world, second-hand, wherever curiosity and English occur together . . . It will automatically make the eye stop and the hand reach out."

On the advice of such raves, readers bought Ripley's book in vast quantities. It flew off bookstore shelves and via mail order. Kids and adults loved it; cartoon aficionados and history buffs loved it—all drawn to the promise of the enticing subtitle, "A Modern Book of Wonders, Miracles, Freaks, Monstrosities and Almost-Impossibilities." Ripley wisely mailed scores of autographed copies to former colleagues, reporters, and editors, which earned even more press.

Rube Goldberg praised Ripley's "striking innovation," telling him, "You have no peer." The wildly influential Walter Winchell devoted a full column in the *Evening Graphic* to "the sort of tome you cannot put down." Everywhere, reviewers hailed "a book that should be bound in leather and saved for future generations to read," as *The Chattanooga Times* put it. Philadelphia's *Public Ledger* compared Ripley's "eye of the child" to that of Voltaire, while the *Saturday Review of Literature* likened him to Poe. The esteemed *Daily News* critic Mark Hellinger said Ripley amused and startled readers in "one of the most interesting books I have ever read."

One reviewer, after reading a hundred pages, dropped the book into his lap and wondered aloud, "What sort of mind has the man who collects so much freak data?" The question was asked again and again—*Who is this guy?*—and the *Evening Post* went so far as to enlist a group of professors to attempt an answer in a series of promotional articles. Ripley's cartoons "are thrill pills," explained Professor Rudolph Pinter. "They give us a quick vicarious thrill." And Professor Clyde Miller said Ripley's *Believe It or Not* drawings "are a blessing to everyday people. In contrast to humdrum life, they are an emotional tonic."

Simon & Schuster kept printing copies and was soon into a fifth printing, then a ninth, eventually reaching forty.

⌒ BELIEVE IT! ⌒

Over the next twenty years, Ripley's books would sell more than two million copies.

✳ ✳ ✳

SUCH SUCCESS INEVITABLY inspired copycat efforts, such as Ed Wolff's *Why We Do It*, which explained the stories behind why people throw rice at the bride, why men tip their hats, why women wear rouge, and how barber poles began. One critic complained that Wolff's book too closely resembled *Believe It or Not*, and that publishers were rushing to cash in on "the fascination of blobs of knowledge."

In truth, Ripley's imitators had been multiplying for years. Bernarr Macfadden's *True Story* magazine (tagline: "Truth Is Stranger Than Fiction") had been around for a decade, and in 1928 a talented young artist named John Hix launched his syndicated *Strange as It Seems* cartoon.

But the competition hardly compared with the original. As Ripley's book climbed the bestseller lists, fans clamored for more of the curious author and Ripley was showered with offers. *Collier's* invited him to contribute a regular cartoon feature to the magazine. A company called Famous Speakers Inc. offered a lecture series, and Ripley signed a contract that would give him half the proceeds from those lectures. He was even offered a nationwide vaudeville tour, and was soon being wooed by radio networks looking for ways to capture the *Believe It or Not* magic on the airwaves.

After twenty years in the newspaper business, he was finally in league with men such as Peter Kyne: an author, a lecturer, a world traveler, a *celebrity.*

While some fans wrote letters marveling at how he "keeps it going" for so many years, Ripley was finding it easier by the day, thanks to Pearlroth, his staff, and his fans. One *Evening Post* contest earned thousands of mailed-in reader submissions, including celebrity entries from Franklin D. Roosevelt, Jack Dempsey, and New York Giants manager John McGraw. With so much assistance, the supply of cartoon material seemed inexhaustible.

Believe It or Not was a self-perpetuating *machine,* and Ripley was suddenly being wooed by the biggest names in newspapers.

* * *

ROBERT L. RIPLEY and *Believe It or Not* were now entwined, indivisible. His cartoons weren't just some widgets he manufactured, they had become extensions of his personality. Yet, the real Ripley remained a mystery. In person and onstage, he seemed jovial and fun, though hardly at ease in public, often coming across as unrehearsed, a bit awkward and clumsy. He had a singsongy, faux-aristocratic voice (not unlike Hearst's), but his buckteeth hampered his articulation. He still stuttered—or, with too much nerve-calming booze, slurred—and his hands seemed to be constantly waving about. Such foibles only endeared him further to fans.

Ripley knew he needed to make himself available to readers and fans, or at least show a version of himself. He hired an assistant to manage his schedule and financial affairs. With a crew of employees toiling behind the scenes, he began spending more time as the public face of *Believe It or Not,* some days only working for an hour on the cartoon and the rest of his day managing offers from those wanting him to sign books or speak to their organization. Requests poured in for product endorsements or charitable donations, and Ripley had a hard time saying no. With an affinity for boys' and orphans' groups, he donated cartoons and cash to the Boys' Work Committee of the Rotary Club, the National Tuberculosis Association, and the Orphans Automobile Day Association.

When the publicity demands slowed, in the late spring of 1929, Ripley felt he could take time off to travel once again. He planned a two-month tour of Central America, but the trip was delayed when Bugs Baer's wife fell ill, and Ripley stayed with his longtime pal in New York. When Marjorie "Cass" Baer died of pneumonia, Ripley attended the funeral, serving as a pallbearer.

Finally, in late May, he sailed to Guatemala, El Salvador, and Honduras. Pearlroth had read about an ancient and primitive Central American civilization that an aviator had recently discovered in Guatemala and, though he hated the idea of flying, Ripley decided to search for the tribe himself. He hired a pilot who told Ripley that he always brought weapons when flying into the wilderness— a shotgun, a machete, and a blackjack—as precautions against the swarms of curious natives who always surrounded his plane. (It's unclear whether Ripley found the tribe he was seeking.)

In Mexico, he traveled deep into the Yucatán Peninsula to tour the Chichen Itza ruins, and would later claim to have "discovered" the origins of basketball there.

℃ BELIEVE IT! ⌐

Pre-Columbian tlachtli *ball courts discovered at Chichen Itza and elsewhere in Central America featured stone hoops built into the walls. Using heavy rubber balls, players competed in a mash-up of soccer and basketball, a game later called* ulama.

In the blistering Yucatán heat, Ripley's exploration was cut short when he contracted an inner-ear ailment and was rushed to Cuba for treatment. By now he had visited dozens of countries, and friends found it remarkable that Ripley never got sick, an accomplishment he attributed to his miles-long New York walks, his rounds of handball, and his steady intake of germ-killing alcohol. Plus, he always traveled with a jar of disinfectant.

When he was released from the hospital and sailed from Havana toward home, Ripley was suddenly eager to get back to work. While traveling, word had leaked of the new job he'd been offered. Reporters and photographers would be waiting for him, having learned that their colleague was about to join the big leagues.

* * *

MONTHS EARLIER, Max Schuster had wisely sent one of the first copies of Ripley's book to William Randolph Hearst. When Hearst finally got around to reading it, he sent one of his men to tempt Ripley with a hard-to-ignore offer.

Hearst, like Ripley, had started his newspaper career in San Francisco, taking charge of his father's struggling four-page *San Francisco Examiner* in 1887. Over the next forty years, Hearst amassed thirty-four other newspapers and assorted magazines, and by 1929 employed twenty *thousand* people. At age sixty-four, he still put in twelve-hour days tending to his massive journalistic empire. His personal fortune, *The New Yorker* magazine had recently estimated, "mounts into nine figures."

Although Hearst's legacy would become that of a spoiled son who squandered his family's fortune in a maniacal quest for acquisition, he was actually a forward-thinking newsman obsessed with hiring the best of the best. "Your search for talent must be incessant and sleepless," Hearst told his editors. He pioneered global syndication and new methods of advertising, such as running ads for his publications in rival newspapers. An early supporter of moving pictures, he had partnered with the Vitagraph company as early as 1915 to distribute newsreels, and later turned a few of his newspapers' cartoons into animated short films. Ripley knew that Hearst had lifted many cartoonists' careers, not only paying them well but bringing their art to animated life on-screen.

To be sure, they had their differences. Hearst never drank, for example, and had stayed married and fathered five sons, despite an imperfect relationship with his wife and a longtime mistress (Marion Davies, Ripley's ex-wife's former Ziegfeld contemporary). But in many ways the two men shared a professional kinship. Hearst had an uncanny sense of public opinion, an ability to predict what the masses wanted to see in his pages. He must have sensed that Ripley knew something about mass appeal too, that he "understands the popular mind," as author Stephen Crane once said of Hearst.

In the spring of 1929, Hearst had sent a two-word telegram to one of his editors in New York: "HIRE Ripley."

✳ ✳ ✳

THE RECIPIENT OF Hearst's directive was Joseph V. Connolly, head of King Features Syndicate, the world's largest purveyor of comic strips, columns, and assorted newspaper features. Connolly's first stop was the New York Athletic Club. Striding up to the front desk, he asked the receptionist, "Where can I find Bob Ripley?"

At that exact moment, Ripley was exiting the elevator, about to step into the lobby. One glimpse of the grim-looking

Connolly, who looked like a lawyer or a cop, told him he didn't want to meet the man. (He'd later say he was worried about an ex-girlfriend's threatened lawsuit.) Ripley slipped out a side exit and disappeared into Central Park. Connolly returned days later, cornered Ripley, and explained that "Mr. Hearst" wanted to hire him.

Due to the huge success of his book, Ripley had met with others like Connolly, men in suits bearing offers from newspapers and syndicates. This time, he sought advice from Bugs Baer, who wrote for Hearst's *New York American* and whose columns were syndicated by King Features. Baer told Ripley that Hearst's kingdom was the best place for him. He retold the story about his overnight stay at San Simeon, Hearst's castle on the California coast: "I left my shoes outside the door and they were gold-plated in the morning." Baer's advice: "Stick to Hearst, Bob."

At the time, nearly one in four Americans read a Hearst newspaper.

* * *

WHILE STANDING in the lobby of the NYAC, just before leaving for Central America, Ripley signed a three-page contract, good for three years. The terms required him to produce six daily *Believe It or Not* cartoons for King Features, starting July 9, plus a new full-page Sunday cartoon. At the time, Ripley was still earning about $10,000 a year. Hearst offered Ripley a base salary worth six times as much. But that was just part of it.

Ripley would also get 70 percent of the net proceeds of *Believe It or Not* sales to non-Hearst newspapers, plus a 50 percent cut of Sunday cartoon sales, with a written guarantee that his share of the profits would be no less than $400 a week. Ripley stood to make at least $100,000 a year.

Walter Winchell, who had recently signed his own contract with Hearst, announced the deal in his new "On Broadway" column in Hearst's *Daily Mirror.* Winchell said Ripley's new six-figure salary "must have made his competitors' heads swim." At the time, the influential gossip columnist was making $500 a week at Hearst's *Mirror*—an impressive salary, but still just over a quarter of what Ripley would be earning.

Ripley's new editor and boss would be one of Hearst's most trusted managers, and one of the more powerful men in news syndication.

Joseph V. Connolly had been a reporter before serving in World War I. He started at King Features as a promoter in 1920 and within three years was running the show. Sensing that postwar readers wanted to know more about the world, but also be entertained, Connolly encouraged Hearst to expand the number of syndicated news and feature stories—and comics. Connolly also played a hands-on role with his cartoonists, helping new artists develop their strips and counseling veterans on how to keep their cartoons fresh. Earlier in 1929, Connolly noticed a new character in Elzie Segar's ten-year-old strip, *Thimble The-atre*, an illiterate, tattooed, and muscle-bound sailor with a good heart whom Segar called Popeye. Connolly advised Segar: "Feature the sailor."

Connolly was also assistant manager of Hearst's other syndicates, International News Service, International Features Service, and Universal Service, whose deep roster of cartoonists included George Herriman (*Krazy Kat*), George McManus (*Bringing Up Father*), Billy DeBeck (*Barney Google*), and Ripley's pal Rube Goldberg, who must have told Ripley that working for Hearst and King Features was as good as it got for a cartoonist.

Ripley had once dreamed of becoming the next Goldberg or Tad, who'd died that May, and whom Ripley called "the greatest influence on my professional life." Though his ascent had been slow, and his path rocky, Ripley was now outearning them all.

✳ ✳ ✳

WHEN RIPLEY ARRIVED home from Cuba on July I, after his abbreviated trip to Central America, word had already spread that he'd be leaving the *Post* for King Features. He was greeted on a Manhattan pier by a crowd of reporters and photographers who clotted around him on the deck of the SS *Orizaba*.

Looking tanned and ebullient in a straw hat and bow tie, posing beside an *Orizaba* life preserver—"like the Ancient Mariner with his tale to tell," one reporter said—Ripley explained that he'd just added four more countries to his checklist and had now visited sixty-seven nations. He was already planning to visit Africa the following year.

On July 9, 1929, Ripley's first day with King Features, Connolly threw a lavish dinner party aboard the SS *Vulcania* ocean liner. He invited dozens of Ripley's friends—artists, journalists, athletes, and actors, including Al Jolson and Eddie Cantor. Cartoonist Harry Hershfield roasted Ripley and crooner Rudy Vallee devoted a new song, written by Irving Berlin, called "Believe It or Not."

It was Hearst's way of saying to Ripley, *Welcome to the family.*

Hearst then followed up his generous salary offer with a barrage of supportive publicity. Via internal memo distributed shortly after he hired Ripley, Hearst ordered his empire: "Please instruct all our papers using Ripley to promote him heavily in full page and half page advertisements in other papers and also on billboards."

In response to The Chief's instructions, Ripley's likeness began to appear in the *Seattle Post-Intelligencer,* the *San Antonio*

Light, the *Detroit Times,* the *Shreveport Times,* the *Asheville Citizen,* and scores of other King Features papers, announcing that Ripley had "joined the staff" or "Rip's coming" or "Ripley starts work tomorrow!" Profile writers dug up and repackaged the story of Ripley's tryout with the New York Giants, many of them claiming Ripley had been a starting pitcher. Hearst's *New York American* ran a half-page ad announcing "another brilliant star to shine on the sports pages."

Though Ripley had worked at three different New York newspapers since 1912, his true home had been Associated Newspapers, and his ultimate boss had been the syndicate's general manager, H. H. McClure, who had played the role of mentor, father figure, and friend. McClure and Ripley's day to day editors, like Walter St. Denis, had mostly given him a long leash, allowing him to do his own thing, to pursue new ideas or write about non-sports topics or sail to Europe on a whim. Connolly would be the first to actively manage Ripley, to mold and shape his magic. And Hearst would be the first to issue edicts and restrictions from on high.

In a mid-1929 telegraph message to "cartoonist Ripley," for example, Hearst insisted that Ripley stop drawing for magazine ads, which "injures the paper and also the artist." He reminded Ripley that his contract required him to "devote all time, attention, and energy" to the cartoon and "not work gratuitously or for hire . . ."

"The effect on your work is something for you to decide but the effect on the paper I can surely say would be unfortunate," Hearst said.

Hearst closed by adding, "We are happy in your association with our papers and hope everything will continue happily."

The message was clear: *Do as I say, and all will be well.*

* * *

THREE MONTHS into his new job, Ripley learned that his Hearst contract was the gift that kept giving.

Connolly informed him in late October that King Features had decided to start selling *Believe It or Not* cartoons overseas. Since this hadn't been addressed in the initial contract, Connolly suggested that they apply the same fifty-fifty split they'd set for profits from the full-page Sunday cartoons. "I believe that we can build up a worthwhile foreign business," Connolly said, adding that *Believe It or Not* could be as big in China and Australia as it was in the United States.

Ripley was given office space at the *New York American* in Lower Manhattan, but he often chose to work from home. The NYAC had opened a new clubhouse in 1927, a block east of its previous clubhouse on Central Park South. (Ripley helped design the new handball courts). As a longtime resident, he was given one of the two-room bachelor's suites, with a front-room parlor that he converted into an art studio and a bedroom in back. Room #1801 was the biggest place he'd lived in since leaving Santa Rosa twenty years earlier.

For someone who considered himself "indolent" and "the laziest man in the world," Ripley was soon working harder than ever. To produce the required quota of cartoons, he honed a new routine: starting work at dawn, drawing sketches in a robe and bare feet, eating a light breakfast, and skipping lunch. Though he always wore suits and ties in public, at home he could be downright slobbish. After a few hours of work, his hands would be caked with ink and charcoal, his fingernails black. When he ran out of socks, he'd rinse a pair in the sink.

He had been a NYAC resident for a decade but still treated

the club more like a hotel than a home, just a temporary stop-over between travels. The apartment had become cluttered with souvenirs and artwork accumulated from overseas trips, some of which he had begun putting into storage. On his Central America trip he had picked up a foulmouthed parrot that he taught to say "Hello, Rip" and "Good-bye, Rip." From its previous owners, the bird had learned more colorful words. As one writer put it, Ripley's pet was capable of as "sulfurous a flow of potent language as ever horrified delicate ears."

When the bird got too loud and raunchy, Ripley turned up his radio. When the apartment got stuffy, he stripped off his robe and worked in gym shorts, chatting with the parrot above the crackling squawk of the radio. Sometimes he invited one of his cute new secretaries up to dictate a letter, all the while listening to his music, sketching at his easel, and taunting his parrot, wearing nothing but skimpy shorts.

As the workload increased, Ripley tried to keep his drinking in check. He established a new rule for himself: no drinks before four or after seven. Under this odd but productive arrangement, Ripley quickly made good on Hearst's hefty investment.

* * *

WITH THE FINANCIAL CRISIS looming that fall of 1929, Hearst feared that readers would have less time to spend on their daily paper. In order to present news "briefly as well as brightly," he gave the *American* a tabloid-like makeover—expanding the Sunday comics page and putting cartoons on the front page— jazzy touches that prompted the *New Yorker* to praise Hearst's "journalistic sixth sense." Hearst seemed to feel that Ripley's jazzy everyman appeal could keep and attract readers, especially working-class and ethnic readers. Ripley's cartoon and sensibilities meshed nicely with Hearst's love of contests and stunts.

↶ BELIEVE IT! ↷

After Lindbergh's 1927 transatlantic feat, Hearst had sponsored a New York-to-Rome flying contest. One of his editors, Phil Payne, joined the crew of a Hearst-sponsored plane, Old Glory, *which crashed into the Atlantic, killing Payne and the others aboard.*

Ripley already knew how to goad readers with a tricky puzzler or far-fetched declaration. On November 3, a week after the stock market crash, as the markets continued their historic plunge, Ripley made this provocative statement in his first Sunday cartoon for Hearst: "America Has No National Anthem."

The sketch featured a chubby man raising a glass, singing to a packed barroom, with a caption that said Congress had repeatedly refused to endorse "The Star-Spangled Banner" as America's official anthem. Furthermore, "The Star-Spangled Banner" melody was based on "a vulgar old English drinking song." According to Ripley (with details provided by Pearlroth), while the lyrics to America's unofficial national anthem were written by Francis Scott Key, the music was based on the song "To Anacreon in Heaven," written around 1780 by members of the Anacreontic Society, a men's club in London. Intended as a homage to Greek poet Anacreon, known for his erotic poems, it became a popular drinking song whose lyrics celebrated wine and women—nine feisty maids, the myrtle of Venus, and Bacchus's vine made cameos.

With the nation's financial system in turmoil, some viewed this as indelicate timing, if not treasonous. One furious columnist called the cartoon "scurrilous" and derided Ripley as "one of the most offensive animals in the Hearst stable of odiferous zebras." Others were tickled, or inspired into patriotic action.

Letters poured in from all camps, demanding that Congress officially adopt the anthem. Within a year, Veterans of Foreign Wars activists and others would collect a petition with five million signatures. A one-sentence bill would make its way through Congress and on March 3, 1931, President Herbert Hoover would sign Public Law 823, making "The Star-Spangled Banner" America's national anthem. (The Hearst machine would credit Ripley in print for this achievement, and Ripley would become a devoted Hoover supporter and friend.)

* * *

IN AROUSING READERS, Ripley sometimes went too far for Hearst's tastes.

"St. Patrick was neither a Catholic, a saint, nor an Irishman! And his name was not Patrick!" Ripley declared in a late-1929 cartoon, which generated more animosity than any Ripley cartoon to date. Besieged by irate phone calls from offended Catholics, Hearst personally telegrammed all King Features papers, telling them to kill the cartoon. But it was too late and only a few afternoon papers were able to scrap it.

An Irish priest editorialized that Ripley should steer clear of religion and stick with "interesting little facts of nature or trick problems in arithmetic." A priest in Hawaii told the *Honolulu Star-Bulletin* the cartoon was "unpardonably inaccurate" and "stupid." When Ripley responded with a letter accurately explaining that Saint Patrick was not born in Ireland and not officially canonized, the priest shot back that "nobody pays attention to the silly cartoons of Ripley to question their exactitude."

It was just the kind of publicity Ripley thrived on, even if it angered Hearst, who was wary of offending immigrant Catholic readers. (In an effort to appeal to Italians, Hearst once hired Benito Mussolini to write a column.) Hearst's support for Ripley barely wavered, though. In fact, King Features launched a series of contests, offering autographed *Believe It or Not* books or cash to readers with the best strange-but-true items.

Submission letters poured in by the tens of thousands. One winner submitted the shortest sentence containing all the letters of the alphabet ("A quick brown fox jumps over the lazy dog"), only to be outdone a week later by a sentence one letter shorter ("Pack my box with five dozen liquor jugs").

Such contests were an ingenious scheme for the man contractually required to produce seven cartoons a week, each containing as many as six unbelievably true tidbits. Ripley's readers were now carrying some of the load and by the end of 1929, as he told one lecture crowd, he had *Believe It or Not* ideas "piled up three years ahead." With such a cache of believe-it-or-nots, he was hoping to get back on the road.

* * *

THOUGH THE GREAT DEPRESSION would soon consume the nation, forcing most Americans to hunker down and travel little or not at all, Ripley would see his fortunes and global travels soar in reverse correlation. His brand of printed entertainment—*See the world with Ripley for just a few cents! A thrill a day for less than a nickel!*—would grow to become just the kind of affordable diversion a troubled nation craved. Now that he was making more money every few weeks than he'd previously earned in a full year, he began planning an expanded list of alien lands to visit—*North Africa! The Holy Land! The Middle East! Russia!*

Back in Santa Rosa, Ripley's former hometown paper summed up his hard-earned success. ROY RIPLEY HAS WON FAME: SANTA ROSA BOY REACHES TOP OF LADDER, blared a *Press Democrat* headline, above a story calling him "one of the leading cartoonists of America, if not of the world . . . while a few years back he was a mere school boy with a hobby."

Ripley's *Believe It or Not* book finished the year ranked among 1929's top sellers, in the elite company of Ernest Hemingway's *A Farewell to Arms* as well as books by Edith Wharton, Bertrand Russell, Sinclair Lewis, Will Rogers, and Ripley's old San Francisco pal Peter B. Kyne, who had encouraged him to move to New York back in 1912.

His path had been rockier than that of his peers, and *Believe It or Not* had hardly been an overnight success. But now, at age thirty-nine, the obsessive pursuit of the aberrations of humanity had at long last become Roy Ripley's entire life. The kooky cartoonist and his kooky cartoon were inextricably entwined.

"Now it looks as though I will never do anything else," he had written in the introduction to his book. "And I don't care if I do."

CHAPTER

13

Within weeks of agreeing to join Ripley's staff, Dick Hyman found himself shivering and trapped in a snowstorm, stranded at a southern Indiana railroad depot, wondering what he'd gotten himself into by agreeing to become Ripley's new business manager and publicity director.

Since meeting Ripley years earlier in Rio, Hyman had been working as a reporter in Rhode Island. When Ripley lured him to New York, his first assignment was to visit the town of Santa Claus, Indiana, to mail thousands of pre-addressed letters just before Christmas, a scheme hatched at the last minute. He learned this was typical of Ripley.

A blizzard had shut the railroad, leaving Hyman stuck far short of Santa Claus. He was forced to travel the final miles by horse-drawn sleigh. When he finally reached the town— population thirty-two—he found the postmaster, who also ran the general store, lugging sacks of potatoes in from the snow. Hyman convinced the man to pose for pictures and to postmark Ripley's letters, then wrote a story about it all for King Features.

When the letters reached their recipients, hundreds of

newspapers around the world published photographs of the envelopes, each bearing a note preprinted on the front—*Believe It or Not, This Is a Letter from Santa Claus*—with an arrow pointing to the now-stamped "Santa Claus" postmark. Hyman learned that Ripley could be disorganized and unpredictable and difficult to work for, but his publicity instincts were impeccable.

"He never missed a beat," Hyman said years later, looking back on the start of his long partnership with Ripley.

Just as Ripley needed Pearlroth's research skills at a critical moment in his career, he now needed someone like Hyman to help him promote and manage himself. In Hyman, Ripley found the loyal aide he'd need to control the coming explosion of his career—the fame, the wealth, and the women.

* * *

BY MID-1930, nearing his first year of employment with Hearst and having just turned forty, Ripley looked back on the headiest months of his life.

The year began with a nonstop publicity blitz. In Akron, Ohio, he spoke to university students and then soared above the city in a blimp, terrified but waving gamely to the photographers. In Michigan, he spent an afternoon with Henry Ford at his Dearborn estate. In Washington, DC, he spoke to a standing-room-only crowd at Central High School, gave a midnight lecture at the Earle Theater, and the next day visited disabled veterans at Walter Reed Hospital. During a three-day visit to Boston, he met the mayor and governor, lectured and signed books, visited sick kids at Children's Hospital, and played pool at the Boston Boys Club, sinking fifteen in a row. Each night he appeared in a vaudeville-style show, outdrawing stage favorites Amos and Andy, who were performing at a rival theater.

Suddenly, everywhere he went, Ripley was trailed by photographers and autograph seekers. A *Boston Daily Record* editorial raved, "Believe It or Not is more than a feature, it's a *craze.*"

Followers began calling themselves Bonfans (*Believe It or Not* fans) or "Rip-O-Maniacs." Even his former paper, the *Post*, acknowledged that Ripley had become "a nation-wide vogue . . . a one-man fad." According to one news report, he received more mail than Will Rogers, Rudy Vallee, and Herbert Hoover. He had received a *million* letters in 1929, nearly three thousand a day, and was considered to have broken all records for mail received by one person. In 1930, he became the target of some of the oddest envelopes ever to pass through the postal system.

One correspondent taped Ripley's photograph to an envelope, pasted on a two-cent stamp, and mailed it with no address. The letter would normally have been dumped into the dead-letter office, but postal workers by now knew where to send it. When King Features published a story about this feat—and awarded the letter writer a cash prize—it triggered waves of mischievous missives. One sent only a stamp, with the address and a forty-seven-word message inked on the back. Another sent an envelope with a drawing of a bird in place of an address. It took a magnifying glass to reveal the words "Robert Ripley" repeated thousands of times in the shape of the bird. Others sent letters addressed in Confederate Army code, in Boy Scout semaphore, or simply addressed to "the damndest liar in the world."

Ripley, meanwhile, was a terrible correspondent, and horribly disorganized when it came to paperwork. For a while, he simply threw it all away, until Hyman suggested it might be good publicity to respond now and then. Ripley then began saving *all* his mail, reluctant to toss it but unwilling to process it. When secretaries tried to categorize the letters, he'd say, "Just put it aside, put it aside. I'll decide later." Occasionally, before heading out of town, he'd grab a stack of letters and stuff it in his bag, with plans to write to a few correspondents. Friends loved to repeat the story about the stack of unopened mail Ripley flung from the window of an airplane above the African plains. Back in New York, the same letters were waiting for him.

Finally, the US postmaster general decided his employees had better things to do than manage Ripley's fan mail. On April 19, 1930, Walter Brown issued a directive to all postal workers, instructing that "such letters hereafter will either be returned to the sender or sent to the dead letter office."

Said Brown: "Postal clerks have had to devote too much time recently to deciphering freak letters intended for Ripley."

When King Features published Brown's directive, word for word, in hundreds of Hearst newspapers, it only inspired the letter writers to get freakier.

* * *

KING FEATURES had exposed Ripley to a massive, global audience, and except for a minority of curmudgeons who considered Ripley's tastes too downscale and creepy—"devoid of conscience or brains or both," said one critic—the public mostly loved him. Hearst had given him a huge new stage, and Ripley found he was ready for the spotlight. No longer a mere reporter, he was now the man *other* reporters sought to interview.

He would invite interviewers up to his NYAC apartment and spend an hour casually answering their questions, whether it was a national magazine correspondent or a student reporter from Julia Richman High School's *Bluebird* newsletter. "Go right ahead, I'm not busy," he would insist, putting aside his nub of charcoal.

"Rip is quite unspoiled," said Hugh Leamy, who interviewed Ripley for the *American* magazine. "One of those soft-spoken, unobtrusive souls who can do a half dozen jobs at once without getting confused or excited."

Ripley worked hard to avoid the business side of his job. Contracts, letters, and phone calls were Dick Hyman's job. But he always made time for friends and fans, even if they put him behind schedule. He felt fortunate to have attracted so many followers, and was grateful for their loyalty. As he told Leamy, "If I hadn't hit on a lucky idea, I'd have been just another cartoonist."

Every day brought new offers. *Billboard* magazine described the "spirited salary-bidding contest" between RKO and Warner Bros., both hoping to sign Ripley to a vaudeville contract. Ripley signed with Warner Bros. for $4,000 per show. That was followed by a similar bidding war between radio networks, which led to Ripley signing with the National Broadcasting Company's Red Network and agreeing to a year of weekly programs, a contract worth $52,000—$1,000 for every fifteen minutes of airtime. *Billboard* said Ripley was the only performer besides Jack Dempsey who could earn so much without singing or dancing.

Becoming a stage and radio performer was a bold move for someone still uneasy with public speaking, and Ripley considered turning down the offers, knowing he was "not very good at it." At Hyman's urging, he began taking speech lessons to improve his elocution and diction. He also started attending theater performances and films, studying how professional actors spoke and carried themselves. "I'm getting better," he told one reporter. "And it's good discipline for the spirit."

It turned out that spirits were also good discipline. Ripley performed best with his paper cup of gin or whiskey nearby. But even with the emboldening assistance of alcohol, he remained a less-than-natural entertainer. His hands shook and his talks were speed-bumped with "ums" and "ahs." He hoped to prove to sponsors and fans, though, that he was a good sport, willing to try anything if it helped the cartoon. "Shyer than a white rabbit," a radio colleague said. "But he threw himself heart and soul into everything he did."

Fans and radio listeners would come to appreciate Ripley's awkward, earnest manner.

As would Hollywood.

*　*　*

WARNER BROS. had been founded by four Polish brothers from western Pennsylvania who, after World War I, began producing their own Hollywood films. After a successful run with the heroic soldier-dog Rin Tin Tin, the brothers bought the Vitagraph Company in 1925 and took over that company's Vitaphone studios in Brooklyn, where they produced "talkies." In 1927, Warner Bros. unveiled *The Jazz Singer,* starring Al Jolson, followed a year later by *The Lights of New York,* considered the first true talking picture. By 1930, Warner Bros. had produced hundreds of experimental short films called "Vitaphone Varieties" or "Broadway Brevities," starring vaudeville stars, comedians, singers, and even media celebrities like Walter Winchell.

ᘓ BELIEVE IT! ᘒ

*In 1930 Vitaphone launched a series of animated cartoons
called "Looney Tunes" that would create such characters
as Porky Pig, Daffy Duck, Bugs Bunny, and Elmer Fudd.
Introduced as Egghead in the late 1930s, the speech-impeded
and stuttering character who became Fudd was believed to
have been partly modeled on Ripley. One cartoon, "Believe It*

or Else,"featured a bucktoothed Egghead wearing a loud suit and spats. The narrator introduces the world's loudest hog caller, the human basketball, and the world's fastest woodcutter. "I don't believe it!" says Egghead. Egghead/Fudd also made a cameo appearance in The Isle of Pingo Pongo, *a faux South Seas travelogue cartoon that was later banned for its racist depiction of black islanders.*

Hearst had been working with Vitaphone for more than a decade, and it's likely that his influence led Warner Bros. to offer Ripley four ten-minute "Vitaphone Varieties" shows, at $3,500 per episode—the start of Ripley's long-term and lucrative relationship with both Warner Bros. and the big screen. Ripley's name began to appear on theater marquees in mid-1930 and the films became instant hits, sometimes prompting applause at their conclusion.

In Ripley's first-ever film, he introduced viewers to a six-year-old Chinese boy from Chicago named One Long Hop, said to have been born the day of Lindbergh's transatlantic flight, and a woman who could speak ten words per second. (The boy was actually the son of Ripley's cartoonist friend, Paul Fung—"One Long Hop" was a nickname; fast-talking Cygna Conly was a romantic interest who would soon come to work for Ripley.) In his next film, Ripley emerged from behind a six-foot mound of letters to thank a few letter carriers for handling so much of his mail. Then he displayed some creatively addressed envelopes, including one addressed in Braille, others in Greek, sign language, and one with a tear in the envelope next to a sketch of Robert E. Lee—*Rip + Lee.*

The films offered the first in-the-flesh look at the famed cartoonist. For many, it likely came as a shock to see how badly his teeth protruded and how significantly they affected his speech.

Like a craggy wall between upper and lower lips, Ripley's misshapen and misaligned teeth prevented him from fully closing his mouth, making it difficult to pronounce certain letters. With the help of his speech lessons (and liquor) he had grown accustomed to compensating, but certain letters and words still sounded awkward—*b*'s sounded like *v*'s, *p*'s sounded like *fee*, and *s*'s emerged in a slushy lisp.

On-screen, Ripley appeared swishy and loose-limbed, almost effeminate—possibly due to his self-prescribed doses of hooch. He walked with a sheepdog's waddle and constantly fiddled with the nubs of charcoal he kept in his pockets. After introducing guests, he'd shuffle to an easel and sketch a cartoon—an "Up-arm Man" from India or the boy who died of old age at six years old or the man-eating tree of Madagascar. He wore nice suits with bow ties and spats over his shoes. He appeared fit and confident, though he was starting to develop a paunch and lose hair, the remnants of which were slicked back and shiny.

The director, Murray Roth (who cowrote *Lights of New York*), grew frustrated as Ripley mangled the scripts. In his *On Broadway* column, Walter Winchell teased, "Ripley, who knows everything, can't remember his lines over at the Long Island studios. heheheh." Speaking before a small audience assembled on a stage designed to look like a ship's lounge or an airplane cabin, Ripley introduced guests and shared film footage of his travels to Morocco or Jerusalem or film clips of real people doing weird things. His human queeriosities included a sixteen-month-old roller skater, a six-year-old boy who smoked, and an armless trombone player. By featuring odd performers from Scranton, Flint, Tacoma, and Toledo, he showed an appreciation for small-town America as well as genuine awe for the fetishes and fixations of those willing to spend years of concentrated effort carving a chain of matchsticks or building a violin entirely of sugar or printing an eighth-of-an-inch copy of the *Rubáiyát of Omar Khayyám*, which Ripley stored inside a pinky ring.

In one episode, Ripley is arrested and tried in a mock court, forced to prove some of his controversial statements: *America had no official national anthem? The Statue of Liberty was built atop a prison?* He patiently defends himself on all charges and once again explains the details of his famous claim that Lindbergh had been the sixty-seventh man to fly across the Atlantic. Finally, the judge intervenes and declares, "Mr. Ripley, believe it or not, you are *acquitted.*"

* * *

HEARST'S SYNDICATES were reaching more Americans than any one news source had at any time in history, which meant Ripley was reaching them, too. But as the financial crisis worsened—Hearst ordered his papers to *never* use the term "depression"—circulation declined, prompting Hearst to aggressively expand his media empire into radio. He told employees that radio publicity was "the greatest promotion in the world today."

Ripley had done occasional radio shows since his 1922 debut, a thirty-nine-minute show on WDY in Roselle Park, New Jersey (the nation's first broadcast station). He had appeared on *The Collier Hour* show in 1929 and in early 1930, but those shows had all been one-time events. By mid-1930, he was ready for a show of his own, and signed with NBC.

Sponsored by Colonial Beacon Oil Company, Ripley's program would air Monday nights in New York and a dozen other cities. As with his Vitaphone films, Ripley would introduce listeners to some of the strange people he'd been featuring for years in print. His first guest was speed-talking Cygna Conly, who read Lincoln's Gettysburg Address in thirty-two seconds— eight and a half words per second. Eventually, by putting sextuplets on the air, a girl who roller-skated on her hands, a legless boy swimmer named Zimmy, a girl named June Bugg, a man who survived being buried alive, a seventy-year-old contortionist, and scores of other "living Believe-It-or-Nots," he would join Jack Benny, Al Jolson, and Kate Smith as a star of 1930s radio.

* * *

WITH *BELIEVE IT OR NOT* on the air and in the theaters, it was getting harder for Ripley's doubters to prove him wrong. Instead of existing as black-and-white newspaper drawings, Ripley's oddities and their feats could now be seen and heard. In time, some of his achievers would become minor celebrities themselves, bringing even more mail from people with odd abilities or physical deformities or unlikely tales, all wanting to become part of Ripley's famous world of the weird.

As a self-described odd duck, Ripley felt justified in encouraging other odd ducks to share with him their peculiarities and abnormalities, even if he knew it might not be in their best interest. Some had accidental talents, such as the Kansas man with the iron stomach who ate glass, newspapers, raw cow livers, and a sack of cement. Others were born with deformities or became disfigured by accident and developed unique new skills, such as the Missouri man who lost his arms and eyesight in an explosion but learned to read Braille with his tongue—an accomplishment worth $5,000 in one of Ripley's contests.

By now, Ripley realized that he owed his success to the "twisted folly" of such volunteers. And at a time of rising unemployment and a malaise spreading like a disease, the escapist distractions of his world travels and his expanding menagerie of misfit characters was the ideal tonic for an ailing nation.

His book was now in its fourteenth printing and still on the bestseller lists, having sold more than 70,000 copies. The *Believe It or Not* brand was succeeding overseas, too, with the book's foreign editions earning rave reviews in Dublin, Cape Town, Stockholm, Munich, Bratislava, Tokyo, and Peking. Simon & Schuster wanted him to write another book in 1931, so he began saving readers' letters to recycle their material. Fans wrote to him constantly, sharing their lives with him. They wanted Ripley to know about their empty rocking chair that rocked each night at the same time. About the man who bowled two games at once—lefty in one lane, righty in the other, scoring 270 in each. About the eight-year-old girl who'd been driving a truck since she was five. About the man who could lift a table and six chairs with his teeth, or the man who had smoked ten cigars a day for sixty-five years, or the sisters who made clothing from newspapers.

Such letters were proof, as the *New York American* put it in a promotional ad, that "there's a little bit of Riplianism in all of us," that everyone harbors a "fascination with the apparently untrue facts of life."

It seemed people needed Ripley's affordable brand of entertainment, treasured it during an otherwise troubled time. America was hunkering down, suffering a Roaring Twenties hangover. But with Ripley in their papers and on their radios, they could experience foreign lands, meet strange and interesting people. Ripley was becoming the country's know-it-all professor of history, geography, science, and anthropology. His offbeat lessons gave people hope.

That's how Norbert Pearlroth saw it too. Ripley's cartoons "show that life is not all cut and dried, that nature is not always so workaday, that it has its own exceptions. Life *does* play strange tricks." While Ripley's lifestyle soared, Pearlroth's remained workaday. He still visited the library each day and came home late each night, despite complaints from his wife and son. He was making about $75 a week by 1930, but he continued to believe that his search for "the marvelous, the incredible" was a worthy mission. In fact, he seemed addicted to the thrill of finding what he called "a good one."

"A really good item," he once said, "is one where your heart has some part of it, where your heart begins to beat."

✳ ✳ ✳

WHEN RIPLEY HEADLINED the National Automobile Show in January 1931, he was preceded onstage by President Herbert Hoover, who assured the crowd that "despite the depression" he was looking forward to "a prosperous New Year." While 1931 would hardly be a prosperous year for most Americans, Ripley's fortunes would mount.

For two years, his life had been a nonstop whirl. He'd tried to keep up his traveling pace, but every trip now carried obligations. If he visited Toronto or Havana, he was expected to do interviews with Hearst papers and radio stations. If he wanted to see Europe, King Features expected stories and cartoons, NBC expected him to make up for his absence from the airwaves, and Vitaphone wanted more film. Such duties rarely stopped him from leaving the country as often as possible, though—often on a moment's notice.

In March of 1931, he and Bugs Baer escaped New York on the SS *Roma*, bound for Northern Africa and the Middle East.

Shadowed by a Hearst cameraman, Ripley toured Morocco, Algiers, Tunis, Egypt, Palestine, Istanbul, and the Balkans. He returned home in May, and while the SS *Leviathan* was moored off Fire Island, still fifty miles from Manhattan, he broadcast a radio show from the ship back to NBC's New York studios, which his producers touted as the first ship-to-shore radio program.

The next day called for another stunt. In order to reach Newark for a radio show that night, Ripley climbed into a lifeboat that was lowered over the side of the *Leviathan*. The boat delivered him to an awaiting seaplane. Looking disheveled in a rumpled three-piece suit and crooked tie, his thinning hair askew, Ripley tipped his hat to passengers crowded along the *Leviathan*'s rails, then climbed inside. As the plane took off from choppy seas, a cameraman from Hearst's Metrotone Newsreel circled above in another plane, filming the whole scene.

What the cameras couldn't see was Ripley's fury. He hated to fly and hadn't been told about the stunt until the last minute. The scheme had been concocted by Dick Hyman, his new business manager and publicity assistant, who rode beside him. During the short flight, Ripley glowered, refusing to speak to Hyman. His anger melted the next morning, though, when he saw the front-page newspaper coverage, including maps, diagrams, and photos of Ripley waving from the seaplane.

The stunt allowed Hearst's papers to declare that Ripley had completed his most recent foreign journey "by liner, boat, plane, train, and motorcar." When Ripley summoned Hyman to the New York Athletic Club that afternoon, he was beaming.

* * *

FIRED FROM HIS first two newspaper jobs and on the brink of unemployment just five years earlier, Ripley was suddenly being described in print as "the highest paid artist in America today." At the time, Arthur Brisbane was making $250,000 as editor of Hearst's *New York American* and was considered to be the country's best-paid newsman. But Ripley's income from King Features, Warner Bros., Simon & Schuster, and NBC actually surpassed that of Hearst's most trusted employee. Ripley's income—an astounding $350,000 a year in 1931—accidentally found its way into print, thanks to a lawsuit.

Famous Speakers Inc. sued Ripley, claiming that the contract he signed in 1929 required him to give lectures exclusively for Famous Speakers. Company president Betty Smythe wanted *half* of the earnings from Ripley's films, radio shows, and vaudeville performances. In his testimony, Ripley revealed to a Supreme Court judge his six-figure income, which was hungrily picked up by the gossip columnists. The judge ruled in Ripley's favor, but the experience spooked him. He realized he needed to be more protective of his lucrative franchise.

After hiring Hyman in late 1929 he hired NYAC handball partner Robert Hyland to manage his finances and legal affairs. Next, he formed a company, Believe It or Not, Inc., and invited his brother, Doug, to help run it.

Now in his late twenties, Doug had lived a nomadic life. After leaving Santa Rosa, he'd briefly lived with sister Ethel and her husband in Sacramento but then quit school and moved to Ohio, staying with his father's relatives and working as a carpenter. That lasted a few years until Doug escaped altogether, moving into the hills to live in a cabin. Ripley had been trying to lure Doug to New York for years. He would visit or send money to the grocery store Doug frequented, but instead of buying a train ticket Doug would buy more supplies and head back to his cabin. By 1931, Ripley had finally convinced his brother that it was time to move to New York and become part of the *Believe It or Not* machine.

Even with Doug added (somewhat reluctantly) to the payroll, Ripley's pace never slowed. He typically arose at dawn to start his twelve-hour workdays. After twenty-five years of cartooning he remained a skilled artist with an almost obsessive focus on the smallest of details. Intense morning sketch sessions were typically followed by film work in the afternoon and radio at night, then a late dinner or drinks. The release of his second book in late 1931 required another round of nonstop publicity. The *New York Times* called it "better, more entertaining, more surprising than his first one." When the book tour ended, he was back in the Vitaphone studios, filming a musical called *Seasons Greetings*.

Ripley hired a clipping service to collect articles in which his name appeared, another effort to keep track of his empire. One clip summed up the dizzying expansion of the Believe It or Not brand, adding: "Fortunately for him he enjoys a strong physique or he would break down beneath the celebrity strain." But at forty-one, the strain was showing. With no time for exercise or handball, he was losing his athlete's physique, losing hair, gaining weight, and drinking too much. He told friends he had started having headaches.

He was an artist, not a businessman, but he now needed to be both. His popularity and fame had grown so quickly, he suddenly found himself with "no time for anything," as he put it in a woe-is-me story for *Reader's Digest*.

> I am blessed with an indolent nature. I detest business. But since the publication of my Believe It or Not book, I have not had time, nor rest nor peace. . . . There are lectures, talking pictures, radio; syndicate features to prepare and

illustrate, more books to write. . . . All this pressure has taught me the necessity of tightly packed entertainment, recreation, self-instruction, into the little, scattered, ten-minute fragments of time that are left to me.

What he needed most was a vacation. And a companion.

14

The boy who once ran from girls was now being chased by them. Even with his bad teeth (which he was thinking of getting fixed, now that he could afford to), he was among the most eligible men in New York, often seen with an attractive young actress, singer, or dancer on his arm. He had come close to proposing a time or two, but always reminded himself he was not spousal material. Monogamy, he had learned, was not his forte.

Three years after Hearst and King Features hoisted him onto a global stage, he had become rich, famous, and beloved. But he also wanted to love and to *be* loved. Or at least not be alone. He had discovered there were plenty of women who wanted to spend time with a needy cartoonist. Even married women.

Part of Dick Hyman's job was to manage the love interests that were playing a larger role in Ripley's daily life. If Ripley wanted to be alone with a lover, they had to meet in hotels, since women weren't allowed at the NYAC. Wary of seeing his name in the gossip pages, he would instruct Hyman to pack a heavy telephone book or two into an empty suitcase, take it to the hotel, then check in under an assumed name. Hyman would later hand a key to Ripley, who would slip into the hotel room later that night, where his girlfriend would be waiting.

Despite such attempts at discretion, one lover refused to stay in the shadows. Her name was Marion Ohnick, but she went by the stage name Haru Onuki. "That delectable morsel of Japanese femininity," the *Los Angeles Times* once called her. Onuki performed on Broadway and in traveling vaudeville shows from 1916 through the late 1920s, making her operatic debut in 1926 as the lead in *Madame Butterfly* with the touring San Carlo Opera Company. The *New York Times* described Onuki's "striking entrance" and "dramatic talent," but added that her voice "was not quite heavy enough for the tragic demands of the role."

Ripley had known Onuki since the mid-1920s and had featured her in a 1926 cartoon, calling her the "beautiful Japanese prima donna" who took a full day to fix her hair. Now thirty-seven, she was past her prima donna days but still regal and glamorous. Ripley had been seeing Onuki on and off for years, and proposed to her in 1931. At least, that's what Onuki would claim. He apparently kept delaying the event and soon started avoiding her. In September of that year, Onuki waited in the lobby of the NYAC, demanding to see "Bobbie." When Ripley repeatedly refused to come downstairs, she lay down on the lobby floor.

"I won't move until I get five hundred dollars from him!" she yelled.

Ripley eventually sent down the cash and Onuki left New York to be with her family in California. Shortly afterward, she sued, accusing Ripley of breaking his promise to marry her and seeking $500,000 in damages. The lawsuit initially went unnoticed by the press until Ripley's lawyer challenged Onuki's lawsuit due to her "diversity of citizenship." (Ohnick's father was Japanese.) A New York State Supreme Court judge agreed to transfer the case to the US District Court, and that's when word leaked to the newspapers—*Ripley sued by scorned lover.*

The breakup and lawsuit were reported in *Time* magazine, the *New York Times*, the *Los Angeles Times*, and others, putting Ripley's love life back in the headlines, ten years after the divorce from Beatrice earned similar notoriety. As before, Onuki wanted Ripley to pay for his alleged wrongs.

"I love Bobbie as much as I did when I first promised to be his little Japanese sister," she told *Time.*

One benefit of his wealth was the ability to quickly escape such troubles. So when Onuki moved back to New York, to the St. Moritz Hotel—right next to the NYAC—Ripley made sure he got as far away as possible. By March 1932, he was on the opposite side of the globe "seeking new incredible facts," as *Time* put it.

He was also seeking love—and Onuki's replacement.

＊　＊　＊

THE SS *MARIPOSA* was a speedy, triple-smokestack liner that, if tipped on its nose, would reach almost halfway up the newly built Empire State Building. She began her maiden voyage on January 16, leaving New York with five hundred passengers. Ripley caught up with the ship in Los Angeles and began sailing toward the South Pacific, to explore "the wonderlands of the south seas," as the travel brochure promised.

With first-class dining halls, a hardwood dance pavilion, a library, two outdoor swimming pools, and the largest promenade deck of any American ship, the vessel would be Ripley's home for nearly three months and thirty thousand miles.

Capt. J. H. Trask, who had been sailing the Pacific for as long as Ripley had been alive, was entrusted with such notable passengers as former Hawaiian territorial governor George R. Carter and filmmaker Howard Hawks, who had just finished work on his latest film, *Scarface*. Ripley's entourage included a small radio crew to help conduct long-distance NBC broadcasts along the way, and a young man from Utah named Joe Simpson, who had been hired by King Features as Ripley's traveling secretary and cameraman. Simpson would film and photograph the journey for use in future Vitaphone films. (Based on the passenger logs of the *Mariposa* and many other ships Ripley had sailed, it seems Norbert Pearlroth never joined Ripley on any of his overseas travels.)

Ripley promised Joe Connolly he'd mail home a steady supply of cartoons. In the meantime, he intended to forget about the pending lawsuit and his near-miss second marriage to the litigious Onuki, and unwind with his feisty young female companion in their two-room suite with a private balcony.

Entrusted to Ripley's care was the woman he referred to in his journal only as "M." An employee would later describe her as "some pretty young thing he was hanging around with at the time" and a friend referred to her as "a beautiful, amusing woman whom he doted upon."

Based on photographs, passenger logs, and other documents, it seems Ripley's "pretty little shipmate" was actually Ruth Ross, a woman he'd met in the late 1920s in Europe who would become a constant traveling companion, employee, and, in time, his secret lover.

She was Eastern European (from either Russia or Hungary; Ripley's friends were never sure) and had left home to study in Paris. By the time Ripley met her she had become a successful antiques dealer. One colleague would describe her as "a flashing-eyed Jewess, handsome, intelligent, and vital." Ripley had initially hired Ross to accompany him during a tour of

France and Germany and to serve as his translator and cultural guide.

During their European travels they fell in love—or, at least, Ripley fell for her. By 1930 she had moved to New York, and friends came to believe Ripley had pulled strings to help her immigrate, though he was vague about her route to America, as well as her country of origin. Her English was good and Ripley adored her accent—"OK" sounded like "oakie," and she frequently used the term "okie-dokie," which he found cute. He nicknamed her Oakie.

Ripley kept a detailed journal, which provides a blow-by-blow account of the trip and, at times, the intimacy he and Oakie shared in their lovers' suite.

* * *

RIPLEY AROSE EACH MORNING around five o'clock to wander the decks barefoot, stopping to read *National Geographic* in the library. By late morning he'd find Oakie beside the pool, slowly turning brown. The two of them spent their days wearing only bathing suits—"or less," he wrote in his journal. By the time they reached Fiji, Oakie's skin had turned deep tan—"that golden brown is so attractive," said Ripley—while his own skin was the "ugly color of sickening pink and white." As on previous trips to Asia, Ripley sometimes felt self-conscious about the extreme whiteness of his skin, in contrast to the exotic darkness of the "natives."

Though Ripley enjoyed the multinational city of Suva, he wanted to see native Fijians, with their wild and reddish hair, whose ancestors were known cannibals. He was never much interested in postcards and typical tourist trinkets, but he did like the idea of bringing a "cannibal fork" home with him.

ꙮ BELIEVE IT! ꙮ

*A Fiji chieftain named Ratu Udre Udre was believed to have
eaten nine hundred people in his lifetime.*

In a rural village north of Suva, Ripley and Oakie toured among grass-roofed huts and watched native "spear dances" and a fire-walking demonstration, then reluctantly agreed to participate in a "kava ceremony." Villagers chewed the leaves of a kava plant, spit the juice into a bowl, and handed it to Ripley, who sipped the leaf-and-saliva concoction, winced, and told his hosts it tasted like soapy water with pepper sprinkled into it, but no worse than the liquor back home.

Before leaving Suva, Ripley befriended a bartender who sold him a few bottles, and over the next few days he and Oakie drank by the *Mariposa*'s pool while Ripley nursed his feet, which had become swollen and sore after his walking tour in Fiji. Ripley and Oakie sometimes spent whole days in their cabin, emerging only for dinner and some nights not dressing at all. Ripley hinted in his journal at Oakie's "free-air fiendishness" and how she'd get so "goofy about Bob" he'd wake up in the mornings with a sore back and neck. One morning he awoke with such a raging headache that he vowed not to allow himself to "be duped with drink and beautiful women."

Of course, Ripley's *Believe It or Not* duties were never far away. While crossing the Tasman Sea, Ripley and his NBC crew set up equipment for a planned radio broadcast to be sent back to New York—billed as the first South Seas–New York radio show. One of his guests was Czech pianist Rudolf Friml, formerly a *Ziegfeld Follies* composer. A known tippler, Friml forgot his lines and cues despite two days of practice. "Well, what do you want me to do," Friml said when Ripley introduced him on-air, but Ripley managed to keep him more or less on track and had him play a few songs.

When the ship stopped in Sydney, Ripley was confronted by a throng of newsmen and spent three days giving lectures and meeting with editors at Hearst's newspaper, *The Sun*. He and Oakie had an awkward dinner with his friend Whupsie Strelitz, the woman he'd dated in Buenos Aires in 1925 and had stayed in touch with. (Oakie was not happy; Ripley told his journal he was tempted to throw her overboard.) His last night in Sydney called for another complicated transoceanic radio broadcast, linking the show to New York via a network of Australian stations. Captain Trask agreed to delay the *Mariposa*'s departure to allow Ripley to finish his broadcast, but the show ran late and Ripley sprinted to the ship to meet the angry stares of passengers and crew.

Over the next month, the *Mariposa* sailed among tropical islands, hopping from port to port as Ripley and Oakie drank gin and dined with Rudolf Friml. In New Guinea, Ripley posed for photos with beautiful narrow-waisted and topless Papuan women, who warned him not to venture into the nearby jungle. A local tribe had recently invited another tribe to a peace conference, but the visitors slaughtered their hosts—"quartered them and ate their flesh," Ripley reported. As guests at the home of the Port Moresby police chief, Ripley and Oakie drank cocktails while watching performances by native dancers, including a prohibited "sex dance." He and Oakie were again the last passengers back aboard the *Mariposa* that night, just barely reaching the gangplank before it was pulled up.

* * *

WHAT RIPLEY LOVED most about traveling were the slow-paced moments of "delightful fatigue," far from New York's madness—walking barefoot on the empty decks at sunrise, hitting golf balls out over schools of flying fish, watching Oakie spread tanning oil on her glistening body.

He also loved visiting exotic locales that felt original and untouched by modernity. He found Bali to be one of the most peaceful, beautiful places he had ever seen, inhabited by "lovable, brown-skinned people" who were "the most artistic on earth." Ripley preferred his "natives" to be authentically *native*—barefoot and bare breasted, living simply in their huts of grass. In Bali and throughout Java, he eagerly captured more film footage of native dances and ceremonial rituals.

In Singapore, Ripley introduced Oakie to John Little's bar, where he had first tasted Singapore Slings in 1923. The bar seemed more run-down than he remembered, though after a few midday Slings he decided it looked pretty good after all. He had to practically carry Oakie back to the ship, where she collapsed unconscious into her bunk, but rebounded for a late night on the town. They got back to the ship at four a.m., and found a monkey and a parrot in their cabin.

Sailing into Bangkok, Ripley watched children diving off the horns of a partially submerged water buffalo. That night, he experienced the "wonderful quality" of Thai opium before watching a performance by Siamese dancers, whose kaleidoscopic costumes were "the most magnificent I have ever seen."

Days later, the *Mariposa* entered Hong Kong Harbor, its pale-green waters jammed with thousands of sampans, fishing boats, and ferries. Thrilled to be back in the Orient, Ripley quickly immersed himself, riding rickshaws down ancient narrow alleys and exploring streets alive with clicking mahjong games and clubs overflowing with the gaudy music of singsong girls—*his* China. After two heady days in Hong Kong he decided he wasn't ready to leave and made a last-minute decision to visit Shanghai. Twenty minutes before the scheduled departure from Hong Kong, he, Oakie, and Joe Simpson packed a bag, disembarked, and watched the *Mariposa* sail away.

The *New York Times* advertisement for the *Mariposa* tour had promised "a dramatic journey with a scintillating prologue." Now, the South Seas prologue of semi-clad native dancers and Singapore Slings was about to be replaced by the drama of war.

* * *

RIPLEY AND HIS COMPANIONS reached Shanghai at a volatile and dangerous time. Seven months earlier, Japanese troops had invaded the Manchuria region of northeast China and just two months before Ripley's arrival Japan had attacked Shanghai. The Chinese Army had pulled back, but sporadic fighting continued and Ripley witnessed evidence of the conflict: corpses and unexploded shells, charred buildings and fifty-foot bomb craters. He was stopped and questioned often by Japanese soldiers, who confiscated his movie camera and film. (Simpson managed to retrieve the camera and Ripley would return to the States with grisly footage of an execution: A group of prisoners is led through the streets, lined up on their knees, then shot in the head by a firing squad. It's unknown whether he purchased the film or if he and Simpson shot it. Years later, Ripley would admit during a lecture, "I have seen numbers of people executed because they disagreed politically.")

In some sections of town, Japanese soldiers dined easily in Chinese restaurants. Elsewhere, machine-gun fire popped and dark smoke curled into the sky. Ripley tried to cheer himself by visiting clubs he'd sampled years earlier. At the St. Georges, he was recognized by American sailors, who bought him a beer. To his surprise, he didn't feel like drinking. At the Del Monte, a group of Japanese naval officers invited Ripley to drink with them. As the Japanese officers drank beer, Ripley sipped coffee, then walked sullenly and alone back to his hotel.

"Felt low all day due to the influence of the war," he wrote in his journal.

The next morning, despite Ripley's fear of flying, he and his companions boarded an American seaplane and flew above a crazy quilt of rice paddies to Nanking. There, they toured past the conference hall where peace talks were being held and past the home of Chiang Kai-shek, who was quietly preparing for all-out war with Japan. Ripley also had dinner with Pearl S. Buck, who had just won the Pulitzer Prize for her novel *The Good Earth*. "It is very tense here," Buck had recently told a friend, and Ripley was about to discover just how tense his favorite country had become.

Unlike his previous visit, touring China was now risky and disturbing. On a crowded train to Peiping (as Westerners called Beijing at the time), Ripley was refused service in the dining car and forced to sit in a passenger car crammed with Chinese men drinking brandy and smoking cigars, many of the men staring intensely at the only white people aboard. He had always considered China peaceful and loving, but now he felt threatened and unsafe—which helped explain the scarcity of other American or Western travelers.

Still, he tried to pretend it was just a vacation and not an error in judgment. He and Oakie toured the Great Wall in sedan chairs and walked through the Forbidden City and the Temple of Heaven, where he was startled to meet two former Santa Rosa classmates. In a market Ripley found a comfortable pair of Chinese slippers for his aching feet, the sight of which earned some laughs from passengers on that afternoon's steamer journey to Dairen.

From Dairen (as Dalian was called at the time), they traveled north to war-shredded Mukden. The city, now under martial law, felt spooky and on edge. On the pier, Ripley was met by a man who called himself Chris Shibuya, who worked for the "News Bureau" and offered to give Ripley a tour. When Ripley explained who he was, the man abruptly turned and walked off. Ripley assumed Shibuya was a spy, and over the next two days felt as if he was being followed.

Mukden proved to be a stressful stop for the American tourists. Just days before Ripley's arrival, twelve suspected bandits had been executed and decapitated, their heads hung from the arch of the city gate. By day, shops remained closed and citizens walked nervously through town, eyeing Ripley with suspicion. Each night, machine guns sputtered. Ripley was forbidden from taking photographs or even scribbling notes. He had to secretly send cables to New York addressed "Dear Elsie . . ." to prevent his messages from being intercepted by the Japanese military.

Despite the dangers and images of war, he left China as enchanted and beguiled as ever. Though besieged by Japanese invaders, the country struck him as resilient and magical, a place "of superstition and religion, of mercy and goodness," as Pearl Buck once put it, "of dreams and miracles, of dragons and gods and goddesses and priests . . ."

Ripley's group left China by boat, traveling to the Korean city of Pusan and then across to Japan, where Ripley spent a few days visiting temples, sitting for interviews with Japanese newsmen, and catching up on his cartoons before reuniting with the *Mariposa* once again for the journey home—to California.

Bucktoothed LeRoy Ripley, age eight. "Everyone at school picked on him because he was so different," a classmate would later say. "Not one of the guys," said another.

"THE VILLAGE BELL WAS SLOWLY RINGING"

Though he'd later claim to have sold his first drawing at age fourteen, Ripley was actually eighteen when this cartoon was published in *LIFE* magazine, in June of 1908. He was paid $8, which inspired him to pursue cartooning as a career.

At far right with the ***San Francisco Chronicle*** art staff, 1912. After moving to San Francisco in 1909, Ripley was fired from his first newspaper job, at the ***San Francisco Bulletin***—"My work was poor," he admitted—but was quickly hired at the ***Chronicle***.

SCAN THIS PAGE TO SEE VIDEOS, CARTOONS, AND PHOTOS ODD**SCAN**
(SEE PAGE IX FOR DETAILS).

Having played in California's bush leagues after high school, Ripley dreamed of playing professional baseball. While covering the New York Giants' 1913 spring training in Texas, he was invited to suit up and try out for the team. An injury would put an end to his baseball career.

At the drawing board, 1915, working for the **New York Globe**, which would be his home for a decade.

A model and a Follies Girl, Beatrice Roberts sang and danced with the **Ziegfeld Follies**. A week after her eighteenth birthday, she married Ripley in Newark, New Jersey, and the couple honeymooned in Atlantic City. The smiles would not last.

Ripley the handball player, showing off his athlete's physique.

MAILED MONDAY, FEB. 5, 192..
From
THE ASSOCIATED NEWSPAPERS
114 LIBERTY STREET, NEW YORK
FOR IMMEDIATE RELEASE

RIPLEY'S
RAMBLE 'ROUND
THE WORLD

Goodbye

By ROBERT L. RIPLEY.

In late 1922, Ripley began his life-changing "Ramble 'Round the World" voyage, a four-month adventure that exposed Ripley to the country that would become his favorite: China— "the vast, old decaying land of the Celestial."

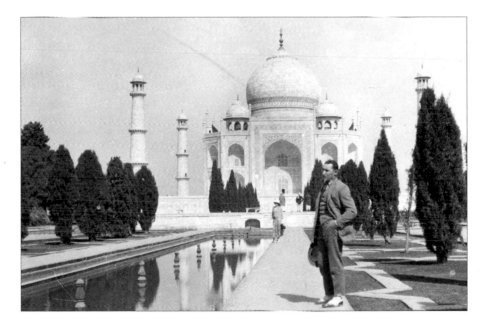

At the Taj Mahal, during his Ramble. Ripley found India to be fascinating and revolting. "Nowhere on earth can you see such a weird cross-cut of human life," he wrote, after a visit to the holy city of Benares. "All this pagan panorama."

SCAN THIS PAGE TO SEE VIDEOS, CARTOONS, AND PHOTOS **ODDSCAN**

THE GLOBE AND COMMERCIAL ADVERTISER, NEW YORK, WEDNESDAY, APRIL 11, 1923.

World's Champions Finally Gets Under Way

IT'S NOT SUCH A WICKED TOWN AFTER ALL

Bob Ripley is back! The Globe's celebrated cartoonist, after a four months' trip abroad, during which time he visited every town and point of interest in the old world, is ready to portray the things that will be uppermost in the minds of sport fans the country over.

Rip, the most famous sporting cartoonist that ever lived, will supply sport enthusiasts with the inside "dope" on all the great events in the sport world scheduled for decision hereabouts this summer, fall, and early winter. He knows, probably more than anybody else, the true import of every sporting event, and gives the fans his views in a clear-minded, unprejudiced, unbiased way.

ABOVE: In April 1923, Ripley returned from his circumnavigation a changed man. Having witnessed the "demented, delusioned, diseased, and devout" of the world, his cartoons grew stranger, more gruesome and eccentric—and more popular.

With his best friend, the writer, humorist, and cartoonist Bugs Baer, mid-1920s. The two Mutt-and-Jeff pals would become rich and famous together.

At the railway station in Hell, Norway, 1928. "It has frequently been suggested that I come here," Ripley wrote in a column for the ***Globe***, describing Hell as "delightful!" and advising his readers, "Go to Hell! I mean it."

Ripley forcing a smile—in truth, he hated to fly.

TO TED STONE
—ALL THE BEST!
from
RIPLEY
and
HIS SEEING-EYE DOG
"CYCLOPS"
BELIEVE IT or NOT

Ripley's one-eyed dog, Cyclops. A habitual collector, Ripley collected pets, too. Some visitors to his mansion felt he seemed more at ease with his dogs than with people.

MERRY XMAS AND HAPPY NEW YEAR! RIPLEY · BELIEVE IT or NOT ·

Outside his mansion on BION Island.

BELOW: Ripley with some of his lady friends, paddling in one of his many boats on the pond behind his mansion. Associates would refer to his collection of girlfriends as his "harem."

With a mummified fetus known as "Atta Boy," featured on the jacket of his second book, 1931. Through the 1930s, Ripley became more interested in human deformities and sideshow freaks, displaying a P. T. Barnum–like obsession with grotesquerie.

ATTA-BOY
6½ INCHES
TALL
REDUCED & MUMMIFIED
HUMAN FIGURE
JIVARO — PERU

BELIEVE IT or NOT—

"BULUM BALUBA" from Ripley
SUVA, FIJI ISLANDS

During an extensive 1932 journey through the South Seas and Asia, Ripley insisted on visiting with a tribe of alleged cannibals in Fiji. He proudly managed to bring home a "cannibal fork," which he would display in his museums and exhibitions.

In Port Moresby, New Guinea, with members of a tribal dance troupe, March 1932.

In a dug-out canoe at Waikiki Beach with the love of his life, Ruth Ross, whom he called "Oakie," February 1932. In his travel journal, he described how much they drank—and how little clothing they wore—during their South Seas cruise.

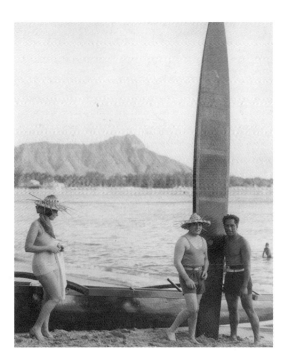

With Oakie and Olympic swimming star Duke Kahanamoku, considered the godfather of modern surfing. Ripley first met Kahanamoku at the 1920 Olympics.

At his peak, Ripley received more than a million letters a year. In 1930, the U.S. postmaster general issued a directive: "Postal clerks have had to devote too much time recently to deciphering freak letters intended for Ripley."

With Arjan Desur Dangar, one of the performers at Ripley's Odditorium exhibition at the 1933 Chicago World's Fair. Just before the fair started, Dangar fought with his manager, who ripped off half his mustache. Ripley sent them back to India.

With lion mask from Bali, 1932. Ripley amassed many crates of collectibles during his years of world travel, and in 1934 he finally bought a home to display his masks, weapons, beer steins, artwork, and other strange collections—including his erotica.

For $100, Ripley bought his first shrunken head from a tribe in Bolivia in 1925. Such heads would become *Believe It or Not* emblems. (The head in the photo was stolen from a Ripley's museum in the 1980s and has never been recovered.)

On a ship with his friend, the writer and radio personality Will Rogers. Ripley once ran into Rogers in the middle of the Syrian Desert at a fortress called Rutbah Wells, on his way to Baghdad, and later sailed home from Europe with Rogers and his wife.

His years as a sports cartoonist led to friendships with boxers (left to right) Jack Dempsey, Gene Tunney, and Floyd Gibbons. Ripley also befriended Babe Ruth and Lou Gehrig.

SCAN THIS PAGE TO SEE VIDEOS, CARTOONS, AND PHOTOS *ODD* 5CAN

Ripley with child movie legend Shirley Temple, mid-1930s.

BELOW: After traveling from Jerusalem to Damascus to Baghdad to Tehran, Ripley entered Soviet territory for the first time. En route from Azerbaijan to Georgia, he insisted on a foolhardy crossing of the Caucasus Mountains—by car. Incredibly, two farmers with oxen were coming across from the other side and pulled Ripley's car free.

Another risky mountain crossing—this one traversing Khyber Pass, from Afghanistan into Pakistan (then northern India), 1936. Ripley eventually had to abandon the car and make the next portion of the trip by camel.

With a Hindu holy man in India, 1936. Ever since his 1922–23 trip around the world and his visit to the holy city of Benares, India, Ripley had been obsessed with the strange things mankind did in the name of their various gods.

Ripley's beloved statue of Hananuma Masakichi on display at the New York Odditorium in 1939. The sculptor, working in the nude and surrounded by mirrors, painstakingly re-created every muscle, wrinkle, and sinew of his body.

One of the *See America First with Bob Ripley* radio shows, this one airing from 850 feet underground in Carlsbad Caverns, New Mexico, June 1939. Left to right: James White, who discovered the caverns as a young boy; New Mexico governor John Miles; Ripley; Carlsbad National Park superintendent Colonel Thomas Boles.

Descending into the Grand Canyon—with a young Barry Goldwater—for another technically challenging *See America First* radio show.

During a 1936 live broadcast from Silver Springs, Florida, Ripley and his snake-handling, crocodile-wrestling host Ross Allen entered a pit full of poisonous snakes. When the lights suddenly went out, Allen yelled, "Let's get the hell outa here!"

First underwater radio broadcast—from the bottom of the shark tank at Marineland in St. Augustine, Florida. One shark got too close and knocked Ripley on his bottom.

Posing with the inaugural 1918 ***Believe It or Not*** cartoon (originally titled "Champs and Chumps"). He hung the cartoon behind a backlit mirror above the massive fireplace in his mansion and loved to flip the light switch that illuminated the hidden cartoon.

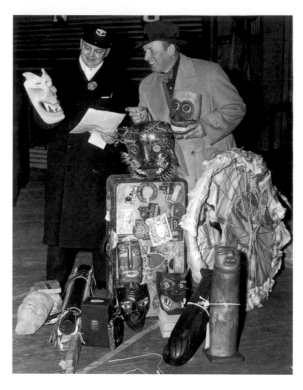

With a customs agent and a collection of masks after his 1940 travels through South and Central America. World War II would curtail Ripley's global travels.

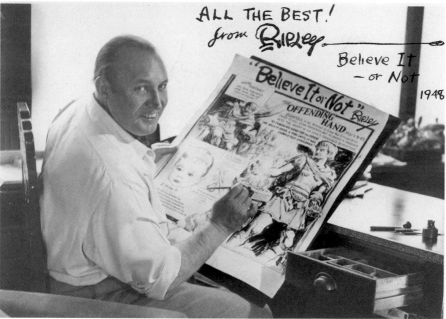

ALL THE BEST! from Ripley.

Believe It — or Not

1948

A King Features Syndicate publicity photo shows Ripley at work on a cartoon. Owned by William Randolph Hearst, the syndicate exposed Ripley to a global audience.

Ripley and his staff, rehearsing a radio show in his Manhattan apartment overlooking Central Park. To the right of Ripley are the two long-time employees who were crucial to his career: Doug Storer and Norbert Pearlroth (on couch).

FAREWELL PARTY
TO
LING AI AND WING AI
N.Y. STUDIO · JUNE 9, 19

With close friend Li Ling-Ai (on Ripley's right) in Ripley's China-themed New York apartment, called Nirvana, which he had purchased from famed travel photographer Burton Holmes.

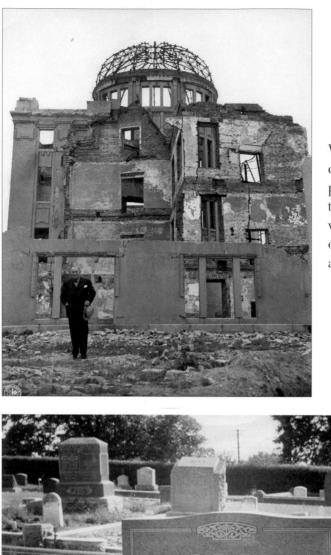

Visiting Hiroshima, during his somber postwar journey through Asia, which would be one of his last adventures.

The Ripley family tombstone in the Odd Fellows Cemetery in Santa Rosa, California. Like his parents, Ripley died before reaching sixty.

His latest big adventure put him in a philosophical mood, and his journal captured his sometimes pessimistic view of mankind, and possibly himself:

Nature is strong and man is weak

The earth turns green and man turns dark

Nature is virulent and man is impotent

* * *

ON FRIDAY MORNING, April 29, thousands of Santa Rosa citizens gathered outside the courthouse to celebrate "Ripley Day," an event timed for Ripley's return from the Orient. Ripley's sister met the *Mariposa* at the pier in San Francisco and drove him straight to Santa Rosa, which he hadn't visited since his mother died.

Bands marched, flags waved, and residents cheered the return of their now-famous former citizen as Mayor George Cadan presented him the keys to the city and Ripley thanked the crowd. At a luncheon, ex-classmates sang high school fight songs and bombarded Ripley with backslaps and bet-you-don't-remember-me's. Ripley told the group that in the seventeen years since his last trip home he had visited Santa Rosa, Mexico; Santa Rosa, Chile; and Santa Rosa, Philippines.

Ripley was escorted by civic leaders to his old grammar school and then to Santa Rosa High, where he told 1,500 students the story of leaving town in 1909 to work at the *San Francisco Bulletin* for $8 a week. He was joined onstage by his former English teacher, Frances O'Meara, whom he embraced in an enormous bear hug. Ripley thanked O'Meara for encouraging his drawing, then gave her a gold-and-jade necklace he'd purchased in China. After the event, O'Meara grew weepy recalling the 1921 fire that destroyed the old high school, torching all of

Ripley's drawings: "Part of me was destroyed in that fire . . . Their loss can never be replaced."

At one last reception that evening, the mayor gave Ripley an unexpected gift—a section of the roof beam from his old Orchard Street house. As a lonely little boy, LeRoy Ripley had sometimes crawled into the attic. He once etched his name into the beam with a pocketknife. The beam had been salvaged from the house and still bore Ripley's hand-carved name. Visibly moved by the gesture, he seemed on the verge of tears. Fortunately, he had the excuse of a plane to catch. He quickly thanked everyone, then drove off in Ethel's car.

∗　∗　∗

IN 1932 ALONE, Ripley estimated that he covered sixty thousand miles—equal to two and a half times around the Earth.

In recognition of his relentless global explorations, he was elected to the prestigious, century-old Royal Geographic Society of London. (Ripley thought it was a prank and initially ignored the society's congratulatory letter.) Joining the society put Ripley in the company of one of his heroes, Burton Holmes, the famed creator of the "travelogue," who for forty years had been telling stories about his globetrotting experiences in popular lectures and films.

Ripley had much in common with Holmes, who harbored a deep admiration for Marco Polo, loved the Orient, slept on a futon at night, and often wore a kimono by day. Ripley likely heard Holmes speak at the San Francisco World's Fair in 1915, or read about Holmes witnessing the eruption of Mt. Vesuvius in 1906. He surely knew of Holmes's much-publicized wanderings, which far outpaced his own. Along the way Holmes had collected massive amounts of art and curios, stored in his numerous residences. He now lived in a sprawling apartment, called Nirvana, overlooking Central Park.

Holmes's motto—"To Travel Is to Possess the World"—seemed to have become Ripley's as well. And while Ripley enjoyed sharing his experiences with the public, he preferred the road to the radio booth or the lecture stage. At the start of 1933 he cut back on his radio and lecture schedule to prepare for even more far-flung travels.

✳ ✳ ✳

BY NOW, Ripley had become something of a wayfaring snob. For foreign lands to be interesting, they needed to challenge him, enlighten him, surprise him, or at least disgust him. South America and Europe had been too ordinary compared to the countries that most fascinated him, mainly India and China.

He was hoping for some surprises from Africa when he booked a last-minute sea-and-air tour from Cairo to Cape Town in early 1933.

As on previous travels through Muslim lands, he found himself troubled by the "fanatical" teachings of Islam and the Koran. He was also annoyed that the "natives" suddenly seemed so *Western*—drinking whiskey, wearing English suits, mixing socially with white Brits and Yanks.

His curiosity was finally aroused when he and Joe Simpson and a camera crew (no girlfriend this time) reached Sudan, where he fell into a typical rhythm. One day he'd be amazed by the sword-wielding Bishari tribe. The next day he'd be repulsed by the "unwashed horde" traveling in the third-class barge towed behind his ship down the Nile. As on other travels, he was shocked at how hard the women worked. "In this country, there are three beasts of burden," he wrote in a dispatch, en route to Khartoum. "The camel, the donkey, and the woman." The men, meanwhile, spent much of their time horizontal. Although he'd sometimes be accused of mistreating the women in his life, there was a complicated duality to Ripley's contradictory attitudes on gender and racial equality. He had fallen in love with Africa, for example, but disparaged African males' work ethic, sometimes referring to Africans as "darkies" and at times claiming admiration for the British "white standard" in its colonies.

"The English know how to run colonies," he wrote, while the Americans "have a knack for spoiling natives."

Friends could never quite resolve the seemingly bipolar attitudes of Ripley the traveler. On the one hand, he was the worldly anthropologist, concerned about women being treated as beasts of burden in male-dominated cultures, and seemingly envious of the simple lives of the poor. (In New Zealand, he had admired the Maori, who seemed peaceful and lived "in the moment.") On the other hand, he was the narrow-minded hayseed, relieved to get off the Nile and into the Grand Hotel in Khartoum, which he called "a first-class white man's oasis in the desert, where they have pink gins, and Scotch and sodas." He was sometimes being ironic in such statements, or self-mocking. Still, it was often hard for Ripley to disguise his unease amid the dark-skinned poor or conceal his fluctuating compassions. In Khartoum, when his car was surrounded by swarms of beggars, he found them menacing but also "curious [and] good natured."

Ripley flew south to the city of Juba and, in his adopted traveling uniform—pith helmet, khaki shorts, and two-toned shoes—he walked through a village of thatched-roof huts shaped like beehives, gathering footage for an upcoming Vitaphone film (in which he would describe the "African Beehive Village"). He filmed some of the topless women, but many rushed to cover themselves when the strange-looking white man approached.

In Nairobi, Ripley toured a Kikuyu village with an Englishman named John Boyes, who had lived in Africa for years and once fought beside the Kikuyus against a rival tribe, afterward declaring himself their king. Boyes was also a known elephant poacher who exploited what he called the "Dark Continent." Discussing colonialism with Boyes gave Ripley the chance to explore topics that had nagged him since his arrival in Africa. He disagreed with Boyes on a few points—for example, that the "savage" native was inferior to the educated Westerner or that the Kikuyu practice of female genital mutilation was acceptable— but felt there was something valid about Boyes's argument that white men had upset the natural order of Africa. Just as he hated to see signs of Westernization in Cairo, Ripley disapproved of what he saw in Nairobi: "stupid white people trying to change the age-old habits of the Africans."

"Missionaries are the curse of Africa, the same as they are the curse of the Islands of the South Seas. The black man of Africa in his savage state is a gentleman," he wrote in his journal. "Only when he starts to become civilized does he lose his character and become diseased, immoral, unhealthy, and criminal."

* * *

ONE APRIL MORNING, Ripley worked in his hotel room in his undershorts, catching up on overdue cartoons while nursing a hangover. He'd been celebrating the previous day, after hearing the news from back home: Congress had voted to repeal the Eighteenth Amendment, and Prohibition would come to an end later in 1933. Nairobi was an expensive city—a pair of socks cost $2.50—but for the price of two socks Ripley managed to buy a celebratory quart of scotch.

Ripley loved to drink when he traveled (and when he didn't), but usually found time to work off the liquor through exercise. Lately, it had been getting harder to squeeze in a swim, a long walk, or a game of tennis or handball, and he worried often about his weight. That didn't stop him from drinking and eating more and more freely. His weakness for alcohol was something else he shared with Burton Holmes, who never smoked but would boast in his autobiography that he "violated the Volstead Act at every convenient or inconvenient opportunity."

Even with the extra pounds and rounded face, Ripley was recognized everywhere in South Africa. He traveled from Mombasa to Zanzibar to Maputo (known then as Lourenzo Marques), then to Swaziland and onward to Durban, where he judged a *Believe It or Not* contest and gave a radio address. During the show, he made frequent trips to the adjacent Durban Club, but later felt "utterly disgusted" with himself. After a visit to Victoria Falls, he again drank too much during a "disgraceful" appearance at the Plaza in Johannesburg and awoke feeling embarrassed about his public drunkenness "and more or less sore at the world in general."

He forced himself out of bed for a scheduled trip to the Robinson gold mine, which turned out to be the perfect hangover cure. He descended by elevator nearly two miles underground into a buried city of railroads, electric lights, blacksmith shops, and hospitals, all squeezed beneath a low ceiling propped up by crooked timbers. He was amazed that man's "lust for gold" had inspired him to dig so deep into the earth's crust. Though overwhelmed by the thick heat, he was grateful for the perspiration, the previous night's scotch seeping from his pores. When he emerged from the elevator and back into sunlight, he felt euphoric.

During a radio interview in Cape Town, he described his experience in the gold mine as "the most thrilling of my life."

* * *

BY NOW RIPLEY had visited 147 countries, traveling "farther than the distance from the earth to the moon," by his estimation. When asked about his favorite country, he usually listed China first, but told a South African interviewer, "at the present time, after my trip from Cairo to Cape Town, I am a little bit in doubt." He flew to Argentina by seaplane— among the earliest transatlantic passenger flights—then flew to New York, lugging many crates of artifacts he'd purchased in Africa.

He also returned home armed with more strange scenes with which to entertain a depressed nation.

In Mombasa, he had watched a two-hour tribal dance that climaxed when one frenzied dancer "stuck the blade of a dagger into his mouth and twisted it around and then spouted blood all over." Just like the holy men of India who tortured themselves, he continued to be fascinated by religious fanaticism. He had come to believe that "the strangest places on earth are the holiest." He was also developing a guilty fascination with disfiguration. In Zanzibar he searched for victims of elephantiasis, offering two rupees to anyone who would expose their large and gruesome limbs to his camera.

While flying (nervously) home from Africa, he had tried describing in his journal what he loved about travel, how the rewards were always worth the hardships:

I don't know what my position in life really is—I don't like to fly, I don't like to walk, I don't like to swim, and I don't like to be underground . . . Yet each time I do either one of these things I am thrilled, but more thrilled after they are finished. Every time I go up in an airplane, I am exhilarated after I am on the ground again.

15

Ripley's fame would soon expand significantly thanks to the promotional instincts of a fellow Santa Rosan named Charles C. Pyle.

Known as "Cash and Carry" or just "C. C.," Pyle was a born promoter. As a boy, he had created a goodwill tour to lure businesses back to Santa Rosa after the 1906 earthquake. In 1925, he became publicity agent for Chicago Bears star Red Grange, considered a first in pro football. Pyle next formed his own football team, the New York Yankees, and founded his own nine-team American Football League to compete with the NFL.

When the AFL flopped and was absorbed into the NFL, Pyle switched sports to promote a 1928 L.A.-to-New York marathon called the Bunion Derby. Most of the runners dropped out along the way, struck by cars or felled by illness, and only a handful made it to New York. Pyle lost at least $150,000.

Another money-losing venture was a sideshow tour with the mummified corpse of a train robber named Elmer McCurdy, which Pyle bought for $50, dubbing him the "Oklahoma Outlaw." Critics—and the police—eventually forced Pyle to bury poor McCurdy.

Ripley had attended grammar school with Pyle's sister and was willing to listen to an intriguing business proposal from a childhood acquaintance.

Pyle's idea was to bring the Believe It or Not franchise to the upcoming World's Fair in Chicago in the form of an exhibit that would display some of the curios and artifacts Ripley had been collecting. The highlight of Pyle's proposed exhibition would be live performances by some of the bizarrely talented people Ripley had featured in his cartoons, films, and radio shows. Pyle would run everything and pay Ripley a licensing fee plus a share of the profits. With Ripley traveling and still overcommitted to his lecture, film, and radio obligations, the arrangement could spread the Believe It or Not brand name without much heavy lifting by Ripley.

Ripley's initial contribution to the partnership was to give the exhibition its name: the Ripley "Believe It or Not" *Odditorium*.

✴ ✳ ✱

RIPLEY TAPPED his Hearst-appointed secretary and frequent traveling partner, Joe Simpson, to help Pyle track down performers and negotiate contracts. Simpson and Pyle sent out scores of letters and telegrams seeking the world's oldest man, the shortest man, contortionists, Hindu ascetics, and other *Believe It or Not* subjects. "We have done our best to trace the Horned Man of South Africa but have been unable to do so," read one reply from an overseas acquaintance.

Performers were offered travel expenses, a $40 weekly salary, and free room and board. Half their pay would be withheld until the end of the fair, to prevent premature quitters. (Delayed payments were implemented after the early loss of a performer from India. When Arjan Desur Dangar learned that his manager/translator was keeping two-thirds of his income, he cracked open the man's head with a brick. The manager fought back and accidentally ripped off half his client's seventy-eight-inch mustache. Pyle sent them both back to India.)

The Century of Progress Exposition opened on May 27, 1933, commemorating Chicago's hundredth birthday and its recovery from the 1871 fire that had leveled much of the city. Spread across 424 acres south of downtown, the fair was scheduled to last five months.

Ripley visited in July for a dizzying three-day Odditorium kickoff. He hosted a huge contest in Hearst's *Herald and Examiner*, gave radio interviews and lectures, and autographed books at Marshall Field's. At a luncheon of the Chicago Association of Commerce, he was introduced as "one of the world's greatest explorers," and he was a special guest at the first-ever Major League Baseball All-Star Game, held at Comiskey Park.

❧ BELIEVE IT! ❧

The All-Star Game was intended as a one-time matchup between the two Major League divisions but would become an annual event.

At Pyle's air-conditioned exhibition hall, visitors walked past display cases with shrunken heads, medieval torture devices, and hundreds of other treasures and trinkets that Ripley finally released from his boxed-up personal collection, including Jesse James's first gun and a "cannibal fork" from Fiji.

Farther inside were sixteen small stages, where entertainers performed vaudeville-style acts. On one stage, an attractive sword swallower plunged a two-foot neon light down her throat, where it glowed. Another performer lifted weights with hooks attached to his eyelids, then used the same hooks to tow a wagon carrying his wife. Other stages featured a man who could smoke a cigarette and inflate balloons through his eye socket, a man who could dislocate his jaw and "swallow" his nose, and a one-man orchestra who could play twenty-one instruments simultaneously.

Some of the two dozen performers had been featured in *Believe It or Not* cartoons over the years, including E. L. Blystone, who wrote more than two thousand letters on a grain of rice, and a man who crammed his huge mouth with four golf balls and a full-sized baseball. As one newspaper writer pointed out, "You'll not have to wonder about these men and women from a pen and ink illustration. They'll be right there in person."

In the first weeks, however, business lagged, and Pyle worried that the Odditorium might be a bust. He considered dropping the forty-cent admission price to lure visitors and shared his nagging concerns with another sideshow operator named Lou Dufour. "I don't understand it," Pyle lamented.

Somewhat audaciously, Dufour had come to the fair with a display of human embryos in jars of formaldehyde, including a two-headed fetus. His other exhibit, "Darkest Africa," was a village of thatched-roof huts inhabited by Zulu and Senegalese immigrants from Harlem dressed in loincloths and carrying spears. "Darkest Africa" also included the hut of a man named Captain Callahan, who had been mutilated during an expedition to the Congo. A show barker told patrons that savages "had decapitated his penis and testicles," and that Callahan would remove his robe to reveal the scars—for an extra fifty cents.

Dufour told Pyle to find better acts, like Callahan. His advice: *less vaudeville, more torture.* "The public loves to suffer," he liked to say. Dufour offered to help Pyle find more interesting performers—a man who could drive long nails into his nose and stick hatpins through his cheeks, one who licked red-hot bars with his tongue—in exchange for 3 percent of the ticket receipts. But Pyle was hesitant to create a blatant freak show.

"People will faint," he protested.

Dufour assured him, "*That's* when the business will start."

Ripley had by this point stepped back to let Pyle take charge, having learned in recent years that he could hardly manage his empire alone, that he was still a better traveling artist than a businessman. Though he had grown wary in recent years of tainting the Believe It or Not brand and was quick to sue anyone who misused his trademark, with a fellow Santa Rosan in charge he freely turned over the "Ripley" name and hoped for the best.

Meanwhile, as Pyle worked to save the struggling Odditorium that summer of 1933, Ripley was in a Jerusalem hotel, wondering how to find the Garden of Eden.

✳ ✳ ✳

RIPLEY COULD BE CYNICAL when he spoke or wrote about religion, but he was still a Christian and believed in the stories of the Bible, which he read frequently. (If caught, he'd claim he was just searching for *Believe It or Not* material, but close friends could tell the book was more than a research tool.) Whenever he found himself at some holy site, he always thought to himself, *Christ was here.* While sitting alone at the King David Hotel leafing through the Bible, he read from the Book of Genesis: "And the LORD God planted a garden eastward in Eden." Suddenly, he decided to see Eden for himself.

Though his initial destination had been the Middle East, he now wanted to push ahead to Iraq and Iran (then called Persia), since Iraq was home to the alleged site of the real Garden of

Eden. He contacted the Persian minister in Washington, whose office arranged for a letter of introduction. Persian consul general Phiroz D. Saklatvala assured Ripley that by presenting the letter to the first official he encountered in Persia, he would "receive courteous treatment."

Ripley first traveled north along the coast to Haifa, then stopped in Nazareth and Cana, where he visited a display of the two clay jars in which Jesus was said to have converted water into wine. In Damascus, Syria, he dined on pigeons and watched a cabaret show but found the beggars "more annoying than ever." Joining up with a caravan of buses and cars headed east, Ripley and his one-man camera crew, Simpson, bounced and bucked five hundred miles through the rock-strewn desert. Their chariot was a modified bus whose twelve balloon tires helped it surf over inches-deep sand. With no sign of anything that could be called a *road*, the whole stifling hot expanse of flat desert was a gritty-dusty highway. Ripley sent home a *Believe It or Not* featuring "The Widest Road in the World! It is wider than it is long!"

The caravan drove all day, stopping occasionally for sandwiches (Ripley preferred scotch and sodas), and finally parking for the night at a sprawling compound in the middle of the desert, the fortress of Rutbah Wells, where Ripley was confronted by the drawling voice of his friend, Will Rogers, who was on his way to Damascus.

The two men ate fish for dinner and spent a few evening hours touring the fortress, walking atop the walls and looking out at the fires of the thousands camped outside.

* * *

AFTER A MUCH-NEEDED BATH at Baghdad's Tigris Palace Hotel, Ripley found a tour guide to help him explore his 152nd country. The guide arrived in a brand-new Studebaker. Folded in Ripley's pocket was the letter from the Persian minister's office, which he hoped would ease his travels through this unfamiliar terrain.

At the police station in Karbala, Ripley pulled out the minister's letter and was provided a police escort through the city, "to protect us from any fanatical outbreak on the part of the devout Mohammedans," he wrote in his journal. He witnessed plenty of devotion on the road to Najaf, clogged with Iraqis delivering their dead—in cars and on donkeys—to the massive cemetery in one of the holiest Islamic cities. But the "magic letter," as he called it, failed to protect him and Simpson in Najaf. A group of men started shouting when they saw Simpson's camera aimed at their Koran studies. Simpson was scratched and punched while shoving his way to the Studebaker.

After the roughing-up in Najaf they toured the crumbling remains of the alleged site of the Tower of Babel, which Ripley found to be "a glorified pigeon house." He was even more disappointed upon reaching the alleged site of the Garden of Eden, which was just a barren patch on the banks of the Euphrates. In a forthcoming *Believe It or Not* panel he would dispute the biblical tale of Adam and Eve and speculate that mankind's original transgression was probably eating a fig, not an apple.

Ripley called rural Iraq a land "where ancient history is written in sweat and blood, where life is mixed with horror." Baghdad, on the other hand, was "a man's town, the most masculine place I have ever seen." He spent two more days in Baghdad, filming circular "guffa" boats bobbing along the Tigris River and learning a few of the thousand words for "sword." After a few German beers at a café, Ripley donned the white robe and headdress he'd purchased at a bazaar.

Later, when photos of Ripley in Bedouin garb were transmitted to Hearst's papers, eager copy editors added a bogus description of how Ripley traveled "in disguise during a trip through forbidden country of Near East." An overnight train ride took him to Persia, where he ate herring and drank beer for breakfast. His magic letter barely prevented his film from being confiscated, and he became mesmerized by Persia's women, swathed in black veils and head-to-toe blouses and pantaloons.

∗ ∗ ∗

RIPLEY'S LETTER from Persia's minister eventually turned out to be an invaluable traveling aid. During the seventeen-hour drive from the Iraq border to Tehran, he was stopped nearly every hour by police. He noted in his journal that even with the letter his passage across Persia became entangled in red tape, and "we almost wished we had never heard of this police controlled country." It took a full day to get permission to visit Isfahan, but he soon appreciated the access to "the most beautiful city in Persia."

As usual, Ripley managed to find a drink in the most unlikely of places. In Isfahan he bought strange-tasting beer for $1.25 a bottle and sampled two local drinks, which he soon regretted. He spent his last day and a half in Persia complaining about "too much *pelo* and *mastique*."

On his final night in Tehran—a "much overrated" city—he attacked his nagging hangover with a bottle of warm wine and cheap caviar. As on many previous travels, Ripley was hardly squeamish about sampling local foods, the more exotic the better. He had particularly enjoyed cold tongue salad and oxtail ragout in Baghdad.

Driving north to the Soviet border for a planned crossing into Azerbaijan, Ripley was again stopped often by police, and at every stop a swarm of beggars surrounded his car. He considered Persian beggars "the raggedest and dirtiest of any place in the world." Of course, they may have been just curious locals— Ripley often viewed rural villagers as "beggars." He was an intrepid traveler but not always a compassionate one.

After exiting the many gates of Tehran, Ripley's car, his bags tied atop, slogged for hours through dozens of small towns and walled cities, bypassing nomadic families and their sheep and camels. As the starry night descended Ripley felt the first reluctant stirrings for the age-old beauty of Persia. Stopping for the night in Zingan (later called Zanjan), Ripley followed a tall blond tourist around town but soon learned she was married. He spent his final hours in Persia sulking on his balcony.

At the Aras River Bridge crossing, Ripley and Simpson were forced to wait for hours—at first held up by sluggish Persian border guards savoring their afternoon tea, then by stone-faced Russian solders on the Soviet side, toting rifles and aiming their bayonets at the unarmed cartoonist and his Mormon sidekick.

Ripley jumped when he heard a loud *pop*. It was only the huge bottle of disinfectant he'd been carrying for the past five thousand miles, expecting to need it in Russia. One of the guards had dropped it on the bridge.

✳ ✳ ✳

BACK IN CHICAGO, C. C. Pyle had enlivened his exhibit with a cast of performers that gave the Odditorium a kinky new reputation. Pyle had dropped all pretense, replacing gee-whiz novelty acts with freak-show entertainers. By late summer, as Lou Dufour put it, the Odditorium was "packing them in like sardines in a tin."

Among the new acts: "Crocodile Man" and "Leopard-Skinned

Man" (both victims of skin disease); "Rubber-Skinned Girl" (Agnes C. Schmidt, whose skin ailment caused thick skin on her hips to droop to her knees); "Mule-Faced Lady" (Grace McDaniels, who had enormous, disfiguring facial tumors); and "The Armless Wonder" (who shaved himself, brushed his hair, lit a cigar, and threw knives at a female model—with his *toes*).

A crowd favorite was Betty Lou Williams, "The Girl with Four Legs and Three Arms." Betty Lou was born two years earlier to a poor family in rural Georgia with the remains of her twin sister's undeveloped body emerging grotesquely from her torso—two lifeless legs, pelvis, and one arm. Odditorium visitors were told that X-rays showed the "perfectly developed" head of Betty Lou's parasitic twin inside her abdomen. Doctors had been unable to remove the extremities of Betty Lou's sister, so her parents agreed to let a sideshow man take her to New York. Pyle paid Betty Lou's parents $250 a week to appear in Ripley's show—more than five times what other performers received. The toddler stood in diapers and white booties, or sat in the arms of a nurse, her deformed body exposed to bug-eyed crowds for twelve hours a day.

Another popular new performer was Martin Laurello, the "Human Owl." Laurello had spent three years in training, twisting his head and neck farther and farther until he could turn his head 180 degrees and look backward. Equally unsettling were the feats of Singlee, the "Hindu Fire Worshipper," who aimed a flaming blowtorch at his face, and Leo Kongee, "The Human Pin Cushion," who nailed pins into his head, sewed buttons into his flesh, and fastened socks to his legs with safety pins.

Then there was adorable Frieda Pushnik, the "Armless, Legless Girl Wonder." A healthy baby, except for her missing arms and legs (the result of a botched appendectomy performed during pregnancy), Frieda grew to be impressively independent, learning to dress and feed herself, to sew, write, and draw using her teeth, chin, and the small nubs where her arms should have been. Frieda traveled the sideshow circuit with her mother and sister but always introduced her own performances, sitting atop a pillow and telling audiences, "I'm Frieda Kathryn Pushnik. I'm nine years old and I attend public school." She would thread a needle and sew a few stitches, piece together a jigsaw puzzle, then write a few words on a notepad by wedging a pencil beneath her chin. Her show lasted just a few minutes, but she repeated it over and over, sometimes sixteen hours a day. Frieda earned extra money signing souvenir photographs in her near-perfect, swooping script, "Best Wishes, Frieda." (Her handwriting had received a national penmanship award from the creators of the Palmer Method.)

Said one newspaper reporter, "At the Ripley 'Believe-It-or-Not' Odditorium her cheery smile has won her a host of friends."

＊ ＊ ✻

RIPLEY OFTEN CLAIMED to detest the word "freak," preferring to think of his religious fanatics and disfigured performers as "oddities" or "queeriosities." But as more spectators sought out Cash & Carry Pyle's revamped exhibit that summer and fall in Chicago, it quickly became obvious that Ripley's Odditorium had become nothing less than a spiffed-up adaptation of a Barnum-esque *freak show*.

P. T. Barnum had launched his own showbiz career by tight-roping between entertainment and exploitation, starting in 1835 when he toured with a blind, emaciated slave billed as George Washington's 161-year-old former nurse. Barnum gave his acts catchy names, nearly identical to the ones Ripley now used—"Human Pincushion" and "Armless Wonder"—while avoiding the term "freak." Barnum preferred to call his performers "living wonders" or "human curiosities."

After Barnum's death in 1891 (and the death of his partner, James Bailey), his shows were bought by five Wisconsin brothers named Ringling, who turned the Ringling Bros. and Barnum & Bailey Circus into the largest purveyor of human oddities during the first decades of the 1900s. Many Ringling Bros. sideshow performers were featured in a controversial 1932 film called *Freaks,* whose graphic portrayal of Siamese twins and fat ladies, half boys and armless girls disgusted critics and viewers alike. Some theaters posted warnings: "Children positively not admitted. Adults not in normal health are not advised to see this picture." The film was banned in many cities, which may have heightened the public's curiosity and lured them to Ripley's 1933 show.

Burton Holmes roamed the fairgrounds, too, filming and photographing the sites—"Midget Village," nudie shows, the smallest couple in the world, and "the world's tallest man"— having "the time of my life," as he put it, collecting footage for a travelogue about the fair that he'd present in 1934.

With the Odditorium costing forty cents and most exhibits and rides costing a quarter, *Variety* magazine called it all "a poor man's carnival." There was plenty of traditional wholesomeness— carousels, Ferris wheels, and the midway; roving clowns and jugglers; nightly fireworks. But the dominant theme was guilty pleasure, with the most popular concessions and nightclubs peddling sexuality or freakishness. Even Texas Guinan, Ripley's friend and speakeasy matron from New York, brought a troupe of beautiful, barely clad women to her "Dance Ship" exhibit.

✳ ✳ ✳

BUGS BAER, in his Hearst-syndicated column, called the Odditorium the fair's highlight. "Rip has collected every amazing freak in the world," Baer wrote.

Ripley later claimed he had to keep six beds on hand for the hundred people a day who fainted. Despite the exaggeration, people *did* faint after seeing some performances, and Pyle stowed cots in an alley, a makeshift hospital where a nurse cracked smelling salts beneath the noses of queasy or unconscious patrons.

Though Ripley wouldn't learn the details until returning from his travels later that fall, the Odditorium was an unexpectedly huge success, earning $400,000—proof that makeshift sideshows were another lucrative outlet for his Believe It or Not franchise, even if it also earned some harsh accusations of exploitation. Syndicated *Chicago Tribune* columnist Westbrook Pegler had mercilessly mocked Pyle that summer for his "exotic educational innovations." Pegler reminded readers of Pyle's failed Bunion Derby and his ownership of the Oklahoma Outlaw corpse, calling Pyle "an insidious teacher who stoops to conquer ignorance." The implication was that, by association, Ripley was insidious as well.

Until now, Ripley had mostly avoided any close affiliation with the sideshow world of the deformed and the abnormal. If his cartoons featured people with birth defects or disfiguring injuries, they were often long dead or distant foreigners—the Chinese man with two sets of pupils, for example, or the horned African. But by leasing his name to Pyle's show, he had crossed a boundary, moving further away from athletes or prodigies or even religious fanatics as his hard-to-believe subjects.

In truth, the terrain had beckoned for years. Ripley's contorted teeth had fostered a kinship with those afflicted by bodies or faces that had failed them, sometimes horribly, but who still managed to live useful or at least hopeful lives. It's that attitude that allowed Harry Overdurff, whose bones had fused and turned his body stiff and boardlike, to earn money at Ripley's Odditorium as the "Ossified Man." To Ripley, such people were the ultimate underdogs, wonders of nature and worthy of attention.

Now that he was famous enough to pursue personal obsessions, he had grown comfortable filling his cartoons, radio shows, and now his Odditorium with such people. He had also grown more comfortable exploiting the legions of devotees who did bizarre things to their bodies in order to gain Ripley's attention. If these people were willing to invest the time necessary to learn how to swallow three gallons of water and regurgitate it into a jar, Ripley had no problem giving "The Human Fountain" a moment in the spotlight.

"A man may be too foolish for his own good, but not for mine," he once said. "Their folly is my fortune. I'll get rich off the ridiculous yet."

* * *

ALTHOUGH IT OCCURRED during one of the lowest points in the Depression, the Century of Progress Exhibition succeeded far beyond its organizers' hopes. Even recently inaugurated president Franklin Roosevelt went so far as to encourage Chicago officials to resurrect the fair for a second year. Ripley's Odditorium was among the concessions that would be invited back for an encore run in the summer of 1934.

Instead of sending his performers home until mid-1934, Pyle quickly put together a traveling show, loading entertainers onto buses and driving to Cleveland, where a temporary downtown Odditorium was created, and from there onward to Pittsburgh and Washington. A Pittsburgh sports editor who had previously worked with Ripley wrote, "Who would have thought that the young Bob Ripley we knew as a sports cartoonist some years ago would put together a show such as this one? Bob was such a quiet, bashful guy, and now he's knocking the world's eye out with his amazing exhibit."

At that moment, Ripley had finally embarked on the last legs of his most exhaustive—and controversial—journey in years, performing his part in the broader *Believe It or Not* show. Because, while freaks onstage were clearly profitable, for the formula to succeed Ripley needed to maintain his reputation as an outlandish traveler.

*　*　*

AFTER BEING FORCED to wait for hours in no-man's-land, halfway between Persia and Azerbaijan, Ripley was finally allowed to cross into Soviet territory. His bags were delivered late that night by ox-pulled dray to an inn, where he and Simpson dined hungrily on canned salmon and slept a few hours in a dirty room, then awoke before dawn to board a train. They immediately fell asleep, but woke at sunrise to catch Mount Ararat out their window as they passed through Armenia.

The slow-moving train was filthy, the toilets backed up and black, and there was no food or water available during the daylong trip into Georgia. Ripley and Simpson were joined by two official escorts from InTourist, the Soviet travel agency created four years earlier by Joseph Stalin. The view outside their windows was a sprawling blur of concrete buildings that Ripley joked was the Soviets' "last word in modern housing." During layovers in small towns, the best Ripley could find to eat was cabbage soup and black bread. At each town he saw gaunt-looking families hovering around the station collecting scraps of food. With the help of some vodka, he managed to sleep and to avoid the rainy, homely landscape outside. He would soon publish his initial assessment of the Soviet Union, describing "the filthiest train I have ever seen in 158 countries" and impoverished citizens who never smiled.

During an overnight stop in the Georgian capital of Tiflis (soon to be renamed Tbilisi), he had to maneuver his way across a treacherous train platform maligned by missing planks and rotted holes toward a smelly hotel room. In Tiflis, Ripley decided to abandon the train and drive into Russia, against the advice of his InTourist guides, who warned that the Caucasus Mountains had received eighteen inches of snow the previous night and the pass might be closed.

When Ripley insisted, his escorts reluctantly found a car and a chauffeur, but the car broke down a few hours into the next morning's drive. While waiting for a replacement, Ripley and Simpson ate lunch with a family of "peasants" (Ripley's word) as dogs and pigs scurried beneath their legs. The driver returned with another car and they continued into the mountains, but at a crowded mountainside inn they were warned not to proceed, that they'd all freeze and die. Ripley agreed to wait until morning and drank vodka with his hosts until he grew sleepy, then curled up on a cot still wearing his clothes and overcoat.

The next morning, his driver inched through deep snow toward the pass, the car sliding on and off the serpentine road. The driver had forgotten to bring tire chains, but it looked like they might have enough momentum to climb the final mile—until they were stopped short by a farmer's horse-pulled wagon, stuck in the snow and blocking the pass. Ripley and Simpson helped the farmer push his horse cart aside, but then the car refused to budge and it looked as if the previous night's warnings had been correct, that they'd perish up there at 7,800 feet. Incredibly, four hours later, two poor farmers came plodding through thigh-high snowdrifts with a team of oxen. The men hooked their oxen to the car and slowly pulled it over the top, with Ripley and the others pushing and shoveling. In film footage of the dangerous crossing (recorded by Simpson), Ripley appears giddy, almost euphoric, having the time of his life.

Later that afternoon, they snaked down the north slope of the Caucasus range into a mining village and ate their first meal of the day—cabbage soup. Ripley wisely decided to ditch the car and catch a train. A mile from the station, though, the driver pulled over with a flat. Hearing a train whistle, Ripley and Simpson grabbed their bags and ran to the station, only to learn their train would be five hours late.

It would take another month to reach New York, an extended anticlimax after the experiences of Iraq, Persia, and Georgia. Ripley briefly visited Moscow ("a hard, severe, unromantic, and inartistic city") and Leningrad ("clean and dignified"), where he was given a tour of a hospital and watched Russian surgeons perform an abortion. He was surprised by Soviet health care, especially the free contraceptives. Two things he admired: Russia's vodka and its liberal sexual mores. "Sexual intercourse in Russia is not looked down upon at all, as it is in our conventional country, but is regarded purely as a human necessity and treated as such," he wrote, revealing his own view.

Still, he was hugely relieved to reach Finland, which felt instantly cleaner, more civilized, and friendlier. It seemed as if everyone on the train sighed and smiled with relief "to be out of Sovietland." During two weeks in Russia, he had seen few smiles.

⁕ ⁕ ⁕

RIPLEY OFTEN JOKED that he traveled so much—two-thirds of the past five years spent on the road, by his estimate—to stay ahead of Prohibition agents and find a good drink. While roving the world he had swilled gin slings in Singapore, chota pegs in Bombay, cold Champagne in Panama, and even cold beer in Iraq. Days after his return from Russia, however, the Twenty-first Amendment was ratified, repealing the Eighteenth Amendment and finally putting an end to Prohibition.

Burton Holmes was among those who cheered the end of "the dark fourteen years." With Prohibition good and dead, Ripley no longer needed Manhattan's speakeasy scene to accommodate his drinking bouts. That scene had been diminished anyway by the passing of Texas Guinan, who died in November at age forty-nine, a month shy of seeing the conclusion of America's experiment in abstinence.

During the same fourteen years of Prohibition, Ripley had been living at the NYAC, in what one interviewer described as a newspaper's city room—"if a city room had hats and shirts and things strewn around it as well as crumpled newspapers and such." Until recently, it had been all the home Ripley needed, since his real home had been foreign hotel rooms or ocean-liner cabins. But the NYAC—and even the city itself—had begun to feel a bit tight.

By early 1934, Ripley had come to the conclusion that, at age forty-four, it was time to move out of the NYAC, and even out of Manhattan, leaving the handballer/bachelor/Prohibition-violator lifestyle behind to find a residence suitable for a middle-aged millionaire.

CHAPTER

16

Five years after the Wall Street crash, President Roosevelt ramped up his New Deal efforts to get hungry and unemployed Americans back to work. Violent dust storms scoured the Great Plains. Farmers lost their homesteads to foreclosure. Factory workers were striking.

And Robert Ripley flourished, making money seemingly without trying. Unscathed by the lumbering events of the Depression, cash and new contracts and profitable new offers found him, practically *chased* him, and his income kept dancing skyward. Even Uncle Sam threw money at him, issuing a much-publicized $20,000 Treasury Department refund after Ripley complained he'd been overtaxed in 1931.

Though exact numbers are elusive, his income from newspaper, radio, books, endorsements, film, and his Odditorium was believed to be at least half a million dollars a year (the equivalent of nearly $9 million in 2012 dollars). He was far outearning any cartoonist in the business. One columnist referred to him as "the six-figure gent."

"Last year was the worst year of the depression but it affected cartooning very little compared to other industries," said a 1933 article in *Modern Mechanix* magazine titled "How Comic Cartoons Make Fortunes," which featured Ripley atop the list of "big money makers in the funnies," ahead of Rube Goldberg, George McManus, Bud Fisher, and even Walt Disney. "Why? Because editors wanted more and more 'funnies' to cheer people and help them forget their troubles."

For two decades he had lived and worked in the heart of a metropolis that featured more floodlit glitz than any similar patch of land. But with the means to live wherever and however he chose, he decided to leave the island of Manhattan and buy an island of his own, trading his cramped apartment for an over-the-top residence twenty-five times larger.

Using his acronym for "Believe It or Not," he called his grandiose new home BION Island.

* * *

THE DECISION TO LEAVE New York surprised many friends, who assumed he would be content to live at the NYAC forever. Said one columnist, shortly before Ripley moved north, "Those close to him perceive no indication that he'll ever move into more commodious quarters. Probably he feels that to keep two rooms littered is work enough."

Yet, as he would explain in a magazine article, Ripley had been feeling rootless—"like the proverbial sailor who is always a-sea but looks forward to the time when he may have a home of his own, to be embellished with mementoes of his sea travels." Traveling so far and so often, he had accumulated too many artifacts and collectibles, stashing them in warehouses but frustrated by the inability to *do something* with them. He was finally ready to free that booty from its storage crates, to put it on display, and enjoy it.

Ripley had been visiting Mamaroneck and surrounding Westchester County for years. The NYAC had built its Winged Foot Golf Club there in 1922. Joseph Connolly, Ripley's boss at King Features, and Max Schuster lived in Westchester County, as did other newspaper and radio friends.

An old town, full of odd historical facts and characters, Mamaroneck was an ideal fit. An ethnically diverse home to shipbuilders, textile workers, and fishermen, it began attracting theatre people after D. W. Griffith, director of the 1915 film *Birth of a Nation*, bought an estate there and built a studio, turning Mamaroneck into a miniature Hollywood. Mary Pickford and Lillian and Dorothy Gish moved there, as did Ethel Barrymore, who wrote in a memoir that Mamaroneck was just twenty miles from New York but "might just as well be a million miles."

Trolleys ran up and down the main street, an old Indian trail now called the Boston Post Road, and Manhattan was less than an hour away by train. In a sense, it was like an East Coast version of the Santa Rosa–San Francisco link of his youth, with Ripley living in the country village an hour north of the big city.

Ripley's island was at the end of Taylors Lane, which branched off Boston Post Road. He bought it for $85,000 from John Eberson, an architect who had designed movie theaters but lost his fortune as the Depression took its toll on the film business. A stone causeway led out to three acres of lawns, gardens, tall pine trees, rocky outcroppings, and swampy marshes. The centerpiece was a twenty-eight-room English-style manor of stucco and stone, built in 1910 atop a rock mound at the center of the island. The homestead also contained a smaller house, a garage, and a boathouse, all of it surrounded by a tidal pool that had been severed from Long Island Sound by a dam.

With oak floors and dark-wood paneling, the mansion's shadowy interior resembled an elegant lodge or the NYAC's dining hall and saloon. Scattered across three stories were bedrooms, sitting rooms, a solarium, a dark room, a steam room, and a gymnasium. Windows were scarce, but drafty. Ripley soon learned the old house was difficult to heat in the winter, musty in summer.

A Gothic living room looked out onto the Sound, always busy with boats and gulls. Above the huge fireplace, Ripley hung the 1918 "Champs and Chumps" cartoon in a frame, with the original title crossed out and "Believe It or Not" written beside it. Later, he would encase the cartoon behind a mirror and surprise guests by flipping a hidden switch that turned on a light, revealing the cartoon that had started it all. He now had a place to display the beam he'd received from his childhood house. He hung it in his favorite room: the basement bar.

He began unpacking crates that had been in storage, some of them for years. In time, the mansion would become his personal Odditorium, more a museum than a house and surely one of the more bizarre dwellings in all of New York. At first, it was an absolute mess, the rooms cluttered with javelins, mastodon and elephant tusks, boomerangs, skeletons, and war drums. Hand-carved cabinets of teak and mahogany set askew. Turkish and Oriental rugs piled up on the floors. In the garage were scores of crates, boxes, and trunks stuffed with wooden statues and carvings, musky-smelling python skins and stuffed animals, a huge bell from Japan that could ring for twenty minutes, all waiting to be unpacked.

There wasn't much time to get settled, though. He first had to loan some of his souvenirs to the Odditorium in Chicago, where C. C. Pyle's exhibition was reopening for its encore season at the Chicago World's Fair.

✳ ✻ ✺

RIPLEY PLAYED a more aggressive role in the 1934 Odditorium, promising in a King Features press release that the new Odditorium would be "bigger and in every way better . . . the greatest congress of oddities and curios in the world today."

After the surprising success of the 1933 Odditorium, Ripley followed Pyle's lead and willingly crossed more fully into Barnum territory, advising Simpson by handwritten letter: "No sword swallowers. Too Coney Island." Instead, he wanted an "Up-Arm man" from India, a "Sun-gazer," and a "Hindu sitting on nails." He wanted the seven-foot-nine-inch Buddhist monk from Korea and Kikuyu women wearing plate-sized earrings from Africa. He wanted men who ate glass, drank boiling water, stuck knives through their cheeks or spikes in their noses. He wanted a horned girl.

Ripley considered himself and his sideshow more reputable than P. T. Barnum, who was known for fakery and deceit. Instead of Exit signs, Barnum sometimes posted signs that said Egress, luring rubes and illiterates outside and forcing them to pay to reenter. Barnum sometimes claimed that the public *liked* to be tricked, that it was all a game. Ripley disagreed, once telling an interviewer, "Barnum was wrong. The public doesn't like to be fooled. And I'm happy to say I've never fooled my public. Not that the public always thinks so."

Among those returning for the 1934 Chicago show were Frieda Pushnik ("The Little Half Girl"), Leo Kongee ("The Human Pincushion"), Singlee ("The Fireproof Man"), and Betty Williams, who had learned to walk and could display the gruesome remains of her twin sister while standing on two of her four feet. New acts included a man who puffed cigarettes through a hole in his back and one who could break six-inch nails in half with his teeth. Ripley hired Swami See Ram Lai, a Hindu ascetic he'd met in Benares, who skewered his tongue with a long needle, then meditated. Ripley called him "The Great Tongue-Tied."

His proudest oddity was a recently purchased statue, a freakishly lifelike and anatomically correct self-portrait of a Japanese artist.

Diagnosed with tuberculosis in the mid-1800s, Hananuma Masakichi had intended for the sculpture to be a dying gift to his lover. Working in the nude and surrounded by mirrors, he painstakingly re-created every muscle, wrinkle, and sinew of his body. Starting with his feet and moving upward, he glued together thousands of wood strips, then etched and sanded his likeness into the wood. He crafted startlingly realistic glass eyes and then—Ripley loved this part—drilled tiny holes to match each pore on his body and filled them with strands of his own hair. Upon completion, with hair on its arms, legs, head, face, and genitals, the statue looked like its creator in every way. Some newspaper stories later falsely claimed that the artist even pulled out his own fingernails, toenails, and teeth and inserted them in his statue.

After finishing his masterpiece in 1885, Masakichi held exhibits, standing perfectly still next to his creation as viewers tried to figure out which wiry figure was statue and which was man. Masakichi died ten years later at age sixty-three.

Ripley had known of the statue for years, having seen it at a curio shop when he'd first moved to San Francisco. When he learned it was still there, he arranged to have it shipped to Chicago—one worker shrieked when they unpacked the crate. (In one retelling, Ripley claimed to have bought the entire store from the reluctant proprietor in order to get the statue.) Ripley called it "the greatest piece of art in the world."

Missing from the May-through-October fair would be Lou Dufour's "Darkest Africa," the victim of an NAACP antidiscrimination campaign, and the girly joint run by Texas Guinan, now dead. But the fair's second season would be as popular as the first, with more than forty million visitors during the two seasons combined. Ripley's Odditorium would draw more than two million and Pyle's final balance sheet showed a profit of $500,000.

What Pyle didn't reveal was the $10,000 he'd paid Lou Dufour for helping to restyle the show. Dufour felt he deserved more, complaining that Pyle had agreed in 1933 to pay him 3 percent of the *gross* ticket sales. Pyle refused. Since they only had a handshake deal, Dufour accepted the $10,000 but promised to get revenge someday.

The half-million-dollar success of the partnership inspired Ripley and Pyle to create an ongoing series of Odditoriums, a self-perpetuating side business. Pyle started making plans for the next World's Fair events: San Diego in 1935, Dallas in 1936, and Cleveland in 1937.

* * *

AFTER CUTTING BACK on his radio schedule to travel during the previous two years, Ripley returned to the airwaves in 1934 with a global gimmick that made headlines and earned him another new partner.

He assembled a team of sixteen linguists and squeezed them onto a stage. Surrounded by rows of microphones, they translated Ripley's show into their respective languages. The show was broadcast using a transmitter linked to radio networks and shortwave transmitters in other countries, allowing Ripley to claim he had performed the first radio show to be broadcast simultaneously around the world.

RIPLEY TALKS TO WHOLE WORLD, said the next day's headlines, noting that the show had been picked up in China, Japan, Italy, Germany, Sweden, Holland, Argentina, Persia, and beyond. The man behind the curtain on that record-setting broadcast was Doug Storer, a self-taught master of such gimmicks.

Born near Harlem in 1899, Storer had graduated from Dartmouth with a medical degree but ditched his doctoring plans to run the radio department at a Chicago ad agency. He left advertising to manage a cousin's radio stations in Toledo and Detroit, then became director of radio for the Blackman Company, producing shows for the United States Rubber Company, Procter & Gamble, and Hudson Motor Car.

Ripley had first met Storer a couple years earlier during an appearance on NBC's *Saturday Night Dancing Party* radio show, which Storer helped produce. An hour before airtime, Storer was running around the studio, handing out scripts and barking orders. He saw Ripley sneak quietly through a side door and would never forget Ripley's outfit: a pale-blue shirt, an orange batwing tie, a plaid jacket, tan slacks, and black-and-white shoes.

"*You're* Bob Ripley?" Storer asked.

Ripley bowed slightly, "grinning like an embarrassed schoolboy," as Storer later put it. He suspected Ripley had been drinking.

All Ripley had to do that night was read a brief introduction to a dramatic reenactment of one of his *Believe It or Not* cartoons, which would be performed by actors. At the microphone, he stammered through the introduction, his voice shaky, his hands shakier. He dropped the script and, when he bent to retrieve it, almost knocked over the microphone. After the show, he went straight to the control room.

"H-how'd I do?" Ripley asked Storer, who couldn't believe the celebrity cartoonist cared what *he* thought.

Feeling obliged to be honest, Storer said, "You need a little practice."

Storer was shocked to find Ripley so shy and self-conscious, yearning for approval. But he was impressed that Ripley seemed game for anything, especially broadcasts that accomplished something new and unique. Storer knew of Ripley's previous exploits over the airwaves: transmitting a cartoon from London to New York (1926), broadcasting from ship to shore (1931), and broadcasting from Australia to New York (1932).

It had been Storer's idea to hire translators and attempt the simultaneous worldwide broadcast, which served its intended purpose and earned Ripley a new radio show.

On Hudson Motor Car Company's *Terraplane Program,* with bandleader B. A. Rolfe conducting the "Terraplane Orchestra," Ripley played a smallish role introducing live reenactments of scenes depicted in his cartoons. Sometimes Bugs Baer served as emcee—he was a natural—and Ripley had a scant few lines. Storer felt that with more speech lessons and practice, Ripley could land an even bigger sponsor. Ripley agreed and invited Storer to work for him full-time, offering Storer 10 percent of all his radio income. Storer soon proved worth his commission. When the *Terraplane Program* ended in 1935, he convinced NBC that Ripley was ready for a show of his own. He landed a deal with the *Baker's Broadcast,* sponsored by food conglomerate Standard Brands. The show would air in prime time on Sunday nights, with Ripley as the host, assisted by a sidekick/bandleader named Ozzie Nelson and Nelson's soon-to-be wife, the singer Harriet Hilliard.

Storer made sure the new Ripley-and-Ozzie-and-Harriet

partnership received plenty of newspaper ink, and telegrammed congratulations poured in. "You're the nuts," the actress Beatrice Lillie wired, and Jimmy Durante wished him "good luck." Jack Dempsey wrote, "You're a knockout to me." Storer became a true believer in the Believe It or Not brand and, like Norbert Pearlroth and others, another moonstruck apostle eager to lash his career to Ripley's.

Storer loved Ripley's lack of pretense or polish, his unrehearsed authenticity. The public seemed smitten too. "In fact, the pubic *liked* Ripley's awkward manner," Storer said later, describing him as "boyish and appealing, so earnest and honest."

It was that same boyish, earnest appeal that had drawn Pearlroth to Ripley a decade earlier. Back in 1923, as Frank Munsey tore apart the newspaper network that had been Ripley's support base, Pearlroth was Ripley's most loyal accomplice. Lately, though, as Joseph Connolly and Ripley's brother and now Doug Storer came aboard, Pearlroth felt a distance growing between him and his boss. Yet, even as he felt shoved aside a little, he was unwilling to walk away from his "dream job."

Storer, meanwhile, seemed to have found his own dream job. He felt that his previous careers, as adman, radio producer, and talent agent, had all been leading him to Ripley.

Like Ripley's other benefactors—Max Schuster, William Randolph Hearst, and C. C. Pyle—Storer possessed a keen sense of what the audience wanted, even if he sometimes tested sponsors' patience. He and Ripley pitched one show in which circus performer James Mandy—alleged owner of the hardest head in the world—would head-butt a goat. When a humane society accused Ripley of cruelty to animals, NBC officials nixed the idea. Ripley and Storer also once considered the proposal of a terminally ill man who wanted to kill himself on the air—for $5,000.

Though they declined the offer, Ripley told Storer, "It would have been a helluva show."

* * *

HEARST CONTINUED to be a tolerant patron, letting Ripley push the boundaries of radio and indulging his cartoonist's perpetual traveling and forays into freak shows. Hearst also protected Ripley from the economics of the troubled news business. When King Features proposed cutting costs by reducing the size of Ripley's Sunday cartoons, Ripley complained to Hearst that it would be "harmful" to the Believe It or Not name.

"This is quite true," Hearst wrote back. "We will resume the larger sizes later."

Hearst was less accommodating when Ripley defied him, as he did when he continued to accept offers to endorse products in magazine ads, or when Ripley willfully crossed into territory that might cost Hearst subscribers.

Ripley had grown more politically conservative by the mid-1930s, distrustful of Roosevelt's New Deal and suspicious of Communist-friendly politicians and policies. He and Storer tussled frequently over Ripley's spontaneous pontificating on the air. When Upton Sinclair lost his 1934 campaign for governor of California, Ripley congratulated his birth state for its "good sense in rejecting a man who would turn [California] into another Soviet state."

As fear of communism and socialism slowly infected America, Ripley became more vocal in airing his views on the dangerous shortcomings of the Soviet way of life. His tiff with the Soviet empire had begun in late 1933, following his trek through Azerbaijan, Georgia, and Russia. Months later, he'd written an article for Hearst's *International Cosmopolitan* magazine, describing his Soviet travels as the most miserable of his life.

"It is always misty in Russia . . . the sun never shines," he wrote, claiming that citizens had grown dour and fearful after more than a decade of Soviet rule. "There is no God in Russia. Lenin has taken the place of Christ," said Ripley, who called Lenin "the Deity of the Downtrodden."

True, Ripley had been reluctantly impressed by Russia's social liberalism, free health care, and liberal sexuality, and he even worried that "Sovietism" might catch on, that the USSR could become "one of the strongest nations in the world." In early 1935, however, he shared a more critical account of his Russian visit in a speech to the Crusaders, an organization initially created to fight Prohibition that had grown into an aggressive anti-Communist consortium. Ripley claimed that Russians never smiled or laughed because they were *starving to death*. The Soviet government stole farmers' grain, he said, forcing people to "subsist on dogs, cats, weeds and grass." Ripley's address was broadcast on radio and reprinted on the front page of Hearst's *New York American*. The headline: "I SAW STARVATION IN RUSSIA," SAYS BOB RIPLEY.

His accusations were extreme. And, as they appeared to give voice to Hearst's own outsized fears of communism, they raised some eyebrows:

"Everybody in Russia is a prisoner of the government."

"Russia is a gigantic poorhouse where millions of people are on the verge of starvation."

"Outside of Moscow and Leningrad—the Soviet showplaces—starvation stalks through squalor and filth."

The *Daily Worker* newspaper, published by the Communist Party of America, ridiculed Ripley's claims, pointing out that he was only in-country for two weeks and spent most of his time on trains. The writer called Ripley a "well-known Hearst stooge" and a "phony."

It's unknown whether Hearst, no fan of communism himself, played any role in Ripley's tirades. Hearst complained often of Roosevelt's "socialistic" tendencies and felt the New Deal nurtured a socialist movement in America, and he'd recently argued that his media empire needed to "make a powerful crusade against Communism . . . if we want to retain our liberties." So it's plausible that Hearst and/or Connolly lurked behind Ripley's vocal accusations.

Still, Ripley's scuffle with Russia might have petered out if he hadn't mischievously attempted another visit to "Sovietland."

* * *

IN EARLY 1936, Ripley began planning yet another around-the-world trip and applied for permission to enter Siberia, in far eastern Russia. When his visa application was denied, he complained to the US secretary of state, whose office responded: "It is not the practice of this Government to intervene in such matters." Ripley then sent copies of his letter, as well as the secretary of state's response, to the media and members of Congress, igniting a political firestorm.

Legislators tripped over themselves to denounce Ripley's "ban" from Russia. Congressman John McCormack of Massachusetts, who chaired a committee investigating un-American activities, called it "a suppression of the truth" that would "crystallize American opinion" of the failures of communism. One New York representative defended Ripley as an "outstanding American cartoonist whose honesty has never been questioned."

Such foot stomping made Ripley an instant hero among

nationalists and right-wing organizations. Harry Jung, head of the American Vigilant Intelligence Federation, thanked Ripley on behalf of his "group of patriots" and encouraged him to "Go after the Bolsheviks!" Ripley suddenly had to consider how far to exploit this new renown. He asked Joe Simpson to look into a possible series of anti-Communist radio broadcasts, but Simpson warned that it might alienate advertisers and listeners. "Not on a commercial radio program," Simpson advised. "Also doubtful of NBC letting it on the air."

Ripley kept stoking the anti-Communist theme. In one Sunday-night broadcast he complained about his inability to visit Russia and promised to discuss the reason for the ban the following week. He immediately received a letter of admonishment from the advertising firm J. Walter Thompson Company, warning that the show's sponsor, Standard Brands, wanted no mention of "Russia, Soviet or Communism." Ripley then petulantly fired off letters directly to Standard Brand executives and board members, scolding them while also imploring them to reconsider.

"I am astounded that Standard Brands takes this attitude, because I feel everyone should do all possible to combat the un-American institutions," he wrote.

When a Standard Brands executive replied that his company had to remain "non-partisan and non-political," Ripley appealed to a higher authority. In a telegram to Hearst, he wrote:

I cannot understand such attitude of men who would be first to lose their shirts and heads should Communism succeed in America STOP I would like to write a speech like one I did April fourth last year and broadcast special half hour program over National Broadcasting nationwide STOP Would appreciate your suggestions and assistance.

Hearst's response, if any, is lost to history, but Doug Storer soon received an urgent letter from NBC vice president John Royal. "Be sure Ripley doesn't say anything about Russia in any way, shape or form on Sunday night," said Royal, advising Storer that "everyone will be saved embarrassment."

Ripley complied, but found other ways to snipe. At St. Thomas Episcopal Church in Mamaroneck, he delivered an address titled "How God Is Worshipped All Over the World." With religion banned in Russia, he said it was vital for other lands to explore "the mystery of whence we came and whither we are going." The many religious customs he'd witnessed over the years "are all pointing in the same direction," he said. "They are trying to make the pathway of life more pleasant."

He continued: "The greatest thing in life is faith. . . . Whatever your religious belief is, believe in it very much."

A nonpracticing Christian, Ripley never made it clear exactly where his own faith lay, except maybe a deep belief in the strange truths of life. And in himself.

＊　＊　＊

IN JANUARY OF 1936, Congress released a report on the previous year's highest-paid Americans. While not a definitive list, the report found that sixteen people had earned more than $300,000; nine were General Motors employees, with GM president Alfred P. Sloan Jr. topping the list at $561,311. Ten movie and radio stars reported income in excess of $200,000, with Gary Cooper making $370,214.

Ripley was not mentioned, possibly because his income came from various sources and no single corporation. Nonetheless, the curious cartoonist from Santa Rosa was now earning as much as GM's president and ranked among the highest-paid men in America.

He was also, by at least one measure, one of the most popular.

The Boys Club of New York conducted a nationwide survey that spring of 1936, asking thousands of boys between the ages of eight and eighteen one question: "If you had your choice of all the jobs in the world, whose job would you want?" Walter Winchell ranked tenth—"because he knows everything before it happens," one boy wrote. President Roosevelt was seventh, boxer Jack Dempsey sixth. Such notables as Henry Ford, golfer Bobby Jones, and aviator Charles Lindbergh didn't even crack the top dozen. Movie star James Cagney ranked third, preceded by FBI director J. Edgar Hoover.

Overwhelmingly, the boys preferred the job of that buck-toothed cartoonist, world traveler, and radio and film star Robert L. Ripley—who must've felt an extra thrill to have beaten Roosevelt. Among the boys' reasons:

> "He gets 'round a lot."
>
> "He is so busy with his radio speeches, drawings, and trips that he doesn't have time to get into mischief."
>
> "He meets interesting people and freaks." (Rube Goldberg noted in his column that President Roosevelt also met many freaks, "only he keeps quiet about it.")

The widely publicized survey set off a flurry of editorials seeking to make sense of the values of America's youth. "He is engrossed in life, as shown by a desire to go places and see things," said the *Nashville Tennessean*. A *Columbus Dispatch* editor said, "Ripley makes a great deal of money just doing the things which the youth would like to do."

Boys recognized in Ripley a kindred spirit, a whimsical child in a man's body who displayed "that priceless quality of naive and youthful wonder," said a columnist friend of Ripley's.

"The wide-eyed, innocent curiosity that started Bob Ripley along the trail of fame more than 15 years ago burns as brightly today as ever," O. B. Keeler wrote. "He is still a youngster . . . and he can never grow old, for the freshness of life is an eternal dew in his heart."

LeRoy Robert Ripley was becoming a real-life Peter Pan.

Later that year, the New York Boy Scout Foundation honored Ripley at a star-studded benefit dinner chaired by Hearst and held at the Waldorf-Astoria in New York. Among the attendees were Lou Gehrig, Walter Winchell, and many of New York's top cartoonists. More than two thousand people paid $10 apiece to attend, raising scads of money for Ripley's favorite charity, the Boy Scouts of Greater New York.

Ripley had been traveling and arrived, theatrically, just in time for dinner. Wearing white socks with his dark suit, Ripley was surrounded by autograph seekers, patiently signing copies of his book, the backs of envelopes, scraps of paper. As if striving to live up to recent accolades, he told the attendees about his latest exploration throughout Greece, Africa, India, and Afghanistan.

But the world as Ripley knew it had begun changing. Due to political upheaval and the storm clouds of war, lands he had recently visited were shifting allegiances and changing names. Latvia had become a dictatorship. Persia had become Iran. Adolf Hitler, Germany's hawkish president, was expanding his army, building an air force, conspiring with Italy. In China, Mao Tse-tung's Communist Army had been forced into retreat by Japan's Imperial Army, even as many rural Chinese, left hungry and homeless by famine and civil war, wondered if communism might save them. Across Europe and Asia, nations were realigning—Communist or Socialist or Fascist—teaming up and choosing sides.

None of which was good news for a man who, as fourteen-year-old Leroy Smith had put it to pollsters, "goes all around the world, has brains, and is always having adventures."

The future for adventure was looking bleak as Ripley's foreign playgrounds tilted toward war, one after the other. For Ripley, it was like watching a curtain slowly close. And he worried: If he couldn't travel at will, what would fuel his cartoons? If he couldn't experience the wonders of the world and translate and reinterpret them in print and on air, what would stoke his followers' dreams?

As one of the most popular men in America, Ripley reigned among the most eligible, with an international playboy's reputation nurtured in the gossip pages.

"Almost always in public he is squiring with much gallantry something especially slick and saucy," columnist O. O. McIntyre wrote in the *New York American*.

"Who are the most beautiful women in the world?" a teenager shouted one night after a lecture at a Connecticut boys' school, and Ripley professed an appreciation for Icelandic women: "Blond and blue eyed, with beautiful skin and marvelous figures." The boys wanted to hear about French and Spanish women, but Ripley said Europeans were "overrated" and that Oriental and Arab women were the most lovely and mysterious.

Then again, he added, "You can see more beautiful women any day in the week in one New York block than you can find anywhere in the world."

With newspaper and magazine photography now commonplace, Ripley was often caught in the act of sharing drinks or dinner with actresses and dancers. Long gone were the requisite ball games and boxing matches, replaced by Broadway parties, charity balls, or cocktails at midtown nightclubs, often in the company of his raspy-voiced sidekick, Bugs Baer. Pictures of Ripley and Baer appeared regularly, posing with some attractive unnamed woman at a table with Gene Tunney or Babe Ruth. Ripley always looked dapper, in tailor-made suits, bright-colored shirts, bow ties, and his trademark black-and-white wing tips. He wore a pinky ring and twirled a walking stick. Columnists stoked his reputation as a fop. "All shyness disappears as Ripley goes to town sartorially," said one writer. "High colors are his choice—green that is green, red that is red."

Yet, Ripley suspiciously remained a bachelor, and the question lingered—*Why aren't you married?* "Women have a way of falling in love with Ripley," wrote a female reporter who spent a weekend at BION Island while researching a story for *Radio Stars* magazine. "Popular, wealthy, fabulously famous, extremely attractive to women—and still not married!" Ripley usually explained that his hectic travel schedule limited his marital prospects to women who were extremely tolerant, adventurous, or both. "If she didn't like to travel," he said, "she'd be a widow most of the time." He told another reporter that he sometimes dreamed of having children and "growing old at BION." But it seemed that anytime he fell in love he would leave for a trip and return to find his lover betrothed to another.

In truth, he had already found the ideal partner, beautiful and loving, adventurous and tolerant . . . yet married.

* * *

RUTH "OAKIE" ROSS had for years been the mystery woman of Ripley's life, the one who appeared and disappeared and reappeared again without anyone ever catching her full story, even as she became his constant traveling companion and a paid employee of Believe It or Not, Inc.

Through the mid-1930s she had frequently joined in his travels, including the 1932 South Seas and China adventure. In 1934 they had toured throughout Northern Africa—Morocco, Tripoli, Libya (then known as Cyrenaica), Algeria—and on to Northern Europe. Though she was listed on his payroll as "secretary," Ripley once introduced her to reporters as "Mrs. Ripley" during a visit to the Shetland Islands. At the end of that trip, he and Oakie sailed home with Will Rogers and his wife.

When Ripley bought BION Island in 1934, Oakie helped organize the messy contents of his new mansion. She lived in Manhattan but spent many days and nights at the Mamaroneck house. Their lives were woven tightly together and at times they lived practically as man and wife. One contemporary called her "a combination social secretary and companion [who] earned the right to move in and out of Ripley's life as she pleased."

But sealing the deal by proposing was apparently never a consideration, largely due to dark memories of his failed marriage to Beatrice. In one of the why-aren't-you-married stories, a reporter asked if he ever *had* been married. "Oh, nooooooo," he said, then quickly admitted, "I guess I was once. But she's married and got children."

Ripley had occasionally run into Beatrice over the years, once while searching for Mayan ruins in Mexico. The captain of Ripley's ship had introduced him to the owner of a hemp plantation, who invited Ripley to stay the night. At dinner he introduced his wife—it was Beatrice. Ripley later told Bugs it felt "a little creepy." In another version of that story, Beatrice sent him a note later that night: "Roy, you'll always be the only one I love." An employee would later claim that the run-in was no accident, that Ripley knew Beatrice was living there and staged the encounter with her husband in order to see her.

Ripley so rarely talked about Beatrice that her true identity would become mixed and muddled. For decades, *Believe It or Not* fans thought she was the same Beatrice Roberts who became a Miss America contestant, a small-time actress, and Louis B. Mayer's lover. Based on census records, Ripley's marriage license, Miss America documents, and newspaper articles, it turned out they all had the wrong Beatrice. After divorcing Ripley, Beatrice returned to Massachusetts to live with her family. She eventually married a Cuban man and lived with him in Cuba, but her husband died of tuberculosis, leaving her with two children. She moved back to Massachusetts, and Ripley helped by continuing to send occasional checks to his widowed ex.

Beatrice wasn't the only ex-lover who'd remained part of his life. After Haru Onuki (aka Marion Ohnick) sued him in 1932, Ripley settled out of court, paying an undisclosed sum. She eventually moved back to California, and Ripley would visit during trips to Los Angeles. He once received a cable from Onuki, who had lost her purse while traveling and wondered if her "Bobbie" could wire some money. Though his attorney smelled "a frame," Ripley complied.

A collector and sentimentalist, Ripley seemed unable to sever ties to the women he once loved, and had even continued to contact his high school love, Nell. But he had at least learned not to remarry, that he could "never make a wife happy," as he once put it. Besides, there were too many beautiful women in the world. Ripley was no braggart, but he once told Doug Storer that he intended to have sex in every country he visited and wasn't far off that goal. One of his proudest conquests was still his tryst in Hell, Norway—"Just for the hell of it," he told Storer with a wink. A self-professed connoisseur of the female form, he wrote in his third *Believe It or Not* book that he adored Nordic women ("pure unadulterated beauty"), Eurasian women ("always beautiful"), and Turkish women ("lovely"), adding, "I doubt if anyone ever saw anything cuter than a Javanese."

In Oakie, he found someone possessing the best features of all the world's women. Though he appreciated slim, dark-skinned women—especially Asian women—Ripley also liked intelligent, independent, and worldly women. Oakie was all of that.

At thirty-eight she was older than most girlfriends, but carried herself with poise and assurance, always well-dressed, a confident strut, often grinning. While in the tropics, she wasn't shy about removing her top and sunning herself. In one of Ripley's home movies, he and Oakie are lounging on a boat someplace steamy, Ripley sweating in just white skivvies and Oakie with her bathing suit pulled down to her waist, her head thrown back to soak up the sun.

Elsewhere in Ripley's home movies the two seem perfectly at ease walking along cobblestone streets or beaches, sharing a pedicab or a meal or a dance. With her, Ripley seemed carefree and happy, and friends could tell there was something special about their relationship. Other serious partnerships had ended in divorce, lawsuits, headlines, allegations of abuse—indications that Ripley preferred drama and conflict in his liaisons. With Oakie, he sought simplicity and domesticity. Though he would remain secretive about the details of their affair, it became obvious to those close to him that he truly loved her.

But there was that one complication in their otherwise romantic love story, which compelled Ripley to be furtive. His lover was a married woman.

* * *

FRIENDS WOULD LATER say that Ripley declined to marry Oakie, so she eventually wed someone else, sometime in the mid-1930s. Others assumed she had been married all along, and that Oakie gave Ripley the ideal duty-free relationship. The particulars would remain murky, as would the identity of Oakie's husband. However it came to be, the strange arrangement might have been for the best.

Until meeting Oakie, Ripley had seemed incapable of fully sharing his life with just one woman. He admired the male-dominated cultures of certain countries, even those practicing polygamy, and he complained often about American-style marriages. In one interview he declared his admiration for Muslim-style marriages. "Men are left to enjoy themselves," he said. "Women aren't making noise all the time with court litigation like they do here." Oakie apparently decided there was no sense in forcing Ripley to commit. She simply married another and became Ripley's favored mistress. They seemed to have made a pact, each agreeing to the ruse in which their separate lives sometimes overlapped.

At BION Island, Oakie left her imprint everywhere. She had initially helped him find and hire domestic help—cooks, chauffeurs, gardeners, and maids—and then began arranging his antique furniture and artwork. By 1936, Ripley was living and working there nearly full-time, roughly two years after buying the place.

* * *

WITH HIS VARIOUS collections now on display across BION Island, he loved to show off his extraordinary and eccentric estate to guests. With Hitler stirring up conflict in Europe, it wasn't an ideal time for overseas passenger travel anyway, which meant Ripley couldn't venture too far abroad. He tried to take at least one long vacation each summer (usually with Oakie), but scaled back from his two or three global trips a year, and was forced to stay away from Europe and parts of Asia. He compensated by displaying some of the world's weird artifacts on his private island, reminders of previous adventures that helped him relive life on the road.

In 1937, he visited Alaska, then stopped at Ye Olde Curiosity Shop in Seattle, where he spent $1,000 on more BION decorations, including totem poles and a "man-eating" clamshell. He decorated his island with Buddha sculptures, Japanese bells, African idols, and covered nearly every inch of floor space in thick rugs from India, China, Turkey, and Persia. (Ripley's feet frequently ached and swelled, and he preferred to walk barefoot across rug-draped floors). Oakie helped fill rooms with velvet-covered chairs and a hodgepodge of dark-wood, hand-carved furniture. Walls bristled with weapons—spears, masks, torture devices, and pieces of armor—giving the house a medieval warlord motif. Here and there, Ripley added sentimental touches. In addition to the ridgepole hanging above the bar, he had purchased the front door from his childhood home, handmade by his father and with the metal numbers of his old street address still attached. He installed it as the entrance to his bedroom.

On weekends, he'd invite friends, employees, newsmen, sports stars, and celebrities to his island. He hosted swimming, boating, and seafood feasts in summer, ice-skating and bonfires in winter. His brother and a carpenter built a new bar in the boathouse, and Ripley purchased (or relieved from storage) boats to use on his pond, including a sealskin kayak from his Alaska trip, a boat of woven reeds from India, a dugout canoe from Peru, and a circular guffa boat from Iraq. Columnist O. O. McIntyre, after a weekend ride in a guffa, raved about Ripley's "moated castle."

Guests lingered in the low-ceilinged basement bar, cool and dark as an Irish pub, where Ripley happily played barkeep. He stocked the bar with fine wines from California, many of them sent by the mayor of Santa Rosa. He'd serve drinks beneath the flags of countries he'd visited, scores of them dangling from the walls. Shelves were cluttered with unusual souvenirs, sheep's bells and bullwhips, a collection of rare goblets, steins and tankards, a narwhal tusk, and the dried penis of a whale. When guests asked what *that* was, Ripley would explain, "Let's just say it was very dear to the whale." When the mayor of Hell, Norway, passed through New York, Ripley threw him a party and hired waiters dressed as monks to serve hell-themed dishes like deviled eggs and sizzling meats.

In one rock-walled, grotto-like basement room, which was off-limits to most visitors, he displayed his erotica: pictures, statues, books, and carvings from around the world. One visitor described the collection as "ranging from the revolting to the exquisitely executed." In this dimly lit room he also stowed a few of the gruesome photographs he'd acquired over the years—men being tortured in China, elephantiasis victims in Africa.

He began collecting pets, too. His first dog, a cocker spaniel named Dokie (as in *okie-dokie*), had been joined by Suzy the Dalmatian; Flash the collie; Sin and Virtue, both spaniels; and others. Some visitors observed that Ripley seemed more at ease with his animals than his guests.

✳ ✳ ✳

HIS KOOKY HOME became his primary workplace, where six to ten employees tended to the Believe It or Not realm. For nearly thirty years he had worked in either a newspaper office, his NYAC apartment, or hotel rooms and cruise-ship cabins. By 1937, he had developed a new set of work routines.

Before eating or even dressing, he'd begin drawing cartoons at dawn in the spacious studio he created on the top floor. Barefoot and clad in a kimono, he worked feverishly to catch up on his quota of cartoons. By late morning, with a few sketches completed, he'd eat a light breakfast in the massive kitchen, where he employed two full-time chefs from China. (He favored oxtail soup.) Then he'd return to the studio with snacks and work until dusk, while staffers scurried around on the floors below. In warm weather, he kept the studio windows open and scattered nuts and cracked corn on the sill to attract squirrels, chipmunks, and birds. On midday walks around the island, he always kept a stash of nuts in his pockets, to feed the rodents.

Norbert Pearlroth still worked at the New York Public Library and would send *Believe It or Not* ideas to the island. Robert Hyland continued to work as Ripley's financial manager, Dick Hyman as publicist, and Joe Simpson as traveling secretary, while C. C. Pyle oversaw the Odditoriums, and Doug Storer managed his radio shows. Ripley's domestic staff included a personal assistant named Mac, Joe the chauffeur, Barry the gardener, Elinor the housekeeper, and his chief secretary, Cygna Conly, the speed-talker featured in cartoons and on the air. Another ten employees worked at the King Features offices in New York, managing the daily deluge of mail.

Ripley's brother, Doug, was now a full-time fixture in Believe It or Not, Inc. He'd spent a few years living in New York after Ripley first lured him away from his cabin in the Appalachian hills of Ohio. Now living at BION Island, he preferred working with his hands, fixing things or assisting the carpenter or gardener, but Ripley kept giving him business duties, such as delivering cartoons into New York. Doug was a quiet, moody presence among the others, seemingly immune to his hardworking brother's work habits and more at ease with the household staff than the newsmen. He drank a lot—sometimes even more than Ripley—and occasionally scuffled with King Features staffers. He developed an especially scrappy relationship with Ripley's boss, Joe Connolly, a regular visitor to BION Island. Doug once called Connolly a "freeloader" and kicked him off the island. Connolly retaliated by barring him from Hearst's offices in New York.

Ripley usually defended Doug, trying to make good on his long-ago promise to their mother. He must have sensed Doug's unease amid the hubbub of his celebrity lifestyle. When Ripley got permission to build a pier off the island, he bought Doug a yacht, and Doug would disappear for days at a time, motoring all over Long Island Sound. In time Doug learned to navigate the tricky waters around Manhattan and would shuttle his brother into New York. Some nights Doug would wait at an East Side pier to take Ripley back home, but he'd end up waiting past midnight before realizing his brother wasn't coming. Doug would head back to Mamaroneck alone. He eventually sold the yacht and bought a speedboat.

*   *   *

AS A DISORGANIZED MANAGER of his own affairs, notorious for running late, losing keys, and forgetting important phone numbers, including his own, Ripley relied on his brother and his staff more than ever. He communicated by intercom, sometimes testily calling downstairs for more paper or ink, food or drink. Employees became the buffer between Ripley and King Features. They stayed in touch with the downtown office by phone or mail, sending requests for more art supplies and arranging for the delivery of Ripley's sketches, which were often behind schedule. Editors wrote back regularly asking Ripley to *please* send more cartoons.

Unlike other big-name cartoonists, Ripley continued to draw

his own sketches. "That's fundamental," he once said. But he had begun to allow other King Features artists to ink the captions. He would send drawings to New York with instructions on how the captions should be arranged. In the coming years, Ripley would turn more artistic duties over to subordinates, even though he would publicly insist that he drew every last cartoon with his own hand.

Despite some tensions caused by Ripley's move to Mamaroneck, Believe It or Not remained a profitable enterprise for King Features, which now sold Ripley's cartoons to hundreds of papers. In late 1937, when Ripley agreed to extend his partnership with Hearst for three more years, Joe Connolly sent a personal note expressing his pride in a partnership that "has been so satisfactory and so personally pleasant to me." As Ripley's most vocal advocate, Connolly used all his resources to promote *Believe It or Not,* instructing reporters and photographers to give coverage to all of Ripley's travels and radio shows.

At a time when he had begun to feel threatened by rivals and competitors, Ripley needed to stay in the public eye.

* * *

JOHN HIX, whose cartoons featured unusual historical facts and scientific phenomena, had been nipping at Ripley's heels for a decade. Ripley initially viewed Hix's *Strange As It Seems* as both a blatant knockoff and a sign of flattery.

By the mid-1930s, however, Hix had become a true threat, his cartoon getting picked up by more and more papers. Hix had expanded into comic books and radio, his show closely resembling Ripley's, with curious tales dramatized in reenactments. But Hix wasn't the only competitor. A cartoon called *Screen Oddities* featured odd facts about actors, actresses, and other celebrities. Bernarr Macfadden's *True Story* magazine now reached a circulation of two million, prompting Macfadden to create more stranger-than-fiction offspring: *True Romances, True Ghost Stories, True Detective.* Other knockoff magazines included *Amazing Stories, Weird Tales,* and *Science Wonder Stories.*

Rivalry was advancing on all fronts. The Depression had become a heyday for cartoons, launching such soon-to-be favorites as *Dick Tracy, Flash Gordon, L'il Abner, Prince Valiant,* and *The Gumps.* Many of those cartoons had also earned their own radio shows.

With Hix and other competitors on the radio, in comic books, and in newspapers, Ripley realized he needed to protect his brand at all levels. When he heard about a Massachusetts theater show featuring performers who had appeared in his cartoons, he sued, accusing the show of copyright infringement. He also sued the "House of Mirth," carnival and its sideshow, titled "Robert (Believe It or Not) Ripley's Freaks." One act featured men and women of "abnormal sex nature," which Ripley's lawyers called "indecent, lewd, immoral, disgusting." A judge agreed and sent sheriff's deputies to halt the show's railroad cars in Connecticut.

Ripley complained to a *Popular Mechanics* writer that he felt "besieged by lawsuits, taxes, and imitators." One columnist, in a mid-1930s Ripley profile, said, "He has more imitators—some of them extremely good—than any other artist of his type the world ever saw. But there is only one 'Rip.' He combines with the gift of his art that glowing spark of curiosity and the beautiful quality of wonder as no one else ever has."

Despite the competition, *Believe It or Not* continued to inspire boys and artists. When a young Minnesota cartoonist noticed his dog's propensity to eat broken glass and sewing needles, his first thought was Ripley. The boy drew a picture of his dog Spike and mailed it to New York. In early 1937, Ripley published the sketch inside a *Believe It or Not* panel with a caption explaining that C. F. Schulz's dog "eats pins, tacks, screws and razor blades."

Charles F. Schulz, whose ill-mannered dog became the cartoon legend Snoopy, was just fourteen.

* * *

AFTER NEARLY THIRTY YEARS of cartooning, Ripley's newspaper panel could feel as constrictive as a cell. He sometimes preferred the excitement of NBC's radio studios at Rockefeller Center over the solo grind of the drawing table. This was partly thanks to Doug Storer, who by 1937 had begun managing Ripley's radio career with brio.

When a successful two-year run with Ozzie and Harriet ended in July of 1937, Storer sought a new sponsor with deeper pockets. He signed with General Foods, which was promoting a new breakfast cereal called Huskies. "Believe It or Not Featuring Robert Ripley" would air over NBC's Red Network.

In addition to Ripley's $3,500 weekly salary, General Foods agreed to fund an annual vacation of eight to thirteen weeks, at $1,500 a week. The thirty-minute show was set to air Friday nights but soon switched to the prime eight p.m. Saturday slot, temporarily easing Ripley's concerns about upstarts and imitators.

Ripley felt restricted by his previous show and had urged Storer to find a more progressive sponsor. He'd developed a sense of the growing power of radio and hoped to take his show in a new direction, attempting more groundbreaking broadcasts from remote locations, such as airing from the Cave of the Winds beneath Niagara Falls, where he would interview the man who in 1928 had soared over the falls inside a huge rubber ball.

Storer encouraged the concept, impressed by Ripley's enthusiasm for radio adventure. In Ripley's view, he *needed* to take risks to keep a step ahead of his rivals. Just before launching his new show, Ripley told a reporter that as a former baseball and handball player, he'd retained a competitive streak. "I take a great delight in competing on the air as a radio artist, not as a cartoonist," he said. "It makes me very happy to be a success in radio, for it's the last thing I'd ever imagine I could do."

His new shows, beginning in mid-1937, featured two types of segments. The first were interviews with Ripley's "living Believe-It-or-Nots"—the blind woman whose sight was restored, the woman who had lived for years inside an iron lung, and the story of a man who survived getting blown by pressurized air through a hole in the roof of an underwater tunnel. The other segments were dramatic reenactments of Ripley's cartoons, including the story of a Mexican man who survived a firing-squad execution and whose scarred flesh still carried the bullets. But Ripley and Storer constantly reached for fresher, weirder ideas, offering to pay the expenses of anyone with a good story who was willing to come to New York and bare their soul on NBC.

Occasionally, Ripley welcomed celebrity guests—Shirley Temple or Somerset Maugham or Lou Gehrig, whom he interviewed within hours of Gehrig's record-breaking two thousandth game. Gehrig accidentally veered off script and said his favorite breakfast cereal was "a big bowl of Wheaties"—a competitor of the show's sponsor. When Ripley invited the mayor of Hell, Norway, onto his show, he proudly persuaded Lorentz Stenvig to state on the air, "It's hotter than Hell in New York!"

Toward the end of the first twenty-six-week season, with a hiatus upcoming in early 1938, Storer convinced Ripley to finally allow a dentist to attempt to fix the offensive teeth that had been a lifelong handicap. Public-speaking lessons had greatly improved Ripley's stuttering, and he rarely went on air anymore

without a nerve-calming cup of liquor. But the teeth had continued to mangle certain letters and words.

His dentist felt it wasn't possible to corral them with braces,
that Ripley's situation required more drastic measures. He
yanked out the front teeth and replanted them at a less disfiguring angle. (Ripley asked not to make them *too* straight, since
the imperfection was part of his brand.) After the procedure,
his teeth were held in place for weeks by thin wires, and they
slowly settled back into the gums. Ripley was soon back on the
air, though not without months of pain and discomfort.

One columnist wrote that "the sudden oratorical ease of
Robert L. Ripley over the radio is the celebrity accomplishment
of the hour . . . He devoted a year to it and now has everything
under control."

* * *

RIPLEY'S MOST POPULAR SHOWS were those in which
unknown people shared their most personal stories. He reunited
a sister and brother born seventy years earlier, allegedly in a set
of sextuplets, who hadn't seen each other for twenty-five years.
Another show reunited twin sisters who had been separated at
birth and adopted by different families. "Marjorie, meet your
twin sister Shirley," Ripley said, as the estranged sisters tearfully embraced.

One show featured a couple who got married forty-four years
after their original wedding date. They had fought that day, canceled the wedding, and later married others. When their respective spouses died, they found each other again and wed. Ripley
also introduced listeners to "The Modern Adam and Eve," who
married after the woman was injured in a car accident and the
man donated a rib to help surgeons repair her injuries.

It turned out that Ripley was well suited to moderate family reunions and on-air retellings of odd marriages and divorces, of reunited twins and orphans. He was a patient and empathetic interviewer, whether his guests were disfigured or handicapped or from some distant land. As one who had suffered humiliation and loss in his own life, he seemed to understand the discomfort of others. As one who had mingled with all classes, he seemed to possess some reserve of compassion, coming across as gentle and nonjudgmental. Guests responded by speaking honestly and emotionally, as they would decades later with Phil Donahue or Oprah Winfrey.

* * *

IN JULY OF 1938, a pilot named Douglas Corrigan touched down in Ireland after allegedly flying across the Atlantic by accident. Within hours, "Wrong-Way Corrigan," as the press would soon call him, received a call from Doug Storer, and the next night he was live on NBC discussing the Brooklyn-to-Dublin flight with Ripley.

"A fellow can't help it if he gets mixed up, can he?" Corrigan asked Ripley.

A month later, Ripley hosted an even more memorable show starring an Indian "mystic" named Kuda Bux, known for performing such stunts as firing a gun at targets with his eyes taped shut. Storer invited Bux to attempt a far more impressive stunt: to walk barefoot across a bed of flaming coals.

Workers dug two ten-foot ditches in a parking lot beside Radio City Music Hall, filling them with bags of charcoal topped by stacks of oak wood. By the next night, the fiery coals had reached 1,400 degrees. Thousands of onlookers crowded around the site as ambulances and fire trucks stood by. From his studio high above the fire pits, Ripley explained to listeners: "In my travels to the Orient, I have always been fascinated by the unexplainable miracles that the holy men of India perform."

As Bux removed his shoes and rolled up his pant legs, some in the crowd covered their ears or pinched their noses, afraid to hear or smell burning flesh. Ripley signed off briefly and descended from Rockefeller Center to street level. Announcer Graham McNamee took over the play-by-play, describing "red-hot coals that shine brightly in the night," and then excitedly announcing Ripley's approach. "The crowd is milling about now . . . the cameras are grinding," he enthused. "And, O-*ho*! Here comes Bob Ripley. He has a police escort and he's getting nearer; he's fighting through the crowd and here he comes!"

When Ripley took the microphone, he described Bux as "completely cool and unruffled." A team of doctors—New York's health commissioner; a skin specialist; and Doug Storer's father, a doctor—examined Bux's feet to make sure there were no abnormal calluses or chemical coatings, and pronounced his feet to be normal. Then, before anyone could stop him, the diminutive man in the turban scampered through the smoking-red pits, hiking his pant legs and sinking ankle-deep in glowing coals. When the sluggish cameramen realized they'd missed the money shot, they encouraged Bux to "do it again, do it again." So he did.

Afterward, doctors found a small burn where a coal had become embedded in his heel, but otherwise no scars. Bux's body temperature was normal and he seemed pain-free. Ripley called it "the most amazing thing I have ever seen."

When the crowd and the cameramen settled down, Ripley sat beside Bux and asked the obvious question—*How?*

"It is faith, Mr. Ripley," replied Kuda Bux. "It is faith I have that allows me to do it."

"Well, Kuda Bux, it must be faith," said Ripley. "Because

that fire was so hot that none of us here could get within three feet of it."

✳ ✳ ✳

MONTHS LATER, radio listeners tuned in for a Halloween-night drama by Orson Welles on WABC. In a reenactment of H. G. Wells's *The War of the Worlds,* fake newscasters read mock news flashes about aliens landing in metal cylinders in New Jersey and tentacled Martians killing residents with death rays. Across the New York metropolis, people ran from their homes, fleeing to parks and police stations, believing America was under attack, despite the three (albeit brief) announcements that the performance was fictional.

Already edgy from a recent hurricane that had ravaged New York and New England, radio listeners were furious, accusing Welles of intentionally causing a panic. Welles weathered the outrage, which helped launch his career. But he'd upped the ante in the game of bold radio achievement.

Radio had become America's favorite pastime, the nightly schedule packed with plays and music, comedy and baseball. At the time of Welles's headline-grabbing feat, however, Ripley was no longer in the game. He had lost his radio show weeks before.

Two years earlier, Ripley's *Baker's Broadcast* with Ozzie and Harriet had been one of America's favorite shows, in league with the top-ranked shows of Jack Benny and Bing Crosby. But his Huskies-sponsored program had struggled to find an audience. Its initial Saturday-night success in 1937 slumped when General Foods moved the show to Tuesdays. When the show switched to Mondays, ratings dipped further and his sponsor pulled the plug.

He was still earning a mid-six-figures income, but he hated to be off the air when John Hix and other cartoonists *were* on the air. Cartoons and comic strips had continued to infiltrate American culture, becoming what *Fortune* magazine described as America's "adult dream life." *Action Comics* had debuted in mid-1938, its cover dominated by a flying strongman called "Superman." *Believe It or Not* had changed little over the years, and Ripley worried constantly that the whole concept might grow stale. He was desperate to find more stunts like the Kuda Bux show to keep things fresh.

In December of that year, Ripley celebrated his cartoon's twentieth anniversary. Though the original hadn't been called *Believe It or Not* and was a sporadic feature until the mid-1920s, King Features had established 1918 as its birthday. The syndicate ran commemorative ads, prompting an outpouring of celebrity telegrams. Babe Ruth wrote that he "learned a lot of things from following [Ripley's] work" and Kate Smith sent congratulations to "my favorite cartoonist." Rube Goldberg, noting that they had both been Hy Baggerly's trainees in San Francisco, wrote: "I believe Ripley has done more for the profession of cartooning than any one man in our time. May his great influence for good both in the entertainment and educational worlds continue for many years to come."

But his entertaining influence seemed to be waning, and Ripley the pioneer ended the year searching for a new radio sponsor, only to find potential advertisers skittish as Europe edged closer to war. Normally, during times of stress and anxiety, he'd hit the road and attempt to outrun his troubles. But it was not a promising time for world travel. Indeed, America was about to clamp shut, caging Ripley like an animal and separating him from his playground.

CHAPTER

18

In early 1939, the planet seemed to be at war with itself. Civil war raged in Spain. Thirty thousand were killed in a Chilean earthquake. Ripley's favorite country, China, was now eighteen months into full-on bloody warfare with Japan. Germany had taken over parts of Czechoslovakia and was planning to invade Poland, while Italy was planning an attack on Albania. These were dark days for world travelers.

Unable to cross the Atlantic or Pacific, Ripley and Oakie started the New Year in the Caribbean, having sailed there just before the holidays for a month-long escape. Ripley wanted to see the tribe on the San Blas Islands off Panama that celebrated Christmas with cockfights, adding San Blas to the list of countries he'd visited, even though it wasn't really a country. (San Blas, later renamed Kana Yula, was an autonomous territory and part of Panama.)

Still, *Time* magazine dutifully reported that "buck-toothed Ripley" had visited two hundred nations and was now "more widely traveled than Marco Polo, Magellan, and any other human being that ever lived." By Ripley's count, he needed to visit thirty more countries to have visited them all.

After Panama, Ripley and Oakie visited Haiti and Jamaica, where he received an urgent telegram from Doug Storer. By phone, Storer told Ripley that he had finally found a sponsor for a new weekly *Believe It or Not* program, starting in March 1939. Due to a muffled connection, Ripley thought his sponsor was Coca-Cola, and he and Oakie spent the next few days celebrating with rum and Cokes. Ripley wouldn't learn until arriving back in New York that his sponsor was actually Nehi Corporation's *Royal Crown* Cola. He was hardly disappointed, however, when he learned that he'd be paid $7,500 per show.

By now, Ripley had entrusted Storer with more duties. In his role as agent, adviser, and personal manager, Storer had negotiated other deals to keep Ripley busy—endorsements and magazine ads in which Ripley (despite Hearst's earlier warning) would lease his name and drawings to Macmillan Oil Company, Flexo Tray ice-cube trays, Parker Pen Company, Gillette razors, and Realsilk socks. Even better, Storer was in discussions with Twentieth Century Fox, which wanted to produce half a dozen short Movietone films about Ripley's travels, netting Ripley $3,000 per film.

Storer even managed to score Ripley a college diploma, convincing his alma mater, Dartmouth College, to give Ripley an honorary degree recognizing his "artistic contributions." Weeks later, Ripley the high school dropout received an honorary *doctorate* from Missouri Valley College, and president Thomas Bibb's proclamation read like a eulogy, touting "Ripley's contributions to human knowledge; his stimulation of widespread interest in science, history, literature, and the arts . . . and his own achievements in overcoming personal handicaps to become one of America's and the world's best-known and best-liked personalities."

After the ceremony, Ripley somberly shared with a reporter his concerns that the world had become "topsy turvy . . . a very difficult world of depression, millions of unemployed, the outlook is not very encouraging I will admit."

When the reporter asked Ripley to describe the most unusual thing he'd ever seen, Ripley said he hadn't seen it yet: "If I had, I would lose my ambitions and I would not travel any more."

* * *

WITH THE DOOR closing on overseas travel, Ripley decided a key feature of his new radio show would be "on-the-spot" broadcasts from remote locations, allowing him to explore more of his own country. He was ready, for a change, to see America.

One of his first *See America First with Bob Ripley* shows took place deep inside New Mexico's Carlsbad Caverns in the summer of 1939. Engineers unspooled a thousand feet of electrical and audio cable to allow Ripley to conduct a live interview with Jim White, the man who discovered the caverns in 1901.

"I am now speaking to you from 750 feet below the surface of the earth, from the most inspiring place of beauty in the world," Ripley reported. A Fox film crew recorded the event for one of Ripley's Movietone films, and a *Look* magazine photographer snapped pictures. Back in New York, B. A. Rolfe called it "one of the most thrilling broadcasts ever heard" and NBC estimated that twenty million listeners tuned in.

Seeing more of America awakened Ripley's patriotism and public spirit, and he began donating time and money to an increasing number of charity events and humanitarian organizations, such as the Finnish Relief Fund, established by Herbert Hoover to assist Finland after an attack by Stalin's Red Army.

But his favorite charities remained orphan groups, youth organizations, and scout troops.

In mid-1939, to raise money for the Boys Club of New York, he co-hosted a charity softball game at Madison Square Garden, serving as captain of the celebrity-packed "Believe It or Nots" team, which included Babe Ruth, Jack Dempsey, Rube Goldberg, and Jimmy Durante. The opposing "Nine Old Men" team, captained by writer/broadcaster Lowell Thomas, included Walter Winchell and boxer Gene Tunney. A crowd of fourteen thousand watched Ripley's team emerge from the dugout wearing comically baggy uniforms of pantaloons and turbans. The *New York Times* said Ripley and Bugs Baer "looked entirely out of place and most uncomfortable."

Ripley, in a reprise of his bush league days, pitched the first two innings. He gave up two runs, but Babe Ruth swatted their team to a 7–2 lead. Frequent interruptions for "refreshments" in the dugout caused the crowd to grow restless, and the umpire, New York mayor Fiorello La Guardia, called the game after four innings. The *Times* said the event raised $12,000 for the Boys Club and "a grand time was had by all."

＊　＊　＊

WHEN IT CAME TO GIRLS, meanwhile, he associated with a very different kind of club— the deformed, the disfigured, the armless and/or legless.

Ripley's traveling Odditorium show had visited half a dozen cities in recent years, and in 1939 his cast of entertainers was called upon to appear in *two* Odditoriums at once. C. C. Pyle put together an exhibition for the upcoming Golden Gate International Exposition in San Francisco, at the same time organizing an even bigger show for New York's 1939 World's Fair. Ripley was looking forward to having Odditoriums on both coasts.

Two weeks before the San Francisco fair opened, Pyle suffered a stroke at his Los Angeles home. The fifty-six-year-old showman hadn't finished setting up the two Odditoriums and his partner struggled to launch both shows simultaneously.

Ripley then learned that New York officials decided they didn't need his Odditorium after all. Lurking behind this last-minute decision was Lou Dufour, who after the 1933–34 Chicago fair had vowed to exact revenge on C. C. Pyle. Dufour felt he deserved more than the $10,000 he received for helping Pyle fix his ailing show in Chicago, and had promised to "get my compensation in some other manner."

That day had come. Dufour partnered with John Hix to produce a "Strange As It Seems Show" and museum, a near replica of Ripley's Odditorium, replete with razor-blade eaters and contortionists. Hix soon launched a new CBS radio show too. A *New Yorker* magazine profile of Dufour that summer referred to Hix as "Ripley's bustling young rival," and said Ripley was "peeved by the affront to his prestige."

With performers and exhibits already lined up for the New York fair, Ripley decided to create his first *permanent* Odditorium in a vacant restaurant building at Forty-eighth Street and Broadway. There, he would present exhibits from his personal collection on the ground floor, and live performers on a second-floor rotating stage.

Ripley and an investor sank $2 million into renovating the building and creating display cases for his collection of curiosities, including shrunken heads, a box made of human skin, the lifelike Masakichi sculpture, and the shoes of the world's tallest man, Robert Wadlow.

Huge neon signs hung off both sides of the corner building, welcoming visitors to Ripley's "exhibit of curioddities from 200 countries" and "40 living Ripley radio oddities." For the grand opening, a piano player named Bill Hajak sat out front, insisting he'd play nonstop for a month. He lasted two weeks, setting a world's record for marathon piano playing, but quit after missing his daughter's birth. Inside, sword swallowers, glass eaters, superhuman contortionists, and unfortunates with physical deformities performed their acts of self-mutilation or pseudo-torture from noon until one a.m.

Shortly after the grand opening, though, the crowds thinned and the museum began to falter. Busy with cartoon and radio duties, Ripley had turned the museum over to his financial manager, Robert Hyland, and his brother, Doug, whose blue-collar skills didn't translate to running a business.

Shy and solitary, Doug drank to find courage in social settings. Too often he crossed the line. He frequently scuffled with Robert Hyland over management of the Odditorium, and Hyland accused Doug of always being late and/or drunk. Hyland hired his teenage son to pick up the slack, but his son and Doug regularly argued and often came close to blows. Patrons sometimes overheard the shouting, and Ripley's financial partner started asking why he hadn't seen any returns. By the fall, other creditors came knocking, and the Odditorium, $100,000 in debt, seemed headed toward insolvency.

The only good news in the whole mess was that Hix's World's Fair exhibition also flopped. Fair organizers invited Ripley to replace Hix and bring a *Believe It or Not* show to the fair's second season, in 1940. The San Francisco fair also planned an encore season in 1940 and invited Ripley back as well. This time, Ripley would put Pyle's partner, Frank Zambreno, in charge of both Odditoriums. Even in death, Pyle found a way to make money for Ripley.

* * *

AS HIS BROADWAY MUSEUM floundered, Ripley fled, making a trip in early 1940 to the only countries still safe enough to visit. He and Oakie covered ten thousand miles during three weeks in South and Central America, then joined Herbert Hoover on a tour through the southern United States to raise money for the Finnish Relief Fund. At each stop Ripley showed movies of his recent travels and tribal masks he'd purchased in Brazil and Mexico.

His restlessness inflamed, Ripley asked Storer to expand the *See America First with Bob Ripley* radio series and strive for even more technically complex broadcasts from remote corners of the nation. Ripley even announced plans to take his on-the-spot broadcasts to Europe and South America, that he would start sending shortwave radio reports from war zones and even the North and South Poles. More realistically, Storer reached an agreement with the Department of the Interior to begin touring America's national parks, starting in the summer of 1940 with trips to the Grand Canyon and Yellowstone.

But first, Ripley and Storer took their *See America* show to Florida.

Marineland, the world's first "oceanarium," had opened two years earlier in St. Augustine and quickly became one of Florida's most popular tourist destinations. Ripley's crew arrived with plans to broadcast part of the show underwater. Ripley fed a couple porpoises, which leapt out of the water to snatch fish from his hand, then milked a female porpoise that was lifted from the water in a webbed harness. A Marineland attendant had to cut a harness strap so Ripley could reach his hand around the porpoise's teat, but in doing so accidentally cut the porpoise. A spurt of blood splattered onto Ripley's diving suit.

Next, Ripley put on a huge diving helmet, which fit over the headphones and microphone that would allow him to broadcast from a huge pool containing sharks and porpoises. Burdened by the cumbersome suit and helmet, Ripley and a Marineland expert slowly descended to the bottom of the pool. Ripley had grumbled about this stunt all day. He was not a good swimmer and was anxious about speaking on the air without a script. One of his writers quickly prepared a few remarks, but Ripley snapped, "How do you expect me to read underwater!"

On the floor of the pool, Ripley and his attendant, a professional diver, tried to feed a pair of sharks, using a long stick to shove dead mullets into their mouths. For some reason, the sharks weren't interested. They began circling Ripley and one shark bumped him backward onto his butt. The diver grabbed Ripley's arm and dragged him to the stairs, where he was pulled from the water. The diver figured the sharks must have picked up the scent of porpoise blood on Ripley's suit. The experience frightened and infuriated Ripley, but the show was a thrilling hit.

His encounter with a hungry shark did little to dampen Ripley's intrepidness. When he heard about a snake and alligator farm at Silver Springs, Florida, he wired his New York office: "Change next week's schedule." He wanted to milk a rattlesnake on the air. He moved the radio team inland, where he began his broadcast on a boat with Ross Allen, founder of the Silver Springs Reptile Institute. "Don't be frightened by that noise you hear in the background," Ripley told listeners. "It is just the bellowing of the alligators, who are all excited by this broadcast from their homeland!" He then described how, moments earlier, Allen had dived into the Silver River to wrestle a ten-foot alligator.

"Ross, how did you conquer that alligator?" he asked Allen, who stood beside him still dripping in his swim trunks.

"I tired him out," Allen said. "You've just got to understand them."

Allen and Ripley next climbed down a ladder into a pit slithering with five hundred poisonous snakes. The plan was for Allen to grab a rattlesnake and show Ripley how to "milk" it and collect its venom. Ripley wore thick rubber boots, while Allen remained barefoot.

"Nervous, Bob?" Allen asked.

According to the script, Ripley was supposed to say that after man-eating sharks and deadly snakes, "these *Believe It or Not* programs will be the end of me yet." He didn't get the chance. Just as he and Ross lowered themselves into the pit, the lights went out.

"Let's get the hell outa here!" Allen yelled, his words barely audible over the air. (Allen later found that muskrats had chewed into the wiring.)

He and Ripley fumbled their way out of the pit, and Ripley managed to turn the show over to his New York studio.

"Take it away, B. A. Rolfe!" he ad-libbed.

After the sunny Florida broadcasts, Ripley returned to BION Island, which was immediately slammed by an ice storm that turned every surface into an icicle. For days Ripley and his staff lived without heat or electricity, warming the mansion by keeping the fireplaces stoked. As was usually the case when confronted with adversity, Ripley was dazzled by the freak storm, walking childlike and wide-eyed around the island with his dogs, filming the surreal, glimmering beauty.

People frequently disappointed him—women, employees, even his brother—but nature, and his dogs, rarely let him down.

✳ ✳ ✳

IN MAY OF 1940, a special railroad car was attached to the back of the *20th Century Limited* and the *Believe It or Not* radio crew rolled west for a month-long tour. (Instead of Oakie, Ripley brought along a new Japanese girlfriend.) The highlight would be a broadcast from the bottom of the Grand Canyon. To achieve this, engineers would have to transmit the audio signal up to the canyon rim, send it along the nearest town's lone telephone line, then relay the show to ninety-two CBS stations.

Crew members grumbled that the whole idea was nuts, even as they marveled at Ripley's willingness to attempt the impossible. It took thirty mules to carry actors, writers, guides, and two thousand pounds of equipment down the seven-mile trail to the canyon floor. Ripley, in cowboy garb atop a white mule, kept waving his hat and yelling *yee-haw*. The crew was divided into thirds. One group would set up a dramatization around a fire pit, using local cowboys as actors. Another crew would record the sounds of the Colorado River, using a boom microphone stretched over the water.

The third and most complicated piece of the broadcast was a live report from a river guide as he shot through a section of rapids. Emery Kolb had been navigating the river for decades, but rarely at night, and never with expensive radio gear. Kolb suggested to Doug Storer that they hire an announcer to accompany him and operate the shortwave radio. Ripley grew concerned when he saw the announcer Storer had chosen: six-foot-two and over two hundred pounds.

"Why didn't they send a little guy?" Ripley grumbled. "This fellow will sink the boat."

Thus was Ripley introduced to a young department store manager and aspiring Phoenix politician named Barry Goldwater.

The first half of the show went according to plan. But during the shoot-the-rapids sequence, Goldwater and Kolb missed the flash of a lantern that was to be their signal to start downstream. As per the backup plan, they started rowing at what they believed to be the correct time. Ripley and his engineers waited to hear Goldwater describing the rapids, but at first all they heard was a police dispatcher asking fellow officers to be on the lookout for a stolen green Chevrolet—the radio signals had gotten crossed. Fifteen long seconds later, Goldwater's voice came through, but his report was brief. Water had begun slopping over the gunwales, threatening to short-circuit the equipment and sink the boat. Goldwater reacted quickly. "Take it away, Bob," he said. "I can't talk. I have to bail."

Ripley picked up the description of the moonlit action, but in doing so missed his own cue to throw a rope out to the boat, which swept past the sandbar where it was supposed to pull out. Ripley watched helplessly as Goldwater and Kolb rolled farther downstream.

❧ BELIEVE IT! ❧

Five months later, Goldwater joined pioneering river-runner Norman Nevills on the first-ever commercial paddling trip through the Grand Canyon. Goldwater wrote to tell Ripley about it, and Ripley invited him to New York. The two men hit it off (like Ripley, Goldwater was a foe of Roosevelt's New Deal), and Ripley encouraged Goldwater to use his photographs to create a slide show and lecture. While delivering his travelogue presentation to packed audiences, Goldwater discovered a knack for public speaking and, after serving as a pilot in World War II, entered politics, eventually making his run for the presidency of the United States.

✳ ✳ ✳

AFTER A MONTH on the road, the *See America* train returned east, stopping in Birmingham, Alabama, for another unique broadcast, from the National Air Races.

"Ladies and gentlemen. Now I shall present a *Believe It or Not* which has never been done on the air before," Ripley announced at the start of the show. "Jack Huber is a young man who will make a parachute jump of twelve thousand feet—almost two and one half miles—and actually describe his sensations to you as he falls."

Storer had convinced Huber, a Hollywood stuntman, to jump from a plane with a clunky twenty-pound radio transmitter strapped to his chest. Later, no one could ever say for sure whether Huber actually "spoke" during his 160-mile-an-hour plummet to earth. All that listeners across America heard was the muffled shush-and-whistle of air whipping across the microphone attached to his harness. One reason for Huber's lack of commentary was that his main parachute failed to open and ripped away from the harness. Unknown to those in Radioland, Huber spent a few terrifying moments plummeting toward his death until his backup chute finally bloomed open.

Even with his backup chute, Huber had lost altitude and slammed into the ground. His wife, watching nearby, burst into tears as an ambulance sped toward the drop zone. Doug Storer got there first and found Huber slumped at the edge of the field, certain that the daredevil was dead.

Ripley, back at the makeshift studio, improvised: "You have just heard, in his own words, Jack Huber's sensations as he made a twelve-thousand-foot parachute drop . . . And I must say that I, for one, never heard a more thrilling description in my life." Ripley announced that at any moment Huber would be on the air "to prove that he landed safely, and that all is well." Storer was relieved to find that all actually *was* well—Huber was alive, having only had the wind knocked out of him.

* * *

BY NOW, Ripley's Odditorium on Broadway was in its death throes. Doug Ripley and Robert Hyland had tried to revitalize the show with a two-headed baby from Sumatra, but the deal fell through and attendance slumped further. Ripley's main investor sued, forcing the money-losing venture toward closure. The museum's parent company, International Oddities, of which Doug Ripley was president, would soon file for bankruptcy.

When Hyland learned that a sheriff's deputy was planning to confiscate Ripley's collectibles, he asked Doug to intercept the officer and stall while he secreted Ripley's valuables out the back and into a moving van. Doug helped by getting the officer drunk, giving Hyland enough time to deliver Ripley's stuff back to BION Island.

Ripley had been anxious during his museum's final weeks, terrified that the papers would write about the biggest financial flop of his career. He blamed Hyland for mismanaging the enterprise but defended his brother, bringing an end to his longtime friendship with Hyland, who quit.

The Odditoriums at the San Francisco and New York World's Fairs, meanwhile, had performed surprisingly well. Yet, by the time those shows closed in the fall of 1940, fewer Americans were in the mood for that type of entertainment. Freaky sideshows had been a welcome diversion during the Depression but now seemed out of place at the troubled start of a new decade.

* * *

ON OCTOBER 30, 1940, a farmer living on an island in the Bahamas watched a small wooden boat wash ashore. Inside, he found two emaciated and disoriented men, sailors from a British cargo ship that had been sunk by German torpedoes off the coast of Africa.

Germans had strafed the ship's life rafts but seven crewmen, including Roy Widdicombe and Robert Tapscott, escaped in an eighteen-foot "jolly boat." Their craft contained just a few portions of food and water. Within a week, four men died. A week later Widdicombe wrote in a journal, "2nd cook goes mad dies. Two of us left." Rainstorms provided some drinking water, but the food ran out and Widdicombe broke his teeth trying to eat a shoe. In one log entry he wrote: "Getting very weak but trusting in God to pull us through." Days later: "All water and biscuits gone but still hoping to make land."

That was the final journal entry. Five weeks later, the farmer found Widdicombe and Tapscott on his beach, nearly three thousand miles from where their ship sank. When they recovered enough to speak, the men explained that flying fish had landed in the boat one day to provide nourishment. Small bits of seaweed helped too, but they often went days without water, sliding in and out of consciousness. Widdicombe lost eighty pounds, Tapscott lost sixty. Both were severely sunburned. Doctors called it a miracle that they'd survived.

When Doug Storer heard the story, he immediately made plans for a live broadcast from the Bahamas. He, Ripley, Oakie, and a technical crew flew to Nassau to set up the show. While getting his script approved by Bahamian officials, Storer was introduced to the former king of England. Now known as the duke of Windsor, Prince Edward had been sent to the Bahamas to serve as governor after abdicating his throne to marry an American divorcée.

The day before the broadcast, the duke unexpectedly offered to join the show—a potential coup for Ripley and Storer, since

the ex-king had never spoken on commercial radio. His participation remained uncertain until just hours before airtime due to
CBS concerns about Rolfe's orchestra, stationed in New York,
playing both "The Star-Spangled Banner" and "God Save the
Queen." CBS didn't want to give the appearance that the United
States was allied with England, now at war with Germany. The
duke learned about CBS's concerns (Storer suspected his phone
had been tapped) and offered to withdraw, but Storer begged
him not to cancel. Hours before the show, Ripley paced his hotel
room in a loose robe that kept flapping open, unconcerned that
he was flashing Storer's former secretary, Hazel, who had become Storer's wife.

"You're crazy," he kept telling Storer. "He'll never do it."

The broadcast began that night at ten o'clock in the ballroom of the Royal Victoria Hotel. After Ripley interviewed Widdicombe and Tapscott about their ordeal at sea, and the two men
gamely answered questions about the slow deaths of their crew-
mates, the duke approached the microphone. He read a brief
prepared speech, calling the sailors' journey "an extraordinary
adventure up to the standard of Mr. Ripley's famous feature."
The show was rebroadcast to ninety stations across North America, and the next day's papers were filled with reports about the
biggest scoop of Ripley's radio career.

⌇ BELIEVE IT! ⌇

Widdicombe would not enjoy his miraculously spared life for
long. After recovering, he traveled to New York, then sailed
toward England to reunite with his wife and child. With
Liverpool in sight, Widdicombe's ship was torpedoed and sunk.
All were killed. Tapscott recovered and enlisted in the Canadian
Air Force, then rejoined the Merchant Marine. He served at sea

for twenty years, until his premature death at age forty-two.
Hellmuth von Ruckteschell, the captain of the German ship that
had attacked Widdicombe and Tapscott's ship, was convicted of
war crimes and died in prison.

Satisfied with the publicity, Ripley and Oakie left the Bahamas the next morning for a seaplane ride to the island of San Salvador, to tour the site where Columbus allegedly landed in the New World, believing he'd circled the earth and reached Asia.

But for Ripley and Oakie, it would be their last adventure together. As they would learn within a few months, Oakie was sick. Incurably so.

* * *

AS 1940 WOUND DOWN, Ripley must have exhaled, having survived a year of tumult. Threatened by rivals such as Hix and enduring the financial distress of his Odditorium failure, he never slowed down, and in fact kept pushing himself further, always striving to reinvigorate his oft-mimicked brand.

That fall he earned a glowing two-part profile in the prestigious fifteen-year-old *New Yorker* magazine, whose writer, Geoffrey Hellman, summarized the Ripley legend and touted the cartoonist's astronomical wealth, his $500,000-plus annual income, the thirty annual lectures at $1,000 a *pop*. Hellman rehashed vignettes of Ripley's charmed career, like the time he fell into an orchestra pit during a lecture, couldn't find the stairs, and had to exit the theater and pay admission to reenter . . . or the time a group of Nicaraguan kids chased him down Managua's streets shouting, *"Reep-lee! Reep-lee!"*

A late-1940 Advertising Research Foundation survey found

that *Believe It or Not* had become the second most popular newspaper feature. Only the front page was of more interest to readers. Ripley had survived imitators' threats, lovers' lawsuits, and risky radio shows.

Now he had to find a way to keep his career alive through another world war.

Though frustrated by the global wartime travel limitations, Rip ley managed to transfer some of his excess energy into further sprucing up BION Island and hosting his increasingly audacious parties. Among the many impressive skills the once-shy cartoonist had developed was the ability to throw a bash. In New York he emceed star-studded galas for politicians, sports stars, military leaders, and visiting royalty, from Malaysian princesses to Spanish and Portuguese counts. On BION Island, he entertained as if ringmaster of his own circus.

At scores of dinners, luncheons, barbecues, wedding showers, and even christenings, he spent freely on the best food, drink, and entertainment. For summer cookouts he'd have six chefs grilling meats and seafood while magicians or musicians entertained the crowd, including his lovely new accordion-playing friend, Gypsy Markoff. Sometimes Bugs Baer would entertain guests with ad-lib comedy routines, and Ripley was always ready to initiate a game of softball or badminton or a dance on the outdoor dance floor. Any holiday was reason enough for a party—St. Patrick's Day, the Fourth of July, Chinese New

Year. Ripley loved to hustle around, bossing his staff, introducing guests to one another, giving speeches and toasts.

Not every party went according to plan. Ripley once invited newsmen to honor a seventy-year-old bride and her twenty-four-year-old husband, whom he'd featured in a radio show. He forgot it was his kitchen staff's day off, so his housekeeper and gardener had to prepare and serve lunch for thirty. Another time, Ripley invited a Boy Scout troop for a luncheon but neglected to tell the staff, who scrambled to prepare a suitable feast. Then there was the Sunday morning when his brother announced he was marrying his German girlfriend, Crystl, that afternoon at four. Doug preferred a simple affair, but by five his brother had invited guests and launched a fully catered party.

Ripley often strained his staff's tolerance by calling a dozen friends over for impromptu get-togethers or making impulsive plans to roast whole pigs or sides of beef all day on a spit. "Rip never cared for being alone," Doug Storer's wife, Hazel, once said. One housekeeper later said, "I cannot remember a dinner without at least one or two guests . . . one or two *lady* guests."

Ripley had installed a wiring system for lights and an outdoor sound system. During daylong affairs he would make announcements over the loudspeakers before the start of a swimming or boating contest, a softball game, or a toast. Some parties brought a hundred guests or more and Ripley stocked the guest bathrooms with extra bathing suits, slippers, robes, towels, and sun lotion. At larger parties, if anyone drank too much—or, in one case, started a fight—Ripley was quick to enforce order. "Throw that bum out!" he bellowed late one night after a scuffle between guests. "Throw *all* those bums out!"

By 1940, magazine writers and photographers had learned that Ripley's strange abode and massive parties made for good copy. Visitors included *LIFE* magazine (headline: BELIEVE IT OR

NOT: THIS IS WHERE ROBERT L. RIPLEY LIVES), *Radio Guide* (AT HOME WITH RIPLEY), *Liberty* magazine (WHERE A GLOBETROTTER HANGS HIS HAT), and even *Good Housekeeping*, which interviewed his housekeeper (IF YOU WERE HOUSEKEEPER TO MR. RIPLEY).

In the summer of 1940, *LIFE* co-hosted a party at BION featuring a dozen Odditorium performers. Guests arrived in limousines and the day's events were captured in a four-page spread. One photo shows Linda Lee, a singer on Ripley's radio show, pouring a beer beside a sword-swallower in mid-swallow. In another photo, a woman lights a cigarette while sitting on the chest of a man lying on a bed of nails. One particularly creepy picture shows Martin Laurello (The Human Owl) getting a drink at the bar, his head turned gruesomely backward. By afternoon, "the novelty of examining one another's peculiarities had worn off," as *LIFE* put it, and guests went swimming, spun around the pond in Ripley's boats, and played musical chairs. A fire breather tried to cook hot dogs on a skewer.

Also at that party was one of Ripley's heroes, Burton Holmes, who sat in a wheelchair nursing an injured foot. Ripley wheeled Holmes around the island, showing off his totem poles, bronze statues, and his boat collection. During the tour, Holmes mentioned that his injury had lately kept him from enjoying Nirvana, his bi-level apartment beside Manhattan's Central Park. He was thinking of selling the Asian-themed place, which would come fully furnished with artifacts Holmes had collected from the Orient. Holmes wondered: *Was Ripley interested?*

Weeks later, Ripley called from New York to tell his housekeeper, Almuth Seabeck, "I have found the apartment I have been looking for." Ripley's chauffeur delivered Seabeck to Sixty-seventh Street and Central Park West and they spent the afternoon inspecting Holmes's ten-room apartment, the dark hallways, ornate teak molding, two-story living room, and the balcony overlooking Central Park. A week later, Ripley was moving in. Employees dubbed it his "new baby."

Ripley rationalized that he could now work in the city during busy weeks of radio shows and lectures, then spend weekends at BION Island. His staff knew the arrangement would be more complicated than that, and would surely involve extra work for all. Seabeck, a middle-aged woman who had traveled the world before settling in America, had been Ripley's housekeeper since 1938 and had come to predict and even appreciate Ripley's frenetic pace and his antics.

She immediately ordered duplicates of Ripley's favorite clothes—one set for the city, one for the country.

* * *

BUGS BAER and other longtime friends found it astonishing that a man who'd spent so many years living out of a suitcase had become consumed by his domestic surroundings, to the point of obsession. Baer had even begun worrying about Ripley's health now that he'd stopped exercising. "Bob walks twice around that island of his and collapses," Baer told the *New Yorker*, which remarked on Ripley's "increasing tendency toward plumpness."

A doctor tried to impose a diet, but regular parties thwarted doctor's orders. At age fifty—the same age his father died— Ripley had become downright beefy. Though he tried to eat right, preferring vegetables and rice over steak and potatoes, his decade with King Features had enriched him at the expense of his athlete's physique. The youthful obsession with fitness had been fully sacrificed on the altar of fame. The former champion, once touted as someone who "plays handball as well as he draws," hadn't danced across a handball court for a decade, and the effects were mounting—high blood pressure, stress, sleeplessness, and fatigue. He'd previously held a new religious belief in the curative effects of exercise. Now he clung to the hope that if he just kept busy, kept traveling and having fun, he'd outrun his father's fate.

It wasn't just work that prevented Ripley from exercising so much as a transference of obsessions. Instead of good health he'd become fixated on good housekeeping.

Incapable of turning all household duties over to his staff, Ripley could be finicky about the smallest of domestic details. He once grew furious when an actress visited for a weekend at BION Island and clogged the plumbing with her blond hair, calling her "the dirtiest female I have ever known." He constantly relocated furniture and artwork, often redecorating entire rooms on a whim. He would tell a staffer to start working on a remodeling project that seemed important one day, but the next day he'd change his mind, telling the same housekeeper, gardener, or carpenter, "Drop it, it's not important!"

* * *

AS A BOY, Ripley once paid a hard-earned nickel for a postcard-sized duplicate of a painting by a Russian artist named Konstantin Makovsky, titled *The Boyar Wedding Feast*. When he couldn't convince his mother or sister to pose, he would sketch the postcard for practice, over and over.

One day, Seabeck found two rolled-up canvases in an attic, one of which appeared to be the original *Wedding Feast*. She framed and hung it in Ripley's New York apartment. The other painting was a portrayal of a Russian nobleman selecting a frightened girl to become his wife. Unaware of Ripley's complex views of wedlock, Seabeck encouraged him to hang *The Choosing of the Bride* in his mansion, and for some reason he decided to devote an entire room to the painting. He had the domed ceiling painted blue, to match the painting, and had the floor tiled in black and white, to match the tiled floor in the painting. When guests entered the room, the effect made it seem as if they were entering the choosing-the-bride scene itself—an oddly sentimental gesture for someone who claimed never to have been in love.

Among his more ambitious projects was digging a tunnel beneath his house, to connect the basement bar to an outdoor rotunda. Workers soon discovered they'd have to blast through bedrock to get the job done, but Ripley gave the go-ahead and put his brother in charge. Crews spent weeks boring into rock with pneumatic drills, setting off small explosives that shook the house and caused spiderweb plaster cracks in the ceilings. The tunnel eventually reached its destination, but was quickly neglected, a rarely used passageway that became a dimly lit space for Ripley to display his collection of tribal masks, which the staff called the Mask Room.

Some visitors didn't understand this need to convert a home into a museum. One writer, after a tour, said that walking through Ripley's house felt "like getting lost in the mummy section of a museum after its been closed for the night. It's just plain creepy."

Creepy or not, people loved to visit BION *and* to be around Ripley, whose quirks of dress and personality could be endlessly entertaining. Ripley had always been an oddball, but his eccentricities seemed to amplify with age. He walked quickly and pigeon-toed, with a slight butt-waggle. He sucked his teeth and twiddled his now-necessary eyeglasses. He wore a small sketch pad on a cord around his neck and was always scribbling ideas or doodling. When someone told him an interesting story, he would pop open his mouth and bug out his eyes in exaggerated astonishment.

After so many years on radio and in film, onstage and before audiences, he had become an unexpectedly adept performer, though he now sometimes performed more than necessary. In social settings, he could be pedantic and a bit of a bore. Some visitors were put off by his know-it-all history lessons, his stories about some artifact he had discovered in Bolivia or Afghanistan or Egypt. "Listening to Bob was sometimes like attending a lecture," Seabeck once said. But longtime friends and employees tolerated Ripley's monologues as fair trade for his vast generosity, for his willingness to turn his home into a carnival for *their* entertainment.

* * *

THOUGH GENEROUS and compassionate, Ripley could be atrociously forgetful. B. A. Rolfe once bumped into him on a date with a beautiful blonde, and Ripley pulled Rolfe aside to ask, "Do you know the name of the girl I'm with?" Still, he seemed able to remember anyone who had assisted him along the path to success.

Over the years he had stayed in contact with Carol Ennis, who helped him get his first newspaper job in San Francisco. If he visited San Francisco, he would always treat her to lunch or dinner, and if Ennis visited New York he would make sure she had a chauffeur-driven limousine to squire her around town.

Norbert Pearlroth, though sometimes feeling underappreciated by King Features, remained as devoted as ever to Ripley after twenty years. Pearlroth once mentioned to Ripley his frustration over the cost of his daughter's private-school tuition. The next day, Ripley handed him a $500 check, then another check each of the following six days. When Pearlroth thanked his boss for the $3,500, Ripley said, "Next time ask me something really tough."

Ripley seemed aware of his good fortune, the beam and

front door from his Santa Rosa house reminding him how far he'd come. He always showed guests the original "Champs and Chumps" cartoon hidden behind a backlit mirror above his fireplace, telling them with a gesture toward his paintings, rugs, and furniture, "If it weren't for that [cartoon], these wouldn't be here." He also seemed to feel grateful for the years of support and loyalty of longtime friends, especially Bugs Baer.

While traveling, he would often send postcards to friends, and though he might forget the day of the week he rarely forgot birthdays. He'd send hand-drawn cards, like the one drawn for Baer's fiftieth that showed Baer's head growing out of a long stem, above a caption that read "Long Life to the Half Century Plant."

Ripley frequently invited friends to stay at BION for a night or two, including his King Features boss Joe Connolly, or Doug Storer and his wife, or Vyvyan Donner, who had made him feel so welcome during his first years in New York. (It helped that Donner, as fashion editor for *Movietone News,* often brought along pretty young models.) Donner would laugh at Ripley and Baer, both now past the half-century mark, calling them "overgrown boys." Seabeck the housekeeper noticed that, whether it was softball or drinking, a political argument or girl talk, Ripley and Baer went at it "with the eagerness of two youngsters playing hooky from school."

Maybe to compensate for his abbreviated boyhood—the premature departure from high school and his teenaged entry into the workforce—Ripley performed well in the role of heedless adolescent. He loved to play pranks, such as hiding the nude Masakichi statue in guests' closets and then waiting outside for their shouts of terror.

Friends assumed there was something *chemical* at work, that

Ripley was neurotic and compulsive, perpetually sophomoric and impetuous, that he simply couldn't help himself or control his urges. Empty floor or wall space? It seemed to make him uncomfortable and needed to be filled with a statue or a weapon or a chair or a painting. Uncluttered ledges? The shelves surrounding his bar were now jam-packed with figurines, carved tusks, pistols, tureens, and old currency.

This pathology extended to his collection of pets. He now owned collies, Dalmatians, spaniels, and cats, including a six-toed Manx named Peter who loved to hide under the fridge, waiting for a dog to walk past to attack. Ripley still owned his foulmouthed parrot and had recently obtained a twenty-eight-foot boa constrictor as thick as a Dalmatian.

One weekend, on an early-morning stroll around the island, Joe Connolly practically tripped over the fat snake, named Gertie, who had gotten loose from the pen.

"Don't worry, Joe," Ripley said. "He's a friend of mine."

Though Ripley fed Gertie a steady diet of rabbits, the snake escaped regularly. Baer especially hated Gertie, and Ripley once created a barrier of broken glass around the snake's pen, assuring Baer, "A snake won't cross broken glass."

"Neither will I," Baer replied, vowing not to come back to BION while Gertie was still on the loose. (The snake was later shipped off to a zoo.)

✷ ✳ ✴

WHEN HE WASN'T OCCUPIED with his curiosities and his pets, he used BION Island to nurture his nostalgia for the boozy Prohibition-era NYAC/bachelor's lifestyle. He installed beer kegs in the bar so that even during the workweek he and his staff could slip downstairs to draw a cold pint. Whenever

B. A. Rolfe visited, the tubby bandleader would immediately grab a quart-sized tankard from Ripley's collection and insist that it never be allowed to dip toward empty.

Everyday life at BION was like a fraternity party, with a Keystone Kops aspect to the workaday. Ripley's desk was surrounded by file drawers, stacks of papers, reference books, sticks of charcoal, leftover food and drink, and two phones. While drawing he'd reach for a phone to ask a secretary to find some tidbit at the library or call some scholar—or Pearlroth—to verify an elusive fact. He was always falling behind schedule, always late for meetings. Trips to New York escalated into madcap flurries. Thursdays were the worst, since Ripley was due for rehearsals for his Friday-night radio show. Everyone scurried about collecting script pages, cartoons to deliver to King Features, Ripley's glasses, extra clothes for the New York apartment, drawing materials, and maybe a bottle of sherry for the drive south.

Still, Ripley seemed immune to the persistent backlogs, almost amused by the never-ending demands and the sometimes-angry insistence from King Features to "send more cartoons!" At the worst possible moment he would call for a spontaneous softball game or tell staffers to meet on the front lawn to help assemble some new boat he'd ordered from India. He managed to find time for fishing, boating, sunbathing, and afternoon naps. He believed in the healthy effects of a good sweat, and liked to lie in the hot sun, then cool off with a glass of beer. He took steam baths before dinner, and after dessert would lead guests downstairs to the bar for cordials, radio, and conversation. He rarely went to bed before midnight, often ending his night with a drawn-out card game, a glass of milk, or a late-night snack in the kitchen.

Seabeck the housekeeper often complained to Ripley about

his collections of curios "with no place to put them" and about the odors his crates and boxes emitted, especially anything from Tibet, which smelled like "rancid butter." One night Seabeck retired to her bedroom, exhausted as usual. She was about to climb into bed when, with a shriek, she discovered the Masakichi statue tucked beneath her bedcovers.

Over time, Ripley's staff became its own semi-functional family. Years later, friends and staffers would wonder whether the parties and gags, the dog and snakes, were Ripley's way of staving off a festering sadness.

＊　＊　＊

ONE NIGHT IN 1941, the staff sat in the kitchen, drinking and reading aloud from some of the bizarre letters submitted to Ripley's latest contest. They were laughing their heads off when Ripley, who was supposed to be in Central America, walked through the kitchen door with terrible news.

After nearly fifteen years as his most consistent female companion, his traveling partner and not-so-secret lover, Oakie, was dead.

When Oakie had gotten married—sometime in the mid-1930s, though no one seemed sure when or where—Ripley became even more vague with friends about the details of their relationship, though it was hard to ignore that they continued to spend enormous amounts of time in each other's company, on BION Island or touring the world: Morocco, Tripoli, and Libya; Germany, France, and Italy; Mexico, Brazil, and Bermuda. They once visited the Mediterranean island of Djerba, which in Greek mythology had been home to the lethargic Lotus Eaters, whose diet of lotus leaves brought them peace. He and Oakie had plucked a few leaves and fed them to each other, and Ripley declared, "One taste of this plant and man forgets all his troubles."

Over time Oakie had apparently come to accept his particular views of love and fidelity, and she seemed to agree with Ripley that America's moral standards were out of whack. Ripley felt the American preoccupation with monogamy was to blame—the same moralistic fixation that led to Prohibition. "You can't force people *not* to drink," he told one reporter—just as you can't force people to love only one person.

And yet, though he had chosen not to marry her, and allowed her to wed another, he would later confess that Oakie was "the only woman I ever loved." He had assumed she would be his covert love forever. When she succumbed to breast cancer, it clearly rattled him.

In his mourning, Ripley launched himself into a project that he hoped would honor her memory. He began designing a room that he planned to endow to a New York hospital, a place where women suffering from cancer might live during their treatment—or during their final days. He wanted the room to have soothing colors, inspiring paintings, and comfortable furniture, "to delight the eye of the sufferer." (He would work on this project off and on over the next few years, but it seems as if he never saw it through to fruition.)

After Oakie's death, Ripley seemed to resort, almost desperately, to his collector's habits. Having amassed a small zoo of pets, *four* homes (he still had his NYAC apartment and had purchased a beach house in New Jersey), plus enough employees to field two baseball teams, he began to add more and more beautiful women to his cluttered and manic life.

✳ ✳ ✳

NO ONE COULD SAY for sure when and where he found some of his companions. A random woman would show up one day, introduced as a new "secretary" or "housekeeper" or "publicist." She'd stay for dinner, then be at the breakfast table, then still around the next night, until she was part of the BION Island family. Later, there would be another new arrival, and another. Almost all were young immigrants, predominantly Asian, some in seemingly murky roles—they worked for him, lived with him, and sometimes shared his bed.

Among the first to commit herself unreservedly was a quiet and fragile Japanese woman named Ming Jung, referred to by one colleague as "an exquisite creature." As was often the case, no one at BION seemed to know the woman's full story, but Hazel Storer would sometimes chat with Ming and in time learned that she had been married to a man who had worked as a cameraman in Los Angeles. The couple split after their only child died, and Ming kept the baby's ashes in a lacquered box.

Ming accompanied Ripley on a few trips, and at parties she was often dressed in a snug-fitting Chinese gown. She became part of a rotating cast of Ripley companions who, by the early 1940s, began regularly occupying BION's guest bedrooms.

Toshia Mori, an actress whom *Time* once called "a sloe-eyed Japanese girl," was hired as a "research assistant" for Ripley's Movietone films and soon moved in. She once fainted after wandering into the secret basement room where Ripley kept his erotica and torture photos. Ripley had added to this collection over the years, including a shrunken head from Ecuador that had arrived by mail with a note: "Please take care of this, I think it is one of my relatives." One ghastly photo showed an African family, all ten of their legs terminating at the knee, and another featuring a man whose testicles were so swollen by elephantiasis he had to carry them in a wheelbarrow.

"Oh those terrible things," Toshia whispered as one of Ripley's staffers carried her to a couch and gave her some brandy.

Ming and Toshia were joined by a pert young assistant

housekeeper from Spain who napped constantly, and a histrionic Japanese singer who sought Ripley's attentions with halfhearted suicide attempts. She once swallowed half a bottle of aspirin and another time threatened to stab herself in the heart—with a bread knife. One night, she leapt dramatically off a balcony, but the four-foot drop was only enough to inflict a bruise.

Women came and went, some semi-famous, though it was never entirely clear who was friend, girlfriend, or just a curious visitor. Gossip columnists found euphemistic ways of referring to Ripley's female coterie without naming names: "a very charming friend of Ripley's" or "tall, quite dark, and full of sparkling vitality." One frequent guest was Ann Sheridan, a redheaded actress and pinup girl who was between marriages when she befriended Ripley and became a fixture at his dinner parties, occasionally photographed by his side in magazine profiles. Another regular was singer and actress Anna May Wong, a Chinese American beauty who had pulled away from Hollywood to raise money for Chinese war refugees and, in Ripley, found a sympathetic supporter of her causes.

⚬ BELIEVE IT! ⚬

Known for her dragon lady and diva roles of the 1920s and '30s, Wong had appeared with Toshia Mori in Streets of Shanghai *and* Mr. Wu *in 1927. Laws against interracial marriage prevented both actresses from becoming leading ladies, since they weren't allowed to kiss white men on-screen.*

There were others: Daniel Boone's great-granddaughter; a leggy blond Hungarian actress, Ilona Massey; singer/actress Marion Hutton, whose mother was a bootlegger and speakeasy proprietress; Marquita Nicholi, a model who lived at the famed Barbizon Hotel for Women. Ripley had little tolerance, though, for women who didn't make themselves useful in some fashion. A publicist named Kay Lawrence was another regular at BION, always drinking white wine and giggling. Ripley called her the "goofy blonde" until she mishandled a magazine story that Ripley felt was less than flattering, after which he called Lawrence "half-assed."

Sometimes these girlfriend-secretary-housekeepers would leave, to be replaced by another. Sometimes they overlapped and two or three would be living on BION Island at once. "The ones with gumption and pride left him," Hazel Storer would write years later. "Those that stayed found plenty of compensations— easy living, easy money, not too much work, and plenty of liquor."

Ripley kept bedrooms and bathrooms stocked with necessities, as well as fragrant soaps, talcums, oils, and lotions. One writer speculated that Ripley stocked his life with women so he wouldn't have to choose just one. The women had their reasons to appreciate his attentions. Though he dressed sloppily during the day—no shoes, bathrobes, charcoal-covered fingers—he cleaned up well and dressed elegantly at night. He could be funny, charming, and wildly generous. And he doted on them, sometimes taking three or four women shopping at once.

One night Doug and Hazel Storer visited to find Ripley reclined on a chaise in his living room, wearing only a robe and framed by four gorgeous women—Hungarian, English, German, and Russian. Two sat on silk pillows, massaging his feet, while two rubbed his neck and shoulders. "It looked just like a harem," Hazel recalled, and would later claim that Ripley (who had now become her boss) "lived in open concubinage."

One of Ripley's radio writers referred to them as his "Broads Brigade." If Ripley announced he was headed to New York for the day, the women would declare they'd been planning to go there too. If he was headed out of town they'd try to position themselves to be chosen to join him. Once, Ripley was headed to the Caribbean and told a girlfriend (probably Ming) that she couldn't come along because he was visiting a British colony and, since she was Japanese, she wouldn't be permitted. She saw Ripley off at Penn Station and by Philadelphia he had hooked up with the woman who *would* accompany him.

Ripley knew plenty of women were desperate to become Mrs. Robert L. Ripley. They competed with and undermined one another and sometimes went too far. A married woman from Buffalo sent a torrent of love letters and warned that if Ripley didn't write back she'd show up at BION Island. When her furniture and suitcases arrived, Ripley had to pay to send everything back. (The husband apologized for his wife's behavior.) Another fan sent a barrage of valentines, telling Ripley she was unhappy with her husband and her life. When she died, the woman's teenaged daughter took up the letter writing. One girlfriend cornered him at a train station in Vienna, a minister in tow, and Ripley hid in an empty rail car until the hopeful bride gave up.

By now, he had learned from past mistakes. Lovers who had sued or threatened to sue upon realizing a proposal wasn't forthcoming had taught him to be careful with his affections. As Hazel Storer would tell a writer years later, "He liked, needed, and distrusted women." He would admit as much, telling one interviewer, "Women are wonderful, simply wonderful— in their place." At BION, he actually took the extreme precaution of having some female guests sign a one-page waiver, in which they acknowledged that they were living on the island "voluntarily."

Slow nights featured just the "intimate circle," as Seabeck the housekeeper put it in an unpublished memoir: Ripley's brother and his wife, Crystl, plus two of Ripley's handpicked women, one on his left, one on his right. Some nights the women jostled for the more respectable position to Ripley's right.

Sometimes the arrangement flat-out collapsed. Ripley once invited Bugs Baer and others for Christmas dinner, but Baer had plans and Ripley found himself alone with just four guests: a widowed ex-girlfriend and her teenage son, a French actress, and an Asian girlfriend. As Ripley later described it to Baer, the ex-girlfriend propped a framed photograph of her late husband next to her plate while her skinny son sulked. The two other women glared at each other silently through the meal until one of them reached into the Christmas turkey, grabbed a fistful of chestnut stuffing, and threw it in her rival's face.

Ripley called Baer the next day. "It's just as well you and Louise didn't come," he said. "You probably wouldn't have had a very good time."

* * *

IN 1941, Ripley installed two massive bronze Chinese warrior statues at the end of the causeway crossing to his island. Mounted on stone pedestals, each menacing figure weighed a ton, and he would tell guests they were to ward off evil spirits. With America edging closer to war, he wasn't taking any chances.

Ripley had desperately wanted his country to remain neutral, for political and personal reasons. Earlier in 1941 he had given a radio address encouraging President Roosevelt and Congress to do everything possible to avoid the war. Former president Herbert Hoover, with whom Ripley had become friends, thanked Ripley for his efforts. "Believe it or Not, that speech has surprised me in the effect which it has had," Hoover wrote. "Your opportunities to help are very great." Hoover's encouragement prompted Ripley to write to congressmen, some of whom wrote back with promises of neutrality. Ohio senator Robert Taft replied, "It is always encouraging to hear from those who feel as I do on this issue."

Of course, the events of December 7, 1941, changed everything. By early 1942 Ripley had immersed himself emotionally and professionally in the war and in relief efforts. He began spending more time at his New York apartment, to be closer to the radio studios, and even bought the top two floors of the building to gain extra space for guests, staffers, and offices. He continued decorating Holmes's former Nirvana with Asian artifacts, including a Chinese bridal bed and a sedan chair. At one of his Chinese-themed parties, he parked the chair in the living room with Ming Jung sitting inside most of the night. Guests wondered if she willingly stuffed herself in the passenger compartment or if Ripley had encouraged it for theatrical effect.

Oddly, it seemed as if Ripley's female companions were all from lands at war—Japan, Russia, China, and Germany. Shortly before the bombing of Pearl Harbor, Ripley had hired a tall and striking new secretary, a German immigrant named Lieselotta Wisse. She was nineteen when she joined Ripley's stable of female "employees," although, unlike some others, she was a hard worker and a well-organized secretary who was soon managing Ripley's social and business schedules. *Liberty* magazine called Liese, as she was known, "a disarming-looking brunette." When Liese received her citizenship papers, Ripley threw her a party at his New York apartment. She and twenty friends arrived to find a huge Nazi flag laid out on the living room floor. Ripley toasted Liese's citizenship and, gesturing to the flag, told her to "stomp on it." He meant for it to be a cathartic event, but guests felt embarrassed for Liese as she jumped on the flag.

Ripley's hatred for Hitler was soon far outweighed, however, by mounting worries over the land that had established itself through the years as his favorite: China.

CHAPTER 20

It had been a decade since Ripley and Oakie witnessed firsthand the evidence of Japan's brutal invasion of China—the craters and rubble, the corpses and executions.

By 1942, word had reached the United States of China's many years of suffering. Eleanor Roosevelt had begun encouraging Americans to host "Bowl of Rice" parties to raise money for humanitarian aid to Chinese refugees. Ripley hosted one such charity luncheon at his apartment and invited an elegant and witty Chinese American divorcée named Li Ling-Ai to speak to guests about the United China Relief program.

Li had been raised in Honolulu and studied theater and dance in China. The war with Japan and a failed marriage inspired a move to New York in the late 1930s. She lived in near poverty in a closet-sized apartment until she was hired to run the Chinese Pavilion at the 1940 World's Fair (along with Anna May Wong). Li then helped produce and finance a 1941 documentary that exposed China's struggles against its Japanese invaders. *Kukan: The Battle Cry of China* won an honorary Academy Award and Li was invited to the White House for a special viewing with President and Eleanor Roosevelt. Soon Li was being invited to give lectures and performances, and she used her newfound fame to raise money for aid to China. She even took flying lessons, in hopes of delivering food to war-torn Chinese villages.

After seeing *Kukan* and reading about Li, Ripley invited her to his luncheon that day, one of many such fund-raisers he hosted during the early 1940s. Ripley was instantly impressed by her eloquence, humor, and charm. And it was hard to ignore that she was stunningly beautiful. Li designed her own clothes and jewelry and was always dressed as if she were a costumed stage actress, wearing shapely, intricately embroidered gowns, bejeweled headdresses, and flowers in her hair.

Li found herself drawn to Ripley, too. Though he was surrounded by other women "all the time," she found him to be "a rough diamond, but a gentleman." In an interview decades later, she recalled their first meeting: "This man, I looked at him and I thought, a real gentleman in the Chinese sense."

Ripley introduced his new friend in a cartoon as a "celebrated Chinese actress, author & lecturer." The cartoon contained a close-up sketch of Li's pretty face and the statement "Chinese eyes do not slant!! It's an illusion." (She was mad at first, since he hadn't asked for her permission.) Elsewhere in print she was described as a noted Chinese feminist, dancer, dramatist, designer, and aviatrix. She was soon being featured in *Harper's Bazaar* and *Vogue*. When Li sang at one of Ripley's dinner parties, gossip columnist Louella Parsons wrote about Li's "sweet, low, throaty voice . . . I never saw such a personality."

In no time Li became one of Ripley's "favored lady friends," as Seabeck put it, and he asked her to join his staff, giving her an impressive title: Director of Far Eastern Research. She became a regular on BION Island and at the New York apartment, and the others could tell from the start that there was something different about their relationship. They would co-host parties together, cooking up Chinese meals dressed in matching costumes. Sometimes she would pick him up in her beat-up Chevrolet and squire him to some small family restaurant in Chinatown, or she'd arrive unannounced at the mansion and he'd demand, "Hurry up and make something good to eat." A self-described "sassy girl," Li was the only one who could get away with teasing Ripley, arguing with him or making fun of him. It helped that she could match him drink for drink.

Ripley loved to spar with Li. War had caused his political views to skew further to the right, which was at odds with the left-leaning bent of some of his guests, particularly Li. At a party for Li's film he embarrassed guests by raising a toast to "that son of a bitch" Roosevelt. Often he'd instigate a political argument, taking a contrary position, egging on both sides, and it was sometimes unclear whether he felt strongly or just wanted to rile things up. At dinner tables Li would mischievously take the position of the stubborn liberal and never backed down. Ripley would get up from the table and, with a smirk, turn his radio up to full volume.

Friends couldn't quite tell if Ripley and Li were lovers or just pals, but it was hard to ignore the similarities between her and Oakie. Just as Oakie had left a war-ravaged homeland after World War I, Li was a refugee of sorts—her hometown of Honolulu had been attacked, as had her adopted homeland of China. Like Oakie, Li was sophisticated, independent, and educated, worldly and multilingual. And most important to Ripley, she was strong-willed and passionate.

Commenting years later on their friendship, Li said, "He likes to argue, likes when you argue back. He's annoyed by stooges and yes men."

Ripley and Li began traveling together—to an air show in Cleveland, lectures in Boston, and "Chinese Night" in Mamaroneck, among other destinations—to promote Li's film and to raise money for British and Chinese relief agencies. With help from Ripley and the Hearst publicity machine, Li was soon becoming famous herself. She and Ripley were frequently photographed together—a Boston newspaper photographer captured them eating cheek to cheek from a shared bowl of rice—and writers began referring to Li as "China's leading dancer."

A beautiful partnership had blossomed. Li would later describe how Ripley had given her a break when nobody else would. He encouraged and supported her, provided a leg up. She believed that, through her, he was repaying a favor to those who had helped him. She called such gestures the "reflection of the heart."

Ripley preferred people who served a purpose—those who were either funny or smart or talented or beautiful. If someone didn't enrich his life somehow, they weren't useful. He cherished those who enhanced *Believe It or Not* in some way too. And while there was a price for admission to Ripley's inner circle—he was obsessed with work and impatient with distractions—there were also rich rewards. "He pretends to be tough but he's always doing little things for people," Li told a reporter at the time, describing her new friend's loyalty and generosity.

In that manner, Li viewed Ripley as an American with a Chinese soul. She liked to think he viewed her as a Chinese with an American soul.

Though Ripley was pleased with this new relationship—especially so soon after losing Oakie—by 1942 the war had completely closed off most of the planet, sealing him inside US borders. It was a harsh blow to his wanderlust. Ever resilient, however, he managed to find a new and reliable source of unbelievably true stories for his cartoons: *war.*

✳ ✳ ✳

AFTER PEARL HARBOR, the Nehi Corporation exercised a clause that allowed it to kill Ripley's RC Cola radio show in the event of "dire international calamity." With the country about to devote all its resources to a two-front war, it seemed Ripley's decade-long run on the air might come to an end. But then his years of vocal pro-Americanism paid off in a surprising way, as did his trust in Doug Storer, who negotiated a new program with the biggest sponsor of all: Uncle Sam.

By now, Storer's own career had progressed, thanks to the exposure he'd earned as Ripley's manager and radio producer. He'd taken on other clients—self-help guru Dale Carnegie, King Features writer Bob Considine, and bandleader Cab Calloway, for example—and by late 1941 had been named head of programming at NBC's new Blue Network. Wielding his new title, within days of the Pearl Harbor attack Storer had reached an agreement with the coordinator of inter-American affairs for Ripley to broadcast twenty-six half-hour episodes featuring pro-American, war-related believe-it-or-nots. Just as he had drawn patriotic cartoons for the US government during World War I, Ripley would lend his artistic talent to the current war effort.

There was one catch: the deal had to remain a secret. The coordinator of inter-American affairs, millionaire Nelson Rockefeller, wrote to demand that Storer and Ripley never publicly mention Rockefeller, nor his department, nor the US government "as sponsoring or in any way being connected with or responsible for carrying out the project." NBC would air the shows with no reference to the real sponsor.

The Coordinator of Inter-American Affairs Office (CIAA) had been created within the State Department to disseminate news reports, films, advertising, and radio to Latin America, an effort to counteract pro-Italian and pro-German propaganda there. By 1942, CIAA had a $38 million budget and a staff of a thousand, all devoted to shaping South America's public opinion in favor of its neighbor to the north. Walt Disney performed duties similar to Ripley's on CIAA's behalf, notably a 1941 South American goodwill tour that produced the film *Saludos Amigos* ("Hello, friends"). Rockefeller's reaction to the film—"exceeds our highest expectations"—prompted Disney to produce more thinly veiled propaganda films for the CIAA.

⌁ BELIEVE IT! ⌁

US intelligence later discovered that the CIAA Office had been infiltrated by Soviet intelligence. Federal employees at the CIAA were sharing information with Soviet spies, whose code name for the CIAA was "Cabaret."

Ripley's directive was to broadcast positive stories about Americans at war and promote the United States' commitment to "Western Hemisphere defense." The primary goal was to comfort South America, as Ripley's $1,500-per-show contract put it, with stories of "every-day life, history, famous institutions, science, heroes, soldiers, statesmen, artists." Rockefeller's office, the War Department, and the State Department would be allowed to review Storer's scripts and veto guests.

See All the Americas with Bob Ripley launched in January of 1942 on Saturday nights. An announcer told listeners that "our modern Marco Polo, the most traveled man in history" would "make you better acquainted with the twenty neighboring republics to the south of us." Each show highlighted a different country, and Ripley told stories of visits to Quito, Rio, and Buenos Aires. "The principal delight in my Believe It or Not work is the pleasure of traveling," he said in one show. "But if someone should ask me where I have derived the greatest content, I would have to say, truthfully, South America." (*Truthfully,* Ripley preferred Asia to South America, having once scorned Bolivians as "stupid" and "weak.")

Ripley was proud to be playing a role in the war effort and intoxicated by the covertness of the project. Plus, he would now be able to verbally attack communism and fascism on the air without fear of being muzzled. The new show was important to Ripley, who felt he was doing something more valuable with his passionate patriotism than just entertaining. Ever the competitor, he was doing something heroic for his home team.

✳ ✳ ✳

RIPLEY'S FIRST THIRTEEN-WEEK season was extended for thirteen more weeks, and Nelson Rockefeller wrote to thank him for doing such a "marvelous job."

Then Ripley received a letter of censure from the Office of Censorship, slapping his wrist for identifying the location of a US fighter squadron in the South Pacific. Soon after that, he received a letter from President Roosevelt's radio department thanking him for "the valuable service you have rendered to the government" but informing him his contract would not be renewed. Ripley wondered if his opposition to Roosevelt was partly to blame.

Thus began a yearlong period in which Ripley would not be on the air, the longest such gap in a decade. He tried to stay busy, lending time to war efforts and charities. He cooperated with the Office of War Information by donating *Believe It or*

Not sketches—of Medal of Honor winners or star athletes in the military—which were reprinted as posters or in military newspapers. He performed onstage for servicemen headed overseas and even agreed to draw sketches for a military booklet warning soldiers about venereal disease. Still, he felt a growing need to devote more of himself, somehow, to the war.

"I wanted to get into this war," he would soon tell a reporter, concluding that radio might be "my greatest opportunity for serving my country." Storer assured Ripley that he was searching for new shows and sponsors, but there were limited opportunities "with the war picture as it is."

In late August 1942, he received more bad news. Linda Lee, the sultry-voiced singer who had performed for years on his show with B. A. Rolfe's orchestra, was dead at age twenty-seven. Lee had been under a doctor's care for "a nervous condition" and had been fretting over her husband's enlistment in the Army. She fell to her death—or possibly jumped—from the low-silled window of her seventh-floor apartment on Central Park South. Wearing a nightgown, she landed on the sidewalk across from horrified diners at the Hotel St. Moritz café.

Lee's death was the latest in a series of personal losses for Ripley, starting with the 1940 death of his high school teacher Miss O'Meara. (Ripley wrote a letter that was read at the funeral, avowing that O'Meara's teachings "will be cherished throughout my life.") That was followed by the devastating death of his lover, Oakie, and then the unexpected death of his travel secretary, George Wieda.

Even his dogs had begun dying. Barking and roughhousing had become part of everyday life at BION Island. Ripley raised Dalmatians and donated his pups to Mamaroneck's fire department. He adopted a shaggy-haired English sheepdog named Rhumba, and for promotional photos and holiday cards he would comb Rhumba's hair over one eye and pose beside his one-eyed dog, Cyclops. With so many dogs and their offspring on the island, he often gave puppies to friends as gifts.

Inevitably, not all the pets survived. Ripley's first dog, Dokie the cocker spaniel, had been killed by a delivery truck. A spaniel named Virtue crashed through the ice and drowned in the pond. His collie Flash was killed by the gardener's Saint Bernard. Ripley buried his dogs in a pet cemetery on a knoll atop BION Island. One pet's headstone read, HE LIVED A DOG'S LIFE.

As he was absorbing the deaths of colleagues and pets, he received the heartbreaking news that his companion Ming Jung had been sent to an internment camp, one of the detention centers into which Japanese Americans were forcibly relocated, beginning in 1942. It's unclear how she ended up there, since Executive Order 9066 applied primarily to Japanese Americans living on the West Coast. Ripley acted quickly and used his influence to secure Ming's release, but she'd gotten sick at the camp and had to be hospitalized. The details of her illness remained unknown to friends, but Ripley once told Storer that she'd developed problems with her circulation, that her blood pressure dropped to dangerously low levels and at one point doctors thought she'd die. Ripley fretted during her months in the hospital and visited her often. Ming eventually recovered and moved back to BION Island, but the internment and illness had taken a toll. She would spend hours paddling alone on the pond and rarely spoke about her imprisonment or illness.

By 1943, it seemed as if everything in Ripley's life had been upended by war. Newspaper friends were headed off to war assignments, trusted chauffeurs and butlers were being drafted or enlisting, and other employees found stateside jobs related to the war effort. When Almuth Seabeck's husband enlisted, the housekeeper resigned and Ripley decided to shutter BION Island for a while. It was too difficult to keep the place running without a full staff, so he hosted one last party—a farewell for Seabeck and her husband—then mothballed his mansion and moved into the New York apartment.

* * *

MONTHS EARLIER, Storer convinced NBC to allow him to create another new Ripley show to promote stories about aviation and encourage youngsters to become pilots. Sponsored by the Junior Air Reserve, with the support of the air forces of the US Army and Navy, *Scramble* would broadcast coast to coast each Friday.

Ripley aggressively took up this new cause, advocating the future of flight to America's youth. Lending his voice to the aviation community was a natural fit. He'd always had an interest in flying, and he realized that he owed a portion of his success to the airplane—his Lindbergh cartoon remained one of his best known, and the Wrong-Way Corrigan interview had been among his earlier radio coups. Over the years, he'd befriended famous flyers, including Eddie Rickenbacker, a frequent BION visitor whom he'd known since Rickenbacker's pre–World War I days as a race car driver.

Scramble gave Ripley an opportunity to tap into his memories of a world before war, to describe to radio listeners his actual visits to the places that were now gory battlefields—in China, North Africa, the South Pacific, and Europe. "When I was in Tripoli . . ." began one such episode.

Ripley's success with *Scramble* prompted the National Aeronautic Association in 1943 to name him "special assistant" to its Air Youth Division, and he embarked on a nationwide tour. He spoke to junior aviation groups, high schools, Boy Scout troops, and orphanages, encouraging young men and women to pursue a career in aviation. "The air age is on us," he told a group in St. Louis. "The airplane has made the world so small and drawn the peoples of the world so close together that in a not very long time they all may speak the same language and wear the same clothes." Fifteen years earlier, Ripley had been terrified of flying. Now he was declaring throughout the Midwest that aviation would "bring about lasting peace."

Finally, with Ripley so much in the public eye, Nelson Rockefeller contacted Doug Storer to say his office had decided to renew Ripley's CIAA show. Rockefeller said Ripley's return, with more episodes on Latin American countries, "would be in the best interest of the United States." Through the fall of 1943, Ripley was back on the air, and Rockefeller wrote in a letter, "You are certainly making a real contribution toward better understanding between the Americas."

Just as Ripley had thrived during World War I and during the Depression, he was flourishing through the second world war, at least career-wise. The year ended on a professional high note, with a twenty-fifth *Believe It or Not* anniversary party at the Waldorf-Astoria. Max Schuster couldn't attend but sent a gushing telegram: "After twenty-five years of awed and breathless admiration I am more convinced than ever that the greatest Believe It or Not of them all is the story of Bob Ripley."

✳ ✱ ✴

BACK IN LATE 1942, a German U-boat had torpedoed a British merchant ship off the South American coast and only one of the fifty-four crewmen survived.

Poon Lim, a Chinese steward, had grabbed a life vest and dived overboard, then climbed into a life raft stocked with enough food for sixty days. Lim drifted for twice that long before being rescued by fishermen off the coast of Brazil. His 133 days alone at sea—nearly twice as long as the castaways Ripley had interviewed in the Bahamas—was an all-time record.

In January of 1944, Ripley interviewed Poon, a slight and quiet man who described singing folk songs to pass the time and, when his food ran low, making a fishhook from the spring of a flashlight. On the air, while actors dramatized his plight, Poon could be heard in the background, sobbing. In his column the next day, Walter Winchell listed the emotional broadcast among his weekly "headliners."

Ripley's new show, *Rhythm, Romance, and Ripley,* sponsored by Pall Mall cigarettes and airing over the Mutual Network, became an instant hit. It was also Ripley's most lucrative radio partnership, with Pall Mall coughing up $4,000 a week for Ripley's salary. Airing five nights a week at 9:15 p.m., the fifteen-minute broadcasts focused exclusively on hard-to-believe war stories. "Amazing wonders culled from a world at war" was how publicists described it.

One night Ripley profiled a soldier whose pet monkey saved his life on a North African battlefield, and he later featured a man who was honorably discharged for snoring too loud. One show introduced listeners to Ray and Curtis Ewing, a father and son from Bellingham, Washington, with an inconceivable story. Curtis Ewing's army base in northern Australia was bombed in 1942, and while picking through rubble he found a chunk of shrapnel with his father's name etched into it. Ray Ewing, a Boeing airplane mechanic, had years earlier chiseled his name into the engine block of the family car. The scrap metal from the old car had somehow ended up in a Japanese bomb factory.

With his new show up and running, Ripley hired a press agent, and the gossip columns were suddenly packed with

Ripley stories and snippets. He earned ink in the columns of Hedda Hopper, Louella Parsons, Louis Sobol, Dorothy Kilgallen, E. V. Durling, and, on a regular basis, Walter Winchell. Some writers said Ripley was thinking of taking his strange life story to Broadway, working with a writer on a *Believe It or Not* play. Others rehashed certain facts (some questionable) about Ripley's life so frequently, so consistently word for word, that it was obvious they were writing from press releases: *born on Christmas Day . . . visited 201 countries . . . designed tombstones as his first job . . . likes the company of chipmunks . . . first man to broadcast around the world . . . still uses the front door of his boyhood home . . . only wears bowties.*

Columnists raved about evenings spent at "one of Ripley's fabulous parties," with guest lists ranging from Jimmy Durante, Jack Dempsey, and Carmen Miranda to Chiang Kai-shek's personal physician. Louella Parsons described the "heartwarming" birthday party Ripley threw for his longtime boss and friend, Joe Connolly, who had been ill. When Bugs Baer, Eddie Rickenbacker, Vyvyan Donner and others sang happy birthday to the famed King Features president, Parsons pronounced the evening "one we'll all remember."

* * *

THOUGH PARSONS PRAISED RIPLEY as "a grand host" for celebrating Connolly's fiftieth, the relationship between Ripley and his superiors had in fact become quite strained.

Ripley's radio show often stretched him to the breaking point, and his obligations to King Features got pushed down the priority list. In addition to prepping for five weekly shows, he was still drawing seven cartoons a week. And while columnists sometimes gushed that Ripley remained "one of the few famous cartoonists who still does his own drawings," the truth was that a growing stable of young King Features artists was drawing more of Ripley's cartoons.

Ripley had become overwhelmed by obligations many times before, and always emerged intact. A sheepish shrug seemed to repair all ills. Lately, however, with trusted staffers off to war and Ripley neck deep in one of the busier periods of his career, something had to give. Too often it was the cartoon. King Features executives regularly wrote or wired, from 1942 through 1945, about "your late schedule" or "further complications" or being "weeks behind our war-time schedule."

At one point, with Ripley a month behind schedule, one of Connolly's associates, Brad Kelly, pleaded: "Something has got to be done quickly . . . Won't you remedy this situation imme- diately and supply two weeks [of cartoons] every five days until you are on the war-time schedule?" The situation grew worse when mail restrictions forced Ripley to send cartoons an extra week ahead of schedule. "The situation is serious," another King Features executive wrote.

Ripley's secretary, Cygna Conly, tried to help him avoid the $5,000 fines King Features began threatening for missed deadlines, but her boss seemed almost intent on sabotage. In late 1944, desperately itchy to travel, deadlines or no deadlines, Ripley escaped to Cuba for the Christmas holidays. When he returned to New York, King Features colleagues must have all slapped their foreheads as they read headlines about Ripley's lat- est effort—trying to buy a Mexican volcano.

At a New Year's Eve party in Cuba he'd learned about a volcano that had mushroomed up from a cornfield in Mexico. A fissure in the cornfield began vomiting up lava and ash in 1943 and within weeks it had bulged to a five-story mound. By 1944 it was a 1,100-foot cone of steaming cinders called Paricutin, which continued to belch smoke and lava. Ever since the 1906 California earthquake, Ripley had been fascinated by natural disasters and the violent tics of the earth. Earlier in 1944, Italy's Mount Vesuvius had also erupted, the first such eruption since 1906, inciting Ripley's obsession with owning his own volcano.

When he learned about Paricutin, he began telling dumbfounded friends that owning it might fill a spiritual void, or that the volcano might contain minerals that would be a good financial investment. After returning from Havana, Ripley began negotiating by phone and mail with the farmer, whose claim to the land turned out to be somewhat vague. Mexican authorities finally told Ripley they weren't keen on having an American own Mexican land, and the legislature hastily passed a bill making the volcano state property.

"I could have charged admissions and made money off it," Ripley complained, vowing to search for another volcano elsewhere and proposing a *Believe It or Not* volcano contest.

Soon after the failed volcano purchase, Ripley learned that Joe Connolly, his mentor for more than fifteen years, had died. Connolly and his wife were coming home from a movie when Connolly suffered a heart attack. He died later at the hospital, in April of 1945, a week after President Roosevelt's death.

Connolly had been in poor health for years, but never slowed down. Six hundred people attended the funeral, at which Ripley served as pallbearer. Connolly's replacement at King Features, Brad Kelly, told Ripley, "You were his pride and joy."

Ripley's own health had been in continual decline. The man once called America's most eligible bachelor, who in 1942 had ranked sixth in a columnist's "Catch of the Season" list, was now described in print as "stocky" and "a heavyset middle aged man with dark laughing eyes."

He had recently learned that one culprit behind the years of suffering from sore and swollen feet was a heart condition that caused poor circulation and dropsy. When he told Li Ling-Ai about the diagnosis, she could tell he was shaken, knowing that his father had died young of a heart attack. And while there is no record of it, Hazel Storer would say years later that Ripley also suffered a small stroke in the mid-1940s—"in a hotel out in the Midwest on a lecture date."

After attending so many funerals in recent years, Ripley had to be contemplating mortality during this period, especially as America tallied its dead at the conclusion of four years at war. As World War II finally ended, Ripley tallied his own losses— friends, bosses, dogs, and even the luxury ships he had once sailed upon. War's end seemed to bring Ripley little peace, and friends worried that the years of global conflict had strained his ties to the exotic lands he'd so obsessively pursued.

"We want to be a part of somebody and something," Li Ling-Ai later observed. "We might fall in love to say we're a part of somebody's life. But to be a part of humanity, the world . . ."

Li knew Ripley well enough to sense that a man so attuned to the weird, wide world around him needed, now more than ever, to be part of *something*.

Until 1941, Ripley had stubbornly pretended that World War II wasn't spreading like a cancer, that Earth wasn't becoming a battlefield. He kept lobbying for neutrality while poring over maps and atlases, making lists and notes and lofty travel plans. Even as it became obvious that America would join the fight, he had obsessively compiled possible itineraries, optimistic but unlikely tours of Greece, Romania, Turkey, Egypt, Italy, France, West Africa, and the South Pacific.

In fact, just a year before the attack on Hawaii, he had communicated by mail with the Japanese Tourist Industry, which offered to cover the expenses for a railway tour of Japan. His travel secretary at the time, George Wieda, advised Ripley that some of his ideas were "impractical."

Now that the war was over, he couldn't wait to get back overseas after five years of wartime restrictions. Unfortunately, the travel industry was hardly ready to accommodate him. Indeed, many of the beautiful vessels that had once delivered him to exotic ports had been lost during the war and now lay in pieces on the ocean floor.

The SS *Santa Luisa*, aboard which Ripley had sailed to South America in 1925, had been sunk in the Aleutian Islands. The *Conte di Savoia*, which carried him home from Europe in 1932, had been set afire and bombed by the Germans, sinking in the English Channel. The *Savoia's* sister ship, the SS *Rex*, which ferried Ripley back and forth across the Atlantic a few times, had also been sunk, by the British.

He had tried to explore close-to-home waterways during his decade at BION Island, paddling his pond in his international collection of boats from Iraq, Alaska, and Peru, or occasionally commuting into Manhattan on his brother's yacht. Though Ripley had championed the power of aviation, he preferred being on the water. And when he learned that no luxury liners would be available for passenger travel anytime soon, in early 1946 he decided that he was ready for a boat of his own.

As usual, no ordinary purchase would suffice. For $7,500, he bought the strangest and least practical vessel on the eastern seaboard.

*　*　*

THE *MON LEI* had been built in 1939 for a wealthy Hong Kong businessman. (Ripley always referred to him as a "war lord.") According to one version of the story, when the Japanese invaded China, they captured the boat and sold it on the black market to British employees of Dollar Steamship, who were stranded in Hong Kong. The new owners sailed with a Chinese crew across the Pacific, through the Panama Canal, and up to Baltimore, where Ripley found the boat. In another version, the boat was sailed across to California, to keep it out of Japanese hands, and was later found sunk in the mud in Florida.

Ripley invested $40,000 to restore and repaint the worn-out

vessel. He installed a powerful new diesel engine and, in recognition of a Chinese belief that boats are propelled by the spirits of dragons, had eyes, teeth, and whiskers painted on the engine. In the wheelhouse he painted a Chinese saying that translated as "May she sail like a flying dragon and move like a leaping elephant." For the boat's flag, he chose the entwined yin and yang symbols. He installed a gong to ward off evil spirits and, because Chinese sailors believed that only a golden anchor could hold fast, he gold-plated his anchor accordingly. Belowdecks, there were sleeping cabins with six bunks and a tiled bathroom with a shower stall. He refinished the elaborately hand-carved teak wood, and the paint scheme throughout was heavy on gold and red lacquer.

Ripley loved to explain how the name *Mon Lei* (in a Cantonese dialect) meant "ten thousand miles" or "infinity," that it was sometimes used to imply "bon voyage." She was a fishing boat known as a "junk," fifty feet long, seventeen feet wide, and her draft—the depth of the hull below the waterline—was just shy of five feet. The flat-bottomed boat was designed for the shallow waters of the lower Yangtze in Shanghai. Rather than carve through water, "she slides over it," Ripley liked to explain. Of course, that made the *Mon Lei* ill suited for the chop around New York and along the East Coast. But it wasn't so much navigational proficiency he valued as the exotic worldliness his boat represented, and the freedom from US shores she offered.

Though it had been built for sailing, the three scalloped sails were now decorative, made obsolete by the new engine. But Ripley insisted on keeping the sails up, and local boaters snickered at the diesel smoke coughing from the alleged sailboat's rear. On weekends, Ripley would invite friends aboard for floating parties around Long Island Sound, serving cocktails and

Chinese food in his captain's outfit—a double-breasted jacket, white pants, and sailor's cap. Ripley hired a real captain and crew to navigate, but he loved to dress the part. He'd invite guests belowdecks to rub the belly of Ho-Tei, his statue of a Chinese good-luck god. He kept a prayer wheel aboard with 1,000 prayers inside a cylinder that, when spun, was said to release the prayers toward heaven. One writer said that descending belowdecks "is like entering a different world, one in which grinning Buddhas, flaming-mouthed dragons, and prayer wheels are necessary accoutrements."

Ripley soon grew bored with the waters of greater New York and began planning more distant *Mon Lei* adventures. Though global hostilities had mostly ended, it was still risky for civilian vessels to sail beyond American waters, so Ripley came up with routes that would allow him to safely play captain for weeks at a time. He rationalized that these trips would perform double duty as colorful *Believe It or Not* publicity campaigns. In April of 1946, he and his crew sailed to Florida, stopping in a dozen ports along the way. Liese Wisse and Ming Jung joined him on the sluggish journey south—the boat was only capable of 11 knots. When the *Mon Lei* finally arrived in Miami, a newsman said she "looks like something between an Orange Bowl float and an opium dream."

On one trip to Connecticut, Ripley was scheduled to be feted by the *Hartford Times*. The publisher and editor waited dockside with a King Features publicist named Joe Willicombe, all of them looking down the Connecticut River for the *Mon Lei*. Willicombe finally excused himself and drove south until he found the *Mon Lei* docked in Middletown, fifteen miles away. When Willicombe asked why they weren't in Hartford, the captain insisted, "This *is* Hartford!" Willicombe found Ripley relaxing below and convinced him that they were still an hour's sail from Hartford, then drove him north to the day's festivities.

The next day, the rival *Hartford Courant* teased, RIPLEY ERRS, MISTAKES MIDDLETOWN FOR HARTFORD.

In a similar display of Ripley's nautical naiveté, he agreed to sail up the Hudson River for a day of festivities in Albany. The *Mon Lei* was expected by ten a.m., to join a flotilla of yachts and Navy ships. Hundreds lined the shore, awaiting the flamboyant boat and her owner, but by noon there was no sign of them. Joe Willicombe again found himself nervously driving downriver, where he found the *Mon Lei* bobbing lifelessly. Her engines had died and the captain had no luck attempting to sail the final miles. Willicombe wired a message to Albany and a Navy boat sped to the rescue, hooked a rope to the *Mon Lei*'s bow, and towed her into port.

For a day trip into Manhattan to view a flotilla of Navy ships, Ripley, Baer, Li Ling-Ai, and others dressed in Chinese costumes and swilled cocktails as the *Mon Lei* chugged south, passing beneath drawbridges. When a bridge tender asked Ripley's captain to identify himself, Baer taunted, "We can't tell you. We're smuggling in dope from the Orient." At another bridge, Ripley pointed to Li Ling-Ai and yelled, "You better let us pass, we have Madame Chiang Kai-shek aboard."

When the *Mon Lei* sailed too close to the USS *Missouri*, which President Truman was scheduled to visit by helicopter, a Coast Guard patrol boat motored up and began nudging the *Mon Lei* away. An officer ordered Ripley's crew by megaphone to "pull to the Jersey shore," and the party came to an end with Ripley, unable to talk himself out of trouble, being interrogated and paying a fine.

* * *

THE *MON LEI* quickly became Ripley's refuge, and his favorite toy. After hiring a full-time captain, a first mate, and a cook, he spent as much free time as possible exploring East Coast ports. Ripley found the deadlines, the phone calls, and the demands of his fame all melted away while sailing.

Over the years he had often told reporters that he sometimes imagined himself as the reincarnation of a Chinese warlord, or that he wished he could come back in his next life as "a Chinaman." On the *Mon Lei*, he could live out such fantasies. When he brought girlfriends along, he expected them to dress their part. In newspaper and magazine photographs, Ming Jung, Liese Wisse, and other female friends and secretaries are usually wearing embroidered Chinese dresses. He'd invite well-known Chinese entertainers aboard, including actresses Anna May Wong and Jessie Tai Sing. For one magazine photo shoot he hosted beautiful dancers from the China Doll nightclub, and his itinerary for press tours always included a request for "Chinese girls for pictures." (Joe Willicombe actually received a letter from King Features with the exact instructions: make sure good-looking Chinese women are always aboard, and reserve hotel suites for Ripley and his "secretaries.")

Li was a frequent passenger, always dressed in elegant Chinese garb. She even put together a stump lecture about the *Mon Lei*'s features and oddities, which she would deliver to visiting journalists. During a trip to Greenwich, Connecticut, Ripley left the *Mon Lei* at the pier to play golf with Samuel F. Pryor, a vice president with Pan American Airways. Pryor delivered his mother and her friend to the pier and Li gave the older women a tour. One of them asked about the large symbol over Ripley's bed and Li explained, "It means 'I wish you one thousand lays.'" The older women nodded their heads, thinking of leis, the flowery Hawaiian wreaths.

That fall, he docked the boat in Long Island and put Ming Jung in charge of an overhaul, which included adding a barroom and converting one of the cabins into a bedroom/art studio. Ripley then spent most of the winter of 1946–47 living and working aboard the *Mon Lei* (with Liese Wisse along as his companion) traveling south to Charleston, Savannah, Miami, and Key West, where newsmen gawked at Ripley's "pretty secretary," who felt woozy after weeks at sea. Ripley never got seasick, Wisse said with a pout to the reporters: "It makes me *mad.*"

The *Mon Lei* sailed up Florida's west coast to St. Petersburg, where he signed autographs at the pier for hours.

His staff would later learn that he had signed something else on aboard the *Mon Lei* that spring in St. Petersburg. The "Last Will and Testament of Robert L. Ripley" was witnessed and signed by Liese Wisse and the *Mon Lei*'s skipper, William L. Platt, on April 4, 1947.

After Ripley signed the document, he hid it aboard the *Mon Lei*, hoping its services wouldn't be required for years to come.

✳ ✳ ✳

LATE THAT YEAR, he concluded another season of radio and sailed once more to Florida for the winter. When the *Mon Lei* arrived in Miami in the final days of 1947, she was surrounded by so many curious onlookers that Ripley (and Liese) had to check into a hotel to get some rest. A reporter cornered Ripley and asked him to describe "the greatest oddity," but Ripley said he was still looking.

"When I find it, I'll retire," he said.

Having been diagnosed with high blood pressure and warned by doctors to take better care of himself, he must have sensed that retirement was near. During the Christmas holidays, he decided he liked the idea of sunshine in winter, and bought himself yet another house—a Spanish-style mansion called Hi-Mount—in Palm Beach. He immediately had a special dock and boathouse built for the *Mon Lei*, right on the shore of Lake Worth, a lagoon that connected to the Intracoastal Waterway.

His first night at Hi-Mount, in early February 1948, was spent eating take-out food on the floor with a girlfriend and Doug and Hazel Storer. Two employees were still driving south from New York with furniture. The only items in the house were a couple of chairs and cabinets, a Chinese rug, and a beat-up wooden drawing table from the *Mon Lei*, which Ripley had been using for thirty years. He set up a small buffet on the table and they all sat on the rug eating cold cuts and drinking Michelob beer.

The Storers thought Ripley seemed more at ease than he'd been in years. Far from the demanding New York lifestyle, Florida seemed to relax him.

He certainly wasn't thinking about his recently signed will that first night at Hi-Mount. The will that named those who'd befriended him or hired him or worked for him or slept with him over the years. The will that listed in detail the amount of money each of the most important people in his life should receive when he was gone. The will that named his brother and sister, as well as an inventory of current and former secretaries, housekeepers, and lovers.

"He was utterly happy that night," Hazel Storer later said. "He was happy and relaxed and felt free to be completely natural."

When the Storers left for their hotel, Ripley and his companion curled up in a pile of jackets on the Chinese rug and fell asleep.

Within weeks of that happy first night in his new Florida home, Ripley was back in New York, back to the lifestyle he'd been denied during the war. He reopened BION Island, started hosting parties again at his New York apartment, and was back on the air. Ripley's *Believe It or Not Radio Odditorium* had broadcast three times a week in 1947, but NBC decided to bump the show to five days a week for the 1948 season.

Just as quickly, he was back to planning his long-delayed escape from American soil. By now—two and a half years after the war—the full onset of peace meant Ripley could travel once more. The *Mon Lei* and the new Florida house had been exciting distractions, but apparently not enough.

He suddenly, *urgently,* wanted to return to Asia, especially China. Ripley had first mentioned this surging desire to Doug Storer at a Christmas party. "How about you and Hazel going to China with me?" he had asked. Weeks later, he invited Storer to his apartment, ostensibly to discuss details of the radio show. Instead, Ripley again raised the topic of China. He'd been reading news reports about his favorite country's tilt toward communism after World War II and felt the need to act fast if he wanted to see China again.

"It won't be long before the Reds gobble up the rest of the country—gobble it up and close it up," he said. "This will probably be our last chance to go back."

Storer reminded Ripley of his contractual obligations—the NBC program and the cartoon, to name two—and that he couldn't just sail off to the Orient. But Ripley seemed insistent, almost desperate, and suggested that they broadcast radio shows by remote along the way, as they had during the *See America* series. Storer said he'd look into it, doubtful that he could pull it off but worried that Ripley wouldn't let it go.

A solution practically fell into Storer's lap. He spotted a *New York Times* ad for the upcoming maiden voyage of the SS *President Cleveland*, which would be making a speedy tour through the South Seas, China, and Japan. Storer immediately called the head of American President Lines and pitched an idea: Robert Ripley would air his weekday radio show from aboard the *President Cleveland*. Fully warming to Ripley's harebrained adventure, Storer suggested bringing a technician along so they could create audio travelogues from each country. The fifteen-minute shows could be performed in foreign ports or at sea from the ship's deck, recorded, and transmitted back to New York.

Storer convinced the president of the cruise line that the gimmick, and Ripley's presence aboard ship, might be good publicity. The president finally agreed to host Ripley and his party free of charge. The ship would leave San Francisco in April, giving Storer less than a month to prepare the Believe It or Not machine for the road.

✳ ✳ ✳

RIPLEY KNEW THE drill. As with his regular trips before the war, he promised King Features he'd mail cartoons and promised NBC he'd send radio shows, even if such commitments would make for an exhausting vacation with little time for unplanned diversions. As usual, there were girlfriend issues to manage. Liese Wisse, Ripley's longtime secretary (and part-time lover), insisted on coming along. Ripley initially didn't want her aboard, having already invited Li Ling-Ai, who was out west and would meet him in San Francisco. Ripley recklessly instructed Storer to tell Wisse the trip had been canceled, but of course she discovered the truth, and Ripley relented. She packed a huge trunk full of dresses and joined him on a westbound train.

Storer, meanwhile, arranged to have his wife, Hazel, come along to help with radio scripts, and an NBC production manager named Ed Dunham to set up the radio equipment. Liese would help photograph everything—Storer wanted to make sure he captured it all on film, knowing that Ripley's return to Asia might be his last.

But first, the entourage had to stop in Los Angeles, to offset the cost of Ripley's troupe's ride to China. As part of a complex scheme Storer had worked out with NBC, Ripley had to appear on the *Truth or Consequences* radio show before earning his free passage on the *President Cleveland*.

✳ ✳ ✳

GEORGE MCMILLIN was a young stockbroker from Chicago whose father had recently died. When George's girlfriend dumped him, George moved to Los Angeles to live with his widowed mother and twin brother, and to pursue his dream of breaking into radio. When a friend gave him a ticket to the *Truth or Consequences* radio show, George was plucked from the audience as one of the show's contestants.

The host, Ralph Edwards, instructed McMillin that his challenge was to exit the studio and convince the first person he met that he was the cartoonist Robert Ripley. In the studio hallway he met a man named Roberts, from Des Moines (actually Ripley in disguise), and tried selling himself as Ripley, but quickly gave up and confessed that he was "just George McMillin." Edwards then asked McMillin if he'd like to meet the *real* Ripley, and McMillin said, "Sure!"

"Well, shake hands with him," said Edwards. "He's right in front of you!"

When McMillin recovered from the shock, he was told that he'd been chosen to spend an expenses-paid trip with Ripley, leaving from San Francisco in less than a week. McMillin would receive a spending allowance of $600 a week, and in a note to his mother he gushed that he'd won a trip to the Orient "with the most traveled man in the United States—and they are going to *pay* me to go."

The ship left port on April 9, and as McMillin settled into his bunk he couldn't sleep a wink, thinking how lucky he was. "How can this all happen to me?" he wrote in his diary. "I'm not that good a boy. I will be from now on, tho." McMillin learned the next day that his trunk had been left on the San Francisco pier, and that he was headed to China with just the clothes on his back. He had to borrow $50 from Ripley to buy clothes from the ship's store.

Also aboard the ship was Ripley's composer/conductor friend Rudolf Friml. The two men reminisced about their travels to the South Seas together in 1932. Friml was accompanied by two beautiful Chinese "secretaries," and McMillin told his diary that Friml's companions were the prettiest women aboard.

McMillin's first days on the *Cleveland* were spent half-drunk beside the pool, ogling Friml's friends; earning a blistery sunburn; dancing (badly) on the wooden dance floor; sharing late-night cocktails with Li Ling-Ai, who could hold her liquor better than most men; and sweating off hangovers in the ship's gymnasium with Doug Storer.

Ripley, meanwhile, made himself scarce, holing up in his stateroom, scratching out cartoons while sipping gin and grape-fruit juice. Sometimes he emerged full of mirth at cocktail hour and joined the others for dinner, after which they'd roll games of dice. One night they all crowded around a radio to listen to a rebroadcast of the *Truth or Consequences* show.

McMillin found Ripley to be generous and entertaining, always willing to offer a bottle of beer or a sandwich. He also glimpsed the melodrama of Ripley's VIP lifestyle. Ripley once blew up when he learned that his favorite masseur had missed the ship at San Francisco. Storer had to hunt down someone to attend to Ripley's sore back, and to the rescue came a bass player in Friml's orchestra who was studying to become a chiropractor.

Still, Ripley spent most of his days inside his darkened cabin, possibly to avoid Liese Wisse, who hadn't learned until San Francisco that she'd have to share a cabin with her perceived rival, Li Ling-Ai. During the first days of the journey, Liese made frequent visits to Ripley's cabin, where she and Ripley launched into terrible arguments like an embittered married couple. No one was quite sure what they were fighting about, but their shouts spilled into the hallways.

* * *

IN HAWAII, the "land of romance and happiness" where Ripley once imagined himself retiring, he finally emerged from his stateroom for an eighteen-hour layover packed with the duties and obligations of fame.

He reunited with former Olympic swimming champ and

famed surfer Duke Kahanamoku, who was now fifteen years into his term as Honolulu's sheriff. Duke escorted Ripley's group to the Outrigger Canoe Club at Waikiki Beach, where Ripley recorded one of three radio shows scheduled for his short Hawaiian visit. He then climbed into an outrigger canoe with McMillin, Wisse, and two beefy guides. The fivesome paddled offshore, surrounded by Duke and other local surfers. When a big swell approached, the guides yelled, "Paddle! Paddle! Paddle!" Ripley's boat caught the wave, as did the nearby surfers, and they all surfed the curl toward shore.

Ripley had surfed in an outrigger canoe during his memorable South Seas trip with Oakie sixteen years earlier. Now he threw his head back, lifted his oar in the air with both hands, and laughed giddily as water sprayed over the sides. It would be one of the purest, happiest moments of the trip.

During that night's radio show, Ripley interviewed a local boy with the shortest Hawaiian name (Mi) and a girl with the longest (eighty-one letters). In another show, Ripley gave an impassioned plug for Hawaiian statehood and interviewed Li Ling-Ai's parents, both doctors for fifty years. Li's parents threw a dinner party, after which Ripley made an emotional toast to his Hawaiian hosts, who escorted Ripley's entourage back to the *Cleveland* for its midnight departure.

For the next twelve days, Ripley mostly retreated to the sullen cave of his stateroom while the rest of his entourage fell into a lazy schedule, the leisurely life-at-sea pace Ripley once loved. McMillin, the Storers, Wisse, Li, and the others sunned themselves by the pool, played tennis and shuffleboard, ate buffet lunches, and on the rare cool days sipped hot bouillon. Tea was served at four each afternoon, followed by highballs at five, then dinner and a carefree night of card games, slot machines, or bingo. One night the ship's staff threw a costume ball and the men in Ripley's group borrowed clothes from Wisse and showed up in drag. (Liese brought along so much clothing her trunk blocked the bathroom entrance. During a cabin inspection, the ship's captain asked Li how she got in and out past Wisse's trunk. She winked at him and said, "Easy. I go Chinese fashion—sideways." Li's quip later got back to Ripley, who bugged out his eyes and roared with laughter.)

As the days wore on, Ripley's absence from most activities began to feel awkward. McMillin noted Ripley's truancy in his journal: "Very seldom see Mr. Ripley during the day. He is usually working in his stateroom . . . Once in a while he gets up on deck for a couple of hours of sun." Ripley seemed to spring to life just before his broadcasts, and performed dutifully. Then he'd disappear back to his room. With windows shut and shades drawn, it became rank with leftover food, fruit peelings, unwashed clothes, and empty cocktail glasses. In a rare display of hospitality, Ripley hosted a cocktail party one night for thirty guests, all of them getting bombed and silly. Li sang "When Irish Eyes Are Smiling" and Storer and McMillin performed a mock *Believe It or Not* radio show that had Ripley howling.

"Gosh, life is wonderful," McMillin declared in that night's journal entry. But as the *Cleveland* steamed toward the Philippines, Ripley's laughter was again replaced by quiet solemnity.

Ripley one day asked the ship's florist to prepare a wreath of flowers. He'd arranged with the captain to visit the spot where a Japanese ship carrying American POWs had been accidentally bombed by US planes. One of those killed was the son of Ripley's friend in New York, and Ripley had offered to toss a wreath atop the spot where the so-called hell ship went down. Coincidentally, another passenger aboard the *Cleveland* had prepared a similar ceremony for his twin brother, who was lost on the same ship. Ripley and the other man stood beside the railing as the *Cleveland* slowed to a crawl. A small crowd gathered as a priest said a quiet prayer and they each tossed their wreaths overboard.

Ahead in Manila waited more celebrity duties and more reminders of war: a city in ruins, buildings and churches gutted and crumbling, pocked with battle scars. In port, children swarmed around Ripley's group, begging for coins and Cokes and shrieking, "Hello, Joe!" Ripley, drenched in sweat, swatted them away, looking stricken as he scanned the gaping wounds and lopsided buildings of the downtown skyline.

With special permission, Ripley's crew received a tour of Corregidor Island, at the entrance to Manila Bay. Douglas MacArthur had used the island's tunnel network, Malinta Tunnel, as his headquarters at the start of America's entry into World War II, but the island fell to Japanese invaders in 1942. When it was retaken by US forces in 1945, many Japanese soldiers committed suicide to avoid capture, detonating explosives that brought sections of the tunnel down on top of them. Across nearly five years of battle, Corregidor had been shelled to rubble. Only Filipino demolition squads and some American soldiers lived there now, and the island remained a dangerous place, rigged with land mines and booby traps. Just weeks earlier, twenty men were killed by an explosion in Malinta Tunnel, their bodies still trapped inside. Some of the soldiers stationed on the island believed Japanese fighters were still hiding deep inside the tunnels, unaware the war had ended.

Ripley's tour guide was a young Filipino lieutenant who oversaw the demolition crews. As he drove Ripley inland, the lieutenant said a land mine was found on the road that very morning—Ripley could have been killed. Ripley had brought along a case of cold Dutch beer, but he and his companions hardly felt festive, and the beer quickly turned warm. At the top of the island, they all began climbing a tower, its metal staircase rickety and damaged. Ripley, now a much portlier specimen than the athlete he'd once been, was exhausted and refused to climb the last steps to the top. The others continued up, then looked out over the complete devastation of a once flowery and magical island, silent except for a few birds.

"Once, many people lived over there," the lieutenant said, pointing. "They laughed and danced and the island was very alive. Now, there is nothing here but death."

On the boat ride back to Manila, one of the engines died and the two-hour trip stretched to four. Ripley arrived shamefully late for a banquet with Army officers and orphans who had been held during the war at nearby Santo Tomas Internment Camp.

In the next day's radio show, Ripley solemnly described the "extent of the damage done by the Japs."

* * *

AFTER A ONE-DAY VISIT to Hong Kong, during which Ripley visited the Wo Hop shipyard where the *Mon Lei* had been built a decade earlier, the SS *President Cleveland* steamed into Shanghai, finally delivering Ripley back to Chinese soil. The arrival wasn't nearly as cathartic as he'd hoped.

Ripley had first visited Shanghai twenty-five years earlier and it had always ranked atop his list of most fascinating cities—"the Paris of the Orient," he'd called it. Now he found chaos, poverty, and anti-American angst. The city had taken a steady beating since the Japanese bombing in 1932, shortly before Ripley's visit that same year. After so many years of battle, the recent postwar economic collapse, and the rising influence of the Communist Party, Ripley hardly recognized Shanghai. As one employee later put it, for Ripley it was like meeting "an old flame who had become soiled and shabby with age, illness, and misfortune."

"Shabby" didn't come close to describing what had occurred in Shanghai after Japan's more aggressive second invasion in 1937. More than 200,000 Chinese soldiers were killed and thousands of civilians raped or beheaded. Eleven years later, Ripley found himself dumbstruck by Shanghai in her wrecked and soiled postwar state.

In a radio broadcast he announced that every time he turned a corner his eyes popped from his head, that he was in a "continual mental tailspin." He was sorry that the man-powered rickshaws had been replaced by pedicabs, and it almost hurt to see the ruined swimming pool at the French Club, which had been used to store Japanese bombs. The city's economy was in turmoil, the exchange rates fluctuating hourly. At one point an American dollar was worth a million Chinese dollars. Ripley described for Radioland how near-worthless $1,000 Chinese bills blew down the streets, how a newspaper cost $50,000 and a single cigarette cost $6,000. In order to buy a new suit from his favorite tailor, Ripley had to hire two men to lug wheelbarrows of Chinese currency from Chase Bank.

Despite the eye-popping distractions, Ripley stuck to the work schedule, drew his cartoons, and spoke into his microphone to NBC listeners. But he seemed disturbed by China's sad state of affairs. During a dinner party at the ambassador's residence he learned that the Communist Army was literally at Shanghai's city gates. He gruffly excused himself and went back to his hotel. Hazel Storer, who had once lived in Shanghai, could tell that Ripley was a wreck. "Shanghai was all but unrecognizable . . . a ravaged caricature," she would write years later. "The whole city seemed to be covered in a thin, gray scum.

The people were silent, indifferent . . . He knew that he would never see China again." Ripley would later describe how it was "beyond all belief" for him to watch the citizens of Shanghai "sit idly in the streets waiting for the Communist armies to roll in and take over."

The next day, Ripley told Doug Storer he wanted to leave Shanghai immediately and fly ahead to Tokyo, to prepare for their planned broadcast from Hiroshima. He argued that he and Storer could use the extra days ahead of the *Cleveland*'s arrival to ensure that their stay in Japan was fruitful. Storer agreed, and he and Ripley caught a hastily arranged flight.

In Tokyo, Douglas MacArthur's staff arranged for Ripley to broadcast from Radio Tokyo, the infamous station where Tokyo Rose had aired her taunting wartime propaganda. MacArthur's PR officer then helped Ripley visit Hiroshima. Security was tight, so Ripley traveled alone, carrying his own camera to film the spot above which the atomic bomb "Little Boy" had detonated nearly three years earlier. He taped his radio show from that site, interviewing survivors of the US attack. Surrounded by mounds of rubble and a crowd filled with injured and sick victims, Ripley told radio listeners that vegetation had begun to grow again and that residents "look very well and they're beginning to wear their bright clothes again." But his voice seemed shaky and unsure.

Meanwhile, back on the *Cleveland*, the others were having "a gay old time," as McMillin put it. He and Li one night competed in a "chug a lug" contest of martinis. When the ship reached the port at Yokohama and they all reunited, Hazel Storer became worried at how "sobered and saddened" Ripley seemed after Hiroshima.

He was becoming more somber as the trip progressed.

✳ ✳ ✳

ONE NIGHT, the ship's captain hosted a dinner and invited Ripley to sit beside him at the head of the table. Ripley began drinking heavily, and was soon grousing about Franklin Roosevelt, a tirade that escalated into shouts about "that son of a bitch."

The others at the table—including congressman Emmet O'Neal, a Democrat from Kentucky, who'd been appointed ambassador to the Philippines—later said Ripley acted like "a wild man," cursing and waving his arms, his face turning purple. Friends were never entirely sure of the source of such venom. Ripley had for decades lived among wealthy men who had resisted Roosevelt's New Deal. He then became one of those millionaires who hated the idea of sharing his income with the government. He could be generous with charities, he was patriotic to a fault, but he didn't trust the US government with his tax dollars.

Ripley had once met Roosevelt, in the 1930s, and initially claimed to like the man. He served on a March of Dimes committee at one point and sketched a few *Believe It or Not* cartoons that were sympathetic to Roosevelt. Over the years, however, his animosity grew, and even three years after Roosevelt's death his hatred was on full, fuming display that night at the captain's table. Years later, friends would speculate that maybe the poverty of Ripley's youth fueled his belief that the New Deal helped people who should be helping themselves. Li wondered if it had something to do with China—Roosevelt's hesitance to help China during its war with Japan, or maybe Ripley's pride in the fortitude of the Chinese. "He liked China because he saw people working despite poverty, working in spite of war," she said. Ripley seemed to believe the New Deal prevented people from finding their inner strengths (as he had) and made them "beggars forever."

Whatever the complicated reasons, Ripley seemed to know he'd gone too far that night. The captain, Hobart Ehman, finally rose and put a hand on Ripley's shoulder, then whispered in his ear. Ripley hung his head and excused himself from the table.

*　*　*

HOMEBOUND TOWARD SAN FRANCISCO, the *Cleveland* stopped once more in Honolulu, where Ripley received special permission and a military escort to tour the devastated naval yard at Pearl Harbor. Here again he came face-to-face with lingering scenes of the war's most terrible moments.

Many of the ships that had been wounded or destroyed on December 7, 1941, had been scrapped or sunk, leaving only the towers, turrets, and antennae of the USS *Arizona* visible above the waterline. Ripley told radio listeners the *Arizona*'s remains looked "like bony skeleton hands." More than 1,100 men had died on the *Arizona*. Ripley was shocked to learn that most of the bodies were still entombed inside.

Standing above the rusting battleship, trying to describe on-air what he was experiencing, Ripley's voice quavered and he struggled to proceed. The others stood back nervously and watched him peer down into the water, the *Arizona*'s deck visible just feet below the surface. He seemed so sad.

"You have no idea how shocking was the sight of that twisted, tortured steel," Ripley said at the close of his broadcast. "I'm sure that all my listeners will join me in tribute to the heroes of Pearl Harbor."

Li Ling-Ai had decided to stay in Honolulu with her parents, and as the *Cleveland* left she stood on the pier waving up at Ripley and the others, wiping tears from her eyes.

While sailing toward home—just ahead of warnings that a tidal wave was roaring toward Hawaii—Ripley told Storer that he wanted to design a memorial for the *Arizona*, some monument that could become a national shrine and forever honor the men who had died there. Ripley even hoped to convince the Navy to raise the *Arizona* and give the dead sailors a proper burial. Storer promised he would get the idea and a few drawings into the right hands, and Ripley began sketching various designs during the final days of the three-week, 26,000-mile journey.

* * *

ON THE LAST LEG to San Francisco, the Storers, McMillin, and Ed Dunham (NBC's radio manager) held a small party for Ripley in his stateroom. Dunham performed a mock radio skit, pretending to be Ripley celebrating his ninety-second birthday. But the party was cut short by stormy seas; not quite the predicted tidal wave but a violent thrashing that tossed the ship and caused Ripley to miss his final radio broadcast, scheduled for that night in San Francisco. It was the only show he missed during the journey.

In San Francisco, as he often did during visits there, he stopped briefly at McAllister Street to look into the basement windows of his first apartment. He and the others then traveled by train to Los Angeles for one more *Truth or Consequences* show. That night, Ripley invited McMillin to dinner at the Brown Derby, along with two beautiful blond Hungarian actresses, Mitzi Bruce and Ilona Massey. Massey gave McMillin her phone number and told him, "Call me sometime."

McMillin had fallen in love a dozen times during his weeks abroad, and noticed that Ripley—who "dresses colorfully and in good taste for a big man"—seemed to attract beautiful women, seemingly without trying. The trip had been a young man's fantasy and McMillin filled his diary with giddy descriptions of all the stunning women he'd met. Though he had seen little of

Ripley during the cruise, he was suddenly sitting at Ripley's side in the company of two Hollywood starlets.

Ripley left the next morning for a train ride to San Simeon, to meet with William Randolph Hearst. McMillin, meanwhile, was soon back with his widowed mother, unemployed and planning to look for a job. Yet, as he put it in the final line of his diary, he'd always be able to say, "I went to the Orient with Bob Ripley.

"I could learn more facts in 10 minutes of conversation with Mr. Ripley than I could in reading a whole volume of Book of Knowledge. What a guy."

CHAPTER
23

Those who'd watched Ripley grow moodier and more unpredictable in recent years had hoped that the trip to Hawaii, the Philippines, China, and Japan would refresh him. Instead, he returned home crankier and more volatile than ever.

He snapped at employees and friends. He fired and rehired one of his personal secretaries, Bill McDonald, almost weekly. Once during a dinner party he barked at Ming Jung, telling her not to speak to the other guests, saying, "Get off to your room." He even took his frustrations out on Doug Storer. When one show ran behind schedule, Storer interrupted Ripley during the final moments in order to reach the commercial break in time. Ripley seethed for days and then sent Storer a furious letter. "I don't recall being so disturbed or humiliated as I was on the last program when you cut me off on the air," he wrote, complaining that the dramatic sketches were too long. "This definitely I will never permit again under any circumstances whatever."

Storer dutifully wrote a lengthy letter of apology, blaming the director and promising, "It won't happen again."

King Features was also a target of Ripley's wrath. In a 1948 memo to his editor, Brad Kelly, he complained about changes to a cartoon in which an artist who drew the caption had covered up a small portion of the drawing and, in Ripley's view, ruined the whole thing. "I seriously object to any change being made in the Sunday cartoon," he wrote. "Certainly the greatest newspaper feature in the history of the newspaper business should not be cut down at any time."

Doctors had continued warning Ripley to work less and lose weight, to relax and slow down. Instead, he kept plunging into new projects, including one that he hoped might outlive him. It seemed Ripley had begun giving serious thought to his legacy, to what he would leave behind, and for the past few years he'd been looking for a location for a permanent Believe It or Not museum, ideally one in his former hometown.

In 1945, he had come close to buying a building on the former Santa Rosa estate of Luther Burbank (who'd died in 1926), but the deal fell through. Then, just before the ship left San Francisco for his 1948 Far East trip, Ripley made a quick drive north to Santa Rosa with his sister, Ethel. They visited their parents' graves at the Odd Fellows Cemetery and their mother's church, which was in bad shape. Ripley told Ethel he was thinking of buying the run-down Church Built of One Tree and turning it into his personal museum. It could be a memorial to Lillie Belle, he said, and a place to display his thousands of collected curios.

Back in New York in mid-1948, he contacted Santa Rosa's city manager and offered to pay half the cost of restoring the church, if the city would pay the other half. He suggested moving the building to a new location and adding a special museum wing while keeping the original church intact. The city council initially agreed to the idea, but then a new city manager was hired and argued that the church was too old and would cost too much to move. "Besides," said the new city manager, Ed

Blom, "the building is not fireproof and not a good place for housing valuable curios."

While waiting for his hometown to make a final decision, Ripley continued to work on his Pearl Harbor memorial.

He'd initially proposed raising the *Arizona* and removing the bodies, but the secretary of the Navy's office informed him by letter that it had already decided that recovering the bodies would inflict "needless cruelty" on the victims' families. Ripley agreed to modify his proposal, the design for which included a marble causeway that would give visitors access to the *Arizona* from land. He even wrote to William Randolph Hearst, seeking help with the costs.

"I feel so very deeply about this," he told Hearst, adding that he was ready to appeal to readers and listeners for support.

Storer felt that, with Hearst behind the memorial and Ripley promoting it on radio, it could be "a monument of great importance." He encouraged Ripley in letters through the summer of 1948, reminding him that the Navy was receptive to his idea and that top Navy officials were awaiting Ripley's sketches. Storer nudged him to "send them along shortly." When Ripley finally finished his designs, Storer sent them to Rear Admiral John J. Manning, head of the Navy's yards and docks bureau, who called Ripley's idea "most commendable" and "one that would give me great pride."

Manning offered to provide $8.7 million in military funding, but suggested that the memorial become one that honored not just those killed aboard the *Arizona* but "all of the heroic Pearl Harbor dead." He further suggested building the memorial in a different location, so it could be viewed by ships entering Pearl Harbor, the Hawaiian equivalent of the Statue of Liberty.

Storer then watched in frustration as Ripley slowly, inexplicably backed away from the project through the latter half of 1948, distracted by other tasks and apparently unwilling to modify his designs to meet the Navy's suggestions. Ripley also pulled away from his plans for a Santa Rosa museum after the city hesitated to cooperate.

In no time, both opportunities were lost.

☙ BELIEVE IT! ❧

It would take another fourteen years for the USS Arizona *to be declared a national shrine. A memorial would be built above the ship's sunken remains; instead of Ripley's causeway, the memorial is now reached by boat.*

* * *

TOWARD LATE 1948, at the end of his current radio program's cycle, Ripley made plans to travel once again, arranging to join a four-day trip around the world by airplane. By now, however, it had become clear that his hair-trigger temper and angry outbursts weren't solely emotional but were physical manifestations of his increasingly bad health. His doctors refused to allow him to make the trip. Doug Storer wondered if the small stroke Ripley had apparently suffered a few years earlier was partly to blame for his erratic behavior.

Then again, in his recent travels Ripley had discovered the world to be a much different place. His cruise on the *Cleveland* had taken him to or past the battlefields and morgues of the Pacific war, all of which had ruffled and saddened him, as had China's unstoppable slump toward communism. He'd returned home in an exhausted state but continued to work at a frenzied pace, and now the doctors were telling him: *No more traveling.*

What he needed most was to take a *real* vacation and recuperate. To escape to Florida and lounge beside his pool. To dawdle aboard the *Mon Lei,* which now sat docked behind his house like a neglected toy. Instead, he added yet another massive commitment to his perpetually overbooked life: a television show.

* * *

THOUGH TWENTY YEARS of live radio had prepared Ripley reasonably well for a transition to television, it turned out the mediums were hardly interchangeable.

As Ripley sat on a soundstage behind a hand-carved desk and cameras began to roll during the filming of his pilot episode, he seemed startled when co-host Norman Brokenshire (a popular radio announcer) appeared beside him, accompanied by a spectacularly beautiful young woman. *"We-elll,* who's this pretty lady," Ripley asked, and Brokenshire introduced Nellie Jane Cannon, a cover model whom *LIFE* magazine referred to as one of "New York's loveliest girls." Ripley seemed flustered and promptly mangled her name, welcoming "Miss Jennie Ling" to his show. It's possible he'd leaned too heavily on his radio-show crutch and tossed back too much drink.

When Brokenshire asked Ripley if he still actually drew all of his own cartoons, Ripley insisted that he got up at six o'clock every morning to draw. Brokenshire dared him to prove it, and Ripley turned to Nellie/Jennie and asked what she'd like him to draw.

"How about the strangest man you've ever seen?"

Ripley walked over to an easel, picked up a piece of charcoal and quickly slashed a few thick lines, then scratched some waves and squiggles that seemed to be hair. As he stroked and swished, the vague shape of a man's face appeared. Ripley smeared parts of his drawing with his fingers and palm and, as if by magic, the disjointed black scribbles came into focus. The man was clearly African, practically a caricature, with a wide nose and high forehead.

It was an impressive impromptu drawing, but as Brokenshire quickly pointed out, there didn't seem to be anything strange or unique about the face. Ripley then explained: "The reason he really is so strange is because on his head he has *horns . . ."*—and here he drew on his man's forehead a long, black horn—*"twenty . . . eight . . . inches . . . long!"* Ripley said that years earlier in Africa he had met the humble man, who shed his horns the way deer shed antlers.

"Each year they grew again," Ripley told Nellie Jane. "He is without a doubt the strangest man I've ever seen."

Despite Ripley's awkward hesitations and occasional stumbles, NBC executives decided they liked what they saw in the pilot, which also featured Nellie Jane gamely choking down a bite of a hundred-year-old Chinese egg that Ripley fed her with a spoon. The network decided the Believe It or Not brand was ready for prime time and offered Ripley a weekly show that would launch on March 1, 1949.

While Storer was thrilled to introduce his best client to the untested waters of broadcast television, he was worried about Ripley, who was clearly unwell. Ripley promised Storer he'd take it easy during an upcoming Florida vacation. But first he closed out 1948 in style, dressed in a checked suit and sporting a fake mustache.

In mid-December, King Features hosted a massive celebration for the thirtieth anniversary of Ripley's *Believe It or Not*. The Gay Nineties–themed costume party was held at Toots Shor's on West Fifty-first Street. Ripley and Baer had become fans of the restaurant/bar and its wisecracking owner, Bernard

"Toots" Shor, a rough-edged storyteller beloved by such celebrity eater-drinkers as Jackie Gleason, Frank Sinatra, Orson Welles, and Ernest Hemingway.

All the top King Features executives attended, as did many syndicated Hearst columnists and cartoonists. Dressed in a baggy houndstooth suit and wearing a derby and his fake mustache, Ripley posed for silly pictures and signed autographs for King Features employees who'd worked for him for years but who rarely got the chance to see the man in person. Liese Wisse looked stunning in an extremely low-cut burlesque outfit and Li Ling-Ai came dressed as a sexy Chinese peasant. Surrounded by so many friends and colleagues—Vyvyan Donner, Cygna Conly, Bugs Baer, and many others—Ripley drank and sang and danced all night, having the time of his life.

* * *

EVER SINCE HIS STEEP RISE to fame in the 1930s, Ripley had been nursing a plan. He'd explained it in a 1935 interview with one of his first editors, Harry B. Smith, who was still working as a columnist at the *San Francisco Chronicle*. During the interview, Smith asked about the sudden wealth and renown, remembering Ripley as so shy and seemingly vulnerable to exploitation. But Ripley assured Smith that stardom didn't trouble him because once he'd earned enough money he would buy a dream house on the Atlantic coast and, as he put it, "spend his last years in leisure and ease."

Fourteen years later, he'd found the house but not the leisure and ease.

Into 1949, he spent busy weeks obsessively sprucing up Hi-Mount. He'd already moved some of his household staff down from New York and now had ten people working at the house or on the *Mon Lei*. His longtime carpenter came south to install new cabinets and fixtures throughout the house, to build a special ramp beside the saltwater swimming pool, to help Ripley's dogs get in and out of the water. It was all in preparation for what Ripley intended would soon become his permanent relocation to Florida, the dream he'd described to Smith.

Doug and Hazel visited for a few weeks so that Ripley and Storer could discuss the upcoming TV show. At first, Ripley seemed like his old entertaining self. He invited another couple to visit and they all rang in 1949 together, swimming in the pool and strolling on the vast lawn that sloped down to Lake Worth.

Ripley one day invited a dozen friends over for a floating cocktail party on the *Mon Lei*, handing everyone colorful straw hats as they boarded. Despite heavy winds and protests from his captain, Ripley insisted on sailing beyond Lake Worth, through an inlet into the Atlantic. Waves battered the flat-bottomed boat and Ripley's guests were nearly tossed overboard. The captain quickly returned to the calmer waters of Lake Worth and the party continued on Ripley's dock. That night, the Storers watched Ripley slip into a sodden funk. He complained that his guests had taken the valuable Chinese hats he'd handed out, thinking they were souvenirs.

Soon, there were more signs of instability. One day, Hazel walked into the living room to find Ripley's secretary, Cygna Conly, holding a hand to her face and seething with anger. Conly and Ripley had argued about some business matter and he'd slapped her. He later apologized and bought Conly a mink coat—not the first time a mink served as an apology. (Ripley once enlisted Li Ling-Ai's help in buying *twelve* mink coats for "the ladies that he went out with once in a while," as Li put it years later. When Ripley gave Li the money to make the purchase, he told her, "Choose one for yourself.")

Among his many messy, overlapping relationships, the one with beautiful Ming Jung remained especially mysterious to those who witnessed Ripley's occasionally harsh treatment. Hearst sportswriter and columnist Bob Considine and his wife once spent a summer living across the pond from BION Island. They visited frequently for cocktails, despite some competitive tension between Ripley and Considine (who would write a less-than-flattering and wildly inaccurate mini-biography of Ripley in 1961). The Considines were visiting the night Ripley ordered Ming, "Off to your room," and Millie Considine went to comfort Ming, who talked about keeping her child's ashes in a lacquered wooden box. "They are not there now," Ming allegedly told Considine. "When Bob gets mad at me he hides them."

Millie Considine would see Ming paddling alone on the pond and wondered what made Ripley's women stay. Millie came to believe that "once Ripley took an interest in a girl there was a bond between them forever after—no matter what." Hazel Storer would similarly wonder about the women who stayed, later writing, "How some of those gals took what he handed out in the way of abusive and contemptuous language I'll never know."

Just a year earlier, in an interview with *American Weekly* magazine, Ripley had shared his ongoing belief that "the only time women are happy is when they are completely under the domination of men." Now, though, even Ming had had enough of Ripley's domination. She'd finally given up on him, moved out of BION, and married a man who ran the Mamaroneck auto and marine service station that refueled and repaired the *Mon Lei*.

Ripley was rarely without companionship, however. At Hi-Mount he presented a sexy new Cuban girlfriend to the Storers and other visiting friends, and for a few days they all had a grand time, taking turns riding Ripley's new motor scooter or his tandem bicycle around the lakeside path. They went to the movies one night and Ripley snored through *A Tree Grows in Brooklyn*. (Notorious for sleeping in theaters, and for snoring like a diesel engine, Ripley once annoyed a crowd by loudly sleeping through a performance of Rodgers and Hammerstein's *Allegro*, despite much hushing from an usher and the audience.) Ripley's girlfriend was soon joined by an attractive blonde who flew up from Havana bearing bottles of rum and an adorable springer spaniel puppy. Rum punches lasted until dawn, but the fun ended the next day.

Worried that the puppy seemed sick, Ripley suggested to his owner that she take the dog to a vet. She promised she would, but instead corralled the dog inside the kitchen. A household staffer found the dog there, sicker than before, and took him to the vet, where he died. Ripley was furious. To make amends, his Cuban girlfriend and her guest offered to make dinner. They clattered around in the kitchen while the Storers and another couple got dressed in upstairs guest rooms.

Ripley sat drinking rum, getting madder the more he drank. Hazel was the first to come downstairs and found Ripley alone at the dining room table, his head in his hands. She touched his shoulder and Ripley jumped up and exploded with a tirade about the death of the puppy and his visitor's carelessness. Hazel went to the kitchen and found the two women locked in an embrace, clearly terrified. Moments earlier, Ripley had apparently gotten fed up with the giggling and burst into the kitchen, yelling at his girlfriend's friend, accusing her of treating the puppy like "a toy." He'd terrified both women, and possibly himself.

And yet, Hazel doubted that Ripley's love of animals was the true source of his anger that night. She suspected some undiagnosed illness was to blame.

✸ ✳ ✳

THE STORERS STAYED with Ripley a few more weeks. Doug Storer wanted to make sure his client and friend was emotionally and physically ready for the upcoming television season. Though Ripley was often surrounded by eager employees and devoted girlfriends, he had few truly close friends with whom to share his deepest troubles. This became apparent during the last days of the Storers' final visit at Hi-Mount.

One night they went to a quiet French restaurant in Palm Beach and Ripley relaxed and spoke freely, telling them the full story of Oakie, about his sorrow in losing her to cancer before the war. He broke into tears at the memory of the one true love of his life. Another night, Ripley sat alone with Hazel on the back deck and talked for two hours about his tenuous relationship with his brother, and their most recent schism.

He'd tried over the years to find the right fit for Doug in his world. Doug had done some work at King Features, until his conflicts with Joe Connolly got him fired. Doug's role as captain of Ripley's yacht hadn't lasted long either, and Doug mostly ended up doing manual labor around BION Island, more comfortable with chauffeurs and carpenters than his brother's newspaper friends. Doug was extremely introverted and often felt overwhelmed by the social scene that swirled around Ripley. In trying to relax and fit in, he usually drank too much. Tensions led to occasional fights between the brothers, with Doug once telling Ripley, "To hell with you!"

One frequent houseguest said Doug "changed from mouse to lion as the level on the bottle went down" and Li Ling-Ai thought Doug seemed "always high." ("He was a blue-collar guy who was caught up in a white-collar world," one of Doug's two sons, Robert, said decades later. "There were a lot of temptations there, be it alcohol or women.") Ripley eventually bought Doug and his wife a house in Mamaroneck and Doug ventured out on his own, working blue-collar jobs, including a stint at a naval shipyard. Even so, Ripley always tried to lure his brother back, calling and asking, "What are you doing? C'mon over."

Ripley explained to Hazel Storer that night in Florida how one particular fight with his brother had not yet healed. They'd been at Ripley's New York apartment and Ripley was on a ladder arranging some of his shelved curios. Doug had been drinking and the brothers began to argue about something. Voices were raised, arms flailed, and Doug knocked over the ladder, which nearly hit Ripley in the head as it crashed to the floor. Stunned, Ripley shouted, "Out!" He pointed to the door and told Doug he wanted him out of his life. He told Hazel he was thinking of cutting off any future financial support.

Ripley could be quite generous with friends, and in fact had recently loaned Doug Storer $1,000 to carry him through a financial rough patch until the new TV show began. He once bought Li a new car, as thanks for the many rides she'd given him in her beat-up Chevy. (She asked him to return the car.) Li wondered if Ripley, in the role of surrogate parent, had high expectations for his brother and didn't believe in "handouts." Ripley sometimes felt that Doug wasn't willing to care for himself, at least not in the manner that Ripley, as father figure, expected. Ripley set high standards for everyone who worked with him, and Doug had clearly fallen short. In his rant that night with Hazel, Ripley said he considered Doug "no brother of mine." Hazel tried to be sympathetic, but she was shaken by Ripley's bitterness.

* * *

AFTER THE STORERS left Hi-Mount, Ripley traveled to Cuba, possibly to reconnect with the girlfriend he'd scared off.

While in Havana, he concocted a new plan: to buy the property next to Hi-Mount and turn it into a studio from which he could broadcast television shows.

He mailed Doug Storer drawings of what the studio might look like, along with an enthusiastic letter: "I have many more and different ideas . . . What do you think?" Storer replied, in the kind of patient tone one might use with a child, "We don't know whether it would be mechanically possible to broadcast from that spot," adding that there might be restrictions that would prevent such a business from operating in a residential neighborhood.

After Havana, Ripley returned to New York, and a few weeks before the first TV show he invited a group of friends to his apartment for a party.

When the Storers arrived at Ripley's place, he was waiting anxiously at the elevator that opened directly into his tenth-floor apartment. He immediately grabbed Hazel by the hand and led her into his bedroom. He'd developed a kinship with Hazel, who assumed that Ripley took a special interest in her because she'd lived in Shanghai in the 1930s. Hazel could tell he was unusually distraught and had been drinking heavily. He sat at the edge of his huge bed and began to cry, tears dribbling onto his white dinner jacket. He'd read earlier in the day that the Communist Army had finally overtaken Shanghai.

Over and over, he told her, "We'll never see China again. *Never!*"

Hazel knew, as did Li Ling-Ai, just how passionately Ripley felt about China. "Rip really loved and admired this remarkable country and its people," Hazel once said. He had surrounded himself with women, employees, art, food, and furniture from his adopted land. Impressed by the Chinese ability to find happiness in poverty and war, he admired their resilience, believing that the survival of life's hardships made people stronger and more creative.

Li once said the Chinese "made him remember his own youth and feel good that he survived too."

It made sense, then, for Ripley to become so emotional the night he learned of China's latest setback. The Communist Army had taken control of all but southeast China, and it was just a matter of time before Chiang Kai-shek's US-supported Kuomintang forces fell to Mao Zedong's Soviet-backed People's Liberation Army.

For a man so inspired by all things Chinese, it also made sense that the decor and tone of his TV show would be distinctly Asian, a televised culmination of his lifelong obsession.

* * *

ON MARCH 1, 1949, at 9:30 p.m., anyone on the East Coast with a television set tuned to the NBC network would have seen their black-and-white screens fill with the image of a young Chinese man banging a gong, who then welcomed viewers to one of the more surreal programs in the short history of broadcast television.

After achieving such massive success in newspapers, publishing, radio, and film, Ripley the media pioneer was hoping the Believe It or Not magic would translate to this latest medium. His first show launched with a comedy duo, Ming and Ling, veterans of New York's cabaret scene who worked at the China Doll club and were known for their Chinese hillbilly routine and their Frank Sinatra impressions. (They'd soon score a radio hit with their song "Eggroll Eatin' Mama.")

Ripley then introduced his lovely sidekick, twenty-four-year-old Peggy Corday, a World War II pinup girl. Ripley bragged that Corday had recently been named "Miss Television of 1949." Her first moment as Ripley's on-air assistant was a shrill scream of pretend shock as she opened a closet door to find Ripley's lifelike Masakichi statue staring back at her. Corday was bright-eyed and quick on her feet; her role would in part require her to keep the unpredictable host on track.

Until now, Ripley had achieved celebrity as a mostly invisible cartoonist and radio personality. Across the first half of 1949, he became an in-the-flesh television star.

While the show sometimes featured actors performing the same type of dramatic sketches he'd aired on radio, those acts now took a secondary role to Ripley's on-screen persona. He'd been in the public eye for three decades, but hadn't appeared in a film—or on a screen of any kind—since before the war. On the grainy screen of a Motorola set, he seemed older and paunch-ier than the global adventurer viewers may have expected. (His teeth looked better than ever, though. He'd had another aggressive surgical procedure to further straighten them, so much so that his upper lip, after a lifetime of protrusion, now dipped *inward.*)

Viewers liked what they saw. At the end of the first six episodes, NBC had a chance to back out but instead affirmed its commitment to a full thirteen-episode season. Most shows featured Ripley interviewing special guests, war heroes, and interesting people he'd profiled over the years, including a paralyzed Canadian artist who painted with a brush in his teeth. Ripley usually sketched a favorite cartoon, such as the self-mutilating holy men he'd seen in India or African Kikuyu women.

"I always like to draw pictures of the young ladies," he said flirtatiously to Corday.

He seemed most at ease during those pure moments of drawing at his easel while talking breezily about his travels. Ripley was still a supremely talented artist and NBC weaved plenty of on-air sketches into each script, with Ripley drawing scenes that he'd "bring to life for you" in segments called "Ripley's Sketchbook."

Ripley's favorite dramatic reenactment involved the story of a melancholy Italian man who could never laugh "because the whole world is ugly and unhappy." His doctor's prescription was to find laughter at the circus, where the famous Grimaldi the Clown performed. It turned out that the doctor's patient was Grimaldi himself, who eventually died of "melancholia." Said Ripley, "The funniest man in the world was also the unhappiest."

Turning to Peggy Corday, he added, "The difference between joy and sadness isn't so very much after all." Friends would note the irony of Ripley's affinity for Grimaldi's story.

As he'd done since breaking into radio in the early 1930s, Ripley drank whiskey or gin before each episode. Sometimes it helped, and he appeared smooth and calm. Other nights he seemed awkward and clumsy, forgetting guest names and mangling lines and, if one listened closely, slurring and swishing his words. While introducing a lord and lady from Scotland who were to perform a traditional Scottish dance—a surreal jig alleged to be the only time British nobility performed such a thing in public—Ripley told the couple, "Well, you'll have the joint a-jiving—or something like that."

Though he seemed to be finding some momentum, the shows were taking an emotional toll, and colleagues worried about Ripley's increasing agitation, how he often looked so drawn and tired. On May 4, he fired off one of his scathing telegrams, this one aimed at NBC executives. "This is a formal protest against the dreadful way in which the 'Believe It or Not' TV show has been mismanaged," he wrote, signing it "Believe It or Not Ripley."

Two days later, NBC received another telegram, this one from Liese Wisse, telling NBC that Ripley refused to come to the studio the next day. "Mr. Ripley is entertaining guests in New York apartment. Will not be available for rehearsal," Liese wrote.

NBC had to wonder what it had gotten itself into with the temperamental cartoonist.

✶ ✳ ✶

PEGGY CORDAY WAS PAID $100 per episode and turned out to be worth every penny. Smooth and professional, even a bit sassy and flirty, she often ad-libbed when Ripley flubbed one of his lines or maimed some guest's name, deftly covering up the host's gaffes. She was the perfect and perky offset to the sometimes confused and distracted Ripley, who seemed to enjoy having her by his side during his tenuous venture into television.

Even with Ripley's lack of polish, the show became instantly popular, at least among the limited number of households with televisions. Ripley could be clunky while interviewing others, but his unease somehow helped guests relax, as it had on radio. Like the daytime TV hosts who would later become megastars using a similar formula, he gently coaxed guests to open up, to share their emotions and vulnerabilities, often with surprisingly moving results.

He again interviewed Poon Lim, the sailor who'd drifted for 133 days in a life raft. He told Ripley, "I was never afraid." Ripley introduced viewers to a Philadelphia man who was injured in a car accident and, told that he'd be wheelchair-bound for life, trained himself to walk again—on his *hands*. Another guest was born blind and had taught himself to play piano—at age *two*. One show celebrated National Hospital Week and Ripley interviewed Army nurse Katherine Dollison, who'd been on

Corregidor when it fell to the Japanese. She broke down while describing her three years in a Japanese prison: "Well, Bob. It was pretty awful."

Off-screen, however, the troubles continued. He became disproportionately angry when NBC approved, then overruled, a guest list he and Storer had put together—*after* the guests had already been paid. Ripley also complained about the injustice of one writer (George Lefferts) getting full credit for writing the show when others (including Pearlroth and Storer) had been doing much of the work. In general, Ripley seemed burdened by this foray into TV land. A week shy of the final episode of his first thirteen-week season, Ripley bade his audience farewell with an impromptu and heartfelt prayer, concluding: "The blessing of the Lord be upon you."

Though frustrated with aspects of NBC's handling of the show, he appreciated those who worked on it, and in late May threw a party at a German restaurant for the cast and crew, just before the May 24 program, which would unexpectedly turn out to be his last.

CHAPTER 24

Thirteen weeks into the season, Ripley fans knew when and where to tune in. At nine thirty on Tuesday night, May 24, viewers saw the familiar introductory shot of a Buddha, followed by the sound of a gong. Announcer Fritz DeWilde explained that tonight Ripley would bring to life a dramatization of "the true story behind the world's most famous bugle call." With Memorial Day a week away, Ripley had decided to feature a patriotic tribute to taps.

First, Peggy Corday joined Ripley at his desk to introduce a reenactment of a Hungarian man and wife being separated during World War II and sent to concentration camps. Each thought the other had died and after the war they both moved to New York. While riding the subway one day, the man met another Holocaust survivor, Marcel Sternberger. As the two men talked, Sternberger realized that he knew the man's wife and he helped reunite the couple.

Calling it "one of the most touching love stories ever recorded," Ripley interviewed Sternberger, whom he called the couple's "guardian angel."

In the next segment, Ripley and Corday looked through his collection of crown jewels, gem-crusted replicas of crowns, and scepters from England, France, India, and Africa. Ripley explained how the duke of Windsor chose not to wear a crown during his brief reign as king of England (before abdicating to marry his American girlfriend). He added that he'd recently seen the duke in Palm Beach, and instead of a crown and scepter he wore a golf cap and wielded a golf club.

Suddenly, Ripley's eyes glazed over and he grew quiet, still holding one of the crowns in his hand. Corday realized something was wrong and quickly stepped in.

"Bob, they're beautiful," she gushed, and held a jeweled crown up to the camera. "Henry the Sixth!"

Standing offstage, Doug Storer knew something was wrong too, even though the rest of the crew didn't immediately react to the sudden stillness of the host. Storer had seen it before, these brief Ripley blackouts. But the show was live, with a studio audience, and couldn't be interrupted.

"Bob, they're absolutely astonishing," Corday continued, trying to keep the show rolling.

As Ripley slumped slightly, his eyes still open, Corday stepped closer and put her arm on his shoulder, to prevent him from falling over. Storer was amazed at Corday's poise but knew he needed to intervene. Just as he was about to walk onto the stage, Ripley emerged from his stupor and, with Corday's help, haltingly carried on.

After mumbling an introduction to a dramatization on the life of King Henry the Fourth, Ripley groggily introduced the planned reenactment of the story behind the funereal bugle call taps. He repeated the oft-told but apocryphal version of the song's origins in which a Union captain found the music in the pocket of his dead son, a Confederate soldier. (Taps was actually composed by Union general Daniel Butterfield in 1862 and later played by buglers at both Union and Confederate funerals.)

Instead of closing the show with his usual good-night prayer, Ripley looked into the camera and explained in a somewhat shaky voice that the program would end with the playing of taps, in honor of all the veterans whose ultimate sacrifice to their country was being commemorated that Memorial Day.

"May this call be a requiem not only for our dead but for the very act of war which took their lives," he said. "And to that all mankind must say *Amen*."

As the program began fading to black, a lone bugler played the familiar notes of taps, his figure silhouetted against a backdrop of clouds.

When the final note expired, the show closed with the sound of a gong.

* * *

IT'S UNCLEAR what exactly happened to Ripley onstage that night—there is no known film footage of the episode, and eyewitnesses later shared differing accounts of what occurred next. Some witnesses said Ripley grew weary again after the show, passed out, and fell to the floor. Others said he collapsed on the air and was rushed to the hospital. One employee speculated that Ripley had suffered a small stroke, while others assumed that his heart problems had caused a temporarily sluggish flow of blood to his brain. (As a producer for the show, Doug Storer witnessed the entire scene, making his version the most reliable.)

In a detailed account written years later, Storer said he cornered Ripley in the studio while crews disassembled the set and the audience filed out.

"Stop," Storer said. "I want to talk to you about something."

Storer knew Ripley was physically in bad shape and that his doctor had been warning him to get a more complete checkup.

"You've got to go into the hospital and get those checkups," Storer said. "You're going to do it this week."

"No, no. I'm not going to do it this week," Ripley said. "Maybe next week."

"Bob, I don't care if we cancel the show. I'm not going to have you do what you did tonight and make it permanent," Storer insisted.

Storer was a few inches shorter than Ripley, who patted him on the shoulder as if he were a child and said, "Oh, Doug, Doug, stop worrying."

But Storer was familiar with Ripley's often-irrational optimism and well-honed delay tactics. He made Ripley promise to visit the hospital as soon as possible.

"You win, Doug," Ripley finally agreed. "I'm going to the hospital for a checkup at once."

But Ripley didn't check in the next day. Instead, he threw a party.

When Ripley called Li Ling-Ai the next morning and told her he wanted to host her birthday party, she told him he'd mixed up the dates and it wasn't her birthday yet. But he seemed desperate for an excuse to defer his promise to Storer, so Li relented. She could tell Ripley was nervous about the hospital visit and assumed he wanted to enjoy one more get-together with friends before letting doctors poke and prod him.

The day after that—Thursday, May 26—Ripley checked into Harkness Pavilion at Columbia-Presbyterian Medical Center, where technicians administered tests that confirmed what he already knew: like his dad, he had a bad heart.

His condition was hardly critical, though, and Ripley remained in fairly good spirits, even when doctors decided to keep him overnight for more tests. That night, Bugs Baer paid a quick visit, sneaking in a bottle of booze to ease his friend's discomfort.

The next morning, Ripley used his bedside phone to call other friends and start making plans for the weekend. One doctor, Ralph Boots, then arrived with two well-known heart specialists, who agreed that even more tests were needed. The specialists administered an injection of some kind, but Ripley insisted he still felt good and expected to be released soon. Li had promised to stop by for lunch and Ripley told his nurses that Madame Chiang Kai-shek was going to pay him a visit. When Li arrived, the nurses assumed she really was Madame Chiang until Ripley confessed to the gag.

But Li grew worried when she saw Ripley. Liese Wisse was already there, having volunteered to spend the day by Ripley's side, and she seemed troubled too.

"His face was a little lonely," Li said years later. She tried to cheer him up by ordering lunch from a nurse, asking if they had pheasant lips on the menu. Ripley laughed but then got back to business. He had previously asked Li to enlist a group of scientists and doctors for an upcoming episode about believe-it-or-nots in medicine and, specifically, Chinese herbs. Li said she was meeting with two scientists and a doctor that very night. When she left him, she could tell Ripley seemed anxious.

"I sensed an unease," she later said, recalling that he was "a trifle scared."

Still, Ripley tried to convince himself it wasn't serious and continued making future plans. At around five o'clock, at the end of his second day in the hospital, he called Baer, who now lived in Connecticut, not far from Ripley's home in Mamaroneck.

Ripley told Baer he was still suffering through his doctor's "checkup," but that he expected to be home for the weekend and wanted to see him.

"I'm going to get home this week," he said. "I don't care what happens. I'm going to go home and *be* home."

"Come on," Baer offered. "Join me. We'll do something."

Ripley seemed thrilled with the idea. "I'll be out to your farm tomorrow afternoon," he said.

When Ripley hung up the phone, he asked Liese to take some dictation, then suddenly clutched his chest and began to convulse.

Liese jumped from her seat and rushed to his side, calling out wildly for help. When no one responded, she raced down the hall to beckon a nurse, who quickly found the doctor on call. They all sprinted back to Ripley's room, but it was too late.

LeRoy Robert Ripley was dead, the victim of a massive heart attack. He was fifty-nine.

* * *

WITHIN THE HOUR, Liese found herself all alone and tasked with making a series of painful, tearful phone calls—to Ripley's brother, to Norbert Pearlroth, to Robert Hyland, Doug Storer, and many others.

"Mr. Ripley is dead," she told each one, over and over. "He's *dead*."

Liese next reached Cygna Conly, who in turn broke the news to Li Ling-Ai. Li couldn't believe that the man who'd just hosted her premature birthday party, who seemed so full of jokes and optimism just hours earlier, was dead. She gripped the phone in shock. *How could Ripley be gone?* "It is no good to be that famous and work that hard," she told Conly. "Because you die young."

A group of friends gathered that night at the hospital. Amid the gloom, Pearlroth quietly commented on how strange it was that Ripley's final broadcast had been his thirteenth, that the show had featured the story of a funeral song. He further told the others that ten years earlier Ripley had actually predicted his life might end in 1949.

They'd been having dinner together when Ripley observed that his life had thus far gone in ten-year cycles. Ever attuned to a hard-to-believe story, he explained how he'd started his cartooning career in 1909, had launched his *Believe It or Not* series ten years after that, and in 1929 had joined King Features. Ripley told Pearlroth that night in 1939 that he hoped Providence would allow him "another ten years of the same life."

Li told the others how Ripley once spoke to her about his hope to be reincarnated—in China. She said she believed Ripley had "the Chinese attitude."

"We are all born lonely," Li said. "We are all what we create."

Bizarrely, the day Ripley died was also a day of death for China. The last of the Nationalist Army troops retreated from Shanghai while others surrendered to Mao's soldiers, who then marched them off to POW camps. The world's fourth-largest city was now fully in the hands of the Communists.

⁎ ⁎ ⁎

NEWS OF RIPLEY'S DEATH spread quickly. Hazel Storer was listening to music on the radio when an announcer broke in with a news flash. When Bugs Baer learned that his friend was dead, he immediately started writing a column, which would appear the next morning in Hearst's *New York Journal-American* and across America, via the International News Service.

"This one is tough to believe," it began. "The Believe-It-Or-Not man will not answer the gong [on his TV show] Tuesday night. It rang for the last time Friday afternoon when Ripley dissolved into the mysterious past whence came his amazing truths."

Baer had known Ripley for more than thirty years. They had grown up together, become famous and rich together. They'd shared innumerable drinks, laughs, and women. Baer had been with Ripley the night he created his first "Believe It or Not" (that is, "Champs and Chumps") cartoon, and the night he'd met Beatrice. Ripley had been with Baer when his first wife died, and earlier in 1949 had hosted a New York Heart Association fund-raiser for his second wife, Louise, who was ill. Now Ripley was gone and Baer was in mourning. But print was his life, his outlet, as it had been for Ripley, so he forced himself to mourn publicly. His column continued:

> He had the pride of craftsmanship in his drawings and the authority of knowledge in his statements. Nobody ever proved him wrong. If Ripley told me I had two heads, I would go out and buy two hats. And tip them both to the greatest cartoonist in the history of American journalism.

* * *

FOUR DAYS LATER, a funeral service was held at St. James Episcopal Church, a half-dozen blocks from Ripley's apartment. Though he'd nurtured a lifelong fascination with religion, he was never a churchgoer. The Episcopal church had been Storer's idea, and he asked the Rev. Dr. James W. Hyde to officiate.

More than four hundred attended, with hundreds more waiting outside. William Randolph Hearst's son, William Jr., served as an honorary pallbearer, alongside publisher Max Schuster. Former heavyweight champs Gene Tunney and Jack Dempsey attended, as did famed aviators Eddie Rickenbacker and James

Doolittle; numerous celebrities, journalists, and athletes; and a large contingent of artists and cartoonists, including such long-ago colleagues as Paul Terry and Herb Roth.

One by one, Ripley's lovers arrived, including Ming Jung, now married. She and a few other former BION Island inhabitants (the voluntary signers of Ripley's waiver) sat together in a pew, weeping behind black veils, an awkward reunion. Eight men carried the coffin, staggering at one point and almost losing their grip. Thousands lined the streets to watch the bronze, rose-covered casket roll toward Grand Central Station, where it would begin traveling by rail back to Ripley's native California. A group of his companions, including Liese and Ling-Ai, entered a black limousine behind the hearse as onlookers rubbernecked to see who was behind the veils.

One man on his lunch break turned to a man beside him and said, "They must be his models." A woman nearby made a crude joke ("You mean his whores?") and they all shared a laugh. Hazel Storer overheard and scowled at them.

Ripley then began his final transcontinental journey, loaded onto *The Chicagoan*, accompanied by his brother and sister. In Chicago, his body was transferred to a *City of San Francisco* train for the two-day trip west, back to the town where his cartooning career had begun. Nell Griffith, Ripley's first friend and first love, met the casket at the San Francisco depot and traveled in the hearse, led by police escort, for the last fifty-mile leg back to Santa Rosa. It was a suitable final journey.

* * *

SANTA ROSANS TURNED OUT by the thousands to say farewell, lining the streets and spilling out of Lillie Belle's Church Built of One Tree.

Classmates and neighbors told stories to the papers about

young Ripley the obsessed doodler, the aspiring ballplayer; how he never forgot his hometown, especially Miss O'Meara; how proud they were of the rangy and curious barefoot boy who left town and followed his whimsical dreams.

Nell Griffith wrote a story for the *Santa Rosa Press-Democrat,* describing the LeRoy Ripley she once knew: "a shy and rather awkward boy . . . a boy dressed in a brown suit with knee pants . . . a boy with a great gift and a driving ambition." Nell's husband had died two years earlier. Now widowed and raising her children alone, Nell said of Ripley's death, "It shouldn't have happened so soon."

Compared to the average Joe, Ripley seemed to have lived the life of twenty men. He had also poured everything he had into *Believe It or Not,* which became his life, his identity, his true religion. That commitment had fully consumed him, professionally and personally, leaving little room for anything or anyone else.

Some, like Hazel Storer, believed that losing China to a Communist regime had contributed to Ripley's ill health. (Mao Zedong would officially establish the People's Republic of China five months after Ripley's death.) His sister, Ethel, on the other hand, wondered if his inability to create a museum and a legacy in the Church Built of One Tree had been a factor. "He felt pretty bad about not being able to make it a memorial for his curios," she told a reporter after the funeral.

The likeliest reason for Ripley's health problems and turbulent behavior was one he'd been hinting at in print for decades.

An insatiable, incurable romantic, he loved women so much (and, apparently, so often) but had never managed to find his one true love—except Oakie. In fact, his physical and emotional decline seemed to have begun in full after Oakie died. In a

revealing 1947 interview with *True Confession* magazine, entitled "Ripley Wants a Wife!" he admitted that for all the material
success he had gained, what he still lacked was "the one thing
that really matters to a man."

"I've discovered that fame and good fortune don't mean a
thing unless you can share them with the right woman," he
said.

After a prayer service at Lillie Belle's church, the church
Isaac had helped build, LeRoy Ripley was buried beside his
father and mother at Odd Fellows Cemetery, less than twenty
blocks from his childhood home. Li stood beside his grave,
tearfully praying that he'd get his wish to be reincarnated.

"He was such a mystery, like the Chinese. He loved the
mystery of an idea," she said. "He loved life so much."

On one of his final *Mon Lei* trips, while moored in Savannah, Ripley told a reporter that his staff was so well organized he expected *Believe It or Not* to continue "many, many years after I die." In the weeks following his death, however, there were no guarantees Ripley's legacy would survive, let alone thrive. In fact, it seemed as if everything he'd built up might collapse into rubble without his stewardship.

At first, the television show limped ahead, airing Tuesday nights through the summer of 1949. A bearded announcer named Robert St. John introduced himself as the new host and "guest custodian" of Ripley's sketch books. Joined by Li Ling-Ai for a few shows, they'd flip through pages of Ripley cartoons, then introduce a dramatic reenactment, with no on-air mention of Ripley's demise. (The show would last another year. It would be revived in the 1980s, hosted by Jack Palance, and again in 2000.)

The daily cartoon also lurched onward. King Features editor Ward Greene announced that the cartoon would continue because Ripley's research files contained so much "interesting material." Norbert Pearlroth kept mining the library for hard-to-believe facts, as he had for twenty-six years, and Paul Frehm became the lead artist.

ℭ BELIEVE IT! ℌ

Ripley's Believe It or Not *remains one of the longest-running cartoons in history. In 2012 it was being drawn by John Graziano.*

Even with the television show and cartoon on seemingly stable ground, the rest of Ripley's empire—all the strange objects, peculiar people, and amazing performers he'd collected—began splitting apart and dispersing, and it seemed as if the magical Believe It or Not world might disappear altogether.

Earlier in 1949, when a secretary overheard a loud argument with Doug Storer, Ripley had ominously warned, "You think that was bad? It's nothing compared to the arguments and fights and lawsuits that will take place after I've gone." Indeed, a power struggle erupted within days of Ripley's demise as various factions, including Doug Ripley and Doug Storer, competed for control of the orphaned remains of Ripley's kingdom.

* * *

PARTLY THIS WAS Ripley's fault for never officially designating a successor. Months before his "many, many years" prediction to a Savannah reporter, he had signed his will and stashed it aboard the *Mon Lei,* where it was found in the days after his death. In it, Ripley was very specific about cash awards—bequests ranging from $500 to $5,000 to longtime employees and friends—but excruciatingly vague about what should be done with the lucrative brand he'd created.

The names in the will read like a guest list to Ripley's biggest party, among them patrons who'd helped early in Ripley's career—Carol Ennis, Vyvyan Donner, and his old editor Walter St. Denis; secretaries, housekeepers, and female companions; such longtime employees as Norbert Pearlroth, Doug Storer, and two captains of the *Mon Lei;* as well as close friends such as Bugs Baer and Li Ling-Ai.

Ripley instructed that the rest of his estate be formed into a trust, whose income and profits would be shared by his sister and brother.

Though Ripley did not specify who should actually run things, Doug had hoped to take charge of the company and keep his brother's menagerie of peculiarities intact. But he soon allowed the lawyers to auction off the estate, then watched in horror as moving vans pulled away from BION Island, loaded with Ripley's curios and collectibles. Unable to keep the employees on board, Doug watched them disappear too.

Three months after Ripley's death, nearly a thousand artworks and curios—collected from BION, the New York apartment, the Florida house, and the *Mon Lei*—were sold during a four-day session at the Plaza Art Gallery in New York. Scores of bidders competed for Ripley's totem poles, beer steins, Buddhas, Ugandan masks, opium pipes, and shrunken heads, along with the Makovsky paintings and the lifelike Masakichi statue. Among the bidders was Francis Cardinal Spellman, who was outbid for a statue of Saint Patrick, and a young couple from Queens vying for statuettes and brass dragons. "Oh what an apartment we're going to have," the woman whispered to her fiancé. "I can hardly wait till we're married."

The auction, featured in the pages of *LIFE* and *The New Yorker*, netted $90,000—no small sum, but a fraction of the booty's true value. The main bidder was John Arthur, who *LIFE* said was "trying to step into Ripley's shoes." Arthur spent

$50,000 for "several vanloads of stuff," as *LIFE* put it, and paid another $5,500 for the *Mon Lei*.

BION Island sold for $50,000 to Ferruccio Tagliavini, a Metropolitan Opera star, who never moved in. The mansion was sold a few years later and razed to make room for two new houses; the site remained vacant for years.

Proceeds from the auction and the sale of Ripley's homes netted $500,000 for Doug Ripley, who was forced to buy back from the estate any items of sentimental value. In 1951, he and Storer together purchased all shares of Believe It or Not, Inc., with Storer taking over as company president and Doug chairing the board of directors. It was an uneasy partnership from the start, and through the mid-1950s both men scuffled in court, as did Robert Hyland and John Arthur. When Doug Ripley was diagnosed with cancer, Storer saw a chance to take over, and Doug Ripley seemed to realize he'd been outplayed.

"He didn't know what to do without Roy," Doug's granddaughter, Rebecca Ripley, said decades later, using the family name for Robert/LeRoy. Doug's son, Robert, said his father was never entirely comfortable in his big brother's world. "I don't think it was my father's cup of tea," he said. "I think he was out of his element there."

Doug Ripley died in 1956. His sons, Robert and Douglas Ripley, were still living in Mamaroneck in 2012.

Storer took sole possession of the company, calling it "a frightening responsibility." He managed the cartoon and sold comic books and published new editions of *Believe It or Not* books, which sold hundreds of thousands of copies through the 1950s.

But the legal battles continued, as Ripley had predicted they would. In 1959, Storer sold out to John Arthur, the man who'd purchased so much of the estate at auction. Arthur had put his purchases on permanent display in an Odditorium-style museum housed in a former castle in St. Augustine, Florida, which opened in 1950 and was followed by Ripley museums in Las Vegas, Atlantic City, and Times Square. Arthur had also hoped to create a floating museum aboard the *Mon Lei*. But storage and repair costs, plus a threatened lawsuit, prompted Arthur to sell the boat, which fell into private hands.

In 1969, a Canadian named Alec Rigby bought out Arthur, moved the headquarters from New York to Toronto, and began expanding the company, opening museums in Niagara Falls; San Francisco; Chicago; Gatlinburg, Tennessee; and Myrtle Beach, South Carolina.

In 1971, Lillie Belle's church was finally restored and turned into the museum Ripley had once hoped for. Among the displays: a two-headed calf with six legs. The church/museum closed in 1998 and fell into disrepair; it was restored in 2010 by the city of Santa Rosa, which turned it into a community meeting hall.

In 1985, Rigby sold the company to Jim Pattison, one of Canada's wealthiest men, whom Toronto's *Saturday Post* credited with resurrecting Ripley's "multimedia entertainment conglomerate." The newly named Ripley Entertainment, Inc., relocated to Orlando and opened more museums and other attractions.

There are now dozens of Ripley-themed attractions worldwide—haunted houses, aquariums, mini golf courses—in Australia, England, South Korea, Thailand, and even India.

✳ ✳ ✳

THROUGHOUT THE VARIOUS POST-1949 corporate iterations, Ripley's core staff scattered, and no one seemed to keep track of the whereabouts of his many secretaries, housekeepers, chefs, butlers, and lovers such as Liese Wisse, Cygna Conly, and Ming Jung. Though the brand had survived, quite impressively, the strange and international and eccentric family Ripley had gathered together on BION Island and beneath his Believe It or Not umbrella did not.

In 1959, after selling his interest in Believe It or Not, Inc., Doug Storer founded his own brand, Amazing But True, an attempt to reinvent himself as the new Ripley, with a similar multimedia array of books, radio shows, and newspaper columns. Using Ripley as his model, Storer traveled extensively through the 1960s and '70s, collecting stories and photographs. He eventually retired to Florida, where he died in 1985, at age eighty-six. His wife, Hazel, died in 2005 and bequeathed to the University of North Carolina Doug's trove of Believe It or Not materials (now known as the Doug and Hazel Storer Collection).

Norbert Pearlroth's association with *Believe It or Not* lasted longer than even Ripley's. He continued to work for King Features, visiting the New York Public Library daily to dig up new material for the cartoon. In 1972, he told the *Wall Street Journal* he never got bored. "It's just like being an explorer," said the man Ripley referred to as "the human encyclopedia." Pearlroth retired in 1975, at the age of eighty-one.

But after a fifty-two-year commitment to *Believe It or Not*, Pearlroth missed his days at the New York Library. ("He *lived* there," said grandson Jonathan.) Pearlroth died in 1983, a month before the ninetieth-birthday party scheduled for him at the library.

Li Ling-Ai, after co-hosting the *Believe It or Not* TV show, worked briefly with Doug Storer as his *Amazing But True* "Far East consultant." In 1973, she published a book about her parents, *Life Is for a Long Time*, whose mottoes and maxims seemed to be part commentary on Ripley's life. (Example: "Learn what it is to be a whole person in this new world.") Li also wrote children's books and over the years gave lectures and spoke regularly on radio and onstage about Chinese history, cooking, and culture. She died in 2003 at age ninety-five.

Before her death, in an interview for a documentary about Ripley's life, Li described him as "a special institution" who found his life and the world around him endlessly interesting and exciting, who felt compelled to share that shameless enthusiasm with his fans—and with anyone else who'd listen.

"He understood the psychology of the American public," she said. "He didn't really have hobbies. He liked to draw. He didn't talk about the stock market or good scotch or wine . . . because it doesn't matter whether you have caviar and Champagne or mink coats. It is life that is exciting and interesting, no matter what.

"That's all," said Li. "That's Ripley."

✳   ✳   ✳

WHILE BELIEVE IT OR NOT has endured, as Ripley predicted it would, the brand is safeguarded by the spirit of its long-dead creator. This haunting has actually been more of a boon than anyone might have anticipated, an added mystique to Ripley's lasting appeal. At tourist-packed Believe It or Not museums on Fisherman's Wharf in San Francisco or Times Square in New York, Ripley is a spooky presence, a beneficent ghost, his face grinning from deep within faded black-and-white photographs.

Then again, he is something of a cardboard mascot. In today's world, it's hard to imagine an incarnation of such a man, a shy, goofy, portly, bucktoothed stutterer who becomes a world traveler, a multimedia pioneer, a rich and famous ladies' man, and one of the most popular men in America. Consumers of the twenty-first century are a jaded lot. In the belief that there's nothing new to discover, purveyors of popular culture created reality TV instead. The revelations that made Ripley gasp—burning ghats in India, shrunken heads in Ecuador, armless/legless girl wonders—seem archaic compared to the intentional extremes of shows like *Jackass* and *Survivor,* the exploits of the masses on *Fear Factor* and *American Idol,* or the televised Burton Holmes–esque travels of Andrew Zimmern in *Bizarre World* and *Bizarre Foods.*

And yet, the phrase Ripley coined remains part of the English lexicon nearly a century later.

In 2011, "believe it or not" appeared more than twelve thousand times in the *New York Times* and on its website, and a mid-2012 Google search landed more than seventy *million* "believe it or not" hits. The spirit of Ripley lives on in shows like *MythBusters* and *River Monsters,* on *America's Funniest Home Videos* and all across YouTube. Also thriving, on the Internet, on TV, and on radio, are the aspirations that Ripley embodied—to show people something they didn't know, to entertain and educate and titillate, to question and challenge the truth—as are the driving passions of voyeurism, exhibitionism, and the base appreciation of freakishness, oddities, and pranks of nature.

The man who considered himself a rube and a farm boy, who indulged in a lifestyle as risky as that of any character in his cartoons, who taught readers to gape with respect at the weirdness of man and nature, who contributed to the adoption of America's national anthem and the creation of the Pearl Harbor memorial and so much more . . .

LeRoy Ripley, it turns out, may have been the most unbelievable oddity of all.

AUTHOR'S NOTE ON SOURCES

On Friday, August 24, 2007, while skimming the *New York Times*, I came across a story that diverted me from the book project I'd been working on and set me on the five-year path that led to this book. Headlined O, BELIEVERS, PREPARE TO BE AMAZED!, the story profiled a new museum that had opened in Times Square: the Ripley's Believe It or Not Odditorium. Reporter Edward Rothstein seemed genuinely shocked at the "entertaining and provocative" displays inside, and described the "voyeuristic sense of gaining entry to a forbidden, exotic and at times unsettling realm."

Channeling Ripley, Rothstein mused a bit about the people and places that celebrate the freakish: "The freakish is the ultimate avant-garde, a finger in the eye of the buttoned-up bourgeois vision of ordered life, like a tattoo parlor in the midst of a holistic spa."

Midway into the story, Rothstein introduced the proprietor of the metaphorical tattoo parlor—"a cross between the Coney Island barker and the cultural anthropologist"—and cited the 1936 newspaper poll that had ranked Robert Ripley as the most popular man in America.

As a former newspaper reporter and a lifelong newspaper

reader, I had read and known about Ripley's cartoons since childhood. But I'd never stopped to consider the man behind it all. I grabbed a pen and started underlining the *Times* reporter's words—"something refreshing about Ripley's enthusiastic refusal to homogenize humanity's extremes . . . his gaze roamed across his own culture's peculiarities too, treating them with the same amazement."

My curiosity aroused, I visited Amazon.com and quickly learned that there existed no definitive biography of Ripley. In fact, it seemed as if the only biographical retelling of any kind had been a slim 1961 volume, *Ripley, the Modern Marco Polo*, by Bob Considine, a used copy of which I ordered from Amazon. Unable to wait a few days, I scoured the Internet and in minutes found and began printing a PDF of that same book. By that afternoon, I was in awe of the life Ripley had lived, and soon decided to attempt to write the first full story about the freakish man who celebrated the freakishness of the world.

My early research led me to the Orlando-based Ripley Entertainment Inc., which manages the Ripley empire and publishes those fat and weird annual *Believe It or Not!* books. Through the generous cooperation of VP Norm Deska and archivist Edward Meyer, I was granted unfettered access to the climate-controlled room containing the company's archives, a one-stop-shopping trove of Ripley's personal and business papers, journals, photographs, home movies, letters, and more. It's no exaggeration to say this was a reporter's jackpot—this project could never have happened without the help of Ripley Entertainment, especially Meyer.

Six months after immersing myself in Ripley's life, almost by accident I learned about the Doug and Hazel Storer Collection at the University of North Carolina at Chapel Hill. Doug Storer, Ripley's business manager, had died in 1985, and his wife Hazel died in 2005, after which the family's papers were donated to UNC. After two years of being organized and catalogued, the collection was opened to the public in 2008. I spent many long hours in the manuscripts department at Wilson Library, taking digital photographs of thousands of documents that proved invaluable to this project.

In addition to gaining access to such long-buried treasures at Ripley Entertainment and UNC, I was grateful for the cooperation I received from Sidney Kirkpatrick, who had previously begun exploring Ripley's life and who agreed to share with me his many boxes of research. I'm humbled by his generosity.

Last but not least, I'm very thankful that Ripley's nephew Robert and grandniece, Rebecca, graciously accommodated my many phone calls and finally agreed to speak with me about Ripley and his brother, Doug. Their cooperation helped shed some light on one of the mysteries of this story, and I hope my portrayal of the brothers and their complicated but loving relationship is accurate. Any errors are my own.

NOTES

For more information on sources—including samples of Ripley's personal journals, business letters, travel photos, home movies, and more—visit www.nealthompson.com/books/curiousman.

KEY

Ripley Entertainment archives = RE

Ripley personal scrapbooks (Note: exact titles, dates, and even publication names are occasionally missing) = SCRAP

Doug and Hazel Storer Collection = DHS (http://www.lib.unc.edu/mss/inv/s/Storer,Doug_and _Hazel_Anderson.html)

Believe It or Not cartoon (and/or essay) = BION

Sidney Kirkpatrick papers = SID

Gaye LeBaron Collection = GLB (http://library.sonoma.edu/regional/lebaron/)

Sonoma Historian, journal of the Sonoma County Historical Society = SH

Santa Rosa Press Democrat = SRD

San Francisco Chronicle = SFC

San Francisco Bulletin = SFB

New York Globe = NYG

Associated Newspapers = AN

New York Post = NYP

New York Times = NYT

King Features Syndicate = KFS

The Incredible Life and Times of Robert Ripley: Believe It or Not, TBS Productions, Turner Home Entertainment, 1994 = TBS

CHAPTER I

On Ripley's childhood and family, see the following: RE "Ripley's Ramble 'Round the World," *Associated Newspapers,* December 4, 1922; "Strange Things Under the Sun," by Hugh Leamy, *The American,* October 1929; "Famous Cartoonist Tells Story of His Life," by Robert Boyd, *The Success Magazine,* January 1926; SH ("Robert Ripley, His Own Greatest Oddity," by H. Lightfoot, Fall 1967); SCRAP (untitled profile by Edgar T. "Scoop" Gleeson, *San Francisco Bulletin,* 1915; "Where a Globetrotter Hangs His Hat," *Liberty Magazine,* May 11, 1946); GLB (Ethel letter to Roy); SID (interview with Bruce Bailey, January 14, 2002); SID (interview with George Proctor, May 12, 2002); SID (interview with Nancy Jo Black Cafo, February 15, 2002); "I Remember When," unpublished essay by Clara VanWormer Black, 1958; SRD (Ripley obituary, May 28, 1949); SRD ("As Nell Wilson Knew Him," May 28, 1949); SRD (August 24, 2005); Li Ling-Ai interview with TBS, 1993; RE

("How to Draw," unpublished Robert Ripley manuscript, n.d.); "Recollections of Ripley," unpublished essay by Frances O'Meara; GLB (assorted SRD columns); "Believe It or Not, Ripley Was Almost as Odd as His Items," by Donald Dale Jackson, *Smithsonian*, January 1995; *Ripley, the Modern Marco Polo*, by Bob Considine, Garden City, NY: Doubleday & Co., 1961 (hereafter referred to as MMP); DHS (interviews, letters, and handwritten notes by Hazel Storer).

Note on Ripley's birth date: Census records from 1900 and 1910 show Ripley's birth year as 1890; so does his headstone. Family photos further confirm Ripley's birth in early 1890. A photo taken in July 1890 says "at six months."

Santa Rosa history: *Santa Rosa: A Twentieth Century Town*, by Gaye LeBaron and Joanne Mitchell; *How Plants Are Trained to Work for Man*, by Luther Burbank, PF Collier & Son, 1914, NY; *Images of America, Santa Rosa*, by Simone Wilson, Arcadia Publishing, 2004; *Santa Rosa California in Vintage Postcards*, by Bob and Kay Voliva, Arcadia Publishing, 1999; SH (Volume I, 2006); *The Garden of Invention*, by Jane S. Smith, Penguin Press, 2009.

CHAPTER 2

Santa Rosa history and earthquake: SRD (assorted clips); GLB (SRD columns and *Santa Rosa: A Twentieth Century Town*); author interview with Jeremy Nichols; SRD (anniversary story, April 19, 2006); assorted unpublished memoirs; "The Story of an Eyewitness," by Jack London, *Collier's*, May 5, 1906; RE "Ripley's Ramble 'Round the World," December 10, 1922; SRD (June 13, 1908); SH ("1906 Earthquake Issue," 2006).

Note on the higher death per capita compared to San Francisco: Santa Rosa had 64 to 100 deaths and 6,700 to 8,700 residents—1 in 80 died; San Francisco had 500 deaths and 400,000 residents—1 in 800.

Ripley at school, and home life: SH ("Robert Ripley, His Own Greatest Oddity," by H. Lightfoot, Fall 1967); SID (interview with George Proctor, May 12, 2002); SRD (Ripley obituary, May 28, 1949, including recollections by Helen Proctor and others); DHS (interviews, letters, and handwritten notes by Hazel

Storer); "Recollections of Ripley," unpublished essay by Frances O'Meara; "Panther Profile," Santa Rosa High School newsletter story, 1989; "Famous Cartoonist Tells Story of His Life," by Robert Boyd, *The Success Magazine,* January 1926; SCRAP (untitled profile by Edgar T. "Scoop" Gleeson, *San Francisco Bulletin,* 1915; SCRAP (untitled *Pittsburgh Chronicle Telegraph* story, date unknown, circa spring of 1916); "Odd Man," by Geoffrey T. Hellman, two-part profile in *The New Yorker,* August 31, 1940 and September 7, 1940.

Comics: *The Ten-Cent Plague: The Great Comic-Book Scare and How It Changed America,* by David Hajdu, Picador, 2009; *The Comics: Before 1945,* by Brian Walker, Harry N. Abrams, 2004.

CHAPTER 3

Moving to and living/working in San Francisco: "The Village Bell was Slowly Ringing," *LIFE,* May 18, 1908; DHS (Carol Ennis letter to Bob Considine); MMP (pp. 20–21); "Famous Cartoonist Tells Story of His Life," by Robert Boyd, *The Success Magazine,* January 1926; "Pictures from the Past," by John Baggerly, *Los Gatos Weekly,* September 19, 2001; SRD (March 2, 2009); SCRAP (*Saturday Evening Post* profile, 1932); GLB; RE (Ripley's Ramble 'Round the World, December 11, 1922); "Timeline of San Francisco History," www.sfhistoryencyclopedia.com/articles/timeline/index.html [accessed September 30, 2012]; US Census, 1910; SFC (June 10, 2009); *The Comics: Before 1945,* by Brian Walker, Harry N. Abrams, 2004; *Rube Goldberg: His Life and Work,* by Peter C. Marzio, Harper, 1973; SCRAP (untitled profile by Edgar T. "Scoop" Gleeson, *San Francisco Bulletin,* 1915; SID (Ripley letters to Nell, August 15, 1909 and October 6, 1909); DHS (notes by Hazel Storer).

Believe It! sidebar (TAD): *New York Times* obituary, May 23, 1929.

Note: Different versions of the end to Ripley's *San Francisco Bulletin* career would endure. He'd sometimes claim he was fired after a week. Other times he lasted a year, until an office boy tipped him off that Baggerly was thinking of bagging him and he quit. Occasionally he'd claim he was shown the door after demanding a two-dollar-a-week raise.

CHAPTER 4

Ripley at the *Chronicle:* 1909 San Francisco city directory; author interview with Bill Beutner, research assistant, San Francisco Architectural Heritage, July 29, 2009; "Famous Cartoonist Tells Story of His Life," by Robert Boyd, *The Success Magazine,* January 1926; SCRAP ("Ripley's Life a Believe It or Not," by Gladys Baker, *Birmingham News-Age-Herald,* May 12, 1936); RE and DHS (untitled, unpublished article by Herbert Corey, based on his interview with Ripley); RE (*How to Draw,* unpublished Ripley manuscript); "Believe It or Not," by Jack Banner, *Radio Guide,* November 9, 1935.

Note on baseball: Although Ripley would later claim to have been Ping Bodie's teammate and to have played in California's minor leagues, I was unable to find records in any Pacific Coast League archives to support this, and neither is he mentioned in any minor-league baseball stories in the *Bulletin* or *Chronicle* between 1908 and 1912. He may have continued to play at the semi-professional level, as he had in Santa Rosa—there were scores of "bush league" teams in the Bay Area. He once claimed to have played a season for "the Oakland team of the California State League." The Oakland Coasters were part of the State League, considered an "outlaw" minor league. Sources include books on the Pacific Coast League; e-mail interview with Dick Beverage; NYG ("Bodie Fans with Ripley," August 21, 1912); SCRAP ("Getting Acquainted with Rip," by Robert L. Ripley, *Strength* magazine, December 1929).

Ripley and Nell: SID (Ripley letters to Nell, August 15, 1909; October 6, 1909; December 9, 1909; and April 24, 1910); SRD ("As Nell Wilson Knew Him," May 28, 1949).

Reno and fight: "Struggle for His Soul," by David Remnick, *The Observer,* November 2, 2003; SFC (assorted 1910 clips); NYT (assorted 1910 clips); "Famous

Cartoonist Tells Story of His Life," by Robert Boyd, *The Success Magazine*, January 1926; International Boxing Hall of Fame, www.sweetscience.com; *Unforgivable Blackness: The Rise and Fall of Jack Johnson*, by Geoffrey C. Ward, Vintage, 2006 (also the PBS film with Ken Burns); MMP, p. 23.

Leaving San Francisco: "Believe It or Not Here's Ripley," by Lee Bevins, *Pageant*, October 1948; "Believe It or Not," by Jack Banner, *Radio Guide*, November 9, 1935; DHS (Hazel Storer notes); "Famous Cartoonist Tells Story of His Life," by Robert Boyd, *The Success Magazine*, January 1926; "Strange Things Under the Sun," by Hugh Leamy, *The American*, October 1929; SCRAP ("Ripley's Life a Believe It or Not," by Gladys Baker, *Birmingham News-Age-Herald*, May 12, 1936); RE ("Ripley's Ramble 'Round the World," December 11, 1922); SCRAP (*Pittsburgh Chronicle Telegraph* story, date unknown, circa spring of 1916).

Route to New York: Ripley likely left San Francisco on either the Western Pacific's Feather River Route or the Union Pacific and Southern Pacific's Overland Route, both of which offered daily departures (www.sfmuseum .org/hist1/skeds.html); route details and $85 trip cost estimate from Clifford Vander Yacht—best name ever!—editor of the Railway and Locomotive Historical Society newsletter, whom I interviewed on July 28, 2009.

CHAPTER 5

Story about arriving in New York: SCRAP (untitled profile by Edgar T. "Scoop" Gleeson, *San Francisco Bulletin*, 1915).

Believe It! sidebar (yellow kid): *The Chief: The Life of William Randolph Hearst*, by David Nasaw, Mariner Books, 2001; *The Ten-Cent Plague: The Great Comic-Book Scare and How It Changed America*, by David Hajdu, Picador, 2009; *The Comics: Before 1945*, by Brian Walker, Harry N. Abrams, 2004.

Looking for work in New York and starting at *New York Globe*: DHS (Hazel Storer notes); "Famous Cartoonist Tells Story of His Life," by Robert Boyd, *The Success Magazine*, January 1926; "Strange Things Under the Sun," by

Hugh Leamy, *The American*, October 1929; SCRAP ("How to Be a Cartoonist," *Saturday Evening Post*, October 19, 1940); SCRAP (Herb Corey, article manuscript, date unknown); "Odd Man," Geoffrey T. Hellman, *New Yorker*, 1940; *America's Oldest Daily Newspaper, The New York Globe*, by James Melvin Lee, *The Globe*, 1918; *The Encyclopedia of New York City*, edited by Kenneth T. Jackson, Yale University Press, 1995; NYG (assorted clips, February and March, 1912–1913); "Ripley, Believe It or Not—A Real Success Story," by Harry B. Smith, *San Francisco Chronicle*, February 13, 1935; "Friends Honor Bob Ripley," *Rochester Times-Union*, January 5, 1944; NYT (1949 obit.).

Believe It! sidebar (Yankees): "Red Sox vs. Yankees," Harvey Frommer, 2005, p. 266.

Assorted details about cartoons and comics: *The Ten-Cent Plague: The Great Comic-Book Scare and How It Changed America*, by David Hajdu, Picador, 2009; *The Comics: Before 1945*, by Brian Walker, Harry N. Abrams, 2004; *Over 50 Years of American Comic Books;* by Ron Gaulart, 1991; *Stripper's Guide*, http://strippersguide.blogspot.com/2008_04_01_archive.html [accessed October 1, 2012]; Billy Ireland Cartoon Library & Museum, cartoons. osu.edu [accessed October 1, 2012]; *Men of Tomorrow: Geeks, Gangsters, and the Birth of the Comic Book*, by Gerard Jones, Basic Books, 1995; author interview with Allan Holtz, March 25, 2009.

Ripley playing for the New York Giants: NYT (assorted clips, including "M'Graw Goes South," February 17, 1912); "Odd Man," Geoffrey T. Hellman, *New Yorker*, 1940; "Famous Cartoonist Tells Story of His Life," by Robert Boyd, *The Success Magazine*, January 1926; SCRAP ("Getting Acquainted with Rip," by Robert L. Ripley, *Strength* magazine, December 1929); SCRAP ("Ripley's Life a Believe It or Not," by Gladys Baker, *Birmingham News-Age-Herald*, May 12, 1936); MMP, pp. 33–34; "The Brighter Side," *Charleston Gazette*, January 15, 1939; "Believe It or Not," by Jack Banner, *Radio Guide*, November 9, 1935.

Believe It! sidebar (jazz): "I Remember the Birth of Jazz," Edgar Gleeson, *San Francisco Call-Bulletin*, September 3, 1938; Gleeson article, *San Francisco*

Call, March 6, 1913; "Art Hickman and His Orchestra," by Bruce Vermazen, www.gracyk.com/hickman.shtml [accessed October 1, 2012]; "How Baseball Gave Us 'Jazz,'" by Ben Zimmer, Boston.com, 3/25/12.

Ripley and Santa Rosa and family: SFB ("Ripley Returns to Scenes of His Early Triumph," Edgar Gleeson, circa 1915); RE (Ripley telegrams); DHS (Hazel Storer notes); "Odd Man," Geoffrey T. Hellman, *New Yorker,* 1940; interview with Bob, Doug, and Rebecca Ripley (nephews and grandniece of Ripley); NYG ("Ripley Interviews Ritchie," August 9, 1915).

CHAPTER 6

Settling in New York, and meeting Bugs Baer: *Green Book Magazine,* July 1916, http://historicalziegfeld.multiply.com/photos/album/252 [accessed October 1, 2012]; NYT (1949 obituary); NYT ("Bugs Baer Dead," May 18, 1969); NYG (April 7, 1915, and January 8, 1916); *Unforgivable Blackness: The Rise and Fall of Jack Johnson,* by Geoffrey C. Ward, Vintage, 2006; "Odd Man," by Geoffrey T. Hellman, *New Yorker,* 1940; MMP, pp. 27, 31–32.

Details on cartoonists and Disney: SCRAP (*American Magazine* story, 1916); *The Comics: Before 1945,* by Brian Walker, Harry N. Abrams, 2004; *Walt Disney: The Triumph of the American Imagination,* by Neal Gabler, Vintage, 2007; RE (*How to Draw,* unpublished Ripley manuscript).

World War I cartoons: NYG (December 6, 1915; August 16, 1916; July 28, 1914; September 8, 1914; June 2, 1914; July 18, 1918; and April 2, 1918); RE (*How to Draw,* unpublished Ripley manuscript).

World War I details: *How We Advertised America: The First Telling of the Amazing Story of the Committee on Public Information That Carried the Gospel of Americanism to Every Corner of the Globe,* by George Creel, Kessinger Pub. Co., 2008; National Archives, www.archives.gov/research/guide-fed-records/groups/063.html [accessed October 1, 2012]; assorted links from the Wikipedia page for the Committee on Public Information (http://en.wikipedia.org/wiki/Committee_on_Public_Information); NYG (letter to editor, August 20, 1917).

Champs and Chumps: "The Incredible 'Believe It or Not,'" by Robert Ripley, *Popular Mechanics*, February 1936; DHS (Hazel Storer notes, and letters to Hazel); "Strange Things Under the Sun," by Hugh Leamy, *The American*, October 1929; "Odd Man," Geoffrey T. Hellman, *New Yorker*, 1940; RE (*How to Draw*, unpublished Ripley manuscript); "The Story of Believe It or Not," by Mel Heimer, King Features Syndicate Biographical Series, No. 29.

CHAPTER 7

Bernarr Macfadden and Freddie Welsh: bernarrmacfadden.com [accessed October 1, 2012]; *Occupation: Prizefighter: Freddie Welsh's Quest for the World Championship*, by Andrew Gallimore, Seren, 2006; author interview with Allan Holtz, November 2, 2009.

On women: RE (typed manuscript of "The New Beauty for Women," by Robert Ripley—unpublished?); SCRAP ("Getting Acquainted with Rip," by Robert L. Ripley, *Strength* magazine, December 1929); SCRAP ("Why I Am Not Married," by Betty Brainerd, for her "We Women" column, date unknown).

Life at the NYAC and playing handball: *The First Hundred Years: A Portrait of the NYAC*, by Bob Considine and Fred G. Jarvis, 1974; New York Athletic Club, nyac.org [accessed October 1, 2012]; author interview with NYAC historian Tom Quinn, August 20, 2009; "Famous Cartoonist Tells Story of His Life," by Robert Boyd, *The Success Magazine*, January 1926; *Spalding's Official Handball Guide*, by Robert L. Ripley, American Sports Pub., 1923; "The New Beauty for Women," by Robert Ripley; SCRAP ("Getting Acquainted with Rip," by Robert L. Ripley, *Strength* magazine, December 1929); NYT (obituary, 1949); MMP, p. 38; SCRAP ("Ripley Owns an Egg Pen Now," undated article); "Believe It or Not, Ripley Was Almost as Odd as His Items," by Donald Dale Jackson, *Smithsonian*, January 1995.

Marriage to Beatrice: in addition to obtaining Beatrice's birth certificate and Ripley and Beatrice's marriage license, the details of their marriage are based on assorted articles found in Ripley's scrapbook (many from 1922 and 1923, and others undated), as well as letters from Ripley to his sister; "No One Would Believe It," by Ruth Biery, *Radio Stars* magazine, May 1936; and "Why I Am Not Married," by Betty Brainerd. At the time of their marriage, a few newspapers referred to Beatrice as Beatrice Carlisle. As I explain in chapter 17, for many years there was confusion over the true identity of Ripley's wife.

Ziegfeld and the *Ziegfeld Follies: Ziegfeld: The Man Who Invented Show Business,* by Ethan Mordden (2008).

Olympics: *The First Hundred Years: A Portrait of the NYAC,* by Bob Considine and Fred G. Jarvis, 1974; NYT (July 19, 1920); NYG (August 25, 1920); Official Website of the Olympic Movement, www.olympic.org [accessed October 1, 2012]; *Flanders Today,* flanderstoday.eu [accessed October 1, 2012].

Troubles with Beatrice: "No One Would Believe It," by Ruth Biery, *Radio Stars,* 1936; MMP, pp. 39–41; SCRAP (assorted stories about the court proceedings and divorce, 1921 and 1923); NYT (April 13, 1923); "The New Beauty for Women," by Robert Ripley.

CHAPTER 8

All details of the Ramble are based on Ripley's personal travel journals and his cartoons and essays that appeared in the *New York Globe* and other newspapers. [Note: Though the actual journey began in early December of 1922, some papers wouldn't start running the illustrated articles until January of 1923.]

Believe It! sidebar (Titanic): author interview with Tom Quinn.

CHAPTER 9

Frank Munsey: "Mr. Munsey Buys," *Time,* June 4, 1923; "Another Buy," *Time,* February 4, 1924; author interview with Allan Holtz; *Forty Years, Forty Millions:*

The Career of Frank A. Munsey, by George Britt, Farrar & Rinehart, 1935; NYT (Munsey obituary, December 29, 1925); "The Classic Era of American Pulp Magazines," by Peter Haining, www.crimetime.co.uk/features/peterhaining .php [accessed October 1, 2012].

More troubles with Beatrice: NYG (April 14, 1923); NYT (April 13, 1923); "No One Would Believe It," by Ruth Biery, *Radio Stars* magazine, May 1936; SCRAP ("Why I Am Not Married," by Betty Brainerd, for her "We Women" column, date unknown); SCRAP (assorted stories about the court proceedings and divorce, 1921 and 1923); NYP (Ramble 'Round South America, January 27, 1925).

Details about Doug and Ethel: interviews with Rebecca and Robert Ripley; RE (letter to Ethel, April 15, 1923).

Death of the *Globe*: NYT (Munsey obituary, December 29, 1925); *America's Oldest Daily Newspaper, The New York Globe,* by James Melvin Lee, *The Globe,* 1918.

Norbert Pearlroth: "In Search of the (Nearly) Miraculous," by Susan Lydon, *Village Voice,* October 22, 1979; "You Better Believe This," by Dan Carlinsky, *Modern Maturity,* 1974; Pearlroth obituary, *Time,* April 25, 1983; "Believe It or Not," by Kenneth Turan, *The Washington Post,* April 1, 1973).

Miscellaneous: NYP (Ramble 'Round South America, March 23, 1925 and January 27, 1925); The Circumnavigators Club, www.circumnavigatorsclub .org [accessed October 1, 2012]; SCRAP ("Why I Am Not Married," by Betty Brainerd, for her "We Women" column, date unknown).

CHAPTER 10

All details of the Ramble are based on Ripley's personal travel journals and the cartoons and essays that appeared in the Associated Newspapers and various other newspapers throughout early 1925. Additional details: MMP; DHS; RE.

CHAPTER 11

Munsey's death: *Forty Years, Forty Millions: The Career of Frank A. Munsey,* by George Britt, Farrar & Rinehart, 1935; NYT (Munsey obituary, December 29, 1925); "Uncensored Commentaries," by Theo Lippman Jr., *Baltimore Sun,* March 31, 2003.

Handball note: Ripley played at the 1927 National Championships in St. Paul but lost by a few points, in a best-of-three series against the eventual champ.

Believe It! sidebar (Curtis's income): *Time* (June 19, 1933); NYT (Curtis obituary, September 6, 1925); *Outliers: The Story of Success,* by Malcolm Gladwell, Little, Brown and Company, 2008.

Starting at *New York Post*: "Circulation Figures," *Time,* October 22, 1923; NYP ("Ripley's Returned," August 16, 1926); author interview with Jeff Pearlroth.

Macfadden: *Winchell: Gossip, Power, and the Culture of Celebrity,* by Neal Gabler, Vintage, 1995, pp. 72, 74, 77.

Lindbergh cartoon, lying accusations, and Marching Chinese cartoon: "You Better Believe This," by Dan Carlinsky, *Modern Maturity,* 1974; *Ripley's Believe It or Not!: In Celebration . . . A Special Reissue of the Original!,* by Robert Ripley, Ripley Publishing, 2004, p. 39; MMP, pp. 52–53; SCRAP ("Celebrated Caricaturist Entertains with Sketches and Interesting Facts," exact date and publication unknown; "Ripley to Talk . . . ," unknown publication, April 9, 1928; and "Ripley Loves to Have Fans Call Him Liar," *New York Herald,* day unknown, 1929).

Lectures and letters, and verifying facts: SCRAP (untitled clip, March 22, 1927; untitled article, by Joseph M. Ripley, *American Press,* 1929; miscellaneous clips); NYP (letter from Mabel Henry, October 1, 1928; letter to editor, April 12, 1928; assorted Ripley cartoons and essays); SCRAP ("Getting Acquainted with Rip," by Robert L. Ripley, *Strength* magazine, December 1929); *Ripley's Believe It or Not!,* by Robert Ripley, Ripley Publishing, 2004; MMP, pp. 45, 49, 50, 59.

Ripley lifestyle versus Pearlroth lifestyle: SID (Rube Goldberg letter to Bob Considine); "You Better Believe This," by Dan Carlinsky, *Modern Maturity*, 1974; "In Search of the (Nearly) Miraculous," by Susan Lydon, *Village Voice*, October 22, 1979; "Believe It or Not," by William Allen, *Saturday Review*, February 1973; "Believe It or Not," by Kenneth Turan, *Washington Post*, April 1, 1973; DHS (letters, notes).

Goes to Hell: "Ripley Goes to Hell," *The Troy Times*, May 7, 1928; SCRAP (untitled, *Time*, March 26, 1928).

CHAPTER 12

Simon & Schuster and book reviews: *Only Yesterday: An Informal History of the 1920s*, by Frederick Lewis Allen, Harper Perennial, 2000, pp. 144–45; Simon & Schuster, simonandschuster.net [accessed October 1, 2012]; "Simon & Schuster Inc. History," www.fundinguniverse.com/company-histories/Simon-amp;-Schuster-Inc-Company-History.html [accessed October 1, 2012]; RE (Schuster letter to Ripley, October 31, 1927); DHS (Ripley's contract with Simon & Schuster); SCRAP (untitled, by Harry Hansen, *The First Reader*; "Behind the Backs of Books and Authors," by Mary Rennels, *New York Telegram*, day unknown, 1929).

Lawsuit: NYT ("Sue Ripley," May 20, 1930).

Travel to Central America: SCRAP (untitled, *Peddie News*, date unknown; untitled, *San Antonio Light*, date unknown; "Believe It or Not, but Ripley Is Home," unknown publication and date); NYT (Cass Baer's obituary, May 11, 1929); RE (October 23, 1933 journal entry).

Signing on with Hearst, working with Connolly: "Notes on an American Phenomenon," by John K. Winkler, *The New Yorker*, April–May 1927 (5 parts); *The Chief: The Life of William Randolph Hearst*, by David Nasaw, Mariner Books, 2001, pp. 237, 322–23, 379–80, 387); *The Uncrowned King: The Sensational Rise of William Randolph Hearst*, by Kenneth Whyte, Counterpoint, 2009; MMP, pp. 15, 37; SID (letter to Bradley Kelley, October 29, 1964); author interview with Tom Quinn, NYAC historian; DHS (contracts); *Winchell: Gossip, Power, and the Culture of Celebrity,* by Neal Gabler, Vintage, 1995, p. 104; kingfeatures.com/about-us/king-features-history; NYT (Connolly obituary, April 18, 1945); SCRAP (assorted undated clips, including "Robert L. Ripley Is Guest of Honor"); "The Press: Average Man," *Time,* November 26, 1945; RE (Connolly letter to Ripley, October 29, 1929).

Living at the NYAC: SCRAP (assorted undated clips, including "Ripgrams," 1930); author interview with Tom Smith; *Terrible Honesty: Mongrel Manhattan in the 1920s,* by Ann Douglas, Farrar Straus and Giroux, 1996; DHS (notes by Hazel Storer).

Believe It! sidebar (plane crash): *The Chief: The Life of William Randolph Hearst,* by David Nasaw, Mariner Books, 2001, p. 380.

Early King Features cartoons . . . and controversies: SCRAP (including "Catholic Father Declares Ripley Shows His 'Tremendous Ignorance,'" *Honolulu Star-Bulletin,* undated; "Believe It or Not," *The Northwest Review,* edited by Rev. SJ Ryan, 1929; "Ripley Contest Has 7 More Days," *San Francisco Examiner,* 1929; and "Best Sellers of Year Reported by Publishers," by Fanny Butcher, *Chicago Tribune,* December 21, 1929).

CHAPTER 13

Hyman working for Ripley: DHS (Hyman letter to Considine, 1959).

Fans and fan mail: NYP (untitled story, by Norman Klein, 1929); SCRAP (untitled *Boston Daily Record* story January 11, 1930); MMP, pp. 10, 15, 37. "Odd Man," by Geoffrey T. Hellman, *New Yorker,* 1940; part 2, p. 27; "Strange Things Under the Sun," by Hugh Leamy, *The American,* October 1929; RE (original letter).

Fame, radio, and movie offers: SCRAP ("Ripley, True Pioneer," *Kansas City Star,* 1929); "Believe It or Not," by Sylvia Covino, *The Bluebird,* Julia Richman High School, 1930); "Strange Things Under the Sun," by Hugh Leamy, *The*

American, October 1929; "Ripley Target of Circuit Bids," *Billboard,* February 22, 1930; "Odd Man," by Geoffrey T. Hellman, *New Yorker,* 1940, part I, p. 22; "The Most Unforgettable Character I've Met—Robert Ripley," by Douglas F. Storer, *Reader's Digest,* June 1959, Vol. 74, No. 44623.

Elmer Fudd and Vitaphone films: *Winchell: Gossip, Power, and the Culture of Celebrity,* by Neal Gabler, Vintage, 1995, p. 112; SCRAP (untitled *Variety* story, June 25, 1930, and untitled *Chicago Herald Examiner* story, June 8, 1930); *Believe It or Else,* directed by Tex Avery, written by Dave Monahan, Warner Bros. Pictures, 1939; NYT ("Cartoons of a Racist Past Lurk on YouTube," by Daniel Slotnik, April 28, 2008).

Hearst and radio: *The Chief: The Life of William Randolph Hearst,* by David Nasaw, Mariner Books, 2001, pp. 389–90, 405, 437; SCRAP ("Ripley to Lecture for Radio Fans at Roselle Tonight," publication unknown, undated, 1922).

Letters and Pearlroth: DHS (Hazel Storer notes); *Dear Mr. Ripley: A Compendium of Curiosities from the Believe It or Not! Archives,* by Mark Sloan, Roger Manley, Michelle Van Parys, and Robert Ripley, Bulfinch Press, 1993; SCRAP ("Ripley's Career Began When He Was Fourteen," *New York American,* 1929, exact date unknown); "Believe It or Not," by Kenneth Turan, *Washington Post,* April 1, 1973; "You Better Believe This," by Dan Carlinsky, *Modern Maturity,* 1974.

Travels: "Telephone Remarks to the National Automobile Chamber of Commerce," January 6, 1931, by Herbert Hoover, The American Presidency Project, www.presidency.ucsb.edu/ws/index.php?pid=22999 [accessed October 1, 2012]; Sideshow World, sideshowworld.com [accessed October 1, 2012]; SCRAP (unnamed article, "Ripley's Home by Sea and Air," *Memphis Press Scimitar,* May 27, 1930, and uncredited *International News* photos March 6, 1931 and May 22, 1931); MMP, pp. 74–76.

Lawsuit and Doug Ripley: NYT (May 20, 1930); author interviews with Robert and Rebecca Ripley.

CHAPTER 14

Onuki and women: "No One Would Believe It," by Ruth Biery, *Radio Stars* magazine, May 1936; DHS (Hyman letter to Considine); NYT (September 19, 1926 and February 25, 1932); MMP, p. 76; *Time*, March 7, 1932; *Los Angeles Times*, May 5, 1918 and February 25, 1932; www.strippersguide.com.

Details of *Mariposa* trip: RE (Ripley's travel journal); KFS (assorted cartoons and essays); original travel brochure; assorted NYT clips; *Los Angeles Times* (February 4, 1932); "Fiji's Cannibal History," www.fijiancustomculture .com/2009/10/fijis-cannibal-history.html [accessed October 1, 2012]; SCRAP (untitled article, *Daily Democrat News*, May 29, 1939); *Pearl Buck in China: Journey to the Good Earth*, by Hilary Spurling, Simon & Schuster, 2011, p. 201; Zhenjiang Pearl S. Buck Research Association, www.pearlsbcn.org/e/ (Buck's speech at Nobel Prize Award Ceremony) [accessed October 1, 2012].

Introduction to Ruth "Oakie" Ross: DHS (Hazel Storer notes, and Bill MacDonald letter to Doug Storer, 1962); RE (interviews with Edward Meyer); TBS interviews with Li Ling-Ai; MMP, pp. 72–3.

Santa Rosa visit: SRD (Ripley obituary, May 28, 1949); SCRAP (assorted clips).

CHAPTER 15

Charles "Cash and Carry" Pyle: SRD (February 5, 1995); *Chicago Daily Tribune* obituary, February 4, 1939; SH; *Sports Illustrated*, May 2, 1955; SCRAP (untitled columns by Westbrook Pegler, *Chicago Tribune*, July 29, 1933 and November 7, 1933).

Odditorium and Chicago World's Fair: RE (letters and contracts); "Chicago's World's Fair Remembered," by Ray Weiss, *Chicago Tribune*, May 7, 1984; "Baseball's First All-Star Game," by Jennie Cohen, June 13, 2010, www.history.com/ news/baseballs-first-all-star-game [accessed October 1, 2012]; Sideshow World, www.sideshowworld.com [accessed October 1, 2012]; "Masters of the Midway," by A. J. Liebling, two-part series, *The New Yorker*, 1939.

Travels to Iraq and Persia: RE (Ripley's personal travel journal); KFS (cartoons and articles); SCRAP ("The Name Believe It or Not Is Familiar," by Mary Morris, unknown New York newspaper, unknown date); "Bob Ripley Writes This Week's Guest Column," *Will Rogers Field News*, March 5, 1943; DHS (Hazel Storer notes).

Odditorium performers, sideshows, and P. T. Barnum: Sideshow World, www.sideshowworld.com; *American Sideshow*, by Marc Hartzman, Tarcher, 2006; "1934 World's Fair," Sideshow Ephemera Gallery, http://missioncreep.com/mundie/gallery/gallery8.htm [accessed October 1, 2012]; "Frieda Pushnick: Armless and Legless Wonder Girl," http://missioncreep.com/mundie/gallery/gallery21.htm [accessed October 1, 2012]; The Human Marvels, www.thehumanmarvels.com [accessed October 1, 2012]; "Masters of the Midway," by A. J. Liebling, two-part series, *The New Yorker*, 1939; *Freak Show: Presenting Human Oddities for Amusement and Profit*, by Robert Bogdan, University of Chicago Press, 1990.

CHAPTER 16

Decision to move to Mamaroneck: SCRAP (undated "News and Views" and "Ripgrams" clips; Ripley profile in *Hobbies: The Magazine for Collectors*, July 1940); interviews with Greg Daugherty; NYT (Ripley obituary, 1949); DHS (notes and letters by Hazel Storer and Bob Considine); SCRAP ("Ripley's Life a Believe It or Not," by Gladys Baker, *Birmingham News-Age-Herald*, May 12, 1936); MMP, pp. 41–43.

Odditorium, continued: RE (telegrams and letters, press releases and brochures); SCRAP ("Barnum Was Wrong, Says Ripley," *Boston Advertiser*, 1930, day unknown); "Which Is the Real Masakichi?" www.anomalies-unlimited.com/Death/Masakichi.html [accessed October 1, 2012]; "Century of Progress Exposition," *Encyclopedia of Chicago*, www.encyclopedia.chicagohistory.org [accessed October 1, 2012].

Doug Storer and radio: RE (publicity press releases); DHS (assorted notes, letters, and articles); "The Most Unforgettable Character I've Met—Robert Ripley," by Douglas F. Storer, *Reader's Digest*, June 1959; "To Be or Not to Be Like Bing," by Alton Cook, *World Telegram*, October 17, 1935; MMP, pp. 114, 120.

Ripley and Russia: RE (telegram, Hearst to Ripley, June 15, 1935; copies of letters to legislators; undated memo from Joe Simpson to Ripley, "RE: Anti-Communist Broadcast"; Ripley telegram to Hearst, March 18, 1936; Ripley letter, March 10, 1936; John F. Royal letter to Storer, March 14, 1936); DHS (Hazel Storer notes on Ripley's "politics"); SCRAP (untitled *Daily Worker* article, April 6, 1935; *New York American* clip, March 3, 1936); *The Chief: The Life of William Randolph Hearst*, by David Nasaw, Mariner Books, 2001, pp. 484, 493–94); "Russia Afraid of Ripley, say Legislators," Associated Press, March 4, 1936; "Appeal for Religion," *New York American*, June 5, 1936.

Ripley's income and popularity: NYT ("Highest Salaries Paid in the Nation Are Listed by House Committee," January 9, 1936); "How Comic Cartoons Make Fortunes," by Alfred Albelli, *Modern Mechanix and Inventions*, November 1933; SCRAP ("A Laugh with Rube Goldberg," April 19, 1936; "Believe It or Not," column by O. B. Keeler, date unknown); DHS (Hazel Storer notes on "travel").

CHAPTER 17

Female relationships, especially Oakie: SCRAP ("New York, Day by Day," by O. O. McIntyre, June 16, 1937; "Ripley Discovers a New Republic," *Sunday Republican*, Waterbury, CT, June 30, 1935; "Ripley Pins His Faith in Future on Aviation," by Frances Wayne, *Denver Post*, January 14, 1943; "Search for Oddities Leads Robert Ripley to Visit 181 Countries," by Harriet Mencken, unknown publication, 1936; "Mr Ripley Visits Shetland," *The Shetland Times*, September 15, 1934; "The Name Believe It or Not Is Familiar," by Mary Morris, unknown New York newspaper, unknown date; "No One Would Believe It," by Ruth Biery, *Radio Stars* magazine, May 1936); ships' passenger logs, including the SS *Ile de France*, September 28, 1934; MMP, pp. 72–3, 41–3; RE (1962 letter from Bill McDonald to Doug Storer); DHS (extensive notes by Hazel Storer about Ripley's "women"); according to the US Census, Ross was born July 11, 1899, and lived at 112 W. 59th Street, also Park Avenue, Central Park South, and Beekman Place.

Details about life at BION Island: *1001 Curious Things: Ye Olde Curiosity Shop and Native American Art*, by Kate C. Duncan, University of Washington Press, 2001; MMP, pp. 41–43, 72–73, 169; *Just a minute, Mrs. Gulliver*, by Millie Considine, Prentice-Hall, 1967, reprint edition; RE (unpublished memoir by Ripley's housekeeper, Almuth Seabeck); DHS (Hazel Storer notes); "Ripley's Boat Draws Visitors," by O. O. McIntyre, unnamed newspaper, New Castle, PA, June 25, 1937; "Ripley Was Crazy About Dogs," by Greg Daugherty, *Bark*, Nov/Dec 2007); SCRAP (undated "News and Views" clips, 1933–36); author interviews with Robert and Rebecca Ripley; RE (Cygna Conly memos to KFS; Joseph Connolly memo to Robert Ripley, March 3, 1938).

Hix and other competitors: "How Comic Cartoons Make Fortunes," by Alfred Albelli, *Modern Mechanix and Inventions*, November 1933; *Everything Was Better in America: Print Culture in the Great Depression*, by David Welky, University of Illinois Press, 2008, pp. 93–4; www.bernarrmacfadden.com/macfadden5.html; *Men of Tomorrow: Geeks, Gangsters, and the Birth of the Comic Book*, by Gerard Jones, Basic Books, 1995, pp. 29–33; DHS (copies of lawsuit filings); SCRAP ("Believe It or Not," column by O. B. Keeler, date unknown); *Schulz and Peanuts: A Biography*, by David Michaelis, Harper Perennial, 2008, p. 93.

Radio shows with Storer: RE (assorted Storer/Ripley letters and contracts; BION radio script, August 2, 1938; Kuda Bux film footage); DHS (assorted Storer/Ripley letters and contracts); MMP, pp. 84, 112–113; SCRAP ("Search for Oddities Leads Robert Ripley to Visit 181 Countries," by Harriet Mencken, unknown publication, 1936; "New York, Day by Day," by O. O. McIntyre, 1934; "Fire on Air," *Time*, August 15, 1938; undated Crossley ratings clip, 1936);

Daily Life in the United States, 1920–1940: How Americans Lived Through the Roaring Twenties and the Great Depression, by David E. Kyvig, Ivan R. Dee, 2004, p. 90; *Everything Was Better in America: Print Culture in the Great Depression,* by David Welky, University of Illinois Press, 2008, p. 67; SID (letters: December 2, 1938 and December 15, 1938).

CHAPTER 18

Prewar radio and travel: MMP, p. 114; DHS (legal contracts from 1930s; Hazel Storer "chronology" notes); SCRAP (untitled *Daily Democrat News* clip, May 29, 1939; "Ripley Broadcast Carries Cavern Publicity to Entire World," *Eddy County News,* June 9, 1939); NYT ("14,000 See Ruth Smash Soft Ball as Celebrities Play in Garden," by Louis Effrat, May 10, 1939).

Note on female performers: Betty Lou went on to have a successful sideshow career, earning enough money to send her twelve siblings to college. She died in 1955 at age twenty-two. Frieda Pushnik spent six years with Ripley and in 1943 joined the "Congress of Freaks." She entered semi-retirement in the 1950s, but appeared occasionally in films, including 1963's *The House of the Damned.* Frieda died in 2000 at the age of seventy-seven. (Sources include *American Sideshow,* by Marc Hartzman, Tarcher, 2006, p. 230; "1934 World's Fair," Sideshow Ephemera Gallery, http://missioncreep.com/mundie/gallery/gallery8.htm [accessed October 1, 2012]; "Frieda Pushnick: Armless and Legless Wonder Girl," http://missioncreep.com/mundie/gallery/gallery21.htm [accessed October 1, 2012]; The Human Marvels, www.thehumanmarvels.com [accessed October 1, 2012]).

Odditoriums (San Fransisco and NYC), Lou Dufour, and Doug Ripley: Virtual Museum of the City of San Francisco, www.sfmuseum.net/hist1/index0.1.html [accessed October 1, 2012]; "CC Pyle Dies," *Chicago Daily Tribune,* February 4, 1939; www.sideshowworld.com/SSNL-Spring-2008-P5.html; "Masters of the Midway," Liebling, *New Yorker;* DHS (Hazel Storer notes, and assorted letters and documents); author interview with Robert Ripley (nephew).

Traveling radio shows: SCRAP (International Newsreel photo, January 1, 1940; "Words and Music," by Sid Weiss, *Radio Daily*, February 8, 1940; "Bob Ripley Program at Grand Canyon," by Kenneth Webb and Charles Speer, *Santa Fe Magazine*, unknown date); MMP, pp. 124–126; RE (radio scripts).

Believe It! sidebar (Goldwater): RE (letter from Ripley to Goldwater, October 7, 1940); Joan Nevills Staveley and Sandra Nevills Reiff interview, Cline Library, Northern Arizona University, September 12, 1994.

Odditorium flop: "Odd Man," by Geoffrey T. Hellman, *New Yorker*, 1940; DHS (Hazel Storer notes, and Odditorium documents and court files).

Believe It! sidebar (Widdicombe and Tapscott): "The Log of the SS *Anglo Saxon*'s Jolly Boat," Imperial War Museum, www.iwm.org.uk/upload/package/7/anglosaxon/log.htm and "Landfall," Imperial War Museum, www.iwm.org.uk/upload/package/7/anglosaxon/landfall.htm [accessed October 1, 2012]; DHS (Hazel Storer notes and letters); MMP, p. 130.

CHAPTER 19

Ripley's parties and life at BION: SCRAP ("America's Catch of the Season," by E. V. Durling, *Boston Evening American*, March 3, 1942; "Where a Globetrotter Hangs His Hat," *Liberty Magazine*, May 11, 1946); "If You Were Housekeeper to Mr. Ripley," by Nanete Kutner, *Good Housekeeping*, 1942; *You're Right Mr. Ripley*, unpublished manuscript, by Almuth Seabeck (Ripley's housekeeper); DHS (Hazel Storer notes on "parties"); "Life Goes to a Party," *LIFE*, July 8, 1940; "Odd Man," by Geoffrey T. Hellman, *New Yorker*, 1940; MMP, pp. 101, 104, 108; "Believe It or Not," by Jack Banner, *Radio Guide*, November 9, 1935.

Note: One of the more revealing articles I came across was an undated clip found in the Ripley archives—"The Name Believe It or Not is Familiar"—written by Mary Morris for an unnamed New York newspaper. Morris describes the day she spent with Ripley, at one point asking him what he liked most about the East. "Love, marriage, romance," he said. "In the Mohammaden countries there are no fights between husband and wife, no divorces. Men are left to enjoy themselves. Women aren't making noise all the time with court litigation like they do here." In the United States, he added, "Our moral codes, or standards, are all wrong."

TBS: I managed to review the unedited interview that TBS conducted with Li Ling-Ai, during which Li mentions Ripley's relationships with Fannie Hurst, Babe Murray, and others, including Oakie. (In the same interview, Li declined to say whether she and Ripley had been lovers.) TBS also interviewed Hazel Storer, who also discussed Ripley's love affair with Oakie. (Li died in 2003, and Storer died in 2005.)

Losing Oakie; other women: RE (interviews with Edward Meyer; Ripley's will); SCRAP ("Ripley Returns with Brand New Believe It Or Nots," International News Service, September 25, 1936; "The Name Believe It or Not Is Familiar," by Mary Morris); DHS (detailed handwritten notes by Hazel Storer on "women"); TBS (unedited interview footage, Hazel Storer); MMP, p. 72; "Tosia Mori," *Canadian Ken,* http://canadianken.blogspot.com/2008/06/toshia-mori .html; *Just a Minute, Mrs. Gulliver,* by Millie Considine, Prentice-Hall, 1967, reprint edition; *You're Right Mr. Ripley,* by Almuth Seabeck (unpublished manuscript); *Liberty Magazine,* May 11, 1946; "Believe It or Not Ripley," by Jack Stone, *The American Weekly,* June 22, 1947.

Believe It! sidebar (Wong and Mori): *Anna May Wong: From Laundryman's Daughter to Hollywood Legend,* by Graham Russell Hodges, Hong Kong University Press, 2004.

Wartime: RE (Hoover letter to Ripley, May 1941; Taft letter to Ripley, September 19, 1941); *Liberty Magazine,* May 11, 1946; MMP, pp. 92, 104, 108; passenger list for the SS *President Cleveland,* 1927.

CHAPTER 20

Li Ling-Ai and China Relief efforts: Charles Pearson press releases (from Robin Lung); TBS interview; SCRAP (*New York Journal* article, date unknown);

Liberty Magazine, May 11, 1946; "The Name Believe It or Not Is Familiar," by Mary Morris; author interviews with Robin Lung.

WWII radio shows . . . and CIAA spies: RE (contract, January 10, 1939; BION radio show scripts); "The Most Unforgettable Character I've Met—Robert Ripley," by Douglas F. Storer, *Reader's Digest*, June 1959; DHS (assorted letters and contracts, 1941–43); *Walt Disney: The Triumph of the American Imagination*, by Neal Gabler, Vintage, 2007, pp. 372, 394–95; www.waltandelgrupo.com; "Ripley Pins His Faith in Future on Aviation," by Frances Wayne, *Denver Post*, January 14, 1943); "Nelson A. Rockefeller's Office of Inter-American Affairs (1940–1946) and Record Group 229," by Gisela Cramer and Ursula Prutsch, *Hispanic American Historical Review*, 2006; "Coordinator of Inter-American Affairs," http://en.wikipedia.org/wiki/Coordinator_of_Inter-American_Affairs (external references and links); The Venona Project, http://sovietspies.blogspot.com.

Deaths: "Seven Story Fall Kills Linda Lee, Radio Singer," *New York Evening Journal*, August 25, 1942; DHS (letters and Hazel Storer notes); *You're Right Mr. Ripley*, by Almuth Seabeck (unpublished manuscript); "Where a Globetrotter Hangs His Hat," *Liberty Magazine*, 1946.

Radio, parties, and troubles: "Ripley Finds Aviation Way to Brotherhood," *St. Louis Post Dispatch*, February 11, 1943; SCRAP (NYT, May 25, 1943); "Big Town Heartbeat," *Atlanta Journal*, January 30, 1944; "Father Carves Name in Engine," *Herald Advance*, Milbank, SD, February 17, 1944; "The Voice of Broadway," Dorothy Kilgallen column, February 28, 1944; "In Hollywood," by Louella Parsons, *Pittsburgh Sun-Telegraph*, February 10, 1944; "Does His Own," *Radio Life*, February 20, 1944; "Believe It or Not," *Time*, January 29, 1945; "Believe It or Not Here's Ripley," by Lee Bevins, *Pageant*, October 1948; "On the Side," by E. V. Durling, *Boston Evening American*, March 3, 1942; "Ripley to Sail Chinese Junk," by Priscilla Endicott, *Westchester Times*, July 31, 1947; RE (assorted letters and memos, 1942–44); TBS interview with Li Ling-Ai; NYT ("JV Connolly Dies," April 18, 1945); DHS; MMP, p. 101.

CHAPTER 21

The *Mon Lei:* DHS (letters, Hazel Storer notes); *You're Right Mr. Ripley,* by Almuth Seabeck (unpublished manuscript); RE (Bill McDonald letter to Doug Storer, 1962; Cygna Conly letter to Joe Willicombe, March 18, 1966; Willicombe itinerary, 1947); SCRAP ("Ripley Arrived Today," by Sidney Epstein, December 1, 1947, publication unknown; "Ripley to Spend Vacation Here," by SW Matthews, *Miami Daily News,* date unknown; "I Found the Lost Weekend," by Louise Baer, *DAC News,* date unknown; *Key West Citizen* article, February 14, 1947; "Ripley to Sail Chinese Junk," by Priscilla Endicott, *Westchester Times;* "Planes and Yachts Greet Ripley Today," by Jack Leary, *Albany Times-Union,* August 8, 1947); MMP, pp. 176–77.

CHAPTER 22

Most of the details of Ripley's final trip to China come from a detailed journal written by George McMillin, found at the Ripley archives. Other sources include: RE (letters, 1947–1949, including Ripley to Storer, February 27, 1948, Ripley to Ward Greene, October 11, 1948, and Storer to Ripley, July 25, 1948; also 1949 BION show scripts); MMP, pp. 193, 197; DHS ("Partnership Leads to Believe It or Not," by Hazel Geissler, *St. Petersburg Evening Independent,* March 29, 1979; Hazel Storer notes and letters); "Ina E. Ohnick, Magnate's Widow Who Survived a Wartime Prison," by Peyton Whitely, *Seattle Times,* September 18, 1992); *The Man Who Loved China,* by Simon Winchester, Harper, 2008, pp. 46–7, 50–1; SCRAP ("Ripley Aboard President Cleveland," *Honolulu Star-Bulletin,* date unknown); TBS interviews with Hazel Storer and Li Ling-Ai.

CHAPTER 23

Ripley's volatility, declining health, disputes with brother: RE (numerous letters to and from Ripley, 1947–1949; Cygna Conly memo, January 20, 1947; KFS inneroffice memos); interviews with Robert and Rebecca Ripley; MMP, pp. 193, 206; *Just a Minute, Mrs. Gulliver,* Millie Considine, Prentice-Hall, 1967, reprint edition; SRD ("Robert Ripley Will Be Buried in City of Roses," May 28, 1949); DHS (Hazel Storer notes and letters; Doug Storer business letters and memos); "Believe It or Not Ripley," by Jack Stone, *The American Weekly*, June 22, 1947; SFC ("When Fights Were Fights," by Harry B. Smith, February 13, 1935); TBS interviews with Hazel Storer and Li Ling-Ai; SID (notes on Ming Jung).

CHAPTER 24

Ripley's final days and death: RE (Doug Storer letters; BION show scripts; BION film footage); NYT ("The Battle for Shanghai Ended Today," May 27, 1949; Ripley funeral, June 1, 1949); DHS (Hazel Storer notes); TBS interviews with Hazel Storer and Li Ling-Ai; MMP, pp. 210–211; author interviews with Robert and Rebecca Ripley; "One Man's Junk Is Another Base's Treasure," by Andy Stephens, *Air Force Print News Today*, December 7, 2006; "The Most Unforgettable Character I've Met—Robert Ripley," by Douglas F. Storer, *Reader's Digest*, June 1959; SRD ("Robert Ripley Will Be Buried in City of Roses," May 28, 1949).

Note: According to an essay written by Ripley employee Kay Lawrence (which I found in the Ripley archives), Ripley was dictating something to Liese Wisse when he started to convulse. Lawrence arrived at the hospital soon after he was pronounced dead, and found Wisse hysterical and sobbing. A doctor told them it was a heart attack. They were soon joined by Cygna Conly, Robert Hyland, and Doug Ripley. Lawrence writes that all of them except Doug Storer were grief stricken. Storer, she said, was "nonchalantly twirling his watch chain . . . talking about what he planned to do in the future regarding the business."

EPILOGUE

The aftermath and the legacy: SCRAP ("Ripley to Sail Chinese Junk," by Priscilla Endicott, *The Westchester Times*, July 31, 1947); author interview with Allan Holtz; RE (undated essay by Kay Lawrence); author interviews with Robert and Rebecca Ripley; "Ripley Auction," *LIFE*, September 12, 1949;

"With or Without Dragons," *The New Yorker*, September 1949; author interviews with Edward Meyer; "Believe It or Not," by Kenneth Turan, *Washington Post*, April 1, 1973; "Believe It or Not Going Strong at 33," *Editor & Publisher*, December 15, 1951; SRD ("A Big Tree, A Little Church, A Restoration," by Gaye LeBaron, December 25, 2010); "Would You Believe Louis XIV Never Took a Bath?" by Jill Millikin, *Wall Street Journal*, February 1, 1972; "In Search of the (Nearly) Miraculous," by Susan Lydon, *Village Voice*, October 22, 1979; TBS interviews with Hazel Storer and Li Ling-Ai; "Li Ling Ai," *Village Care News*, Spring 2003.

Note: Other *Believe It or Not* writers and artists included Lester Byck; Paul and Walter Frehm (Paul would win a National Cartoonist Society award in 1976); Don Wimmer; Joe Campbell; Art Sloggatt; Clemens Gretter; Carl Dorese; Bob Clarke; Clarence Thorpe; and Stan Randall.

ACKNOWLEDGMENTS

Supreme gratitude to Norm Deska and Edward Meyer at the Ripley Entertainment company for opening your doors to me, allowing me inside the archives, entrusting me with your treasures, and for giving me a chance to tell the full story of LeRoy Robert Ripley. Without your help, this book could not have been written.

Also at Ripley Entertainment, I'm thankful for the support of Jim Pattison Jr., Amanda Dula, and Anne Marshall, as well as Anthony, Viviana, Amy, Natasha, Angela, and Todd, and everyone who made me feel so welcome during my many visits to your Orlando HQ.

I'm deeply indebted to Sidney Kirkpatrick, who mined portions of Ripley's story before me and, in an act of humbling graciousness, agreed to share with me his research. Thank you, Sidney (and Nancy).

To the Ripley family—Ripley's grandniece, Rebecca; her father, Robert; and her uncle, Doug (Ripley's nephews)—thanks for putting up with my phone calls and letters, and for speaking with me so graciously and openly about your memories of the Ripley brothers.

Acknowledgments

Many thanks to Greg Daugherty, for the Mamaroneck tour; Tom Van Pelt, for sharing his Ripley collection; and to both men, for welcoming me into their homes. In Santa Rosa, I'm grateful for the assistance of the wonderfully gracious and funny Lee Torliatt and the rest of the crew at the Sonoma Historical Society, and Santa Rosa's longtime columnist and semi-official historian, Gaye LeBaron. Thanks to John Hacku, who oversaw Santa Rosa's sadly short-lived Ripley museum.

At the New York Public Library, I count myself once again among the fortunate writer-researchers to have benefited from the skills and generosity of Dave Smith—thanks! And though I may not remember all the names (nor you mine), my humble thanks go out to the sixth-floor microfilm crew and others at the Seattle Public Library. I'm also thankful for the time I was able to spend at the library's Scandiuzzi Writers' Room—thank you, Chris Higashi.

Robin Lung, I appreciate the help you offered with the story of Li Ling-Ai and her relationship with Ripley. (Best of luck with your film, *Finding Kukan*—nestedeggproductions.com.) For assistance with the history of comics, my thanks to Allan Holtz, Cole Johnson, and the excellent website Stripper's Guide (www.strippersguide.com). To the Pearlroth family, Jeff and Jonathan, thanks for speaking with me. And to Tom Quinn, thanks for sharing bits of the history of the NYAC.

With each of my books, I've been fortunate to have friends and family willingly read and critique sloppy drafts; thanks to Katherine Reed, Pauline Trimarco, and Brian Klam. I'm grateful to New Jersey records sleuth John Mooney for tracking down Ripley's marriage license. And, since writing is often such a solitary pursuit, I'm thankful to those who made the job less solitary or offered advice or support, a well-timed cocktail, or a bed: Jack and Deirdre Timmons, for the loan of the Vashon

Acknowledgments

Island retreat; Lisa Loop, for coaching and editorial input; Andrew Chapman, for moral support and lunches; Reid and Lucas Adams, for bourbon and a bed while researching at UNC; Joe D'Agnese, Denise Kiernan, and Tom and Rebecca Gholson, for being there from the start; Spencer and Man Cohen, for Chinese translations; and Phil Thompson, for loaning me the Mini during my Florida visits, and for much more.

To William Langewiesche, thank you for taking a look at an early draft and offering advice. And my gratitude to Richard Florest, for providing outstanding editorial input at a crucial stage.

Heartfelt thanks to Michael Carlisle for getting this project rolling and, especially, to my agent, Rob Weisbach, thank you for believing in and championing the project. I look forward to many more.

At Crown, I'm incredibly grateful to my editor, Rick Horgan, and his assistant, Nathan Roberson, for their diligent, smart, and relentless efforts in shaping and elevating this story, as well as to copy editor Rachelle Mandik for regularly saving me from myself. And my sincere thanks to everyone at Crown—designers Jaclyn Reyes and Nupoor Gordon, production editor Robert Siek, and especially Tina Constable, Christina Foxley, Ellen Folan, and Kristen Fleming—for believing in Ripley's story.

Finally, to Mary, Sean, and Leo, my unbelievable believe-it-or-not family.

INDEX

ABOUT THE AUTHOR

Neal Thompson (www.nealthompson.com) is a veteran journalist and author of three previous books: *Light This Candle: The Life & Times of Alan Shepard, America's First Spaceman; Driving with the Devil: Southern Moonshine, Detroit Wheels, and the Birth of NASCAR;* and *Hurricane Season: A Coach, His Team, and Their Triumph in the Time of Katrina.* Thompson and his books have been featured on NPR, ESPN, the History Channel, Fox, and TNT, and his stories have appeared in *Outside, Esquire, Sports Illustrated,* and the *Washington Post Magazine.* He lives in Seattle with his wife and two skateboarding sons.

THE PALACE OF LAUGHTER

JON BERKELEY

ILLUSTRATED BY BRANDON DORMAN

SIMON &
SCHUSTER

London · New York · Sydney · Toronto

A CBS COMPANY

SIMON AND SCHUSTER

Published in 2006 by HarperCollins Children's Books
A division of HarperCollins Publishers, New York

First published in Great Britain in 2006 by Simon and Schuster UK Ltd
A CBS COMPANY

Africa House
64–78 Kingsway
London WC2B 6AH

1 3 5 7 9 10 8 6 4 2

A CIP catalogue record for this book is available
from the British Library

ISBN 1-416-91071-9
EAN 9781416910718

Printed and bound by
LegoPrint Spa, Italy

This is for Orna,
who makes the magic happen round here

CONTENTS

CHAPTER ONE

A BOY IN A BARREL

On a blustery October night the Circus Oscuro
came to town. It was clear from the start that this
was no ordinary circus. It did not roll into town with fan-
fares and cartwheeling clowns. No one handed out flyers or
announced the show through squawking loudspeakers.
Instead, the circus came in the dead of night, when all the
townspeople were asleep. Its wagons crept and rumbled
down the winding road and across the old stone bridge
while the town's fat mayor, who normally had to give his
permission before anyone could set up as much as a fruit
stall, was snoring in his bed. The circus wagons turned in to
the long field at the bottom of the hill that overlooked the

town of Larde, and creaked to a halt in neat rows with barely a sound.

From the wagons and trucks a strange crew emerged into the moonlight – great muscled men with sun-darkened faces, a tattooed giantess with a booming voice who could lift three of the men at once, small wiry boys dragging coils of rope and buckets of sawdust. They began to set up their enormous tent there and then by the light of flickering lanterns, with the wind whipping at the stripy canvas and cracking the ropes across the men's hairy arms. Their shouts and curses were snatched from their throats by the wind and flung up over the hill. Two elephants were led from one of the wagons and set to work, lifting wooden poles into place and pushing them upright with their stubbly foreheads. Acrobats ran up the swaying poles like monkeys, fixing ropes and leaping from point to point as though they were only inches from the ground, gripping lanterns in their strong teeth. A thin man on stilts 20 feet high checked blocks and pulleys and shouted orders to the men below. Slowly the huge tent rose from the grassy field like a great beast awakening, and still the townspeople slept, and the fat mayor's snores ruffled his walrus moustache and rumbled through his wife's dreams.

There was just one witness to the arrival of the circus. A small boy, huddled in a large wooden barrel high on the side of the hill, watched the raising of the big top, awakened from his sleep by the shouts of the circus people and the occasional trumpeting of the elephants. The boy's name was Miles, and the barrel was his home.

Now if you are picturing a shivering boy standing knee-deep in slimy rainwater in an upright barrel, you will need to turn that picture sideways and let the water run out for a start. This barrel lay on its side under a low-spreading pine tree, which provided shelter from the wind and the rain. It was an enormous barrel that had once held a fine vintage wine, and Miles could almost stand upright in it, although he was nearly eleven. It was dry and warm inside. In the barrel was an old mattress that had been thrown out by Piven, the baker, and which still gave out a cloud of fine flour when you sat on it. A candle stub in a fat bottle served as a lamp, and an old biscuit tin with the paint worn off as a larder.

Miles had lived in his barrel on the side of the hill since escaping (for the seventh time) from Pinchbucket House, the county orphanage. He shared his wooden home with a small stuffed bear named Tangerine, no larger than a tall man's hand. When Tangerine wasn't out and about with his owner, he lived in a deep pocket of the old overcoat that Miles used as a blanket. Some of Tangerine's stuffing had escaped, which made him a little floppy. His fur, which had once been the colour of a tangerine, was now a kind of orangey grey. His mouth wore a crooked smile, and although he never said a word, he was a good listener.

Under a silver moon Miles, curled up in the mouth of his barrel, watched as the circus tent grew fatter and taller and the thick ropes that anchored it grew tauter. The hypnotic ringing of sledgehammers on iron pegs and the snatches of strange music that floated from the trailers made his eyes heavy and his head nod with sleep. He pulled the old overcoat tighter around him, and closed his eyes for a moment.

When he opened them again he did not know how much time had passed, but everything seemed strangely still. Not an owl's hoot or mouse's rustle broke the silence, and the pine tree stood silently, undisturbed by the faintest breeze. Miles rubbed his eyes and looked out to see if work on the circus tent had ceased, but his eye was caught by something that had not been there before. A large shape crouched in the grass not twenty paces from where he sat in the mouth of his barrel. A shape with a huge head, enormous paws and a long striped tail. It was a fully grown Bengal tiger, stretched out motionless except for the tip of his tail, which twitched from side to side in the silvery grass.

The tiger was so close Miles could almost count his whiskers. His inky stripes seemed to shift and breathe as the thin clouds swept across the moon. Miles held his breath. It was no use crying out; no one would hear him. He had never been face to face with a tiger before, but he was pretty sure that to the magnificent striped beast who sat a stone's throw from his barrel, he must look like a sandwich whose bread had fallen off.

The tiger yawned, his teeth like yellow knives in the red cave of his mouth, and gave a loud but oddly human sigh that made his whiskers shiver. His massive head turned and he stared directly at Miles with his amber eyes. The world turned and the grass grew, and still the tiger regarded the boy silently. Although he had never seen a tiger before, Miles found his gaze strangely familiar, like an echo of a dream often visited and always forgotten. He could feel his heart thumping, and realised that he had not taken a breath since the tiger had appeared.

"Most people run," said the tiger at last, in a deep smooth voice. He flicked the tip of his tail.

Miles said nothing for a moment. Obviously the tiger could not really have spoken to him. Everyone knows that tigers can't talk. Except for the tiger himself it seems, who was waiting for an answer.

"I have nowhere to run to," said Miles, his voice barely

above a whisper. "So if you are going to eat me," he added after a moment, "please make it quick."

The tiger gazed at the skinny boy, wrapped in an over-sized overcoat and curled up in the mouth of a barrel. "Now that you mention it," he said, "I do get a little peckish at this time of the morning, but you wouldn't make much of a snack."

"You're right about that," said Miles in a slightly stronger voice. "I am very thin, and . . . and my feet smell terrible! I don't think you'd like them at all, unless you like strong cheese."

The tiger made a rumbling noise, which might have been a chuckle, or the sound of an empty stomach. "I've eaten far fouler things than you, tub boy," he said. "I once ate a health and safety inspector, clipboard, bowler hat and all. I had stomach cramps for a week."

"D-didn't that get you into terrible trouble?" asked Miles.

"On the contrary," rumbled the tiger. "I was given a week off from performances, and a whole wagon to myself."

He got to his feet and stretched himself, five hundred pounds of teeth and muscle rippling in the moonlight. "All this talk of food is making me hungry after all," he said, taking a step towards the barrel and fixing Miles with his steady gaze. "And one can't be too choosy when there's only one item on the menu."

Miles shrank down into the overcoat, trying to look stringy and unappetising. He had often wished he were anywhere but inside a wooden barrel on the side of a hill, but it had to be better than being inside a large tiger's stomach. He groped desperately behind him on the untidy floor of the barrel. His fingers closed on the stub of a candle. No good. He dropped it and groped again, finding one of his threadbare socks. "Maybe I can stink him to death," he thought as the tiger padded closer. He was only a few whisker lengths away now. His hot musty breath warmed the boy's face, and his eyes burned like cold fire, but Miles could not look away. The tiger stopped, the rising sun giving him a halo of fur the colour of flame.

"You can stop scrabbling, little tub boy," he said. "There are some hungers too deep to be satisfied by skin and bones." His nose twitched slightly. "Besides," he said, "I never had a taste for circus people."

"What do you mean?" asked Miles, the words barely escaping his dry throat.

"What I say," said the tiger. "I can smell the circus in you, though you don't look like you could even stand on your head."

"I can't," said Miles, "and I've never even been to a circus."

"Believe what you will," said the tiger, and he turned slowly and began to pad down the grassy slope without a backward glance. The circus was quiet now, its people hidden in their wagons as the town began to stretch and wake in the dawn. The only sound from below was the faint cracking of the long black pennant that fluttered from the peak of the big top, and the squeaking of a rusty wheelbarrow in which a tiny man carried large slabs of red meat between the animal cages, shoving them through the bars with a stout pole and whistling softly to himself.

Miles rubbed his eyes, which smarted from lack of sleep. He shook his head and looked down the hill, but the tiger was nowhere to be seen, and the wheelbarrow sat empty and unattended in the shadow of the farthest wagon.

Miles woke again when the morning sun was already high in the sky. He was stiff from sleeping curled up in the mouth of his barrel, and his hungry stomach grumbled. He looked down to the bottom of the hill, half expecting to see nothing but an empty field, but there it was, the enormous black and red tent with its rows of silent wagons. "At least that part wasn't a dream," he said to Tangerine, whose head poked from the overcoat pocket. Tangerine just smiled.

In the daylight Miles could see more clearly what a strange circus it was. The wagons were painted in dark and lurid colours, with patterns that were spiky and tangled.

Their wooden wheels were studded with iron hobnails. The largest wagon was decorated with an enormous clown's face, his eyes and black-lipped mouth wide open in a silent laugh, and his electric-blue hair standing out from his head, like a hungry crocodile that had been struck by lightning. There was a painted scroll beneath the clown's head, and Miles squinted as he read the letters. "The Great Cortado," said the scroll. The name was somehow ominous. *The Great Cortado.* He shivered in the thin sunlight.

The two elephants were tethered to a tree at the edge of the field, where they stood patiently resting from their labours of the night before. Other beasts could be half seen in their cages. Several monkeys screeched insults at the haughty camels next door. Another wagon housed a pair of zebras whose stripes blended with the shadows of the bars, so that you could only see them when they moved. A long scaly tail hung through the bars of one cage almost to the ground. Miles searched for any sign of a tiger.

There was one wagon set apart from the others in a corner of the field. It was painted entirely in red, except for black frames on the door and on the tiny barred windows. The door was fitted with three strong bolts, each with a padlock the size of a man's fist. The dogs that ran in circles, barking at the flapping canvas and stealing scraps of meat that had dropped from the cages, steered well clear of the corner where the red wagon stood. It seemed a strange sort of housing for a tiger.

"As soon as it gets dark," said Miles to Tangerine, "we're going to sneak into that circus, and we're going to find that tiger, if he really exists."

CHAPTER TWO

A BAG OF BONES

Miles Wednesday, barrel-dwelling, unwashed and tiger-visited, made his way through the narrow streets of Larde until he reached the warm smelly butcher's shop in Sausage Lane. Haunch the butcher was chopping ribs with a shiny cleaver, flipping them over on his worn wooden block behind the marble counter and grumbling to his customers as he chopped. He saw Miles in the doorway and scowled.

"You again," he said in his big bassoon voice. "It's no good scrounging off me. I've got nothing for you."

"I'm not scrounging," said Miles. "I'm looking for work. You must have something you need doing."

The butcher grunted and went back to his chopping and complaining, while the women queuing for his paper parcels of meat clucked sympathetically. Miles waited patiently, his arms folded and his feet planted wide in the doorway, making it difficult for the butcher to ignore him.

"Well don't just stand there," he growled eventually, as he handed a packet of sausages to a big square woman with a head scarf knotted under her chin. "Out the back with you and get scrubbing. And mind you make a good job of it or you'll feel the toe of my boot."

Miles slipped through the forest of women in their scratchy woollen coats, out into the butcher's yard, where halved carcasses swung from steel hooks, and the smell of old blood made it hard to breathe. He filled the wooden pail with soapy water and began to scrub the cracked tiles with a worn brush. The water was cold and his hands were soon red and raw, but he scrubbed and dunked and scrubbed again. The last time he had cleaned out Haunch's yard he had been paid with a dozen leftover sausages. He could almost smell them now, sizzling plumply on the end of a stick, the drops of fat hissing on his little campfire under the pine tree on the side of the hill.

As he scrubbed the smelly yard he thought about the tiger. Its steady gaze burned so clear in his memory that a couple of times he glanced over his shoulder, half expecting to see the huge beast stretched out in the corner, watching him. His head buzzed with the strange sounds of the circus, and when his hunger made him dizzy, the patterns in front of his eyes were spiky and tangled like the decorations on the wagons. He could not wait for nightfall, when he would sneak into the circus and look for the tiger's cage, just to see if he was real. Darkness seemed a long time away, and he scrubbed even harder, as though it would make time pass more quickly.

A burst of laughter came from the butcher's crowded shop, the cackling of the customers like a flock of geese startled by the distant thunder of the big man's guffaw. Miles edged towards the back door to see what was happening. Laughter had been strictly banned in Pinchbucket House, and it always made him curious. The butcher was wiping his eye with the corner of his apron. "There's not enough laughter in this world," he said, and he brought his chopper down hard on a chunk of meat. His customers nodded and sighed, their shoulders sagging and the tiredness returning to their faces. Miles went back to work.

By the time he had finished, the floor tiles were gleaming, and the pail had been emptied of water and filled with the big blue-knuckled bones that had littered the yard.

Haunch came to the door and scowled at the scrubbed floor, as though it were knee-deep in rotting meat.

"Hmff," he grunted.

"I'd like my sausages please," said Miles. His stomach was rumbling at the thought.

"No sausages," grunted the butcher. "Sold out of sausages. Sold out of everything. You can have some bones."

"Bones?" said Miles. "I can't eat bones!"

"Boil 'em up. Make soup," said the butcher. "Bones is all I got." He shook open a paper bag and scooped a few hand-fuls of bones from the wooden pail, rolling the top of the bag shut and thrusting it into Miles's arms. "Hold it under-neath," growled the butcher, "else them bones will fall out the bottom."

As Miles left the butcher's shop, his bag of bones clutched in his numb fingers, the butcher called after him. "Shouldn't of never left that orphanage. You'd've got properly fed there."

"I'd have got properly poisoned there," Miles shouted back over his shoulder, "if I'd stayed much longer."

A pale sun hung low in the afternoon sky, and the sound of barking dogs carried on the breeze from the city pound. The smell of the butcher's bones seeped from the soggy brown bag, making Miles turn his head to the side just to breathe clean air. "I can't make soup from these," he thought.

"Even Mrs. Pinchbucket's gruel would be better than that."
He stopped for a moment, shifting the weight of the bag in
his aching arms.

A smile crept over the boy's face. If you knew Miles well
(which few people did) you would have recognised that
smile as the one that always appeared on his face when a
plan was hatching in the back of his mind. The smile grew
wider, and he turned to head for the pound, following the
noisy barking of the mongrels of Larde.

The city pound was a narrow yard beside the police station, surrounded by a high red-bricked wall. Right now it
was full of shaggy, limping, drooling dogs, the result of
Mayor Doggett's annual roundup of the town's stray mongrels. The order had been telephoned to Sergeant Bramley,
who had listened with his little raisin eyes screwed up in
his porridgy face. Sergeant Bramley and his two trusty constables had dropped their official duties (searching the
newspapers for evidence of crimes, especially in the crossword clues, and making hot sweet tea in a battered tin pot
in case of emergencies), and had marched out purposefully
into the street with a large net on a pole, and two big cloth
sacks.

The sergeant and his constables, who worked in a crack
team of three, had rounded up the dogs of Larde and taken

them into custody for the Good of Public Health. They knew the mayor's fickle attention would soon turn elsewhere, and the dogs could be quietly released "back into the wild", as Constable Wigge put it, and in any case it made a change from the crossword.

The barking grew louder as Miles approached the pound. Thirty mongrels and more were in full throat at the sound of his footsteps and the reek of tasty bones carried on the breeze. Miles laid the bag carefully outside the pound, leaving the smell to creep over the high wall, and climbed the worn stone steps of the police station next door.

The police station was small and cluttered and stuffy. It contained two old wooden desks, an ancient typewriter with several keys missing, a cast-iron potbellied stove, three very unhappy policemen and a little old woman with a green umbrella. The end of the umbrella was a dangerous metal spike, and its owner was waving this under Sergeant Bramley's shapeless nose. She was yelling at him angrily, but what she could be yelling about it was impossible to tell. The pokey office was so full of the din of barking dogs that there was no room for any other sound. Indeed the old woman might have been barking herself and no one would have been any the wiser.

Sergeant Bramley had his hand cupped behind his good

ear. He was trying to lean close to hear the old woman's words without getting the point of her umbrella up his nose at the same time. He turned and bawled something at Constable Wigge, but Constable Wigge could hear nothing, as his ears were plugged with soft wax from the candle on his desk. He was frowning at the crossword, trying to think of a seven-letter word beginning with "B" and meaning "dog speech".

Constable Flap, who had once done a short course in lipreading in *Modern Constable* magazine and could read the sergeant's flabby lips like a large-print book, leaped from his seat instead, and opened the side door that led into the pound. The noise of the dogs was deafening. Constable Flap opened his mouth and yelled "QUI-ET!" but his mouth was small and his voice was reedy, and the dogs ignored him completely. He shut the door again and flopped back, defeated, into his chair.

Miles climbed onto a stool beside the high counter, where he found a yellow pencil stub and some squares of paper. He thought for a moment, then wrote carefully with the neat letters that his friend Lady Partridge – who lived up a tree – had taught him:

I CAN STUP THE DOGGS BARKENG

He slid the note over to the sergeant. The old lady was still shouting at the top of her voice, despite the barking of the dogs, and the sergeant's glasses were flecked with old-lady spit. He removed them from his nose and wiped them with his handkerchief. He read the note twice, then turned it over to see if there was more.

He squinted at Miles for a moment, then he reached into his pocket and held up a silver coin. Miles nodded and left the police station, being careful to close the door behind him. He picked up the bag of bones and selected the biggest one. This he wrapped in paper torn from the bag and wedged it into his pocket. Then he began to toss the rest of the bones, as quickly as he could, over the wall. The barking turned to snarling and yelping as the dogs fought and nipped and shoved, then one by one they fell silent, until the only sound was the crunching and cracking of dog teeth on butcher bones, and the occasional growl as a dog warned his bone not to try any funny business.

Back inside the police station the silence seemed almost as deafening as the barking had been. Constable Wigge had removed the candle wax from his ears and was writing in his crossword, his tongue sticking out with the effort: B-A-R-K-I-N-G. The sergeant stood and stared, his pudgy fingers still holding the coin in the air. Miles climbed onto the stool, plucked the money from his fingers, said thank you, and jumped down again. The old lady jabbed Sergeant Bramley in the chest with the point of her umbrella.

"Well?" she shrieked. "What are you going to do about it?"

"About what?" asked Sergeant Bramley.

CHAPTER THREE

THE TINY ACROBAT

Miles Wednesday, wind-swayed, bread and cheese in hand, sat in the fork of a tall tree outside Pinchbucket House. He had bought his dinner with the sergeant's shilling, but it was not yet dark enough to sneak into the circus. With time to kill, his feet had found their way through the familiar lanes to the grimy building that had once been his home.

Pinchbucket House was a squat grey building with row upon row of small, mean windows. Steam belched from basement-level gratings, creating a permanent fog around the lower floors. Any children of Larde or the surrounding area who had the misfortune to lose their parents would sooner or later find themselves hauled to the doorstep of Pinchbucket House. Once inside those grey metal doors, they would have their hair shaved off (Mrs. Pinchbucket sold it to the wigmaker in Calvo Lane), and their nice clothes (if they had any) exchanged for a set of worn and faded pajamas. Anything of value in their pockets would end up in the locked tin box under Mrs. Pinchbucket's rickety iron bed.

In return the child would be given a name taken from the day on which he arrived, and set to work in the sweltering laundry that steamed and rumbled all day long in the basement of Pinchbucket House. The only child in the whole building who was not named after a day of the week was Hettie November. She had been found, half frozen in a cardboard box on the orphanage steps, while Mrs. Pinchbucket was in the hospital having a stubborn trace of generosity removed. Her husband, Fowler Pinchbucket, who could not tell one day from another, had put the child in the boiler room to thaw out and forgotten all about her, until one of the older girls heard her whimpering and rescued her from the sooty basement. Miles himself had been brought there as a baby, and could remember no other home.

From his perch in the tree Miles had a clear view through the lit windows at all the little Fridays, Mondays,

Saturdays and Tuesdays who sat in shaven-headed rows at the two long tables that stretched the length of the dining hall. Mrs. Pinchbucket, as thin and dry as a pencil, stalked between the tables, rapping her knuckles on the skull of any child who was not spooning gruel into his or her mouth as fast as possible. Miles imagined he had a powerful cata-pult and a smooth stone in his hand, and squinted through one eye. Mrs. Pinchbucket's nose, like a pink shark's fin dividing her sour face, made a tempting target.

Fowler Pinchbucket was kneeling by a square hole in the wall, a screwdriver between his crooked teeth. A tangle of brown and black wires stuck out of the hole, and Fowler frowned stupidly as he looked at them. Fowler fixed every-thing in Pinchbucket House to save money, and once something had been fixed by Fowler the Growler it was never the same again.

Miles had finished his bread and cheese and was about to climb down from the tree, when Fowler Pinchbucket reached a decision on his electrical problem. He grabbed a thick black wire and a crumbling brown one with his hard square fingers and twisted them together. There was a loud bang and all the lights in the orphanage went out. The lumpish silhouette of Fowler Pinchbucket flew backwards through the dining hall in a shower of sparks.

As the lights flickered back on, a singed figure could be

seen rising unsteadily to his feet. His hair stood out from his head like blackened corkscrews, and wisps of blue smoke escaped from the collar and cuffs of his shredded shirt. One of his shoes had landed upside down in Ruben Monday's soup bowl, the other was steaming in the mop bucket. He swayed on his stockinged feet for a moment or two, squinting at Mrs. Pinchbucket as though trying to remember who she was.

At the sight of the singed Fowler Pinchbucket the children burst into laughter, and the sound seemed to fill the drab dining room with warmth. Now you might remember that laughter was strictly forbidden in Pinchbucket House, and at the sight of the laughing orphans Fowler's face turned even blacker. He took a wild swipe at the nearest table, knocking a small child clean off the wooden bench and smashing a couple of plates. At the other end of the table Mrs. Pinchbucket boxed a few ears for good measure. The laughter died at once, leaving only the ceaseless clanking and belching from the laundry below, and the scraping of benches as the children scrambled to their feet, ready to be marched to their dormitory.

Miles sat in the fork of the tree a moment longer, feeling the same knot in his stomach that had awoken him every cold morning in Pinchbucket House. He pictured himself now, bursting in through the grey doors on the back of a magnificent tiger, leaping the stairs in a couple of bounds and prowling into the dining hall, where the tiger would swallow the Pinchbuckets whole, to the cheers and whoops of the orphans.

He thought of his barrel on the side of the hill, where he would curl up later that night with only a stuffed bear and the hooting of the owls for company, and quickly turned his mind to the circus instead. Dusk was falling, and he had an appointment to keep. He scrambled down the tree, and his feet skipped on the worn paving stones as he trotted down the hill toward Beggar's Gate, feeling the weight of the bone that he had kept for the tiger swinging in his jacket as he ran.

The strange smells of animals from foreign lands drifted through the narrow streets at the edge of town. The towns-people were making their way in a steady stream towards the circus, which was dressed in a million red and yellow lights. They pushed and jostled, and their children pulled eagerly on their hands as they followed the jangly music and the rolling of drums. Brightly coloured posters were tied to every lamppost. Some showed daring trapeze artists flying through painted air; from others the proud face of a tiger snarled, his great paws raised in menace. Miles joined the crowds, hoping to slip in unnoticed among them, but at the circus entrance he spotted Constable Flap standing on tiptoes to shout in the ear of the tattooed giantess, who loomed over the policeman as she collected the tickets at the turnstile. Miles remembered Constable Flap's Special Ear Pinch Arrest Method, which he had also learned from a short course in *Modern Constable* magazine, and decided to find another way into the circus.

He made his way around the edge of the moonlit field, where the outer trailers squatted silently in pools of darkness. Miles slipped in among the wagons, looking for anything that might betray the presence of a tiger. As he darted between the shadows he saw two men walking toward him, deep in conversation. One was a dwarf wearing a shiny round helmet decorated with flames. The other was a big square man with a high old-fashioned collar and a bowler hat. His huge bloated belly hung out between his braces, and the ends of his trousers stopped several inches short of his ankles, as though he were expecting a flood.

"Now look here, Mr. Genghis," the dwarf was saying. "I need a proper flying suit for this stunt."

The big-bellied man gave a wheezy laugh. "A flying suit, is it? We ain't shooting you to the moon, you pocket-sized prima donna."

"You can laugh," said the dwarf testily, "but last show I was blown clean out of my trousers by the gunpowder, and it's no fun sailing over five 'undred people in your second-best underwear."

Miles ducked down just in time and slipped under the canvas of the circus tent where a missing rope left it flapping loosely in the breeze. He found himself under banked rows of wooden seats, his boots squelching slightly in the trampled mud. The orchestra had struck up for the start of the show, and Miles moved forward quietly, crouching down as he came to the lower benches nearest the ring.

Looking for a clear view through a forest of ankles, he caught a glimpse of the elephants that he had seen the night before. They wore ornate blankets with swinging tassles now, and a man in shiny knee-length boots was cracking a whip and shouting commands at them in an unfamiliar tongue. Miles could only see the bottom half of the elephants, their wrinkled knees bending as they performed some trick that he could not see. The crowd applauded, and the shiny-booted man bellowed something more at the elephants. Their big round feet began to trot around the ring. A clown's baggy trousers and battered boots appeared, the feet leaping high as he ran in front of the elephants. The townspeople laughed and clapped some more.

As Miles hunkered down to watch, a generous scoop of

ice cream dropped through a gap between the benches and fell straight down the back of his shirt collar. His gasp was drowned out by a child's wail from the seat above him. The upside-down, ice cream–smeared face of a small girl appeared below the bench. Her eyes widened when she saw Miles. "Give me back my ice cream," she yelled at him. Several voices shushed her. She shouted louder.

"Mum – a mucky boy has my ice cream! Dad! There's an escaped ice cream thief under the seats!" As Miles scrambled away in the gloom a few more heads appeared below the level of the seats and peered about, like ducks foraging for river weeds.

If you've ever had to crawl through cold mud with half a pound of strawberry-vanilla ice cream creeping down your spine, you will know why Miles felt that his first visit to a circus was not going according to plan. As soon as he had put a safe distance between himself and the scene of the crime, he sat down in the muddy grass below the banked backsides of the people of Larde, and removed his shirt and jacket. He rolled the sodden shirt into a ball and crammed it into his remaining jacket pocket, then put his jacket back on and buttoned it up tight.

He turned back to face the ring, and found himself a gap between a pair of pin-striped trousers and some very tall high heels, which gave him a clearer view of the performance.

The elephants and the clown had gone, and in the centre of the sawdust-carpeted ring sat a large frosted white ball. Balancing on the ball was a coloured pyramid, and on top of the pyramid wobbled a cube, and on top of the cube another frosted ball, and on this ball a steel table was balanced on its side, and as Miles craned forward, he could see more and more shapes piled up in a teetering tower that stretched up almost to the pointed roof of the circus tent.

At the very top of this precarious tower stood a tiny girl in a sparkling white outfit. Thirty feet from the ground she balanced on tiny feet, with her arms outstretched and her head held high. No one watching dared to draw a breath. Every eye in the tent was fixed on the little girl, who looked no more than six years old. Her short blond hair was tucked behind her ears, and though she was lit by a spotlight she seemed to give off a soft glow of her own. To Miles she looked like a magical creature, more like a dream than the tiger he had dreamed of the night before. As he watched, transfixed, he saw her glance down at the crowd far below her, and Miles was sure that she looked straight at him, hidden in the gloom between the ankles of the people of Larde.

And then it happened – the tower began to fall. A ball halfway up began to wobble off the pyramid that supported it; the cylinder on top of the ball tipped the other way, and the whole fabulous balancing act came undone in slow motion and began to cascade to the ground. The crowd gasped in horror as the tiny girl began to fall to earth, her eyes wide with fright, and neither net nor cushion to catch her.

CHAPTER FOUR

THE NULL

Miles Wednesday, ice-cream-chilled and mucky-booted, saw the tiny acrobat fall from the toppling tower. Before he knew what he was doing, he was scrambling through the gap between the bench and the walkway as though he could catch her in his arms, but as he clambered over the seat in front of him the crowd gave another gasp, this time in wonder. Halfway to the ground the girl's fall had suddenly slowed. A pair of delicate pearly wings sprouted from her shoulders, fluttering minutely as she floated gently to the ground.

Her feet touched down so lightly that they left no mark in the sawdust. Her wings folded and tucked themselves away, and a tiny smile crossed her face as the last of the coloured shapes crashed to the ground around her and bounced to a standstill. In the stunned silence she looked directly at Miles, who was suspended half in and half out of the darkness. She looked into his face with her clear blue eyes and gave him a tiny bow, before being scooped from her feet and set on a beautiful piebald horse, which carried her proudly from the ring and through the star-strewn velvet curtains at the back.

Forgetting altogether that he was not supposed to be there, Miles picked himself up from the dusty planking, and stared at the swinging curtain through which the horse and his rider had disappeared. He was not the only one. At the other end of the curtain stood the ringmaster, a small neat man in red trousers and high black boots, and he too was staring after the tiny acrobat, stroking his blue chin beneath his enormous moustache and frowning to himself.

Some of the townsfolk broke into halfhearted applause, but others were confused and angry.

"Shouldn't be allowed to give people frights like that," said a woman with a fur collar.

"Nearly gave me a heart attack," said another.

"If you ask me she's far too young to be performing dangerous stunts," said her husband. "You can be sure they're breaking some law putting her up there. Probably breaking a dozen of them."

"It's all done with mirrors," said a man in the row behind. "You'll find she never left the ground in the first place, if I'm any judge."

"I prefer the clowns, anyway," said the first woman. "I get enough of balancing just doing me finances of a Monday."

Miles was about to say that it was the most magical thing he had ever seen, but he never got the chance to speak. A hand gripped his collar tightly from behind. He twisted around to see the man with the enormous belly and too-short trousers glowering down at him.

"Got your ticket, then?" said Genghis, giving his collar a shake for good measure. His voice was high and wheezy like a broken whistle.

"Lost it," said Miles, looking him in the eye.

"Cobblers!" said the man. "You never came in the front door at all, you little weasel, but that's the way you're going out." His swollen purple nose stuck out between his battered bowler hat and his stiff white collar, and he smelled of stale cigar smoke. He marched Miles toward the entrance, the boy stumbling as he tried to keep up. When they reached the flap of the tent, Genghis grasped the seat of Miles's trousers with his free hand and tossed him through the air like a sack of coal. He landed in the mud with a splash, and picked himself up just in time to avoid the toe of Genghis's boot.

"Next time I see your dirty face around here I'll feed you to *The Null*," said Genghis as he turned on his heel and went back into the tent.

Miles headed for the exit, but as soon as he was sure the fat-bellied man had disappeared, he doubled back and began to slip between the wagons again. The second half of the circus show had started, with a clashing of cymbals and banging of gongs, and he was still determined to search for a tiger's cage. He peered into a wagon with barred sides. A reptilian eye stared at him unblinking from the smelly darkness. "Not that one," he whispered to Tangerine, and crept on. Cage after cage he visited, some empty and some occupied. The zebras he had seen that morning stamped and whinnied. The next wagon contained long-necked wooly animals he had never seen before. The last one in the row was full of parrots and macaws, who screeched insults at him in several languages.

A little distance away he spotted a single red wagon standing apart from the others. It was the one he had seen that morning, the one that even the dogs steered clear of. Making sure he was not watched, he ran lightly across the grass and slipped into the shadows beneath the red wagon. He took from his pocket the bone that he had kept for the tiger, and unwrapped it carefully. He wondered what would happen if he dropped it in through the small barred window above his head.

Miles did not know that this decision, along with the bone itself, was about to be taken out of his hands. The creature that lurked in the wagon above him was no tiger, nor anything that had been given a name. It was known only as "The Null", a word that means "nothing". It was a dark and terrifying beast, the sort of being that haunts the deepest corners of your blackest nightmares. The Null was large and squat and hairy and immensely strong, with red-rimmed eyes and bone-crushing teeth. Some said it was a kind of ape, or even a yeti from the unexplored reaches of the Himalayas. Others whispered that it had once been a man, turned into a monster by powerful witchcraft. Whatever was the truth, few had ever seen The Null face to face, for it could be neither tamed nor trained. The last man to try had ended up in Saint Bonifacio's Hospital for the Unhinged, and had not spoken a coherent word for seven years.

As Miles removed the last shred of soggy paper from the bone, an immense knotty black arm swung down from the small barred window, snatched the heavy bone in its clawed hand, and withdrew with it into the darkness.

Crack! The Null's mighty jaws split the bone with ease, and it slobbered and gulped as it sucked the marrow from inside. Its great teeth ground the bone to splinters in seconds, and a belch like a blast on a tuba made the wagon dance on its iron springs. Miles crouched, trembling, under the monster's cage. He had no idea what kind of creature lurked in the wagon above him, but it was not the tiger he had expected, and he knew that if it once got hold of him it could crack his skull like a boiled egg.

Miles Wednesday, bone-bereft and shaken, crouched behind the wooden spokes of the red wagon. He was afraid to leave his hiding place, and just as afraid to stay in it. As he huddled out of reach (he hoped) of the monster's hairy grasp, he saw two figures emerge from the back of the circus tent, one large and one small. The bigger one, a black shadow with a bowler hat and an unmistakable belly, was pushing in front of him the tiny acrobat from the toppling tower. Her hands were tied behind her back. The moonlight shone in her hair and winked from her sparkling outfit. Genghis opened a small wagon with a key from the large ring hanging on his belt. He lifted the girl, threw her bodily into the wagon and locked the door. He turned and stumped over to the Great Cortado's trailer with its crazed clown's face, and disappeared inside.

"It's time we got out of here," whispered Miles to Tangerine.

Tangerine said nothing, but Miles knew what he was thinking.

"If they catch us, we'll be fed to The Null," he said. Still Tangerine kept silent.

"We *can't* get her out," he hissed, beginning to feel annoyed. "The door is locked, and there are bars on the windows. Besides," he said, forgetting to whisper now, "it's none of our business."

At the sound of his voice the red wagon tilted on its creaking iron springs. The Null's hairy claw appeared and began to grope between the spokes of the wheel. It had enjoyed its starter, and was looking for the main course. A curved yellow nail scraped Miles's bare ankle, and with that he was out from under the wagon like a greyhound from a trap and flying across the muddy grass. In his panic he headed for the cover of the nearest wagon, and only when he reached it did he realise it was the small one in which the tiny acrobat was imprisoned. He groaned quietly.

"Who's there?" came a small voice from the barred window.

"Me," said Miles.

"Can you get me out of here, Me?" said the voice.

"Not Me, Miles," said Miles.

"Who's Miles?" asked the voice.

"I am," said Miles. "And I can't get you out. The door is locked."

"Then you'll need the key," said the girl.

"Genghis has the key," said Miles.

There was a shuffling sound from inside the trailer, and the top half of the little girl's face appeared in the window, peeping over the wooden sill.

"Oh!" she said in surprise. "It's you! You tried to save me when I fell."

Miles blushed in the darkness.

"I'm glad it's you," said the tiny acrobat. "You are very brave. I'm sure you can get the key and let me out."

Miles sighed, and looked up at the girl. She looked small and frightened in the darkness of the wagon.

"What's your name?" he asked.

She hesitated for a moment, then said, "Little."

"All right, Little," said Miles. "I'll try to get the key. Get down from the window and stay quiet."

Little nodded. Her face stayed at the window.

The large wagon that Genghis had entered stood a short way from the one where Little was locked up. It was a dark midnight blue, edged with silver decorations that curled and twisted like thorn bushes. The door to the wagon stood ajar, and a dim red light and the sound of muttered conversation escaped from inside. Miles crept forward and hid himself beside the wooden steps. His heart was beating like a drum.

A man's voice came from inside the wagon. "The older one is going down a storm at the Palace of Laughter. His trick with the firebolts works a treat, though I still haven't figured out how it's done."

"You reckon we can trust him?" asked Genghis's reedy voice.

"As long as we keep his little sister here at the circus, he'll do as he's told."

"What about her then . . . that business with the wings?"

There was a long silence, followed by a cloud of smoke that curled out through the half-open door and was whipped away by the breeze.

"There's more to that little one than meets the eye," said the first man finally. "We'll have to get to the bottom of this before someone gets too curious, and the sooner the better. See that she gets some sleepwater with her supper tonight."

Miles raised himself up quietly and risked a glance over the top step. Through the gap in the doorway he could see a slice of the wagon's interior. The two men sat in leather armchairs, their faces out of sight, their legs stretched beneath a black marble table that stood in the centre of the thick red carpet. Big Belly's too-short trousers revealed lemon yellow socks peeping over the necks of his boots. Miles recognised the other man as the ringmaster by his black knee-length boots and red trousers with the yellow stripe. Lazy plumes of cigar smoke drifted back and forth in the dim red light, as though each man were trying to out-smoke the other.

An ebony carving of the laughing clown's face hung on the trailer wall, just inside the door. A mirror was set in the clown's wide-open mouth, and below it was a row of hooks. An enormous key ring, carrying at least forty heavy keys, hung from the nearest hook. Miles felt his heart beat even faster. He had just made up his mind to run up the steps as quietly as he could, when Genghis leaned forward and placed his empty glass on the table. Miles froze.

"Well," said Genghis, squinting through the smoke at a large pocket watch, "show's just about over." He put his cigar butt in his mouth and sank back out of sight, in order to make the biggest smoke cloud he could manage by way of a finale.

The orchestra in the circus tent reached a crescendo that sounded like several angry cats doing battle with a buffalo in a hotel kitchen. Miles seized his chance. He ran up the wooden steps of the Great Cortado's luxurious wagon and reached for the heavy keys that dangled from the hook. As he did so he glanced in the ebony-framed mirror, and found himself looking straight into the eyes of the Great Cortado himself.

CHAPTER FIVE

A BLACK HOLE

Miles Wednesday, mud-caked and red-handed, stared at the Great Cortado through a cloud of cigar smoke and an ebony clown's mouth. At first glance, the only thing great about the ringmaster was his moustache. It was a fine, thick moustache that swept outwards from his face like wings and curled up to two needle-sharp points. It far outmoustached Mayor Doggett's droopy whiskers. By contrast, everything else about the Great Cortado was small. He had a small round head like a marble, with hair slicked back and curling behind his ears. His delicate red lips held a fat cigar, and blue smoke curled from the nostrils of his neat button nose. He looked almost like a child with a blue chin and false moustache, but his pale eyes seemed to over-flow with wisdom and humour.

Genghis hoisted himself from his armchair with a grunt, and the Great Cortado spoke.

"We have a visitor, Genghis," he said. "Bring him inside."

Miles froze for a second. His gaze was still held through the mirror by the Great Cortado's clear grey eyes. Had Cortado guessed what he had been reaching for? Should he grab the keys and make a run for it? But by the time these thoughts had flashed through his mind it was too late; Genghis had reached him in two strides. He grabbed his arm and hauled him roughly into the trailer.

"Genghis, please!" said the Great Cortado, with a smile in his voice. "Is that any way to treat a guest?"

Genghis released his grip, but not before giving Miles a hard pinch. "Not sure if 'guest' is the word for this 'un," he said sullenly. "I've already turfed him out of the show once tonight. Caught him sneaking around under the seats. Told me he'd lost his ticket, the little weasel."

"Is that so?" said the Great Cortado, his eyes wrinkling with amusement. Miles felt himself relax a little under the small man's steady gaze. "Perhaps you would go and see the punters off, Genghis, while I find out from this lad why he is so drawn to our circus that he is undeterred by the mere lack of a ticket."

Genghis shot Miles a dirty look and clumped down the trailer steps. The Great Cortado stubbed out his cigar and waved Miles into the empty chair. Miles felt scruffy and out of place in these comfortable surroundings. He sank down into the soft leather upholstery, and held the collar of his jacket closed so that Cortado could not see that he wore it over his bare skin.

"Well," said the Great Cortado at length. "Do you have a name?"

"Yes," said Miles.

There was a moment's silence, then the Great Cortado laughed. "Would you like to tell it to me, or is it top secret?"

"It's Selim," said Miles at once. He was not sure why he said this, although he knew from his spelling lessons with Lady Partridge that Selim was his own name spelled backwards. "Perhaps it was that mirror," he thought, "that made me think back to front."

"Tell me, Selim," said the Great Cortado, "what did you think of our circus? Was it worth watching from under the seats?"

"I didn't see much of it, to be honest," said Miles. "And I was hoping there would be a tiger."

"A tiger?" The Great Cortado took another cigar from the box on the table, and tapped it twice on the lid. His clear grey eyes fixed their gaze on Miles. "Why a tiger, Selim?"

"There's one on your poster," said Miles. He did not think it wise to tell the Great Cortado of his moonlit conversation with a tiger the night before.

"So there is," said Cortado, "so there is. But that's an old poster, and a traditional design. There has not been a tiger in this circus for many years."

"Maybe you should get one, since you still have one on the poster. If I'd bought a ticket, I would have been disappointed."

The Great Cortado's face cooled, and the smile disappeared from his eyes. "There are not many people who would speak to the Great Cortado like that," he said quietly. "I wonder, is it courage or foolishness that makes you so bold?"

"Maybe it's a bit of both, Mr. Cortado," said Miles.

"Perhaps it is," said the Great Cortado. He lit the cigar that he had been turning over in his fingers. "In which case," he said, "you would have precisely the qualities needed in a circus performer."

"That's what I wanted to talk to you about," said Miles. He was becoming anxious about Little, waiting for him in the locked trailer, and an idea was beginning to form in his head.

"I thought it might be," said Cortado. He leaned forward in his seat. "Let me show you something that might change your mind." He unbuttoned his shirt, and opened it to reveal a long white scar that stretched diagonally across his chest and abdomen, from collarbone to hip. The skin around the scar was puckered and bore the traces of large clumsy stitches. "This," he said, "is the mark of a tiger, a tiger that I adopted from another circus and cared for as though he were my own. This is how he repaid me." He buttoned his shirt again. "The circus is a dangerous place, my boy, and if it is the life you choose, you had better be strong enough to stay on top. What would your parents have to say about this idea, I wonder?"

"I wouldn't know," said Miles. "I've never met them. I live by myself, and I make my own decisions."

"I see. And in the absence of a tiger to tame, what do you feel you could bring to a show as spectacular as the Circus Oscuro?"

"Oh I wouldn't want to tame any tigers. I was thinking more of a disappearing act."

"A disappearing act? Is that it? Every nickel and dime show has a disappearing act, Selim."

"Not one like mine. Mine is different."

The Great Cortado raised one eyebrow.

"Mine is completely unexpected," said Miles.

The Great Cortado leaned forward again in his seat, and fixed Miles with his unwavering stare. The smile had returned to his face, but it did not reach his eyes. "Would this act simply consist of you disappearing from my trailer, by any chance?"

"That wouldn't be very spectacular, would it, Mr. Cortado?"

"No it wouldn't," said the Great Cortado. He sat back. "In that case, when will I have the pleasure of seeing this fabulous act?"

"I can show you now, but I will need to go outside and make some preparations."

The ringmaster considered this for a moment, then he said, "You look tired and hungry to me, Selim. So this is what we will do. I will fix you a drink from an old recipe that we circus people guard jealously. I guarantee you it will take care of all your hunger and fatigue. While I do this, you will have a minute or two to make your preparations. But I warn you, I am the Great Cortado, and people who waste my time end up very sorry indeed. This trick of yours had better surprise me."

"I think I can promise that," said Miles.

He stood up and went to the door. A glance in the ebony mirror showed him that the Great Cortado had turned his back and was fixing his special drink at the marble bar in the end of the trailer. Miles lifted the heavy key ring gingerly from the hook and slipped it inside his jacket. His heart was beating so loudly that he was sure the ringmaster would hear it. He went quickly down the steps and ran across the grass to the trailer where Little was being held. The keys clinked together as he took them from his jacket.

"Is that you, Miles?" whispered Little through the keyhole.

"It's me," said Miles. "But I don't know which is the right key. There are a lot of them to try."

"Come to the window and show them to me," said Little. Her face appeared over the sill again. Miles climbed onto the wheel rim and held them up for her to see. She examined them for a moment. "That one," she said. "The one with the twisted stem and the curly end."

Miles put the key in the lock and it turned with ease. Little slipped out through the door. Her wrists were tied behind her back by a long rope, wrapped several times around her waist for good measure, and Miles had left his pocketknife in his barrel. She held a thin blanket behind her back. Miles wrapped it around her to hide her bound wrists and sparkly suit, and she stood on tiptoe on the wooden step to whisper in his ear.

"We have to go quickly," she said. "These are bad, bad people."

The circus show had ended and the crowd began to spill out into the night air, laughing and jostling. Miles could see

Genghis tying back the flaps of the tent. The big man barked something at one of the circus boys, who was waiting for the townspeople to go home so that he could search for their loose change under the wooden benches. Genghis turned towards Little's wagon. "Quickly!" said Miles. He pulled Little down into the shadow beneath the wagon and crawled in after her. As they crouched in the darkness, a faint glimmer of light caught his eye. Some sort of ticket lay in the long grass. It shone faintly as he picked it up and slipped it into his pocket with barely a glance. He saw Genghis's windswept ankles appear by the bottom step and stop there.

"Hell's teeth!" hissed Genghis's voice. He ran up the steps and peered into the empty wagon. The door slammed behind him as he stomped back down the steps. "Now I'm for the high jump," he muttered, as he strode off in the direction of the Great Cortado's wagon.

As soon as he was gone, Miles and Little crept out from under the trailer and slipped into the crowd that was streaming past them toward the exit. A large woman swirled by with a gaggle of small children hanging on to her skirts, and Miles and Little joined them, trotting to keep up. As they passed the Great Cortado's wagon they could hear the ringmaster's raised voice through the curtained windows.

"Then get after them, you great barrel of pork! I want

the girl back in her wagon within the hour, or you'll find yourself starring in a disappearing act of your own!"

"What about the boy?"

The Great Cortado spat in disgust. "Give him to The Null."

"*Give* him to The Null? But it'll tear him to pieces!"

"Stop whining, Genghis," barked the ringmaster. "The boy's no use to me, and nobody will miss him. It will be the last time he tries to play games with the Great Cortado."

Genghis emerged from Cortado's trailer, and at the same time the large woman in whose skirts Miles and Little were hiding stopped to pick up one of the children who had tripped and fallen. It took her some time to stop the child's crying, and Miles had to bite his tongue to keep from telling her to hurry up.

As they neared the circus exit they could see a bare-chested fire-eater standing by the ticket box, belching balls of flame over the heads of the departing townspeople. The people ducked to avoid having their hats set on fire, and as they did so, the dwarf with the helmet (who had managed to keep his trousers on this time) was handing them silvery tickets like the one Miles had found under Little's wagon. "Congratulations," he told each one in turn. "Another lucky winner." Beyond the fire-eater Miles could see fat-bellied

Genghis, who had stationed himself at the exit and was scanning the children in the crowd for escapees.

"Not that way," said Miles. He steered Little out of the crowd into the shadow of one of the cages. He peered around the back of the wagon, but one of the circus boys stood there, holding a snarling dog on a short lead. The dog strained and growled, and it took all the boy's strength to hold him.

"He's had a splinter in his back paw for weeks," whispered Little, "and no one has noticed it. That's why he's so mean."

"How do you know?" asked Miles

The girl looked at him in surprise. "He told me," she said.

Something warm and wet slopped against Miles's ear, making him jump. The llamas had crowded against the door of their cage, and one had stuck his tongue out between the bars. Little giggled. "I think you should let them out," she whispered to Miles. "They want to go for a little gallop."

She nodded at the iron bolt on the cage door. It was unlocked. Miles eased it open and slid the door back. Immediately a woolly mass of llamas leaped out of the cage and charged happily into the shrieking crowd, sending people diving into the mud. One knocked against the fire-eater, who belched an extra-large fireball straight at

Genghis's head. Genghis leaned backward in the nick of time, but not quickly enough to save his cigar and the front of his hat brim, which both went up in smoke. He roared and swung a fist at the fire-eater. In the confusion Miles and Little darted behind Genghis and in among the hurrying townspeople on the road. Miles held Little's arm in case she tripped. She seemed to weigh nothing at all.

"Where are we going?" she asked as they ran.

"To see Lady Partridge," said Miles. "She'll know what to do. But first we'll go to my barrel to get my knife and cut that rope off you."

"Why do you keep it in a barrel?" said Little.

"I live in the barrel," said Miles, lifting Little over the ditch and starting up the hill. "It's my home."

"Oh," said Little. "Does Lady Partridge live in a barrel too?"

"Of course not," said Miles. "She lives up a tree."

Little gave a sudden gasp as she twisted her ankle on a loose stone. She sat down on a tussock and grimaced with the pain. Miles pulled up some cold dock leaves and wrapped them around her ankle. "We're nearly at the barrel," he said. "You can rest there for a few minutes before we move on."

He helped her hop up the last part of the slope. She winced with each hop.

"It's a pity you don't have those circus wings on," said Miles. "You could fly the rest of the way."

Little laughed her musical giggle. "You're funny!" she said.

Once inside the barrel he took his pocketknife from under the mattress and cut the rope binding her wrists. "They weren't taking any chances with you, were they?" he said.

"They never tied me up like this before," she said. "I think something bad would have happened tonight, if you hadn't helped me escape."

Miles wrapped her in the overcoat, and she watched him silently as he coiled the rope and put it in his pocket, along with his last apple and his pocketknife. He went to the door of the barrel and looked down the hill to see what was going on below.

"Are they looking for us?" asked Little.

"I don't think so," said Miles. Darkness stole over the field as a cloud covered the moon, leaving the swaying strings of coloured bulbs to cast a dim light over the scurrying circus people as they rounded up the last of the reluctant llamas. When the moon emerged again, Miles noticed a knot of people gathered around the red wagon in which The Null was housed. Two boys carried lanterns, and there were several strongmen holding long poles and heavy chains. Two of them held up what appeared to be a net. Genghis stood to one side of the wagon door. It looked as if he were removing the padlocks.

Miles felt the floor of his stomach fall away. "Oh no," he whispered.

"Oh no what?" asked Little.

"It's The Null," said Miles. "I think they're letting it out."

"Oh *no* oh no," said Little. "We have to go now, at once. Far away."

"You can't walk, and I can't go fast enough carrying you," said Miles. "You'll have to stay hidden here, and I'll draw them off."

Little shook her head. "But I . . ." She paused, looking uncertain. "Are you sure I'll be safe here?"

Miles covered her completely with the overcoat. "You'll be fine," he said. "Just keep out of sight, and whatever you do, don't make a sound until I come back for you."

"Be careful," came a muffled voice from under the overcoat.

"Don't worry," said Miles. "I know this hill inside out, and they're strangers, even if they do have a monster with them." He wished he felt as confident as he sounded.

He slipped back down the way they had come, peering through the shifting darkness for any sign of the circus men and their beast. The moon was hidden behind another cloud, and the wind gusted up the hill, flattening the grass and stealing the breath from his mouth. A strong odour like rotten bananas reached his nose, mixed with the stale cigar smell that surrounded Genghis like an invisible fog, and he heard the clink of chains and the nervous shouts of the strongmen. An eerie barking laugh made the hair stand up on his scalp.

He left the path and pushed through the bushes, heading directly away from the barrel. As he half ran, half slithered down the side of the hill, he strained his ears for any sign that the circus men and their beast were following him. He remembered the smaller children he had tried to bring with him on his failed escapes from Pinchbucket House, and the beating they would all receive from Fowler Pinchbucket on their return. Miles had a feeling that Little's fate, if his diversion should fail, would be something far worse. The men's shouts were getting closer now, and he could see the lanterns swinging crazily as the boys who held them clambered over the rocky ground. They had picked up his trail all right, and they were gaining on him.

Deep beneath the town of Larde, an ancient stream flowed through a dark tunnel before emerging through a stone arch below Beggar's Gate. Miles had used this underground stream in two of his failed escape attempts, and it was to the stone mouth of the tunnel that he was headed now, along the slippery bank of the stream. He knew his footprints in the mud would make him easy to follow.

The moon came out again as he reached the tunnel mouth, and as he ducked down into the darkness, he risked a glance over his shoulder. The Null was no more than twenty yards behind him, a hideous shadow that seemed to suck the moonlight into itself like a black hole. It had shaken off the strongmen, and its three stout chains dragged loose behind it from its iron collar. The creature's red mouth opened wide in the blackness and its manic laugh followed Miles into the tunnel.

The tunnel was clammy and pitch black, and cold water soaked Miles as he ran through the shallow stream. The faint moonlight from behind was blocked by the huge beast that splashed through the water on all fours, almost at his heels. A little way up the tunnel was an iron gate, and he knew from his Pinchbucket House escapes numbers three and five that he could just about squeeze himself between the bars. He was struck by the awful thought that he may have grown too big since the last time he tried this, and a moment later he was struck by the bars themselves as he ran full tilt into them in the inky darkness. His head met the iron gate with a loud clang, and he almost fell backwards under the feet of his pursuer. With stars exploding in front of his eyes, he stumbled to one side and began to wedge himself into the narrow space between the bars. He breathed in, and turned his head sideways, but it was no good. He was stuck fast.

In the cold darkness, deep below the sleeping town of Larde, The Null hit the centre of the gate like a giant hairy cannonball, almost wrenching it free of the crumbling stone walls. The impact buckled the gate, pulling the bars apart slightly and releasing Miles from its rusty grip. He fell through the gate and onto his knees, and began to crawl through the water, his head throbbing. The Null was rattling the bars and screeching with rage. Between its shouts he could hear Genghis's wheezy voice echoing up the tunnel.

"You, Knoblauch and Kartoffel, get in there and see what's going on."

"Not me, sir, I ain't going into the dark with that thing."

"You'd better get in there, you haddock-brained half-wits, or I'll have you boiled in vinegar," shouted Genghis.

"You'd best heat up the vinegar then, sir, 'cause I ain't going in no tunnel with that devil-thing."

There was more shouting and cursing, mixed with The Null's angry gibbering, as Miles felt his way along the left-hand wall, looking for the rusting iron ladder that led up to the drain in Crooked Street. The ache in his head was subsiding, and he felt pleased with himself. The Null would keep them occupied for a while, leaving him to slip back to the barrel, collect Little and bring her to Lady Partridge. She would be safe there, and Lady Partridge would know what to do.

Miles climbed the ladder and pushed at the heavy grating above his head. It was jammed shut with dirt, and he had to work at it with his pocketknife for some time before the grate would open. He clambered through the opening and crept through the winding alleys, shivering in his thin jacket. He had lost the heavy keys somewhere in the darkness. He kept to the shadows as he passed the circus, dark now except for the glow of lamplight from some of the trailer windows. Somewhere a concertina played a cheerful tune, and there was the sound of laughter and the clinking of bottles. There was no sign of The Null or its reluctant handlers. "It must be back in its wagon by now," he whispered to Tangerine, who was cold and damp too, and not feeling talkative.

When he came within shouting distance of his barrel, he stopped. Something was wrong. He could smell the rotten-banana smell again, and there was harsh laughter coming from the direction of his home. Miles sank down and began to crawl through the long grass, his heart thumping. As he neared the spot where the tiger had sat the night before, the moon emerged from behind a cloud and shone on a terrible scene.

The Null had not been returned to its barred wagon at all. It sat among the smashed ribs of Miles's barrel like the black heart of some ruined animal, tearing chunks from the mattress and stuffing them into its mouth. The strongmen had a tight grip on the chains again, and the boys with the lanterns leaned against the trunk of the pine tree, smoking the cigarette butts that the strongmen had thrown aside. Genghis kicked through the ashes of old campfires, a cigar glowing beneath his singed bowler hat. A handful of gnawed bones lay in the grass next to The Null, and there was no sign of Little anywhere.

CHAPTER SIX

LADY PARTRIDGE

Miles Wednesday, homeless and headstruck, wormed through the long grass in a wide circle around his smashed barrel. His head throbbed from the impact of the iron gate, and fear crawled over his skin like a swarm of icy centipedes. He found a vantage point behind a small twisted bush, and tried to blank out the pictures that ran through his mind of what The Null might have done to Little. The beast had tired of chewing the mattress now and was beating it with a curved rib from the barrel. Tufts of white stuffing rolled up the hill before the breeze.

Genghis blew his nose on a large grey handkerchief that he had pulled from his sleeve. "Knoblauch! Kartoffel! Get that creature to its feet and let's get it back into its box," he said. "And don't let go of it this time." He gave the ashes an angry kick.

"Wasn't our fault, sir," said Knoblauch, his white hair standing up from his scalp like a yard brush. "Monster was 'ungry."

"It hunts better when it's hungry, you bonehead," said Genghis. "But it's supposed to be hunting runaway brats, not flocks of sheep."

"It only ate two, sir."

"Ought to have the beast put down," muttered Kartoffel. "Gives me nightmares, it does."

"Course it does," said Knoblauch. "It's meant to. That's why the boss keeps it, innit? Keep everyone in line."

"Stop flapping your gums and get moving," barked Genghis. "We have to get The Null back into its wagon before the Lardespeople roll out of their beds and find something's been snacking on their mutton."

The strongmen yanked on the chains, and The Null whipped around in the remains of the mattress and gave a cackle that made the hair stand up on Miles's neck. Two of the strongmen pulled it after the retreating figure of Genghis, while another couple hauled from behind, stumbling and slipping as they struggled to keep the creature from mauling the men in front.

Miles waited behind the rock a few minutes more, shivering in his wet clothes. He stared at the bones that lay scattered in the grass. If The Null had been eating sheep, he thought, perhaps it had not devoured Little after all. But if not, where was she? She could not have run away with her twisted ankle. Perhaps she was under what remained of the mattress, squashed flat by the weight of the monster. He crept forward and stood before the mattress, summoning up the courage to look underneath. He bent and flipped it over. It was lighter than before, having lost most of its stuffing, and there was nothing underneath but splintered wood and his old biscuit tin, entirely flattened. The overcoat lay in the grass where it had been tossed aside.

Miles flopped down on the disembowelled mattress and put his head in his hands. "This is what happens," he muttered to Tangerine, "when we meddle in things that aren't our business. Now the girl is missing, and we have nowhere to live." There was no answer from Tangerine.

A pinecone fell from the tree above and bounced off the back of his neck. Another one hit the top of his head. Miles looked up at the tree. "That's right, drop your cones on me," he shouted. "Do I look like I don't have enough troubles already?"

"I'm sorry," said the tree in a familiar voice. "I just wanted to make sure it was safe."

"Little?" said Miles.

A pale face appeared in the darkness between the branches. "Have they gone away?" asked Little.

"They've gone away," said Miles. A wave of relief rose from his frozen feet and swept through him like laughter. "You can come down now."

Little scrambled down the twisted trunk. Her skin was scratched by the bark. Miles shook out the overcoat and wrapped it around her. It trailed on the ground like a royal train.

"Are you okay?" he asked her.

"Yes," she said. "I know you told me to stay out of sight, but I heard someone coming, and I knew it wasn't you. You don't smell *that* bad. So I hid up the tree."

"You're lucky you got up there before they saw you," said Miles. He looked at the small girl, who reached no more than halfway to the tree's lowest branches, and wondered how she had managed to get up there at all.

"Let's go," said Miles. "I'll carry you on my back."

Little did not seem as light as before, but Miles suspected that his old overcoat counted for much of the weight. He followed a familiar path between the rocks and gorse bushes, over the brow of the hill and down into the small wood on the other side. Dry leaves whispered under his feet, and overhead the wind rustled through the treetops, making the branches creak. Out of sight of his smashed home he could imagine that it was still there, warm and dry, waiting for him to return. To push the picture of the demented beast out of his mind he thought about the tiger who had visited him the night before.

"Little, is there a tiger at the Circus Oscuro?"

"I've never seen one," said Little. "Why?"

"I dreamed about one last night. At least I think it was a dream, but it seemed almost more real than real life. I was sitting in my barrel and a tiger came and sat near me. He looked like an ordinary tiger, but he spoke to me. He told me that he could smell the circus in me, but I've never been to a circus until tonight."

"If a tiger said it, it must be true."

"But it was only a dream," said Miles.

"Tigers don't lie," said Little. "Not even in dreams."

They came to a high stone wall, ivy bearded and crumbling with neglect. Miles made his way along the wall to a place where it had collapsed, leaving a gap like a missing tooth, and clambered across the tumbled stones.

Once inside the wall, he let Little down gently. They stood waist-deep in a swaying sea of weeds, among old trees of various shapes, some twisted and wild, others tall and dark like pillars holding up the night sky. The hulk of a derelict mansion stood with its back to them, empty windows staring blackly across the overgrown garden.

In the centre of the garden stood an enormous beech tree. It was a strange tree, with two trunks growing from the mighty roots, joined together by a web of branches that clasped each other like the arms of wrestling giants. Perched among these branches was the dark jumbled shape of a tree house. It was made from an assortment of old furniture, floorboards, and tea chests, as though it had been washed up into the tree by a freak tidal wave. Little saw a cat stalk along one of the branches, and as her eyes became accustomed to the dark mass of the tree, she saw there were others – three, five, twenty and more cats, staring down at them, or washing their paws and pretending not to notice them.

Miles grabbed the lowest rung of the rope ladder that dangled from a hole in the tree house floor, and called up the tree. "Lady Partridge! It's me. I've brought a friend."

"So they tell me," called a voice from above. "Bring her up, my boy."

He lifted Little to the ladder and she hopped up it on one foot. Miles followed behind.

The inside of the tree house was unlike anything you've ever seen, unless you live in a curiosity shop with branches growing up through the floor. A large Persian rug covered the uneven floorboards, and a fire glowed in an ornate iron fireplace that was set into the crooked walls. The walls themselves consisted largely of a jumble of bookcases, kitchen dressers, and chests of drawers, stuffed to overflowing with books, fat candle stubs, prickly cacti, and jars filled with herbs, polished stones, old coins, dried fruit, broken jewellery, boiled sweets, nuts and bolts, dried petals, hairpins, seashells, and a thousand other strange things whose use could only be guessed at. There were so many books that they flowed from the lower shelves and piled themselves around the edges of the floor, among the umbrella stands, snake baskets, ships in bottles, milking stools, chopped logs, hookah pipes, china elephants, brass divers' helmets, ornate vases, butter churns, whalebones, sewing machines and parrot cages, not to mention a large stuffed crocodile that stared with a glassy eye from a dark corner by the potbellied stove.

A broad hammock was strung between the two trunks, where they passed through the tree house on their way to the sky. A large woman sat in the hammock, peering at Little over her crooked spectacles. In her lap sat a heavy book. She wore a black silk Chinese dressing gown decorated with red dragons, and her grey hair was piled up on her head with the help of several tortoiseshell combs that seemed on the verge of falling out.

"Well well," she said. "And who do we have here?"

"I'm Little," said Little.

"And I'm a great deal Larger than I ought to be," said

Lady Partridge, and she burst into a great guffaw of laughter. Little glanced at Miles, who grimaced back.

"Well sit down, my dears," said Lady Partridge, dabbing at her eyes with a lace handkerchief. "If you can find a space."

Finding a space on the floor was not as easy as it sounds. The room was almost completely carpeted with cats. Tabbies, tortoiseshells, Siamese and Persians, cats as black as coal at night and as white as sugar in a china bowl. They swarmed over the tumbling piles of books, perched on every shelf and draped themselves across Lady Partridge's hammock. A small orange cat sat squarely in the middle of her book, smoothing his ears with licked paws. The whole tree house purred.

Little picked her way around the edges of the room, keeping her weight on her good foot. She peered into every nook and cranny, lifting things from shelves to look at them more closely. She listened to the ocean's call from the seashell, and held up a jar of amber nuggets to let the light pour through. On the shelf behind the jar was an old photograph with curling edges, in which a young man with a freshly scrubbed face stood by a large and fabulous contraption of wheels and pistons and jagged teeth. "Who is this?" asked Little, picking it up as she replaced the jar. She held out the photograph to Lady Partridge.

"That," said Lady Partridge, peering down through the spectacles balanced on the end of her nose, "is my late husband, Lord Partridge. He was a handsome chap, as you can see, with a head full of bright ideas. At least that's what I believed."

"Is that one of his ideas behind him?" asked Little.

"I'm afraid so. That was his all-in-one tree converter. If you fed it enough coal and ink it could chop down a forty-foot tree, chew it up and convert it into fourteen school desks, eight hundred triple-column accounting ledgers, and enough matches to keep fifty stevedores chain-smoking for a year and a half. By the time he had perfected the machine it could get through half an acre of trees in just over an hour. He called it Geraldine, although I was never quite sure why."

"It says 'Geraldine XIV' on the side," said Miles, looking at the photograph over Little's shoulder.

"Yes, they were all called Geraldine. There was a fleet of twenty-four of them at one stage, and no timber merchant could hold up his head unless he had at least two. It all came to an end when they realised they had made a dozen school desks for every man, woman and child in the land, and that the ledgers they had produced would not be used up before the middle of the next millennium. But by that time Dartforth — that was my husband's name — was very wealthy indeed. He had set up several other businesses and seemed to have completely forgotten about Geraldine."

"Did you live in the big house then?" asked Little.

"We did, my dear, and we had a butler and two cooks and a team of gardeners. We had swans on the pond and peacocks on the lawn, and for many years I never bothered my head about Dartforth's businesses and what they might be making. Not until he was killed by an exploding pudding in one of his factories did I think to look at them more closely, I'm afraid."

"An exploding pudding?" said Miles, looking at the photograph with renewed interest. There was nothing in the young Lord Partridge's bearing or his cheerful face to suggest that he might be on course for such a sticky end.

"An exploding pudding," said Lady Partridge. "It was a prototype they were developing in secret for the army. It was cunningly disguised as an enemy ration tin, and was designed to be sneaked behind enemy lines by undercover cooks. They tried to keep the accident quiet of course, and offered me a pension that would have kept me in luxury for the rest of my days, but all I wanted was to find out the truth about how Dartforth had died. I hired an investigator, and little by little he discovered what kinds of businesses my husband had been involved in."

She sighed. "He was not a bad man, Dartforth. I believe

he really thought that everything he did was for the best, but he was always in such a hurry to get on with the next brilliant idea that he had no time to see the consequences of the last one. He invented a cereal that was supposed to make children grow big and strong, but some rats broke into the storeroom and feasted on it for a week. Soon there were rats the size of sheep rampaging around the country-side and a team of python handlers had to be brought up from the south to hunt them all down. Then there was the Saltifier, for making lakes more like the sea so people didn't have to travel far to the beach, and the Jumbo-sized Cocktail Sausages that made people's fingers and toes swell up. Everything he turned his hand to seemed to produce poisonous gases, or terrible nocturnal noises, or two-headed chickens. After Dartforth died, there was only one thing to be done. I spent most of the money he had made over the years putting right the damage that he had done. I had some factories converted to making things that people really did need. Others, I'm afraid, simply had to be dynamited, in the hope that someday the grass will be able to grow over them."

"You must have been very sad," said Little.

"I was rather angry really," said Lady Partridge, "but it had to be done."

"I mean when he died," said Little.

The question took Lady Partridge by surprise. She was quiet for a moment, gazing at something beyond the tree house and many years ago. Then she took off her glasses and dropped them into a pocket in her dressing gown. "Well, we don't talk about that," she said briskly, tipping the orange cat from her book and placing it on top of a teetering pile that conveniently reached her left elbow.

"Who doesn't?" asked Little.

"Well . . . people in general, I suppose."

"Then how do people make each other feel better?"

Lady Partridge seemed completely stumped. Little put the photograph back in its place and walked over to where she sat on the edge of her hammock. She climbed the precarious stack of books, put her arms around Lady Partridge's neck and gave her a big kiss on the cheek. Lady Partridge hugged her back, then lifted her down gently.

"Well, here I am wittering on, and I'm sure you're both hungry," she said, dabbing her eyes quickly with a silk sleeve. "Sit down . . . um . . . somewhere, and I'll make you some soup."

Miles shifted a plump cat or two, to make space for Little and himself. His damp jacket steamed in the warmth of the fire. Little hopped gingerly over to where he sat.

"You're limping, my dear," said Lady Partridge.

"She twisted her ankle," said Miles.

"Well why didn't you tell me?" said Lady Partridge. "We must get you bandaged up at once." She stepped down from the hammock into a pair of worn purple slippers and produced a rolled bandage from a wooden box on the shelf behind her. She knelt down on the Persian carpet with a great deal of huffing and sighing, and began to bandage Little's ankle with a practised hand.

"Why did you leave your house to live in a tree?" asked Little, wincing a little.

"Oh, I built this tree house over the years, with the help of my gardeners, from old furniture we no longer used in the house. Dartforth was forever ordering newer and grander furniture for the manor, but I hated to part with the old stuff. In the days before those dreadful Pinchbuckets took over the orphanage I used to have all the children around for picnics on Saturday afternoons. It was nice and cool in the tree house, and they could play up here when the sun became too high. The Pinchbuckets stopped all that many years ago. I don't think they ever let the poor things out nowadays, except for their annual trip to the cement quarry. After Dartforth died I began to spend more and more time up here myself. It was a good place to sit and think. All the staff had long gone, and I had sold almost everything in the house. It became too big and lonely, and I simply couldn't bear to be there anymore, so I moved my last few things out here where it was small and cosy. The grocer's boy comes once a week and the coal man delivers too, so I hardly need to venture out at all. Anyhow, it's rather appropriate that I should live in a tree with two trunks. That makes me a Partridge in a pair tree!"

Lady Partridge bellowed with laughter at her own joke, causing a fat tabby to wake with a start and fall off the shelf where he had been perched.

"And now, my dears," said Lady Partridge when she had calmed down, "I had better stop rambling on and see about that soup I promised you. A good tale never fares well on an empty stomach, and I can see that you both have a story to tell."

CHAPTER SEVEN

FALLING THROUGH THUNDER

Lady Partridge, book-bound, dragon-gowned, and mistress of a hundred cats, rummaged among the tins and jars on the dresser by the stove. As she did so she muttered to herself, or perhaps to her cats. She filled the belly of the stove with a shovelful of glowing coals from the fireplace, and placed a pot of soup on top.

While the soup bubbled in the pot, Miles told her a story that you and I have heard already. He told her of the strange circus and the mysterious tiger, of how he had seen Little fall, and later rescued her from her locked trailer under the nose of the Great Cortado. Over bowls of steaming soup he spoke of the nameless beast that had pursued him through the night, and how it had reduced to splinters the barrel that had kept him warm and dry for three winters under the pine tree on the side of the hill. Lady Partridge listened, and her cats listened too.

"Well well," said Lady Partridge at length, when his story had taken them up the ladder and into her tree house. "You must both stay here for the night, and in the morning we'll see what's to be done." She peered thoughtfully at Little. "Would you mind, my dear, if we took a look at those wings of yours?"

"She doesn't have them on now," said Miles. "They're back at the circus."

But Little had slipped off the heavy overcoat. The thin straps of her glittery costume left her shoulders almost bare, and as she turned her back to Lady Partridge Miles saw to his astonishment a pattern of gracefully curving lines traced faintly across her shoulder blades. As he looked closer he could see in the pattern the outline of a pair of neatly folded wings. Little gave her shoulders a shake, and the wings opened out. They were a little longer, from the bend to the tips of the primaries, than her upper arm from shoulder to elbow. They looked even more magnificent in the cluttered tree house than when he had seen them in the circus. The firelight gave a pearly glow to their fine, closely fitting feathers.

It took Miles a moment to find his voice. "They're *real*?" he croaked. "Where . . . where did they come from?"

"I think the real question," said Lady Partridge, "is where did Little come from?" She smiled at Little, who had folded her wings so neatly against her back that they seemed almost to melt back into her skin. "We should very much like to hear your story, my dear," she said. "I'm sure it would make the time fly!" She was overcome by a fit of laughter. Little and Miles smiled politely as she dabbed her eye with the corner of her dressing gown.

"I'm not really supposed to tell," said Little hesitantly.

"You can trust us, dear," said Lady Partridge. "We won't breathe a word to anyone."

Little chewed her lip thoughtfully for a moment. "Well . . . ," she began slowly, "I suppose the trouble started when I followed Silverpoint down through a cloud tunnel."

"Silverpoint?" echoed Lady Partridge.

"Silverpoint is a Storm Angel," said Little. "He's older than me, perhaps a thousand winters old. I used to watch him and the other longfeathers rolling thunderballs across the cloud fields and dodging one another's lightning. It was fun to watch, and a bit scary too. They were as quick as thought when they played, and the sound of their thunder made my head shake. Sometimes my hair would all stand up on end and you could hear it crackle, when they got too close."

"Did you say a *thousand* years old?" interrupted Lady Partridge.

"That's what he told me."

"Good gracious! Then how old are you, my child, if that's not a rude question?"

"I'm not sure," said Little. "Silverpoint once said I had lived more than four hundred years, but the seasons come and go, and I've never had much time for counting."

"Well," said Lady Partridge, pushing her spectacles up on her nose. "I certainly hope I'm as sprightly as you when I'm four hundred years old," and she chuckled to herself while Little continued her story.

"Silverpoint is the quickest of them all, and his lightning is strong and blue and always finds its mark. He would get angry if he saw me watching, because I wasn't supposed to be there. He told me that someday I would get fried, and my song would never be heard, but I still used to watch whenever I could find a hiding place.

"One day I saw Silverpoint and Rumblejack heading for the cloud fields, so I followed them at a distance. They gathered up some thunderballs, and I hid myself to watch, but they didn't play in the usual way. Rumblejack began rolling the thunderballs in a circle. Round and round he rolled them, faster and faster, and a sort of whirlpool began to form in the clouds underneath. The noise was like a thousand giants roaring. The centre of the cloud sank lower and lower, like a tunnel heading downwards. All at once Rumblejack shouted something to Silverpoint, and flew off back the way he had come. I saw Silverpoint look around to see if anyone was watching, so I sank down lower. He didn't see me. Then all of a sudden, he took a long run and dived into the hole. Just like that.

"Without thinking for a moment I got up and ran after him. It was a silly thing to do, but I just wanted to see where he had gone, to see that he was all right. But as I got near to the tunnel the wind began to pull me. I tried to stop then, but the pull was too strong, and the tunnel swallowed me like a huge mouth."

The coals shifted in the fireplace, sending a shower of sparks up the dark chimney. The ginger cat had returned to Lady Partridge's ample lap, and sat licking its paws among the red dragons on her dressing gown.

"What was it like in the tunnel?" asked Miles.

"It was white, and cold," said Little. "I was sliding very fast, twisting and turning, until I didn't know up from down. I tried to slow myself, but there was nothing I could hold on to. The tunnel became darker, purply grey, and darker again until it was almost black, and I was going faster still. I couldn't see Silverpoint anymore. My shouts were lost in the sound of the thunder, and the wind was racing through the clouds and spinning me around as it passed. Then suddenly there was no cloud, and I was falling from the sky in a rain of hailstones. When lightning flashed I thought I saw Silverpoint far below me, but the hailstones were so thick I couldn't be sure."

"Why didn't you use your wings, like in the circus?" asked Miles.

"I did!" said Little. "I opened my wings before I even left the tunnel, but the storm was too strong. I'm only a soft-wing, and in a hailstorm like that even a longfeather needs all his strength and skill. The wind took me and threw me this way and that, and though I did slow my fall I couldn't control where I was going, not even if I could have seen what was below me.

"Just when I thought I would never stop falling, I saw the shapes of trees rushing up to meet me, and other shapes – a huge striped tent and a circle of trailers. I flapped with all my strength to slow myself down, then I fell into a big pile of hay in the back of a wagon. Right into the centre I dived, and the hay covered me up completely. I didn't know whether anyone had seen me, so I lay as still as I could for a while, waiting to get my breath back. That hay was really itchy!" She wriggled her shoulders at the memory.

"The stalks of hay poked up my nose and in my ears, and the little seeds tickled me all over. I wriggled over to the side of the wagon and looked through the wooden slats to see if there was anyone around." Little giggled. "To tell the truth, I didn't know what kind of monsters I might see. I'd never been to the Hard World before, but I had heard all sorts of stories."

"Really? What kind of stories, my dear?" asked Lady Partridge. Her precariously piled hair had been gradually undoing itself, and looped in grey coils over her ears and down her neck, but she didn't seem to notice. The ginger cat played with a long strand, biting the end and swatting it with his paws.

"Oh, all sorts. I heard that people have no wings, which was true, and that they might have two heads, or hairy faces. Bluehart, the Sleep Angel, told me that some people eat without stopping until their insides explode, and others walk like skeletons and eat seeds from cracks in the earth. The first man I saw, looking out from the hay, had a white face and a round red nose like a ball. His hair was purple and it stood up on end. He was beating a pig with a long stick.

"I couldn't understand what was going on. The pig was on four legs and had no hands to hold a stick of his own. He was covered with big green spots, but they were washing off in the rain. He was tied to the wheel of a wagon, and could do nothing but stand there and squeal. I could hardly even make out what he was saying."

"Do you mean you can understand animals?" exclaimed Lady Partridge.

"Of course," said Little. " I am a Song Angel, and every language is an echo of the One Song, even the sigh of the wind and the groan of the mountains. Everything speaks. You just have to know how to listen.

"Anyway, the poor pig was crying as the man beat him. I thought I heard him saying 'not again', then he said some things about the man that were so rude I would have laughed, if it wasn't so horrible. Nobody came to his help, so I had to do it myself. I climbed out of the hay (and anyway, I couldn't have stayed in there a second longer), and I told purple-head to stop at once."

"That was very brave of you, my dear," said Lady Partridge. "What did the man do?"

"He turned around and stared at me. He had one real eye. The other was made of glass and could see nothing. He turned back and gave the pig an extra-hard whack, then he walked over to me and raised his stick high in the air.

"Just at that moment there was a loud crack, and the man's purple hair burst into flames. He dropped the stick then, and he let out a yell. He began to run around in circles, flapping his hands at his head and shrieking. The pig was shouting, "My turn gone, your turn now! My turn gone, your turn now!" For a moment I thought the pig had somehow done it to him, then I saw Silverpoint standing there with his hands on his hips and thunder in his face, and I understood. The man with the flaming head tripped over an iron peg and fell straight into a big bucket of paint. That put the fire out all right, but when he stood up his whole head was white and dripping, and he stepped straight into something the elephants had left behind. It was really very funny." Little giggled at the memory.

"Silverpoint was angrier than I had ever seen him. I didn't know if he was more angry with me or with purple-head. He grabbed my arm, and there were sparks still coming from his fingertips that made my skin hurt. He said, 'Come!' But before we could leave, a man stepped out of the shadow of the tent."

"He was a small man, no taller than Silverpoint himself. You have met him, Miles, I think. He is called the Great Cortado. He spoke to us from behind his great moustache, and his words were kind. 'That was a very impressive trick, and funny too' was what he said to Silverpoint. The purple-haired man had wiped the paint from his eyes, and he bent to pick up his stick, but then he met the Great Cortado's eye and he dropped it again, and slunk off with his head down.

"Silverpoint thanked the Great Cortado politely and told him that we really must be leaving, but Cortado insisted that we go into his trailer to have some supper and to dry off. Silverpoint tried to refuse, but Cortado wouldn't take no for an answer. While he went to have supper made for us, we sat in his wagon and Silverpoint told me off for following him. He said that it was very foolish, but now that I was here, there were things that I must remember. He said that humans could not be trusted. I mean *he* said . . ." She hesitated.

"Don't worry, my dear," said Lady Partridge. "In some cases I'm afraid he's right, but we're not all bad! What else did he say to you?"

"He said that people must never find out who we really were. He told me never to let anyone see my wings, and above all never ever to sing my real name."

"Isn't Little your real name?" asked Miles.

Little laughed, and her laugh itself was like music. "Of course not," she said. "Little is just the name that Silverpoint gave to me, when the Great Cortado asked who we were. It's far too short a name for a Song Angel!"

"You must excuse our ignorance, my dear, but what exactly is a Song Angel?" asked Lady Partridge.

"Song Angels are the voices of the One Song," said Little.

"And what is the One Song?" asked Lady Partridge.

"It's hard to put into words," said Little. "I've never had to explain it before." She stared into the fire for a minute, a small frown on her face.

"The One Song is the music that runs at the heart of everything. It keeps the world spinning and the stars shining. Everything that exists, every insect and rock and river and flower, has a name in the One Song. Love and Sorrow, Laughter and Anger and Courage all have their places too, and they must be kept in harmony. When one of these strands is taken out from the rest, that is when bad things happen, like a rope beginning to unravel. Each Song Angel must learn a part of that song. We keep it alive and guard it, and in the end we must each add our own name to it so that the Song keeps growing and the world keeps moving along its path."

"But why can't you use your real name, instead of Little?" asked Miles, who had not understood much of what she had just said.

"If I sang my name here, its power would be spent. I would be bound to Earth, and would never be able to return home." She laughed. "Besides, my real name would not come to life on the clumsy tongues of people."

"Is Silverpoint a made-up name as well?"

"Well . . . yes and no. A Storm Angel's name is a different thing, and does not have the same power. Silverpoint is something like his real name, but shorter and simpler. It's a name he uses when he visits Earth."

"And why did Silverpoint come down through the

clouds, my dear?" asked Lady Partridge. She was trying to rebuild the unruly pile of grey hair on her head, and she held a tortoiseshell comb and several hairpins between her lips. Her question sounded more like, "Und fwoy did Filverfoint come down shoo du cloudsh, wy dear?"

"I didn't get the chance to ask him that, because the Great Cortado returned with our supper before we had finished our talk. He asked us many questions, but Silverpoint answered them cleverly and told him very little. Cortado's voice was soothing and his eyes were kind, and after a while even Silverpoint seemed more at ease. At the end of our meal we had a hot, sweet drink that glowed like fire inside us, but this was the worst mistake of all. I saw Silverpoint's head start to nod as he swallowed his last mouthful, and before I could even put down my own cup, I fell into a sleep without dreams.

"When I woke up I didn't know if it was night or day. I was in a small trailer, and a huge woman, as tall as a tree and with pictures on her skin, was wiping my face with a wet towel. She told me her name was Baumella, and that Silverpoint had sold me to the circus and gone away. I didn't believe her, of course, but I said nothing. They gave me a sparkly costume to wear, and began to teach me to walk on a rope and to balance on things. When I wasn't practising or performing they kept me locked up all the time. Baumella treated me well enough, but she never let me out of her sight.

"I tried to find out where Silverpoint was. He wasn't any-where in the circus. I asked the animals whenever I got the chance. One of the monkeys told me he heard the parrots say that Silverpoint had been taken to the Palace of Laughter, but none of them knew where that was. That was all I was able to find out."

Little fell silent for a while. In the firelight Miles could see tears shining in her eyes.

"I haven't seen Silverpoint since that night," she said quietly. "I don't know what's become of him, but it's all my fault. If I hadn't followed him he never would have had to save me, and we would never have been captured. I have to find him, somehow."

Miles looked at the small girl sitting among the cats and the bric-a-brac. She had pulled the overcoat back around her, although it was warm in the tree house, and was wiping her eyes with the back of her hand. Her skin still gave off that faint pearly glow, only visible in dim light. She looked lost and alone.

He thought about his smashed barrel and his disem-bowelled mattress. There was really only one choice to make. Whatever the dangers of her search for Silverpoint, he would go with her. He could not let her face such a journey alone, even if she did have wings and was four hundred years old. Besides, he thought, it would surely be more exciting to set off into the unknown in search of a Storm Angel, than to look for a new barrel to crawl into.

He knew what Tangerine would think. He put his hand into his inside pocket to check on the bear. Beside the familiar straggly fur his fingers felt something smooth and strangely cold. It was a card of some sort, and only when he had taken it from his pocket did he remember the silvery ticket he had picked up from the muddy grass beneath Little's wagon at the Circus Oscuro.

CHAPTER EIGHT

THE SILVER TICKET

Miles Wednesday, soup-filled and fire-warmed, held the ticket up to catch the light from the candle flames that flapped lazily on the shelves. In the centre of the ticket was the laughing clown's face from the side of the Great Cortado's wagon, and around it looped the words "The GREAT CORTADO PRESENTS for your AMUSEMENT the FUNNIEST SHOW on EARTH. For ONE NIGHT ONLY at the PALACE OF LAUGHTER. As performed before the CROWNED HEADS OF EUROPE. Admit two. Train leaves at dawn tomorrow.' The ticket sparkled in the light.

"The Palace of Laughter," said Miles. "Isn't that where you said Silverpoint was taken?"

"That's what the monkeys told me, and they don't miss much," said Little. Miles handed her the ticket. She frowned at the writing, and turned it over in her hands. "I can't read," she said. "Does it tell you where to find it?"

"No. It just says that the train leaves at dawn tomorrow."

"Then you shall have to try and catch the train if you are to find your friend," said Lady Partridge. "We'll find a way to disguise you, so you won't be so easy to spot. Perhaps Miles will go with you."

Miles did not answer. He was trying to remember where he had heard of the Palace of Laughter before. Crouching by wooden steps, breathing the smell of cigar smoke. That was it! The Great Cortado had mentioned it in his conversation with Genghis. Miles pictured a rambling palace, the doors standing open and the sound of laughter flooding out on the warm firelight. The thought of it made him smile. Somewhere out in the distant night, this place really did exist. He began to look forward to the adventure that was unfolding before them.

"You can't come with me," said Little. "This is trouble that I made for myself, and you've already done enough for me. The Great Cortado is a dangerous man, and he'll be very angry with you for helping me to escape."

"Then I'd better keep out of his way," said Miles. "But you can't go on your own, and anyhow the Great Cortado owes me a new home. If I can't ask him for one, I'll find another way to make him repay me."

"Quite right," said Lady Partridge, "but you shall both have to be very careful. I don't like the sound of this Circus Oscuro at all. Giantesses. Bone-crunching beasts. It's not my idea of a circus."

She sighed, stroking the ginger kitten on her lap. "I used to bring the orphans to Barty Fumble's Big Top. Now that was a wonderful show. It used to pass through here every summer, and we never missed it. It was small and friendly, and you could see that everyone really enjoyed themselves, right from the prop hands to the ringmaster himself. Barty Fumble was a real gentleman. You could tell by the way he held himself. It was said that he looked after all his performers, whether on two legs or four, as though they were his own children. I remember his pride and joy was a tiger named Variloop . . . Voopilar . . . some foreign name that I never could pronounce. There were many wonderful acts but that magnificent tiger was always the highlight of the show."

"What happened to Barty Fumble's Big Top?" asked Miles.

"I'm not really sure, my dear. It merged somehow with a larger circus, but that was years ago now. Rumour had it that Barty Fumble disappeared shortly after that, and his tiger along with him. I've never heard anything more of them since, and no other circus has passed through here for years, not until this Circus Oscuro arrived.

"Anyhow, that was all a long time ago," said Lady Partridge, "and what you both need now is a good night's sleep, or you won't be going anywhere at the crack of dawn, not if I have anything to do with it." She slipped into her purple slippers, which waited as usual below her hammock, and began to rummage in a wide drawer for bedclothes, muttering to herself as she did so. "Pillows, pillows, not in this one . . . nor that one. Now where did they go? . . . Shoo, you big furball. . . . Ah, here's Great-aunt Boadicea's embroidered cushion, that will do. . . . Now let me see . . . blankets . . . Don't get many visitors these days, you see. . . . Where did I put the dratted blankets?"

By the time she had found all that she needed, Little and Miles were asleep. She gently slipped pillows under their heads and covered them with warm blankets, then with a deep sigh she damped down the fire and shuffled through a purring sea of cats to her hammock.

Now imagine for a moment that you are an owl, drifting silently over the garden of that deserted mansion in the middle of an October night. Your sharp hunter's eyes would see the strange jumble of Lady Partridge's tree house, nesting in the tree below you. A thin wisp of smoke is rising from the crooked pipe that serves as a chimney, before being pulled apart by the night breeze that rocks the tree house gently in the arms of the twin beech tree.

If you should perch on one of the higher branches, you would see through the single dusty window in the tree-house roof the outlines of three sleeping figures, and the twitching shapes of a hundred dozing cats. Inside every one of those sleeping heads is a world of dreams.

The dreams of the cats are much as you would expect them to be. Insects buzz through the dry grass of a summer's day, always just out of reach, and sometimes a whole fish will jump out of nowhere and land in a shower of sparkling droplets, right at the surprised dreamer's feet.

Curled up under a tartan blanket, Miles dreams of the basement laundry in Pinchbucket House. He is working with the other children, hauling damp sheets from a giant washing machine. On top of the machine sits the Bengal tiger, calmly cleaning his whiskers as though the laundry were his natural habitat, and not the jungles of Asia. Miles turns to drag his full basket over to the dryer, and sees to his horror that Fowler Pinchbucket is feeding his orphan brothers and sisters, two at a time, into the mouth of a huge machine in the corner. His mean face wears a grin of satisfaction. Miles turns to the tiger, who is paying not the slightest attention. He points at Fowler Pinchbucket and opens his mouth to shout, but no sound comes out. Two by two the children disappear, while the tiger licks his paws and the machines rumble on.

From your perch in the branches you would see Miles turn over in his sleep, rubbing the arm he has been sleeping on, while Lady Partridge snores gently in her swaying hammock. She is dreaming of a hot summer afternoon, her hammock strung between the twin beech trunks in the shade below the tree house. Her cats are swarming over her, rubbing their cheeks against her chin and mewing loudly. She feels groggy from the heat, and she brushes them off irritably. When she opens her eyes they have disappeared, every last one of them. She has an uneasy feeling that they were trying to tell her something important, but it is too late to ask. She groans in her sleep, and the dream slips away.

But what of Little? The vast dreams that fill her sleep are beyond anything you or I have ever imagined. She is soaring high above the Earth, riding the speeding winds among bright billowing clouds that tower above her as thunder rumbles deep in their bellies. All around her the One Song, of which we have never heard more than a lost echo, fills the skies of her dreams like a braided river of light. She sings as she swoops and climbs, feeling the thrill of speed in her stomach, and the wind sings with her. She becomes aware of two angels, riding on either side of her. They still the wind and silence the Song, and the clouds dissolve into a grey fog. "Silverpoint," says one. "Where is he?"

"Where is Silverpoint?" echoes the other, and he reaches out and lays a cold hand on her forehead. Little whimpers quietly in her sleep.

And now, if owls are as wise as they say, you will know that it's time to leave in search of that crunchy mouse you fancied for supper, for the tree in which you are resting is home to a hundred cats. They have begun to slink out along the branches and drop to the ground, and Little is waking from her sky-blown dream.

CHAPTER NINE

THE COUNCIL OF CATS

Miles Wednesday, sleep-muddled and blanket-warmed, woke to find Little shaking him by the shoulder. The tree house seemed quieter and draftier than before. The only sound was the creaking of branches and the soft snores of Lady Partridge, and he realised that the cats had all left.

"Where have they gone?" whispered Miles.

"To their Grand High Council, in the gazebo. They hold it every third full moon. We should go and see what they're saying."

Miles stretched and rubbed the sleep from his eyes. He pulled Tangerine from his inside pocket, to check that he was all right. Little watched him as she pulled on the old overcoat. "What do you call him?" she asked.

"Tangerine," said Miles. "He used to be bright orange once, but he's not too keen on baths."

"Have you had him for a long time?" said Little.

Miles nodded. "I've always had him," he said. "He's the only thing I have that my . . . that I had when I came to the orphanage."

"Your parents gave him to you?" said Little softly.

"I suppose so," said Miles. It was something he did not like to talk about, and he shifted uncomfortably on the creaky floorboards. Mrs. Pinchbucket had told him that his parents had left the orphanage laughing and driven away in a shiny car, leaving him on the doorstep. She told this to all the children, and Miles did not believe it. It was hard to imagine what kind of monsters could leave their children with nasty Mrs. Pinchbucket and her brutish husband, and he preferred to believe that his parents were dead. They had been swallowed by time, and his only link to them was Tangerine.

"Can I see him?" Little reached out her hand. Miles hesitated. He had never parted with Tangerine, not even for a moment. It felt strange to be handing him to someone else. Little took the small bear gently and propped him on her knees. She looked into his clouded glass eyes for a long time, as the tree house creaked gently in the breeze, then she leaned close and whispered something into Tangerine's ear. She whispered very quietly, and as she did so Miles felt a strange sensation, like the warm breath of some invisible giant, passing through the tree house walls and ruffling his hair before disappearing into the night.

Little smiled to herself, and put Tangerine down on the floor. Instead of flopping straight over, Tangerine kept his feet, and as Miles watched in disbelief he began to totter across the Persian carpet toward him. It was a wobbly path that he traced, and he fell over several times, picking himself up each time until he reached Miles's knee. He began to climb, and Miles reached down instinctively to help him. His threadbare fur and saggy stuffing felt the same as they always had, but he wriggled in Miles's hand, and when Miles tried to help him into his pocket, Tangerine clung to him and squeezed, just as Miles had hugged him ever since he could remember. Suddenly he felt warmer in his thin jacket. He looked at Little, who was watching him with a smile. "How did you do that?" he whispered.

"I found his name in the One Song," she said, "and I sang it back to him. Don't ever tell Silverpoint. He'd be very angry."

"Can you do that with just anything?"

Little shook her head. "Everything has a name in the

One Song, but I am only learning, and there are many things whose names I don't know. I found Tangerine's real name there because you brought him to life in your imagination, and you made his name strong and bright, even though you didn't know it."

Tangerine wriggled into his accustomed place in Miles's pocket. With his head swimming, Miles buttoned his jacket carefully and followed Little down the rope ladder into the swaying weeds below. She set off around the empty mansion, still limping on her bandaged ankle. On the far side of the house the path curved away between the trees and around an old pond, choked now with weeds and long since abandoned by the swans. A small ornamental house with an open front perched on the edge of the pond, where Lady Partridge and her visitors had once sat on summer afternoons, fanning themselves and watching the swans sail among the water lilies. This was the gazebo, and in its dilapidated ruins the last few stragglers were just arriving to attend the Council of Cats. Lady Partridge's hundred cats had been joined by several stocky mousers from the surrounding farms, a number of strays, and a delegation of town cats from the tall houses of Larde.

Little put her finger to her lips and beckoned to Miles. He followed her to a willow tree beside the pond, whose feathery branches hung to the ground, making a sort of

leafy cavern. They ducked under the tree and sat themselves on a carpet of dry leaves. Between the branches that
trailed in the water's edge, they could see across the pond
and into the gazebo, which was so packed with cats that
those on the lip of the pond were in danger of falling into
the water. A beam of moonlight shone through a hole in
the roof and picked out a large tomcat. He was completely
white except for a black tail and ears, as though he had
been dipped in ink at both ends. He sat on top of an
oblong of sandstone, carved with a tangle of leaves and a
horned face, that stood on its end in the middle of the
gazebo.

The black-eared cat opened his mouth and let out a low
yowl, which silenced the others for a moment. Little sat forward as though to hear better. For some minutes the cats
meowed and growled back and forth as cats will, especially
when they are outside your window and you are trying to
get to sleep. Miles listened as carefully as he could, but he
could make no sense from the sounds the cats were making.
"What are they saying?" he asked Little. She put her finger
to her lips again, and leaned over to whisper in his ear. "We
must be quiet. We would not be welcome if they knew we
were here."

"I can't understand a thing," said Miles.

"You are listening too hard. You must stop trying to

listen before you can hear. The voices are there, and they're not that different from your own."

Miles tried to grasp what she was saying, but it made little more sense to him than the mewing of the cats. He sat and listened for a while longer, but soon became sleepy and bored. He felt in his pocket for Tangerine, who grabbed his finger and lifted himself out. Miles put him down, and Tangerine crawled about happily, rummaging among the crackling leaves and tossing the furry willow seeds at Miles when he found them. In the distance a voice was saying, "The circus cats have a right to hunt our fields, provided their stay is short."

Somehow Miles knew, without even looking, that this voice belonged to the black-eared cat perched on his sandstone throne. He forgot Tangerine for a moment and stared in amazement at the moonlit figure in the centre of the gazebo. The cat's voice sounded just the same as it had before, and he couldn't understand why the meaning had not been clear to him all along.

"What right is that?" called a bony black cat who was wedged into a corner at the back. "There's three and more big cats hunting our fields since yesterday. Fat fellows they are too, living well enough on circus leftovers. Why they need to be muscling in on our pickings is beyond me."

A large cat, stretched out on the gazebo roof, chuckled

quietly at this. "No one tells us where we can hunt and where we can lie. We are citizens of the road and guests of every town. Besides, as you say yourself, there are plenty of scraps to be had at the circus, if you have the teeth to ask for them."

Several of the cats that crowded the roof and the surrounding trees sat up to look at the speaker. One hissed at him and stalked to the other end of the roof, his tail held high. "I wouldn't share food with a circus cat, nor would I turn my back on one for a second. I've heard it said . . ." He hesitated.

"Go on," said the circus cat, in a slow voice with a hint of amusement. "What's the chatter among the gutters and alleys?"

"It's no laughing matter," said the other, whose name was Tiptoe. "I heard that . . . that a king of cats was killed in that circus, some years ago."

The circus cat was on his feet in a flash, and had swiped at Tiptoe before he had a chance to move, almost knocking him from the roof. "You heard wrong. There are no tigers in this circus," he hissed, "and there never were."

"I thought," said a fluffy cat from a low branch in a nearby tree, "that the lion was the king of cats."

The entire council erupted into yowls of laughter at this. There were cries of "Shame!" and the unfortunate cat began to clean his whiskers busily, pretending that it was someone else who had spoken.

"You've spent too much time among humans," said Blackears. "Every cat knows that the tiger wears the mark of royalty. Lions are braggarts with big hair, but there is no royal blood in their veins, no more than in mine or yours. However" – he looked up through the broken roof to where the circus cat stood – "this is a serious allegation, and it is the council's decision that you will come down here and present your case before the bench. You will not find yourselves welcomed among the local cats while such suspicions hang over your kind."

The circus cat dropped through the roof onto the carved column, right beside Blackears. He was a heavy grey cat with a large head, and he put his face close to the other cat and sniffed at him, before dropping casually to the ground. The other cats made a space for him hurriedly.

"Well?" said the circus cat.

"Is it true," said Blackears, "that a tiger met an unnatural death in your circus?"

"It's not my circus. And there has been no tiger there in my time."

"And how long might that be?"

"I'm three and more winters old," said the grey cat, who in common with all cats could count no further than three.

"Surely you would have heard of such a terrible crime."

"No doubt," said the grey cat, yawning. "Which simply bears out that it never happened. There never was a tiger with the Circus Oscuro."

"There's a tiger on the poster," said the bony black cat in the corner. "They're all over town."

"That's right," said Tiptoe. "How do you explain that?"

The grey cat got to his feet and began to thread his way through the crowd towards the door of the gazebo. "It's obvious you know nothing about the ways of the circus," he said over his shoulder. "Every circus, even if it consists of nothing more than a pair of poodles and a clown, has a tiger on its poster. It's tradition, and circus folk would sooner blow themselves from a cannon than depart from tradition."

The circus cat left the gazebo and made his way around the edge of the pond, his tail high in the air. Blackears called the council to order and began a discussion on the strange rumours of a sheep-eating monster that some of the stray cats had reported. Miles picked up Tangerine, who appeared to have fallen asleep, and put him back in his pocket.

"Come on," he said to Little. "We had better get back. The sun will be up in a couple of hours." They made their way back through the overgrown garden and climbed the ladder to the tree house. Little fell asleep almost immediately, but Miles sat quietly by the fire, his head abuzz with strange happenings. Outside the tree house a chorus of birds sang the sun into place, just below the rim of the world.

CHAPTER TEN

THE SURLY HEN

Miles Wednesday, clean-shirted and cat-surrounded, spooned hot porridge into his mouth in the half-light before dawn, while Lady Partridge rubbed soot from the hearth into Little's hair. The result was a dirty, dark grey that would pass for black if you didn't look too closely. Against the dark hair her skin was white as a pearl.

Little was dressed in a boy's jacket, shirt and trousers that Lady Partridge had produced from an old leather trunk in the corner. They were a few sizes too big, but with the trousers turned up and the shirtsleeves rolled they fit her well enough. "These," said Lady Partridge, "belonged to Will, the gardener's boy. I used to pass them on to the orphanage when he outgrew them, until I discovered that horrible Pinchbucket woman was selling them to a stall-holder at the market and keeping the few pennies for herself." She had rummaged again in the trunk and found an ice-cream-free shirt for Miles, and a cap that would at least partly hide his face. The shirt felt clean and a little stiff, as he spooned the last of the porridge from his bowl. He felt in his jacket pocket, but Tangerine was sleeping.

Lady Partridge stepped back to admire her handi-work. "You look like you've just fallen off the back of a coal truck, my dear, but I don't think anyone would recognise you too easily." She wiped her hands on an old cloth that hung from the tree trunk beside her. She looked from one to the other. "Now then," she said, "the longest journey begins with a single step. It's time you were going, the two of you, or you'll miss your train." She blew her nose loudly. "And remember," she said from behind her handkerchief, "wherever your road takes you, stick together and look out for each other. Really, if I weren't so generous of figure I would like nothing better than to shin down that ladder and come with you."

They dropped from the ladder into an early-morning mist that blanketed the deserted garden. The dark shape of the old mansion seemed to float among the trees, and the air felt cold and damp after the warmth of the tree house.

Little still limped slightly. They clambered out through the gap in the wall, but took a different route through the woods, skirting around the bottom of the hill until they reached the lane that led to the train station.

They walked quickly along the lane between the tall hedges. Just as they reached the station the sun broke over the mountains, lighting the tops of the ornate chimney pots on the station-house roof. An old train stood at the platform. Its coaches were a dark mossy green and rather tattered. The platform was deserted except for the stationmaster, a tall grey-haired man who walked with a stoop, as though he carried an invisible sack on his shoulders. He was making his way along the platform, shutting the train doors as he went – slam . . . slam . . . slam. He did not seem in any hurry.

Miles opened the station gate. It squeaked loudly, but the stationmaster continued along the platform without a backward glance. "Excuse me," said Miles. The stationmaster slammed another door. "Hello?" said Miles. The stationmaster shuffled onwards, his frayed grey trousers dusting the platform.

"Maybe he's deaf," said Little. The stationmaster stopped. He slammed one more door, then turned around slowly to face them.

"Not deaf, busy," he said. "I've got a lot of doors to close here, in case you hadn't noticed."

"We just want to know if this is the train for the Palace of Laughter," said Miles.

The old man sucked his teeth. He had very few teeth left, and when he sucked them, his wrinkled lips wrapped around them like grey curtains. "The Palace of Laughter," he repeated.

"That's right," said Miles. The stationmaster scratched his head. Miles produced the silver ticket from his pocket and held it out. The stationmaster barely glanced at it. "Says tomorrow," he said.

Miles looked again at the ticket. "Train leaves at dawn tomorrow," it said along the bottom. "But this *is* tomorrow," he said. "I got the ticket yesterday."

"Today is today, son," said the stationmaster patiently, "and tomorrow is tomorrow. Least it was when I went to school. Train leaves at dawn tomorrow."

"But tomorrow this ticket will still say 'tomorrow,'" said Miles. "Tomorrow is always tomorrow!"

"Aye," said the old man. "You're catching on, lad. And dawn tomorrow is when your train leaves."

"How can we be sure?" persisted Miles.

The stationmaster sighed, his lips flapping slightly in the draft. "Because it says so on the ticket. But don't take my word for it, ask them odd folk at the circus. Them's the ones who give out the tickets. Now if you don't mind, I have a busy day ahead of me." He turned and slammed another door. It was a long train, and there seemed to be no one aboard.

"What do we do now?" asked Little as they walked back along the platform.

"I don't know," said Miles. "We can't wait around another day, and it might be a good thing if we could get to the Palace of Laughter before the train does anyhow."

"It might, but we still don't know where it is."

"I think," said Miles, "our best chance might be for me to sneak into the circus again, and see if I can find out anything more. You'll have to keep out of sight when we get closer. They might recognise you, soot or no soot."

They followed the rutted road as it curved around the base of the hill towards the long field. Birds chattered and sang in the trees by the roadside, but the sun had not yet begun to warm the air. As they came within sight of the field, Miles stopped dead in the long shadow of a poplar tree. The red and black tent was nowhere to be seen, and the trucks and wagons of the strange circus had packed up in the night, as silently and unexpectedly as they had arrived. Not a hoop or a bucket or a rusty peg remained. A large oval patch of trampled ground was all the evidence that was left of the Circus Oscuro – that and the tangle of wheel ruts that curved from the field and out along the road towards the mountains.

"They've gone," said Miles. He turned to look at Little, but she was staring at the tree where the elephants had been tethered the morning before. Her face, if it were possible, looked even whiter than usual. Miles followed her gaze. For a moment he could see nothing, then he became aware of a figure standing in the shadow of the tree. Although he could not make out any features, nor even if it was a man or a woman, he was sure the figure was staring straight at them.

"I'll go and ask him," said Miles, "or her. Maybe they know where the circus has gone."

Little grabbed his arm, and though she was light as a feather her grip was painfully tight.

"No," she said urgently, "let's go." She pulled him by the elbow, turning in the direction of the disappearing wheel ruts.

"Wait," said Miles. The figure under the tree seemed to be moving towards them. He felt a strong urge to see the person's face, which still seemed indistinct. It was not that the distance between them was great, but his eyes felt heavy and he found it strangely difficult to focus.

"Stay awake!" hissed Little, pinching his arm so tightly now that he tried to pull himself free of her grip. "Please, Miles." She seemed on the point of tears, and he looked at her in surprise. "Come with me, now," she pleaded.

He began to walk slowly along the road. He suddenly felt as though he had not slept for a year. "Walk faster," urged Little. He turned to look over his shoulder, and again she pinched him hard. "Don't look back," she said. "Just keep walking."

Miles forced his leaden legs to keep pace with Little, and they walked quickly and silently towards the distant mountains. A cart passed them on its way into town with the muffled clanking of full milk churns, and Miles could no longer resist the temptation to look back the way they had come, but the figure was no longer anywhere to be seen.

In the shortening shadows of the late morning, Miles and Little walked along the centre of the road, farther from the town of Larde than Miles had ever been before. They had followed the muddy tracks of the circus wagons until they faded into the road, and continued walking, with no plan left to them but to find the circus wherever it stopped next. Besides, as Miles had pointed out, the road followed the train tracks, more or less, which must lead eventually to the Palace of Laughter.

As they walked, Miles thought about the figure they had seen in the circus field. Little, who seemed incapable of remaining upset or anxious for long, was laughing at the chattering of the birds in the hedgerows, and he felt almost reluctant to bring the subject up, but his curiosity would not leave him alone. The tiredness he had felt had melted away, leaving only the ache of his feet in their cracked boots.

"Who was that, back there in the field?" he asked.

Little fell silent for a minute before answering. "Someone I thought I recognised," she said.

"Someone from the circus?"

Little shrugged. "Maybe," she said. "It was better not to risk it." She gave him a sidelong glance, then turned her eyes quickly back to the road.

"Look," she said, pointing ahead of them. "There's a river crossing the road."

Miles shaded his eyes and looked where she was pointing. He knew she was not telling him all she knew, but it was obvious she wanted to change the subject, and he did not see any point in pressing her further. He shook his head. "That's just a mirage," he said.

"A mirage?"

"Lady Partridge explained them to me. It looks like water, but it's just the hot air bending the light."

Little laughed. "It looks like water because it is water," she said. She sounded so convinced that Miles almost expected to find himself shortly wading through a stream, but when they reached the slight rise where the mirage had appeared, the road was dry.

"See?" said Miles. "Dry as a dragon's tongue. The water was just an illusion."

"The water was here, and it still is," insisted Little. "It just doesn't want to be seen."

"If you say so, Little," he said, but she had picked up a praying mantis and was staring into its green bug eyes as it perched grandly on her outstretched finger, the subject of disappearing water already forgotten.

Around midday they arrived at a small hamlet, little more than a cluster of farms and a small village square with a row of shops and a tiny church. A sign by the side of the road said: WELCOME TO HAY. POP. 481. TWINNED WITH CARTHAGE. At the far end of the square stood a rambling inn with benches and tables outside. The inn was called the Surly Hen, and it appeared to have been built over several generations by owners with very different notions of what an inn should look like. The main part had two steeply pitched roofs rising to sharp points, with leaded windows set into white plastered walls that were divided into neat shapes by a web of black beams. Growing out of that was a low, small-windowed extension, roofed with an untidy thatch that looked like it needed a haircut. There were several other additions ranging in style from mock Gothic to simply indescribable.

The long tables outside the inn were crowded with local farmers and travellers at lunch, shovelling chunks of bread and sausage into their stubbly faces and washing them down with pitchers of dark wine. Miles looked at them curiously. An air of resigned misery seemed to surround them like a fog, and hardly a word was spoken as they ate. Two small girls chased each other among the tables, laughing, but no one paid them any attention. At the nearest table sat a stocky man in a shapeless hat, and a plump woman with several chins. They had a large feed spread out on the rough boards before them, and they were working their way through it with a kind of sad vigour. A half-demolished pie sat in front of each of them, and with a large forkful of steak and pastry on its way into her mouth it looked like Mrs. Farmer was ahead in that particular race. Between them on the table sat a basket piled with crusty bread, and a bowl of green olives that Mr. Farmer was tossing in handfuls between his thin lips after every mouthful of pie. Two plates of sausage were all but done for.

Miles felt a yawning cavern in his stomach at the sight of all this food. His morning bowl of hot porridge seemed a lifetime ago. Mrs. Farmer caught sight of him standing in the road, transfixed at the sight of her enormous lunch. She stared sadly at him for a moment, then returned her attention to her food. As Miles contemplated the best way to get himself and Little fed, without so much as a brass penny between them, the landlady of the inn bustled out among the tables. By contrast to her customers she wore a broad grin, and sang snatches of some tune that must have sounded considerably better in its original form, or it would have been strangled at birth.

She planted her tray on the end of Mr. and Mrs. Farmer's table. "Now, ducks," she said happily. "One jug of wine and a bottle of Tau-Tau's." She took from her pocket a small bottle with a bright green label, which she uncorked and emptied into an earthenware wine jug. She picked the jug up, swirled its contents around for a moment, then slopped a generous measure into two glass tumblers, which she plonked on the table. The farmer and his wife picked the glasses up greedily and emptied the contents in unison. The farmer refilled them at once.

They carried on eating with no less gusto, but it seemed that Mrs. Farmer's cheeks were growing redder by the moment. She glanced in Miles's direction again, and stopped in mid-chew, a ribbon of cabbage hanging from the corner of her mouth. She nudged her husband sharply in the ribs. He had just put his tumbler to his lips, and took more wine up his nose than into his mouth. While he coughed and spluttered into a grubby handkerchief, Mrs.

Farmer beckoned to Miles. "Come here, come here," she called, a smile breaking out on her plump face. "Don't be shy, lad."

The farmer glared at Miles as he shoved his handkerchief back up his sleeve. "No beggin' allowed here," he grunted, tearing off a chunk of bread and wedging it into his cheek to allow other food free passage through his mouth.

"Oh put a sock in it, George," said Mrs. Farmer, whose mood seemed to be brightening by the second. "Can't you see the boy's 'ungry? Looks like he's never had a proper feed in his life. Where'd you come from, lad? Call your little sister over – there's plenty 'ere for both of you."

Mr. Farmer stared over Miles's shoulder in puzzlement. "What little sister, woman? There's only another young lad there."

"Don't be daft, George! Them's just boy's clothes. Anyone can see it's a little girl what's wearing 'em, ain't that right, lad?" Miles nodded. "She's shy," he said.

"Bless 'er," said the plump woman, chuckling, it seemed, at nothing in particular. She emptied some of the bread basket into her pie dish, filling the empty space with the remaining slices of sausage and a lump of rank cheese.

Mr. Farmer grunted, but the miserable expression seemed to be melting from his face too, like winter snow.

"I don't spend the day breakin' my back to feed every 'ungry urchin that 'appens by," he muttered, though none too loudly.

"You don't spend the day breaking yer back at all, you lazy old coot, unless it's liftin' a beer tankard you're talking about." She handed the bread basket to Miles, throwing in the last few olives for good measure. "'Ere, lad, this'll stop your ribs knockin' together. Take it over to your sister and mind you share it, eh?"

"Thank you," said Miles. He hesitated by the table.

"Well?" said Mr. Farmer. "What is it, sonny? Want me socks and britches as well?" He laughed loudly at his own wit.

"I was just wondering if you knew where I could find a place called the Palace of Laughter."

The reaction to Miles's question was not what he had expected. Mrs. Farmer's face went strangely blank, yet at the same time her mouth stretched in a sort of strained grin that was quite unlike the sunny smile she had worn a moment before. A strangled whinny came from the back of her throat. Mr. Farmer stared fixedly at Miles, as though he were trying to remember where he had seen him before. "Never 'eard of it," he said eventually. He picked up the wine jug and emptied it down his throat, then he and his wife got up from their bench without another glance at

Miles, for all the world as though he had become invisible. They walked a slightly meandering path to their battered old car, giggling like a couple of schoolchildren, and drove away in a cloud of dust.

Miles stood for a moment staring after them. He noticed that some of the people at the nearest tables were looking at him with suspicion, so he took the basket of leftovers and hurried over to where Little was waiting for him. She sat on the rim of a stone fountain that stood in the centre of the small square, dangling her fingers in the cool water. "Why did those people leave so suddenly?" she asked.

"I don't know. I asked them if they knew the way to the Palace of Laughter, and they reacted very strangely. They said they'd never heard of it, but I don't think they were telling the truth. I suppose I could ask someone else."

Little put a piece of cheese in her mouth. She pulled a face and bit off a chunk of bread to dilute the sour taste, and shook her head. "I don't think anyone here is going to tell us. As long as we can still see the train tracks we must be going in the right direction."

They ate in silence for a while. The midday sun was hot for October, and after they had quenched the thirst of their long walk with handfuls of clear water, they sat down on the warm paving stones, leaning against the fountain's smooth rim. With his belly full and the sun on his face,

Miles felt sleepy. He looked around him for a moment, half expecting to see the strange figure the circus had left in its wake, but there was no one to be seen but the chuckling landlady, her melancholy customers and the two small girls, who had been joined by a blond boy and were squatting in the dust making patterns with pebbles. "We'll rest here for a few minutes before we go on," said Miles, but Little was already asleep.

Miles felt in his pocket for Tangerine, who gave his fingers a squeeze. He seemed tired too, although he had done none of the walking. A fly buzzed somewhere above their heads, and wood pigeons hooted softly in the trees beside the inn. Squinting through his eyelashes, Miles noticed a circus poster tacked to a pole across the square. Beneath the words "CIRCUS OSCURO", the tiger, magnificent and fierce, reared in the centre of a flaming hoop, while a fearless boy in a red suit with gold epaulettes brandished a whip in the background. He wondered whether he would ever again meet the tiger he had spoken to in the moonlight. It seemed such a long time ago.

Miles felt his head nodding, and the tickle of Little's soot-blackened hair as she leaned against his shoulder. "She weighs nothing at all," Miles thought as he drifted into sleep. "She must have hollow bones, like a bird."

CHAPTER ELEVEN

TANGERINE

Miles Wednesday, stone-warmed and Tangerine-less, blinked in the afternoon sun and wondered for a moment where he was. He lifted Little gently upright and . . . just a moment . . . Tangerine-less? His hand dived into his pocket, but somehow he already knew what he would find there. A silver ticket to the Palace of Laughter, and no bear. Where had he gone? He shook Little's shoulder.

"Little – wake up! Have you got Tangerine?"

"No," she yawned. "Isn't he in your pocket?"

Miles shook his head. He stood up and looked into the fountain behind them, but there was nothing in the water besides a few yellow leaves. He had a panicky feeling, as though the ground were falling away beneath his feet. The square itself was almost empty. At the inn tables the crowd had thinned out, but there were still clusters of people, hunched over beer tankards and talking of horses and hoes and the storms that came down on them from the mountain. Small bottles with green labels stood empty on some of the tables, and if Miles had not been searching so anxiously for Tangerine he might have noticed something odd. Unlike the other knots of silent, grey-faced diners, the people sitting at those tables laughed and chatted as you would expect people enjoying a long lunch and good company to do.

Miles shaded his eyes with his hand and searched the shadows beneath the tables for a sign of Tangerine. He spotted him after a moment. A wave of relief swept over him. The bear was ambling between the table legs toward the door of the inn. Miles took from his pocket the cap that Lady Partridge had given him, and pulled it low over his eyes. He made his way among the tables to the point where he had last seen Tangerine. No one paid him any attention. He bent and looked quickly beneath the table next to him. Tangerine was not under that one, but he could see him in the shadow of the table behind that. The bear had come face to face with a large tabby cat, who stood frozen with his tail fluffed, and stared at him with unblinking green eyes.

Miles ducked under the table and crawled between the muddy boots towards Tangerine. The cat hunched lower and shifted his paws, preparing to spring. Miles wriggled over a crossbar between two table legs, desperately trying to reach Tangerine, who had decided that hide-and-seek must be the cat's game, and was trying to hide himself behind a pair of ankles.

The ankles that Tangerine had chosen to hide behind were dressed in lemon yellow socks, plainly visible beneath too-short trousers. As he stuck his threadbare orange head between the ankles and stared at the slightly bemused cat, two things happened at once. A hand reached down from above the table, and the cat sprang. The tabby cat and the owner of the lemon-yellow ankles reached the small bear at the same moment, and the cat's claws sunk themselves into the man's hand instead.

Genghis (for who else would wear lemon-yellow socks?) staggered to his feet with a yell. The bench fell with a crash. He let fly several strange curses that you would only hear in a circus, and not very often at that, but he did not let go of Tangerine. He aimed a kick at the cat, who bolted for the nearest tree and ran straight up the trunk until he disappeared among the rattling brown leaves. Miles clambered out from under the table, the panicky feeling growing stronger in the pit of his stomach. Genghis was sucking the torn knuckles of his right hand, and holding Tangerine tightly in his left. Miles cleared his throat loudly, the cap still pulled low over his eyes. Genghis turned to him with a face like thunder.

"That's my bear," said Miles. He could see Tangerine pushing feebly at Genghis's thick stubby fingers. He frowned at him desperately to try and get him to lie still, but Tangerine took no notice.

Genghis took a good look at Tangerine for the first time. His sly eyes widened as he saw the bear struggling in his grasp. "Not anymore it ain't," he said. "Now take a hike before I polish my boot with your backside."

"Give him to me!" shouted Miles, grabbing Genghis's wrist. People stared from the surrounding tables, but Miles didn't care. All the love that a luckier boy might have given to his parents, Miles had given to Tangerine, and he was not about to let him go.

Genghis reached over with his bleeding right hand and grabbed Miles by the collar in a grip that was starting to feel too familiar by half. He tried to squirm from Genghis's hold, and the cap was knocked from his head. Genghis gave a start. "Well skin me alive!" he said. "It's you again, you little weasel. You seem to be everywhere, except when you're nowhere to be found, that is." He shoved Tangerine into his overcoat pocket and leaned closer to Miles, his words floating on stale cigar breath. "My boss would like a word with you, little weasel. And I don't think he'll be offering you no job, neither."

The landlady of the Surly Hen had emerged again from the inn's dark interior to see what the commotion was about. "Leave that young 'un alone, you big lummox," she said. "'E's just a boy."

"Get lost," growled Genghis, swinging around to face the landlady. As he did so, Miles twisted in his jacket, sinking his teeth into Genghis's hand at the base of his thumb and stamping on his foot with all the strength he could muster. Genghis yelled and let go of Miles's collar. He stuck his clawed and bitten hand back into his mouth and aimed a clumsy swipe at Miles with his other. Miles ducked, but not fast enough. The big man's fist hit him squarely in the ear, sending him sprawling on the dusty paving stones. Through the ringing in his ears he could just hear the land-lady squawking at Genghis, her face red with anger and her finger stabbing the air in his direction. The diners were glaring at Genghis now too, and from the shadows of the inn door a large bearded man was emerging, hitching his gravy-stained cook's trousers up to an imaginary waist and squinting in the light. He had a large meat cleaver in his hand, and did not look happy to be disturbed in his work. "What is it?" he growled.

"This big lummox is pickin' on that boy, Ted," said the landlady. The sight of Ted, who was an even bigger lummox and with a meat cleaver to boot, was enough for Genghis. He turned on his heel and strode around the side of the inn to the patch of trodden and rutted earth where the carts and tractors of the inn's patrons were tethered.

The landlady opened her mouth to speak to Miles, but before she could utter a word he had scrambled to his feet and was running after Genghis, desperately hoping that Tangerine would manage to wriggle unnoticed from the big man's pocket, as he had from his own. Genghis was climbing aboard a battered blue van as Miles turned the corner of the Surly Hen. He saw the words "THE PALACE OF LAUGHTER" painted in silver letters on the side, as the engine coughed into life and the van made a sharp turn out of the lot. With no thought but to stay close to Tangerine, Miles ran after the van, but before he could reach it the battered vehicle bounced into the road and roared away up the hill, leaving a cloud of dust and the trace of a smell that might have been rotten bananas in its wake.

Miles stood for a minute, bruised and panting, staring after Genghis's van as it disappeared over the brow of the hill. He felt a strange tug, as though something deep inside him had been hooked by an invisible fishing line and was being pulled away along the dusty road. He closed his eyes and tried to fix a picture of Tangerine in his mind. "Sit tight," he said silently to the bear. "I'll come and get you." He opened his eyes again and suddenly remembered Little.

She was no longer to be seen at the fountain, or anywhere else in the square. He hoped she had had the sense to hide herself at the first sight of Genghis, and he looked around the trampled field for any sign of her. A forest of dark conifers began at the edge of the field and ran along the right-hand side of the road that the van had taken. Shading his eyes, Miles spotted Little among the nearest trees. She was standing half hidden behind the trunk of a tall fir, but she was not looking in his direction. She was staring at something a little farther into the shadows. He followed her gaze and saw to his surprise that someone seemed to have hung a circus poster well inside the wood, where it was barely visible in the mossy gloom. He could just make out the dull orange glow of the tiger's stripes, but he could not see the boy with the whip, or the flaming hoop.

In the shadows of the trees the tiger appeared to be moving. Miles walked over to where Little stood, to get a closer look. Without turning, she put her finger to her lips. He could see the tiger more clearly now, and there was no longer any doubt that he was moving. He was walking slowly towards them, his enormous paws making barely a sound on the carpet of pine needles. There was no poster after all, just a large and magnificent Bengal tiger, and this time Miles knew for sure that he was not dreaming.

CHAPTER TWELVE

SUNFLOWER AND STORMCLOUD

Miles Wednesday, bruised, bemused and bearless, held his breath as the tiger approached them in the stillness of the afternoon. The twittering birds had fallen silent, and the sound of cows lowing on the hillside had ceased. He could see the tiger more clearly now, and he recognised the pattern of markings on his face, and the deep gaze of the great beast's amber eyes. At ten paces the tiger stopped. Little glanced at Miles, as though waiting for him to speak, but what do you say to a Bengal tiger who is staring at you from springing distance, and with no bars between you?

The tiger spoke first. "What's the matter, tub boy?" he rumbled. "Cat got your tongue?"

"No," said Miles. "Genghis got my Tangerine."

The tiger seemed to prick up his ears at this, but all he said was, "I've never had much time for riddles."

"It's not a riddle," said Miles. "I have a stuffed bear called Tangerine, and a fat man called Genghis has stolen him and driven away in his van." He pointed in the direction that Genghis had taken. "I have to get him back."

"A stuffed bear?" said the tiger. "You're wasting my time, tub boy. I could be finding myself a tasty meal right now."

"I didn't ask you to come here in the first place," said Miles, rather shortly. He had many questions he wanted to ask the tiger, but at the moment the bearnapping of Tangerine was uppermost on his mind. With every passing minute Genghis was getting farther away, with Tangerine trapped in the pocket of his smelly overcoat, but how could he explain the importance of this to the tiger?

The tiger paced slowly toward him until his eyes were just inches away. His tiger smell was musty and strong. The black markings over his eyes gave his face a slightly quizzical expression, but the eyes themselves were steady and clear. His nostrils flared slightly as he took in Miles's smell.

"Maybe so," he said. "And maybe not." He turned to look at Little.

"Who's your friend?" he said, still speaking to Miles.

"This is Little," said Miles.

"Little," said the tiger. "That's apt, I suppose. There's barely enough of her to go on a cracker."

"The kitchens are just over there." said Little, ignoring the tiger's comment and pointing through the trees to the back of the inn. "I'm sure you could find something to eat, if we could distract the cook for a minute. You'll need all your strength and speed to catch up with Genghis."

The tiger stepped back a pace and looked Little up and down.

"So you can speak," he said. "I prefer my meat on the hoof, little girl. And besides, what makes you think I would go haring over the countryside chasing a fat man with a stuffed bear?"

"I was hoping you could carry us on your back," said Little. "We're not heavy, and you are strong."

"Do I look like a donkey to you, little girl?"

"Not at all," said Little. "You look much faster, and even if a donkey could catch up with Genghis I don't think he would scare him much."

The tiger gave a deep rumbling laugh that seemed to come all the way from his hungry belly. "I suppose a little run might be enjoyable," he said, "and it so happens I was headed in that direction anyway. As for you, you may sit on my back if that's what you wish; I will not even notice you are there. But you should understand that I am not a beast of burden, and staying on will be your own concern. It doesn't matter to me if you fall off and are lost."

The tiger turned to face the distant mountains. Miles was just a shade taller than him, although he would have had to stand on his toes to see over him. He lifted Little from the ground and helped her onto the tiger's back, where she settled just behind his powerful shoulders. Then he grabbed a handful of the tiger's short pelt and hauled himself up behind her. Before he could seat himself, the tiger started off through the thin trees at the edge of the wood, and Miles had to hold on tight until he could swing his leg over and sit up properly. He had no doubt the tiger meant what he said about leaving him behind if he fell off.

If you have ever sat on the back of a fully grown Bengal tiger, you will have noticed that a tiger's body has a leaner shape than that of a horse. Whereas some horses, and especially the kind of ponies you get to ride on your holidays, can be distinctly barrel shaped around the middle, a tiger is basically a long slender slab of pure muscle, which makes gripping a tiger with the knees a little easier, especially if you are a first-time tiger rider.

Miles had no experience of riding either animal, and for the first few minutes he concentrated hard on keeping his balance with nothing for his hands to hold on to. When he became confident enough to look back over his shoulder, the hamlet of Hay and the Surly Hen had disappeared from view, and there was no sign of the horde of policemen and out-of-work zookeepers that he had half expected to see pursuing them along the road.

The tiger's stride lengthened and he began to run. Miles gripped tighter with his knees, but at each bound he felt himself lift in the air, the wind whistling past his ears. He was sure that he would part company from the tiger at any moment and find himself somersaulting through the air. Little, by contrast, sat easily at the tiger's shoulders, looking about her with delight as the sunlight flashed through the passing trees. Miles held her around the waist, as though some of her confidence might flow into him.

The tiger kept to the edge of the woods, a little way in from the road so as to keep out of sight. They had reached the top of the hill over which Genghis's van had disappeared and descended into the valley below. Between the trees they could see a small village in the valley floor, with a tall grey spire rising from a jumble of red roofs. Neatly tended fields climbed gently up the slopes of the surrounding hills. Far off to their left there was a glint of sunlight on the railway, which curved gently away and ran out of sight into the hazy distance.

They came to a break in the trees, where a stone bridge crossed the stream that wound along the edge of the wood, and here they stopped. Miles's legs felt stiff as he slid off the tiger's back, but the tiger showed no sign of tiredness. A bend in the stream kept them out of sight of the town, and there was nobody about. They drank from the clear water that ran over the smooth brown rocks of the riverbed, then Miles and Little flopped down in the lush grass of the stream bank while the tiger waded out into the water and stood there as still as a statue. For two or three minutes he did not move a muscle, then suddenly he gave a short lunge and ducked his head into the water, coming up a moment later with a large trout flapping between his teeth, while sparkling drops of water shivered on his whiskers like dew on a spider's web. Little laughed, and the sun came out from behind a cloud. Everything seemed so new to her, and Miles wondered how she must feel to be so far from the world she knew.

"What's it like, where you come from?" he asked her.

"It's bright," said Little, "and cold, and very beautiful."

"Do you miss it?"

"Of course." She picked a flower from the grass and twirled it in her fingers. "It's very strange down here. Especially people."

"How do you mean?"

"They do funny things." She propped herself up on her elbow and looked at him intently with her sky-blue eyes. "Like you. You are helping me to find the Palace of

Laughter, even though you lost your home and the Great Cortado wants you dead because of me. And you know that when I find Silverpoint I'll be going home."

Miles felt an unexpected lump in his throat. He did not want to think about the moment when Little would leave. "I have to find Tangerine," he said.

"That's not the only reason," said Little. "You tried to save me when I fell. Then you rescued me from the circus, and from The Null. All that happened before you lost Tangerine. It doesn't make sense."

Miles looked at her. There was only curiosity in her eyes. "That's what friends do," he said. "Silverpoint's your friend, and you're going to find him, aren't you?"

Little looked puzzled. "Silverpoint is a longfeather and a Storm Angel," she said. "I am just a Song Angel."

"But you're trying to rescue him," persisted Miles.

Her gaze dropped to the flower that she twirled between her fingers. "I can't return home without Silverpoint," she said. "I led him into a trap, and now I am bound to find him."

The tiger stepped back onto the riverbank, having filled his belly with fresh fish, and shook himself, showering Miles and Little with cold water. He turned to look at them. "I beg your pardon," he said. "I thought you were just a couple of rabbits there in the grass."

Little tucked the flower carefully into her pocket and put her finger to her lips. "Something's coming," she said.

The tiger's rounded ears swivelled in the direction of the road. He turned without a word and padded along the bank until he was out of sight under the stone bridge, where he lay down in the shade. Miles and Little followed him quickly, as the sound of hooves and cart wheels from the road above grew louder. Over the noise of the approaching cart they could hear the sound of laughter. The wheels of the cart rumbled overhead, and Miles saw a small object spinning through the air to land with a plunk in the water of the stream.

When they were sure the cart had gone, the tiger stood and stretched himself. "You'd better climb aboard if you're coming," he said. "We have some catching up to do."

"Wait a moment," said Miles. He was curious to see what it was that had been thrown from the cart. He pulled off his boots and rolled his trousers to the knee. The stream was cold and the stones slippery with weed. He waded to the spot where he had seen the small object hit the water, and found it almost immediately, lodged between two rounded stones. It was a small square bottle with a green label, like the ones the landlady of the Surly Hen had been dispensing. He fished it out and read aloud: "Dr. Tau-Tau's Restorative Tonic. Restores the natural humour and lifts sagging spirits. Just two spoonfuls of this miracle remedy will bring the laughter back into your life. Do not operate heavy machinery or perform surgery for six hours after dosage."

"The tiger is leaving," said the tiger. "Are you finished prospecting for rubbish?" Little was already perched behind his shoulders. Miles nodded, and slipped the bottle thoughtfully into his pocket. He pulled his socks and boots back on over his wet feet, and climbed onto the tiger's back.

The forest through which they had been travelling ended at the stream. On the far bank was a field of sunflowers. They stretched into the distance like a tall green army, their yellow-fringed heads heavy with seeds and drooping slightly. Beyond the fields the mountains rose steeply, their lower slopes terraced with vineyards. The sunflower fields, still lit with the late-afternoon sun, showed a dazzling yellow against the purplish black rain clouds that hung low over the mountain.

"The railway turns away to the north here, but the road looks like it continues straight over the mountain," said Miles.

"Of what concern is the railway, tub boy? I understood your were pursuing a fat man in a van."

"We are" said Miles. "We're also looking for a place called the Palace of Laughter. The train goes there. But it looks like the van might be going there too."

"Then the obvious thing would be to take the shorter route, which would appear to be over the mountain," said the tiger.

Miles and Little nibbled on sunflower seeds that they managed to snatch as they passed through the tall flowers with their thick hairy stems. In the distance they saw a lone farmer, staring in puzzlement at the sight of two children's heads travelling at some speed, just above the level of the sunflowers. They waved at him, and he blessed himself and turned quickly away. The sunflowers seemed to go on forever, but eventually the ground began to rise, and they emerged into the lower terraces of the vineyards. To their left they could see the road beginning to loop from side to side as it climbed the steep slopes towards the gathering storm. The tiger made better speed now, following the paths of packed earth at the edges of the vineyards. When he reached the next terrace he paused for a moment, and Miles could feel he was gathering himself to spring. Little took hold of his pelt, and Miles held her around the waist, and the tiger jumped, soaring through the air to land with his huge paws sinking slightly into the loose earth. Miles, who had slid back almost onto the tiger's tail, pulled himself forwards again as the tiger took off toward the next level.

The tiger leaped from terrace to terrace, and Miles

learned to grip tightly with his knees and lean forward at the moment of the jump. Little laughed with delight as they sped through the bushy vines. Miles had never heard anything quite like this laugh. It seemed to be made of sunlight and sweet air, all the things he had never felt in Pinchbucket House, or in the leaden laughter of the tired people of Larde. There was something else there too, a feeling that he imagined might be the thrill of flying. He looked over his shoulder and was surprised to see how high they were. The town was already a distant jumble threaded on a silver stream, where the dark green of the forest met the gold of the sunflower fields.

Ahead of them the vineyards were coming to an end, and the rocky mountain, dotted with scrubby vegetation and isolated pines, rose into the dark stormclouds. As they left the last neat rows of young vines, fat drops of rain began to fall, and in a few moments they were riding through a heavy downpour that soaked them to the skin. The rain battered the earth with a hissing roar and stung their faces, but the tiger's pace did not slacken. He ran on, bounding from rock to rock and forging through wild shrubs as though the storm were a figment of their imagination.

They could not see far through the curtains of rain, but presently the ground levelled off and they began to descend. Before long Miles realised they were climbing again, and he guessed that the moutain rose in a series of peaks, each one higher than the last.

The sky began to lift at last, and the rain eased off. A cold breeze made them shiver in their wet clothing. The tiger stopped, and they found themselves on the highest ridge of the mountain, looking down the other side. A little way down the far slope an almost circular lake lay in a hollow like a giant cauldron, and beyond that a hilly plain stretched away into the darkness. Miles felt strangely like a small giant, perched on the mountain ridge with the sun setting behind him, and before him a thousand possible futures waiting for him in the mountain's shadow.

CHAPTER THIRTEEN

VARIPPULI

Miles Wednesday, rain-soaked and tiger-carried, stood on a windy ridge at the top of Mount Bareknuckle and surveyed the twilit hills beyond. To his left stood a Bengal tiger, and to his right a girl, smaller than he was but several centuries older, who had fallen from the sky. He felt light-headed and free, as though he could step out onto the wind and sail down from the mountain like an untethered kite.

He tried to make out the course of the road they had been following, but as it wound down from the ridge it soon disappeared into the shadow of the mountain. They made their way down towards the circular lake, which shone faintly with the last remaining light. Miles walked to loosen his legs, while Little sat sidesaddle (but without a saddle, of course) on the tiger's back. A dense pine wood bordered part of the lake, and in the wood they found a small clearing that opened on one side onto the still waters. In the centre of the clearing stood three enormous stones, with another flat slab laid across the top. The standing stones were about three paces apart for a tall man, and the ground between them was dry, sheltered by the stone roof.

"We will spend the night here," said the tiger. "I suggest you build a fire, while I go and catch myself some supper. After all that running I could eat a small village."

Under the pine trees there was plenty of dry wood. They piled it just outside the standing stones, and Miles, who always kept an old brass lighter in his pocket, soon had a good fire blazing. They sat on the dry ground between the stones, and their clothes steamed in the heat. The waters of the lake were now as dark as night. The sky was cloudy still, and only a few patches of stars could be seen here and there. Miles stared into the embers of the fire, glowing orange and black like the tiger's flanks. The ground beneath him seemed to sway slightly, echoing the rhythm of the tiger's muscular back that had carried him through the afternoon. He wondered where Tangerine was now. He pictured him somewhere on a tavern table, being poked and prodded and laughed over by drunkards and fools, and he hoped at least that he was still hidden in Genghis's stale, smoky pocket.

The tiger emerged from the darkness and settled himself in the grass beside the fire. His stomach no longer rumbled, and now and then he licked his lips and sighed deeply.

The questions Miles had been storing up for the tiger came crowding back into his mind. He hardly knew where to start. "Do you have a name?" he asked.

"Yes," said the tiger.

Miles smiled to himself. He felt unaccountably pleased that the tiger had given him the same reply that he had given the Great Cortado. "My real name is Miles," he said to the tiger.

"I prefer 'tub boy'," said the tiger.

"But why?"

"It's hard to eat someone with whom you are on first-name terms," said the tiger, "and you never know when the larder will be bare. If we start exchanging names you might get the notion that we are friends."

Miles looked at Little. She seemed to be miles away, smiling to herself in the soft glow of the fire. He thought of the night before, surrounded by cats as Lady Partridge told stories of her husband, his untimely death by exploding pudding, and the circus that used to visit Larde each year.

"Did you ever hear of Barty Fumble's Big Top?" he asked the tiger.

The tiger made no answer.

"Barty Fumble owned a tiger who was the star of his circus, but I don't know what he was called," persisted Miles. "I just thought you might have heard of them."

"The tiger's name was Varippuli," said the tiger, "and Barty Fumble did not own him. No tiger can be owned by a man. You will find it was the other way around."

"So you did know them?" said Miles.

"I know something of the story," said the tiger.

"Will you tell it to us?"

The tiger sighed. "I suppose I won't get any sleep until you have heard it," he said.

In the glow of a pine fire by the edge of the dark lake, the tiger told Miles and Little what he knew of the story of Barty Fumble and Varippuli. His rich, deep voice brought the tiger and his man alive in the night, and the story he told went something like this:

"Barty Fumble was a dark-haired, barrel-chested man with a huge beard and a laugh that could rattle windows. His eyes laughed all the time beneath his thick black eyebrows, and when his mouth joined in, it was impossible not to laugh with him. The circus had been in his family for five generations, and he treated everyone in it as one of his own children. From his most famous clown to his smallest parrot, from the elephants to the tent boys, they were all family to Barty Fumble, and for this he earned their undying respect and love.

"Barty's circus followed a well-tried route through the country, and its arrival was eagerly awaited in every small town along the way. Indeed, some towns were almost emptied of people when Barty Fumble's Big Top was camped nearby, as all but the most miserable souls crowded into his patched tent to marvel at his majestic animals and lose their worries in the antics of his clowns, who were generally considered to be without equal. But the greatest attraction without a doubt was the famous tiger, Varippuli."

The tiger got up and moved around to the other side of the fire to escape the smoke. He settled himself with a sigh. "Varippuli," he said, rolling the name like distant thunder. "Now there was a magnificent beast. The tiger is the king of cats, as I'm sure you know, and Varippuli was a king among tigers. He could wrestle a bull elephant to the ground, and when he roared, small birds fell stunned from the sky. He was the handsomest and noblest of animals, and though he would suffer the ownership of no man, nonetheless his loyalty to Barty was as strong and enduring as the mountain beneath us.

"One year a cold wind from the east blew all through March, and with it came the Circus Oscuro. It was a big circus, with over a hundred wagons. There were animals from every dark corner of the world, and death-defying acts that could amaze and terrify in equal measure. It was said that this circus had swallowed up other, smaller circuses, and that was how it had grown so large. Whether or not that was true, it was certainly swallowing up Barty Fumble's paying customers. When Barty Fumble's Big Top arrived in Arktown, they found that the Circus Oscuro had rolled out the night before, and their posters were still hanging on every lamppost. No more than a handful of people came to see Barty's Big Top. It was the same in Shallowford and in Nape, and when they arrived at the village of Botox they were met by the sergeant of police, who told them they could move right along, and had better arrive earlier next spring, as one circus a year was quite enough."

"Why didn't they take a different route?" asked Little.

"They did, little girl. Barty was no fool, at least so I heard, and had been in the circus all his life. He struck off to the west, but found himself still chasing the new circus's tail. He doubled back and tried the coastal towns, but the Circus Oscuro had already been there too. He tried taking a short cut over the mountains to Frappe, but even before he got there he could see the dark snake of the Circus

Oscuro winding out of the town in the first light of dawn.

"Now Barty Fumble was a resourceful and optimistic man, but even he was beginning to get very worried. They had not had a successful show in over two months, and the kitty was empty. The animals were short of food and of temper, and the acts were losing their spark from playing to empty houses. What's more, Barty's wife was expecting their first child, which made it the worst possible time to be facing ruin.

"The time came for Barty to make a difficult choice. He got up from his bed well before dawn one morning, and rode ahead on his favourite horse without a word to anyone. He returned late that night with whiskey on his breath and a deal in his pocket. The following morning he gathered his performers together and announced that Barty Fumble's Big Top would merge with the Circus Oscuro for the summer season, and that when winter came they would once again go their separate ways. Some of the performers were not entirely happy at the news, but they knew that the situation was becoming desperate. They trusted Barty's judgment, and many of them realised how hard it must have been for him to swallow his pride and go cap in hand to a larger circus."

The tiger yawned and fell silent. Miles fed the fire from the pile of branches he had collected. The dry wood crackled and spat, and sparks flew dizzily up into the darkness. Crickets creaked in the grass just beyond the circle of firelight, telling their own stories back and forth in the night.

"I heard that Barty and his tiger . . . I mean Varippuli . . . disappeared after his circus joined with the Circus Oscuro," said Miles.

"More questions, tub boy? You should stop bothering me and get some sleep before the sun comes up."

"But I'm curious. You seem to know the story well, and I'm very interested in tigers."

The tiger gave a long sigh. "Then perhaps you're not as foolish as you might be," he said. "And you are certainly as persistent as a mosquito. All right, I will tell you what I remember, but if you're hoping for a happy ending you will be disappointed.

"The combined circus had a very successful summer. They were playing to bigger audiences than ever, and many of Barty's performers forgot their doubts about the wisdom of his deal. In time Barty himself became friends with the Circus Oscuro's ringmaster, who called himself the Great Cortado, but Varippuli never took to him."

"Why not?"

"I don't know, tub boy, I am simply relating what I heard. Now are you finished with the interruptions?"

"Yes, for the moment."

"Very well, then I will continue. Barty's son was born on a rainy autumn night in a small town named Iota, but what should have been a happy event turned to tragedy. His young wife died in childbirth, and neither the midwife nor the town quack could save her. The child was a fine, healthy boy, but Barty was driven out of his mind with grief. He stayed with the circus for a while, but he never uttered another word. In the end he left in the night, taking his infant son with him. I never met anyone who has seen or heard from Barty, from that day to this."

The wind had changed direction once again, and the tiger got up and circled the fire. He padded silently to where Miles and Little sat between the standing stones, and settled himself behind them on the dry ground. His head was less than an arm's length from Miles's right ear, and although Miles had felt a little sorry for the rabbits who had laid down their lives for the tiger's supper, he couldn't help wishing that a few more might come and join them in case he got peckish in the night.

"Did Barty take Varippuli with him?" he asked.

"Of course not, boy," rumbled the tiger in his ear. "Only a fool would wander the countryside with a fully grown tiger. Besides, Varippuli met his end on the same night that Barty disappeared."

"How did that happen?" asked Miles.

The tiger said nothing for some time, then he sighed deeply and continued. "After his wife's death, Barty Fumble retreated into his grief, and there was no one in the circus who could persuade Varippuli to perform again. The Great Cortado, who did not understand the mutual respect that the tiger and the man had shared, became impatient with him. He starved Varippuli for days at a time, and then tried to make him perform for food. Naturally the tiger would never give in to such an ignoble trick. He ate nothing, and he bided his time. When one night the Great Cortado entered the tiger's cage with a whip and a bellyful of whiskey for courage, Varippuli attacked, and opened the little man's chest from neck to navel."

Miles shuddered at the memory of the scar that the Great Cortado had shown him the night he had helped Little escape from the circus. "How did he survive that?" he asked.

"Ah," said the tiger, "nature gave the tiger a most fearsome set of weapons with which to defend his honour, but though men are weak and soft at the edges, they were given the weapon of cunning. While Varippuli gathered himself to finish Cortado off, the little man managed to crawl into his trailer and get hold of his blunderbuss. As the tiger entered the trailer, he cut the magnificent beast down with a blast from the gun at point-blank range. It took two surgeons and a visiting tailor from Marrakech to stitch the Great Cortado together, so I heard, and over a year passed before he could stand on his two feet and wave a whip about again. When he was well enough to listen, he was told that Barty had left the circus, and none could say where he had gone."

The tiger fell silent for a while. Miles turned the story of Barty and Varippuli over in his mind, as the stars wheeled slowly overhead. Little had fallen asleep against the tiger's warm flank. The jacket had slipped from her shoulder, and her pearly skin shone faintly in the firelight. Miles leaned over and pulled her jacket back around her.

"That's a remarkable little friend you have found yourself," said the tiger. "She has more wisdom than you would expect to find in such a small parcel, and you will be glad of it before your journey is done, or I'm a tree frog."

"I'm not sure if she's my friend, exactly," said Miles, thinking back to their conversation by the stream. "She'll be leaving soon, anyway."

"A friendship should be judged by its depth, not by its length," said the tiger. "And not many adventures are better followed alone, unless of course you are a tiger."

"Do you always travel alone?" asked Miles. "Didn't you arrive with the Circus Oscuro?"

The tiger snorted. "I would sooner eat a putrid donkey than perform tricks for that outfit."

"But you were once with a circus yourself, weren't you?"

The tiger gave a low growl. "That was a long time ago, tub boy, and another story entirely. Now if you have any more questions you will have to swallow them again, because I don't care much for talking, and tonight I've done enough to last me through the winter and into next summer."

The tiger settled his head between his paws, and the crickets wound down gradually in the darkness. Miles sat beneath the roof of stone with his arms wrapped around his knees, gazing into the embers of the fire. Tales of acrobats, rolling roads and tiger-striped revenge played themselves out in glowing shapes before his tired, smoke-stung eyes, until at last he drifted into sleep.

CHAPTER FOURTEEN

BALTINGLASS OF ARABY

Miles Wednesday, dawn-chilled and hungry, woke with a pale sun peering at him from just above the horizon. Little was kneeling by the lake, splashing cold water onto her face. The tiger was gone.

His first thought was to build up the fire, but then he remembered that they had nothing to cook on it. His stomach was as empty as the pocket where Tangerine lived. He put his hand in the inside pocket anyway, as if by some miracle he might find Tangerine back in his accustomed place. There was nothing there but the silver ticket. He sat up and shaded his eyes. The pale snake of the road looped down the wooded flank of the mountain, visible here and there between the trees. It was the trail down which Genghis had passed the day before with teeth marks in his hand and Tangerine in his pocket – a trail growing colder with each passing hour.

"Where did the tiger go?" he asked Little as she returned from the water's edge.

"I don't know. He was gone when I woke up."

"Then we'd better get going. We must be at least half a day behind Genghis as it is."

When Miles had quenched his thirst they left the lake and started down in the direction of the road. The slope of the mountain was covered with patchy forest giving way to frequent clearings. They scrambled down a steep slope of mossy boulders and tree roots onto the road. On the far bank the tiger sat, looking down on them with an air of mild amusement.

"You're going to walk all the way? You'd better get a move on."

"We will," said Miles. As he strode down the road he called back over his shoulder, "I can see you're too busy licking your paws to offer us a ride."

There was a soft thump as the tiger's weight landed on the packed earth of the road, and a moment later he was walking beside them.

"As it happens, tub boy, I am also headed this way. And

before you ask, it's none of your business. I might consider letting you ride today, especially if your little friend with the better manners were to ask me."

Little laughed. "Please, King of Cats, lend us your speed and strength, and may the world turn ever toward you," she said.

The tiger stopped. "You see?" he said to Miles. "A little poetry goes a long way. Now climb on before I change my mind."

Once on the tiger's back, Miles felt as though he had been riding tigers all his life. Little sat in front again, and the tiger set off at a steady pace down the centre of the road. They ran in silence for a while. The morning sun began to warm the air, and soon it was abuzz with insects. From time to time they caught a glimpse of the mountain's foothills between the knotty trunks of the tall pines.

"Shouldn't we get off the road?" asked Miles.

"No need," said the tiger. "After all, what stringy peasant would dare stand up to the king of cats?"

"One with a blunderbuss," said Miles.

He could feel the tiger's muscles stiffen beneath him. "Some day you'll be bitten by your own mouth, tub boy," he said, but all the same he left the road a little farther on and entered the cover of the trees.

They made good speed through the patchy forest. The

tiger bounded over twisted roots and dodged between trees with obvious enjoyment. Sometimes he almost seemed to be flying. The clearings became larger and more frequent, and as they reached the lower slopes the woods dwindled into isolated copses rising from the long grass. Here the tiger went more cautiously, threading a path through the longest grasses and pausing before leaving the cover of each copse.

Below them they could see a range of low, gently rounded hills stretching to the horizon. The road wound between the hills like a dusty river. Not far ahead of them it swung to the right and climbed a small hill that was crowned by a village of whitewashed, red-roofed houses.

"We need to get something to eat," said Miles.

"If you're thinking of going to that village," said the tiger, "you'll be going on your own."

"That's what I plan to do. There's an olive grove on the slope, just below that tower. You and Little can wait for me there."

"As you wish," said the tiger.

Miles and Little dismounted from the tiger as they approached the village. An occasional donkey cart appeared on the road, rocking through the potholes and moving with no apparent hurry, and once a tractor chugged by with a train of beige dust. They kept their distance from the road, and when anyone passed by, the tiger simply froze like a statue, so that even from a few paces he was invisible in the tall grass.

They reached the olive grove, which lay at the foot of the village in broad terraces. Rows of olive trees stood on twisted trunks in welcome pools of shade. Not a breath of wind stirred the leaves. Built into the wall of the second terrace was a sort of man-made cave where the olive pickers could rest and eat in the shade. The tiger stood at the mouth of the cave, his whiskers twitching as he investigated it with his nose. Once he was satisfied he disappeared inside.

"I'll come with you," said Little. Miles shook his head.

"It's better if I go alone," he said. "You wait here with the tiger. I won't be long."

The road wound steeply up into the village. It was lined with a parade of crooked houses, with small windows and little courtyards with electric-blue walls and shady trees. He came to a long high wall on his right-hand side. Behind that wall, although he couldn't see it, was a small apple orchard. What Miles could see was the long branch of an apple tree hanging right out over the wall, weighed down by a handful of ripe green apples. If you've ever travelled for miles on a dusty road in the hot sun with a Bengal tiger and a four-hundred-year-old girl, you will be able to imagine just how cool and tasty those apples looked. He stopped in his tracks and stared up at the branch, trying to figure out a way to reach them. He felt in his pockets for something to throw. The apples looked ready to fall at the slightest touch.

"It'll never work," said a voice behind him, making him jump. "They don't fall off so easy."

A plump boy about his own age sat on a low wall across the street. He had close-cropped hair and eyes that looked too small for his face. He smiled, and tossed a large apple core over his shoulder.

"How did you get that one?" asked Miles.

"Easy," said the boy. "I can tell you how to get a sackload of them without breaking a sweat. He's got so many he doesn't know what to do with them."

"Who has?"

"Old Baltinglass of Araby," said the boy. "That house with the apple orchard belongs to him. He used to be a famous explorer, or so he says, but he's been blind as a bat ever since I can recall. He's lived in that house for years, with no one but a dozen chickens and a garden full of apple trees."

The boy jumped down from the wall and crossed the road. He lowered his voice. "All you've got to do is knock on the door and say you're Rufus and you've come about the apples. That's my name, Rufus Weedle. My mam sent me to pick up a bag of apples from old Baltinglass, but if you pretend to be me he won't know any different."

"Why don't you get them yourself?" asked Miles suspiciously.

"Well," said the boy, putting his plump arm around Miles's shoulder as though they'd been friends for years, "there's a small snag. Baltinglass's chickens have the run of the orchard, and they lay their eggs wherever they like. Baltinglass likes his eggs, but he can't go and collect them himself, on account of he's as blind as a bat, like I said. If he went looking for them he'd only step on them, and end up with a load of scrambled eggs, wouldn't he?"

"I suppose so."

"Exactly. So usually my mam picks them up for him on her way to the bakery, and he gives her a bag of apples in return, only today she says her knee is giving her hell and her kidneys feel like they've switched places, so she sent me instead, even though she knows I can't go near chickens."

"Why not?"

Rufus took a step backward and stared at Miles as though he had two heads. "Why *not*? Cause they're 'orrible, that's why not. The way they walk, like little broken machines with feathers, pecking at your ankles. And crawling with vermin too. They give me the creeps! But if you tell him you're Rufus Weedle you can pick up the eggs and be out of there in no time. My mam says there's only a dozen to find, and it never takes more than five minutes. Then we'll split the apples between us, because if I go home to my mam on a bad-kidney day with no apples, I might as well be going home to a crocodile without a dead pig under my arm."

Miles shrugged. "All right," he said. "But I don't see why I can't just tell him that your mam sent me instead."

"Because he's expecting me, not you, dummy!" said the boy in a loud whisper. "And he's not just as blind as a bat, he's as batty as one too. He thinks foreign agents are combing the land for him, looking for some priceless treasures he brought back from the Orient. He once chased the new postman halfway down the street with a sword because no one remembered to tell him that the old one had died. As long as he thinks you're me, he won't slice you in half, will he?"

Miles looked doubtfully at the weathered door of the old house. It was studded with square iron nails. A worn horseshoe hung in the centre, and a knotted rope hung to the right of the door. He thought about Little, waiting in the olive grove, and pulled the rope. A jangling din came from inside the house, as though there were a few pots and pans instead of a doorbell on the other end of the bell rope.

A muffled shout came from within the house, and after

a minute a tap-tap-tapping could be heard on the other side of the door. A bolt rattled, and the door opened abruptly.

"Whaddya want?" barked Baltinglass of Araby. His wrinkled head stuck horizontally out of his shirt on a neck like a cluster of ropes. He wore a knitted hat despite the heat. On either side of a large beaky nose his milky eyes stared, in slightly different directions, into the fog of his blindness.

"I'm Rufus Weedle," said Miles, hoping he had remembered the name right. "I've come about the apples."

"Ah, Weedle junior!" said Baltinglass. "I used to know your grandfather, though I don't think my life was richer for it." He stepped back once, twice. His house was dim inside. The small high windows were filthy and let in hardly any light. Miles could just make out a cluster of pots and pans hanging on the end of the bell rope.

"Well, step inside and be quick about it," said Baltinglass sharply, "before all the air gets out."

Miles took a deep breath and stepped across the stone lintel. The old man slipped around behind him and slammed the door, locking it with a key that he produced from a chain around his scraggy neck. As the door shut, Miles caught a glimpse of the real Rufus Weedle making a mock salute, a funny little smile on his face.

"Now!" barked Baltinglass of Araby, in the dimness of

his musty hallway. "The mightiest task begins with a hitch of the trousers, young Rufus. You get stuck in right away and work like a bull ant's nephew, and you should be finished and free in three days flat!"

CHAPTER FIFTEEN

APPLE JELLY

Miles Wednesday, apple-hungry and self-kidnapped, stared in dismay at the wrinkled features and toothless grin of Baltinglass of Araby.

"Did you say three *days?*" he asked, hoping he had misheard.

"That's what I said, boy. Three days. Sun comes up, sun goes down again!" He swished his cane up and over his head as he said this, hitting the candleless chandelier and showering himself with dust. "Up again! Down again! Up one more time, and if you're still working like a team of mules you'll be all done by sundown on the third day, barring sandstorm and snakebite. But if you're going to stand there gawping like a fish, it'll be four days at the least, so put your best boot forward, young Weedle."

He turned and stumped away into the darkness. Miles followed, his head spinning. He could dimly see an impressive collection of swords, crossbows, and grimacing masks arranged on the walls of the drawing room. A human skull with ornate silver decorations sat on a small round table. Yellowed newspaper cuttings hung in crooked frames near the French windows. One showed a picture of a much younger Baltinglass standing by a rectangular hole in a rocky bank. The headline read GULLIVER P. BALTINGLASS DEFIES THE CURSE OF THE EMPEROR'S TOMB. They stepped out into the blinding light of the orchard.

"How can it take three days to find a dozen eggs?" asked Miles.

Baltinglass stopped in his tracks and swung around to face him, his sightless eyes staring at the source of Miles's voice. "Are you trying to be funny, Weedle?" he bellowed.

"No sir!"

"Where would I be getting eggs from, since you stole my prize-laying chickens and wrung their necks?"

"But Ru . . . but I can't go near chickens!" said Miles in surprise.

"Listen to me, young Weedle," said Baltinglass, stabbing his cane in Miles's direction. "We may not have crossed swords before, but it's my eyes that are blind, not my wits, and if you take me for a fool you might just end up on a wooden plaque on my wall. I've heard all about your lies and your trickery. You were caught red-handed selling my chickens for boilers. How you got your thieving little hands on them I don't know, but it's time to settle your debt and you ain't going to worm out of it."

He marched into a corner of the orchard and pulled out a rickety wooden stepladder. "There's nine trees here, and at least two hundred apples on each. That's eighteen hundred apples, as you'd know if you ever bothered to show up at school. You've got to pick every last one by nightfall. Tomorrow you'll peel and core 'em. Day after that you'll be boiling them up for Baltinglass's Famous Homemade Apple and Thyme Jelly. If I had my way you'd be laying eggs for me too, but Justice O'Hooey felt that'd be a bit too much to ask of a young lad, so count yourself lucky."

He shook the old stepladder open as though he were wrestling a crocodile, his cane clamped between his teeth like a hunting knife. "Grab a basket and up you go, lad. I've got blades to polish, and it's time for my gin and tonic. Keeps the malaria away, you know." He leaned toward Miles like a blind turtle and shouted in his face, "If the malaria jumps on my back you'd better run and hide, boy. Tends to make me lose my calm demeanour altogether."

He turned on his heel and disappeared into the gloom of his house. Miles picked up a large wicker basket and climbed the wobbly ladder. It was not the first time he had visited an orchard in his life, and he was something of an expert in twisting apples quickly from their stems. As he filled the basket, his mind worked overtime. What was he to do? He couldn't possibly stay here for three days. Little and the tiger were expecting him back at any moment, and with each passing hour his chances of finding Tangerine were growing slimmer.

He took a good look at the wall that surrounded the garden. It was high and smooth, and topped with nasty-looking spikes that curved inward and looked almost impossible to get over. He could try telling Baltinglass that he was not Rufus Weedle at all, but as the old man was busy polishing his swords, it might not be the best time to interrupt him with this startling news. It was hard to tell if Baltinglass really was mad, or whether this had all been part of Rufus's ruse. His face flushed hot at the thought of the mock salute the chubby chicken thief had given him as Baltinglass slammed his front door. "I'll flatten his nose for him, if ever I see his fat face again," he muttered to himself.

The basket was getting too heavy to hold. He climbed down the ladder and tipped the apples into a large barrel in the corner. Already his right arm and shoulder ached from picking the apples above his head, and it looked as though he had cleared less than a quarter of the first tree. The garden was filled with the drone of bees, but on listening closer he could hear that it was mixed with another sound. It was the sound of snoring, coming from inside the house. He put the basket down quietly and tiptoed to the open doors that led into the drawing room. Baltinglass of Araby sat in a high-backed cane chair, a straight-bladed Chinese sword across his lap and his head nodding onto his chest. His wide mouth hung open like a torn pocket, and long stretched-out snores escaped from it.

Miles stepped over to the barrel and filled his trouser pockets with as many apples as he could stuff into them. He crept back into the drawing room and over to where Baltinglass slumped in his chair. One of his milky eyes was half open, and Miles had to remind himself that it could see nothing. He held his breath and reached for the silver chain that hung around the old man's neck, the one that held the key to the front door. He drew the key as softly as he could from Baltinglass's shirt. His snores didn't falter, and Miles allowed himself to take a breath. He paused for a moment before attempting to slip the chain over Baltinglass's woolly-hatted head. As he lifted the key the old man sprung like a bear trap, and Miles found his wrist caught in a surprisingly hard grip and the sharp tip of the Chinese sword pressed up under his chin.

"Hah!" bellowed Baltinglass, both eyes wide open now and inches from his own. "Thought you could catch me napping, eh, Weedle? I can grab a sand viper as he strikes, boy, and twist his head so he bites his own backside!"

"I didn't think snakes had backsides," said Miles with difficulty. The pressure of the sword in his throat was making him feel sick.

"Ignorance is a wide sea," said Baltinglass, flecks of spittle on his wrinkled lips, "and you're a very small fish." He withdrew the sword and made a grab for Miles's pocket. Two apples fell out and rolled across the dusty floorboards. "Just as I thought," he bellowed. He struggled to his feet without loosening his grip on Miles's wrist. "Not content with pinching all my chickens — first chance you get you're trying to escape with an armload of my apples too. You're a slippery little savage, young Weedle, but you're not slippery enough to escape Baltinglass of Araby. Now give me one good reason why I shouldn't run you through here and now."

Several good reasons flashed through Miles's mind: Justice O'Hooey was one, the mess that would have to be cleared up was another, and there were always the eighteen hundred apples waiting to be jellied. Instead he said simply, "I'm not Rufus Weedle."

"Not Rufus Weedle, eh? Who are you then – the Sheikh of Djibouti? You told me who you were yourself, in case you've forgotten."

"I lied," said Miles, "My real name is Miles Wednesday."

"And I'm the king of the baboons. You'll have to do better than that, my lad." He let go of Miles's wrist, and opened a glass-fronted cabinet in a shadowy corner. He took out a large glass jar and held it out to Miles. "Know what this is, Weedle?" he barked. "This is the finest apple jelly money can buy. You'll find jars of Baltinglass's apple jelly on the tables of all the world's royalty, the ones with any class at least. But it doesn't make itself. It's taken me years to perfect the recipe. One of the miracle ingredients is hard work, and this year you're going to do the hard work for me, whether you like it or not."

Miles took the jar and read the label aloud: "Baltinglass's Famous Homemade Apple and Thyme Jelly. Excellent for fevers and disorders of the intestine, and a fine accompina . . . accompaniment to lamb dishes."

Baltinglass raised his bushy eyebrows in surprise. "Well blow me down! You've been lighting your fires underwater, young Weedle. The judge told me you were as thick as yesterday's porridge and hadn't caught more than a fortnight's schooling in your life. Where'd you learn to read like that?"

"I told you, I'm not Rufus Weedle, I'm Miles Wednesday. A friend of mine called Lady Partridge taught me to read from her encyclopedias."

At this Baltinglass's eyebrows disappeared altogether into his woolly hat, and he dropped his cane with a clatter.

"Lady Partridge? You mean Lady Gertrude Partridge of Larde?" he barked. "How the devil do you know her?"

"I live near her. I once brought her a litter of abandoned kittens, and we became friends," said Miles. "She found out that I couldn't read, so she decided to teach me."

"Well skin me alive and cure me in salt!" said Baltinglass. "You mean to say you've *really* come all the way from Larde? You must be something of an explorer yourself, Master Wednesday. In that case I expect you'll know my nephew too, Radovan Flap."

For a moment Miles could not imagine who he was referring to, then he realised that it must be Constable Flap. His ear could feel the skinny constable's hard pinch at the mere mention of the name.

"Yes, I know Constable Flap." He thought about the nights he had spent locked in the cell at the back of the police station. "In fact I've accepted his hospitality several times."

"Well well, young Miles. It seems we've got off on the

wrong foot altogether. You had better tell me what you're doing here, and why the blazes you would ever want to be Rufus Weedle of Cnoc."

They sat on a rough wooden bench in the sunny orchard, and Miles told Baltinglass of Araby his story, but he was as brief as he could be, and left out many details. He made no mention of the tiger, nor did he say much about Little except that they were searching for a friend of hers, and that Little herself was waiting for him to return with some food so they could continue their journey. When he got to the part where Rufus had tricked him into changing places, Baltinglass snorted in disgust.

"Rufus Weedle, eh? Rufus Weasel, more like!" he said. "I'll say one thing for the little savage, for all his lack of schooling he has an agile mind. He's managed to stitch the two of us up like a pair of ballet slippers. But you're a bold lad, why didn't you just knock on my door and ask for a few apples yourself?"

"Because Rufus told me you might slice me in half with one of your swords."

Baltinglass stroked his stubbly chin. "He's got a point there," he said.

"Do you think I could have a few apples to bring with me?" asked Miles. He had mangaged to eat one as he picked them, but his stomach was still rumbling. Baltinglass leaped to his feet. "By the trousers of the Sphinx!" he bellowed. "Your friend is waiting, and the sands are running on your mission, while we're sitting here nattering in the sun like two old men. Come to think of it, I am an old man, but you've got a fate to catch. By all means take as many apples as you can carry, my boy. You'll find a bag in that cupboard there, and while you're loading it I'll have a rummage in the supply depot and see what else I can provide you with. An ill-equipped explorer is like a camel with no hump. . . ."

Miles took a bag and began to fill it with apples. He took as many as he could fit in.

". . . and only three legs," shouted Baltinglass from the darkness of the house, amidst the clattering of tins and the squeaking of corks in bottles.

He emerged after a while with an assortment of foods – dried sausage, bread, cheese and olives, a jar of his apple jelly and a bottle of elderflower wine. "Open up another one of those bags, my boy, and I'll drop these in. They should keep you going for a while."

"Thank you," said Miles.

"Not at all, not at all. I have a very fine Berber sword I could lend you too, with a hilt of black horn, or a Gurkha knife if that's more your size. Just in case you come across that Weedle lad. He'd get up to no more mischief if he were diced like a carrot."

"I don't think that would be a very good idea," said Miles.

"You don't, eh?" said Baltinglass, sounding slightly disappointed.

"You need him to pick and peel all those apples, for one thing."

"Ah, you've got a point there. I used to do it all myself, you know, but I'm getting a little stiff around the joints for that sort of thing nowadays."

"How did you manage to do it on your own?"

"Well the ladder's not hard to find, my boy. I fall over the blasted thing every day. The trees are always where I left them last, and the apples smell so sweet I can almost see them in front of my face. They have a green smell, Master Wednesday. The greenest smell there is."

He led the way to the front door and unlocked it. Miles stepped out into the empty street, the sack of provisions and the bag of apples slung over his shoulder. He turned and shook Baltinglass's hand. "I'm sorry I lied to you," he said.

The old man wiped a tear from the corner of his eye. "Tactical necessity, my boy. Think nothing of it. I only wish I was able to come with you. My heart is like a swallow in this old rib cage, Master Wednesday. Now you get on with your adventure before it leaves without you, and may good luck dog your heels."

"Thank you," said Miles again. As he hurried down the dusty street toward the olive grove, he heard Baltinglass bellow after him: "And give my regards to Gertrude when you see her. Tell her she could have seen the farthest corners of the world with me, if she hadn't married that benighted fool Partridge."

CHAPTER SIXTEEN

BIG LAUGHING HEAD

Rufus Weedle, sly-eyed and slick-witted, sat in the lee of a haystack boring a hole into one arm of a forked stick. The stick was thick and smooth, cut from a branch of ash with the bark stripped off. With a length of strong elastic it would make a lethal catapult, and woe betide any small bird that showed its beak once he had it finished. He heard someone walking through the hay stubble, and wormed his way quickly back into the haystack, but not quickly enough.

"There you are!" said Miles. "I've been looking for you." He could tell that Rufus was more than a little surprised to see him.

"Looking for me?" said Rufus. His small eyes squinted nervously up at Miles.

"Of course. How else can I give you your share of the apples?" He swung the bulging sack off his shoulder and held it up for Rufus to see.

"But . . . how did you get them?"

It was Miles's turn to act surprised. "Exactly as you said. I collected his eggs for him and he gave me the apples. Gave me lots of other stuff too, but I forgot to ask for another bag to put your share in. Look – my friend is waiting over there in the olive grove. Come over with me, and we'll sort everything into the two bags so you can have one to take home with you."

Rufus stood up and shook the hayseeds from his collar. He looked baffled to find that his tall story had somehow twisted itself into reality, but curiosity had got hold of his devious little mind, and he followed Miles down among the olive trees. They reached the shelter in the stone wall. Miles poked his head into the shadows and said, "It's me. I've brought you some lunch." He stood aside and motioned Rufus in before him.

We will never know who the boy expected to meet in the darkened cave, but it's a safe bet that he was not expecting to find himself face to face with a Bengal tiger. This tiger was staring at him with interest, and he appeared to have already caught a small girl. Rufus let out a sort of whimper, and tried to reverse out of the shadows, but Miles was standing right behind him. He winked at the tiger over Rufus's shoulder, although he was not at all sure that winks worked on tigers.

"Well that's very gracious of you, tub boy," purred the tiger. "It's nice to see you bring back someone with a bit of meat on him for once. I don't suppose you've got any sauce, have you? I do like a bit of relish with a plump boy."

Rufus let out a long moan of fear. His knees had gone wobbly and he had to support himself on the wall with one hand. The apples he had stolen from the tree must have been bad. Not only did the tiger sound like he was talking, but the little girl appeared to be grinning at him.

"I've got some Baltinglass's Famous Homemade Apple and Thyme Jelly," said Miles. "Apparently it's a big favourite with royalty."

"That sounds like just the thing," said the tiger, but at this point the terrified Rufus found his voice.

"A-a-actually, n-now that you mention it, I ha-have to help an old m-man to make some apple j-jelly," he stammered.

"So you do," said Miles. "He mentioned something about that. Eighteen hundred apples' worth, I think he said."

"What a pity," said the tiger. "It's not often we have someone for lunch. Are you quite sure you have to go?"

"P-p-positive," said Rufus. He turned and shoved past Miles, his face drained of colour, and took off at a fast if shaky pace toward the house of Baltinglass of Araby. He didn't once look back.

"I trust he deserved that, whoever he is," said the tiger.

"More than you can imagine," said Miles. "Would you really have eaten him?"

The tiger met his eyes with his cool gaze. "You should not play games with a hungry tiger," he said, "if you care what happens to the players. And now I think we had better get back on the road before the whole village comes out with their best pitchforks."

"You don't have to worry about that," said Miles. "If he does tell anyone, they won't believe a single word."

Miles and Little ate their fill of the food that Baltinglass of Araby had given them. They offered some sausage to the tiger, who looked at it as though it were a rotten egg and politely declined. After washing down their meal with a little elderflower wine, Little wandered out of the shelter, while Miles set about repacking what remained into one sack.

When he stepped out into the sunlight he could see Little sitting in the shade of an olive tree a little way off. She appeared to be talking to a tiny old man with a big nose, his hands clasped behind his back. As he got closer, Miles could see it was not a miniature person at all, but an ancient and bedraggled crow. The bird was almost completely bald, and most of his feathers were gray, as though summers beyond counting had all but bleached the night out of them.

If you have ever heard crow talk, you will know that it sounds like an old witch with a sore throat who has just caught her fingers in a door, and this old crow's voice was hoarser and wheezier than most. Little was speaking to him in his own language, of course, but the sound of her "Crow" couldn't have been more different. She somehow made it almost musical, and unlike the old crow's speech, Miles could get at least a vague sense of what she was saying. He crept forwards slowly, afraid that the old bird might take fright and fly away, but the crow ignored him.

"He says that he knows of a place that he thinks might be the Palace of Laughter," said Little to Miles. "He calls it 'Big Laughing Head', and he says it's in the big city, about two days away as the crow flies."

"Two days?" said Miles in dismay. "That's farther than I thought."

"Are you sure it's that far?" Little asked the crow. He wheezed something, nodding at a tree a few feet away.

"He says it depends on which crow is doing the flying.

He's over twenty years old, and he can barely make it to that tree over there without having a little sleep to recover. He says a young crow would make it in an afternoon."

She turned back to the crow. "Which way is it?" she asked. The bird croaked a long reply.

"He says keep the sun behind and to the left in the afternoon, pass two wooded hills on our right, look for a rock that looks like a three-headed turtle, bear a little to the left and keep going downward until the ground begins to rise. If we reach the old cork tree we've gone too far to the east, and should go back about five hundred paces and bear farther left, heading straight for the hill that looks like it has been cut in half. When we get to the birch woods we should cut through them in a southeasterly direction, crossing two small streams and turning to the right after the second one. When we come out of the woods we will be near the top of a small ridge, and from the top of that ridge you can see the city below. In the middle of it is a wheel that's bigger than the biggest tree, and beside that is Big Laughing Head."

The crow said something else.

"Or we can just follow the road. It goes straight there," said Little.

The bedraggled crow took a couple of hops to one side, and cocked his head as though to see around Little. Miles followed his gaze and saw that the tiger had emerged from

CHAPTER SEVENTEEN
HALFHEADS

Miles Wednesday, saddle-sore and sun-browned, felt the breeze in his tangled hair as the tiger ran on through field and forest. He had become so used to travelling on tigerback that he wondered how he had ever been satisfied with walking. The smooth rhythm of the mighty animal's pace, which was somewhere between running and a sort of long leaping, was hypnotic. Sometimes it seemed as though they were not moving at all, but were suspended over a river of grass and wildflowers that flowed fast beneath their feet. "This must be the next best thing to flying," thought Miles.

"Is this as good as flying?" he asked Little.

She laughed, and looked over her shoulder at him. "This is fun!" she said. "But flying is living."

The hills stretched before them like irregular green waves. They passed a large rounded rock perched near the top of a hill. Smaller outcrops of stone were clustered around its base, and Miles could make out the shape of a tortoise with three heads. "We must be on the right track," he said to Little, but she was lost in thoughts of swooping between the bright clouds, and gave no answer.

As the afternoon wore on, the sky paled and a cold breeze began to blow. The tiger followed the road into a birch wood. They ran through fern and forest, leaping each of the two streams with a single bound. Up ahead Miles could see the trees begin to thin out toward a rocky ridge that was silhouetted against the sky. He knew from the old crow's directions that the city was near, but nothing could have prepared him for the sight that would meet them from the top of the ridge.

Below them the city of Smelt spread across the floor of the valley like a lake of red roofs and tall steeples and grey chimneys and bridges, and stone buildings with more windows than you could count. It seemed to go on forever. A broad river wound through the heart of the city, glinting yellow in the late afternoon sun, and here and there columns of smoke stood like purple pillars, all tilting at the same angle and rising silently into the pale autumn sky.

Miles whistled. "It must be fifty times the size of Larde," he said.

"It certainly smells fifty times as bad," said the tiger, wrinkling his nose. "Not that it's any surprise. Nature never intended any of its creatures to live in boxes with a neighbour at the end of each whisker."

"Look," said Little. "Is that the big wheel that the crow told us about?"

Miles shaded his eyes and looked where she was pointing. Away in the distance he thought he could see a shape like a spoked wheel rising out of the haze and the grey buildings. He could not imagine what it might be for.

"I'm not sure," he said. "We'll have to go down through the city to reach it."

"Then I suggest you start without delay," said the tiger. "The farther you can get before nightfall the better."

Miles felt his stomach fall. "Aren't you coming with us?" he asked.

The tiger shook his massive head. "This is as far as I go, tub boy. From here on, you must rely on your own mettle, and on your little friend's considerable charm."

"But . . . ," said Miles, and stopped. He had known in the back of his mind that the time would come when the tiger would leave them, but the thought of going on without him filled him with dread. He had already lost the comforting feel of Tangerine in his pocket, and now he felt as though some of his own strength and confidence would leave with the tiger and disappear back into the forest.

" . . . couldn't you come with us, if we waited for night to fall?"

"Night or day, it makes no difference," said the tiger. "Cities are not made for tigers, nor tigers for cities, and there's no doubt I would draw unwelcome attention on the streets. Besides, I have other places to be."

"Where will you go?" asked Little, but the tiger gave no answer. He stood a moment longer, looking out over the city below. His nostrils widened and he drew in a deep breath, as though preserving the odour of the city, or perhaps of Miles and Little themselves, for his journey. He turned to look at them. "Now keep your eyes clear and your claws sharp, both of you," he said. "The city is a jungle, by all accounts, though I have more experience of the leafy kind myself. I suspect your journey so far will turn out to have been the easy part."

He turned and padded back towards the forest until he slipped out of sight among the trees, like a dream retreating from the morning sun. Miles felt like a small boy again, exposed on a rocky ridge and about to enter a city that was larger than anything he had imagined, in search of a place he knew nothing about. He looked at Little, who had already begun to slither down the rocky slope into the valley. He knew that when they found Silverpoint she would be leaving him too, but right now she was all he had left, and he pushed thoughts of the future from his mind and called after her, "Wait for me!"

She stopped and waited for him to catch up. "I think we can join the road now," he said. "Genghis must be half a day ahead of us, and like the tiger said, I don't think anyone else will be looking for us here."

They picked their way across the rocky slope until they reached a loop of the road. The road wound down into the valley, and as they walked quickly along it they soon reached the outskirts of the city. There were low square buildings with blind windows on either side that looked like factories, and between them wooden houses with peeling paintwork and sunken steps. On the sides of the buildings were large posters advertising strange things: Type-o-matic Writing Machines, Golden Meadows Rest Home for Elderly Poodles, Cuffe's Shirts of Distinction. They passed several large posters advertising Dr. Tau-Tau's Restorative Tonic. The posters showed ruddy-faced, happy families holding up bottles like the one Miles had fished out of the stream, and laughing as though they hadn't a care in the world. BRING

THE LAUGHTER BACK INTO YOUR LIFE read the slogan, in huge red letters.

There were rails like train tracks that were sunk into the cobbles, running straight down the centre of the road, and a narrow tram with a clanging bell that swung out of a side street and almost ran them over. Here and there were people, walking quickly with heads down, dragging wide-eyed children who stared at Miles and Little as though they had blue skin and horns. Most wore the same expression, tired and slightly sad, that Miles had noticed on the faces of the diners at the Surly Hen.

A little farther on, a small striped tent had been erected over a manhole in the street. Outside the tent a single road-worker warmed his hands at a makeshift stove made from a punctured metal can. Miles felt the warmth from the fire as they drew level with the tent. A wave of weariness crept over him, and he felt a strong urge to curl up inside the warm tent and slip into a dreamless sleep, where all his fears and his tiredness would slip away from him for good. He looked at the man who stood by the tent, but he could not make out his features. It was as if he were looking at someone standing in a patch of twilight, though the rest of the street was lit by the pale afternoon sun.

Miles became aware that Little was saying something to him repeatedly. "Stay awake. Stay awake. Keep walking," she said. She gripped his hand tightly and was almost dragging him along the road. He wanted to turn and ask the man if they could rest in his tent, but Little's voice reached him again through the humming fog in his ears: "Look at me. Stay awake, Miles." He felt as though he were wading through treacle. Little began to sing snatches of some strange tune, a running song. There was a tremor in her voice, but some of the heaviness lifted from his feet and he began to run with her. Their boots clattered on the cobbles, and people stared at them as they ran by.

"Don't look back," said Little. They came to a side street and turned down it without either one saying a word. The road was a short cul-de-sac, ending in a high wall with a pair of rusty iron doors in the middle. The words "Scrap Metal" were painted in clumsy white letters across the doors. They were closed with a heavy padlock and chain, but a smaller door was set into one of them. Miles tried this door and it opened with a push. They stepped inside, and he bolted it behind them.

The junkyard looked like a miniature city of rusting iron, built by a colony of cross-eyed lunatics. It was another world. Every kind of broken-down car and carriage, printing press, machine and motor was piled up in row upon untidy row, with narrow passages running between them, littered with bolts and tires and bottles and pipes. They turned quickly down the first passage, staring up at the piles of silent junk that towered over their heads. At the end they turned left into another passage, and then right into another, trying to keep an idea of their direction. Somewhere above them a large iron wheel broke loose and bounced heavily down the stack before plunging into a muddy puddle, making them jump.

Miles turned to look behind him. The junkyard was deserted. "Who *was* that person . . . ," he began, but Little interrupted him, a determined look on her face.

"What are all these things doing here?" she asked.

"They're scrap," said Miles patiently. "Things that people don't want anymore."

"Can't they make them into something else?"

Miles shrugged. "I suppose they could, but it's easier to throw them away and make new stuff."

"But won't the whole world fill up with these things in the end?"

Miles didn't answer. He had stopped dead at the end of the row and was staring at something that drove the strange figure from his mind. An enormous and oddly familiar-looking machine squatted in a corner of the junkyard. A forest of pipes sprouted from a copper tank that was mounted on the front (or was it the back?), and there were two massive mechanical arms, one ending with a giant pincer and the other in a rusting circular sawblade. Empty sockets gaped where more arms had once been. Pistons, cogs and other spare parts lay scattered around where they had been torn off and discarded. The machine looked strange and silent, like a sober monument to a man of great curiosity – a man who had been killed by his own exploding pudding.

"It's Lord Partridge's big idea!" said Little.

Miles hoisted himself onto the broken caterpillar track and rubbed some of the rust from the nameplate on the machine. "It's Geraldine XIV," he said. "The very one that's in the photo with him." He poked his head into one of the empty arm sockets. "Hello!" he called. He expected nothing back but an echo of his own voice, but instead he saw a blur of movement in the darkness, and something blunt poked him hard in the chest. A wild idea flashed through his mind, that this was Lord Partridge himself, back from the grave and hiding in the ruins of his own creation. He gave a gasp of surprise, lost his footing and fell backward off the track. Before he could get to his feet, a head appeared through the opening. It was not Lord Partridge's head, of course, but that a boy of about Miles's age.

The boy looked down at Miles. "Hello," he said.

Miles stared back. The right half of the boy's head was shaved, leaving a tangle of black hair on the left side with a number of small grey objects knotted into it. He jumped out of the machine and dropped to the ground beside Miles. His clothes were stiff with dirt, and he carried what looked like a large leg bone in one hand. A bandage was wrapped tightly around one end of the bone, to give him a better grip.

"What was that for?" asked Miles, scrambling to his feet.

"What, this?" asked the boy, giving Miles another hard poke with the end of the bone. Miles made a grab for it, but the boy jumped back. "Halfhead challenge is what it is," he said. "What's yours is mine. Empty your pockets or name yer weapon."

"I don't want a fight," said Miles. "We're just passing through."

"We?" said the boy. He turned and looked Little up and down. "Very handy! I'll have her too. Need a new creeper, and there aren't many windows she wouldn't fit through. Chimneys, neither." He turned back to Miles. "You haven't emptied your pockets yet."

"There's nothing in my pockets that you'd want," said Miles, "and I wouldn't give Little to you even if she was mine to give."

The other boy laughed. "You're not from around here, are yeh?" he said. "You look like a peasant to me. Live in a barn, do you, pez? Well you're in Halfhead territory now, and there's no such thing as passing through, so I'll say this one more time. Empty yer pockets or name yer weapon." He jabbed the bone at Miles again, but this time Miles was the one to skip backward.

There was a laugh from behind him. "You're gettin' slow, String. Can't even clobber a pez now!"

Miles turned, keeping half an eye on the boy with the bone. Another boy with a half-shaved head sat on top of the junk pile behind him, and another to his right, and more were appearing from among the scrap with every second. Little moved closer to Miles and away from the newcomers.

"Ten against one's not fair," said Miles.

"You really don't know anything, do you, pez?" said the one called String. "Fights with outsiders is always one-on-one. If you lose, I keep all your stuff and you run as fast as you can until you're off our turf. That's if you can run at all by the time I've finished with you."

"And if I win?" said Miles.

"You don't need to worry about that," said String, "'cause you're not going to win."

"Get on with it, String," shouted the other boy. He also carried a bone, and a scar ran from the corner of his mouth across his left cheek. "You're nattering like an old woman, and I'm getting hungry. I bet the pez has some grub on him."

String turned to answer him, but he never got a chance. The moment his attention shifted, Miles reached out and jerked the bone from his grip. Before String could recover himself, Miles hit him with the bandaged end, knocking him sideways. He jumped on the boy and sat on his back before he could get to his feet.

"Bone!" shouted Miles. "Or should I have named it first?"

String twisted like an eel and tried to sink his crooked teeth into Miles's leg, but Miles pinned him with the bone across the back of his neck. The boy struggled and spat. Miles was just wondering what was considered a win, when a loud clang sounded from above him.

"Twelve seconds," called the boy from the top of the junk pile. He swung his own bone again and hit the end of a metal drum beside him. "Halfhead out, Halfhead in."

"Halfhead out, Halfhead in," repeated the other boys in unison.

String stopped struggling for a moment. Miles got off him cautiously, keeping a wary eye on his opponent and a firm grip on the bone. String got to his feet and spat. "Gimme my bone," he said.

"Not till I'm well out of your reach," said Miles.

"Not then either," said the boy with the scar, clambering down the junk pile. "Bone's yours now, pez, and he knows it."

"I don't want his stinking bone," said Miles. "I just don't want to be hit with it again. He can have it back as soon as we're gone."

"No he can't, pez," said the other boy, "'cause he's not a Halfhead no more. He's out. You're in. Them's the rules, and Halfhead rules don't bend nor break."

"Look," said Miles, "I don't want his place. I just want to get to the Palace of Laughter."

The scar-faced boy looked at him as though he were planning to visit the moon. "Hear that?" he shouted. "Pez thinks he's going to the Palace of Laughter."

The Halfheads roared with laughter, all except String. "Let him go then, Jook," he said sullenly. "Fight wasn't fair anyhow. It don't say in the rules that an outsider can use a Halfhead's bone in a fight."

"It don't say that he can't, neither," said Jook. "Face it, String. The pez fought smarter than you. He's in. You're out."

"Fine," said String. For a moment his tough face crumpled, and he looked on the verge of tears, then it hardened, and he fixed Miles with a look of pure malice. "I'll see you again, pez," he said, and without another word he turned and disappeared down one of the junkyard alleys.

CHAPTER EIGHTEEN

BONEYARD

Miles Wednesday, chest-poked, half-shaved and hungry, sat on a stone slab in a ruined church as a small boy named Henry tied bones into the remaining half of his hair. His scalp was stinging from the razor, and his stomach rumbled. Little sat quietly beside him.

"Toe bones," said Henry. "Least, they're supposed to be, but it's hard to find real toe bones anymore so these are mostly just from back of the butchers." His quick little fingers knotted as he spoke. "Jook, he got real toe bones back in the old days, when there was still bones left in the broken graves. That was before I became Halfhead. There was another Jook then, but he got took by the cops and then they growed him up. Now he's a cop himself. I seen him in his brass buttons and coat, and he's just as mean as the rest now. Meaner even."

As Henry chattered on, Miles tried to think his way out of the situation they found themselves in. They seemed to have escaped the shadowy figure for the time being at least, but it did not look likely that the Halfheads could be persuaded to let them continue on their way. Henry had told him that now that he was Halfhead, any attempt to leave would be considered desertion, which carried a punishment of a week locked in the sheds behind the junkyard. "Not many has tried it," he said, "and no one's ever got away with it neither."

A fire crackled in the centre of the ruined and roofless church, keeping back the twilight. Around the fire sat a dozen Halfhead boys on large stones. Jook, the boy with the scar across his cheek, was eating some of the food that the creepers had stolen from the pantries and kitchens of the big houses on Elm Hill that day, and the others had to wait until he had finished before they would get their share. The creepers were generally the smaller boys, who could fit through narrow windows or scurry unnoticed under tables. Henry was one of them, and when he wasn't being a creeper he was a nonstop talker.

"Boneyard, junkyard, and bullring, them's the three

corners of Halfhead territory. No one passes through here but answers to us. Any Halfhead that catches an outsider has to challenge him. Mostly Halfhead wins, and he gets everything outsider has on him, and runs him to the borders. But if outsider wins, like you did, Halfhead loses his place to outsider. Them's the rules."

Miles said nothing. It seemed the only sure way to escape the gang was to lose a fight with an outsider, but he could hardly wait around until a suitable candidate happened by. Even if the opportunity came quickly and he lost the fight, he was not sure if they would let Little go. "We have to escape tomorrow," he told himself, but he did not want to risk spending a week locked in anyone's shed. They would have to keep their eyes clear and their claws sharp, as the tiger had put it, and wait for the right moment.

"What will happen to String?" asked Miles.

Henry yanked at Miles's hair. "Don't say that name again – it's not allowed," he whispered. "Once Halfhead's gone, he's gone, and his name goes with him."

"But wasn't he your friend?" asked Miles, twisting around to look at Henry's face in the flickering firelight. Henry looked at him defiantly. "Once Halfhead's gone, he's gone," he repeated. "And yer bones are all done, pez."

He jumped down from the stone slab and took his place by the fire. Little leaned in close to Miles and whispered in his ear with a voice that was tiny and clear. "I'm not hungry," she whispered. "Keep them talking. I'm going to take a look around." Miles nodded. "Be careful," he said under his breath, and he got up to join the other boys.

Jook had finished eating, and the food was being passed around. "Sit, pez," said Jook, sucking meat juice from his fingers. Miles could feel his stomach rumble. He looked at the other boys who sat around the fire. They passed the food back and forth – half-eaten chops, apples and onions, stale bread and sausages – and they talked and laughed as they ate, an odd brotherhood of the unwanted and the lost. "In other circumstances," thought Miles, "I could feel at home here." He emptied his own pockets and passed around the half bottle of elderflower wine and what remained of the food that Baltinglass had given him.

Jook took a swig of the wine. He looked at the bottle (although it had no label) and nodded wisely. "Now," he said to Miles, "tell me where you was *really* headed."

"I told you," said Miles to Jook. "We need to get to the Palace of Laughter urgently." The other boys laughed again, but Jook rapped on a stone with his bone, and they fell silent.

"You'd never get near the Palace of Laughter, pez. Why do you want to go there anyways?" asked Jook.

"We lost a friend of ours, and we think he's been taken

there." He did not mention Tangerine. A stuffed bear that could walk would require too much explanation.

"If your friend is in the Palace of Laughter," said Jook, "he won't be the same no more. And like I said, you'll never make it there."

"Well we're not afraid, even if you are," said Little. She had returned from her investigations, and when Miles looked at her she gave her head a tiny shake. "Come on, Miles," she said.

Jook laughed again. "The kid can go if she wants," he said, addressing Miles as though it were he who had spoken, "but you're Halfhead now, and you ain't going nowhere. Besides, the Palace of Laughter is in Stinkers' territory. They'd tear you to pieces."

"Stinkers?" asked Miles. "Who are they?"

Jook turned to Henry and gave him a rap on the head with his bone. "Didn't you learn him nothing, Henry?"

Henry stood up, his cheek stuffed with meat, and began to recite the missing parts of Miles's Halfhead lesson, spitting crumbs of food into the fire as he spoke.

"Halfheads, Gnats, and Stinkers. Them's the three gangs. Halfheads got the yards, Stinkers the bad-egg factories and the fun park, and Gnats got the alleys. Crossing to another territory is a raid; raid means war, war means prisoners, prisoners means Pigball."

"What if I just fought one of the Stinkers, like I did with . . . like I did today?"

Henry swallowed his last mouthful and stood up again. "One-on-one is for outsiders. You're Halfhead now, pez, and if you step into Stinkers' territory, it's a raid. That means they all got a right to fight, no matter if there's one of us or twenty-four. And that means a war, cause no Halfhead gets left to fight solo."

Henry sat down, his speech finished. He yawned and stretched, then settled himself by the embers of the fire. "Sleep before creep," he said. Most of the other boys were curling up in their favourite sleeping spots. Jook produced a small box of blackened wood from his pocket. There were several half-smoked cigars of various thicknesses inside. He selected a fat Havana that had hardly been smoked, and lit it. They sat and watched the slow blue smoke, listening to the crackling of the flames and the hiss of sap bubbling from the firewood.

"That kid your sister?" said Jook after a while, nodding his head at Little as though she were deaf.

"No," said Miles. "She's . . . my friend."

"Friends come and go," said Jook. "You got to get rid of her tomorrow."

"What do you mean, get rid of her?" asked Miles, trying not to sound too alarmed. He glanced at Little, who looked more indignant than worried.

"What do you mean, get rid of me?" she echoed.

"What I say," said Jook to Miles. "There's never been a girl Halfhead, and that's not going to change on my watch. Long as she's here she's using up food, and if it comes to a raid or a war she'll slow us down. Tomorrow you got to run her off the territory. I'll send some of the boys with you, make sure it's done right."

Miles frowned. He did not like Jook's attitude towards Little. He tried to think of how it might be turned to their advantage.

"I thought she was to be used as a creeper," he said.

"Did you?" said the older boy, blowing out a column of smoke and looking sideways at Miles. "And what gave you that idea?"

Miles knew it had been String's suggestion, but he was not about to fall for that one. "She's small and quick," he said, "and she moves without a sound. You know she'd bring more food than she eats."

"I don't know nothing of the sort, pez," said Jook.

"Maybe you could try her out," he said quickly. "You might be surprised." He winked at Little, and she gave him the ghost of a smile. Jook smoked his cigar silently, until Miles began to think his suggestion would simply be ignored. Eventually he took a last pull on the cigar and flicked the butt into the fire, then he reached out with his bone and gave Henry, and another small boy curled up beside him, a sharp poke each.

"Henry. Ignatz. Wake up. Got a job for you," he said. Henry opened his eyes at once, as though he had slept a full night on a feather mattress. The other boy sat up and yawned.

"Time to do your rounds, boys. You're taking the pez's girl with you, see if she's got the makings of a creeper." He turned to Miles. "Not a Halfhead, mind. A creeper."

"You mean right now?" said Miles. His suggestion had been a delaying tactic, and he had not meant Little to be sent out to sneak into sleeping houses before they even had a chance to formulate a plan.

"Why not?" said Jook. "You waiting for her to grow wings and a tail?"

Miles thought that question would be best left unanswered. "Are you sure this is a good night for creeping?" he asked instead. "There's no moon."

Henry laughed. "That's what makes it a perfect night for creeping," he said. "Cloudy sky, and no wind for blowing things about when the windows is opened. Just the night for breakin' in a new creeper."

"Maybe I should go with you," said Miles. Little smiled at him, but in the flickering firelight he could read nothing more in her expression.

"You're too big for creeping, pez," said Jook. "And I don't

fancy having to come and prize you out of a tight window."

Little stepped forward to whisper in Miles's ear. He expected to hear something she had spotted on her brief investigation, but instead she whispered, "Am I really your friend?"

"Of course," said Miles, taken aback. Little nodded. "Then I'll be fine," she said, and she turned and disappeared after Henry and Ignatz into the darkness.

The fire died down, and he moved closer by degrees as the pool of warmth shrank towards the ashes. He pictured Little creeping through the night with the two boys, and all the dangers that might be waiting to ambush her. He chewed his nails, and missed having Tangerine to confide in. Talking to the bear made things clearer in his head. "What now?" he muttered to himself, trying to imagine that Tangerine was listening from his inside pocket, but the only answer was the snoring of small boys, and the faint hissing of the dying fire.

Miles slept fitfully on the hard ground, waking at every sound. The night seemed to drag on forever, but it was still well before dawn when he heard someone dropping from the window onto the broken tiles of the church floor. It was Ignatz, and he was alone and limping, and smelled of something indescribably rotten.

Miles sat up at once, straining for a sound of Little or

Henry. "Where are the others?" he asked Ignatz. "And what happened to you?"

"Got jumped by Stinkers, up near the borders," panted Ignatz. "We was outnumbered, and the other two got taken. They would've got me too, only I can run like a snotty nose."

Miles felt his heart plummet. "We have to go after them," he said.

"No point," said Jook. He and Lob, his lieutenant, had awoken at the sound of Ignatz's return. "They'll be well inside Stinker territory by now."

"You can't just give up on them!" said Miles.

"Course not, pez. Henry's our best creeper. We'll have to win him back at Pigball."

"What exactly *is* Pigball?" asked Miles.

"Pigball's played in the bullring," said Ignatz, who was beginning to get his breath back. "It's real simple. Each team has a big oil drum, up on the top terrace. You got to get the ball into the other team's drum to score. That's all there is to it."

"Then we have to play for both of them," said Miles. "Henry and Little."

"The girl's not Halfhead. Pigball's never played for outsiders, and there's nothing in the rules says they have to give her back," said Jook.

"Rules were made to be broken," said Miles.

"Not our rules, pez," said Jook. "Pigball game starts at midday after prisoners are took, and you're on the team, so you better get some sleep."

"But I've never played before!"

"Don't matter," said Lob. "You won Halfhead's bone, you get his place on the team."

Miles Wednesday, sleepless and ash-dusted, crept through the back lanes in the morning haze with a gang of half-shaved boys. He gripped a leg bone in his right hand, and his breath fogged the air. Thoughts of Little and the upcoming game knotted his stomach. The rest of the Halfheads, by contrast, seemed unconcerned, and most of them had slept through the morning while Miles fidgeted and practised swinging his bone.

Now Ignatz, limping along beside him, was describing how the three creepers had been jumped by a small party of Stinkers as they crawled through a hole in a hedge, close to the border between the territories. He had been felled by a Stinker club, which he described as a sort of stocking with a ball of hard slime in the end of it, and knocked almost senseless. "It's the stench," said Ignatz. "It's worse than the whack itself. That smell would knock you out on its own." He had crawled free of the ensuing scramble, but they were outnumbered, and Henry and Little had been tied up in a matter of seconds. Ignatz (by his own account at least) had managed to land a few blows with his bone, and with his speed and slipperiness he had escaped the Stinkers and run all the way back to the churchyard.

The mist had almost cleared as they reached the bullring, a dozen bone-wielding Halfheads slipping through the broken turnstiles. Miles looked about him as they entered the dilapidated arena. The Stinkers were waiting at the far side. He could just make out Little and Henry sitting on the crumbling stone terraces, guarded by a couple of the larger boys. He waved at her, but he was not sure if she could see him. Besides the Stinkers, a scattering of small long-haired boys sat around the terraces. Some nudged each other and pointed at the Halfheads as they entered. They were mostly barefoot.

Lob grunted. "Gnats is here already," he said.

Three of the Stinkers were crossing the arena toward them, swinging their clubs in their hands. The top halves of their faces were painted black, as though they wore masks over their eyes. Two of them wore kilts, and the smell of rotten eggs preceded them like an invisible tide. Miles fought the impulse to hold his nose. Jook casually lit a cigar, and stepped forward to meet the chief Stinker.

"Got us one of your creeps," said the Stinker in chief through a broken-toothed smile.

"You got two prisoners," said Jook. "We want to play for 'em both." Miles looked at him in surprise, but Jook's eyes were fixed on his opposite number.

"We got one prisoner," said the Stinker, "and a girl that was with 'em. You taking girls in now, Jook? Your boys not tough enough?"

"She's not Halfhead," said Jook, blowing a cloud of thick smoke at the chief Stinker. "She belongs to one of my boys. You can throw her in with my creeper, and we'll say no more about it."

"Finders keepers, even creepers," said the other boy. "She's not Halfhead, like you said, and we don't have to give her back. Might make a good lookout, if her eyes are sharp. We play one game for the creeper. First to three scores. You lose, you got to play for him again next week." He turned on his heel and began to walk away.

"Wait a minute, slime head," said Miles.

The Stinker in chief whipped around and scowled at him through his painted mask. "I don't know your face, squirt," he spat. "And you're not going to know it either, once this game is done."

He turned to Jook. "I'd teach him to keep his mouth shut if I was you."

"Well you're not me," said Jook, "so you can keep your own mouth shut."

"*I'll* play for both of them," interrupted Miles. "The girl and the creeper. Just me against your team."

There was a moment's silence. Halfheads and Stinkers alike stared at Miles in disbelief, then Ignatz slapped his hand to his forehead and groaned, and the Stinkers burst out laughing.

"You've never played Pigball, have you, squirt?" said the Stinker in chief. He stepped forward and stuck out a filthy hand. "You're on. It'll be a short match, but it'll be fun to watch. Better get a wheelbarrow, Jook."

The three Stinkers walked back across the bullring, still chuckling. Jook let out a long stream of smoke, and stubbed out his cigar butt. "I like you, pez," he said, shaking his head. "That's why I stuck my neck out for you. But that's got to be the stupidest idea I've ever heard."

"It's just a game, isn't it?" said Miles. "How bad can it be?"

"Ever been run over by a tram?" laughed Lob.

"It ain't funny," growled Jook. "You'd better give a good account of yourself in the few seconds you're going to last, pez."

"How many are on a team?" asked Miles.

"How many? The whole gang is a team. You'd have to get the ball across the bullring, up the terraces and into their drum, playing against fourteen of 'em, plus the crowd of course."

Miles felt his stomach sink. "The crowd can play as well?"

"They can't leave the terraces, and they can't score," said Jook. "But they can foul whoever they like."

Miles looked around at the scattering of long-haired boys on the terraces. "They all look very small," he said hopefully.

"That's 'cause they're Gnats, pez. None of 'em's more than six or seven. Some of them's not much more than babies. Henry was Gnats, once. When he got too big we took him as a creeper."

"They shouldn't be too much of a problem then," said Miles.

Jook laughed. "Don't count on it, pez. Gnats sting."

"I think you'd better teach me the rules so I can work out a strategy," said Miles.

"No eye gougin'," said Ignatz, scuffing the dirt with the end of his bone.

Miles waited for a moment. "What about the rest of the rules?" he said.

"That's it," said Ignatz. "No eye gougin'. That's the only rule there is."

CHAPTER NINETEEN

PIGBALL

Miles Wednesday, stomach-knotted and hopelessly outnumbered, looked around him at the crumbling arena with its scattering of tiny spectators. He could just make out the rusted oil drum, painted with black and yellow stripes, on the top terrace at the Stinkers' end of the arena. It seemed impossibly far away. The Halfheads had slapped him on the back and left him alone, forming a huddle to exchange bets. The Gnats fidgeted and squinted in the sunlight, and on the far side of the ring, the Stinkers gathered in a dark huddle, from which laughter broke out from time to time.

A Stinker was dispatched from across the bullring.

"You the new face?" he said. Miles nodded. The Stinker produced a tightly bound ball of rags that looked like it was a veteran of many matches. "You understand the game?" he asked.

"I think so," said Miles.

The boy turned and pointed to the arches that ringed the top of the terrace. "See the black an' yellow drum under the bigger arch?" he said. Miles nodded. "That's where you got to put the ball. Your drum is up there." He pointed to another large arch above where the Halfheads were seated. "That's where we got to put it. Usually a game is first to three, but the chief says you only got to score once. An outsider's not worth three scores, and besides, you'll never make it out of your corner." He spat on the ball and held it out for Miles to do the same.

"The rest of you Halfheads is out of this game, by agreement," said the Stinker. "Otherwise all bets is off, and you don't get the outsider, nor your creeper neither." He turned back to Miles. "It was nice knowin' you," he said. "Game starts in three minutes." Halfway across the arena he placed the ball carefully on the ground, and went to rejoin his team.

The sun was high now, and the heat was beginning to rise from the packed dirt of the arena. Miles took off his jacket, but despite the warmth he felt a cold chill down his spine. He thought of the scoop of ice cream he had unwittingly collected while under the benches at the Circus Oscuro. He paused for a moment, then a smile crept across his face. He moved into the centre of the knot of Halfheads and took off his shirt as well. He rolled it into a ball, knotting the sleeves around it as tightly as he could. He put his jacket back on, and stuffed the shirt into his pocket.

Jook was watching him closely from his seat on the terrace. He took half a cigar from his pocket and put it between his lips, unlit. "I'll bet two toe bones on the pez to score," he said. "Any takers?"

"You're on," said Lob, removing the necklace of bones he wore under his shirt. "I say he never gets to the terraces."

"Get ready for the whistle, pez," said Jook. "Your only chance is to get to the ball first."

A moment later a shrill blast on a whistle echoed across the arena, and Miles took off as fast as he could. His seven escape attempts from Pinchbucket House had made a sprinter of him, and he covered the ground like a whippet. The entire Stinker team, with the exception of the two who were guarding the prisoners, was charging towards him from the opposite side, yelling and whooping and whirling their stinking slime-filled stockings over their heads as they came. Miles carried the bone he had inherited from String, but he concentrated on running and left the whooping and whirling to his opponents. It looked like they would reach the ball at the same time, and Miles tried to block out all thoughts of the coming impact from his mind. He was only yards from the ball now — nine, eight, and the leading Stinkers were almost upon him, eyes staring from their blackened faces, seven, six, tongues hanging out as they ran, the smell of bad eggs turning the air before them. He took a last lungful of clean air at three yards and dived for the ball, still holding his bone in one hand, and a second later he was buried under a pile of smelly boys, scrabbling and grabbing for the ball, and flailing wildly with their slimy clubs.

Miles could feel the ball under his chest. He wormed his fingers in among the knotted rags to tighten his grip. He couldn't breathe for the weight on top of him, and with the weight being composed entirely of Stinkers he wasn't sure he wanted to. A knee dug into his back and a bang on the side of his head made his ear sing. The weight shifted, then eased, as the pile of boys toppled over, and with a mighty wriggle he was out from under them and struggling to his feet. A hand gripped his jacket. He swiped with his bone and felt the grip loosen. He lowered his head and charged a couple of Stinkers who stood in his way, knocking one of them over, and he was free and running again.

He could just see the terraces through a film of sweat that was running into his eyes. He leaped onto the first terrace, hoping that he was heading for the right arch. The Stinkers were hot on his heels. One of their slime clubs wrapped itself around his ankle. He tripped and half fell, then recovered his feet and jumped another few terraces, landing among a crowd of Gnats. Too late he remembered that audience participation was a part of the game. He felt a stabbing pain in the back of his leg, then another, and he fell to the stone terrace with a crowd of small boys swarming over him like wasps on spilled jam.

Once again he was at the bottom of the pile, but this time they were mostly Gnats, although his nose told him that more Stinkers were joining the scrum by the second. His bone was snatched from him, and he could hear it clatter down the steps and out of reach. The real ball was wedged underneath him, and with his free arm he rummaged in his pocket for his balled-up shirt. Instead his fingers found his pocketknife. He was nose to nose with a Gnat who could not have been more than four years old, grinning through his long stringy hair. "Fun, ain't it?" said the boy.

Miles produced his knife, and the boy's eyes widened. "You want this knife?" he gasped. The boy nodded. Miles put it back in his pocket with difficulty. He shoved the ball quickly under the other boy's chest. "Take this up to the Stinkers' drum and wait for me," he said. "Then I'll swap the knife for it."

The Pigball pile shifted and heaved. Elbows were jammed in ears, and feet between teeth, and minor fights and scuffles broke out until the heap of boys collapsed outward onto the terraces. Miles seized his chance. He pulled his filthy rolled-up shirt from his pocket and broke out from the scrum, holding the bogus ball tightly under one arm and leaping down the terraces. He took off at a sprint across the ring, straight toward the Halfhead side. He could hear the Stinkers laughing as they chased him. "Hey, Halfwit," one of them called. "Keep going straight. You're going to score."

Three of the fastest Stinkers were right on his heels. A blow from a slime club stung his ear, and he felt his sleeve grabbed. He spun around as he fell. The three Stinkers were on top of him, shoving him into the dirt. "Here, we'll do that for you," laughed one, then they were up and running toward the Halfheads' drum, one of them with Miles's rolled-up shirt clutched under his arm. Miles scrambled to his feet again. He caught a glimpse of the shocked faces of the Halfhead spectators, and flashed them a grin. He turned and ran as fast as he could towards the terraces. He did not make directly for the Stinkers' end, but reached the midpoint, where the terraces were empty, and leaped onto the first step. His lungs were burning, and his legs stung where they had been cut by the Gnats. The laughter of the Stinkers, and the watching Gnats, echoed across the bull-ring. "He's lost the ball," someone shouted. There was more laughter.

"No he ain't," came a shout from up beside the Stinkers' drum. The Gnat had reached his target unnoticed, but he could see that Miles was on the way with the fine knife he had promised him, and he could contain himself no longer.

"It's up here! I got it!" yelled the boy, holding the ball over his head and hopping with excitement. The Halfheads broke into a roar of delight. Miles leaped the next terrace. The heat and the exertion were making him dizzy, and his legs felt like wet string. The chief Stinker was roaring now too, and not for the same reason. "Get after him, you boneheads! Where's your defense? Flatten the Halfbrain!"

Miles looked across at the Stinkers' end. A crowd of them had started up the terraces to cut him off before he could reach their drum. He was making his way around towards them with each step he climbed, but he was still only halfway up, and the top terrace seemed a lifetime away. The Gnat had stopped jumping up and down now. He had stuffed the ball behind him on the step and was looking worried. The Stinkers were whooping and swinging their clubs as they swarmed up the terraces, the black on their faces smeared with sweat. Miles pushed himself up step after step until he felt his lungs would burst. He reached the top terrace and ran on rubbery legs, following the wide curve beneath the colonnade of arches.

It was cooler up here, where the breeze could reach him and the sun could not. Everything seemed to slow down and fall into place. He could see the Stinkers, clambering up to cut him off, and he could see the Gnat with the ball, looking wide-eyed from him to the approaching horde and back again. He could see Little down below, standing on the terrace between her guards, waving both arms in the air and shouting, and most of all he could hear the roar from the Halfheads, a wave of surprise and delight that seemed to carry him the last few yards to the Stinkers' drum without his feet touching the stone. He grabbed the ball from the Gnat's outstretched hands and paused for a moment at the mouth of the oil drum. The Stinkers were two steps below him, mouths wide as they gasped for air, defeat already in their eyes. He held the ball high, and dropped it into the drum. *Thunk!*

His legs gave way from under him, and he collapsed onto the terrace beside his small accomplice.

"So this . . . is . . . Pigball," he panted as he handed over his knife.

The small boy nodded. "Fun, ain't it?" he said.

CHAPTER TWENTY

A NEST OF ANTS

Miles Wednesday, freshly minted Pigball legend, smiled as he was carried shoulder-high by cheering Halfheads down the bullring terraces. The Stinkers waited below in a surly knot, arguing about the outcome of the game. Tempers flared and scuffles broke out. Little and Henry were still under guard on the Stinker terrace. Jook approached the chief Stinker, and the rest of his gang fell silent.

"Halfheads claim the prisoners back," said Jook.

The chief Stinker shook his head. "Stinkers demand a rematch. Spectators aren't allowed to score."

"The Gnat didn't score," said Jook. "You seen it – our pez dropped the ball in the can."

"Maybe so," said the Stinker in chief, "but he played two balls. That's not allowed."

"The way I heard it, that's only not allowed if one of them is an eyeball," said Miles. "Anyhow, I can't help it if your Stinkers are dumb enough to run off with my best Sunday shirt."

Jook laughed. "Pez is right, and you made a deal. Now hand over the prisoners."

"Or else what?" sneered the Stinker in chief. Some of his fighters began to close in behind him.

"Or else the cops will get you," said Miles.

"What are you talking about, farm boy?" said the chief Stinker.

"Big fellas, shiny buttons, just picked up your two guards," said Miles, pointing over the Stinker's shoulder. The Stinker in chief laughed. "You don't expect me . . . ," he began, but he never got to finish his sentence. Miles was gone, his tiredness forgotten, sprinting in a wide arc around the surprised Stinkers toward the Stinker terraces, where two policemen were hauling Little's guards roughly up the stone steps. Another large meat-faced man made a lunge at Little herself, but she ducked between his legs and jumped down the last three terraces, almost landing on top of Miles as he reached the bottom step.

"Miles!" she said. "You were brilliant!"

"No time for that." Miles grinned. "Here's our chance. Let's get out of here."

The police were streaming out from under the arches and cantering awkwardly down the terraces. They had managed to catch a couple of Gnats by surprise, though the small boys were mostly too quick for them. The arena was suddenly like an ant's nest that had been poked with a stick. Halfheads and Stinkers ran in every direction, pursued by police blowing whistles and shouting – now that the element of surprise had passed – about burglary and painted 'ooliganism, and grabbing whoever they could get their hands on.

Miles took Little's hand and ran towards the mouth of a narrow alley between the terraces. He stooped to grab his discarded bone on the way, and shoved it into his belt. They ran down the alley, through which angry bulls had once charged, rubbing the walls smooth with their coarse flanks and trampling the earth iron-hard beneath their hooves. At the end of the alley their way was blocked by a tall iron gate, topped with curved spikes.

"It's too high," said Little.

"Not for you," said Miles. "You've got wings."

Little shook her head. "I won't go without you." She seemed almost surprised to hear herself say this, but before Miles could answer he felt his ankle grabbed by a small hand, and he looked down in surprise to see Henry's head poking out from a small semicircular window in the alley wall, just above ground level.

"Sssssh," said Henry. "They'll hear you. Get inside!" He disappeared back into the hole, and before Miles could say anything, Little was wriggling in after him. Miles was not sure he would fit, but the pounding footsteps of a heavy man on the terrace above made him drop down and squeeze through the narrow opening, and at the cost of a couple of buttons he was soon crouched in the dank darkness with Little and Henry.

Before long they could see a parade of boots and bare feet passing by the semicircular window. There was a loud clang and the squeal of rusty hinges as the police forced the iron gate open and marched their captives outside and into the waiting vans. The three fugitives huddled in their small cell without daring to whisper.

Some time after all the police boots had passed, and the sound of the departing vans had faded away, they saw the feet of two boys running quietly down the alley towards the gate. There was a rusty screech as they forced the old gate open slightly, then moments later they heard a man's voice shout, "Two more there, Tom," and the sound of a brief struggle, then silence.

"They've left sentries," whispered Henry.

Miles looked about him, but they were in pitch darkness.

"There's no other way out," whispered Henry. "I checked. There's one door, and it's locked. We'll have to wait till the night."

Miles put his head in his hands. His felt bruised and numb and his knees ached from crouching. He would have liked to sit down, but the floor felt slimy under his feet. He patted his pocket from force of habit, as though Tangerine might have magically reappeared, but his pocket was empty. He had had enough of waiting.

"Can't we get back out through the bullring?" he asked.

"Too risky," whispered Henry. "There'll be men on the terraces too, for sure."

"What's outside the gate?" said Miles.

"Cops," said Henry.

"Apart from them," said Miles. "What if we can get past them?"

"I know a way down to the canal," said Henry after a moment. "There's an old pipe. If we can get from the gate to the pipe without being seen, we might get away."

Miles felt impatience rising up inside him. "Let's go then," he said. He poked his head cautiously out through the window. There was no one to be seen in either direction, and he hoisted himself out onto the alley floor. He turned to give Little a hand up, but she was already beside him. He got to his feet and crept along silently to where the gate stood ajar, and peered cautiously through the gap, being careful not to open the noisy gate any farther.

A single police van stood nearby, facing away down the rutted road that circled the bullring. The back doors were locked, and he could see one of the policemen in the cab, pouring himself a steaming drink from a tartan thermos flask.

Miles turned to Henry. "You first," he whispered.

Henry slipped through the gate, silent as a fox, and ran swiftly through the tall weeds in the opposite direction to where the van was parked, with Miles and Little following close behind.

A large concrete pipe ran half buried among the weeds. A little way along it there was a gaping hole where the concrete was broken, and Henry stuck his head in to take a look, before dropping down into the pipe. It had not carried water for a long time. There was a layer of dried silt underfoot, and light filtered in through frequent cracks and holes. They moved rapidly and quietly in the dim light, the pipe sloping gently downward. After a couple of minutes they saw a circle of light ahead, which grew steadily larger as they approached. Henry stopped when he reached the end, and peered out cautiously in both directions. The pipe opened onto the canal, which too was almost dry, with just a thin channel of green water meandering along the mud bottom.

"Where are we?" asked Little.

"Gnats territory," whispered Henry. "I reckon it's safe enough, them being distracted by the cops, but it wouldn't do to get caught here all the same."

"Why are we going this way?" asked Miles.

"I'm taking you to the fun park," said Henry. "That's where you want to go, isn't it – to the Palace of Laughter?"

"Yes," said Miles, "but I thought that was in Stinkers' territory."

Henry nodded. "It is, but this is the best way from here. If we stick to the canal, it'll take us all the way along to the fun park. Used to be a hole in the fence there. If it hasn't been closed up you can get through into the park, and once you're in there you're in Stinkers' territory. I owe you that much for takin' on the whole Stinker team for us, but from there you'll be on your own. Fun park's not a place I'd go to for fun, if you see what I mean."

They dropped from the pipe onto the dried canal bed, and ran along as quickly and soundlessly as they could, keeping close to the stone wall.

"Do you think they'll be all right, the rest of them?" asked Miles as they made their way quickly along the canal bed.

Henry shrugged. "There was lots of cops. More than I ever seen. I reckon someone must've tipped them off."

"What will happen to the boys they caught?"

"They'll try to put 'em in reform school and grow 'em up. Reform school couldn't hold a Halfhead though, not if he wanted to escape."

"How will you get back to the boneyard?" asked Little. She never seemed to tire, and her feet left no mark on the soft mud of the canal bed.

"I know lots of ways that others don't," said Henry. "Been a creeper for nearly two years now, an' Jook says I'm the best he can remember. This whole town's full of holes, like a big cheese, and I reckon I know most of 'em."

The canal took a shallow right turn, and the shape of the big wheel came into view ahead. It was strange and still, like a thick spiderweb nailed to the sky by its rusting cars.

"The fun park," said Henry. He looked nervous. "That big wheel is the Stinkers' HQ. If they catch you, they'll put you right up in the top car for three whole days, no food and nothing to drink but the rain puddles on the floor." He shivered. "Ignatz says people used to pay money to go up on it in the olden days, but I don't believe that."

As they trotted along the canal bed, Miles felt his boots grow heavier with the mud they were collecting. His stomach formed into a knot. He slowed to a walk, letting Henry draw ahead. The sky was beginning to cloud over, bringing a cold wind that whistled along the canal. The wheel grew bigger and bigger as they approached, until it seemed to half fill the sky. Its metal spokes were as thick as tree trunks, and the cars squeaked as they swung in the breeze, rust speckling their faded paint like a brown disease.

Through the spokes of the big wheel he could see a strangely shaped hill looming. In the haze it looked like an enormous head, facing away from them over the outskirts of the city. He remembered the old crow's name for the Palace of Laughter – "Big Laughing Head" – and he knew that this must be the place. It was not as he had pictured it back in Larde, a theatre overflowing with laughter and light. Jook had said that anyone who went in would never come out the same, and now that he could see the menacing outline of the place, Miles found it easier to believe.

"That must be the place," whispered Little. "I don't like the look of it."

Miles took her hand and squeezed it. "It'll be okay," he said.

"You don't have to come with me," said Little. "Silverpoint will know where to look for Tangerine." She laughed. "Though I'll be in trouble for singing his name out."

Miles looked at her in surprise. Rain had washed most of the soot from her hair, leaving it dirty white and tangled.

She smiled up at him, but her eyes seemed to be searching his face for clues.

"I do strange things, remember?" he said. Little nodded. She looked relieved.

"Ssssh!" whispered Henry, who had stopped in front of them. "This is it," he said, almost inaudibly. They were right below the corner of the fence that enclosed the fun park now.

Miles could not see any gap. "Where's the way in?" he whispered.

"There's a hole in the fence behind those bushes," said Henry. "I'll show you which one, then I'm off." He scanned the length of the fence, a small frown of concentration on his grubby face. There was no one to be seen. "Now," said Henry. They climbed up onto the canal bank, and Henry crept along the narrow space between the fence and the bushes that grew beside it, until he came to a place where the wire had been cut. He pulled the broken fence outward and wriggled through the gap. Miles and Little waited, holding their breath. Henry turned and beckoned to them from the shelter of a pile of old tyres, painted in different colours. "Quick," he hissed. Little went through next, and Miles followed, squeezing himself with difficulty through the small hole.

Henry crawled around to the other side of the pile of

tyres. "This is as far as I go," he whispered. "Stinkers can see the whole park from up in that wheel," he said, "so you need to keep out of sight." He pointed to two long rows of old canvas-covered stalls that started near where they crouched, and ran along beneath the wheel towards the looming head. "You can get inside the back of the stalls and run the whole length of them. If you keep under the canvas you'll be out of sight most of the way, then you'll just have to run across the open space till you get to the Palace of Laughter. I don't know how you'll get in there, 'cause I never heard of anyone who's done it, not even Stinkers."

"Don't know why you'd want to either," said a voice behind them. They spun around in unison like startled fish. A boy sat by the gap in the fence, a stem of grass dangling from his lips. What little hair was left on his shaved head was tied up in a topknot, and a black mask was painted across his eyes. He appeared to be on his own. The boy spat out the grass stem and grinned. There was something familiar about him. "Is this a scoutin' party," he asked, "or is it the whole invasion force?"

"That you, String?" said Henry nervously.

The boy's grin widened. "You look worried, Henry," he said. "I'm not going to eat you."

"I was just leavin' anyway," said Henry. He looked around him. "Where's the rest of 'em?"

"My new brothers? The slower ones is in the police cells, waitin' to be reformed. The rest of them is waitin' in ambush down by the railway yards. I told them Halfheads was plannin' a raid along the railway line, but I knew you'd more likely come this way, 'cause I knew you'd most likely be doin' the scoutin', Henry. And being an old Gnat, I reckoned you'd probably come sneakin' up the canal. Looks like I was right too."

"What are you doing here then?" asked Miles.

String's eyes narrowed behind their mask, and his grin faded. "I'm here to help you get where you're goin', pez. You'd have no chance of crossin' this territory without me."

"Why would you do that?" Miles asked suspiciously.

"Firstly, 'cause I don't like you," said String. "And if you're dim enough to want to be swallowed up by that madhouse, I'm only too pleased to help. If you do get in, you'll never come out the same."

Miles said nothing. He had heard that phrase too many times for his liking.

"And secondly," continued String, "when you and your little creeper is safely tucked up in the giant's mouth, me an' Henry here are going back to Halfhead territory, and with you gone I'll get my rightful place back."

"They'll never let you back in! Halfhead's gone, he's

gone," said Henry. "'Specially since you joined up with the Stinkers. Anyway, like I said, I was just leavin'."

String leaned over and pulled back the fence. "Off you go then, Henry. The Gnats is just returning from the bull-ring. I can see a swarm of 'em coming up the canal, and they don't look very happy. Mustn't have been much of a game, eh?" He let the fence swing shut, and grinned. "Look, Henry, it's me, String. We've always been mates, you and me." He glanced at Miles. "The pez, he cheated me, and he's not one of us. Never will be."

Henry looked away, fidgeting with a frayed bootlace. String got to his feet, and the sly grin returned to his face. "I know Jook will see sense on this, 'specially when I tell him what I've learned about the Stinkers. They're not so careful with their secrets once you pretend to join up with 'em.

"Now we'll have to move fast if you want to get over to the Palace of Laughter before sunset. That's when the doors open, and they shut again soon as all the people are inside. If you miss 'em today, you won't get another chance till tomorrow at the earliest, and they don't have a show every day, so I'm told."

Miles stood cautiously and looked around, half expect-ing to find himself surrounded by Stinkers. The park seemed deserted.

"Don't trust me, eh, pez?" said String. "Very smart. You might've made a good Halfhead, eventually. But you're not thinking it through. If I let Stinkers get you, they'll just trade you back at Pigball – after a few nights on the sky wheel – and I'd be stuck in this freaky place with these blackfaced animals for good, wouldn't I?"

He turned and trotted across the short stretch of cracked concrete to the first row of stalls with their faded canvas awnings. He turned and beckoned to them, then he ducked under the loose canvas.

"What do you think?" said Miles.

"I don't know," said Little. "He sings out of tune."

"What about you, Henry?" said Miles. "You know him better. Can we trust him?"

Henry looked uncomfortable. Things were simple once you followed Halfhead rules, but this was outside their scope. The rules said that once a Halfhead was out, he should never be mentioned again, but they didn't say what to do if you met an ex-Halfhead in foreign territory who had pretended to join another gang but wanted to gain back the Halfhead place that he believed he was cheated out of in the first place. Besides, he had known String for a long time, and he'd only known Miles and Little for one day. And Little was a girl, but then, he liked her. And Miles was a Pigball hero. His head spun with all the details. He looked nervously over his shoulder, as though he expected to see Gnats swarming through the hole in the fence.

"I don't know about singin'," he said finally, "but I don't see what choice we got. He's goin' the same way I suggested anyway. I think we should go with him."

Miles looked across at the gap in the canvas through which String had disappeared. A stiff breeze was blowing dark purple clouds across the reddening sky, and the sun was close to the horizon. "Let's go then," he said.

Henry laid a hand on his arm. "Wait," he whispered. "Creeper goes first."

Henry took off, running at a crouch. He was almost as soundless as Little. He did not make directly for the near end of the stalls, where String had disappeared, but ran swiftly along between the two rows until he had reached the third or fourth stall. Here he dropped to his knees, lifted the canvas and peered underneath. He poked his head inside, then quickly withdrew it, but not quickly enough. Several pairs of hands reached out from under the stall and grabbed the small boy. He just had time to shout "Ambush!" before a rag was stuffed into his mouth and he was dragged in under the canvas.

"Run!" said Miles. He took Little's hand and they ran along the alley between the stalls, straight towards the Stinker ambush. There was no point in going any other way.

They were too close to the Palace of Laughter to turn back now, and behind them there were only Halfheads and Gnats. Dozens of Stinkers were wriggling out from under the stalls, their eyes white in their black masks and their putrid clubs in their hands. Miles leaped high over the crawling boys. "I've outrun them before," he thought, "and I can do it again." Little hung on to his hand, and though her wings were hidden away her feet barely touched the ground.

As he ran, Miles felt a sick feeling in his stomach at the thought of leaving Henry to his fate, perched in the sky for three days and drinking rusty water. He hoped that Henry had the story wrong, or that he would somehow manage to escape, but there was no more time to think of this now. As they neared the end of the stalls, a Stinker stepped out in front of them, and in the blur of movement Miles recognised String's sly leer. String was pointing at him with one hand, beckoning the converging Stinkers with the other. "That's him," he shouted. "He's the one that brought the cops on us! I seen him—"

But that was as much as he got to say. Miles had pulled the bone from his belt, and was holding it out in front of him as he ran full tilt towards String. "Here's your bone back," he said, as it dawned on String's face that he had no intention of stopping. The gnarled end of the bone met its original owner square in the chest, and with a gasp of shock the winded boy went down, and Miles and Little leaped over him without breaking their stride.

The big wheel loomed directly over them now. They ran past its gigantic metal feet, fixed to the ground with bolts the size of a man's head. A swarm of painted boys clambered down the wheel with the practice of spiders in a web and dropped to the ground. The Palace of Laughter towered ahead of them, even bigger than Miles had imagined. For the first time he could see it clearly, and it was by far the strangest of all the strange things he had seen since the night the Circus Oscuro arrived in Larde.

Imagine an enormous clown, as tall as a mountain, wading through solid earth up to his chin. If you can picture such a thing at all, you may have some idea what the Palace of Laughter looked like. It was a large, domed hill, carved into the shape of a giant clown's head. His great stone eyes bulged from their sockets and his blue-lipped mouth was frozen in a huge laugh. Set into the open mouth was a pair of huge wooden doors. The crown of the hill was bald and smooth, with a fringe of cedar trees sprouting like fuzzy green hair above the enormous carved ears. Around the hill lay a moat of greenish water, crossed by a drawbridge that looked like a huge wooden tongue.

They ran towards this strange hill, the boy and the angel,

with no idea of how they would get in, indeed with no thought in their heads but to escape the top-knotted, club-wielding army that was hot on their heels. Just before the drawbridge stood an abandoned ticket booth. Miles headed for it instinctively, though it was hard to imagine what protection the dilapidated hut with its glassless windows could offer them.

As they reached the booth and began to scramble through the window, the sound of a great gong rang out from somewhere inside the hill. The enormous wooden doors swung inward, and a moment later a troupe of tumblers and stilt walkers emerged onto the drawbridge, blowing whistles and tooting horns. There were three tiny men in top hats, with whitened faces and each wearing a different-coloured nose. They cartwheeled across the wooden tongue of the drawbridge without losing their hats, followed by two men on stilts so tall that they had to duck to avoid the stone teeth as they left the giant mouth. After them came a number of other clowns, some banging drums and others waving firecrackers on sticks above their heads, and the whole motley procession marched along the cracked concrete path, past the booth in which Miles and Little crouched, towards the wrought-iron gates of the park entrance.

Miles peered back the way they had come, through a

crack in the boards. The Stinkers had melted away at the approach of the crowd. It was as though the park, which a moment ago had been swarming with angry boys, was empty but for Miles and Little, and the strange parade that passed before them on its way to the gates of the fun park.

When they reached the gates the stilt walkers unlocked them and swung them open, and a crowd of people surged in from the street outside, led by none other than Baumella the giantess herself. The clowns and stilt walkers turned and fell in on either side, playing their chaotic music and cartwheeling along beside the people, who shuffled towards the great clown's head as though they had just had a long journey and an uncomfortable night, which indeed they had.

Miles and Little crouched, panting, on the floor of the empty booth, listening to the approach of many feet and the babble of voices belonging to people who were more used to giving their own opinions than listening to other people's. They seemed to have plenty of complaints to get off their chests, and the cheerful tooting and banging of the clowns was having little effect on their mood. Miles could hear snatches of their conversations as the visitors passed close to their hiding place.

"They could have laid on a coach from the hotel, instead of making us walk."

"Hotel, you call it? I'd have swam through thin porridge in me undies to get out of that flea pit, myself."

"Maybe you would, Thacker, but I'd still have liked to be brung on a coach."

"Get on! You've been sitting on your fat behind for the best part of two days. Last thing you need is to sit down some more."

"It's all right for you. I'm a martyr to the gout, and me ankles is still ballooned up with sittin' in that stuffy train."

Whatever Thacker had to say on the topic of gout was lost in the babble of voices as the crowd flowed past. The names were unfamiliar to Miles, but the voices might just as well have belonged to the citizens of his hometown. It seemed that half the population of Iota or Shallowford or Frappe had spent two days and a night cheek by jowl, crawling through the countryside on a crowded train and shacked up in a cheap hotel on the promise of a night of laughter such as they had never seen before. It was a wonder they had not strangled one another.

"I tell you what," said a woman's voice, its owner tottering past on a pair of high heels that were not made for walking on cracked concrete, or for swimming in thin porridge for that matter. "This show had better be as good as it's cracked up to be, or I'll be wanting my money back."

"We didn't pay any money, dear. We won these tickets," said her husband.

The woman snorted. "Us and half the town. It's not a very exclusive prize, is it?"

"Well, you can't expect it to be, if it ain't cost nothing."

"*Didn't* cost nothing, William. You'll never amount to nothing if you don't learn to talk properly."

And so it went on, a parade of grumbling people, tired from a journey that was twice as long as they had expected, and all on the promise of shining a little laughter on the greyness of their lives. The drums and bugles and the sound of footsteps passed by, and Miles risked another look out the window. Baumella had reached the wooden doors, and stood to one side to usher the people in. They straggled onto the drawbridge behind her and began to crowd their way in through the doors.

Miles watched carefully the progress of the crowd. Their only chance would be to try and sneak in at the tail end, just before the doors closed again. They would have to time it just right. The lucky silver-ticket winners were ten deep on the wooden drawbridge, which was fortunately made of very stout oak planks. Many of them were fonder of beer and pastries and pies than was good for them, and had the bridge not been made of such sturdy stuff they might well have found themselves in the moat instead.

As it was, there was a good deal of elbowing and shoving, and those who had not reached their full quota of grumbling earlier were taking the opportunity to squeeze a few more complaints out while they pushed their way inside. It was a strange sight to be sure: an enormous clown's head with green cedar hair and mossy cheeks, its vast stone eyeballs staring out over the city as a long snake of people fed itself into its cavernous mouth. They reminded Miles vaguely of a dream he had had, and not for the first time he wondered what he was doing, far from home and without his Tangerine, staring into the mouth of a nightmare with a four-hundred-year-old girl.

The music of a hurdy-gurdy spilled out from between the stone teeth, mixing with the chaotic sounds the clowns were making. Silver tickets were waved in the air, but no one seemed to be collecting them, and the crowd surged into the mysterious hill without a backward glance, until the last few stragglers were swallowed up and the mighty doors began slowly to swing shut.

CHAPTER TWENTY-ONE

A MOUTHFUL OF NAILS

Baumella the giantess, straight-boned and tree-tall, began to swing the great oak doors shut after the last few people had entered the Palace of Laughter. She had spotted the two little maggots hiding in the ticket booth, yes she had, but she said nothing to anyone. She saw that one of them was the tiny girl she had looked after at the circus, and she guessed that the other might have had a hand in her disappearance. She was surprised to see them here, skulking around the Palace, and rather impressed that they had made it this far. Had they run all the way on their tiny legs? The great doors creaked as they swung closer to each other, and through the narrowing gap she could see the two little ones break cover and run for the drawbridge. They were persistent wee creatures!

She knew they could not see her in the gloom behind the doors, and she chuckled quietly. "I won't turn you in, little maggots, but I won't make it easy for you either," she thought. As they reached the drawbridge, she closed the doors – *kerlunk!* – and smiled to herself. "Let's see what you do now, little ones." She turned to the tall pillars, as cool and unbending as herself, and hauling a large chair from the shadows between them, sat herself down with her back to the great wooden doors.

Miles and Little almost ran full tilt into the hobnail-studded doors. They appeared to have been closing slowly by themselves, and Miles had timed his run to get in at the last possible moment. But they had shut more quickly at the end, or he had misjudged the distance, and now it was too late. He stood with his hands flat on the doors and pushed them with all his strength, but he may as well have been pushing at solid rock. A few flakes of yellowing paint drifted down from the huge stone teeth that lined the top of the doorway. Above the teeth stretched the faded blue lip of the laughing mouth, and above the lip a nose, with its two enormous nostrils like bear caves, jutted out into the sky. Ragged clouds raced over the clown's head, making it look as though the hill were gradually toppling forward.

Miles felt dizzy. He became aware of a deep rumbling sound that seemed to be coming from inside the hill.

"There's thunder trapped in the hill," said Little. She pressed her ear to the doors, and Miles did the same. He could hear the sound more clearly now, a grinding of gears with a regular squeak running through it. Now the ground beneath their feet seemed to be tilting upward. For a moment he thought it was just the dizziness, then he realised what was happening.

"The drawbridge," he shouted. They turned and began to scramble up the wooden tongue, which was rising rapidly, getting steeper by the second. The surface was worn smooth by years of shuffling feet, making it hard to get a grip. By the time they made it to the top, the drawbridge was almost upright. Miles could see that Little was trying to shake her jacket and shirt off her shoulders when the drawbridge stopped with a mighty jolt. He barely managed to keep his balance, but Little, with one wing partly freed, tumbled from the top of the wooden tongue, down into the murky green water of the moat.

Miles hung on for a few seconds, expecting to see Little's head appear above the water. He could see a faint whiteness moving in the moat, caught in the tangled reflection of the big wheel, but she did not surface. He took a deep breath, and jumped in after her.

If you've ever been thrown into a river or a pool by someone bigger and meaner than you, you will know how it feels to be plunged into water against your will. There is the shock of the cold, and the muffled rumble of water in your ears, and a feeling that you should have had the right to choose for yourself when you are dunked into water and when you would rather remain on dry land.

This was exactly how Miles felt as he somersaulted slowly in the moat. His ears were filled with muffled sounds, and he could not tell which way was up. He forced his eyes to open. He was in a swaying underwater forest, and he could just make out the white of Little's skin among the weeds. He righted himself and swam towards her. The oversized jacket that she had been trying to shrug off when she fell had wrapped itself around her at the elbows, and her left foot was tangled in the thick stems of the weeds. She stopped struggling when she saw Miles, and looked at him with wide eyes. He felt that his lungs would burst with the air he was trying to keep in, but there was no time to get to the surface to take a breath. He reached for his knife, then remembered that he had given it to the small boy at the Pigball match. He grabbed the weeds that were wrapped around Little's ankle as near to the roots as he could, and pulled.

The roots of the weeds were tough and the stems slimy,

and they seemed to wriggle out of his grasp as though they had a life of their own. He managed to uproot some of them, and grabbed at the remaining handful. He looked up at Little's face, half afraid that he was too late. He knew that he would have to get to the surface within the next few seconds himself, or take in a lungful of murky moat water. Snowflake patterns were fizzing at the corners of his vision, and through them he could see Little, her mouth slightly open, and her stare becoming fixed. Without stopping his frantic tugging, he glanced over his shoulder in the direction of her stare, and immediately wished he hadn't.

An ugly grey-green face was staring at him from among the weeds, a face with bulging eyes, fat lips and a miserable mouthful of sharp nails. It was an enormous pike, barely an arm's length away. Now a pike is a fish best seen at the end of a long fishing line, or not at all, and certainly not when you are trying to unwrap river weeds from the ankle of a drowning friend and your next breath is long overdue. This particular fish was enormous, mean and constantly hungry. He had spent many years fattening himself on the other citizens of the moat, and he was not used to meeting anything in the water that he could not bite in half with ease. The struggling Little had caught his eye as a particularly tasty dinner, and he was not pleased that Miles had got in his way. The shock of seeing him made Miles lose his lungful of stale air in a rush of bubbles. "I've got to get to the surface now," he thought desperately, and at that moment the stubborn weeds gave way and he grabbed a handful of Little's shirt and kicked hard against the slimy floor of the moat, up toward the light.

Miles Wednesday, weed-wrapped and waterlogged, held on to a ledge of rock at the edge of the moat. As he choked and spat, he felt Little pull free from his grasp and hoist herself onto the rock. He was afraid that the pike would take a chunk out of his leg, but he did not have the strength to pull himself up beside her. When he had cleared out all the moat water from his mouth and nose, he realised that Little was smiling down at him as though nothing had happened. She reached out a hand and helped him climb out of the water.

"You can't breathe when you're underwater, can you?" asked Little.

"Of course not!" coughed Miles. "Can you?"

"Yes, but it's not very nice. It's a bit like being in the middle of a cloud, but much thicker."

"You mean I nearly drowned getting you free and you could breathe all along?"

"Yes, I could breathe. But if you hadn't freed me from the weeds that big fish would have bitten me in half before

I could find his name, and anyway I'm not sure if I could sing it underwater."

Miles leaned back against the rock face and spat out more scummy water. Now that he had recovered he could see that they had come up on the inside bank of the moat and were leaning against the gigantic cheek of the clown-shaped hill. They were on a narrow ledge, barely wide enough to lie down on, which was exactly what he wanted to do. There was still no sign of the Stinkers.

"Do you think they're gone?" asked Little, following his gaze.

"I can't see them," said Miles. "Maybe they think we drowned." He lay back and looked up at the twilit sky. "I just need to rest for a minute, then we'll figure out a way to get back across the moat."

"I could fly over, since there's no one in sight," said Little. "But my wings wouldn't carry you. Besides, why do we need to cross the moat when we want to get inside the hill, and not back on the Stinkers' side?"

"Because we can't get to the door from here," said Miles. "The ledge doesn't go around far enough." He watched the small black shapes of a number of bats darting about in erratic circles against the sky, feeding on the insects swarming around the trees that fringed the clown's giant ear. Some of the bats seemed to be flying in and out of the ear itself.

"It must be where they roost," he thought. There seemed to be more of them coming out than going in. A sudden thought struck him, and he sat up. "On the other hand," he said, "maybe we should have a word in this clown's ear."

Little looked up at the ear for a minute. "It's a long way up," she said.

"It is, but it might be a way in. If it is, it will be better than trying to get through the doors unnoticed."

He stood up and examined the sheer wall of rock in front of him. The rock was relatively smooth, but here and there were small cracks and fissures, and in places tufts of heather grew from them, as though the clown were not very good at shaving. Little took a careful look around, then she removed her jacket and shirt, and tied them by their sleeves around her waist. She still wore the sparkly circus costume underneath. "You never know when it might come in handy, my dear," Lady Partridge had said.

"I'll fly up ahead of you and find the best way to climb," said Little.

Miles looked doubtful. "I'm not sure that's a good idea. Someone might see you." His eyes scanned the sagging stalls and the boarded buildings of the old fun park, but it seemed that the Stinkers had vanished into thin air. "I can't see anyone," he said at length, "but you'd better be careful."

Little nodded. She gave her shoulders a little shake, and

her wings unfolded with a flutter. They were a beautiful pearly pink in the sunset, and to his surprise Miles felt his heart leap at the sight of them. He had not seen her fly since that night in the circus, and he watched with fascination, and a little envy, as she lifted from the ledge like thistle-down and rose above his head. It must have felt good to be flying once again, and she let out a musical laugh as she soared up towards the giant ear, scanning the rock for a path that Miles could take.

Miles sighed, and began to climb. "Come on, slowcloud," said Little, swooping back down towards him. "Go to the right here – there's a place for your feet, and those plants just above you will hold your weight." He grabbed the tuft of heather and hauled himself up. There were not many toeholds, and for some time he inched his way up the rock with his clawed fingers and the tips of his boots. The moat was a long way below him now, but as he neared the top of the clown's fat cheek, it began to slope inward a little more. He could see the huge earlobe almost level with him, and he edged slowly to his right until he could reach it. As he scrambled into the ear's hollow one of his bootlaces snapped and the boot made a break for freedom, bouncing off the stone cheek as it tumbled downwards, and finally kicking off a sharp point of rock and splashing into the dark waters of the moat below.

Miles sat in the huge ear, which was smooth and hollow and comfortable, waiting for his breath to return. He unlaced his other boot with his bleeding fingers, and tossed it after its twin. He was about level with the hub of the big wheel. A small knot of figures was inching up one of the spokes. It looked like two of the Stinkers, carrying Henry between them as they climbed. They were too far away for him to see clearly, and with their backs turned, it was not likely they would see Little. He called to her urgently nonetheless, and she fluttered down beside him and tucked her wings away.

"That was good," she said. "I'm sorry you had to climb."

Miles shrugged casually, "It wasn't that difficult," he lied. He stood up and looked into the dark cave of the ear. The ceiling of the cave was alive with bats, crawling over one another and squeaking like pram wheels. Miles clicked his tongue to listen to the echo. It sounded like the cave went back a long way. He took a few steps into the darkness, the smooth stone cold under his bare feet. His outstretched hands touched nothing.

"I don't suppose you can see in the dark as well?" he said over his shoulder to Little.

"Not very well. I once got lost in a stormcloud, and everyone laughed at me for days." She followed a few paces and bumped into Miles's back.

"I believe you," he laughed. He wondered how they could make a light. The wick of his brass lighter would be soaked with moat water. "We'll just have to go slowly. It can't be dark everywhere in this hill."

They moved cautiously onwards through the pitch darkness, Miles in front with his hands out, and Little hanging on to the tail of his jacket – possibly the only two people in history ever to have been swallowed by an ear.

Outside this strangest of hills, night had swiftly fallen. In the old broken-down stalls with their faded canvas, String was lurking in the shadows, thinking over the things he had just seen. An entrance in the clown's ear, and stranger by far, a girl with wings, who rightfully belonged to him. He would have won her if the pez hadn't cheated in the fight. He did not really want to go back to the Halfheads of course. That had just been a ruse to lure Miles into his trap, and he knew in any case that they would never have him back. But imagine what he could do if he had a scout that could fly! He could become a legend among the Stinkers, among all the gangs. Someday he would be chief Stinker himself. He thought about these things, and he looked at the darkening waters of the moat with a shiver. He steered clear of water whenever he could, and in all his twelve years he could not remember once having a bath. "You won't catch me going in there," he said to himself. "I'll have to try my chances at the front door tomorrow. If that fool Jook is right, they won't be coming out anytime soon."

And so Miles and Little crept deeper into the darkness of the Palace of Laughter, while down below in the watery gloom the nail-toothed mayor of the moat took a bite out of the worn leather boot that had half buried itself in the mud, and chewed it for as long as he could. It was the worst thing he had ever tasted, and he thought with regret of the nice, wriggling white snack he dimly remembered seeing earlier, and spat out the mouthful of tough, smelly leather in disgust.

CHAPTER TWENTY-TWO

BACK TO FRONT AND INSIDE OUT

Miles Wednesday, barefoot and bearless, stopped for a moment and listened. His eyes were smarting from the effort of staring into nothingness, and he had stubbed his toes several times. He had been imagining a faint sound for some time, and now he was sure that it was real, but it was still too far off to hear clearly. The tunnel had begun to rise steadily, and the sound seemed to cascade down towards them like waves breaking against a distant beach.

"Do you hear that?" he asked Little.

"Yes," said Little. "It makes me shiver." She untied her shirt and jacket from her waist and struggled back into them in the narrow tunnel.

Miles strained his ears, but the sound was no more than a faint rushing. "Why does it make you shiver?"

"I don't know," said Little. "There's something strange in it, but I can't hear well enough yet."

They continued through the darkness. A draft of cold air followed them deeper into the hill, and Miles guessed that they were in some sort of air vent. At one point the tunnel became so steep that it was easier to crawl, then suddenly the ground fell away beneath them and began to descend just as steeply. They reached a point where the distant sound became noticeably clearer. It was a strange music, jangly and discordant, and it was coming from somewhere to their right.

"There's another tunnel joining this one," said Miles. He could faintly see a circle of light. "We'll follow the music."

"I don't like it," said Little. "It's . . . back to front and inside out."

Miles listened again. It was certainly unlike any music he had heard before. There were gongs and flutes and other sounds he couldn't name. Somewhere in the middle was a hurdy-gurdy. The notes seemed to fight with one another, and the rhythm would now rush onwards like a strong current, then catch so suddenly that you felt like you had come to a cliff with no time to stop. It made the hair stand up on Miles's scalp, yet it was also strangely funny. He shook his head as though emptying water from his ears, and entered the tunnel. "Come on," he said. "It's only music, and music can't hurt us."

The new tunnel was smaller than the one they had come from, and they had to crawl. There were more openings branching off now. At one point they passed over hollow-sounding wood, as though there might be a trapdoor in the tunnel floor. Now each turn they took brought a little more light, and the music grew stronger until it seemed to be drawing them towards it like an invisible rope.

Suddenly the music rose to a nerve-jangling crescendo and abruptly stopped. Miles and Little stopped too. Silence washed along the tunnel, followed by a voice that was at once familiar and different. It took Miles a moment to identify it as the smooth voice of the Great Cortado. It sounded louder and deeper than it had during his brief job interview in Cortado's trailer. It was impossible to tell how close or how far away it was. He sat back against the tunnel wall and listened. Little was still too. She seemed relieved that the music had paused.

" . . . your Immense Privilege to witness the most spec-tac-u-lar, the most Fan-tas-tical, the most Hil-larious Ex-travaganza of Laughter ever performed," the voice was booming. " . . . Ladies, Gentlemen, Lords and Laddies, Sages and Peasants and Persons of Superfluous Learning, it is my

Pleasure and Delight to present for you this ver-ry night the Funniest, the Wittiest, the most Side-splitting troupe of Fools, Funnymen, Boobs and Bobos, Tumblers and Tricky-Dicks that has ever been assembled in one place since Cortez presented his Hunchbacked Aztec Buffoons to Pope Clement the Seventh."

With a roll of drums, a clash of cymbals and the boom of a mighty gong that sounded more in the chest than the ears, the crazy cacophony started anew, twirling itself like a musical vine around the closing lines of the Great Cortado's introduction: "Tonight, Ladies and Gentlemen, be prepared to be entertained as you have never been entertained before! Tonight the greatest comics in the Wide World will take you Beyond Laughter, and your Lives will be Transformed, FOREVER!"

The music raced and plunged like a wild thing, accompanied by squeaks and shrill whistles that seemed to be hanging on to the music by their teeth. Miles laughed at the sound, despite himself. He began to crawl towards it, but the music seemed to be coming from everywhere at once, and it was difficult to decide which route to take. The swell of laughter added itself to the sound – a great crowd of people laughing at something that was hidden from view. He had to find a vantage point from which he could see this fabulous show. He forgot his bleeding fingers and his stubbed toes, and the clammy chill of his moat-drenched clothes, his mind drawn by the hypnotic music and the waves of laughter that followed it. This, he imagined, would be more like the picture he had first had of the Palace of Laughter, and he felt an overwhelming urge to see for himself the greatest clowns on Earth. The thought of Tangerine slipped into his mind, and he brushed it aside impatiently. There was no point searching for Tangerine while the show was in full swing, he told himself, better to wait until the people had left and the place was quiet. They were nearly there now, he could tell.

"Miles!" called Little from behind. "Wait for me." He glanced over his shoulder. Little's face looked worried and anxious. "What was the matter with her?" he thought irritably. She could find something to laugh at in a cow or a fence post, but now that they were about to witness the funniest show on Earth, she looked as if she were lost on the way to a funeral.

"Just hurry up, will you?" he called. "You're always slowing me down."

His voice sounded sharper than he had meant it to, but they seemed to have been crawling in circles forever, and the show was going on without him. The strange acoustics of the tunnels made the sound confusing. Sometimes it seemed as if people were choking or wailing, then he would turn a corner and it would sound like hysterical laughter again. Little was no longer complaining. She followed him silently, and when he looked back at her he could not read her expression.

The tunnel they were in began to slope downward gently. He turned a corner, and suddenly there was bright light ahead, and the sound became almost deafening. He crawled cautiously to the tunnel mouth and found himself looking out into a huge theatre of some sort, hollowed out of solid rock in the centre of the hill, from a vantage point high on the wall. Above him was a domed ceiling, supported by a circle of massive pillars that were carved from bottom to top with curling vines and strange animals. Just below the tunnel mouth a stone ledge, shaped like a seashell, jutted from the wall, and he dropped down onto it and lay flat on his stomach, peering over the edge.

The roar of laughter washed over him. Some sixty feet below him he could see an enormous circus ring in the centre of the floor, surrounded by banks of stone seats that were packed with people. Miles could see the crowd and the ring through a gantry of bars, pulleys and ropes, suspended from the ceiling at the level of his balcony. The gantry supported rows of spotlights, wired together with cables so frayed and tangled that they looked like the work of Fowler Pinchbucket. One spotlight hung just in front of him, and several ropes were fastened within his reach, each one bound at the end with a different-coloured tape. Sandbags of various sizes dangled from the ends of some of the ropes as counterweights to the props and lights. Little dropped down softly and squeezed onto the narrow space beside him, and together they peered through the gaps in this tangle of metal and rope to get the best view of the performance.

Watching a group of people from almost directly above – through a network of bars, cables and spotlights – can make it very difficult to piece together exactly what they are doing. There appeared to be about twenty clowns on the stage at the same time. He caught a glimpse of the three small clowns with the different-coloured noses. They were trying to oil an elephant's knees with a large grease can. They kept grabbing the can from one another, and slipping and sliding on the spilled grease. The crowd sat in banked circles around the ring, mouths open and tears streaming from their red-rimmed eyes. Miles had never seen people laugh so hard. The sound of it was so infectious that he began to laugh himself.

The ring was full of chaotic movement, but from their vantage point it was almost impossible to make out what was going on. All the time the music looped and raced and clattered around the auditorium like an invisible beast running laps around the walls. The men in the audience guffawed and honked, and the ladies screeched and whinnied. The more he looked at them, the less sure he was that they were really enjoying themselves. It was hard to tell from so high up, but he thought he could see fear in their eyes.

The look of anxiety had left Little's face. She was laughing at something that he could not see. There was something unfamiliar about the sound of her laughter, but he was so distracted by the music, and the little he could see of what was happening below, that he couldn't put his finger on it. Instead he found himself laughing with her. The audience roared. Some seemed to have developed a sort of lockjaw, their mouths fixed open so wide that they could no longer close them. One red-faced woman was cackling so hard that she toppled forward into the ring. Her husband leaned forward to look at her, but seemed unable to help. He slumped back in his seat, clutching his stomach and crying with laughter. The guffawing face of the priest behind him had turned the colour of a ripe plum, and his eyes were fixed on the centre of the ring as though they were glued in their sockets.

Miles turned his attention back to the ring. Through a triangular gap he could just see a pale-faced clown sitting cross-legged in the sawdust in front of an enormous pie and clutching an oversized knife and fork. He had a straight back and a calm expression, and sat in the centre of that whirlwind of hysteria like the eye of a storm. He was dressed in an outfit that was so white it seemed to glow, and wore a very tall chef's hat, as tall again as himself. Suddenly a ragged clown on a unicycle appeared and rode straight through the centre of the pie, hotly pursued by the three tiny clowns, now dressed like undertakers in long black tailcoats and top hats, who trampled what was left of it into the ground. The chef clown leaped to his feet. A small blue bolt of lightning shot from his outstretched finger towards the last of the tailcoated clowns. It hit his top hat fair and square, and the hat flew from his head and burst into flames. The crowd shrieked. Little gave a gasp and grabbed Miles's arm, and Miles knew at once that this must be Silverpoint.

CHAPTER TWENTY-THREE

TOP HAT AND SANDBAG

Miles Wednesday, bootless and buttonless, craned his neck to try and get a better look at Silverpoint. He had marched off in pursuit of the little top-hatted clowns and Miles could no longer see him. Little still held tight to his arm. She was biting her lip.

The music spiralled faster and faster, higher and higher, until it was almost a continuous shriek. In the middle of the ring, a clown dressed as a tramp jumped up from under a sheet of newspaper he had been using as a blanket. The ground beneath him began to shake. He picked up his little white dog with a comical wail and ran hotfoot for the edge of the ring. A trapdoor burst open in a cloud of green and purple smoke, right at the spot where he had been lying a moment before. All over the ring, clowns stopped their hammering and honking and squirting and cartwheeling, and turned as one to face the opening trapdoor. From the fog of coloured smoke a figure rose slowly out of the ground. Miles could just make out the outline of a man sitting on a sort of throne. The hysterical bellowing of the crowd began to subside into a babble of groans and gasps. Some had fallen silent with their mouths still stuck open. Every eye in the theatre was fixed on the throne.

The throne rose on a pillar of steel. It was midnight blue, and on its high back was painted the same laughing clown's face that was on the side of the Great Cortado's wagon, the same face into which the very hill itself had been carved. Looking down on it now, Miles could see it in a different light. The wide-open mouth looked ready to devour anyone or anything that came near, and there was danger in the staring eyes. Seated beneath that manic face was the Great Cortado himself. As the throne reached its full height, he stood up (which didn't make a great deal of difference, it has to be said) and began to speak in the same deep, hypnotic tones with which he had introduced the show. There was no "Ladies and Gentlemen" this time, no "Immense Privileges," no flowery introduction at all. This time the Great Cortado got straight down to business.

"Now you have felt the true power of laughter," he said. "Elemental laughter, that has reached deep down into the centre of your being and cracked you open like a tree root cracks a rock." The audience stared. Their mouths hung open. Miles spotted Genghis sitting at the back, his arms folded and his mouth very definitely shut. His eyes roamed around the stupefied audience, and his face wore a smug look. Miles tried to see his pockets, as though he might catch a glimpse of Tangerine's grubby head peeping out, but it was too far, and too dark, and there were too many things in the way. As though awaking from a dream, he remembered what he was doing here, and he missed the feel of the bear in his pocket more than he could ever have imagined.

"Now you know the weakness of humanity," the Great Cortado continued in a quieter voice. "The debilitating millstone of laughter that hangs around the neck of the human race. Neither beast nor fish nor fowl carries this flaw. It is a cruel trap that nature has made for man alone, for it comes uninvited and saps the strength of whoever is afflicted by it. It distracts and confuses the mind and lies like a thick fog across the path of progress."

The crowd soaked up his poisoned words like blotting paper. Their jaws were slack, their eyes were glazed, and everything the Great Cortado said went in one ear and stayed there.

"Tonight," he continued, his voice growing stronger, "you have finally been set free. With the help of our unparalleled entertainment, you have emptied your souls of every last drop of useless laughter. When you leave this place you will remember nothing of what you have seen, yet so complete is our treatment that you will be cured of laughter forever!"

His voice was as smooth as polished stone and as rich as chocolate, and the audience listened without a murmur. Miles, perched in his balcony, could not help thinking that the Great Cortado's words made a certain sense. Now that the music and the performance had abruptly stopped, he could not quite remember what the point of laughter was, or why it had always seemed such a missing element in his Pinchbucket House childhood. Yet moments earlier he too had been laughing at the mere fractured glimpses he could catch of the performance. He felt confused and a little light-headed, and he shook his head as though to clear it. He knew that there was something twisted about the Great Cortado's words as they wrapped themselves around his thoughts like a snake.

He leaned out from the balcony to see if he could spot Silverpoint. A large sandbag of yellowing canvas blocked his view. It hung from a pulley just above Miles, on the end of a rope that stretched out from the centre of the gantry.

He felt the weight of the sandbag as he tried to push it to one side, and this gave him an idea. He looked at the point where it appeared the far end of the rope was tied. He looked down at the Great Cortado, and he made a quick calculation. The little man seemed to be nearing the end of his speech.

"Ladies and Gentlemen," he was saying, "I, the Great Cortado, have finally got laughter on the ropes. With the help of the learned Dr. Tau-Tau, I have tamed it and bottled it. If ever you find yourself with the foolish inclination to indulge in this intoxicating waste of time, you may purchase it by the bottle (ten cents from all reputable dealers), and cork it when you are done. Collect your free sample on the way out. Thank you for coming."

Miles reached up and began to pry the taut rope over the rim of the pulley wheel. Little looked at him, and her eyes widened. "Are you sure . . . ," she began, but she never finished what she was about to say. The rope came free with a sound that would have to be spelled *"Thungg,"* if it could be written down at all. The bag dropped like a stone, then swung out in a long and graceful arc across the huge auditorium. The Great Cortado was still standing on his throne with his arms outstretched like a letter "Y", and the heavy sandbag was swishing through the air, aiming straight for his head. There was no doubt about it. Little held her breath, and Miles held his. He had time to wonder, as the sandbag curved through the air in slow motion, if this was his most brilliant idea yet, or whether it was an act of foolishness that would have consequences more terrible than any he could possibly foresee.

At the very moment the Great Cortado caught sight of the approaching sandbag, the raised throne jerked into motion and began its descent back into the floor. The sandbag whistled over Cortado's head, ruffling his hair as it passed. He looked up in surprise as it swung over to the other side of the theatre and up, up into the spidery gloom among the bars and wires. It reached the top of its swing and punched the glass out of a large yellow spotlight. The yellow glass rained down in a sparkling shower. Most of it landed behind the outer row of people, but one piece fell, as though it had been given precise directions, and stuck itself into the back of Genghis's right hand, already bandaged where it had been scratched by a cat and bitten by Miles himself. Genghis jumped up with a roar. The stupefied people sitting around him did not even turn their heads.

The sight of Genghis hopping around and holding his injured hand distracted Miles for a moment, but the sandbag was on its way back to him. It curved back across the auditorium, spinning now from its impact with the spotlight, and sailing well over the head of the Great Cortado, whose throne was sinking rapidly into its trapdoor.

As it passed over the ring, the three small clowns in their top hats and tails watched it closely. Suddenly the clown with the green nose hopped up onto the shoulders of his two companions, and without a word or a signal they tossed him high in the air, as though releasing a racing pigeon. Although the circus band had fallen silent, the drummer was unable to contain himself, and began a long roll on the snare drum. Green Nose somersaulted twice and landed on the sandbag as it flew past, grasping it with his legs and flinging his top hat into the air with a shrill blast on his whistle. The drumroll ended with a clash of cymbals. The audience stared, but did not laugh. They seemed to have forgotten how. Genghis watched from below, glaring and sucking his knuckles. The trapdoor in the floor swallowed the Great Cortado, throne and all.

So quickly did all this happen that Miles didn't know what to do. The sandbag that he had released had failed to connect with the Great Cortado's head, and now it was on its way back to him, complete with a small wiry man in a funeral suit and a green nose. If he scrambled to his feet he would be in plain view of Genghis and the other clowns. If he stayed where he was he would be a sitting duck.

"Get back from the edge," he whispered urgently to

Little, but he himself seemed to be glued to the spot. The little man was getting closer by the second. The drummer had fallen silent.

When he remembered afterwards what had happened, it always seemed to Miles that this part had been a dream. As the clown on the sandbag approached the balcony, Miles could see him in sharp detail. His head was covered in black curls that shone like raven's feathers. He had wide, green-painted lips that matched his nose, and bushy black whiskers on either side of his whitewashed face. His glinting eyes were like tiny black olives. The sandbag slowed as it drew level with the balcony, and Miles found himself inches away from the small clown, who was suspended in midair, waiting for gravity to recover its grip. Suddenly he reached out, quick as lightning, and pinched Miles's nose hard with his bony fingers. His mouth opened in a grin of little pointed teeth, and he said something that sounded like "Ommadawn!" Then before Miles could even say "Ouch" he was gone.

CHAPTER TWENTY-FOUR

SILVERPOINT

Miles Wednesday, light-headed and nose-pinched, stared in disbelief at the retreating figure of the clown riding the sandbag like a Wild West cowboy. The clown spun with the sandbag, and whistled as he spun, and all at once he let go. Just like that. He curled into a ball as he fell, and hit the middle of a waiting trampoline as though he had been doing it all his life, which indeed he had. As he bounced high in the air the unicycle wobbled past with his two brothers perched on it, one on the other's shoulders. Green Nose landed on top, and the three clowns did a lap of honour around the ring.

The audience stared, glassy-eyed. They were wiping

their mouths with their sleeves, and patting their pockets as though they had forgotten something, but couldn't remember what it was. The red-faced woman had picked herself up from the ring and was brushing sawdust from her rumpled skirt. Behind her the priest hitched up his black trousers and tucked in his black shirt, and the thin man beside him straightened his tie and ran his fingers back through his floppy hair. They all seemed somehow greyer than they had been before.

Genghis was talking to Silverpoint and a clown dressed as a tramp with a downturned mouth. He pointed up at the balcony where Miles was hidden, then turned and moved out of view. The other clowns led the people out through the doors that stood at intervals around the theatre. A stilt-walking clown stalked among the shuffling people with a tin megaphone. "Don't forget to collect your free gift on the way out," he was calling in a pinched voice. The clowns were still in their bizarre outfits, but now as straightfaced as undertakers, all except for Red Nose, Yellow Nose and Green Nose. They had jumped off the unicycle and were helping to herd the audience out, but there was a skip in their step. Now and then one would steal another's hat or do a quick cartwheel, as though they couldn't help it.

The theatre was almost empty now. Miles sat up and found that Little was gone. He looked up at the mouth of the tunnel. "Little?" he said. Her head poked out of the hole.

"Just hurry up, will you?" she said. He recognised his own words and smiled sheepishly as he scrambled into the tunnel mouth. Little was waiting for him inside.

"We have to find a way to speak to him," she whispered.

"To the Great Cortado?" said Miles.

"No, to Silverpoint. We have to find out what he's doing here."

"I don't think that would be a good idea. He might just bring us to Cortado," said Miles.

Little looked at Miles as though she had been slapped. "You don't know him!" she said. "Silverpoint could never do anything like that."

"But you saw him. He was right in the thick of things. He can hear the Great Cortado just the same as us, and he knows what's going on."

"It doesn't matter. If he's doing it, he must have a good reason."

"Maybe he has," said Miles, "but we will have to be very careful." He could see that it had come as a shock to Little that Silverpoint was taking part in the Great Cortado's scheme, and he didn't want to upset her any further.

"Little . . . ," he said.

She looked at him, her eyebrows raised. Miles searched for the words. He had never been very good at apologies.

"I wasn't very nice to you earlier," he said. "I'm sorry."

Little smiled at him in the gloom. "Forget it," she said. "There is bad music going on here. It turned your soul for a while. I could feel it too."

"It was just music," said Miles.

"There's no such thing as 'just music,'" said Little. "Trust me. Now we have to find a way out of these tunnels. There are so many of them we could be lost in here forever."

"I think we crossed over a trapdoor on our way in," said Miles. "That must lead somewhere."

They went back the way they had come, making the steep climb at the start of the tunnel with difficulty. There was no sound now, except for their own breathing and the shuffling of their hands and knees on the stone floor. Miles found that the way back was easier to find if he didn't think about it too hard and just went with his instinct. The tunnels twisted and turned until he began to feel as though he had been swallowed by a giant snake. Some trick of acoustics made the sound of Little's breathing seem louder by the minute, and Miles had the uncomfortable sensation that she was getting heavier and larger at the same time. A panicky feeling was growing in his stomach. "Are you okay?" he called.

"I'm okay," said Little, "but I think somebody's following us."

A chuckle followed them down the dark tunnel. "She's right you know. Got it in one. Bang on the nail! The cat's on yer tails, little mouses." It was a man's voice with a nasal sound, as though its owner had one of those nasty sore throats that make it difficult to speak.

"Go faster," hissed Miles. Terrified as he was, he would have preferred to let Little get in front, but the tunnel was narrow, and he was afraid that they would simply get jammed.

"Faster, he says," came the voice from behind him. It was getting closer. "Faster's no good. Better if yiz stop now and make it easier on all of us. Well, easier on me anyhow. I reckon youse two are dog meat either way."

Miles could feel his chest tighten. He was sure that they should have reached the trapdoor by now. "Keep with me," he called to Little.

"I'm right here," panted Little.

"Me too, little mouses!" chuckled the man's voice. "Right behind yiz."

Thunka thunka thunk went Miles's hands and knees on the wooden boards. He was moving so fast that he was over the trapdoor before he realised it. "Stop there," he hissed to Little as he squeezed himself around in the narrow tunnel. His fingers scrabbled around the edges of the trapdoor until they felt a smooth brass ring. He yanked at it. Nothing happened. He took a deep breath and pulled again, but the door was stuck fast with time and dirt. "Hurry," said Little.

Miles wished the tiger could have come with them into the dark tunnels. The memory of the smooth power of the animal's muscles working effortlessly beneath him seemed to fill his tired arms with new strength, and he heaved at the trapdoor again. This time there was an unsticking sound, the trapdoor lifted, and light flooded up into the tunnel.

"Gotcha, little mousey " shouted the nasal voice. Little squealed and reached out for Miles across the open trapdoor. Half blinded by the light from below, he could just make out the battered hat and downturned white mouth of the tramp clown behind her in the tunnel, holding on to her ankle. Miles leaned forward and grabbed Little's outstretched hand. He pulled as hard as he could. The man holding her ankles was taken by surprise. He lost his balance and fell forwards through the open mouth of the trapdoor, but he did not let go of Little's ankle, and a moment later all three were out of the tunnel and tumbling through the air. Miles did not have time to see what was below them before the boy, the clown and the angel landed in a heap on the floor.

Unfortunately for the clown, it was he who landed first. Fortunately for Miles and Little, the clown was heavily padded in his tramp's outfit, and it was almost like landing on a rather lumpy sofa. The clown said, "UFFFFF," and lay winded on the floor. Miles grabbed Little's hand again and jumped to his feet, ready to get a good head start before the clown could regain his breath. He turned to see which way offered the best chance of escape, and found himself face to face with Silverpoint.

They were in a long corridor that curved away into the distance in both directions. It was lit at intervals by gas lamps. Now that his eyes were becoming accustomed to the light, Miles could see that in fact the lamps were rather dim. Silverpoint stood right in front of them. Even without the ludicrously tall chef's hat, bent sideways by the ceiling, Miles would have had no trouble guessing that this was the Storm Angel they had been searching for. He was slightly taller than Miles and, forgetting for a moment that he had lived for a millennium or more, looked just slightly older too. His face was pale, almost white, with a thin, straight nose and eyes so dark it was hard to tell if they had any colour. He watched as Miles and Little picked themselves up off the floor, much as an eagle might watch rabbits far below him.

"Well done," he said, and Miles realised he was talking not to them, but to the tramp clown, who had picked himself up and stood panting behind them.

A smile lit up Little's face. "Silverpoint!" she said. Miles gripped her arm, but she did not seem to notice.

Silverpoint looked at her coolly, with no sign of recognition. "There is no Silverpoint," he said.

Little opened her mouth to speak, but Miles squeezed her arm tighter. The smile faded from her face, and she looked down at the floor. "You're hurting my arm," she said quietly.

Silverpoint turned his gaze to Miles, looking him straight in the face for longer than most people feel is comfortable. Miles stared back, determined not to be the first to look away.

"Come," said Silverpoint at last. He turned on his heel and marched down the corridor, his hat swishing against the ceiling. The tramp clown gave them both a shove from behind, but they would have followed anyway. They had, after all, come to this place to find Silverpoint (and Tangerine, of course), and besides, there seemed to be little option. As they walked, Miles looked at Little out of the corner of his eye. She was fighting back the tears.

"We'll get to the bottom of this," he whispered.

"What does that mean?" she whispered back.

"It means . . . we'll find the answer," he said.

"Oh," said Little.

The corridor ended in a pair of lift gates, with the

darkness of the lift shaft beyond them. Silverpoint pushed the brass button, and the cables shuddered to life with a grinding sound inside the shaft. A rectangular stack of iron weights, coated with a layer of grease and dust, slid past them slowly on its way down. The cables continued to move and the grinding grew louder, and still the lift did not come.

"Where are you taking us?" asked Miles.

"Down," said Silverpoint.

The tramp clown, who had been so talkative in the dark tunnel, seemed to have dried up in Silverpoint's presence. It was not hard to see why. Silverpoint, even though he looked like a boy of eleven or twelve, had the air of a person whom you would not question lightly. He folded his arms and looked at Miles again, a slight frown on his face. He no longer seemed to notice Little at all.

The ornate brass roof of the lift came into view, and the grinding stopped as the cage drew level with the floor. They entered and Silverpoint closed the doors after them. Now that they were jammed together in a confined space it became clear that the tramp clown took his disguise very seriously, right down to the smell. Standing close behind him, Miles was reminded of the smell that used to lurk behind the big dirty steam-cleaning machines in the Pinchbucket laundry, with a hint of old fish heads and a dash of ditch water thrown in. He wondered if the clown had been a

Stinker when he was younger. Little nudged him. She was pinching her nose and squinting her eyes. Miles laughed before he could stop himself, and he saw Silverpoint glance at Little in surprise before turning his face away.

Floor after floor slid up past them, and sometimes coils of thick steel cable looped up outside the lift like snakes seeking the higher branches of a tree, and still the lift continued its descent.

Little stood on her toes and whispered in Miles's ear, "Is this what you meant by getting to the bottom of this?"

"Not exactly," said Miles.

Down and down they went, and still the tramp clown shuffled and stank, and Silverpoint's dark eyes stared at something distant that only he could see.

CHAPTER TWENTY-FIVE

A BOX OF STARS

Miles Wednesday, underfed, underground and undeterred, sat beside his four-hundred-year-old friend on a wooden bench, deep beneath the Palace of Laughter. The room they were in had once been a dressing room of some sort. There were faded blue stars painted on the crumbling ceiling. On the wall opposite him was a cracked and fly-spotted mirror, surrounded by singed light sockets. All but three of the sockets were empty, and of the three remaining bulbs only one worked. The room had a sad, abandoned feel.

"You'll get food and water later," Silverpoint had said as he showed them into their makeshift cell.

"What will happen to us?" said Miles.

"Nothing at all, little mouses," said the tramp clown, finding his tongue again. "You'll just get front-row seats to a nice show. Maybe you'll even get popcorn!" He sniggered and wiped his nose on his sleeve as he left the room. Silverpoint said nothing. Without another glance at his captives he locked the door, leaving them with the silence and the dim yellow light from the lone bulb.

They sat on the bench, listening to the fading footsteps of the tramp clown (only now did Miles notice that Silverpoint's feet made no sound). Little stared at the painted stars on the ceiling.

"Why would people make a box underground, then paint the sky on it?" she asked. Looking away from the fading stars, she reached into her pocket and carefully took out the flower that she had picked beside the stream while the tiger was fishing for trout. It was still as bright and fresh as the moment it was picked, despite all it must have been through in the pocket of her jacket. She twirled the stem in her hands and looked thoughtfully into the heart of the flower. "I thought when we found Silverpoint everything would be okay," she said.

Miles could think of nothing to say at that moment that would make their situation seem brighter. "We'll just have to see what happens next," he said. It did not sound like much of a plan. He began emptying his pockets onto the bench. This is what he found:

- The end of a piece of sausage, soaked in slimy moat water
- A brass lighter
- A ticket to the Palace of Laughter, which seemed unharmed by its soaking
- An empty bottle of Dr. Tau-Tau's Restorative Tonic
- The long coil of rope that he had cut from around Little's waist when they reached his barrel
- No Tangerine

It was not much of an escape kit. He had given away his pocketknife, and had long since lost the heavy bunch of keys he had stolen from the Great Cortado's wagon. He pulled out an old hairpin that was wedged behind a corner of the mirror, and went to the door to see if he could pick the lock. A brass plate had been screwed over the keyhole on the inside, and without his pocketknife he had no way to try and loosen the screws. Under its flaking pink paint the wooden door was solid.

Little was looking at the bottle that he had fished from the stream. "What do the words say?" she asked. Miles read the label aloud, and Little shook her head sadly.

"This is not good," she said. "Laughter is a strand of the One Song. It's one of the strongest and brightest, but it lives in harmony with the others. If you tear it out and put it in a bottle, it becomes something else."

She put the bottle down and stared up again at the bogus sky. "That can't be the real Silverpoint." She turned to look at Miles. "Silverpoint is a longfeather. He commands the clouds and drives the wind before him. How could he become a clownmaster's lackey?"

"I don't know," said Miles. He searched for something he could say that would offer a glimmer of hope. "Perhaps he just couldn't show that he knew you in front of the other clown."

Little shook her head. "You were right, in the tunnel. He doesn't even know me."

Miles sat down beside her on the bench. There was nothing they could do, locked in a room far underground. He searched for something to distract her. "Tell me more about what it's like where you come from," he said.

Little closed her eyes again, and leaned back against the wall. "I don't have the words to tell it," she said. "But I'll try."

Miles began to clean the mixture of dirt and moat slime from under his fingernails with the hairpin. This is probably not the politest thing you can do when someone is about to tell you about a world of harsh beauty that is almost beyond your imagination, but Miles had never had much training in manners at Pinchbucket House. Little, at any rate, did not seem to mind. As Miles scraped and flicked, she spoke of her home in the sky.

"I come from a place called the Realm," she began. "It's a place that is never still. Our palaces and halls rise and fall, they grow and move and melt away with the turning of the Earth and with the flow of the wind. You could think of them as ships, but even ships don't join together and break apart as they sail."

"You're talking about clouds!" said Miles. "Are your palaces clouds?"

"That's how they appear to you," said Little.

"If I could go up inside a cloud in a hot-air balloon, would I see more people like you?"

Little shook her head. "You would see nothing but grey mist and half-light."

"Why wouldn't I see them, if they're there?"

Little leaned forward and put her chin in her hands. "Remember the water we saw on the road, walking out of Larde?"

"You mean the mirage?" said Miles.

"We saw water," said Little firmly, "but when we reached it, we saw nothing. It's the same thing with the cloud palaces. Some things are only seen when they want to be."

Miles thought about this for a minute. He could see no point in discussing the nature of mirages again with Little. Besides, he had another question, one that had been lurking at the back of his mind for some time. He was almost reluctant to raise the subject, but the question would not go away.

"Little," he said, "who was that . . . person who followed us in the city?"

"I don't know, exactly," said Little quietly.

"Was it the same person who we saw in the circus field?" asked Miles.

"Yes," said Little. "I mean no." She sighed. "It's hard to explain."

Miles tried a different tack. "Why did I feel so tired when we saw him?" he asked.

Little looked about her, as though someone else might be listening in the tiny, bare room.

"What you saw," she said, "was a Sleep Angel."

"A Sleep Angel?" echoed Miles. "Is that bad?"

Little nodded. "Most people will meet a Sleep Angel only once, and that's a meeting you shouldn't be in a hurry to keep. It's a Sleep Angel who will carry your last breath from you and release it on the wind."

Miles was silent. The room seemed strangely still. He pulled his jacket around him, although the air was stuffy and warm.

"Why was he following us?" asked Miles. He was not sure he wanted to know.

"I don't know why," said Little. "I shouldn't even speak of this – it's not allowed. I'm in enough trouble already." Their meeting with Silverpoint seemed to have washed away her confidence. She looked small and frightened again, as he had first seen her in the locked trailer. "He must be looking for Silverpoint."

"Why did we run from him, then? Maybe he could have helped us."

Little looked at him as though he were crazy.

"Sleep Angels are the highest caste there is. At least the highest I know of. Sleep Angels look after Life and Death. They don't normally make up search parties." She stared unseeingly at the floor between her feet. "If he's looking for Silverpoint, something is wrong."

"Maybe he's a friend," said Miles.

Little laughed. In the tiny room the shine seemed to have gone from her laughter, and somehow it just made Miles feel sad.

"Friendship is an idea that lives down here," she said. "Where I come from there is duty and loyalty. I suppose loyalty is a friendship of sorts, but everyone knows their place in the Realm. It's not a Sleep Angel's place to concern himself with someone from a lower caste."

Miles thought about this for a moment. "Are there many castes of Angels?" he asked.

"Of course! There are Wind Angels, Whitefire Angels, and many others." She seemed glad to leave the topic of the Sleep Angel.

"Whitefire Angels?" said Miles. "What do they do?"

"They draw a map of the One Song on the dome of the night. The map grows and changes as each Song Angel's part is sung. Without it, the Song Angels would lose their way, and the One Song would eventually come undone and all life would be scattered to the darkness. The stars are the crossing points of the Whitefire Map, where the strands of the One Song join each other."

"But the stars are billions of miles away," said Miles. "You couldn't reach them in a hundred lifetimes!"

Little smiled. "The stars are a living map on the dome of the night. I know this because I have helped to sing them into place for as long as I can remember."

Miles's head was beginning to swim. He was not sure whether it was from hunger or the strange notions that Little was releasing in the dimness of the small room.

"I got all my schooling from Lady Partridge," he said. "She has books full of the knowledge of men who have studied these things for centuries. Clouds are made of water vapour. The stars are suns like ours, so far away that their light is millions of years old when it reaches us. Are you telling me all these things are wrong?"

"No," said Little. She twirled the flower she had taken from her pocket, then held it out for Miles to take a closer look. The petals were yellow at the centre, merging to a deep scarlet at their pointed tips.

"Look at this," she said. "What would you call it?"

"I don't know the name of it," said Miles. "It's a yellow flower with red tips."

"Isn't it a red flower with a yellow centre?" asked Little.

"I suppose so. You could call it either."

"Then just because something is one thing doesn't mean it can't be another," said Little.

Miles thought about this for a while. It was hard to get his head around it all. He closed his eyes, which made things a little easier. Fat galleons of cloud began to sail through the blue night of his mind's eye. He could see stars winking between them, some closer than the clouds, some farther away. The picture gave him a feeling that everything was working as it should be in the universe, like a well-made clock with many parts. It made him smile.

He dozed fitfully on the hard bench. How long he slept he could not tell, but he was almost sorry when his dreams were interrupted by the muffled jingle of keys outside the door of their makeshift cell.

His stomach, however, was not a bit sorry. As far as he could tell, it was early morning by now, which made it nearly twenty-four hours since they had eaten. "I hope this is food," he said to Little.

A key turned in the lock with a soft click, and before he had time to wonder who might be outside, the door began to swing open.

CHAPTER TWENTY-SIX

THE ELECTRIC BOY

Silverpoint, pale-faced and long-feathered, stepped into the room in the early hours of the morning, his tall hat sweeping the faded stars. He closed the door softly behind him, took his hat off carefully and placed it behind the door. Little stared at the ground, as though she did not want to meet his eye again and see no sign of recognition. Miles looked at the hat in the corner, wondering if there might be food hidden inside it. Silverpoint walked across the room and stood in front of Little, his hands on his hips.

"And just where do you think you've been, little soft-wing?" he said sternly.

Little looked up at him, and her eyes widened. "Silverpoint?" she whispered. His cool face broke into a smile. Little jumped up onto the bench and threw her arms around him. Silverpoint squeezed Little tightly, and the lone bulb on the wall glowed brighter, as though extra power had surged through the crumbling wires.

He stepped back and held her face in his hands. "I am glad to see you," he said. "How on earth did you get here?"

"Miles helped me. We came on a tiger. We slept up a tree. He stole the keys from under Cortado's nose. Are you all right? A crow told us the way. Didn't you recognise me? Why are you helping them?"

Silverpoint put his finger to his lips and glanced briefly at Miles. "I'm sorry, Little," he said. "When you fell from the ceiling last night I had to pretend not to know you. If that snivelling clown had realised who you were he would have run straight to Cortado himself, and then we would really have had trouble. The Great Cortado has a redder soul than I first realised."

Little laughed with delight and hugged him around the waist. Silverpoint looked at Miles over her blond head. His face was serious again, and his dark eyes searched into Miles's face as before, but this time his gaze was more curious than unfriendly.

"I am in your debt," he said. He looked at Miles a

moment longer, then suddenly held out his hand, as though he had just remembered this was the right thing to do. Miles took his hand. Silverpoint's skin was cool and smooth, but there was a strange tingle in his touch, like the tingle you feel if you are foolish or bored enough to put your tongue on the terminals of a battery. Silverpoint squeezed his hand. Miles squeezed back. It felt like an odd thing to do, particularly with someone who felt like a distant cousin of the electric eel.

Miles took his hand back. Enough was enough. "Actually neither of us could have got here alone," he said.

For a moment they stared at each other silently, then Miles cleared his throat. "I don't suppose you brought any food with you?" he asked hopefully.

"I'm sorry," said Silverpoint. "You must be very hungry. Your breakfast is on its way, but I'm afraid the chefs are a little" – he searched for the right word – "disorganised," he said finally. He disentangled himself gently from Little's arms. "How did you get into the Palace of Laughter without being seen?" he asked.

"We came in through the ear," said Little. "It was Miles's idea. Then we crawled through tunnels for ages. We could hear people laughing, but we couldn't find the show until it was almost over, and we couldn't see properly even then."

"Then you were very lucky. If you had seen the entire

show you would have been lost for good. I have never seen anyone who can resist the power of Cortado's show."

"But *you* can," said Little.

"That's because I take the antidote. All of us who work here are given an antidote before every show. It makes you immune."

"Immune from what?" asked Miles. "What exactly is the Great Cortado doing to all those people?"

"It's a sort of hypnosis," said Silverpoint. "He sucks the laughter out of their souls. After the show they are given a small bottle of liquid and sent on their way. . . ."

Miles felt for the empty bottle of Dr. Tau-Tau's Restorative Tonic and took it out of his pocket. "Like this one?" he said.

Silverpoint looked at him suspiciously. "Where did you get that?" he asked.

"I found it," said Miles. "It was already empty."

Silverpoint nodded. "The tonic brings people back to their normal selves after they've been 'laughtered', as Genghis calls it, but it only lasts a few hours and people soon develop a craving for more. Only the Palace of Laughter produces the tonic, and it has made the Great Cortado a very wealthy man. The more demand he creates for the tonic, the richer he gets."

"But why are you going along with it?" asked Little.

"I had no choice until now, Little. After we were given that sleeping potion at the Circus Oscuro I woke up in the back of a van. I was tied with ropes, bumping about for a day and a night and into the following day. I had no idea where you were. When we got here they said that I would have to do what they told me, or you would be killed."

"Couldn't you have tried to escape?" Little asked Silverpoint. He shook his head.

"I couldn't risk it. Genghis and Cortado go back and forth from here to the circus all the time. It's always on the move, and if I went missing from here they might have got to you before I could find it."

"Did they tell you that I had escaped from the circus?"

"No, of course not," said Silverpoint. "But I knew you were coming anyhow, and when that sandbag got loose I was pretty sure it was your doing. That was a very dangerous thing to do. Cortado was spitting mad. Once the audience had been put back on the train, we were all sent to look for you. It's lucky I was there when you were caught, or you would have been brought straight to the Great Cortado tonight."

"Actually it was me who released the sandbag," said Miles. "I was sure it would hit him. But how did you know we were coming?"

"I knew as soon as I saw that little dancing bear."

Miles almost dropped the bottle that he was turning over between his fingers. "You've *seen* Tangerine?" he said.

"If you mean the bear, of course I've seen him, and I knew at once he was Little's work." He fixed Little with a hard stare, and she lowered her eyes to the floor. "Cortado put him into the act as soon as he set eyes on him," said Silverpoint.

"Tangerine is in the show?" asked Miles in amazement. "I didn't see him. What does he do?"

"He can't be made to do anything, of course, because he's brainless. He just stumbles around and gets in the way. The other clowns fall over him. Why are you so interested in the bear?"

Miles felt slightly insulted on Tangerine's behalf, even though he knew the bear's head was stuffed with sawdust. The idea of Tangerine stumbling around with hundreds of people laughing at him made Miles feel slightly sick. "Tangerine is mine," he said. "I came here to get him back."

Silverpoint turned his dark eyes on Miles, as though searching for something too faint for the human eye to see. "How long have you had him?"

"As long as I can remember," said Miles.

"It will be difficult enough to find a way for the three of us to escape," said Silverpoint after a pause. "We can't jeopardise our chances looking for a stuffed bear."

"You can do what you like," said Miles, "but I'm not leaving without Tangerine."

Silverpoint shrugged. "That's up to you," he said.

"What are they going to do with us?" asked Little. "That smelly clown said we'd be made to watch the show."

Silverpoint nodded, and his face clouded. "It was the only way I could dissuade Cortado from wanting to deal with you right away. I persuaded him that when we found the culprit he should be locked up until the next show. Then he could be put in the front row, and we would have no trouble with him after that. You've seen what the show does to its audience, I think."

"When is the next show?" asked Miles.

"Tonight. There are usually two or three in a row, then Cortado and Genghis go back to the circus."

"Why don't they just take the Palace of Laughter show on the road with the Circus Oscuro, instead of bringing people here?" asked Little.

"Cortado uses the Circus Oscuro to recruit and train performers for the Palace of Laughter," said Silverpoint. "He needs to be absolutely sure of everyone he brings to work for him here. I believe they also like to screen the audience at the circus before handing out the invitations. I don't know exactly how they decide who gets a silver ticket, but you won't find a policeman in the audience here, or a psychiatrist either."

"Then we'll have to escape before tonight's show," said Miles. "You have the keys to this door. If you leave it unlocked when you go, I can sneak out and look for Tangerine. Once I've found him we can go back out through the tunnels, and you can come with us."

"It's too late for that," said Silverpoint. "Cortado has had the trapdoor nailed shut. The only other way out is through the doors, and Baumella guards those night and day."

"She must sleep sometime," said Miles.

"She sleeps on a chair that she puts against the doors. You couldn't open them without waking her."

Miles pictured an elephant gently lifting the sleeping giantess, chair and all, out of the way of the doors. He doubted whether any elephant would be strong enough. "Maybe we can find some way to disrupt the show and escape during the confusion," he said. "Couldn't you knock the Great Cortado out with a firebolt?"

Silverpoint shook his head. "If I hit someone any harder with lightning than I do in the show it would probably kill them, and it is not permitted for a Storm Angel to release a soul. I'll have enough explaining to do as it is, when we get home." He turned another hard stare in Little's direction, but she seemed to be carefully examining her nails.

Miles closed his eyes and tried to rerun what they had seen of the show in his mind's eye, looking for any opportunity there might be to turn Cortado's method against him. He did not get very far before he was interrupted by the sound of someone approaching from the corridor outside. The sound became more puzzling as it got closer. It was hard to tell if there were two people or more, or one person bouncing a large beach ball. Sometimes the footsteps seemed to be running, or even hopping. Sometimes they all marched in step. There was even what sounded like a brief outbreak of tap dancing. As they got nearer, Miles could hear voices chuckling and quietly singing. Another voice said, "Ssssshhh!" and the sounds stopped outside their door. There was a snort of laughter, followed by a sharp rap on the door.

"This will be your breakfast," said Silverpoint, and as he walked to the door Miles heard him mutter, " . . . with any luck."

CHAPTER TWENTY-SEVEN

PROVIDENCE

Miles Wednesday, unwashed and unbreakfasted, stared curiously at the door of the underground dressing room. He could smell food, he was sure of it. Someone out there had some soup. Or maybe a chicken. He pictured Haunch the butcher, standing apologetically with a plate of fat sizzling sausages. Silverpoint opened the door and three small men tumbled into the room as though released from an overcrowded jack-in-the-box. Even if their noses had not still worn traces of red, yellow and green paint, Miles would have recognised them at once. They had changed out of their undertaker outfits into baggy pants and vests, and they fidgeted and hopped as though the floor were burning their feet. Two of them carried plates of stew, and the other a large glass flagon of water.

Silverpoint introduced them as Fabio, Umor and Gila, the famous Bolsillo brothers. Gila, who had ridden the sandbag through the air, winked at Miles and pinched his own nose. He balanced a plate on the tip of his finger and set it spinning, stew and all. Specks of gravy flew from the plate and spattered around the room. Miles could not remember ever having had stew for breakfast, but he was far too hungry to care. A drop of gravy landed on his upper lip and he licked it off.

"That's no way to eat your food," said Gila.

"That's no way to serve it," said Umor.

"Give the boy his supper," said Fabio, cuffing Gila on the back of his head.

"Supper's a bit late, I'm afraid," said Gila.

He tossed the plate, still spinning, up in the air. It missed the ceiling by a whisker, and dropped neatly into Miles's hands.

"The boy's a natural," said Umor.

"Should be in a circus."

"Circus is in him, I'd say."

"Too skinny for that."

The Bolsillo brothers spoke so quickly that it was hard

to follow who was saying what. They had bushy hair that grew low on their foreheads, and small black eyes that glittered under thick eyebrows. When they smiled, their little teeth were pointed.

Umor handed the other plate to Little and bowed almost to the ground.

"Thank you," said Little.

"The pleasure is all mine," said Umor to the floor.

"Then give it back," said Fabio.

Umor straightened up. "Thank you," he said to Little.

"Fabio," said Silverpoint, "we don't have much time, and there are things I need to discuss with Little."

"Of course," said Fabio.

"Say no more," said Umor.

Gila rummaged in the pocket of his baggy trousers and produced a small grey mouse. He put it back, and rummaged again. This time a deck of cards appeared. He shuffled them with a loud snap, and the three little men settled themselves cross-legged in a circle in the corner of the room.

Miles began to devour his stew. He had never tasted anything so good, and it was some time before he could spare his mouth for speaking.

"Maybe," he said through a mouthful of food, "we should play the Great Cortado at his own game."

Silverpoint put his finger to his lips and rolled his eyes in the direction of the three little cardsharps in the corner. "They are on our side, more or less," he said in a low voice. "But I don't know how far they can be trusted."

"What do you mean?" whispered Miles.

"They look out for each other, and care about little else," said Silverpoint, "and they can be a bit light-fingered. They've tried to steal your dancing bear from Genghis at least twice."

Miles glanced over at the Bolsillo brothers. They appeared to be absorbed in their card game. Gila handed the deck to Umor.

"You deal," he said.

"No dice. You deal."

"You're faster."

"Yes, but whenever I deal, you get all the aces. I think you cheat."

"I swear on my grandmother's horse I never did."

"Your grandmother never had a horse. She was a lighthouse keeper."

"It was a sea horse."

"Just deal the cards."

Cards began flipping between the three men. Although Gila was dealing, the cards seemed to be going in all directions. Umor was looking at his and giving back the ones he didn't like, which Gila would pass straight on to Fabio, except for one that he hid in the back of his thick hair while pretending to scratch his head. Miles stared at them in fascination for a moment, then he turned back and spoke quietly to Silverpoint.

"How many times have you heard Cortado hypnotise an audience?"

The Storm Angel shrugged. "Thirty or more," he said.

"Do you think you could do it yourself?" asked Miles.

"I've been thinking of that," said Silverpoint. "If I could gain control of the crowd myself, I may be able to overturn Cortado's plan in some way, but I don't think it's possible."

"Why not?" asked Miles.

"I've watched very carefully what happens," said Silverpoint. "There's a certain point at the end of the show where the pace suddenly slows, and the audience is . . . left hanging in some way. That's when Cortado comes up through the floor. I don't think it would be possible to gain full control over the audience before then. It's all timed very precisely."

"Deuce," cried Gila from the corner of the room.

"Checkmate," countered Fabio.

"Game, set and halftime," said Umor. "Deal again, maestro."

"Maybe there's some way to prevent him from coming

up through the floor," said Miles. "Couldn't you go down and sabotage the throne?"

Silverpoint shook his head. "Nobody's allowed below stage except Cortado and Genghis. That area is kept locked."

"I've been there," said Fabio from the corner. Umor was shuffling the cards, and the three little men were listening in to the conversation. You could almost see their ears wagging.

"You?" said Silverpoint. "What were you doing there?"

"Sleeping," chuckled Umor.

"Fixing," said Fabio. "The throne wasn't working properly. I was fixing it."

"He has a way with machines."

"They do as he says."

"He threatens them with his grease gun."

"How does the throne work?" asked Miles.

"Big electrical engine. Rubber rollers against the steel pole," said Fabio.

"Engine starts up," said Gila.

"Rollers turn."

"Pole goes up, trapdoor opens, Bob's your uncle."

Miles glanced at Silverpoint, then turned to Fabio. "Could you sabotage the throne?" he asked.

"Nope," said Fabio.

Gila clucked his tongue. "That would be treason," he said.

"Treason with a reason," said Umor.

"Why couldn't you? You know how it works," said Miles.

"Because I don't have a key, Master Miles. Genghis keeps the key."

Miles put his empty plate on the floor and scratched his head thoughtfully. There had to be a way around this. "If we can't get below the stage," he said, half to himself, "we'll have to sabotage it from above." He pictured the mayhem that he had glimpsed from his vantage point high above the show. Unicycles. Giant pies. Elephants and grease cans.

"The grease can," he said, jumping to his feet with a smile spreading across his face. "That's how we can do it. The throne is raised by rubber rollers that turn against the steel pole. If the rollers were greasy, the pole would slip and the weight of the throne would make it sink back into the floor."

Silverpoint regarded Miles with his dark eyes. "I'm listening," he said.

Little looked at the excitement shining in Miles's eyes. She didn't understand much about the world she was in. It was heavy and solid and seemed to be full of locks and machines and ugly noises. Nothing changed or moved unless it was pulled or pushed or dragged with a rope, yet Miles seemed to know the secrets of this world as instinctively as she knew the currents of the sky and the tides of the air. If anyone could make this plan work, she decided, it was this thin, coffee-skinned boy who had saved her from the Circus Oscuro.

"Look," said Miles. "Here's my plan. You said you couldn't gain control of the crowd until the final moment anyhow. When the Great Cortado begins to rise up from the floor in a cloud of smoke, we'll be sitting in the front row of the audience, pretending to be brain-fried. I'll jump into the ring—"

"But by then we *will* be brain-fried," interrupted Little.

"I hadn't thought of that," said Miles.

"I have," said Silverpoint. "I will bring you my dose of antidote when I'm given it. We only get them minutes before the show, but if I'm quick I can get down here without being missed."

"But then you'll be unprotected, and we'll have only half a dose each," said Miles.

"I know what to expect, and I will be able to resist the effects of the show," said Silverpoint. He did not look at them as he said this, and Miles had the feeling he was not as confident as he sounded. "As for you, it will dilute the power of the show somewhat, but you'll have to use all your will to block it from your mind from the start. It's the best I can do for you."

"What about their portion?" said Miles, nodding at the Bolsillo brothers. "If we pooled yours and theirs, we'd have four portions between six of us. That would be . . . two-thirds each."

"No!" shouted the Bolsillo brothers in unison.

"No sharing!"

"No dice."

"Bad enough as it is."

"We don't want to be turned into vegetables."

"But if we are, I want to be a turnip."

The brothers looked genuinely frightened at the suggestion. Miles looked at Silverpoint, and he shook his head. "Let's hear the rest of it," he said.

Miles shrugged. "When the smoke goes up," he said, "I'll jump into the ring. Fabio can toss me the oil can, and I'll pour the lot down the steel pole just as the throne starts to rise. With all that smoke around, no one will even see me. The throne will slip back down, and you can take over."

"What about the Bolsillo brothers?" asked Little. "Couldn't they grease the throne themselves?"

Miles shook his head. "We'll need them to distract everyone else. As far as we know, all the other clowns are on the Great Cortado's side. Then there's Genghis, and Baumella if she hears that something's going on. We'll need all the help we can get."

Miles had another reason for wanting to get into the ring himself. He intended to keep a sharp eye on Tangerine throughout the performance, so that he could scoop him up from the smoke and the chaos on his way to sabotage the throne. After the reaction he had got from Silverpoint earlier, he preferred to keep the bear-retrieval part of his plan to himself.

In the corner of the room Fabio had picked up the two empty plates and the water carafe and was practising his juggling. The plates were crossing and recrossing with a dizzying rhythm, and the water bottle spun so fast it was just a blur as it rose and fell, rose and fell from the little clown's busy hands.

Silverpoint stared at the faded stars on the ceiling, his arms folded and a slight frown on his pale forehead as he worked his way through Miles's plan. "What happens when the Great Cortado realises his throne has sunk back down? He'll come up through the trapdoor anyway before we can achieve anything."

"We'll have to block the trapdoor in some way," said Miles. He watched the Bolsillo brothers, who had all joined in the juggling act, and were passing the crockery back and forth as though they were one creature with six arms. The contents of their pockets – a deck of cards, some brightly coloured balls and even the grey mouse – joined the plates and the carafe in their intricate flight. The mouse did not seem to mind at all.

"They can bring their elephant to stand on the trap-door," said Miles, nodding at the juggling brothers, "and you can climb on her back. That way you'll be better able to get the crowd's attention, and the Great Cortado will have to go the long way to get up from underground. You'll just have to get control of the audience before he can return. If we can get them on our side they'll outnumber Cortado's men forty to one."

"Sun's coming up, Silverpoint," said Umor. He had produced an egg timer from his pocket, and the last few grains of sand were whispering through its narrow waist. Gila was feeding crumbs to the mouse, who now sat on his shoulder. Fabio continued to juggle alone.

"We must go," said Silverpoint. "We've been here too long already."

"Wait a moment," said Miles. He was not entirely happy with all the details of his plan, and there would be no second chance to get it right. "How are you going to gain control of anyone if you've given us all your antidote?" he said. "Couldn't you steal some for us instead?"

"I don't know where it's kept," said Silverpoint. "I've been trying to find out since I got here. It's always Genghis who hands it out. He only gives one dose per person, and he never brings anyone with him when he collects it. I offered to help him once, and he became very suspicious."

The crockery spun above Fabio's head with increasing speed. Umor had produced a harmonica and was playing a sad, soft tune. Gila lifted his mouse gently from his shoulder and dropped it into a trouser pocket.

"Ask him!" said Miles.

"None of them know where it is, I've already asked them," said Silverpoint.

"Not the brothers, the mouse," said Miles. He turned to Little. "You could ask the mouse if he knows where the antidote is kept. I'm sure he's done plenty of snooping about in places others can't get to."

"Snooping?" said Gila.

"Investigating, I mean," said Miles.

Gila shook his head. "Too dangerous," he sniffed.

"Please, let me ask him," said Little. "If we don't get some more antidote our brains will be turned to mush. What's his name?"

"Susan."

"Oh! She's a girl. That's much better," said Little.

Gila looked at her suspiciously from under his tufty eyebrows. "Why better?"

"Curiosity, of course," said Little. "Girls like to know everything that's going on. I bet she knows this place inside out."

"Well . . . ," said Gila, "you can ask." He didn't seem to think it strange that Little would be able to speak to a mouse. Perhaps Silverpoint had already told them about her, thought Miles. Gila produced Susan from his pocket and held her out on the palm of his hand. She looked up at Little. Her whiskers twitched. Little leaned forward and squeaked something. Susan squeaked back. Miles tried to remember how he had managed to tune in to the voices of the cats in the garden of Partridge Manor, but he was too worried and excited now to allow the meaning of the mouse's tiny voice to reach him. "What did she say?" he asked.

"Ssh," said Little. She conversed with Susan for another minute, then smiled. Gila and his brothers were watching her intently with their glittering black eyes. "She's done plenty of exploring while you've been snoring, and she thinks she knows where the antidote is kept," said Little. "She saw Genghis filling lots of little glass tubes from a giant bottle in a sort of laboratory. She says it's on the floor below this one."

"I was afraid of that," said Silverpoint. "This floor is the last stop on the lift. The only possible way down is through the iron door at the other side of this corridor, but it's always locked. I saw Genghis go through there once, but I didn't know where it led to."

"Can you ask her how she got into the laboratory herself?" said Miles. "Maybe there's another way."

Little and the mouse sqeaked back and forth for a minute. Unlike her conversation with the crow, the sentences were brief, as though mice did not have time in their short lives for wasting words.

"There's a chimney," said Little. "It runs all the way up from the laboratory, through one of the pillars, and comes out at the top of the hill. They have some kind of a fire in a box down there – I don't know the word for it."

"A furnace," said Miles, who had got as far as "N" in Lady Partridge's encyclopedia, and therefore knew more than most boys of his age about things whose initial letter fell in the first half of the alphabet. He scratched the itchy stubble of his half-shaved head. "How can we use a chimney that comes out at the top of the head," he wondered. "To get into it, we'd first have to get out of the Palace of Laughter, and we can't do that, which is why we need to get into the laboratory in the first place."

"Susan says there are little doors into the chimney every couple of floors. She doesn't know what they're for, as they're too small for most people and she's never come across anyone in a chimney anyhow."

"I suppose they'll be hatches of some kind, so it can be cleaned out if it gets blocked," said Miles.

"If there's one at this level I don't remember ever seeing it," said Silverpoint. "There are dozens of dressing rooms and all the sleeping quarters on this floor, and even supposing we could get into them all, we're fast running out of time."

"Don't worry," said Fabio, who was still juggling with the crockery. "Providence will step in when all else fails."

"What's Providence?" asked Miles, who had not yet reached "P" in the encyclopedia.

"Not sure," said Fabio. "But my mother always said that Providence looks after the foolish, and from the sound of your plan, you would qualify without difficulty." He winked at Miles, taking his eye off the flying plates and the spinning bottle for an instant. An instant was enough. The plates glanced off each other in midair and wobbled in their orbits. The juggling Bolsillo brother said something that sounded like "Hup!" He caught a plate between his pointed teeth and the other under his left arm, but he was too late to catch the spinning bottle, which sailed right over his head and met its own reflection in the yellowed mirror with a splintering crash.

Now the sound of a bottle shattering a mirror can be a strangely satisfying thing, but to the boy, the clowns and the angels it just sounded like very bad timing. They stared, frozen, as the bottle exploded on the floor amid the crashing shards of glass. The sound seemed to go on forever, filling the room and echoing down the empty corridor outside. But it was not the splintered glass that made them stare. Right in the centre of the pale rectangle where the mirror had been, there was a small iron hatch set into the plaster. It stood slightly ajar from the impact of the bottle.

"Well, Master Miles," said Fabio when the last glass splinter had fallen. "Now we know what Providence looks like."

CHAPTER TWENTY-EIGHT
CHIEF GENGHIS

Miles Wednesday, black-faced and burn-fingered, hung from a thin rope in a sooty chimney deep in a giant stone head. The fine black soot had been stirred up by the flapping of Little's wings, and it was making him cough like a seal. The sound echoed and boomed through the metal tube of the chimney, until he was sure that everyone in the Palace of Laughter could hear him. His shoulders felt bruised from squeezing his way through the small iron hatch, and his eyes were smarting from the soot. He managed to force a few words out between coughs. "Go down . . . making . . . me cough," he barked.

"Oh, sorry," said Little. She fluttered downwards and

vanished into the darkness. The soot began to settle, and Miles could dimly see Gila's head poking through the hatch above him.

"You all right?" asked Gila.

"Sort of," said Miles.

"Rather you than me," said Gila. "We have to go now. 'Bye!" His head disappeared like a jack going back into its box.

Miles began to inch his way down the rope. It was the one he had cut from Little's waist when he rescued her from the circus, and had been in his pocket ever since. He wondered if it was long enough to get him to the bottom of the chimney. He could get no foothold in the soot, and his fingers burned from sliding down the rope. In the darkness it was easy to imagine a variety of horrible fates awaiting them below. He pictured a huge set of metal jaws like a bear trap poised to bite them in half, or a pool of acid that would eat them from toe to crown with a loud hiss. "Little?" he whispered. "What's down there?"

"Just me," said Little.

The end of the rope came without warning. One moment he was holding on with two hands, then with one, then his aching fingers gave way and he dropped into blackness. The tunnel began to curve a short way down, and he found himself sliding on his backside until he tumbled into the filthy furnace at the chimney's end with a clatter.

"Shhhh!" said Little from the darkness beside him. "Not so loud!"

"I'll try and remember that next time I'm falling down a chimney," said Miles.

They were in a small, dark iron box, crouched on a thick layer of crunchy ash, still slightly warm from the last time the fire had been lit. The furnace was just big enough to allow Little to sit upright, but Miles's head was pressed against the dusty ceiling. It made the dim dressing room they had come from seem like a room in a five-star hotel. In front of them was the thick glass plate of the furnace door. Miles shuffled forward and looked out through the glass.

The laboratory reminded him a little of the inside of Lady Partridge's tree house, but without the branches growing up through it. There were shelves from floor to ceiling, crammed with beakers, bell jars, boxes, calipers, tinctures, tonics, touchstones, brass scales, sulphur nuggets, rubber tubes, leather-bound books, dried herbs, candles, stirring rods, steam distillers, talismans, tusks, quartz toning vessels, assorted bones, rolled charts, Bunsen burners, pipettes, gold and silver colloids, powdered roots, and on a high shelf, a shrunken head with its hair tied in a knot and a crescent of bone passed through its nose.

In the corner was a wooden cabinet with gargoyle faces

carved on each corner, and on top a pile of dusty books and a bust of Hermes Trismegistos, the father of alchemy. A large solid table with a clean-scrubbed surface stood in the centre of the room. Among the flagons and boxes and stoppered jars on the table, Miles spotted a wooden stand with a row of thirty-six identical vials, each one half filled with a colourless liquid.

"Look," he whispered to Little. "That must be the antidote."

He moved aside so that she could look out through the glass. "There on the table," he said, "in the glass vials."

"I see it," she whispered. "How do we get out there?"

Miles fumbled with the catch on the furnace door. It was difficult to see in the semidarkness, but it was a simple catch and it did not take him long to open. The door swung outward. It was smaller than the hatch through which they had entered the chimney. "I don't think I can get through there," said Miles. "I'm not even sure you will."

Little tucked her wings away and poked her head out into the laboratory. There was no one there. She squeezed through the tiny doorway like a cat through a drainpipe, and dropped to the floor. In a moment she was back with two of the glass vials.

"Well done," said Miles. She smiled and passed one in to him, pulling the stopper from the other.

"Wait!" he said. "How do we know for sure that this is the antidote? It might be some deadly poison."

"Or it might make us twenty feet tall, like Baumella," said Little.

"You might grow a beard," said Miles.

"You might grow wings and turn purple," laughed Little.

"Well, here goes," said Miles. He put the vial to his mouth and swallowed the contents in one gulp. He expected it to taste horrible, or to burn his throat or make his ears hot, but it did nothing of the sort. In fact it didn't taste of anything much, apart from being cooler than he expected in that stuffy room. He could feel it slipping down his throat, and all his muscles relaxed as it passed down through him. In some strange way he thought it tasted blue, and he felt as though he had been holding his breath all his life without realising it, and had only just let it go. Little was looking at him through the open door of the furnace.

"You have turned purple" – she giggled – "and you look a lot better!"

Miles looked down at his hands. They were the same colour they had always been. He turned them over, but they were no different on the other side. "I suppose that was a joke," he said to himself. Out loud he said, "It's safe to drink."

As Little swallowed her dose, it occurred to him that it

might have a completely different effect on her. He was not sure what was inside an angel, or whether their insides worked in the same way as his. It might be anything but safe for her. He shrugged. "It seems to work for Silverpoint," he thought, "and anyway it's too late now."

He handed his empty vial back out to Little. She was licking her lips and looking rather disappointed. "It doesn't taste of much," she said.

"You'd better put the vials back quickly," said Miles.

She held them up and looked at them. "But they're empty. They'll know someone has stolen them," she said.

"I hadn't thought of that," said Miles. He was annoyed with himself. It was an important detail to have overlooked. If two doses were missed, suspicion would be bound to fall on them, or more likely on Silverpoint himself. "Have a look around the room," he said to Little, "and see if you can find the big bottle that he filled them from."

Little placed the two empty vials back in their slots and began searching the clutter on the table, being careful to replace everything where she found it. "Nothing here," she said. She did a slow circuit of the room, examining the items on the shelves. There were bottles and jars with liquids of all colours, and some with clear liquids in which a variety of snakes and lizards were suspended, but they were covered in dust and obviously seldom disturbed.

She came to the wooden cabinet in the corner and tried the doors. They were locked. She rattled them a couple of times to make sure, then moved on to the next set of shelves, wedged between the cabinet and a large porcelain sink. The rattling sound continued, as though someone inside the cabinet were trying to get out. Miles poked his head through the furnace door with difficulty. "Little!" he hissed urgently. "I think there's someone in the cabinet."

Little was trying the brass tap on the sink. She looked over her shoulder at the cabinet and frowned. "Not there," she whispered back. "It's the door."

Miles looked at the dark wooden door in the far corner and realised she was right. A key was rattling in the lock, and now he could hear muffled voices from the other side. "It's too late," he hissed. "Get back in here, quickly!" He shuffled back to make room for her, but instead of heading for the furnace she ran lightly back to the table and lifted the two empty vials from their rack. He heard the key turn in the lock. Little was back at the sink, holding the vials under the brass tap. The tap squeaked as she turned it on, but as luck would have it, the sound was masked by the creaky hinges of the door in the corner, which opened at the same moment. The voices were clearer now. "Is that really as far as your ambitions stretch?" said the Great Cortado's voice.

Little ran back to the table, her feet making no sound, and dropped the vials back into place. They were half full of water, and looked no different from the rest.

"That all depends," came Genghis's reedy voice, sounding slightly defensive. Little ducked down behind the table. The Great Cortado stepped into the room, holding the door open for his big-bellied companion. Miles held his breath. A condescending smirk lurked under Cortado's magnificent moustache. Little reached up from her hiding place and stoppered the second vial just as Genghis came through the door, and at the same moment Miles realised that the furnace door was still wide open. He inched backwards, trying to hide himself in darkness without the thick layer of ash beneath him crunching loudly. As he retreated from the furnace hatch he caught a last glimpse of Little crawling into the tight space under the table, before his view of the room was reduced to a small square of cluttered shelving.

"So you would like to be Mayor Genghis of Smallville," said the Great Cortado's voice.

"Oh no, not me," said Genghis. "You'd be the mayor. I was thinking more of . . . well . . . chief of police."

"I see," said Cortado. "And what town do you feel would be a worthy candidate, Chief Genghis?"

"Well," said Genghis enthusiastically, "I reckon somewhere like Larde would be ripe for the picking. With the money that's been pouring in from Tau-Tau's laugh juice, you could prob'ly buy the whole place, lock, stock and . . . whatever. We could set ourselves up in that big mansion just outside the town. It's a lot fancier than that pokey little town hall, and I reckon nobody'd be sorry if we gave the old loony that lives there her marching orders." He sniggered. "They wouldn't have no choice anyhow, not once you was mayor."

"I'm intrigued," said Cortado in a tone of mock sincerity that Genghis obviously took as genuine. "And what exactly would we do with this small population of peasant half-wits?"

"What would we do?" Genghis sounded a little confused. He began picking up the glass vials and placing them carefully in a worn leather doctor's bag. "Well . . . I could think of lots of things. For starters they would have to supply us all year round with the finest cigars and the best beers available. None of your yellow cat's pee, I mean real beer, with a big frothy head."

The Great Cortado suddenly appeared just outside the doorway of the furnace. Miles froze, afraid that he would look inside, but the moustachioed man just muttered under his breath, "Not the only thing around here with a big frothy head," and closed the furnace door. A momentary updraft lifted the fine ash from the floor and swirled it around the inside of the cramped iron box. Miles pinched his nose to stifle a sneeze, which made his eyes water. The voices in the laboratory were more muffled now, and he had to strain his ears to catch the drift of the conversation.

" . . . bear baiting, for instance," Genghis was saying. "They shouldn't never have banned that – it's just a bit of harmless fun. I used to go with me dad, God rest his soul, when I was no more than a kid. We had a dog ourselves. Snap, his name was. A good fighter, least he was until his back got broken. Eleven fights he made, and we always got ice cream afterward. And cockfights. Used to be two cockpits in Bunkrabble where I grew up. One at the canal dock, and the other in the priest's back garden. We could make 'em legal again, and have an arena built with a bear pit and cockpits, and fifty slot machines in each stand. That fancy church of theirs has a copper roof too, if you don't mind. That would pay for the whole lot if you stripped it down. And then we could have—"

"You'd have not much more than you've got now, but with the wheels taken off," interrupted the Great Cortado. "Genghis, you're a useful fellow at times, I'll grant you that, but I think you should leave the broader picture to me. It's not exactly your forte."

"I was just getting to the best bit . . . ," said Genghis, his voice trailing off. The itch in Miles's nose grew stronger. He could feel that sneeze hanging around, waiting for its chance. He pinched his nose again, wishing they would finish their conversation and leave.

"I can scarcely wait," said the Great Cortado, "but I'm afraid I shall have to. The performance starts in less than an hour, and we have some antidote to distribute, among other things. Have you counted the doses?"

"Thirty-six, Mr Cortado. Got 'em right here in the bag," said Genghis.

"Good," said Cortado. "Then let's not waste any more time."

Miles allowed himself a small sigh of relief as he heard the door hinges creak again. His legs were cramped under him, and his neck ached from bending his head in the small space. He shifted his position slightly, kicking up another small cloud of ash, and that was when his sneeze chose to ambush him. It was a prize-winning sneeze, and when it came out it sounded like a donkey who had swallowed a large dog. It boomed around the metal furnace and echoed up the chimney and out into the evening sky, where it startled a passing tawny owl who had just set out for his night's hunting. A slightly more muffled version echoed around the laboratory just as the door slammed shut.

Miles bit his lip. The door of the laboratory looked solid and heavy, and with the creaking hinges and the loud slam he was pretty sure they would not have heard his sneeze. He debated whether to try and hide himself in the chimney, or to risk a quick look through the yellowed glass of the furnace door to make sure the two men had gone. He wiped his nose on the back of his sleeve and listened. He could hear no sound from the laboratory. Finally he leaned forward to look out through the window in the furnace door, pressing his forehead against the grimy glass.

He could just see Little's foot beneath the table in the centre of the floor. There was no other sign of life, so he was taken completely by surprise when the furnace door was jerked open. It seemed to have grown bigger, and he almost tumbled out onto the floor. A large hand grabbed his collar, and he caught the flash of bright yellow socks and the smell of stale cigar smoke. A moment later he was hoisted through the air and held, dangling like a kitten, in front of Genghis's disbelieving face.

"Hello, Chief Genghis," he said.

CHAPTER TWENTY-NINE

FISH TO FRY

Genghis Big-belly, slack-jawed and dumbstruck, stared at the skinny boy dangling from his fist. The cigar stub detached itself slowly from his lower lip and dropped to the floor unnoticed.

"Can you put me down now please?" said Miles. Genghis let go of his collar, and Miles dropped to the floor. His legs, numb from being curled up in the dusty furnace, almost gave way under him, but he knew that if he fell he might draw attention to Little's hiding place, and he managed to remain standing. He returned the big man's bug-eyed stare steadily.

"It's him," said Genghis in his broken-whistle wheeze.

"It's that little weasel *again*. I swear there must be ten of him."

"So I see," said Cortado, who was standing quietly in the open doorway. His face was white behind his luxurious moustache, and he spoke carefully, as though holding his anger back with some effort. He closed the door softly behind him and walked around the laboratory table, pushing Genghis aside. He grasped Miles's chin and tilted his face up to look at him, although in truth he didn't need to tilt it far.

"Well, Selim," he said, "your little vanishing trick did take me by surprise, I must confess. I was surprised that anyone would be so stupid" – he brought his face closer to Miles and measured out his words like ice cubes dropping into a glass – "as to . . . steal . . . my . . . property . . . from under . . . my . . . nose."

"She's not your property. People aren't anyone's property," said Miles. His legs were shaking now, more from fear of the Great Cortado's anger than from cramp, but he felt that somehow it would be worse for him if he let his fear show.

"Circus freaks," said the Great Cortado, "are not people. You stole her. Now you will tell me where she is."

"I don't know where she is," said Miles. "She left when I cut the rope from her wrists, and I haven't seen her since."

"He's lying, the little snake," said Genghis. He gave Miles a sharp clout on the ear with his bandaged and bitten fist.

"Save it for later, Genghis," said Cortado. "You won't rattle anything out of this boy's head like that." He turned to Miles and dusted some ash from the shoulders of his filthy jacket. The normal colour had returned to Cortado's face, but the smile that lurked beneath his moustache was not matched in his eyes.

"Time enough to return to the subject of the freak later," he said. "As for you, Selim, your disappearing act seems to be surpassed only by your appearing act. Exactly what were you doing in my furnace, and how did you get in here in the first place?"

"I have a ticket," said Miles, producing the silver ticket from his inside pocket. He glanced at the furnace. He could see now that the small hatch through which Little had wriggled was set into a larger door that comprised most of the front of the furnace. It was this door that Genghis had opened in order to haul him out.

"So you do," said the Great Cortado. "But the ticket grants admisson to the auditorium, not to the furnace. And you are wasting my time, Selim."

"I got in through the chimney," said Miles. "I climbed on top of the hill because I didn't want to come in through the front door, and I found the chimney mouth up there. When I tried to climb down it, I fell, and got stuck in this dirty furnace. You should get Genghis to clean it out more often."

"I'll clean *you* out, little snake," wheezed Genghis. He raised his fist again, but stopped himself. "Can I hit him?" he said to the Great Cortado in a wheedling voice. "Just once?"

"I think not," said the Great Cortado. "If you knock him out now he might miss the show, and that would be a shame. After all, he does indeed have a ticket this time, and I'm sure once he sees what a fabulous entertainment we have put together he'll be much more open with us. His story doesn't explain such things as runaway sandbags and tunnel-crawling expeditions, and I am very keen to hear a more accurate version when we've cured him of his stubbornness."

"I could punch him in the kidneys," said Genghis hopefully. "That wouldn't knock him out, as such."

"After I'm finished with him you can do what you like," said Cortado. "From what he tells me, nobody will be sending out a search party. But first I want to find out what he's done with my circus freak, and I don't want him spitting blood onto my clean shirt while he's telling me." He took Miles by the elbow and steered him towards the door. Genghis followed, carrying his doctor's bag and sulking.

The passage outside was short, and ended in a flight of steps that spiralled upward and out of sight. The Great Cortado was in a hurry, and he took the stairs two at a time, keeping his grip on Miles's elbow. Genghis puffed and panted several steps behind them. At the top of the stairs was a heavy iron door such as you might see in a bank vault, assuming of course that you were wealthy enough to have any business at all in the basement of a bank. Miles and the Great Cortado reached the door, and waited for Genghis to catch up.

The larger man was gasping for breath by the time he arrived. He rummaged in his pocket for the key and fumbled it into the lock, beads of sweat trickling down his forehead. He leaned his weight against the door, and it opened onto a curving corridor. Gas lamps hissed quietly in their ghostly globes between the many closed doors, and beside each door was a small wire basket screwed to the wall. "I suppose," panted Genghis, dropping a vial of antidote into each basket as he passed, "that you'd have something grander in mind than a small town like Larde. Maybe like Sevenbridge, or even Turmeric."

The Great Cortado sighed deeply and shook his head. "Did I ever show you the scar that tiger left me before I killed it, Genghis?" he said. Miles pricked up his ears.

"Nasty business," panted Genghis. "What of it?"

"What of it, he asks," muttered Cortado, half to himself. They reached the lift, which stood with its gates open at the far end, and squeezed in. Genghis pulled the rattling iron gate closed and punched the button, and the lift creaked slowly into motion. He opened his doctor's bag and took out the two remaining vials.

"I'll tell you what of it, my boneheaded friend. I came within a whisker of losing my life to that tiger, and once you have stared into the mouth of death you will never look at life in the same way again. The tiger taught me a lesson that I would never forget, even if it were not indelibly written into my flesh. Do you know what that lesson is, Genghis?"

"Stay away from tigers?"

The Great Cortado laughed. He uncorked his vial and swallowed its contents. His laughter ceased at once and a frown took its place.

"I know," said Genghis. "It's 'Never tie your blunderbuss to the wall with wire.' If you'd just hung it on a couple of them big hooks, you'd have—"

"Shut up, Genghis," said Cortado. "If you spent less time blabbering and more time listening, you might learn something."

"But you asked—"

"It was a rhetorical question, Genghis. The lesson the tiger taught me was this. We arrive on this Earth as feeble, mewling bags of spit, and most of us remain little more than that until the day we die. The only thing that makes a real man is power. Without power over other people, and over the dumb beasts themselves, you are nothing." He smoothed the ends of his moustache thoughtfully. "That tiger was left to me by a good friend of mine. He was a man with heart and energy and humour, but none of these qualities were worth a rat's whisker when it came down to it, because he didn't have the power to avert the cruel trick that fate had in store for him."

"Blimey," said Genghis. "That's a bit bleak, ain't it?" He swallowed his dose of antidote and replaced the two empty vials in the bag, belching loudly as he snapped it shut.

"Bleak? It's reality. Before I looked death in the eye, my ambition was simply to own the biggest and most successful circus in the land. I wanted fame and money, but I knew nothing of the importance of power. Power is the only thing that counts, Genghis."

The lift continued to grind slowly upwards through its stone shaft. The Great Cortado's face grew pensive. "I spent years researching the power of laughter, and devoted many more to devising the tools with which to control it. You don't think I spent all that effort just to become an unofficial civil servant in a godforsaken cluster of stone huts like Larde."

"Er, no. Of course not," said Genghis. He frowned for a moment, then said, "Why did you?"

"Because I have bigger fish to fry," said the Great Cortado. Miles paid close attention. The two men seemed almost to have forgotten he was there, but he had listened with interest as the Great Cortado listed what was not included in his ambitions, and now he was curious to know what was.

"Tau-Tau's tonic is more addictive than any amount of beer and bear baiting to someone who's been processed by our little show. More even than those steamed ginger puddings you stuff into your fat face as though there was no tomorrow." There was no sign of a smile on the Great Cortado's face as he said this. Genghis licked his lips thoughtfully.

"Being the only people who know how to make the stuff puts us in a position of considerable power, and that power grows greater with every godforsaken village we put through the mangle. If we were to cut off the supply of Tau-Tau's for a week, we'd have the whole country out in riots. But this is just a start, Genghis. Once I have enough—"

Genghis cleared his throat loudly and jerked his head at Miles.

"What is it, Genghis?" sighed Cortado.

"The boy," said Genghis from the corner of his mouth. "He'll hear you."

The lift ground to a halt, and the Great Cortado waited

for Genghis to open the gates. "What of it?" he said. "By the time he has seen our fabulous show he'll be hard-pressed to remember his own name, and I'm sure this conversation will have slipped his mind altogether." He smiled coldly at Miles. "Open the gates, Genghis," he said.

"Once we have the peasantry hooked, it will be time to reel in the bigger fish," he continued, as he stepped out of the lift. "We will have a season of gala spectaculars at the Palace of Laughter. They will be by invitation only, and we will round up every duke and marchioness and government minister, every bishop and rabbi and general, the prime minister and the chancellor and the entire royal family and God Almighty himself, if we can find his postal address, and we will lay on a show that outshines our most hilarious performances by a factor of three. We will entice everyone with power and influence in the land to spend an unforgettable night under our roof, and before the week is out they will be back in their town halls and palaces, and the power and influence will all be in my pocket."

Genghis let out a whooshing sound that was meant to be a low whistle. "Well I'd have to say that your plan makes mine look like kid's stuff, and no mistake," he said. "You've certainly got the breadth of vision there, that was lacking in my little scenario."

"Elegantly put," said the Great Cortado. "Now let's get

our guest down to the auditorium before the show begins."
They walked along another curving corridor. There was
only one door in this one. It was painted midnight blue, and
the words "Master of Ceremonies" were carefully stencilled
onto it with silver paint. The Great Cortado stopped outside the door and turned to Miles. "This is where we part
for now, Selim. We'll have another little chat after the show,
and I have no doubt you will be more cooperative then.
Genghis, make sure he has a ringside seat." He closed the
door after him, leaving Miles and Genghis alone.

They stepped into the gloom of the entrance hall,
Genghis gripping Miles's elbow with his unpleasant pinch.
Between the tall pillars Miles could dimly see the outline
of Baumella the giantess seated, just as Silverpoint had said,
with her back against the huge double doors. He could not
tell if she was awake or sleeping. They marched towards the
smaller doors that led into the theatre itself, neither of
them noticing the wiry, blackfaced figure of String, who
watched from the shadows behind one of the pillars. His
recaptured bone was tucked into the belt of his trousers,
and there was a glint of malice in his eye.

"Now," said Genghis, tightening his grip on Miles's
elbow, "what was that you said about making me clean out
the furnace?"

"That was just a little joke," said Miles.

"I'm not laughing," said Genghis.

It was on the tip of Miles's tongue to say "That'll be the antidote," but for once he kept his mouth shut. In their hurry they almost bumped into a sour-looking man hobbling on a pair of wooden crutches, his leg plastered from toe to knee.

"What happened to you, Bobo?" wheezed Genghis. "Slipped on the soap, I suppose."

The hobbling man gave off a smell that was every bit as sour as his face, a smell that Miles recognised from the night before, when he and Little had been brought down in the lift to their temporary prison. It was the tramp clown, unpainted today, and certainly still unwashed.

"Very funny," he grunted. "Matter of fact I fell off the high wire, broke me friggin' ankle. I see you're babysittin' one of them little jokers. Who got lumbered with the other one?"

"The other one?" said Genghis. He twisted Miles's arm up behind his back and brought his face down until the burning tip of his cigar was an inch from the boy's nose. "So you weren't alone in that lab, you little weasel. Here, Bobogeek . . . ," he said to the tramp clown. "You just got yourself a new job. Take this one in and make sure he gets a seat in the front row. If he tries anything funny you can hit him with your crutches. You can call it self defense, you being a cripple and all. I've got another one to catch."

"Right so," said Bobogeek, "and try not to let her out-smart you this time, eh?" He let out a nasty whinnying laugh.

Genghis gave no answer. He let go of Miles's arm and aimed a clout at his head. Miles ducked, and the big man's fist landed a hard punch on Bobogeek's arm.

"Oy!" said the tramp clown. "What was that for?"

"For the little weasel," wheezed Genghis. "You can owe it to him." He turned on his heel and hurried back towards the lift.

CHAPTER THIRTY

MANY A SLIP

Miles Wednesday, filthy, front-rowed and (shhh!) anti-doted, sat wedged into a narrow space right at the ringside. On his left sat Bobogeek, his plastered foot stretched out in front and a couple of small but persistent flies buzzing around his head, and to his right sat none other than Haunch the butcher of Larde. Haunch had looked at Miles in surprise as he sat down beside him. "Well well, Master Miles," he said, craning his thick neck to get a better look at the boy. "I didn't see you on the train, nor in the hotel neither, and I thought I'd seen everyone. You was hiding in a luggage rack, I'll wager."

"Not me," said Miles. "I wasn't even on the train. I walked here."

Haunch the butcher guffawed. "That's a good 'un, boy. There must have been something special in them bones I gave you. Reckon I'll double the price on them in future – too good for dogs they are." He chuckled again.

"What on earth is he laughing at?" Miles thought to himself, but then he remembered the stolen antidote he had taken, and he forced a small laugh out of himself for Bobogeek's benefit. It felt like a strange noise to be making.

"Not sure I'd have recognised you, mind, with that funny hairstyle," Haunch went on. "Must be all the fashion, eh? You're the second lad I've seen with a funny hairdo since I came in here. Tell you what," he said, leaning close and tapping his nose with a thick finger, "come round and clean my yard next week, and I'll keep some sausages by for you this time. You're a good little worker, lad." His breath smelled of the brandy that he had had the foresight to bring with him on the journey, which no doubt also accounted for his mood being lighter than usual.

Miles wondered for a moment who it could have been that Haunch saw with an odd hairstyle, and decided that it must have been himself, as Bobogeek steered him down through the seats to the front row. The other seats had been filling up steadily, and the circus band had taken their places among the strange assortment of pipes, horns and gongs in the pit at the far side of the ring. Miles could spot many other faces that were familiar to him from his hometown: Piven the baker and his wife sat opposite him, and behind him was Flifford the bicycle mechanic, difficult to recognise without smears of grey axle grease decorating his face. Father Soutane sat over to the right, listening earnestly to the stream of gossip that Lily the florist poured into his ear. There was not much that Lily did not know about what went on in Larde, and where there were gaps in her knowledge she was happy to fill them in with details that she made up herself.

The boom of an enormous gong signalled the arrival of the clowns, who trotted and cartwheeled down among the seats and spilled out onto the clean sawdust of the ring. The band struck up the same crazy music that Miles and Little had heard from the tunnels the night before. The music looped and squealed, but it did not sound at all funny this time. Miles watched the rest of the audience, some of whom were already beginning to chuckle, and he took his cue from them. When the clowns began an exercise routine that looked like a chaotic kind of tai chi, Miles made himself laugh along with the rest.

He could see Silverpoint, in his tall chef's hat, directing the exercise routine with graceful movements that the other clowns were failing miserably to mimic. Silverpoint glanced over at him, and Miles could see his eyes searching the benches for Little. His face remained expressionless, and after a moment he looked away.

Haunch's shoulders were shaking now with laughter. Miles couldn't remember if his own shoulders shook when he laughed – he had never thought to check. He tried shaking them, but it just felt silly, so he contented himself with producing laughter of the non-shaking variety. Bobogeek was scanning the rest of the audience, his arms folded and his crutches parked by his side. His face wore a miserable scowl.

All of a sudden the music stopped, and the clowns froze with it. In the centre of the ring stood the Great Cortado, his hair slicked back and curling behind his ears, the huge moustache on his small round face perfectly waxed and pointed. He had changed into a dark blue suit with silver buttons, and he spoke without trumpet or megaphone, his voice booming around the packed theatre as though it belonged to a man four times his size. "**Ladies and Gentlemen, welcome to the Palace of Laughter,**" he began. "**Tonight it is your Immense Privilege to witness the most spec-tac-u-lar, the most Fan-tas-tical, the most Hil-larious Ex-travaganza of Laughter . . . ,**" and on he went, word for rolling word, with the opening speech that Miles had heard from the tunnels the night before. The audience listened a trifle impatiently, eager to get past the introduction and on with the promised hilarity. Some tittered at the sight of the Bolsillo brothers, who were not having as much success as the other clowns at staying still, and were having a little spat with much rib digging and eye poking. Fabio was picking the Great Cortado's pocket as he spoke, pulling out a large handkerchief and looking at it with an expression of disgust.

Silverpoint was staring Miles in the eye, as though he could find some clue there as to the whereabouts of Little, and how they had become separated, but Miles could give no kind of signal without making Bobogeek suspicious. The Great Cortado was approaching the end of his speech. " . . . be prepared to be entertained as you have never been entertained before!" he boomed. "Tonight the greatest comics in the Wide World will take you Beyond Laughter, and your Lives will be Transformed, FOREVER!"

The people clapped and cheered. "Didn't they hear what he just said?" Miles thought to himself. "What do they think he meant?" It seemed so obvious to him, squeezed into his seat and waiting for disaster to befall him in one guise or another.

A cloud of blue smoke enveloped the Great Cortado, and when it dispersed he was gone. Miles felt pretty sure he had not disappeared through the trapdoor. He searched in the dimness of the banked seating and spotted Cortado after a moment, slipping out through one of the exits at the back, unnoticed by the mesmerised audience. The band had struck up as he finished speaking and was in full flight again. The music seemed a meaningless babble. In the middle of the ring lay a clown, dressed in a tramp costume and with a downturned white mouth painted on a blackened face, who Miles guessed must be a stand-in for the injured Bobogeek. He was trying to sleep under an open newspaper. Between his feet lay a small white dog, who kept snatching the newspaper in his teeth and pulling it over himself. Each time he did this the clown gave a violent shiver and grabbed it back.

The tramp clown finally got the upper hand. He began to snore like an ox, the band counting out his snores with booms and clashes of their gongs. The Bolsillo brothers, meanwhile, were wobbling at breakneck speed around the ring on their unicycle. While Fabio pedalled, Gila and Umor perched on his shoulders. Umor whistled, and the elephant ambled down through the startled audience and began to chase the unicycle. The people of Larde laughed until they cried, and the music squealed on.

Miles listened to the harsh, ugly laughter and he began to understand now what Little had said about the One Song. The hysterical braying of the audience was not real laughter.

It had been torn from the One Song like a single filament from a rope, and without the harmony of the other strands it could cut through the soul like a taut wire cuts through cheese. He tried to block out the sound and concentrate on the show, searching among the flapping boots and rainbow trousers for any sign of Tangerine. As he forced out a noise that he hoped would suffice for laughter, he worried too about Little. He hoped that she would have wasted no time in escaping up the chimney once they had closed the door behind them. If she delayed too long Genghis would surely find her still there on his return, and without Cortado to control him there was no knowing what he might do. Miles pictured her flying up the length of the chimney and out into the night sky, and holding on to that thought, he forced his attention back to the antics in the ring.

If you have ever had to wait in the wings for your part in a play or a show, you may have some idea how Miles felt as he sat wedged between a large butcher and a smelly clown and watched for his moment. The antidote he had taken certainly quenched laughter, but it did not have the same effect on nerves. His stomach was full of knots, and half of him wished that something would happen that would prevent him from having to leap up on the stage at all. His timing would have to be perfect, and there would be no second chance.

He stole a glance at Bobogeek. The smelly clown was staring at his snoring substitute with a look of sour boredom on his unwashed face. In the ring, the snoring clown was having a dream. Another clown, dressed like a clean and colourful version of himself, perched behind him on a large boulder, holding a small fishing rod. He whistled loudly as he fished, a broad white smile painted on his face. Behind him Miles could see Fabio Bolsillo attempting to oil the elephant's knees. His two brothers were proving more of a hindrance than a help. A lot of oil ended up underfoot, and there was a great deal of slipping and sliding.

The fishing clown suddenly caught a bite, and after a brief struggle a sea lion appeared from behind the rock, the end of the fishing line in her whiskered mouth. The sea lion was dressed in a lime green tutu, and the fishing clown lost his heart to her at first sight. He tumbled off the rock and landed on one knee, clasping his hands and serenading the sea lion with a wordless barking song. The band played on, and the audience howled with laughter.

The tutu-wearing sea lion turned tail and fled, the fishing clown hot on her tail. His hat fell from his head and began to run around the ring as though it had a life of its own. Miles watched it curiously. Suddenly the hat came to rest, and a small orange bear climbed out. Tangerine!

Miles almost leaped from his seat at once. The newly

washed bear had regained some of his bright orange colour, but there was no mistaking his floppy legs and his slightly crossed eyes. Besides, there were not many stuffed bears who could stumble about a circus ring on their own, waving at the audience and tripping up the performers. The people of Larde, purple faced from laughter, clutched their sides and pointed at Tangerine. So much was going on at one time that many of them seemed unable to decide which way to turn. A look of bewilderment began to mix itself with the laughter in their eyes. The music raced ever faster, and the action in the ring became a whirlwind. The fishing clown seemed somehow to have died. The Bolsillo brothers ran out from behind a screen in their undertaker suits, carrying a coffin. It was shorter than the clown, but they wedged him into it. They lifted the coffin, and the bottom fell out, corpse and all. The Bolsillo brothers threw away the coffin and buried the fishing clown in a mound of sawdust. A giant daisy pushed its way up through the mound.

Miles was distracted briefly by a light from the back of the auditorium, and he saw Genghis slipping in from the hallway outside. His face was black with soot and with anger, but he appeared to be alone. Miles looked back at the ring. The elephant had reached over Fabio's shoulder and grasped the daisy with his trunk. He pulled, and the clown came up from the mound, stiff as a board and still clutching the daisy in his intertwined fingers. Miles could no longer see Tangerine. He searched the ring, but the bear was nowhere to be found. The Bolsillo brothers were chasing the resurrected clown, who had stolen their unicycle and ridden it straight through Silverpoint's pie. Silverpoint was shooting firebolts in all directions. His face wore its usual calm expression, but the firebolts seemed to be coming thick and fast, and there was barely a clown in the ring whose trousers, hat or wig wasn't smouldering. The band was playing like a party of dervishes, and the booming, clanging and squealing made Miles feel as though his head itself were one of the gongs.

Genghis was making his way towards him now, pushing the stupefied Lardespeople aside as he clambered over the benches. Miles looked back into the ring in desperation. Silverpoint was pointing straight at him, his cool eyes fixed on Miles's face. A firebolt crackled through the air towards him, finding its mark just above him and to his left. Bobogeek let out a howl of surprise. His eyebrows had disappeared and his tufty hair was smoking. "Oy!" he roared. In the centre of the ring the trapdoor was opening, and from it poured a thick cloud of purple and green smoke. Beside the trapdoor Silverpoint was shouting something at Miles that he couldn't catch. The Storm Angel cupped his hands around his mouth. "You're on!" he yelled.

Miles felt as though he had suddenly been unglued from his seat. He leaped into the ring as the shape of the throne began to emerge from the coloured smoke. The three Bolsillo brothers were leading the elephant around the back of the throne, ready to park her on the trapdoor. Fabio tossed the oil can into the air as Miles ran toward the pillar of smoke. "Mind the holes," shouted Fabio. What holes? The floor was flat and smooth beneath the sawdust. The ring seemed twice as large now that he was in it. A blur of open-mouthed faces filled the surrounding darkness. He caught the oil can and almost dropped it straight through his fingers. The outside of the can was slippery as a fish, and more oil was pouring from at least three different places. *Those* holes! The throne continued to rise. He reached the smoke cloud, still searching for Tangerine, and tried to stop, but the floor was already slick with oil, and though his feet stopped, Miles kept going. He collided with something hard and fell backwards into the greasy sawdust.

As the smoke began to clear, he could see he had hit the edge of the open trapdoor. He scrambled to his feet with difficulty, oil still pouring from the holes in the can. The dark shape of the throne loomed above him, already nearly at its full height. He had lost precious seconds, but it was not too late. The narrow spout would not pour quickly enough, so he grasped the slippery can with both hands, leaned out over the yawning hole, and turned it upside down. For a long second nothing happened, then the last few drops of oil dribbled from the can and began to trickle slowly down the steel pillar.

Miles held his breath. The can was empty. The smoke was dispersing, and he squinted up at the throne that towered above him. It had not slipped downward by so much as an inch. Time seemed to have slowed to a crawl. He could see the Great Cortado high above him, framed in the glare of the lights. "Now you have felt . . . ," the Great Cortado began, and stopped. "Now you . . ." He leaned out from his throne and stared down at Miles, who was suddenly aware of how funny he must look: a failed, half-shaved saboteur coated in oil, soot and sawdust.

He expected to see a look of thunder on the Great Cortado's face, but to Miles's surprise it looked as though two people were fighting for control of his features. Cortado seemed to be struggling not to laugh. Suddenly it dawned on Miles what must have happened. The Great Cortado had not had any antidote! Standing in the creaking lift earlier that evening, he had unknowingly swallowed nothing more than a mouthful of plain water from the brass tap in the laboratory. Now a thousand nights of concentrated laughter were welling up behind his reddening face, looking for a way out, and only Miles could understand what was happening.

He glanced quickly about him. Silverpoint and the Bolsillo brothers were looking at him expectantly. The audience's laughter had begun to falter, and a number of clowns were advancing on him menacingly. He thought of Little, hiding somewhere below, far from the world of light and freedom where she belonged, and the tiger's words echoed in his head: "A friendship should be judged by its depth, not by its length." Miles nodded to himself. It was time to set her free.

He picked up the empty oil can and threw it at Bobogeek's stand-in, who was getting too close for comfort. The can bounced off his head with a loud *toink*, and the tramp clown slithered comically in the grease before losing his balance altogether and landing heavily on his padded backside. "On with the show!" shouted Miles. The Bolsillo brothers exchanged puzzled glances, then sprang into action as though Miles's words had released their overwound clockwork. Gila, rolled into a ball, came careering across the ring and bowled over three of Cortado's clowns like skittles. Umor grabbed the crutches from Bobogeek, who was slithering across the ring on one plastered foot. He hopped up onto the crutches like a pair of makeshift stilts and tottered over to the fishing clown, now the same height as him. "Look at me, I'm normal!" Umor hollered. The audience laughed. He grabbed the fishing clown's nose and tweaked it hard. The clown gave a yelp of pain.

The band, confused, struck up again, and their insane music rattled around the theatre, bringing more laughter in its wake. A clown's curly green wig burst suddenly into flames, and another found the seat of his pants on fire and began to run around the ring shouting for a fire hose. A burly clown with a long red nose like a carrot grabbed Silverpoint from behind. There was a loud crack, and the man staggered backwards with blue sparks flying from his ears. Miles expected to be confronted with an irate Genghis at any moment, but he seemed to have vanished into thin air, yellow socks and all. A strangled sound came from above him, and he looked up to see the Great Cortado pointing at him with a quivering finger.

"This boy . . ." He choked, the words barely escaping his throat. "This boy . . . has ruined . . . my . . . show."

And he began to laugh.

CHAPTER THIRTY-ONE

TIN CAN'T

The Great Cortado, clownmaster and laughter-tamer, stood on his throne high above the people of Larde, and laughed. He threw back his head and opened his throat wide and a volcano of laughter roared up into the Palace of Laughter's domed ceiling. It bounced off the pillars and echoed around the walls until it filled the entire theatre. He doubled over and clutched his stomach, he bellowed and hooted as the tears ran down his cheeks. Year upon year and show upon show, joke after joke after gag after pratfall came back to him in an irresistible rush, and with no antidote to protect him his face turned pink, then purple, and the veins stood out on his forehead like knotted string. His face-painted henchmen stared, openmouthed, as he crumpled to his knees and tumbled slowly from his perch, falling twelve feet to the floor below and landing with a clang, his head wedged tightly in the empty oil can.

There was a moment's stunned silence, then Silverpoint stepped in front of the Great Crumpled Cortado. He raised his arms as he had seen the Great Cortado do every other night for months. "Ladies and Gentlemen," he shouted, but before he could get any further he was interrupted by a growl from Bobogeek, who had struggled to his feet and was standing unsteadily on his good leg. He pointed at Silverpoint and Miles. "Saboteurs!" he yelled in his nasal whine. "Hypnotists! Subversives! They're trying to take over your minds. Don't listen to a word!"

"Ladies and Gentlemen," began Silverpoint again, shouting louder this time. "Now you have seen the true power of laughter. Elemental laughter that can restore your souls to—"

"Don't listen to him!" yelled Bobogeek. "He'll turn yiz into baboons."

At this, Silverpoint's calm expression cracked slightly. He sent a firebolt flying at Bobogeek's chest, knocking him backwards into another clown. Behind them the faces in the crowd were looking confused and angry. They were muttering to one another, and some were shouting,

"Saboteurs! Hypnotists! Baboons!" Somewhere in the middle of the crowd a man was still laughing uncontrollably. It sounded like Genghis.

Silverpoint tried a different tack. "We're on your side. *They* are the hypnotists. You will be safe with us." But without the height of the throne he was just one of a gaggle of clowns trying to shout one another down.

Cortado's henchmen had picked themselves up, and extinguished their wigs and trousers. "Get them," they shouted to the crowd. "Hold them down! String 'em up!"

"He's one of them," shrieked a woman in the audience. Several men, and a little old woman with a sharp green umbrella, had left their seats and were climbing into the ring.

Silverpoint stepped back from the advancing clowns and the irate audience. "What now, plan man?" he muttered to Miles. "And where's Little?"

"She's hiding," said Miles.

"Where?" hissed Silverpoint, but Miles was saved from having to answer. At that moment the main double doors at the back of the theatre burst open and a loud voice said, "That's ENOUGH!"

The audience, the clowns and the saboteurs turned as one and stared up at the double doors. Even Genghis, the unlucky winner of the second vial of plain water, twisted his head and gazed up through streaming eyes from where he sat in the aisle, giggling like a large, fat hyena.

Lady Partridge stood framed in the doorway, her hands on her hips and the red dragons flaming in her coal-black dressing gown. "SETTLE DOWN, ALL OF YOU," she boomed, and she began to march down the sloping aisle toward the ring, stepping over Genghis as though he were a bag of rubbish. A stream of cats followed in her wake.

The big clown with the carrot nose stepped in front of her as she approached the end of the aisle. "Authorised personnel only," he said, raising his palm like a policeman stopping a truck.

Lady Partridge paused and stepped to one side. "Gulliver!" she said, and to Miles's astonishment Baltinglass of Araby popped out from behind Lady Partridge's large silhouette. His woolly hat was still on his head, and several days' white stubble bristled from his chin.

"That's no way to speak to a lady," he barked at the clown, and dealt him a sharp crack on the shin with his cane. The clown let out a yelp and hopped backward.

"Who on earth are they?" said Silverpoint.

"It's okay," beamed Miles. "They're friends of mine." He had never been so pleased to see anyone in his life. Lady Partridge swept towards him across the ring like a monument on wheels. Baltinglass followed in the path that her long dressing gown made through the sawdust. Bobogeek, the only one who wasn't glued to the spot by this unexpected interruption, hop-clunked towards them on the one crutch he had managed to retrieve. Baltinglass of Araby stopped and turned toward the sound.

"You got a wooden leg, lad?"

"No, ye blind fossil," sneered Bobogeek.

"Would you like one?" shouted Baltinglass, and he whipped a sword stick from the centre of his cane. Bobogeek stepped backwards sharply.

Baltinglass wrinkled his nose. "What happened, did you slip on the soap?"

There was a howl of laughter from the aisle. "That's exactly what I said," spluttered Genghis, and he collapsed into giggles again.

The audience had given up trying to make heads or tails of what was going on. They slumped back in their seats with their jaws hanging open, some of them still breaking into fits of laughter.

"Hello, Miles dear," said Lady Partridge as she reached the foot of the throne, and she gave him a wink that only he could see. She looked over at the Bolsillo brothers and their elephant. "Well don't just stand there, boys," she said. "Ask Jumbo to lift me up on this thing." She waved up at the empty throne, as though it had been raised specifically for her arrival.

"The name's Tembo, ma'am."

"Well, Tembo, ask your elephant to give me a lift."

"Tembo's the elephant, ma'am. He's Gila. Hup!"

"Lucky she's been in training," said Gila.

"Manners, Gila," said Fabio, pulling Gila's hat down over his eyes.

Tembo curled her trunk and Lady Partridge stepped onto it. The elephant raised her high into the air. "Hup," said Gila again, and Tembo stood on her hind legs. Lady Partridge wobbled slightly, but if she was nervous she didn't show it. She stepped onto the platform and sat herself on the throne, her untidy pile of grey hair obscuring the manic clown's face painted on its high back.

"Now," she boomed, "would someone please tell me what is going on here? You all look like you've spent a month in the asylum."

"Who are you?" shouted Bobogeek, trying to shake a cat from his leg without falling over. "And why should we tell you anything?"

Lady Partridge glared down at the smelly man. "A gentleman would wait his turn," she said. "However, since you ask, I am Lady Partridge of Larde. In fact, you could say that I'm now a Partridge in a Bare Tree." Some of the audience groaned at Lady Partridge's terrible joke, and even Genghis stopped laughing for a moment.

"Well?" said Lady Partridge, looking down at Miles.

"This man is the Great Cortado," said Miles, pointing at the crumpled heap with his head in an oil can. "He's devised a way of hypnotising people with laughter, so he can get them hooked on a tonic that only he knows how to produce. He plans to gain control over the whole country."

"Is that so?" said Lady Partridge. She sat straight-backed on the throne and swept the audience with a stern gaze, like a schoolmistress with a class full of naughty pupils. "You were about to let this half-pint with a tin can on his head take over the country?" She gave a healthy guffaw that seemed to sweep the remnants of stale laughter from the air. "Tin can't, more like," she boomed.

The audience groaned. Lady Partridge's awful sense of humour was swiftly taking the edge off their hysteria, and only Genghis, who like Cortado had suffered from a massive overdose of Palace of Laughter performances, chuckled on helplessly.

"Well well," said Lady Partridge, searching the gloom beyond the ring, "Hilda Scratch, is that you? Your mascara has all run down to your chin, girl. You look like a badger. And Spivey, your wife has fallen off her chair. Pick her up for goodness' sake, man. What on earth's the matter with you all? One day trip and you go completely gaga. You all plainly need to get out more."

As she spoke, some of Cortado's clowns began to sneak out of the spotlit ring and up through the dumbstruck audience towards the exit doors. It seemed as though the tables had well and truly turned on their leader. They did not know what kind of treatment this formidable woman would have in mind for them, and they did not want to stay around and find out.

"They're getting away," whispered Miles to Baltinglass.

"No they're not, Master Miles," Baltinglass whispered back. "My nephew Radovan and his constabulary have the place surrounded. At least thirty pairs of good boots I heard, and a great deal of whistle blowing, although that had to be stopped when we got near the place. Had to take the whistles off a couple of the younger lads. Excitable chaps, but keen."

"Taking over the country indeed!" continued Lady Partridge from her throne. "I can scarcely believe you could all fall for this mind-control mumbo jumbo. You should be ashamed of yourselves! I don't doubt that you could all do with cheering up, but there are better ways to brighten your lives than the sort of quackery that these charlatans are trying to sell you. You could start by not cheating your customers out of their change, Piven. Everyone knows they come out of your shop a little light in the pocket. And you, Lily Green, why don't you set up a town newspaper so everyone can read your gossip in black and white, and with the same details to boot? You could get that sister of yours to run the florist shop for you."

She scanned the faces in the gloom, and their owners began to straighten themselves up, as though waking from a bad dream. Many were dimly aware that they had seen this lady in the dressing gown somewhere before. They took out handkerchiefs and wiped their chins. They straightened their hair and their ties in case they were next in line to be singled out.

"And you, Father Soutane," said Lady Partridge, "you should be running a choir in that church of yours, instead of cranking out the same dismal tunes week after week from that wheezy old organ. From the sound of the braying I heard on my way in here, you'd have plenty of strong voices to choose from. Maybe if you all got together three times a week to sing a few stirring songs, you wouldn't get so overexcited when you do get out for a day trip."

The Great Cortado began to stir in the shadow of the throne. Miles caught the movement out of the corner of his eye, and watched him closely. He sat up shakily and reached his hand up to feel his head. His fingers walked around the slippery outside of the oil can, then knocked on it once or twice. "Anyone home?" came a muffled voice from inside the can. "Nope," replied the same voice after a pause. "Got a new head then," said the Not-So-Great Cortado to himself, and he began to laugh in a muffled, metallic way.

Lady Partridge peered down at him. "Help him up, there's a good fellow," she said to Silverpoint. The Great Cortado's legs buckled under him a couple of times, but eventually Miles and Silverpoint succeeded in getting him to his feet. The tinny laughter that echoed from inside the can was answered by fits of giggling from Genghis, slumped in the darkness of the aisle. As he lay there helplessly, a small figure with a topknot slipped out unnoticed from behind the seats and rifled through his pockets before disappearing through the double doors at the back of the theatre.

"Take a good look at these two fellows," said Lady Partridge to the people of Larde. "I think we can safely say that they're out of the World Domination business for the foreseeable future. Now perhaps we can all forget about this nonsense, and make our way back home." She looked down at Baltinglass of Araby. "Gulliver, please lead these people back to the Station Hotel, where they can have a good night's rest before making the journey home. Tell the landlord that the Circus Oscuro will be footing the bill."

And so the people of Larde began to gather themselves – butcher and baker, horse doctor and seamstress and librarian and priest, like a crowd of revellers waking from a party that had gone on for far too long. They helped one another into their coats, picked up their neighbours who were still wobbly on their feet, and made their way to the exit doors, herded by the blind explorer, who was not above dishing out the odd rap with his stick to keep things moving at a brisk pace.

At a word from Gila, Tembo lifted Lady Partridge down from the Great Cortado's throne, and with the help of the elephant the Bolsillo brothers joined Baltinglass in rounding up the stragglers and leading them out of the theatre. As the last few Lardespeople left, Sergeant Bramley made his way into the theatre. His uniform was rumpled and he had lost his hat, but he looked pleased with himself.

"Thirty-four assorted villains and one huge tattooed lady apprehended, Lady P," he reported as he marched down toward the ring. "The suspects have been placed under arrest and an agreement has been reached with the city constabulary. Cheeky bleeders, begging your pardon, ma'am, wanted to take credit for the whole operation, but we settled on taking the ringleaders back to Larde to be tried by the district judge, while the lower-ranking scoundrels get locked up here in Smelt North Central."

"Congratulations, Sergeant Bramley," said Lady Partridge. "An excellent day's policing without a doubt."

"Nice of you to say so, Lady P," said the sergeant. "I take it this here is the criminal mastermind?" he added a little doubtfully, eyeing the Great Cortado with his tin-can head.

"He's called the Great Cortado," said Miles. "He's been hypnotising the whole country, bit by bit."

"Is that so?" said Sergeant Bramley, wondering where he had seen this boy with the strange hairstyle before. "Well he won't be doing no more hypnotising once we've got him under lock and key." He took the disoriented Cortado by the arm. "You're under arrest," he said for the tenth time that evening. He had smashed his previous arrest record, which was two vagrants in the same summer, and he was very pleased with himself. "Now," he said, addressing Lady Partridge, "if you wouldn't mind taking these two young lads and vacating these here premises, I'll send in my boys to seal them off for further investigation."

"You go on ahead," said Lady Partridge. "We'll be leaving shortly, and we'll make sure to seal off after us."

"Well . . . ," said Sergeant Bramley, but Lady Partridge fixed him with a hard stare, and he said no more. He marched the Great Giggling Cortado up the aisle to where Genghis lay in a sniggering heap. With the practised use of his truncheon, the sergeant managed to prod him to his feet and arrest him too, and out through the double doors he went, an archvillain in each hand and a beam of satis-faction on his doughy face.

"Well indeed," said Lady Partridge when he had gone. "I'm delighted to see you safe and sound, Miles, but where is Little, and who is this young man?"

"This is Silverpoint," said Miles. "And I left Little hiding in the laboratory, down in the basement."

"A pleasure to meet you, Silverpoint," said Lady Partridge. "And now we had better fetch Little at once. She must be frightened down there on her own."

"Genghis has the key," said Miles, suddenly remember-ing the locked iron door to the basement.

"Which one is Genghis?" asked Lady Partridge.

"The big man with the yellow socks, who sergeant Bramley just arrested."

"Then we shall go outside at once and have the sergeant search his pockets for the keys, and while we're about it I shall persuade him to lend us a van and a driver so we can all repair to Gulliver Baltinglass's house for the night, as soon as we have rescued Little. I can't wait to hear how you managed to storm the Palace of Laughter and tin the Great Cortado all by yourselves."

"I'm staying here," said Miles as a wave of tiredness swept over him. "I can't leave until I've found Tangerine."

CHAPTER THIRTY-TWO

STRING

String the ex-Halfhead, revenge-bent and armed with a reclaimed bone and a dozen keys, crept through the deserted corridors deep below the rapidly emptying theatre. He had sneaked into the Palace of Laughter with the crowd of peasants, wrinkling his nose at the unfamiliar smells they wore, which he imagined must be the smells of cows and sheep and other country things that he had never seen. He had hidden himself behind a pillar in the entrance hall as the audience filed into the theatre. From his hiding place he had watched as Genghis appeared, dragging Miles by the elbow. He saw them meet the man with the broken leg, and overheard enough of their conversation to guess that the winged girl was still hidden somewhere. He had seen Genghis take the creaking lift to a lower floor, and after a while he had seen him reappear, his face as black as thunder, tucking into his pocket a large ring of keys as he entered the auditorium.

It was clear to String what he had to do. He would sneak into the theatre itself and steal the big man's keys while his attention was distracted by the show. He was no stranger to picking pockets, and he felt confident that the hysterical laughter and crazy music he could hear through the doors would provide him with good cover. The real problem lay in getting to the double doors that led into the theatre in the first place. The entrance hall was deserted except for String himself, a giant tattooed lady, and a number of tall pillars. He could dart from one pillar to another if the giantess would just look away, but she sat on her chair against the huge wooden doors, and stared straight ahead of herself until he began to think she might be a statue that had been placed there while he wasn't looking. He was about to risk a quick dash to the theatre doors right under her very nose, when there came a hammering on the main door, and muffled shouts from outside. The giantess stood slowly, and lifted her heavy chair aside as though it were doll's house furniture.

When she swung the great doors open she was

confronted by a woman as impressively large in width as she was in height. The woman was backed by a number of police, and String instinctively pulled back farther into the shadows. "Kindly let us in," said the broad woman in a stern voice.

The giantess shook her head. "No admission without a ticket," she said. The two large women stared at each other, hands on their hips.

A policeman with a pasty white face stepped up beside the broad woman. "Open in the name of the law," he said.

The giantess answered without even looking at him. "No admission without a warrant," she said.

Suddenly a cat appeared at her feet – a large ginger cat who strolled into the Palace of Laughter with neither ticket nor warrant, followed by a black cat with white patches, and a white cat with black patches. The giantess, caught off guard, stared down at them in surprise, and a moment later she was surrounded by dishevelled-looking police with mis-buttoned tunics and stubbly chins – and one even wearing pajama bottoms – like an eagle being harried by starlings. They overpowered the giantess by sheer weight of numbers and dragged her outside, while the large lady and a wrinkly old man with a white stick marched on into the theatre, leaving the doors wide-open and unguarded behind them.

Stealing the keys had been easier than he had expected.

There was chaos of some kind going on in the big ring at the centre of the theatre. The entire audience seemed to be drunk, and the big man with the keys was lying right in the middle of the aisle, laughing like a loon, and did not even notice being relieved of his property.

String had taken the lift down to the lowest level, and was now opening each door in turn and searching the rooms for the winged girl. He needed to find her as quickly as possible so that he could make her show him the way out through the clown's ear, since the main entrance was crawling with police. All the doors he had found so far were unlocked, and he chuckled to himself at the stupidity of their occupants. It was true that there wasn't a great deal of value to be stolen, but his pockets had been steadily filling with a fair haul of loose change nonetheless, and a couple of pocket watches to boot. He had found no trace of the girl, however, and he was just beginning to worry that he would not find her in time, when he came to a heavy wooden door and found it locked.

"Bingo," said String to himself. "Now all I have to do is find the right key." He began to try the keys one at a time. Most fit the lock but would not turn. One turned a fraction and got stuck fast, and he tugged and rattled it impatiently. Time was running out, and there was a nasty smell of rotten bananas from the room he was trying to open that was making him feel slightly sick. Suddenly the key turned, and the lock opened with a click. String smiled. He pictured the girl sitting frightened and alone in the corner of the room. She was small, maybe five or six, and she may even already be tied up. He did not think he would have much trouble with her one way or another.

It would have been better for String if he had pictured an enormous black beast, with eyes like holes in the darkness itself, crouched on the other side of the door and filled with a howling madness, for that was what was waiting for him as he chuckled to himself and rattled the keys in the lock.

He turned the handle to open the door, but as he did so it burst outward and sent him flying across the corridor. He slammed into the opposite wall, knocking himself out cold, and slid to the floor, as the nameless hairy beast barged out of its cell with a barking cackle and loped away towards the lift.

Miles Wednesday, tired, triumphant, but still Tangerine-less, searched the empty theatre for his missing bear. He looked in the discarded clown's hat from which Tangerine had emerged in the first place, and he searched among the other props that littered the ring, but he could find no sign of him. Silverpoint had remained to help him, while Lady Partridge went outside to look for Genghis's keys.

The boy and the angel picked their way slowly around the ring, turning over everything they could find. Miles called Tangerine's name, but the vast empty building seemed to answer with a forlorn cackling, as though the crazy laughter were still leaking from the stone walls themselves. He called again, and the cackle answered. It sounded louder this time, and it made the hair stand up on his neck. He had heard that sound before.

"Silverpoint," he said. Silverpoint straightened up, tucking something quickly into his pocket, and turned to him.

"I think The Null is in this building," said Miles.

"You think what?" asked Silverpoint, frowning. "What do you mean?"

"That," said Miles, pointing over Silverpoint's shoulder with a trembling finger, "is The Null."

The creature crouched there, almost filling the doorway. Its red mouth hung open in the hairy blackness. Silverpoint turned and stared. The Null launched itself down the aisle suddenly, heading straight for him. Silverpoint stepped backward, sending a bolt of lightning toward the beast, which howled with pain but did not stop its headlong charge. There was a rustling sound like someone shaking out a starched sheet, and Silverpoint's magnificent wings spread from his shoulders, tearing through his chef's jacket as though it were wet tissue. The creature bowled into him before he could get off the ground, and they rolled over and over across the floodlit ring, an angel and a demon in a ball of sparks and fury. There was another crackle of blue fire and a roar of rage, and a moment later The Null was charging on towards Miles on its feet and knuckles, smoke rising from its burnt hair, and Silverpoint lay motionless on the floor, his eyes closed and his wings outstretched in the greasy sawdust.

CHAPTER THIRTY-THREE

LITTLE

Miles Wednesday, upside-down and oil-coated, hung by his jacket from The Null's ebony fist, high above the empty ring in the Palace of Laughter. After knocking Silverpoint out, the black beast had come straight at him, grabbing him without slackening its pace, and had begun to climb one of the ornately carved pillars that circled the ring. It climbed swiftly, and Miles dangled by a handful of cloth, hoping at first that the jacket would rip and let him drop, and then that the jacket would hold so he wouldn't fall. He held his breath against the smell of rotten bananas and singed hair. He could see Silverpoint, far below and stretched out still on the floor like a drawing of an angel in flight. He saw a small orange dot clamber from the pocket of Silverpoint's destroyed jacket, and even in the grip of the nameless beast he felt a moment of relief that Tangerine had been found.

At the top of the pillar was a carved capital, with laughing stone faces peering from between curling leaves. With a grunt The Null climbed onto the flat ledge above the capital and hauled Miles up after it. The ring was like a saucer far below. Miles looked at The Null's mighty jaws, and remembered the splintering sound as they demolished the bone it had swiped from him back at the Circus Oscuro. The beast let go of his jacket and grabbed him tightly around the chest with its hairy arms. The breath left his lungs with a whoosh.

Miles felt like a marshmallow in a nutcracker. He pushed against The Null's chest with all his strength, and found himself looking straight into the blackness of its eyes. As the beast squeezed tighter, it seemed that the eyes sucked him into a fathomless universe of pain and howling darkness that was trapped inside its bony skull. He could not bear to look any longer, and he squirmed and wriggled, as much to get away from that terrible void as to try and free himself from the beast's bear hug. He was becoming dizzy from lack of air, and still the beast squeezed tighter. He could hear vague sounds of shouting from below, but he could not look down. As his vision began to fog over he looked across at the laughing stone faces on the next pillar, as though they could somehow help him. He imagined that one of the faces swung open, and he felt an odd desire to laugh. "Now I'm seeing things," he thought.

He saw the face of Little appear where the stone face had been a moment before. The Null squeezed tighter. Little's face was followed by her hands gripping the stonework, and she seemed to pop from the hole in the pillar, wings fluttering in a cloud of soot, and glide through the air towards him. She was calling something to him, but he could not hear her over the sound of his blood roaring in his ears. The Null let out a howl and swiped at Little as she came close, still gripping Miles with its other arm. She dodged the blow, and swooped around to land on the ledge behind them. With the last of his strength Miles tried to free himself from the monster's hold, but his struggling did not loosen The Null's grip in the slightest. He could feel his ribs cracking, and he saw the beast lash out again at Little. It felt as though he were watching from somewhere far away. She tumbled from the ledge, then recovered herself and flew back towards them, hovering just out of reach of The Null's hairy arm. He could feel his consciousness slipping away, but before the blackness could overtake him he had the strange notion that he could hear the sound of singing.

It began like a single voice from a half-remembered dream, and grew stronger and fuller until it swept right through him like a flowing river of light, a sweet blend of birdsong and breeze, of bells and rushing riverwater, and a thousand other sounds of warmth and life and sunlight. It was the most beautiful song he had ever heard, and his pain and fear melted away before it. All the dreams and hopes, the sorrow and simple joy that he had ever felt seemed to be woven into the music as it swirled through him and around him, and the brightest thread of all, the shining sound that held it all together, was the sound of laughter – real, warm laughter glinting through the weave of life and friendship like a thread of gold.

Miles realised that he was breathing again. The Null's deathly grip around his chest had loosened. It let him go, and in his dizziness he almost fell forwards into space. He saw Little smiling at him, still just out of reach, as she came to the end of her song. He knew that the beautiful sound that had quieted the beast and saved him from death must be her real name, the name that she could never utter without binding herself to Earth, but still he did not want the music to end. As the last few notes died away, Little's wings melted into her skin and sadness overtook her smile. Miles watched helplessly as she fell toward the ring far below, just a small girl tumbling over and over with no magic, no wings, no song left to lift her.

The ring was crowded now with people, looking up towards them. He could see Lady Partridge standing there among the blue-uniformed policemen, and the three tiny figures of the Bolsillo brothers, holding between them something that looked no bigger than a coin. Little fell straight towards them, and they shuffled first to one side, then to the other, never taking their eyes off her. After what seemed like forever she landed right in the middle of the trampoline, for that is what they were holding, and bounced high into the air. The assembled policemen broke into applause, and suddenly the whole scene transformed itself into a simple circus act. A troupe of fools dressed in pajamas and misbuttoned uniforms ran in circles around a fat lady, while a tiny acrobat bounced gracefully on a trampoline held by three tiny clowns, and Miles was struck by the strangest of feelings. Perched high above the floodlit circus ring like a trapeze artist awaiting his cue, he felt truly at home for the first time in his life. It was as though he had always belonged here, and the circus had just been waiting patiently for his return.

Miles turned to look at The Null, sitting slumped against the pillar, its fearful eyes closed and its huge jaw slackened into something that looked almost like a smile. He leaned back against the pillar beside the stupefied beast. His cracked ribs began to ache. "And where do you fit in, I wonder?" he asked, as tiredness swept over him and he slipped from consciousness.

Miles Wednesday, monster-squeezed and song-saved, awoke on a lumpy sofa in a firelit room. He could dimly see people sitting around a fire that blazed in the hearth, talking in low voices. He tried to sit up, but a sharp pain shot through his bruised ribs. "Ow!" he hissed.

The talk around the fire stopped, and everyone turned to look at him. "So you're back from the uncharted regions, Master Miles," barked Baltinglass's voice. "I hope you planted a few flags along the way!"

"Sit up carefully, my dear," said Lady Partridge, "and I'll get you a mug of cocoa."

Miles eased himself into a sitting position. He had been bandaged tightly around the ribs and propped on soft cushions, and the bones had been removed from his hair. He could see now that he was in Baltinglass's living room, dimly lit by a couple of candles that the old man had managed to dig out of his supply depot, and the flickering light of the fire in the hearth. Baltinglass of Araby sat in a leather armchair by the fire, a large gin and tonic in his hand in case the malaria chose that moment to ambush him. Lady Partridge rose from another armchair, cats spilling from her lap as she made for the kitchen. Fabio,

Gila and Umor perched on an assortment of stools, and Little sat on the rug in front of the stone hearth, smiling at him for all she was worth and looking none the worse for her fall from the ceiling of the Palace of Laughter.

"Where's Silverpoint?" asked Miles.

"Resting in the bunk room," said Baltinglass. "Had a tussle with a yeti, so they tell me. Could've sworn he had a couple of broken bones when I looked him over at the Palace of Laughter, but when we brought him back here to set 'em, I couldn't find so much as a fracture. Tough as a Magyar, that lad. Hasn't come round yet, though, so we've left him in his cot."

"And Henry!" said Miles, feeling a sudden stab of guilt at the thought of the small boy suspended in the night sky. "We have to go back for Henry. I promised!"

"It's all right," said Little. "The policeman rescued Henry."

"My own nephew, Radovan Flap, rescued the boy," shouted Baltinglass. "Climbed up in the dark with a lantern hanging from his belt and brought the lad down single-handedly. No shortage of pluck, that young Radovan. Gets it from his mother's side, may the gods play a happy tune on her old bones. Would've gone up myself, but the lad wouldn't hear of it."

Little came and sat on the end of the sofa, shooing a

couple of cats out of the way. The soot had been cleaned from her hair, and she was wearing an old dressing gown many sizes too big for her.

"How are you feeling?" she asked.

"A bit bruised, but I'll be fine. But what about you? What about—"

Little put her finger to her lips. Miles lowered his voice to a whisper. "Why did you have to sing your name?" he asked. "You can never go home now, can you?"

Little shook her head.

"Couldn't you . . . couldn't you have found The Null's own name to sing to it, and kept yours to yourself?" whispered Miles.

"I looked for its name," she said, "and I found the place where it should be, but there was only a black hole in the One Song itself, as though the name had been torn out and stolen." She winced at the memory, then smiled at Miles. "Besides, I want to stay here with you. You need a little sister."

Miles searched her face, but could see no sign of regret. He felt a warm feeling spreading from his stomach.

"Won't you miss it? The Realm, and . . . and flying?"

"Of course," said Little, "but I've found something better."

"What could be better than flying, and that beautiful

music?" He could still hear an echo of Little's Song in his ear, and he hoped it would never fade away.

"The One Song is beautiful," agreed Little, "But . . ." She searched for the words. "But up there, I only got to sing it. Down here I can live it. Down here I can have real friends." A smile lit up her face. "And that reminds me . . ."

She reached in her pocket and took out Tangerine. She handed him to Miles. The small bear wriggled out of his hand and climbed to his shoulder, where he snuggled against Miles's ear. The familiar feel of his worn fur seemed to ease the ache in Miles's ribs, and the smile of content-ment on his face stretched even wider.

"Thank you," he whispered.

"Told you so," said Umor from the edge of the fire-place.

"It's really his," said Gila.

"Then it must be him," said Fabio.

"Has to be," said Umor.

"He doesn't look very dead," said Gila. Fabio shushed him with a frown.

"Where did you grow up, Master Miles?" asked Fabio.

"In Pinchbucket House," said Miles. "It's an orphanage. Why?"

"Can you remember where you got that bear?"

Miles shook his head. "I've had him all my life. I know I

had him when I came to the orphanage, because the Pinchbuckets never gave us anything."

"We can remember," said Gila.

"Eleven years ago to the day," said Fabio.

"Which makes it your birthday."

"Happy birthday, Master Miles."

Miles looked at the three tiny men, wondering what kind of game they were playing. "What do you mean?" he said. "Even I don't know when my birthday is."

"It's a long story," said Fabio.

"We thought you were lost, a long time since," said Umor.

"Or dead," said Gila. He rummaged in his pocket for a handkerchief, and finding none, blew his nose on the corner of Fabio's jacket.

"But I've never met you before I came to the Palace of Laughter. How could you know about me?" asked Miles in bewilderment.

"We were there the night you were born," said Fabio.

"We gave you that bear when you were only hours old."

"Before you even had a name."

"Your father, Barty Fumble, was our boss, Master Miles."

"He was like an uncle to us."

"Or an aunt."

"Not really. He was big and strong, with a beard."

"So was the bearded lady."

"Whatever happened to her?"

"I heard she opened a barber shop in Nape."

Miles stared at them with his mouth open. "Barty Fumble was my father?" he said. "Of Barty Fumble's Big Top?"

"Ah, you've heard of Barty Fumble's Big Top?" said Umor.

"Of course," said Miles. "A ti . . . a friend told me the story. But Barty left the circus and took his son with him." He tried to picture the big bearded man in the dead of night, leaving the circus that was his life, stricken with grief and carrying his infant son in his arms. "Me," thought Miles. "Barty Fumble's boy."

"Then . . . what happened to Barty . . . to my father? Where did he go?"

Fabio sighed. "I wish I could tell you the answer to that, Master Miles."

"He left in the dead of night," sniffed Gila.

"And we never heard from him again," added Umor.

"Nor of you, neither, until yesterday."

Miles could scarcely grasp this astonishing news. In the space of a minute he had gained a little sister, and learned that the father he had always believed to be dead was none other than Barty Fumble himself, and that he might still be alive. He was surprised to find tears welling in his eyes as he realised, too, that there was no such hope for his mother. An entire family history had stepped into place behind him. It was a history he already knew something about, and it certainly explained why he had felt so at home perched high above the circus ring in the Palace of Laughter.

Little echoed his thoughts. "That's why the tiger said you had the circus in you," she said, smiling. "I told you tigers never lie."

Miles nodded. It was all too much to take in, and his head swam with the details. Was it just coincidence that Barty Fumble too had counted a tiger as his friend? And why did he leave his child to grow up in the mean grasp of the Pinchbuckets? Suddenly he had answers to questions that he had always carried at the back of his mind, but they brought more questions in their wake, and he was not sure that he wanted them. He had always told himself that both his parents were dead. It was a simple story and a hard one, but knowing the truth seemed to make things much more complicated.

"Don't hold it against your father, my dear," said Lady Partridge. She sat on the arm of the sofa (which creaked in protest) and handed him a mug of steaming cocoa. "We can never understand the decisions people have to face without knowing all the details, and sometimes not even then. In time you may learn more about your parents, and their story will become clearer."

Miles nodded. There were too many things spinning around in his head, and he still had more questions to ask. The Bolsillo brothers dragged the heavy sofa closer to the fire, and there they all sat in comfortable silence, each with their own thoughts: the boy, the lady, three tiny clowns, a blind explorer and a four-hundred-year-old girl with the faint outline of a lost pair of wings etched into the skin of her back.

Silverpoint, marble-skinned and straight-winged, took his leave the following night in Baltinglass's moonlit orchard. He had recovered with remarkable speed from his encounter with The Null, and said that it was time for him to return home and explain his absence, and how he had managed to lose a Song Angel to the hungry Earth. Before he left he had tried to persuade Miles to let him restore Tangerine to his former self. He pointed out that Little was not permitted to give life to any inanimate object, and that the walking, dancing bear was a grave offense against nature. If its existence was discovered, he said, it would make matters even worse. At this, Little flew into a rare temper and refused point-blank to let Silverpoint near Tangerine, and eventually he was forced to let the matter drop.

Silverpoint shook Miles's hand as he had when they first

met, and though Miles was ready for the tingling sensation it still made his hair stand on end. The Storm Angel's dark eyes looked searchingly into his for what seemed a long time, then he turned and embraced Little, lifting her off her feet. As he did so he whispered something in her ear, and his eyes flickered in Miles's direction. Little seemed to stiffen slightly. "Take care, little softwing," said Silverpoint.

"Good-bye," said Little as he put her gently down, and behind the tears that glinted in the light of the moon, Miles thought he heard indignation in her voice.

Silverpoint stood in the stillness of the autumn night among the rows of apple trees, and with a frown of concentration on his pale face he conjured up a storm to cover his departure. Black clouds rolled in from nowhere like pirate ships, covering the moon and throwing the small town of Cnoc into darkness. A sudden torrent of hailstones lashed the roofs and clattered in the leaves of the apple trees.

"Will you be in a lot of trouble?" shouted Miles above the noise.

Silverpoint nodded. "I expect so," he said. "They'll probably have me making drizzle for a century."

The winged boy walked backwards through the trees until he had placed a distance between himself and the others. He looked up into the blackness above. A twisted rope of blue lightning split the sky with a deafening crash and struck the spot where he stood, leaving Miles and Little momentarily as blind as Baltinglass himself. When their sight returned, the black clouds were dissolving like dreams. One of Baltinglass's apple trees was split clean in two, and Silverpoint was no longer there.

The morning after Silverpoint's departure Miles woke late, with the sunlight slanting in through his window. The sky was washed clean by the storm that the angel had created, and the rich smell of damp earth drifted in through the open windows. He found Baltinglass, Lady Partridge and the three Bolsillo brothers deep in conversation on the sun-dappled patio. They were discussing a plan to devise an entirely new show from the remnants of the Circus Oscuro, under the ownership of the Bolsillo brothers themselves, which would reverse the Great Cortado's sinister hypnosis, and wean those people who had been "laughtered" off Dr. Tau-Tau's Tonic for good. Miles thought he heard Little's name mentioned, but the subject seemed to change when he arrived.

He sat himself at the table and listened with his chin resting on his hands, but no one paid him any further attention, and after a while he took an apple from the wooden bowl in the centre of the table and went to look for Little. He found her eventually, after an extensive search of Baltinglass's rambling house, sitting in the window of a small tower room in the roof. She was gazing through the dusty pane at the lightning-split tree in the orchard, and when he asked her if she was all right, she nodded, but did not say a word or turn her head to look at him.

Miles sighed and closed the door softly behind him. He wandered down through the house and out into the orchard, feeling slightly left out. He made his way towards the far end of the walled garden, where the orderly apple trees gave way to a jumbled undergrowth of strange foreign plants with enormous dark leaves, as though some far-off patch of jungle had been unable to part company with Baltinglass and had followed him home. Miles scuffed his feet through the first fallen leaves, and when his toes met the weight of an apple in the grass he gave it a sharp kick, sending it sailing into the undergrowth. There was a low growl, and a tiger's head appeared from the bushes. Miles felt his heart leap.

"Tub boy," grunted the tiger. "I might have guessed. Your manners haven't improved since we last met." He turned and disappeared into the undergrowth, and Miles almost ran to catch up, half afraid that the tiger would vanish as he had before. He found the tiger stretched out in a small clearing in the centre of the miniature jungle. Miles sat down in the grass nearby.

"You found what you were looking for, I take it?" said the tiger.

Miles nodded. He hardly knew where to start.

"I got Tangerine back," he said, "and we found Silverpoint." He picked up the bruised apple and twirled it on its stem. "Lots of other stuff happened too, after you left. We could have done with your help in the Palace of Laughter."

"You still insist on thinking you can call me up like a plumber, I see," rumbled the tiger. "In any case, you seem to have managed all right by yourselves."

"I barely escaped with my life," said Miles. "It was Little who saved me."

The tiger looked at him. "I told you she would prove a valuable companion," he said. "And I am not often wrong. How did she manage to snatch you from the jaws of death?"

"It's a long story," said Miles.

"Then you had better put it in a nutshell for me," yawned the tiger. "They say patience is a virtue, but it's not one of mine."

"She gave up her name for me," said Miles, "and now she can never go home."

"More riddles," said the tiger. "I won't waste time trying to solve it, but it sounds like a noble sacrifice. You had better make sure she never regrets it."

"I'll do my best," said Miles.

"I should hope so," said the tiger. He stretched out in the

grass and flicked his tail idly. "Of course, I may have played a small part in your rescue myself," he said.

"You did?" said Miles. "But I thought you wouldn't go near the city."

"You thought right," said the tiger. "But I'm surprised you haven't wondered about the fortuitous timing of your rescue party's arrival."

Miles frowned in puzzlement. "You mean you told Lady Partridge?"

The tiger chuckled. "You should know I am not in the habit of popping up in people's living rooms, especially if they happen to be perched in a tree. Your ample friend, however, has the good sense to listen to her cats, even if she has little understanding of their speech. It was enough to inform them where you were, and that you were stepping into deep waters. They are resourceful little midgets you know, and plucky too."

Miles considered what the tiger had told him. "Why did you do that for us?" he asked.

The tiger sighed. "Questions, questions," he said. "Life follows its course like a river runs in its bed, tub boy. Perhaps you should just be grateful that things have worked out for you, and leave the chattering to the monkeys."

"I am grateful," said Miles. "Thank you."

"Think nothing of it," said the tiger. "Now I must be on

my way, and it's time you went to cheer up your little friend in the attic. She has been moping at that window since before sunrise, and she has probably had enough of being alone by now."

Miles looked up at the window. He could just see Little's pale face in the gloom, and he wondered if she could see the tiger. A chilly breeze rustled through the bushes, making him shiver as he got to his feet. "Will we see you again?" he asked.

"It's my experience," said the tiger, "that once you have crossed someone's path a couple of times you are bound to cross it again in the future. Unless, of course, you have eaten them," he added.

"So long then," said Miles. He took a last look at the tiger, stretched out and striped in the jungle shade, and pushed his way through the bushes into the cold wind of the autumn day.

CHAPTER THIRTY-FOUR

THE LARDE WEEKLY HERALD

Miles Wednesday, villain tamer and hero of Larde, sat in an old armchair in the rebuilt gazebo by Lady Partridge's pond, and read aloud to The Null from a newspaper. He did not imagine for one moment that the creature could understand what he was reading, but it was still subject to frequent fits of madness, and the sound of his voice seemed to have a calming effect. In any case Lady Partridge had set him the task of reading the paper from cover to cover each week as part of his education, and he found it easiest to concentrate in the peace and quiet of the early morning when he brought The Null its breakfast.

The gazebo had been converted into a sort of fortified

residence for the beast, after a lengthy and boisterous town meeting had debated its fate well into the night. Mayor Doggett was all for having The Null put down at once. He said it was a menace to society, and should be stuffed and mounted and displayed in a prominent place, such as the lobby of the town hall, where it might become a renowned attraction for visitors. This idea had earned him a sharp kick under the table from Mrs. Doggett, who suggested that the beast should be presented to the Smelt city zoo, where it could be reunited with "others of its kind," although she was as vague as anyone on what that kind might be. After many other suggestions had been shouted by the Lardespeople, from harnessing The Null to a plough to training it as a game warden, Miles had stepped up to the podium and the people had fallen silent to hear what he had to say.

He began, in a hesitant voice, by saying that he of all people would have good reason to want The Null stuffed and mounted, or locked away in a far-off zoo. The towns-people nodded as one. Yet despite having been throttled to within an inch of his life by the beast, Miles went on, he could not help thinking that somewhere deep inside its fearsome exterior there lay something like a soul. The townspeople began to look more doubtful at this, but Miles would not elaborate. He was thinking of what Little had

told him about the creature's missing name, and he wondered privately how it could be that any creature could be
left unnamed in the tongues of both men and of angels,
but this was not something he felt he could explain to the
people of Larde. At this point Lady Partridge stood and
boomed that if it was Miles's wish to try and befriend the
creature, that was good enough for her, and she would have
her gazebo converted to provide suitable accommodation.
If there was anyone in Larde who had the nerve to try and
obstruct Lady Partridge's wishes, that person was certainly
absent from the meeting that night.

Now The Null sat brooding in a corner of the straw-
carpeted room, separated by a set of stout bars from the
small lobby with the armchair where Miles sat. The
newspaper from which he was reading was *The Larde Weekly
Herald*, which Lily the florist had set up on her return from
the Palace of Laughter. Like most of the people who had
made the trip, her memory of that night's momentous
events was dim and confused, but she had returned to Larde
with a strange urge to leave the flower business to her sister
Maggie, and go into the newspaper business instead. Taking
full advantage of the town's collective amnesia she
produced a first issue that was so fat with outlandish stories
that it sold out in a matter of hours, and a second edition
had to be hastily printed, followed by a third.

The exploits of Miles Wednesday had featured heavily in the first few issues of the paper, making him something of a local hero. Stories of the Boy from the Barrel who had fought savage tribes in the city and brought down a notorious villain almost single-handedly had been read and reread, until many people were surprised, when they met him, to find that he was not ten feet tall.

Lady Partridge's dramatic rescue mission to the Palace of Laughter had also been covered in some detail. Though she had refused to be interviewed personally (far too busy for that sort of thing) a riveting story had been pieced together from the accounts of various policemen and other witnesses. Apparently Lady Partridge's cats had somehow alerted her to the danger in which Miles and Little had found themselves. How the cats could have known, far less made their anxieties clear to Lady Partridge, no one could say. In any case she had grasped the seriousness of the situation at once. She had intercepted Sergeant Bramley just as he was locking up the police station for the night, and harangued him into rounding up his two constables and setting off for the surrounding villages to collect a rescue party. The half-pyjamaed task force had taken to the highway in a small fleet of battered police vans, and since half the population of Larde had taken a train to the Palace of Laughter the day before, the policemen reasoned as Miles and Little had done, and followed the railway tracks.

If the policemen felt disgruntled at their rude awakening, their tiredness soon turned to excitement as they hurtled through the dawn at breakneck speed. Sometime before midday they had roared into the sleepy town of Cnoc, their whistles and sirens blowing, and screeched to a halt outside the house of Constable Flap's uncle and Lady Partridge's old friend, the famous explorer Gulliver P. Baltinglass. There were many dry throats and full bladders to be dealt with, but to their surprise they found that Baltinglass of Araby had not only met Miles Wednesday, but had provisioned him and sent him on his way two days before. When Baltinglass in turn learned of Lady Partridge's mission, he had torn off his apron and clambered into the lead van, leaving a relieved Rufus Weedle to escape the third and last day of his hard labour, at least for the time being.

There were so many conflicting accounts of what had happened when the rescue party reached the Palace of Laughter, and about how it was that the Boy from the Barrel had already managed to dethrone the Great Cortado and subdue him with a tin can, that Lily had decided they should all be published in the interests of balanced reporting.

As for The Null itself, the exact nature of the beast continued to be the topic of much debate, which led to it being described both as a previously unknown species of hyena, and as a cross between a giant Ivory Coast Baboon and a Tibetan Yeti, in the same issue of the paper. Several policemen from Larde and the surrounding villages claimed that the beast had been attacked by angels as it attempted to strangle the Boy from the Barrel, and that the boy's little sister herself had been one of them, and was over five thousand years old.

These last stories were of course dismissed as complete fantasy. Most people put them down to the long journey the brave constables had undertaken at great speed, which might have rattled their brains somewhat, but they enjoyed reading them all the same. As for the girl herself, there was always a smile on her face and music in her laughter, and the Lardespeople had grown so fond of her that they would not have cared if she had come from the planet Neptune.

The second issue of the *Herald* also featured a detailed account of the mysterious disappearance of Mr. and Mrs. Fowler Pinchbucket from the town orphanage. The paper reported that Miles Wednesday, the Boy from the Barrel, had paid a visit to Pinchbucket House the day after his return from his adventures in Smelt, accompanied by

Sergeant Bramley and his two constables. They had a warrant to search the premises on suspicion that the Pinchbuckets had been stealing the property of the orphans and using the children themselves for slave labour.

To their surprise they had found the orphanage in an uproar. A party had been going on for most of the night, and there was not a sign of an adult in the whole building. None of the children were sure what had happened to the Pinchbuckets, except for two small boys, Ruben Monday and Lawrence Friday. Their outlandish statement told of a huge tiger that had appeared in the orphanage hall in the dead of night. The terrified boys, who had been paying a secret visit to the orphanage kitchen, claimed that the tiger had bounded up the stairs and made his way straight past them to the Pinchbuckets' bedroom. A moment later, the *Herald* said, the Pinchbuckets had emerged shrieking from their room and had stumbled down the stairs and out through the front door of the orphanage, with the tiger in hot pursuit. They had not been seen or heard from since. In the absence of any more reliable witness accounts, the sergeant had filed the incident under Missing Persons, and the case had been closed.

Lady Partridge had been appointed the new director of the town orphanage by Mayor Doggett himself. She had found herself unexpectedly wealthy once more thanks to a miracle cure produced by an obscure factory that her late husband had owned. The chemical in question, which was meant to be a weed killer but had had no effect whatsoever on the gardens of the nation, was discovered by accident to be an excellent cure for insomnia, halitosis, pessimism and nose-drip. It was now selling like hotcakes all over the land, and with the money that had been pouring into Lady Partridge's coffers she had hired a team of skilled craftsmen to restore her mansion to its former glory. Once the restoration work was completed she planned to move the orphanage lock, stock and barrel from its grim municipal building to her newly refurbished stately home.

The *Herald* had reported the appearance of the Once Great Cortado and his accomplice Genghis in court, to answer charages of Attempted Despotism and Accessory to Mind Control Offenses respectively. The two men had been assessed by a leading psychiatrist from Shallowford, who decided they were unshackled from their wits and unfit to answer the charges. They had been committed to the secure wing of Saint Bonifacio's Hospital for the Unhinged, where Cortado would refuse to emerge from his cell for days on end, lurking in the darkness with nothing for company but his own hollow laughter. Genghis, by contrast, had found a use for himself tending the hospital's vegetable garden, between fits of helpless giggling. Inside his Wellington boots he still wore lemon yellow socks.

And so the winter wore on. Lady Partridge's new orphanage took shape steadily. In the mornings the children were schooled by Lady Partridge herself in what used to be the ballroom. Baltinglass of Araby would make the occasional surprise visit to give them a vigorously shouted geography lesson, filled with crocodiles and canyons and endless oceans of white sand, and afterwards he would stomp off to have lunch with his nephew, Radovan, who had adopted Henry once all attempts to trace his family had failed.

In the afternoons the children played in the rambling gardens, and the sound of their laughter, like a genie which had finally been released from the grey bottle of Pinchbucket House, filled the grounds and the rooms of the mansion itself, which the Lardespeople had begun to refer to as "The Real Palace of Laughter." By night the grand bedrooms of Partridge Manor, filled now with brand-new bunk beds and warmed with real log fires, whispered with the soft breathing and the night sighs of its new occupants, mingled with the purring of the cats who curled up at the children's feet.

In the crisp winter nights Miles would often dream of his father, Barty Fumble, the barrel-chested man with the huge beard and the laugh that could rattle windows. He would see him on a lone horse in the mapless canyons of the South, or sunken-cheeked in an eastern opium den, with nothing for company but a burden of sorrow that none could help him carry. In these dreams Miles came to understand why his father had left him in the orphanage on that distant night. He had lost the wife he loved to a fate he was powerless to control, and the fear that someday this might happen to his son was more than his broken heart could bear. Miles would wake from these dreams with an empty feeling. He knew how it felt to face losing someone he loved, but he longed to tell his father what he had learned himself: that a hundred hours of friendship was worth more than a hundred years with a padlocked heart. Lying in his bed he promised himself that one day soon he would follow his father's trail and bring him back, man or bones, to the only family he had left, even if that trail led to the gates of hell itself.

As he waited for sleep to return Miles would think over the adventures he and Little had shared. He pictured them riding on the tiger's back, or crawling through tunnels in a giant clown's head, almost as if it they had been people in a story. He would look at the sleeping face of Little, her skin still glowing faintly when moonlight touched her, and wonder if she dreamed still of soaring through the magnificent realm in the skies, the world that she had given up to save his life. He would think then of the promise that he had made to the tiger at the end of an orchard on a chilly autumn day, the promise that whatever the future might bring, he would do everything in his power to make her life on earth as magical as the one she had left behind.

ACKNOWLEDGMENTS

*Thank you, Mary Waugh,
for the peace and quiet of your yellow boat,
and Eunice McMullen
for your masterful hat trick.*